GAIA

AN ATLAS
OF PLANET
MANAGEMENT

Dedication
To the poor of the world, denied their
share of the world's rich resources.
And to Jim Lovelock, whose Gaia
Hypothesis first alerted us to the idea that
we might inhabit a "living" planet. Gaia,
in ancient Greece, was Goddess of
the Earth.

ABOUT THIS BOOK

This is no ordinary atlas. It maps and analyses a
living planet at a critical point in its history – as
one species, our own, threatens to disrupt and
exhaust its life support systems. It charts the
growing divisions in the human family. And it
proposes that we have the chance to redirect our
course, and become caretakers of our future.

The Atlas of Planet Management is a first
approach to this challenging task. It organizes
the mass of available environmental data,
statistical predictions and often conflicting
opinions and solutions into a simple coherent
structure. It is divided into seven sections: Land,
Ocean, Elements, Evolution, Humankind,
Civilization, and Management; each of these is
considered from three perspectives: Potential
resources, Crises, and Management alternatives.

This structure enables us to examine any
critical area of concern and to weigh up: first,
what it has to offer; second, where, how, and
why things are obviously going wrong; and
third, how we might set about putting things
right, by applying a range of alternative
strategies.

More than a structure for a book, this
analytical formula offers one possible approach
to planet management. We hope it will spur the
rising global debate on our future prospects.

GENERAL EDITOR
NORMAN MYERS
with
John Elkington, Ken Laidlaw, Joss Pearson
PRINCIPAL CONSULTANTS
Erik Eckholm David Hall
Tom Burke Sidney Holt Dorothy Myers Uma Ram Nath David Pimentel Melvin Westlake

Erik Eckholm Overall consultant and reader. Editor of *Natural History*, New York City. Formerly, on the State Department's Policy Planning Staff, Senior Researcher with Worldwatch, and Visiting Fellow at the IIED.
David O. Hall BSc, PhD. Overall consultant and reader. Professor of Biology, King's College, University of London. Chairman of the School of Biological Sciences, London. Project Leader in the EEC Energy Programme.
Tom Burke General consultant, and special adviser on ELEMENTS. Director of Green Alliance. Press Officer, European Environment Bureau, London.
Sidney Holt DrSc. Consultant on OCEAN. Consultant on marine mammals to International Organizations. Former Director of Fisheries Resources, FAO. Holder of the World Wildlife Fund Gold Medal.
Dorothy Myers Consultant on HUMANKIND, CIVILIZATION, MANAGEMENT. BA Research Fellow University of Nairobi. Consultant to the UN Centre for Human Settlements (Habitat). Closely involved with UN Environment and Human settlements programmes, she is widely published on those and related issues.
Uma Ram Nath MA Consultant on HUMANKIND. Lecturer, University of Delhi. Co-editor of *Third World: EEC*, London. Writer, editor, broadcaster on women, health, art and Third World issues.
David Pimentel Reader and consultant for LAND. Professor with the Department of Entomology and Section of Ecology and Systematics, New York State College of Agriculture and Life Sciences, Cornell University.
Melvin Westlake Consultant on CIVILIZATION. Business and Economics editor of *South*. Formerly, Economics writer on *The Times*. Writer and broadcaster on all aspects of finance and economics including Third World policy.

John Elkington contributed his expertise and writing skills to the shaping and polishing of the manuscript. He is a Director of Earthlife UK and of Bioresources Ltd. His published work concentrates on the environmental implications of changing technologies.

Ken Laidlaw was involved in conceptual planning and research for the project from its inception. He is a journalist specializing in environment and development issues, and author of *Crisis decade in the Eighties*, published by ICDA.

Contributors
Peter Adamson MA Writer, journalist and broadcaster for the UN and the BBC on development issues. Co-founder and former Editor of *New Internationalist*. Main contributor to the UNICEF State of the World's Children report.
Stewart Ainsworth BA Lecturer in Education, Jordan Hill College of Education, Glasgow.
Raúl Hernan Ampuero BA MA Course Manager, The Open University, UK. Producer, BBC External Services.
Brian Anson Dipl. Arch. National Planning Aid Officer, Town and Country Planning Association. Consultant for the Irish Government on Environmental Planning.
David Baldock BA Director of Earth Resources Research Ltd, London. Widely published on environmental aspects of Food and Agriculture policy.
Barry Barclay New Zealand environmentalist and film-maker, specializing in genetic conservation and Third World issues.
Frank Barnaby Guest Professor of Peace Studies, Free University of Amsterdam. Director of the World Disarmament Campaign. Widely published on disarmament and peace related issues.
Pamela M. Berry BSc PhD Lecturer, Mansfield College and St Edmund's Hall, Oxford. Demonstrator, School of Geography, Oxford University.
Patricia W. Birnie BA PhD Lecturer in Law at the London School of Economics. Widely published on the Law of the Sea and Environmental laws.
John R. Bowers BA Arch MSc Senior consultant with international development organizations on urban design and environmental land use planning.
Julian Caldecott BSc PhD Researcher, World Wildlife Fund, Malaysia.
William D. Clark MA President, International Institute for Environment and Development, London. Formerly, Vice-President, External Relations, World Bank; PR Adviser to the Prime Minister (UK); Commonwealth Fellow and Lecturer in Humanities, University of Chicago.
Trevor D. Davies BSc PhD Lecturer, School of Environmental Sciences, University of East Anglia. Meteorologist, specializing in pollutants.
Paul R. Ehrlich Bing Professor of Population Studies at Stanford University. Expert on ecology and evolution and widely published on environmental crisis, population control and racial justice.
T. Scarlett Epstein PhD Research Professor, African Studies, University of Sussex. Writer, journalist, documentary film-maker.
Peter G. H. Evans BSc BPhil Research

Population Geneticist at the Edward Grey Institute of Field Ornithology, Department Zoology, Oxford University.
Graham Farmer BSc PhD Senior Research Associate, Climatic Research Unit, Universit East Anglia. Climatologist, specialist in crop-weather modelling and agricultural drough
A. John R. Groom BSc MA PhD Reader in International Relations, University of Kent. Widely published in the field of conflict research.
Jeremy Harrison BSc Head of the Protecte Areas Data Unit of the IUCN Conservation Monitoring Centre, based at Kew, UK.
Paul Harrison MA Writer and journalist specializing in the Third World. Regular contributor to *The Guardian*, *New Society*, *Ne Scientist* and for major development agencie such as WHO and ILO.
Tony Hill BSc Development Desk Program Officer, Catholic Institute for International Relations.
Colin Hines BA Environmentalist and auth Researcher, Earth Resources Research Ltd, London. Coordinator, London Energy and Employment Network.
P. Mick Kelly BSc PhD Senior Research Associate, Climatic Research Unit, Universit East Anglia.
Gillian Kerby BSc Researcher, Animal Behaviour Research Group, Department of Zoology, Oxford University.
Derrick Knight MA Researcher and journa on the staff of Christian Aid. Writer, documentary film-maker with special intere Central America.
Roy Laishley MA Journalist, specialist in agricultural development and commodity is in developing countries.
Alan Leather MPhil Research Officer, Trad Union International Research and Educatic group, Ruskin College, Oxford.
Stephanie Leland Feminist, active campaig in the Green movement. Founder of Wome Life on Earth, UK.
James E. Lovelock Fellow of the Royal Soci Contributor to the NASA space programm since 1974. Author of *Gaia: a new look at life Earth* OUP.
Simon Lyster MA Solicitor, Member of the York Bar. Consultant specializing in International Wildlife Law.
Donald J. Macintosh BSc PhD Research Fe Lecturer, Institute of Aquaculture, Stirling University. Adviser in aquaculture to the O.
Peter Marsh BSc Reporter on the *Financial* and formerly on the *New Scientist*.
Simon Maxwell BA MA Rural developmen and agricultural economist. Consultant for ODA, EEC, FAO.

ugh Miall BA PhD Historian. Energy
nsultant, Earth Resources Research Ltd,
ndon. Gave evidence at the Sizewell B
quiry.

phen Mills MA Writer, film-maker,
ecializing in scientific and wildlife subjects.

rbara Mitchell Research Associate,
ternational Institute for Environment and
velopment, London.

rian R.D. Norman MA MBA Fellow BCS.
nior Management Consultant, Arthur D.
tle Ltd. Adviser to governments on
ormation technology.

vid Olivier BSc Energy Consultant, Earth
sources Research Ltd, London.

er O'Neill BA MPhil Editor of *Third World:*
C, London. Consultant to WHO. Writer,
rnalist, broadcaster specializing in the Third
rld and related issues.

vid C. Pearson MCP Berkeley, Calif., RIBA
ncipal Architect, Technical Services, London
l authority, writer and lecturer.

an Price Honorary Degree, The Open
iversity, UK. Consultant on pollution.
viser to Friends of the Earth.

n Rowley BSc Publications Editor, IPPF,
ndon. Journalist, editor, writer on population
es.

er Russell Honorary Scholar, Cambridge.
nsultant to large corporations on the
velopment of the human mind. Author of *The
kening Earth* Routledge and Kegan Paul.

id Satterthwaite BA Working Associate,
velopment Planning Centre, University
ege, London. Researcher, Human
lements programme, IIED.

tor Sebek PhD Secretary of the Advisory
mittee on Pollution of the Sea. Consultant
ED.

aul Shears MB MSc Refugee Health
rdinator, OXFAM.

than I.R. Simnett BSc MSc Coordinator of
ST, University of Manchester. Director,
nology Research Development Ltd.

in Stainer Journalist. Specialist in
modities.

Stearman BEcon MA Deputy Director,
rity Rights Group, London, an information
research unit on human rights with
ultative status with the UN.

h Synge BSc Head of the Protected Areas
Unit of the IUCN Conservation
toring Centre, based at Kew, UK.

ord Thomas BA Journalist, writer,
nist. Formerly, Deputy editor and
cial editor of *The Guardian*.

Thornback BSc MSc Senior Research
er on the Mammals Red Data Book, IUCN.
ly published on population genetics, sea
conservation biology.

Toffler Author of the celebrated work
Shock Bantam Books. Formerly a
ington correspondent and Associate editor
tune. Visiting Professor at Cornell
rsity, holder of five honorary degrees in
, laws and sciences.

Valentine Writer. Specialist in nuclear
. Participated in the Sizewell B Inquiry.

an Orsdol BA PhD Worked for the New
Zoological Society and the World Wildlife
on natural resource conservation.

V. Tarzie Vittachi Assistant Secretary General,
UNICEF. Associate Editor, *Newsweek*. Journalist,
campaigner, writer, broadcaster, principally on
the Third World, minority rights, the media.
Peter Willets BA MSc PhD Lecturer in
International Relations, the City University,
London. Writer specializing in the Non-aligned
Movement.
Thomas Wilson (Graduate of Princeton
University) Writer and lecturer on environment,
world security, growth policy, human rights.
Consultant, UN Environment Programme.

Help and information were provided by the
very willing staff of many organizations,
including the following:
Amnesty International, London. Art in Action.
BBC. British Oil Spill Coastal Association. BP.
British Library. Canadian High Commission,
London. Channel 4. Commonwealth Secretariat.
Conservation Monitoring Centres, UK.
Cornucopia Project. Council for the
Preservation of Rural England. Earthlife.
Earthscan. Earth Resources Research Ltd,
London. Ecological Parks Trust, London.
Future Studies Group, University of Berkeley.
FAO. Friends of the Earth. Green Alliance.
Greenpeace. IBPGR. ICDA. IFDA. IIED. ILO.
IMMP. IMO. Institute of International
Relations. Institute of Oceanographic Sciences.
Intermediate Technology Development Group,
London. International Coffee Organization.
International Cooperative Alliance. IPPF. IUCN
Environmental Law Centre, Bonn. IUCN,
London and Gland. London School of
Economics. The Minority Rights Group Ltd.
National Maritime Institute. *New Internationalist*.
The Open University, London. OXFAM.
Reading University. *South*. Standard Telephone
and Cables. Survival. Swedish Embassy. Traffic,
UK. Tropical Products Institute, London.
UNEP. UNESCO. UNFPA. UNHCR London.
UNICEF. UN Information Centre, London.
UN University. UN Water Decade. Warren
Spring Laboratory, UK. World Bank, London.
World Conservation Centre, Gland. Worldwatch
Institute. *World Water*. World Wildlife Fund, UK
and US.

Editor's Note
The very making of this book is a tale worth the
telling. One fine summer afternoon, an emissary
from Gaia Books came to see me in Oxford to
tell me about an idea for an Atlas – a project of
such visionary scope that it immediately elated
me. Would I, Gaia Books enquired, care to act as
General Editor?

Since then, the Atlas has dominated the
working hours of a great many people, myself
included. As befits an enterprise of such
demanding concept and scale, it has involved an
enormous number of contributors, consultants,
organizations and researchers, and generated
much argument – sometimes at white heat. The
views expressed here, by no means all my own,
represent as broad a spectrum of opinion and
analysis as we could gather. We have generally
tried to arrive at a practical consensus, and
where we could not we have conveyed those
divergent views with the greatest weight. We
have sifted, organized, checked and rechecked;
searched for graphic solutions; worried over
conflicting data; sent the text to reader after
reader. Sometimes the startlingly gloomy
statistics we were handling have produced bouts
of depression; but as the book has taken life and
form, our spirits have lifted – because the
evidence of new initiatives, and of hope was also
there. As incipient planet managers, however,
the human race has far to go. We have found
that, for all the huge flood of data available,
there are many critical areas where we know too
little, measure the wrong things, or have to rely
on guesstimates. The reader can speculate on
how far this Atlas presents an incomplete
picture of our world, a world we are changing
beyond recognition with every passing day.

So this story concludes with an appeal: write to
us at Gaia Books about those aspects of this Atlas
as of our world that you believe could be more
solidly depicted. The Gaia team, exhausted
though we are, wants nothing better than to get
on with the revised edition.
Norman Myers *August, 1984*

CONTENTS

EVOLUTION
Introduction by Paul R.Ehrlich **138**

HUMANKIND
Introduction by V.Tarzie Vittachi **170**

CIVILIZATION
Introduction by Alvin Toffler **200**

MANAGEMENT
Introduction by William Clark **232**

Foreword

by Gerald Durrell

I am greatly honoured to be asked to write a foreword to such an extraordinary and vitally important book. It explains our place on this planet and the damage we are doing to ourselves. But it is not merely another "gloom and doom" book, for it shows us how we can mend our ways to our advantage.

This is a book that, perhaps, could not have been compiled 20 years ago, since even as recently as that our perceptions about the world we inhabit were, to a large extent, smug, self-satisfied, and ignorant. This book is, in fact, a sort of blueprint for our survival – both for you who are reading this Foreword and I who am writing it. It is an attempt to show what a complex and magnificent world we have inherited, how it works and, most important of all, what bad stewards we often have been, and are still being, of this inheritance. It shows how we are plundering our planet in the most profligate and dangerous way, but it also shows what we can do to redress the situation.

Anyone reading and absorbing the message in this book surely must conclude that nearly all the ills that beset us, from starvation and disease to war itself, can be traced back inexorably to three root causes: overpopulation, political stupidity, and wasteful misuse of the planet's treasures, both finite resources, and renewable living wealth.

We are told that Adam and Eve were banished from the Garden of Eden into the world. We have – ever since we started walking upright – set about the task of banishing ourselves from our own Garden of Eden – our planet Earth. Perhaps banishment is the wrong word to use, for it assumes that there is somewhere else we can be banished to, and in our case, once we have ruined and used up this Eden there is no other, no second world hanging in the sky that we can all blithely move to, as if we were changing houses. This beautiful and endangered planet is the only one we have.

At the present rate of "progress", and unless something is done quickly, disaster stares us in the face. Erosion, desertification and pollution have become our lot. It is a weird form of suicide, for we are bleeding our planet to death. We are led by sabre-rattling politicians who are ignorant of biology, beset by sectarian groups noted for their narrow-mindedness and intolerance, surrounded by powerful commercial interests whose only interest in nature is often to rape it. We are misguided and misled, trotting to oblivion as obediently as the Gaderene Swine. I wonder what the attitude will be if, in a hundred years time, this book is read by our starving grandchildren – and they see that this decimation of their inheritance was recognized, cures for it were available, and nothing was done?

Make no mistake about it, a cure is possible, as is pointed out in this book. But it requires a worldwide effort on everyone's part. We all worry about World War III and the possibility of it being a nuclear war. But instead of wasting billions on a ridiculous and futile arms race, we should use that money to cure some of the ills of the world; ills that, if left to fester, will promote World War III. We are, all of us, regardless of race, colour or creed, facing the same biological problems, all of which directly or indirectly are of our own making. Think of some of the facts revealed here and then ask yourself whether we are not blandly ignoring a threat which may make even nuclear war seem pale in comparison.

By the 1990's, humankind will be exterminating one species (plant or animal) per hour, by the year 2000 one every 15 minutes. These are species that for the most part we know little or nothing about, and could well be of enormous benefit to humanity. Up to now scientists have only examined the potential of one in ten of the 250,000 species of higher plants in the world. By felling tropical forests in the senseless way that we are doing, who knows what riches we are squandering? These tropical forests, once eliminated, can never be restored. They are gone, taking with them untold numbers of foods, drugs, and other products useful to humanity. With them go innumerable birds, mammals, reptiles, and insects, many of which could be of use to us, as the humble armadillo has helped to treat leprosy, and the owl monkey has assisted in treating malaria. We all know people who have attics or cupboards filled with an astonishing assortment of things, preserved because "they might come in useful". Well, the world is *our* attic, and we should preserve everything in it, for we do not know when it will "come in useful".

The world is still an incredibly rich storehouse (our *only* storehouse). It can (if we live with nature and not outside it) provide all of us with all we and future generations need. But we must learn to manage it intelligently. Most of nature – if it is not destroyed or corrupted by us – is a resource that is ever renewing itself. It offers us, if managed wisely, a never-ending largesse. It is our world, but we have yet to learn to treat it with respect and gratitude. Let's hope we do so before it is altogether too late, and we find ourselves breeding like a mass of greenfly on a cinder.

INTRODUCTION
The fragile miracle

The sphere of rock on which we live coalesced from the dust of ancient stars. Orbiting round the huge hydrogen furnace of the sun, bathed by radiant energy and the solar wind, the globe is white hot and molten beneath the crust: continents ride in a slow dance across its face, ocean floors spread. And between its dynamic surface and the vacuum of space, in a film as thin and vibrant as a spider's web, lies the fragile miracle we call the biosphere.

When the first astronauts circled the Earth in their tiny craft, millions of listeners heard them describe the beauty of this planet, "like a blue pearl in space", and were caught up in a moment of extraordinary human revelation. Since then, much has been written about "Spaceship Earth", on whose finite resources we all depend. And the more we explore the solar system, the more singular we understand our world to be. The atmospheric mix of gases, for instance, is entirely different not only from that of nearby planets but from what would be predicted by Earth's own chemistry. This "improbable" state of affairs appears to have arisen alongside the evolution of life, and persisted (with minor fluctuations) despite all possible accidental perturbations of cosmic travel, for perhaps two billion years. Life, by its very presence, is apparently creating, and maintaining, the special conditions necessary for its own survival.

It was a group of space scientists devising life-detection experiments for other planets who first stumbled on this phenomenon of the self-sustaining biosphere – and named it Gaia, the living planet. Since then, we have begun to learn much more about the planetary life-support systems which rule our lives – sadly, mainly by disturbing them.

Within this life realm, every organism is linked, however tenuously, to every other. Microbe, plant, and mammal, soil dweller and ocean swimmer, all are caught up in the cycling of energy and nutrients from sun, water, air, and earth. This global exchange system flows through various transport mechanisms, from ocean currents, to climate patterns and winds; from the travels of animals to the processes of feeding, growth, and decay. Information, too, flows through the biosphere – reproduction transfers the store of genetic coding to new generations and creates new experiments; learning and communication occur between individuals. And throughout the life zone, change and diversity, specialization and intricate interdependence, are found at every level.

It is with this remarkable planet, and what we are doing to it, and to ourselves, that this book is concerned. UFOs apart, we are unlikely to find another Gaia – should we destroy the one we have.

The protective atmosphere
Like the feathers of a bird, the 9 or 10 layers of the atmosphere provide equable surface temperatures, shield life from the "rain" of cosmic particles, and block lethal ultraviolet radiation.

Exosphere

Ionosphere

Photosynthesis

Stratosphere
Troposphere

Planetary life-support systems
The living world, or biosphere, stretches around our planet in a film as thin as the dew on an apple. A hundred kilometres down beneath our feet, the globe is already white hot, at 3000°C. Thirty kilometres up above our heads, the air is too thin and cold for survival. In between, the green world flowers, richest around the tropical zones where the ice age glaciations have never reached. Here, in the tropical forests and the shallow sunlit seas and reefs, much of Earth's living wealth of species is concentrated.

The Earth's green cover is a prerequisite for the rest of life. Plants alone, through the alchemy of photosynthesis, can use sunlight energy, and convert it to the chemical energy animals need for survival. It was the emergence of photosynthesizing algae in the oceans which first released free oxygen into the atmosphere – a cataclysmic event for existing life forms, but a pre-condition for present-day existence. The ocean microflora still supply 70% of our oxygen, and this in turn maintains the protective ozone layer in the upper atmosphere. The oceans act as a "sink" for carbon dioxide from the air.

Plant cover provides the basis of all food chains, mediates water cycles, stabilizes microclimate, and protects the living soil – the foundation of the biosphere. Legions of soil micro-organisms, and of anaerobic microbes in the shallow muds of sea floor and swamp, work ceaselessly to recycle decaying matter back into the nutrient system.

3000°C
100 kilometres down

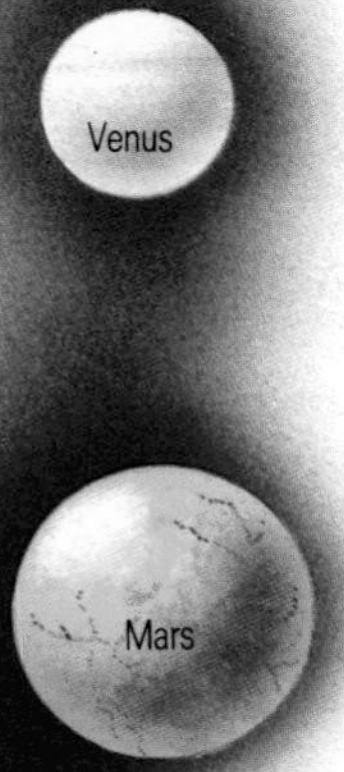

Temperature feedback

Earth's life-support systems are still little understood. Surface temperatures have remained suitable for life for several aeons, despite changes in solar flux. Feedback systems for temperature control are the levels of carbon dioxide and water vapour in the air – both affected by plant cover. Carbon dioxide acts as an insulator – the "greenhouse effect" (pp 116-7). Another is Earth's "albedo" – its shininess.

High albedo from light-covered areas cools the Earth. Most of Gaia's albedo value comes from cloud cover (influenced by vegetation), and from ice caps and oceans. Microflora in the oceans and plants on the land can darken or lighten these areas, thus altering their albedo. Atmospheric pollution raises carbon dioxide levels, while forest clearance and desertification raise albedo. We must act with care.

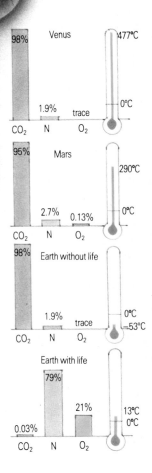

Venus

Mars

	Venus	
98%		
	1.9%	trace
CO_2	N	O_2

477°C
0°C

	Mars	
95%		
	2.7%	0.13%
CO_2	N	O_2

290°C
0°C

	Earth without life	
98%		
	1.9%	trace
CO_2	N	O_2

0°C
−53°C

	Earth with life	
	79%	
		21%
0.03%		
CO_2	N	O_2

13°C
0°C

Illustration labels: Ozone layer · Albedo effect · "Greenhouse" effect · CO_2 · N · O_2 · CO_2 · Earth without life · Water cycle

The unique planet

The most remarkable characteristic of living matter is that it is self-organizing. In contrast with the overall trend towards disorder or "entropy" evident in the universe, life *creates* order from the materials around it, exporting waste in the process. Thus life has the capacity to influence its environment.

When space scientists began devising life-detection experiments, one group suggested that a life-bearing planet might show an unexpected mix of gases in its atmosphere if life's chemistry were at work. When they looked at Earth in this light, their predictions were borne out with a vengeance. Earth's mix of gases, and temperature, were hugely different from what they predicted for a "non-living" Earth, as well as from neighbouring planets (above). The fact that these conditions appeared to have arisen and persisted alongside life led to the Gaia hypothesis – the proposal that the biosphere, like a living organism, operates its own "life-support" systems through natural feedback mechanisms.

Accelerating evolution

Though we wake to a largely humanized world of suburbs and cities, governments and wars, each of us carries within us the birth and death of stars, and the long flowering of Gaia.

Evolution is usually dated from the emergence of life, that "almost utterly improbable event with infinite opportunities of happening" (J. Lovelock). But this event itself was a stage in a process that has continued since time, as we know it, began – when, some 15 billion years ago, the Big Bang sent pure *energy* flooding out into a waking universe.

As this energy dispersed and the universe cooled, a patterning set in, and stable "energy structures" emerged as in a new order, *matter*. Over billions of years, the particles, atoms, and elements of matter formed and were processed and reprocessed in the heart of stars, until a higher order emerged, *life*.

Our probes into space have found life's chemical precursors widely distributed – indeed, space seems to be littered with the "spare parts of life" awaiting the right conditions for assembly. On our primeval planet, these conditions were found: the fierce energies of radioactivity and ultraviolet radiation, the abundant presence of hydrogen, methane, ammonia, and water. In Earth's oceans, the first strands of DNA, and then the self-replicating double helix, must have formed and broken countless times. But once the seed was set, the birth of the biosphere had begun.

Over nearly four aeons, the experiments, the increasing diversity and complexity continued until, as the life-support systems of our planet stabilized, a still higher order of complexity emerged – *intelligence* and *conscious awareness*.

Throughout its 15 billion years, the pace of the universe's development has been accelerating, each new wave of innovation building up to trigger the next, in a series of "leaps" up to further levels of diversification and change. Compress this unimaginable timescale into a single 24-hour day, and the Big Bang is over in less than a ten-billionth of a second. Stable atoms form in about four seconds; but not for several hours, until early dawn, do stars and galaxies form. Our own solar system must wait for early evening, around 6 p.m. Life on Earth begins around 8 p.m., the first vertebrates crawl on to land at about 10.30 at night. Dinosaurs roam from 11.35 p.m. until four minutes to midnight. Our ancestors first walk upright with ten seconds to go. The Industrial Revolution, and all our modern age, occupy less than the last thousandth of a second. Yet in this fraction of time, the face of this planet has changed almost as much as in all the aeons before.

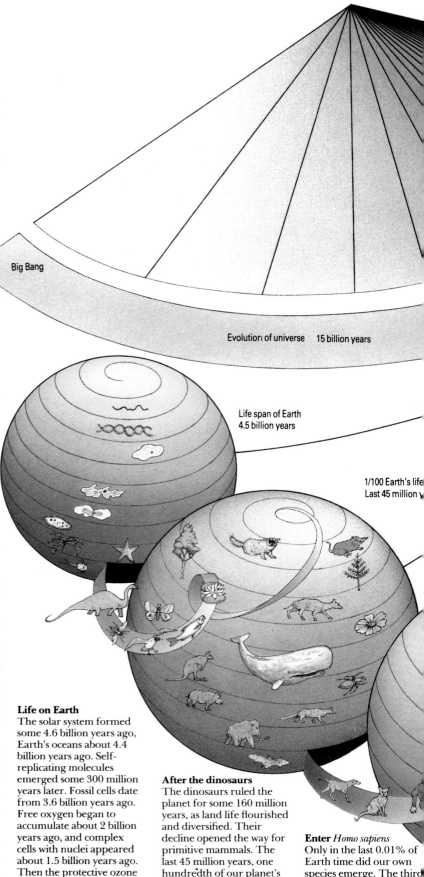

Big Bang

Evolution of universe   15 billion years

Life span of Earth
4.5 billion years

1/100 Earth's life
Last 45 million y

Life on Earth
The solar system formed some 4.6 billion years ago, Earth's oceans about 4.4 billion years ago. Self-replicating molecules emerged some 300 million years later. Fossil cells date from 3.6 billion years ago. Free oxygen began to accumulate about 2 billion years ago, and complex cells with nuclei appeared about 1.5 billion years ago. Then the protective ozone layer formed: life on land, as we know it, occupies only the last 10% of our planet's unique history.

After the dinosaurs
The dinosaurs ruled the planet for some 160 million years, as land life flourished and diversified. Their decline opened the way for primitive mammals. The last 45 million years, one hundredth of our planet's history, have seen the emergence of most of the flora and fauna we know (see second sphere).

Enter *Homo sapiens*
Only in the last 0.01% of Earth time did our own species emerge. The third sphere opens with the taming of fire and early human attempts to shape our Earth.

The momentum of evolution

The fantastic acceleration in the process of evolution is illustrated by these five spheres with "time" winding spirally down them. The first represents the last 4.5 billion years, the entire history of our planet. It traces the evolution of DNA, of the first cells and, much later, of nucleated cells, and of sexual reproduction. The birth of our oxygen-rich atmosphere due to photosynthesizing algae is indicated by the deepening blue tinge. Each successive sphere represents an enlargement of just the last one hundredth of the timescale illustrated in the previous one. The second sphere, represents the last 45 million years, the third the last 450,000 years, the fourth the last 4,500 years, and the fifth only the last 45 years. Yet each sphere shows about as much significant change in this last 1% as in the preceding 99% of time. Emerging in the third sphere, humankind has triggered a further acceleration in evolution.

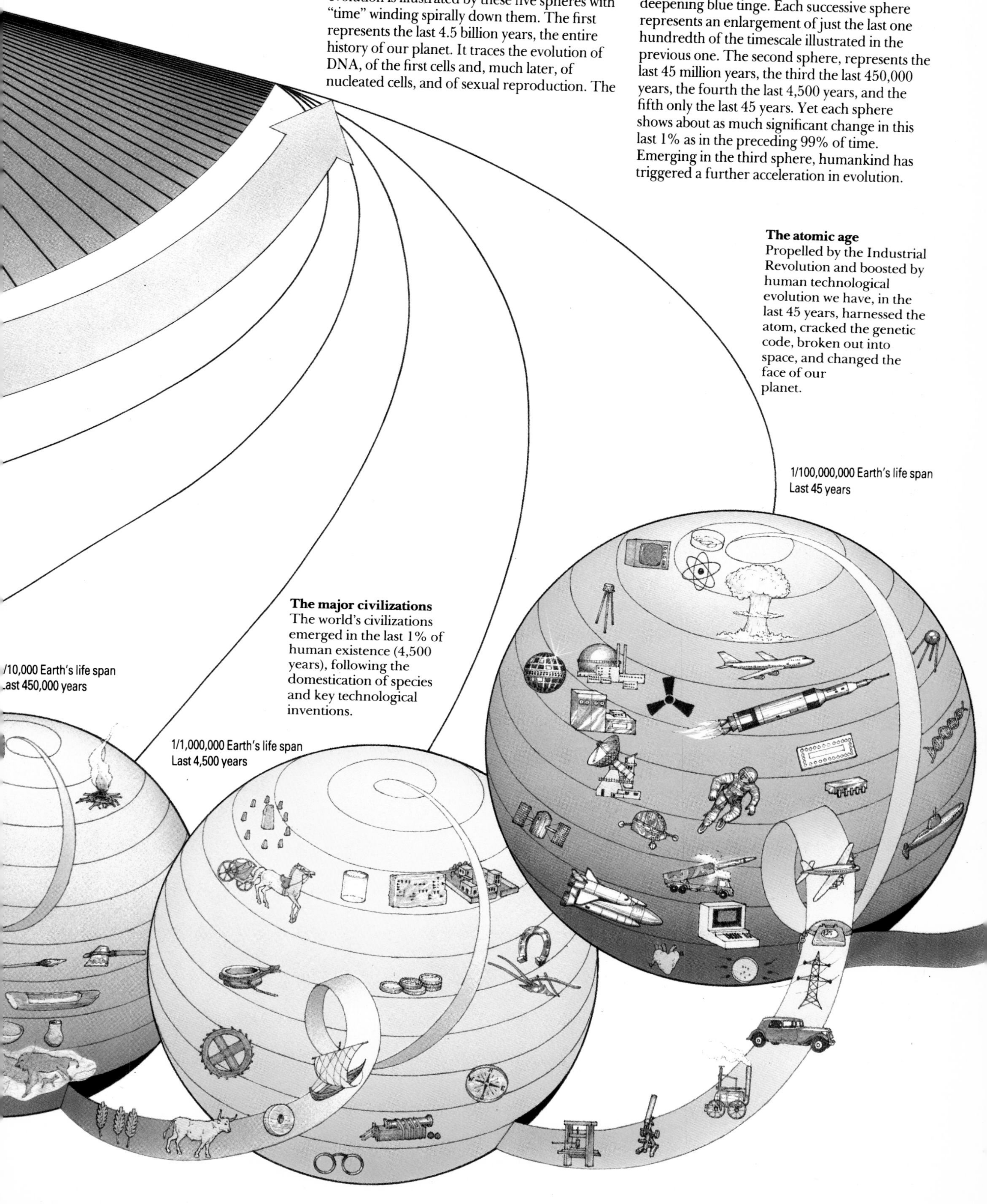

The atomic age

Propelled by the Industrial Revolution and boosted by human technological evolution we have, in the last 45 years, harnessed the atom, cracked the genetic code, broken out into space, and changed the face of our planet.

1/100,000,000 Earth's life span
Last 45 years

The major civilizations

The world's civilizations emerged in the last 1% of human existence (4,500 years), following the domestication of species and key technological inventions.

1/10,000 Earth's life span
Last 450,000 years

1/1,000,000 Earth's life span
Last 4,500 years

Latecomers to evolution

Gaia went its creative way for several billion years, becoming steadily more diverse, complex and fruitful. Then, in the last few seconds of life's "evolutionary day", *Homo sapiens* appeared – a creature that has wrought changes as great as several glaciations and other geological upheavals together, and has done it all within a flicker of the evolutionary eye. The evolution of *Homo sapiens* has produced a being that can think: a being that is aware, that can speculate about tomorrow.

Evolution has also equipped us to create our own form of planetary ecosystem. Whereas natural selection works through a trial-and-error process, undirected and unhurried, we can choose preferred forms of evolution, creating changes that might otherwise have taken millions of years to occur.

The greatest natural development through evolution in terms of energy conversion was the emergence of photosynthesis, two billion years ago. A mere 50,000 years ago we learned to harness fire, and thus to use the stored energy of plants in the form of wood. A few hundred years ago we moved on to exploit coal, then oil. Now, however, we are on the verge of widespread exploitation of the sun's energy through solar cells – potentially as marked an advance for Earth's course as that of photosynthesis itself. Similar breakthroughs include domestication of wild species and genetic engineering: quantum leaps to match the evolution of sexual reproduction.

Among the greatest advances of all is our ability to control disease, and thus to increase our numbers. Within the last 150 years, the human population has grown from around one billion in the 1830s to two billion in the 1930s, to four billion in 1975, and to almost five billion at present – with a further increase to over six billion projected by 1995. Herein we witness the phenomenon of exponential growth, a process that marks not only our increasing numbers, but also our consumption of energy and resources, our accumulating knowledge, and our expanding communications network.

Exponential growth is one of the most important concepts we shall encounter in this book. It is growth that is not simply additive (two plus two equals four and another two makes six); rather it is self-compounding (two multiplied by two equals four, multiplied by two equals eight). Very few people realize its implications for our future existence on Earth. If Africa, for example, maintains its present three percent growth rate until this time next century, its current half billion people will increase to 9.5 billion.

The advance beyond our entrenched expectation for exponential growth in consumption will probably represent the greatest evolutionary leap of all.

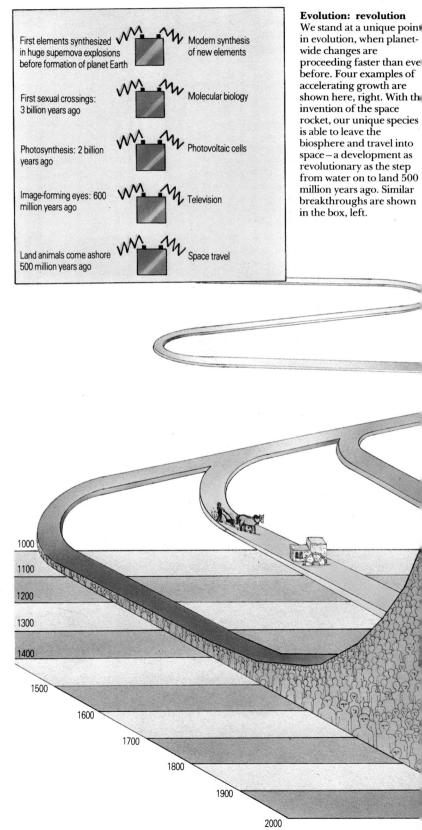

First elements synthesized in huge supernova explosions before formation of planet Earth — Modern synthesis of new elements

First sexual crossings: 3 billion years ago — Molecular biology

Photosynthesis: 2 billion years ago — Photovoltaic cells

Image-forming eyes: 600 million years ago — Television

Land animals come ashore 500 million years ago — Space travel

Evolution: revolution
We stand at a unique point in evolution, when planet-wide changes are proceeding faster than ever before. Four examples of accelerating growth are shown here, right. With the invention of the space rocket, our unique species is able to leave the biosphere and travel into space – a development as revolutionary as the step from water on to land 500 million years ago. Similar breakthroughs are shown in the box, left.

1000
1100
1200
1300
1400
1500
1600
1700
1800
1900
2000

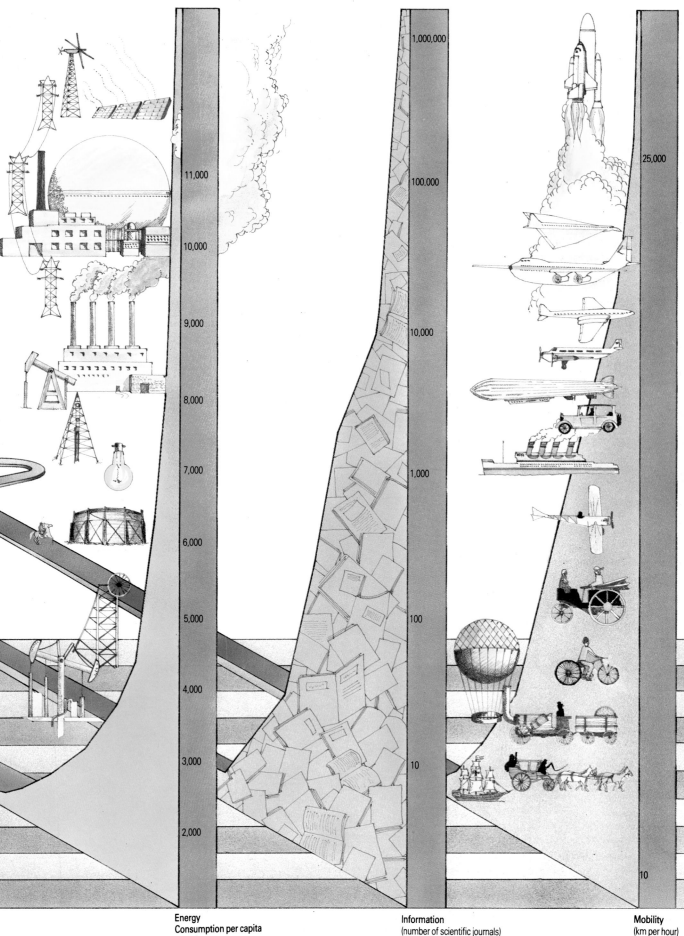

Energy
Consumption per capita
(watts)

11,000

10,000

9,000

8,000

7,000

6,000

5,000

4,000

3,000

2,000

Information
(number of scientific journals)

1,000,000

100,000

10,000

1,000

100

10

Mobility
(km per hour)

25,000

10

The long shadow

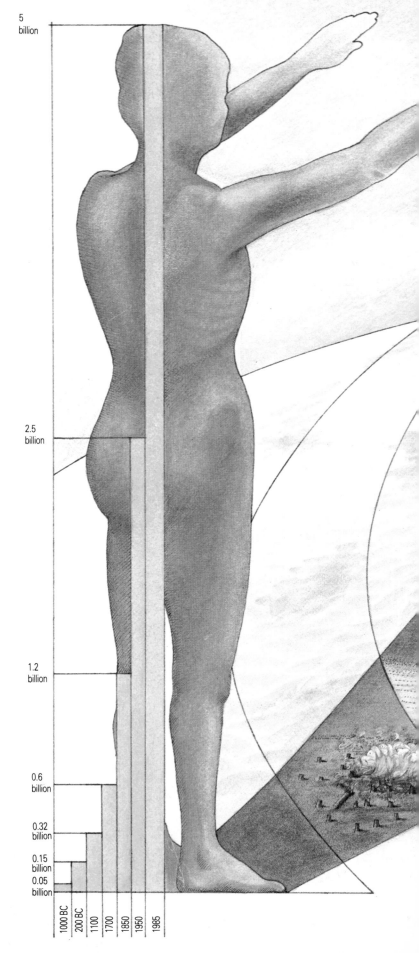

Today, the rise of human numbers casts a shadow over planet Earth. We have reached a total of almost five billion people, and we are plainly failing to feed, house, educate, and employ many of these in basically acceptable fashion. Worse, the human community is projected to reach at least ten billion before the population explosion fizzles out into zero growth early in the 22nd century.

The problem does not lie only in a sheer outburst of human numbers. It lies also in an outburst of human consumerism. One billion over-affluent people enjoy lifestyles that impose a grossly disproportionate pressure on our planetary ecosystem. This consumerism is powered in turn by a sudden expansion in technological know-how, enabling us to use and misuse ever-greater stocks of natural resources – even to use them up. In fact, rather than a "population crisis" or a "resource crisis", we should speak of a single over-arching crisis: the crisis of humankind. The shadow stems from all of us, and it will darken all our lives.

On land, we plough up virgin areas, even though most of them are marginal at best. Soil, one of the most precious of all resources, is washed or blown away in billions of tonnes every year. To compound this tragedy, large tracts of productive cropland are paved over each year, or "developed". Deserts expand, or rather degraded lands are tacked on to them, at a rate threatening a third of all arable land in the next 75 years. Forests in the tropics are chopped down with a zest that will leave little by the middle of the next century. As the forests fall, species in their millions lose their habitats, many of them disappearing for ever.

In the oceans, we ravage one fishery after another. We cause dolphins, seals, and other marine mammals to follow the sad track of the great whales. We pollute the seas, just as we poison lakes and rivers in virtually every part of the world. We use the skies as a dustbin, and we desecrate our landscapes with growing piles of refuse, some of it toxic. In the atmosphere, we disrupt the carbon dioxide balance, triggering climatic dislocations that will upset agriculture worldwide.

Not surprisingly, this overtaxing of the Earth's ecosystem leads to breakdowns of other sorts. As more people seek greater amounts of declining resources, conflicts erupt: more people have been killed through military conflagrations since World War II than all the soldiers in that war. In fact, it is breakdown in our social systems, our economic structures, and our political mechanisms that generate the greatest threat of all. The shadow over planet Earth will never be deeper and darker than when it is lengthened by a mushroom cloud.

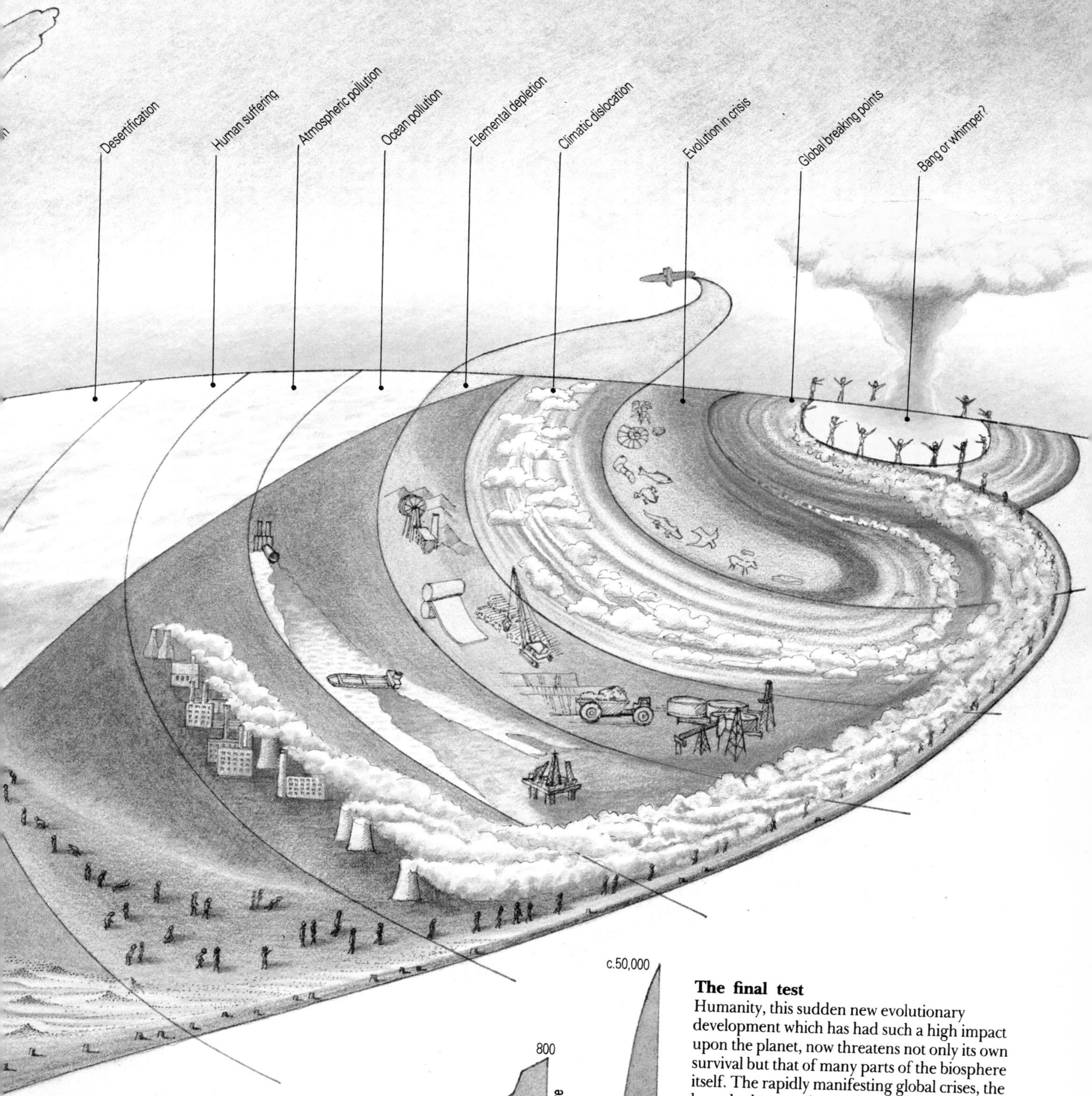

Desertification · Human suffering · Atmospheric pollution · Ocean pollution · Elemental depletion · Climatic dislocation · Evolution in crisis · Global breaking points · Bang or whimper?

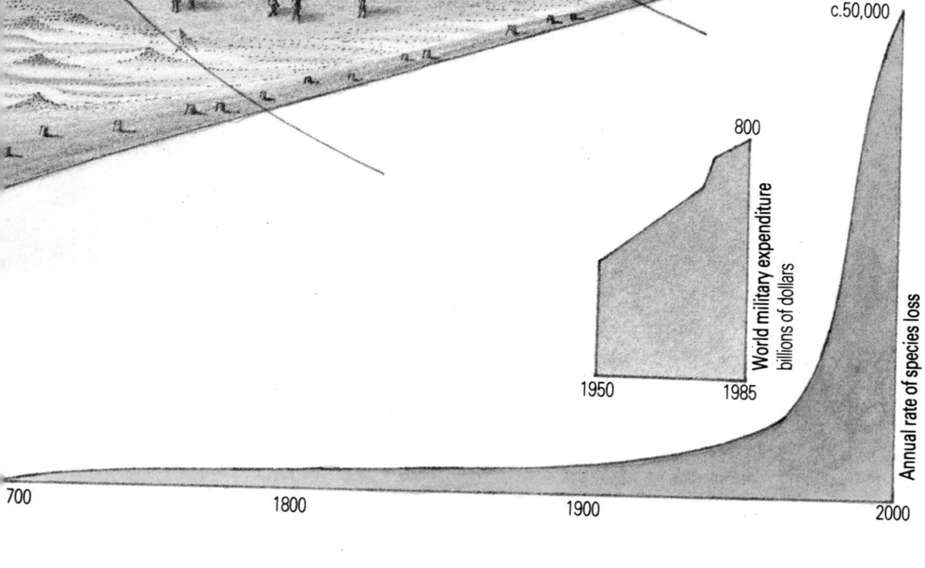

World military expenditure billions of dollars

800

c.50,000

1950 · 1985

Annual rate of species loss

700 · 1800 · 1900 · 2000

The final test
Humanity, this sudden new evolutionary development which has had such a high impact upon the planet, now threatens not only its own survival but that of many parts of the biosphere itself. The rapidly manifesting global crises, the long shadow, cast by the fast-growing figure of humankind, is stretching into the very heart of our biosphere. Since wandering early tribes began to fire the forests, this shadow has spread across land and ocean, through air, water, and soil, into space, and deep into the life-blood of evolution itself.

We might look upon our global crises as a challenge as well as a threat – we are sitting our final evolutionary examination for our viability as a species. Unfortunately, the time limit is rapidly approaching.

Crisis or challenge?

Humankind can be seen as either the climax of evolution's course, or as its greatest error. No other creature is a fraction so precocious. No other can think about the world, plan to make it better, and dream of the best possible. Yet no other reveals such capacity for perverse behaviour – for gross misuse of its habitat and for reckless proliferation of numbers, without thought for the consequences.

In certain senses, humanity is becoming a super-malignancy on the face of the planet, spreading with insidious effect and fomenting ultimate crisis in covert fashion. A cancer cell is unusually vital, since it replicates itself with remarkable vigour; it is also exceptionally stupid, since it ends by killing the host upon which it depends for its survival. But unlike the cancer cell, we are coming to realize the nature of what we are doing. Can we learn fast enough, act soon enough?

This is not the first time that the Earth's community has encountered crisis. Gaia has even benefited from periodic upheavals. Were it not for the dramatic demise of the dinosaurs, there would have been scant opportunity for mammals to become pre-eminent – with all that has meant for the supreme mammal, *Homo sapiens*. Out of crisis can come advance, provided the impetus of change does not "overshoot" into catastrophe. On past occasions, there have been thousands of years, even millions, for the corrective workings of the biosphere to adapt and adjust to new stresses. This time, there are just a few decades, far too short a period for Gaia to work its restorative course, unless it is done with the symbiotic support of humankind.

If we can match up to the crisis, Gaia may well move forward into an unprecedented period of development – development in its proper broad sense, embracing development of Earth's resources and of humanity's capacity for caring. If, however, we fail, *Homo sapiens* could eventually be discarded as an evolutionary blind-alley.

To achieve a breakthrough, we must learn a tough lesson. While it is often all right to adapt through small steps, improving an established course through "fine tuning", there are times when one must do an "about turn", and take more drastic corrective action. The tale of the French schoolchildren and their experimental frog is salutary. They took the frog and dropped it into a saucepan of boiling water, whereupon the frog skipped right out – instant rejection of an environment that proved distinctly unsuitable. But when the schoolchildren dropped the frog into a saucepan of cold water, and slowly heated it up, the frog swam round and round, adapting itself to the rising heat . . . until it quietly boiled to death.

Crises have both positive and negative characteristics. They can represent a threat to the status quo but at the same time can be seen as a symptom that something is wrong. They thus represent an opportunity to correct an imbalance and move on to a new level of organization. This is reflected in the Chinese character "ji" (here painted by a classical Chinese calligraphist) indicating both a crucial point, and an opportunity.

"Once a photograph of the Earth, taken from the outside is available ... a new idea as powerful as any other in history will be let loose".
FRED HOYLE (1948)

LAND

Introduced by Erik Eckholm

US environmental expert

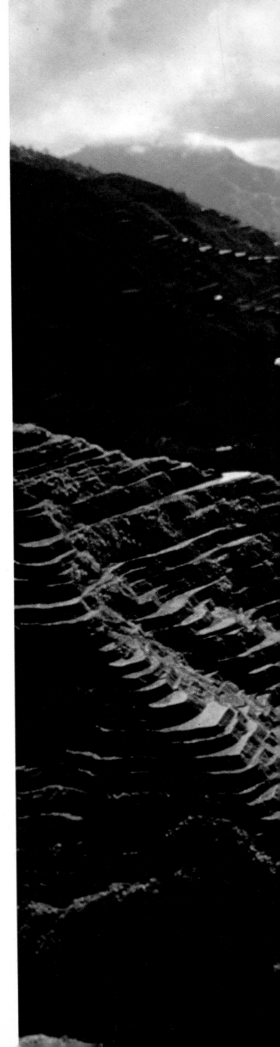

Those who live amid concrete, plastic, and computers can easily forget how fundamentally our well-being is linked to the land. Rural residents of the Third World, by contrast, suffer no such lapses: hundreds of millions still live quite directly off the soils, plants, and animals about them, and regard land ownership as a principal determinant of wealth, status, and power.

Food is only the most obvious link between people and the land. Wood, too, is a basic need. The poorest half of humanity requires wood for cooking, heating, and construction, and wood remains a crucial raw material of modern industrial societies. Less apparent are the critical ecological services provided by forests and wildlife. From the cycling of chemical elements to the moderation of microclimates, the suppression of pests to the renewal of soils, biological systems make the Earth habitable for humans.

Properly managed, the Earth's more fertile lands and its forests could meet everyone's food and wood needs abundantly and indefinitely. The persistent undernourishment of some 500 million people today does not stem from a global scarcity of resources: even as tens of thousands of babies die each day from diseases exacerbated by malnutrition, over one-third of the world's grain is fed to livestock to supply the meat-rich diet of the affluent.

The social and economic failings that permit hunger to persist are also, indirectly, undermining the Earth's ability to support human activity. Millions in the poorest countries are caught in a tragic cycle of poverty and land degradation. Lacking either fertile land or decent-paying jobs, they are forced to scratch a living from marginal lands where soils cannot sustain intensive cultivation. In semi-arid zones, cultivators shorten traditional fallow cycles, transforming ancestral fields to desert. Throughout the tropics, desperate farmers clear forests vital for fuel, goods, and protection of the environment. People are destroying the basis of their future welfare, not out of ignorance, but because their circumstances give them little alternative. A hungry family is not apt to worry much about forests and wildlife. A family without any fuel will strip live trees if necessary.

In recent years there has been a heightened awareness of the crucial contributions of renewable resources to development. Legislation is beginning to curb the damage caused by pellmell industrialization, reforestation is being attempted in many countries, and large natural areas are designated for protection. But in the face of rising landlessness, unemployment, and population pressure, a transition to sound, sustainable land use in the Third World will require changes reaching far beyond the environmental sector.

Citizens of richer countries must ensure that their corporations and consumption patterns do not intensify land-use problems in the Third World. But above all, national and global economic reforms are needed – giving the underclass a chance to earn a living without destroying soils and forests.

Those concerned about the future of the land and its resources have no choice but to be concerned about the politics of global development. For, in the end, the relations of people to the land reflect their relations to one another.

Erik Eckholm

THE LAND POTENTIAL

Marvellous stuff, soil. Sterile and boring as it may appear, often mucky too, this thin layer covering the planet's land surface is the biosphere's foundation, our primary resource.

Soil is as lively as an army of migrating wildebeest and as fascinating, even beautiful, as a flock of flamingoes. Teeming with life of myriad forms, soil deserves to be classified as an ecosystem in itself – or rather, as many ecosystems. One hectare of good-quality soil in a temperate zone may contain at least 300 million small invertebrates – mites, millipedes, insects, worms, and other mini-creatures. As for micro-organisms, a mere 30 grams of soil may contain one million bacteria of just one type, as well as 100,000 yeast cells and 50,000 bits of fungus mycelium. Without these micro-organisms, the soil could not convert nitrogen, phosphorus, and sulphur to forms available to plants.

According to Harvard's Professor Edward O. Wilson, there is far more biological complexity in a handful of soil in Virginia than on the entire surface of Jupiter. Yet we invest more money in exploring the planets than in finding out how our basic life-support systems work here on Earth.

So next time you tread on earth (as opposed to concrete or asphalt), take a look at what lies at your feet. It is likely to be a fairly loose material, half made up of masses of tiny particles, the other half of water and air. This curious assembly of inorganic constituents derives originally from rock which, being weathered by rainwater, atmospheric gases, ice, and roots, has slowly broken down into a form in which it can support multitudes of life-forms. These, in turn, enable it to support plants. Through a constantly self-reinforcing process, the soil becomes enriched with dead organic matter, some of which is called humus – the stuff that helps to make soil fertile.

The process of soil formation is slow. At best, even when sediments build up quickly, formation of 30 centimetres may take 50 years. More usually, when new soil is formed from parent rocks, one centimetre may need from 100 to 1,000 years. So to form soil to the depth of this page could take as long as 10,000 years. Unfortunately, reversing the process by human or natural disturbance is all too quick – soils can be degraded in a fraction of the time they take to form (see p. 41).

Of the Earth's total ice-free land surface, only 1.5 billion hectares (about 11 percent) can be readily cultivated. With human management, however, and

The fertile soil

Not all the soil which covers the Earth's ice-free land surface is suited for growing crops. In fact, of the total area of some 13 billion ha (about one-quarter of the globe), a mere 11% presents no serious limitations to agriculture. The rest is either too dry, too wet, too poor in nutrients (mineral-stressed), too shallow, or too cold.

As much as 28% of the world's land surface suffers from drought (not so surprising, when you consider that the Sahara occupies nearly a billion hectares). Mineral-stressed soils account for a further 23%. Soils that are too thin to be much use cover 22%, while waterlogged soils account for 10%. Permafrost soils (ground that is permanently frozen) cover 6% – and these do not include Antarctica or Greenland.

The illustration shows how the world's soil resources are shared out, each segment of the "globe" showing the percentage of total land area and proportions of soil types for the continent it represents. Notice how the fertile soil is far from evenly distributed, with Europe claiming the largest portion relative to its land area. The pie-charts on the continents show how the land is being used: for forest, grazing, cultivation, or "other" (wild, waste, or urban).

Arable 11%

Potentially arable 24%

Total land area 13 billion ha

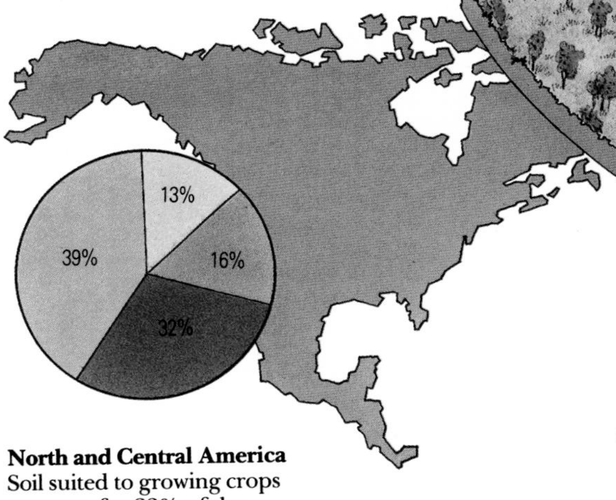

13%
39%
16%
32%

North and Central America
Soil suited to growing crops accounts for 22% of the land, and yet only 13% is actually used as cropland. Between 1945 and 1975, about 30 million ha of land in the US were lost under concrete and asphalt, half of this being arable land.

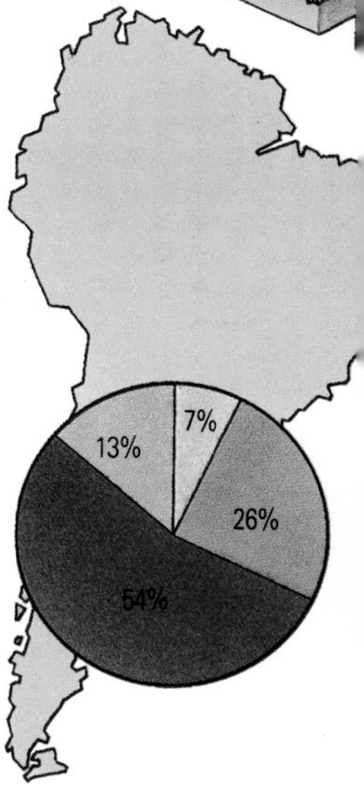

Permafrost

Water excess

Shallow depth

Drought

Mineral stress (poor in nutrients)

No serious limitations for agriculture

Arable and cropland

Grazing land

Forest land

Other land

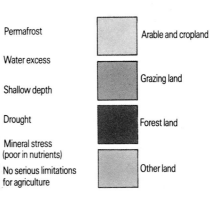

7%
13%
26%
54%

South America
The major limiting factor mineral stress (47%), the areas affected generally being vast tracts of forest. (Tropical forest soils are typically low in nutrients.) Less than half of the fertile soil is used for crops.

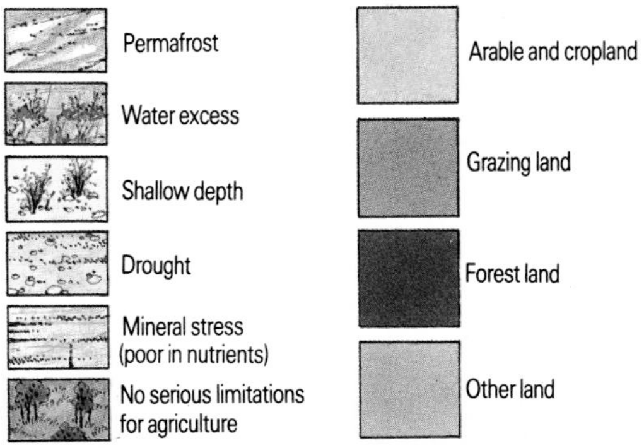

How much land could we cultivate?
We cultivate only 11% of the Earth's surface, and yet some experts believe that as much as 24% could be used for crops.

Litter, humus, and top mineral soil

Coloured mineral soil

Parent rock material

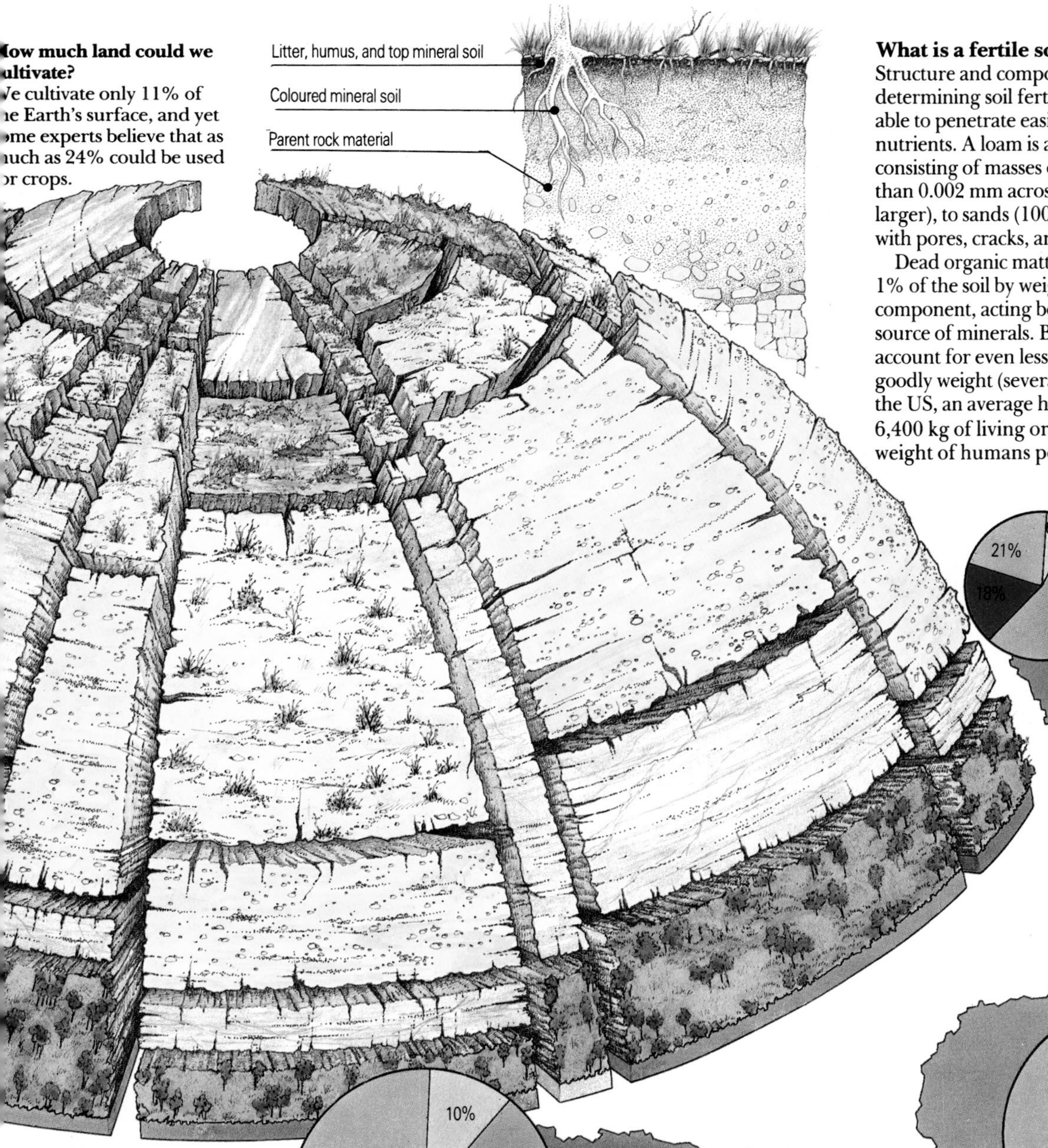

What is a fertile soil?
Structure and composition are key factors in determining soil fertility. Plant roots must be able to penetrate easily to obtain dissolved nutrients. A loam is a naturally fertile soil, consisting of masses of particles from clays (less than 0.002 mm across), through silts (10 times larger), to sands (100 times larger), interspersed with pores, cracks, and crevices.

Dead organic matter amounts to only about 1% of the soil by weight, but it is a vital component, acting both as a sponge and as a source of minerals. By contrast, living organisms account for even less – 0.1% – though still a goodly weight (several tonnes per hectare). In the US, an average hectare of soil supports 6,400 kg of living organisms, while the average weight of humans per hectare is a mere 18 kg.

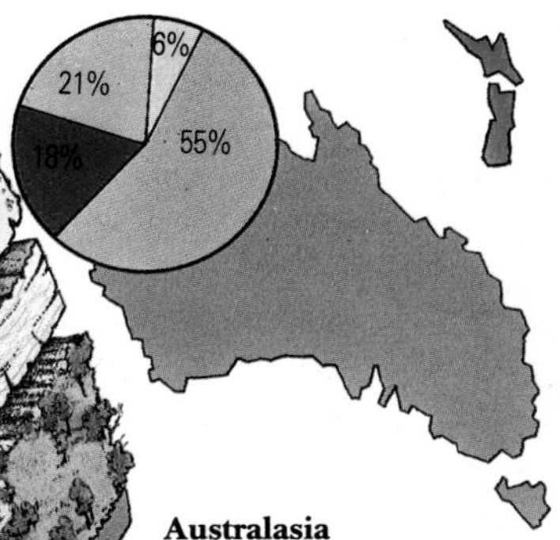

Australasia
As with Africa, drought is the main agricultural constraint, affecting some 55% of land area. Australians do not make full use of their good soil: 15% is fertile, yet only 6% is cultivated.

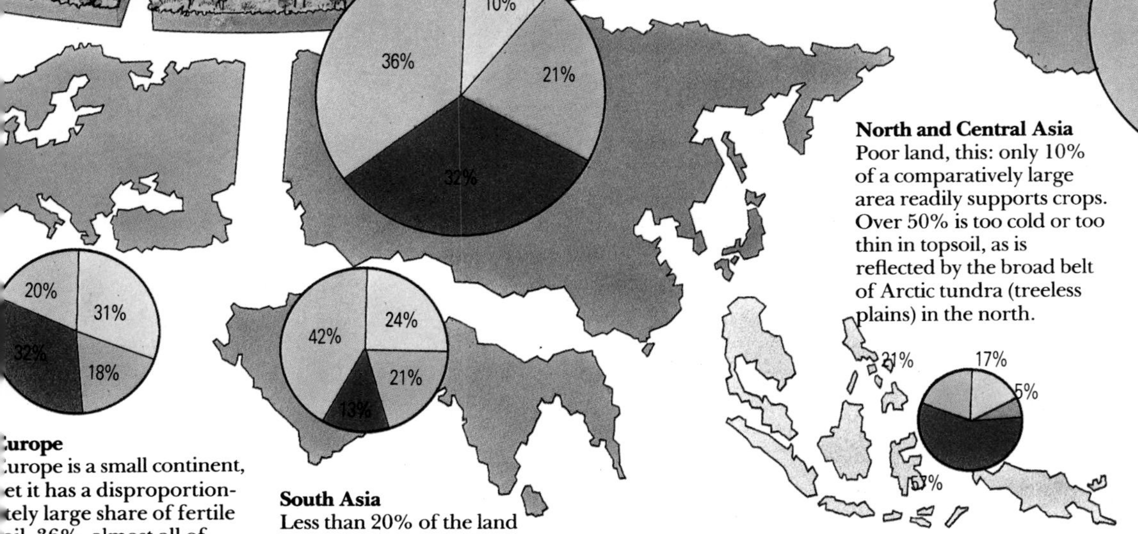

North and Central Asia
Poor land, this: only 10% of a comparatively large area readily supports crops. Over 50% is too cold or too thin in topsoil, as is reflected by the broad belt of Arctic tundra (treeless plains) in the north.

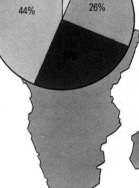

Africa
A huge 44% of the African continent is affected by drought, as is shown by the proportion of land designated "other land". However, 16% is considered suited to agriculture, yet only 6% is actually cultivated.

Europe
Europe is a small continent, yet it has a disproportionately large share of fertile soil, 36%, almost all of which is farmed – 31% of the land area is cultivated. One-third of all soils suffer from mineral stress.

South Asia
Less than 20% of the land is suited to crops, yet 24% is cultivated. This indicates working of unsuitable land (though irrigation can help) – a reflection of the needs of the huge population.

Southeast Asia
Fourteen percent of the land is fertile, yet 17% is given over to crops (cf. S Asia). Note that nearly 60% of the soils are nutrient-deficient, again correlating (as elsewhere in the tropics) with the proportion of forested land.

at very considerable expense, it is estimated that an extra 1.7 billion hectares could be brought under the plough.

Our green planet

In the end, or rather in the beginning, we are all plants. Without the green mantle for our planet supplied by over one-third of a million plant species, animal life as we know it (including *Homo sapiens*) would never have evolved. Millions of years ago, it was the rise of plant life that boosted the stock of oxygen in the atmosphere from a trace gas to the one-fifth proportion that fostered the outburst of animal life. Some biologists believe that the demise of one plant species may eventually lead to the extinction of up to 30 animal species, as the consequences reverberate up the food chains.

Plants convert sunlight into the stored chemical energy on which all animal life depends for food

(and humans for fuel too). The enormous diversity of plants offers adaptations to every conceivable environment, from desert to tundra, the tropics having the richest speciation. We depend on this green wealth at every turn – from indirect benefits for soil and climate to direct supplies to our tables, factories, and hospitals.

How much plant life is there on the planet? And where does it grow most abundantly? Answers to these questions suggest where we might look to increase our growing of crops or our production of fibre. "Phytomass" is the scientific term used to measure an amount of dry plant material (undried plant matter is three or four times heavier), and it is expressed in tonnes per hectare. When we speak of dry animal matter, we use the term "zoomass"; phytomass and zoomass together comprise biomass. Of all biomass on the face of the planet, 99 percent is plant material.

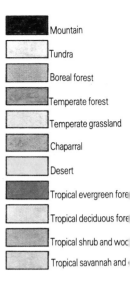

Mountain
Tundra
Boreal forest
Temperate forest
Temperate grassland
Chaparral
Desert
Tropical evergreen fore
Tropical deciduous fore
Tropical shrub and woo
Tropical savannah and

The green potential

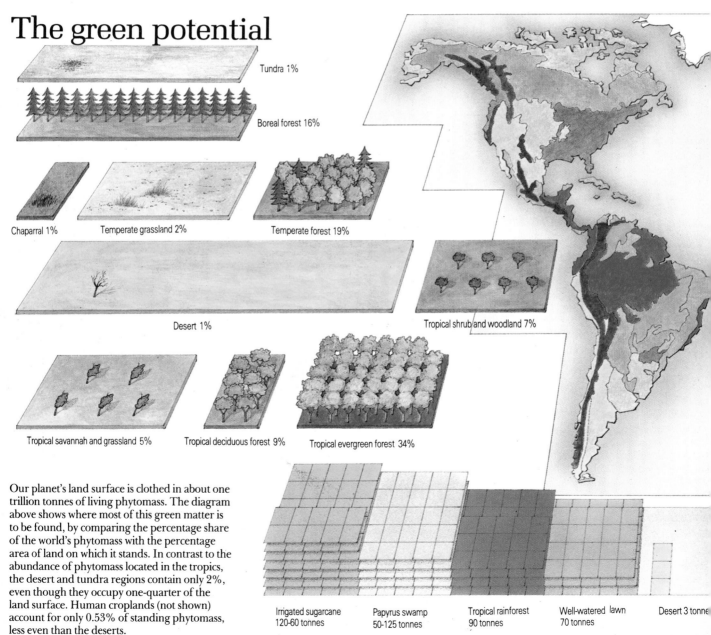

Tundra 1%

Boreal forest 16%

Chaparral 1%   Temperate grassland 2%   Temperate forest 19%

Desert 1%

Tropical shrub and woodland 7%

Tropical savannah and grassland 5%   Tropical deciduous forest 9%   Tropical evergreen forest 34%

Our planet's land surface is clothed in about one trillion tonnes of living phytomass. The diagram above shows where most of this green matter is to be found, by comparing the percentage share of the world's phytomass with the percentage area of land on which it stands. In contrast to the abundance of phytomass located in the tropics, the desert and tundra regions contain only 2%, even though they occupy one-quarter of the land surface. Human croplands (not shown) account for only 0.53% of standing phytomass, less even than the deserts.

Irrigated sugarcane 120-60 tonnes   Papyrus swamp 50-125 tonnes   Tropical rainforest 90 tonnes   Well-watered lawn 70 tonnes   Desert 3 tonne

Not surprisingly, we find that forests contain more than three-quarters of all terrestrial phytomass – in fact some 950 billion tonnes. Of this amount, well over half (or about one-third of Earth's land biomass) is contained in tropical forests, even though they cover less than 10 percent of the land surface. Curiously enough, our cultivated crops amount to less than .7 billion tonnes of standing phytomass, a trifling 0.5 percent, even though they cover more of the land surface than tropical forests.

Comparing the amounts of total living phytomass is only one way of estimating the "green potential" of different ecosystems and regions. Another way is to consider the amount of new plant material generated each year. Again, forests are in the forefront, accounting for 37 percent of Earth's annual production of more than 133 billion tonnes. Tropical forests account for 23 percent. With year-round growth, tropical forests can produce as

much as 90 tonnes of plant material per hectare per year, or almost twice as much phytomass as is generated by temperate forests (and a higher level of productivity than for any other vegetation type except for a few forestry plantations, water weeds such as water hyacinth, ultra-moist savannahs, and high-yielding crops such as sugarcane). Because organic matter is speedily decomposed, however, annual net increment in virgin tropical forest is usually nil. Thanks to intensive agriculture, our crops produce about 15 billion tonnes of phytomass each year (11 percent of the world's total). A good corn crop in the US can generate 15-20 tonnes of plant material per hectare per year, while white potatoes can yield almost 30 tonnes.

In general, the amount of new phytomass produced each year in moist parts of the world doubles as one moves from the boreal to the temperate zones, and more than doubles as one moves from

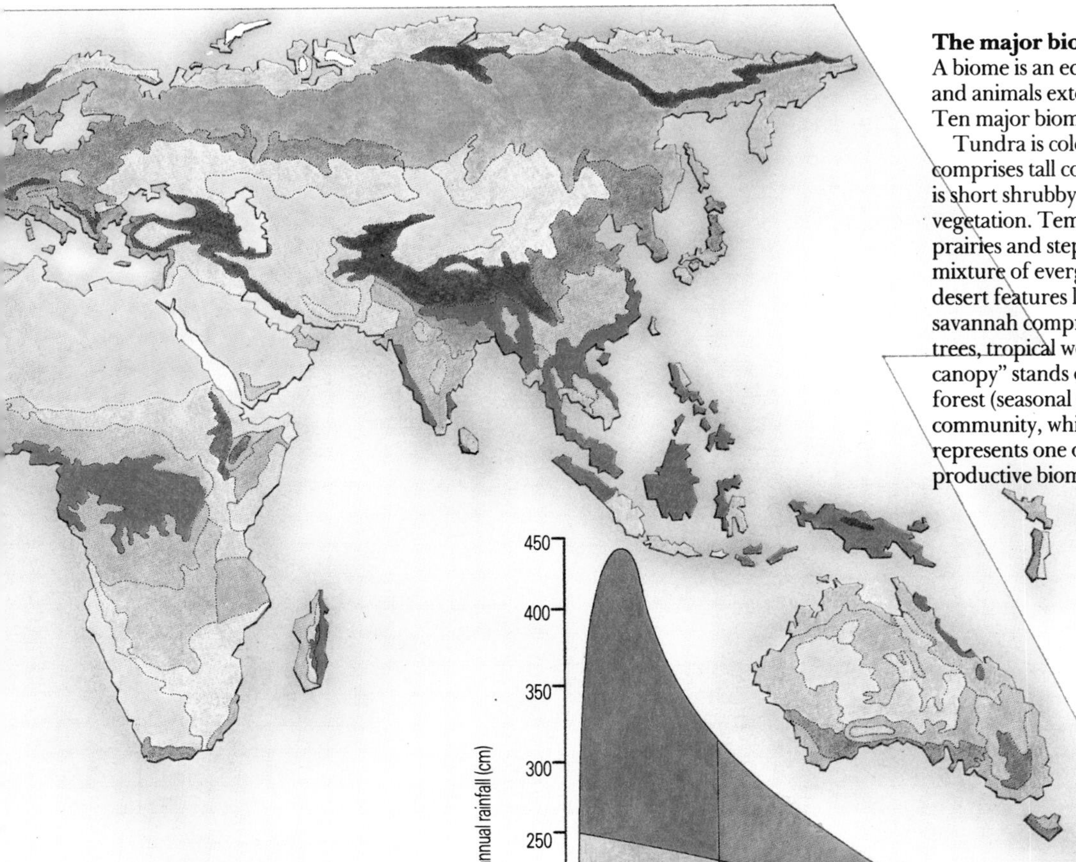

The major biomes
A biome is an ecological community of plants and animals extending over a large natural area. Ten major biomes are shown on the map.

Tundra is cold semi-desert, boreal forest comprises tall conifer formations, and chaparral is short shrubby "Mediterranean-type" vegetation. Temperate grasslands include prairies and steppes, while temperate forest is a mixture of evergreen and deciduous trees. Hot desert features little vegetation, tropical savannah comprises grassland with scattered trees, tropical woodlands amount to "open canopy" stands of trees. Tropical deciduous forest (seasonal or monsoon) is a closed-canopy community, while tropical evergreen forest represents one of the most diverse and productive biomes in the world.

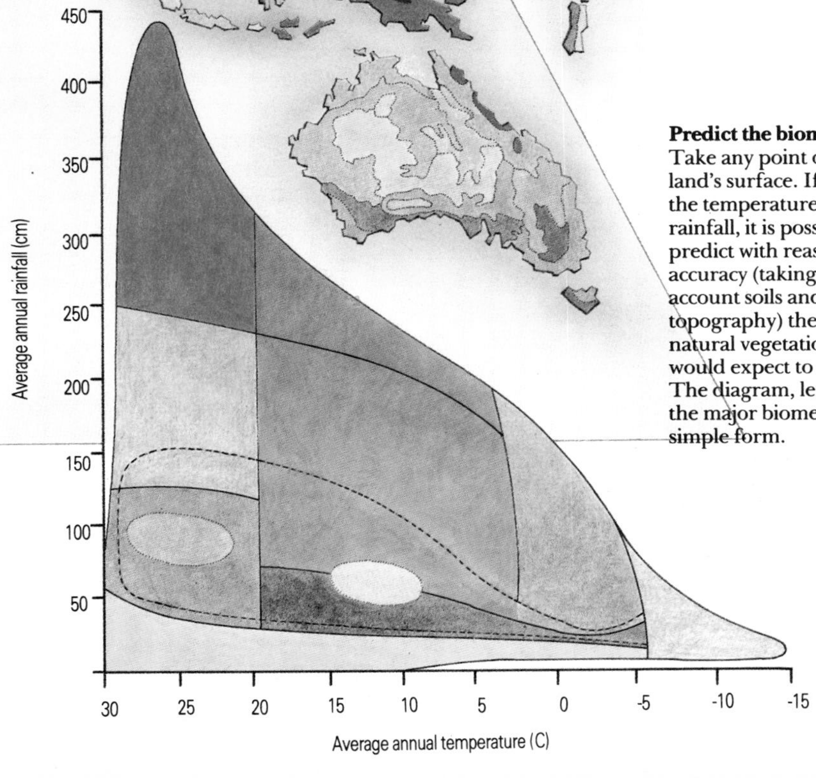

Predict the biome
Take any point on the land's surface. If you know the temperature and rainfall, it is possible to predict with reasonable accuracy (taking into account soils and topography) the type of natural vegetation you would expect to find there. The diagram, left, classifies the major biomes in a simple form.

Growth potential
Plant growth, or "primary productivity", ranges from virtually zero in deserts to vast amounts in tropical forests. Human intervention can modify the outcome more than we may suppose. If we mow a lawn twice a week, holding back the plant growth to its earliest and most vigorous phase, the lawn generates large quantities of plant material. Left uncut, the lawn's growth rate will fast fall away, resulting in only a fraction as much productivity. The diagram, left, compares productivity (tonnes wet weight/ha/year) in five plant communities: a desert, a temperate lawn, a tropical rainforest, a papyrus swamp, and an irrigated sugarcane plantation.

the temperate zones to the tropics. Similarly, ecological complexity increases towards the tropics, from "simple" communities with few species in the polar regions, to communities with great abundance and diversity at the Equator.

Forests and the biosphere

Majestic and diverse, the world's forests represent some of the most exuberant expressions of nature. Whether among the giant Douglas firs of Oregon, the aged oaks of Sherwood Forest in Britain, the vast fir forests of Central Europe, or in a rainforest in Amazonia or Borneo, we feel small and insignificant by comparison. Ranging across some 30 percent of the planet's land surface, forests are the climax ecosystems of a green and flowering world. They tend to support greater stocks of biomass, produce new biomass faster, and harbour greater abundance of species (both plant and animal) than any other ecological zone.

Not only are forests powerhouses of basic biospheric processes, notably photosynthesis and biological growth, creation of fertile humus, and transfer of energy, but their exceptional contribution to the biosphere goes much further. They play major roles in the planetary recycling of carbon, nitrogen, and oxygen. They help to determine temperature, rainfall and various other climatic conditions. They are often the fountainheads of rivers. They constitute the major gene reservoirs of our planet, and they are the main sites of emergence of new species. In short, they contribute as much to evolution as all other biomes.

Among the many goods supplied by forests, the principal one is wood. Wood serves many purposes. It is one of the first raw materials that we use, and it is likely to be our last. It plays a part in more activities of a modern economy than any other commodity, and almost every major industry depends on forest products in at least one of its processes. A house wall built of wood requires about 20 percent less energy for heating and 30 percent less for cooling than a house made of other construction materials. Wood also serves a multitude of purposes as plywood, veneer, hardboard, particleboard, and chipboard. It is competitive too, since substitutes such as steel, aluminium, cement, and plastics need more energy in their production. Furthermore, we use much wood in the form of paper—a key medium of civilization. Not surprisingly, the total of industrial timber that we consume has now risen to 1.5 billion tonnes, an amount that exceeds steel and plastics combined. An average American citizen uses more than twice as much wood as all metals together.

From a human standpoint, we can look upon forests as the great providers and protectors. They maintain ecological diversity for us, they safeguard watersheds, they protect soil from erosion, they supply fuel for about half the world's people, they provide wood for paperpulp and industrial timber,

The global forest

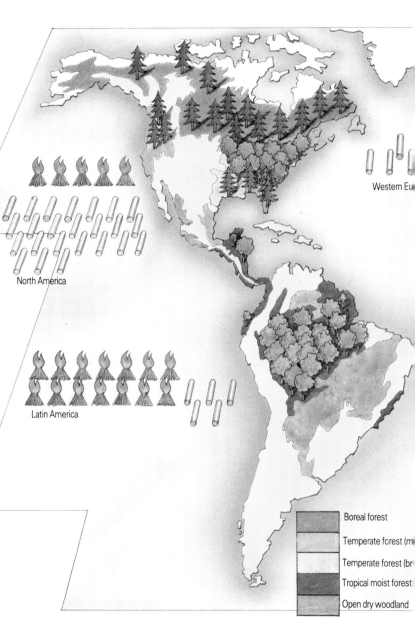

Western Eu

North America

Latin America

Boreal forest

Temperate forest (m

Temperate forest (br

Tropical moist forest

Open dry woodland

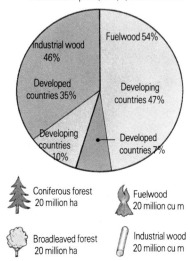

Wood consumption (1980) 3,159 million cu m

Fuelwood 54%

Industrial wood 46%

Developed countries 35%

Developing countries 47%

Developing countries 10%

Developed countries 7%

Coniferous forest
20 million ha

Fuelwood
20 million cu m

Broadleaved forest
20 million ha

Industrial wood
20 million cu m

Land where the crowns of trees cover more than 20% of the area is known as closed forest More than half the world's closed forests comprise broadleaved trees, many of which grow in Latin America. Of coniferous forests, three-fifths are located in the USSR, and over one-quarter in North America.

The tree symbols on the map represent a fixed area of closed forest. The log and firewood symbols in the ocean areas indicate how much wood is used for fuel and industri purposes; combined they give the annual woodcut (1980) for each region.

World wood consumption

Estimates indicate that we now consume 3 billic cubic metres of wood a year, enough to cover a fair-sized city, such as Birmingham (UK), to th height of a 10-storey building. Fifty-five percen of this wood comes from broadleaved trees

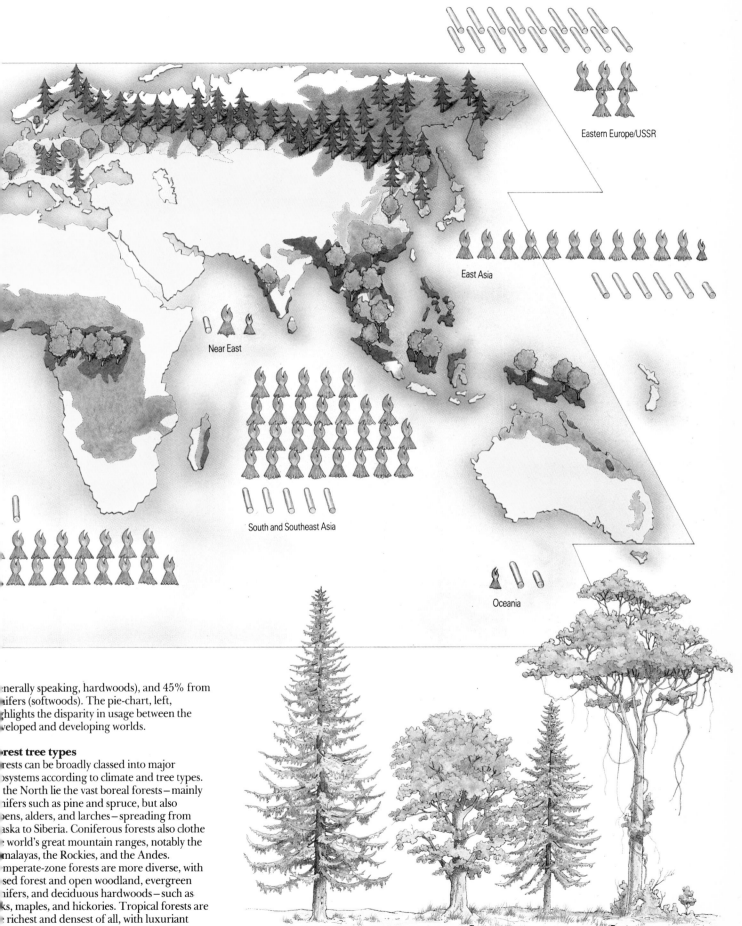

Eastern Europe/USSR

East Asia

Near East

South and Southeast Asia

Oceania

nerally speaking, hardwoods), and 45% from
ifers (softwoods). The pie-chart, left,
hlights the disparity in usage between the
eloped and developing worlds.

rest tree types

rests can be broadly classed into major
osystems according to climate and tree types.
the North lie the vast boreal forests – mainly
ifers such as pine and spruce, but also
ens, alders, and larches – spreading from
aska to Siberia. Coniferous forests also clothe
e world's great mountain ranges, notably the
malayas, the Rockies, and the Andes.
mperate-zone forests are more diverse, with
sed forest and open woodland, evergreen
ifers, and deciduous hardwoods – such as
ks, maples, and hickories. Tropical forests are
richest and densest of all, with luxuriant
wths and great diversity of species.

Boreal forest   Temperate forest   Tropical forest

and they are pleasing to the eye. Without them, our planetary home would be a lot poorer. Yet in certain parts of the tropics, we are losing this heritage at an alarming rate (see p. 42).

Powerhouses of the tropics

Tropical forests form a green band around the Equator, extending roughly 10 degrees north and south. This means that they account for only a small proportion, about 8 percent, of the Earth's land surface. Yet they comprise almost half of all growing wood on the face of the planet, and harbour at least two-fifths of Earth's species (plant and animal)–a genetic resource that increasingly serves our daily welfare via agriculture, medicine, and industry (see pp 146-7). They also comprise the most complex and diverse ecosystems on Earth.

A one-and-a-half hectare patch of forest may hold over 200 different trees alone. They grow in multi-layered profusion: tall "emergents" piercing the canopy; lianas, stranglers, and climbers with aerial roots festooning their buttressed trunks; lichens, mosses, and algae adorning every surface; and an array of fungi colonizing the forest floor. Almost every branch is hung with epiphytic ferns, orchids, or bromeliads, while smaller trees and shrubs compete for light and space below. This intricate plant life supports an even greater diversity of insect and animal life, much of it specialized, with life cycles linked to certain plants.

Yet for all their intrinsic interest, these forests remain almost unknown to us. Scientists have identified less than one in six of their two million species (a minimum estimate). If you were to go into a tract of forest with a net, you would need only a few hours to catch an insect not yet known to science (and to be named after you). We now know more about certain sectors of the moon's surface than about the heartlands of Amazonia–and the moon will be around for a long while to come, whereas tropical forests are being disrupted and destroyed with every tick of the clock. Each time a small area of forest is cleared, several species, perhaps potentially valuable, are lost forever.

Most people (developers included) are surprised to learn that the soils that support the most luxuriant tropical forests are generally of low quality and unsuited for agriculture. Receiving very little of their nutrient supplies from the shallow, impoverished soil, tropical forests have built up stocks of key minerals above the ground, within the vegetation. When leaves fall, or a tree crashes to the ground, decomposer organisms recycle the nutrients within a few weeks, in contrast with the many months required in a temperate forest. Thus tropical forests have an almost leak-proof system to retain nutrients within their living structures. They flourish despite the soils, not because of them.

In so far as tropical forests constitute a kind of benchmark for life processes, we shall not understand life properly until we understand tropical

Tropical forests

The gloom and a solemn silence combine to produce a sense of the past, the primeval–almost of the infinite. The tropical forest is a world in which man seems an intruder, and where he feels overwhelmed by the contemplation of the ever-acting forces, which, from the simple elements of the atmosphere, build up a great mass of vegetation which overshadows, and almost seems to oppress the earth.
ALFRED RUSSELL WALLACE, NATURALIST AND EXPLORER ON HIS TRIP TO AMAZONIA, 1890.

There are four main types of tropical forest: evergreen forest, moist forest, deciduous forest and dry woodland. The first three types have been grouped on the map as moist forest, distinct from open dry woodland.

The pattern of forest regeneration
When large gaps in the forest canopy occur (such as those caused by slash-and-burn agriculture, landslides and typhoons), the microclimate of the mature forest disappears. The forest floor becomes exposed to direct sunlight; the air and soil become dry; and temperatures fluctuate widely between day and night. Certain pioneer species are adapted to take advantage of these conditions, and for them growth is fast and life is short. Most die within 15 years and their timber is light and soft. Second-wave pioneers also demand plenty of light and grow rapidly, but live longer, perhaps more than a century. These trees fix large amounts of nitrogen, playing a most important role in restoring the nutrient bank and thereby setting the stage for the return of the mature-phase species. Bulldozing of all vegetation has serious repercussions. The soils may become irreversibly impoverished. In the end, all that may replace what was once spectacular forest is scrappy, low-grade scrub.

Low-grade scrub   Total forest destruction

Evergreen forest receives at least 4,000 mm of rainfall a year, with hardly any dry season. It is entirely closed at its canopy, and features an abundance of luxuriant vegetation. Occasionally standing 60 m high, the several distinct strata give an impression of "forest piled upon forest". In wetter areas, it is known as rainforest.

Moist forest receives at least 2,000 mm of rainfall a year (no more than 3 months with less than 100 mm). It is very similar to evergreen forest, except that it lacks the ecological complexity.

Deciduous forest receives 1,500 mm of rainfall a year, with 4-6 months virtually dry. Hence the forest loses its leaves for extended periods. Open dry woodland or wooded savannah receives less than 1,000 mm of rainfall, and often experiences prolonged drought.

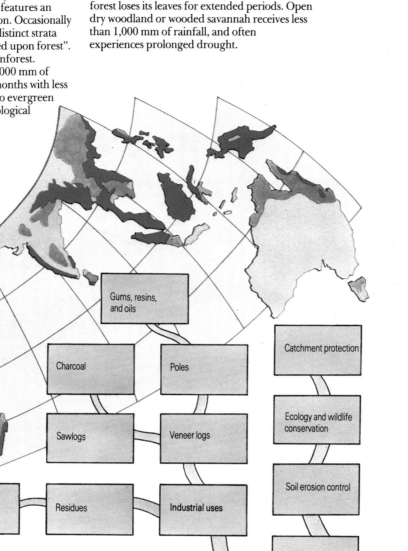

Open dry woodland

Tropical moist forest (evergreen and seasonal)

Gums, resins, and oils

Charcoal

Poles

Sawlogs

Veneer logs

Pulpwood

Residues

Industrial uses

Catchment protection

Ecology and wildlife conservation

Soil erosion control

Ecological effects

Fuelwood and charcoal

Agricultural uses

Building poles

Pit-sawing and saw milling

Weaving materials

Rearing silkworms and bee-keeping

Special woods and ashes

Indigenous consumption

How we benefit from tropical forests
We derive many benefits from the mere existence of tropical forests. Through their watershed effects, they act like a sponge, soaking up rainfall before releasing it slowly and steadily into rivers. They protect precious topsoil. Above all, they regulate climate, whether at regional or global levels.

The "tree" diagram, right, summarizes only some of the goods and services available from tropical forests that already make a solid contribution to peoples' lives. If this diagram were to be redrawn in 20 years' time, how many more boxes would there be?

rest   Forest cut and burned   Farm in use (2-3 years)   Two years later: pioneers established   After 15 years, small primaries emerge   After 60 years, primaries dominate   After 100 years, as uncut forest

forests. They are revealing more about evolution than all other natural environments put together.

The human landscape

Through our agriculture, both crop growing and stock husbandry, we have markedly altered the face of the Earth. For at least 10,000 years, we have been involved in the landscapes around us – to an extent that is often not recognized. When visitors gaze at the autumn foliage in New England, and they marvel at the brilliant colours of the maple trees, they may suppose that they are looking at a specially splendid example of nature's handiwork. But in fact they are delighting in a spectacle more colourful than that which greeted the Pilgrim Fathers.

Through human agricultural intervention in the forest, the species' combinations have been modified in favour of those with the famous foliage.

At the entrance to Serengeti Park in northern Tanzania stands a notice, "Here the world is young and fragile, as it was in the beginning". A beautiful thought, but a far from correct one. Serengeti in 1984 is far different from what it was in 1950, let alone in the time of primeval Africa. In recent decades, local Masai pastoralists, with their expanding herds, have taken to firing the savannahs more extensively at the end of the dry season in order to burn off the dry withered stalks and make way for a fresh green flush at the onset of the rains. As a consequence, much of the Serengeti ecosystem

Humans on the land

When people manipulate the environment, allying nurture with nature, they achieve some remarkable harvests of crops. The first photograph, right, is an example of a highly energy-intensive form of agriculture – through massive investment of money and energy, the Dutch greenhouses achieve year-round productivity in a cool climate. The central photograph shows an experimental desert reclamation scheme in Western Australia. This is an extremely efficient method of growing crops on what would otherwise be barren land: the water is applied directly to the plant, in regulated amounts. The terraced rice paddies in Bali, far right, also represent a form of energy-intensive agriculture, but in this case the energy is supplied by human labour. Irrigated by water from the mountains, these ancient terraces support up to three rice crops each year.

World agricultural patterns

Some communities practise agriculture by relying heavily on machinery and other capital inputs, others must call on human labour as the main contribution. The first approach allows huge areas to be farmed through the efforts of a small proportion of the labour force, the second demands the work of a much larger share of the population (see symbols below for proportions). A prime way to increase productivity is via irrigation: if other countries were to follow the example of China, their existing croplands could generate more food.

The diagram, right, shows the world divided into seven regions. Four elements (proportion of the labour force engaged in agriculture, number of hectares of arable land per worker, number of tractors in service, and proportion of irrigated land) are compared for each region.

Greenhouses glinting in the sun – intensive agriculture in the Netherlands

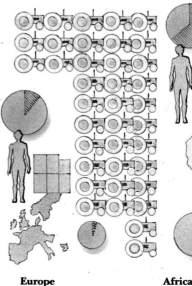

Proportion of arable land irrigated

Proportion of workforce engaged in agriculture

Number of hectares of arable land per worker

10% of world labour force

Number of tractors in service per 500 ha

N America, Japan, Oceania
With the smallest agricultural workforce, this region surpasses all others in food production per hectare.

Europe
This region has the greatest number of tractors per unit of farmland, which reflects its highly intensive agriculture.

Africa
Proportionally, Africa has the biggest agricultural workforce, the smallest number of tractors, and the smallest irrigated area.

contains more, and more vigorous, grassland than it did only a third of a century ago – which is good news for grass-eaters of all kinds, not only cattle but wildebeest, zebras, and gazelles. So much extra grass is now available that the wild Serengeti herbivores have expanded from only half a million to well over four million.

But human involvement with the landscape has not always been so benign. The Fertile Crescent in the Middle East, celebrated in the Bible for its fecundity, is now half barren. Forests virtually everywhere have been mis-used and over-used. In the folklore tales of many human communities, we hear how forests have traditionally been regarded as dark foreboding places.

Not only agricultural interventions have modified our landscapes. Technological intrusions too; when the Suez Canal was opened about 100 years ago, it gave a powerful boost to the tea trade, also to the emergent rice trade. Large tracts of forest were cleared in India, Sri Lanka, Burma and Thailand, to cater for demand for these two crops, among others, in Europe.

Little more than 1,000 years ago, Britain was a sea of forest from end to end; and only a couple of centuries back, a squirrel could have travelled virtually from Lands End to John O' Groats without touching ground. But let us not be too sweeping in our dismay at the clearing of forests. Who, looking out over the ordered fields of rural Britain, cannot

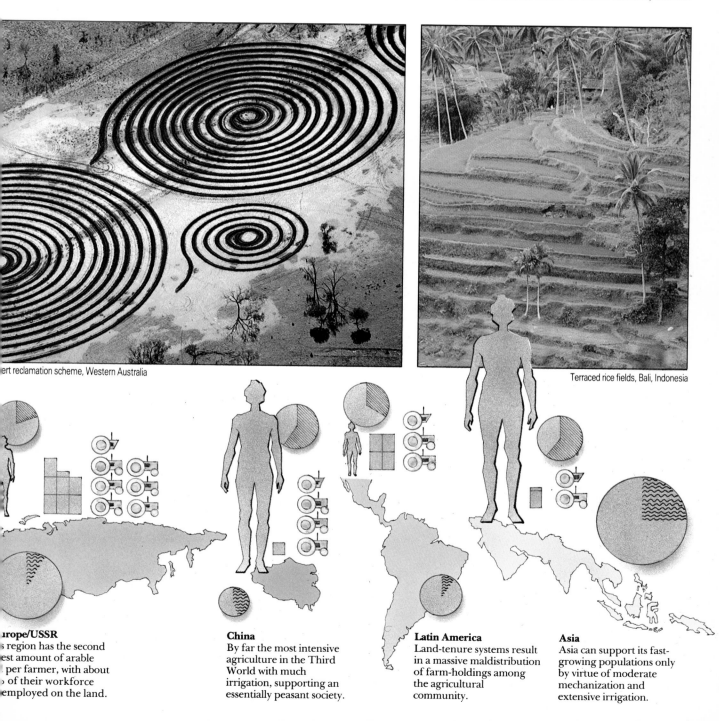

...ert reclamation scheme, Western Australia

Terraced rice fields, Bali, Indonesia

...rope/USSR
...region has the second
...est amount of arable
...per farmer, with about
...of their workforce
...employed on the land.

China
By far the most intensive agriculture in the Third World with much irrigation, supporting an essentially peasant society.

Latin America
Land-tenure systems result in a massive maldistribution of farm-holdings among the agricultural community.

Asia
Asia can support its fast-growing populations only by virtue of moderate mechanization and extensive irrigation.

agree that the farmland vistas are a delight to the eye as well as a boon to the stomach?

The growth of agriculture

The first great developments in agriculture took place some 10,000 years ago in a series of river basins, notably the Nile, the Euphrates/Tigris, the Ganges/Brahmaputra, and the Yangtse (see pp 144-5). In these tropical areas, with their year-round warmth and river-supplied water, people exploited the fertile floodplains to embark on an enterprise that ranks as a human advance to match mastery of fire and the art of writing—and much more important in terms of basic human survival.

Since this first exercise in cropland agriculture, we have dug up a sizeable sector of our planet, one-and-a-half billion hectares in all (the US covers just under one billion hectares). The most productive areas to date have often been the temperate-zone lands, so-called because of their supposedly clement climates. The year-round warmth of the tropics is fine for crop plants, but it is also fine for weeds, pests, and diseases: the tropics lack that great herbicide and pesticide of temperate zones, known as winter. Moreover, many temperate-zone lands feature naturally fertile soils, whereas many tropical soils have lost their nutrients through millennia of tropical downpours that wash out crucial minerals. An area of just one hectare of naturally rich soil in East Anglia (UK) or Iowa can yield as much harvest in one year as ten hectares of naturally impoverished soil in Bolivia or Zambia.

At the same time, temperate-zone farmers, being members of the affluent world, can afford to maintain their soils' fertility by means of ever-growing inputs of synthetic fertilizer, plus capital-intensive machinery and other investments. In other words, temperate-land farmers can now engage in "industrialized agriculture", an option not generally available in the Third World.

On a global scale, our croplands have generated an adequate harvest, more or less, until about the middle of this century. Since that time, we have witnessed the growth of human numbers and of human aspirations, twin pressures that have caused us to concentrate on a handful of high-yielding crop varieties to supply us with the bulk of our dietary needs. Four crops—wheat, rice, maize, and potato— contribute more tonnage to the world's total food production than all other food crops combined. New territories on which to grow these crops have also been opened up: during the period 1950-80, grain-growing areas, which now occupy 70 percent of all croplands, expanded by one-quarter. Half of the expansion was due to Kruschev's bringing the so-called virgin lands of the USSR under the plough, and the rest was divided between the recultivation of 20 million previously idle hectares of US croplands and an extension of arable lands in Brazil, Argentina, Nigeria, and other developing nations. According to the Food and Agricultural

The world croplands

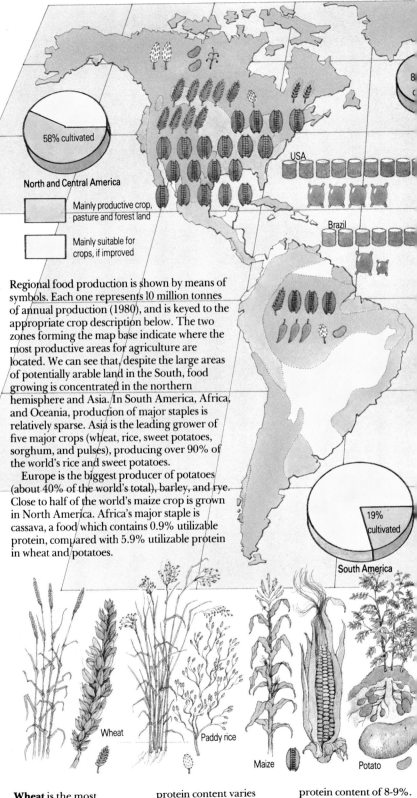

Regional food production is shown by means of symbols. Each one represents 10 million tonnes of annual production (1980), and is keyed to the appropriate crop description below. The two zones forming the map base indicate where the most productive areas for agriculture are located. We can see that, despite the large areas of potentially arable land in the South, food growing is concentrated in the northern hemisphere and Asia. In South America, Africa, and Oceania, production of major staples is relatively sparse. Asia is the leading grower of five major crops (wheat, rice, sweet potatoes, sorghum, and pulses), producing over 90% of the world's rice and sweet potatoes.

Europe is the biggest producer of potatoes (about 40% of the world's total), barley, and rye. Close to half of the world's maize crop is grown in North America. Africa's major staple is cassava, a food which contains 0.9% utilizable protein, compared with 5.9% utilizable protein in wheat and potatoes.

Wheat is the most important cereal in terms of world food production, providing a staple food for over a third of the world's population. It is grown principally in temperate climates and also in some sub-tropical regions. The protein content varies between 8 and 15%.

Rice is the leading tropical crop in Asia. Wet-rice cultivation allows for continuous cropping, so it supports high densities of population. Nutritionally, it is an excellent food, with a protein content of 8-9%.

Maize In the US, the largest producer of maize the bulk of the crop is fed to livestock. As food for people, maize is a staple crop in S America and Africa. The average protein content is 10%.

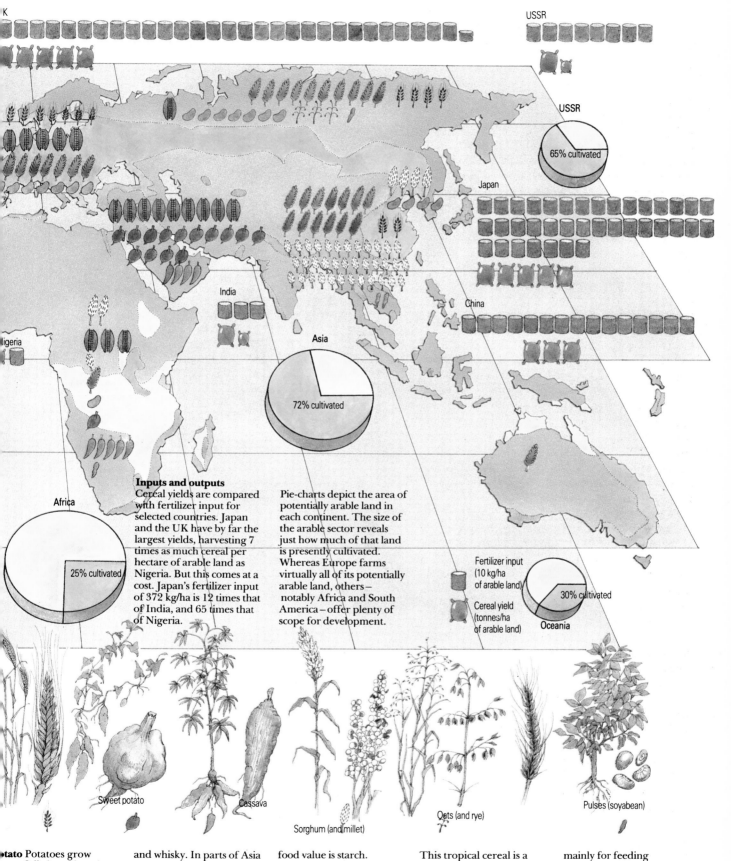

UK

USSR

USSR

65% cultivated

Japan

India

Asia

72% cultivated

China

Nigeria

Inputs and outputs
Cereal yields are compared with fertilizer input for selected countries. Japan and the UK have by far the largest yields, harvesting 7 times as much cereal per hectare of arable land as Nigeria. But this comes at a cost. Japan's fertilizer input of 372 kg/ha is 12 times that of India, and 65 times that of Nigeria.

Pie-charts depict the area of potentially arable land in each continent. The size of the arable sector reveals just how much of that land is presently cultivated. Whereas Europe farms virtually all of its potentially arable land, others – notably Africa and South America – offer plenty of scope for development.

Africa

25% cultivated

Fertilizer input
(10 kg/ha
of arable land)

Cereal yield
(tonnes/ha
of arable land)

30% cultivated

Oceania

Sweet potato

Cassava

Sorghum (and millet)

Oats (and rye)

Pulses (soyabean)

tato Potatoes grow
ccessfully in cool, moist,
mperate regions, and are
taple carbohydrate in
any developed countries.
rley The fourth most
portant cereal crop, it is
d mainly for animal
d and malting for beer

and whisky. In parts of Asia and Ethiopia it is still an important food crop.
Sweet potato Commonly grown in wetter tropical regions, sweet potatoes are generally used as a secondary rather than a staple food. Their chief

food value is starch.
Cassava A very important food crop in Africa, being extremely resistant to drought. It has a very low protein content and should be supplemented with other high-protein foods.
Sorghum (and millet)

This tropical cereal is a staple food in drier parts of Africa and Asia. The grain lacks gluten and cannot be used for bread-making.
Oats and rye Both these crops prefer cool, damp climates. Oats are grown

mainly for feeding livestock, while rye's chief use is for bread flour.
Pulses (soyabean) In poorer regions, pulses may form the principal source of dietary protein. Soyabeans may contain between 30 to 50% protein.

Organization (FAO), we hope to expand our global croplands by a further 15 percent to well over two billion hectares by the turn of the century – but only with sizeable costs to both our energy supplies and our environment.

Animals for food

People began to domesticate animals around the same time as they began to cultivate plants, or shortly thereafter. They probably started with dogs, using them for hunting in return for a dependable food supply. Then as humans learned the arts of crop husbandry, they found it more convenient to herd wild herbivores, and pen them close to settlements. From that early stage, growing crops and raising livestock advanced side by side.

Today we enjoy a range of domesticated animals that includes cattle, sheep, goats, pigs, water buffalo, chickens, ducks, geese, and turkeys. These creatures supply us with high-quality protein, whether in the form of milk or meat. They also supply us with hides, wool, and other material items. Even more important, they provide draught power. However widespread in the developed world the tractor may be, large numbers of people in developing countries still depend upon oxen and buffalo. In India alone, there are over 80 million draught animals – a power output equivalent to 30,000 megawatts. Among certain pastoralist peoples, such as the Masai of East Africa, livestock represents on-the-hoof wealth, and hence a source of social status.

Yet despite our appetite for meat and milk, the number of animal species we have domesticated is a good deal less than that of plants. The nine types of animals represented on the map account for almost all our animal protein from livestock. Production of this protein demands a grazing area of more than three billion hectares, a much greater area than crops (1.5 billion). Note, however, that not all animals graze all of the time: camels, and particularly goats, consume much foliage from shrubs.

In 1980, humankind consumed around 140 million tonnes of meat, or about 30 kilograms per person (about what the average Japanese consumes). The developed nations, however, with just over one billion people, consumed some 90 million tonnes, and the developing nations, with three times as many people, consumed only about half as much. Developing nations possess at least 60 percent of the world's livestock, but people in these countries enjoy only 20 percent of all meat and milk produced. In the US, the average citizen now consumes 110 kilograms of meat per year, in the UK 75 kilograms, the USSR 5l, Brazil 32, China 21, Nigeria 6, and India a miserable 1.1.

This maldistribution is all the more unfortunate in that domestic animals represent a sound way for developing-world people to broaden their food supply. Livestock eats not only grass, foliage, and other cellular plant material indigestible by humans; certain types, notably pigs, chicken, and fish (see pp

The world's grazing herd

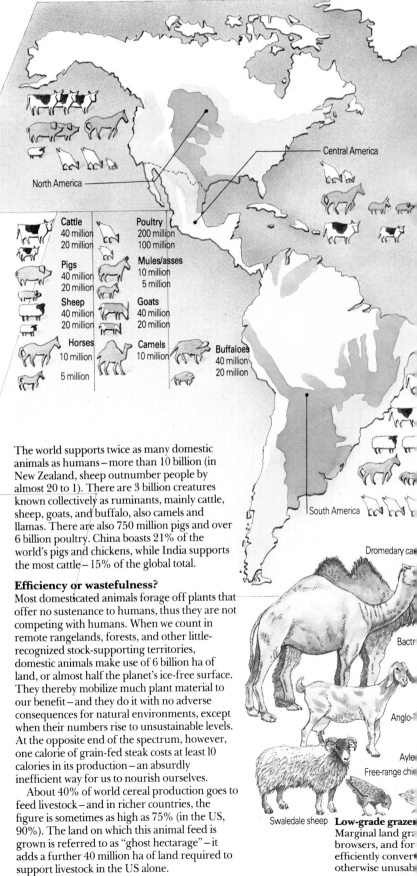

North America

Central America

Cattle
40 million
20 million

Poultry
200 million
100 million

Pigs
40 million
20 million

Mules/asses
10 million
5 million

Sheep
40 million
20 million

Goats
40 million
20 million

Horses
10 million

Camels
10 million

5 million

Buffaloes
40 million
20 million

South America

Dromedary ca

Bactr

Anglo-

Ayle
Free-range chi

Swaledale sheep **Low-grade grazer**
Marginal land gra
browsers, and for
efficiently conver
otherwise unusab

The world supports twice as many domestic animals as humans – more than 10 billion (in New Zealand, sheep outnumber people by almost 20 to 1). There are 3 billion creatures known collectively as ruminants, mainly cattle, sheep, goats, and buffalo, also camels and llamas. There are also 750 million pigs and over 6 billion poultry. China boasts 21% of the world's pigs and chickens, while India supports the most cattle – 15% of the global total.

Efficiency or wastefulness?

Most domesticated animals forage off plants that offer no sustenance to humans, thus they are not competing with humans. When we count in remote rangelands, forests, and other little-recognized stock-supporting territories, domestic animals make use of 6 billion ha of land, or almost half the planet's ice-free surface. They thereby mobilize much plant material to our benefit – and they do it with no adverse consequences for natural environments, except when their numbers rise to unsustainable levels. At the opposite end of the spectrum, however, one calorie of grain-fed steak costs at least 10 calories in its production – an absurdly inefficient way for us to nourish ourselves.

About 40% of world cereal production goes to feed livestock – and in richer countries, the figure is sometimes as high as 75% (in the US, 90%). The land on which this animal feed is grown is referred to as "ghost hectarage" – it adds a further 40 million ha of land required to support livestock in the US alone.

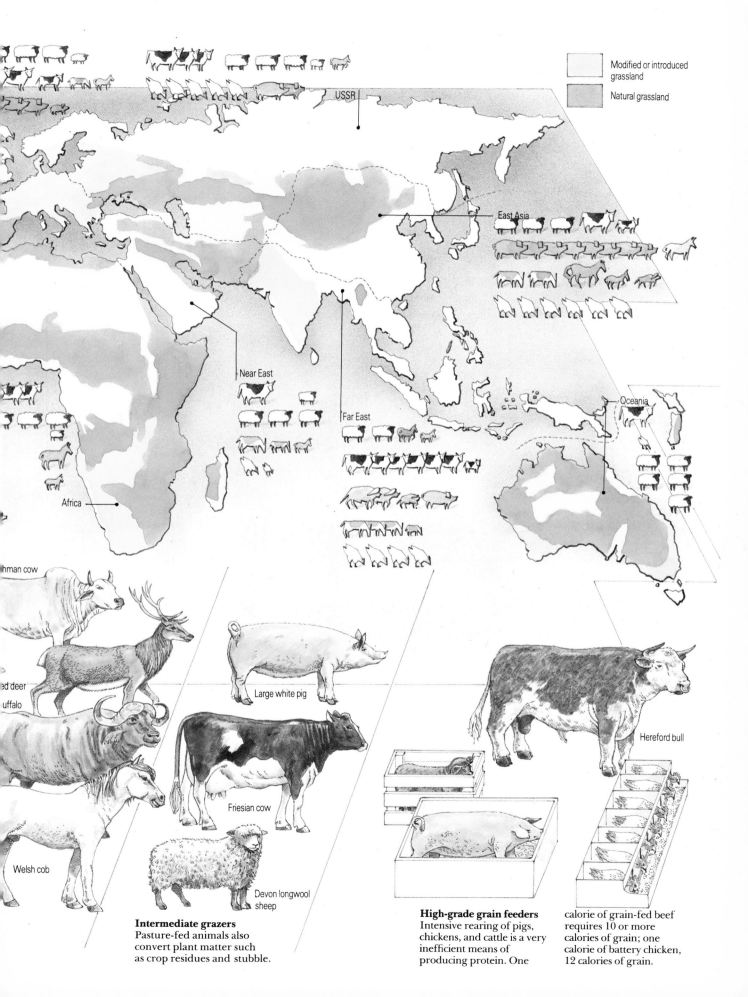

Modified or introduced grassland

Natural grassland

USSR

East Asia

Near East

Far East

Africa

Oceania

Brahman cow

Red deer

Buffalo

Large white pig

Welsh cob

Friesian cow

Devon longwool sheep

Hereford bull

Intermediate grazers
Pasture-fed animals also convert plant matter such as crop residues and stubble.

High-grade grain feeders
Intensive rearing of pigs, chickens, and cattle is a very inefficient means of producing protein. One calorie of grain-fed beef requires 10 or more calories of grain; one calorie of battery chicken, 12 calories of grain.

62-3), consume all manner of material such as farmyard garbage and kitchen refuse.

The ability fo feed ourselves

There is no doubt that we produce enough food to send everybody to bed with a full stomach. Yet tens of millions starve, and millions more are malnourished. The problem is that the Earth is less than "fair" in allocating its land resources. Some sectors are much better endowed with fertile soils than others; some sectors are much more vulnerable to natural injury; and some respond much better to constructive human manipulation. At the same time, we must recognize that we have been less than fair to our Earth. All too often, we have abused it: we have over-worked the soils, we have prodigally felled its forests, we have over-grazed its grasslands, and we have otherwise mistreated the many other gifts of nature. Our meagre sense of husbandry has brought us to a point where, when many more

The global larder

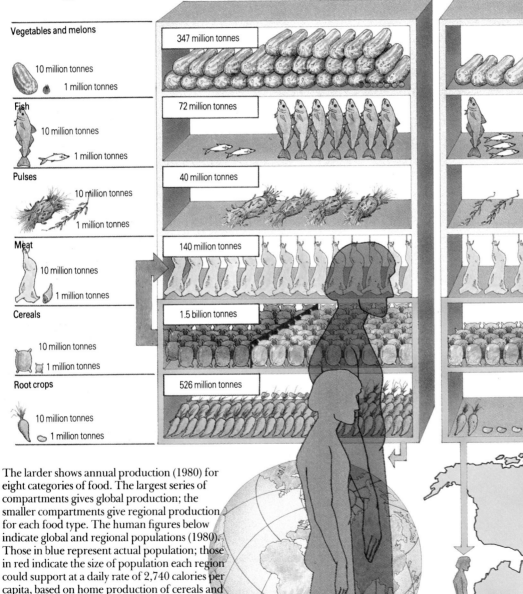

The larder shows annual production (1980) for eight categories of food. The largest series of compartments gives global production; the smaller compartments give regional production for each food type. The human figures below indicate global and regional populations (1980). Those in blue represent actual population; those in red indicate the size of population each region could support at a daily rate of 2,740 calories per capita, based on home production of cereals and root crops (assuming all cereals were fed to humans rather than to livestock). The brown arrow leading from the global cereal shelf to the meat section shows how much grain is presently used as livestock feed.

As the red figures demonstrate, Africa and Asia do not produce enough cereals and root crops to sustain their present populations. Taking figures for the whole world, however, we find that we have enough staples to feed an extra 1.5 billion people.

N America, Japan, Oceania
If grain and root crops were diverted from animal feed to human food, this wealthy group (Japan excepted) could support 3 times their population.

Western Europe
Enough food here to feed almost an extra 300 million people. Nonetheless, the region imports a lot of basic foodstuffs and animal feed

nouths are clamouring to be fed, the resource base self is falling into critical disrepair (see p. 40). Yet ve certainly possess the technological skills and the conomic capacity to supply a rightful place for the ntire human family at Earth's feast table: all we ppear to lack is the ultimate commitment – to say Yes, we shall do it".

But "we shall do it" entails far more than simply loughing up more land, or applying more sensitive gricultural skills. The basic problems are not so much technical and scientific, they are political and economic. Poor people are generally hungry because they lack the financial means to grow enough food, or to purchase it. While a transfer of relief food (and especially of grain used as livestock feed) from the developed world would help to relieve immediate hunger, it would tackle symptoms rather than problems. Poor people need to be able to feed themselves; and to do that, their entire lifestyles need to be upgraded.

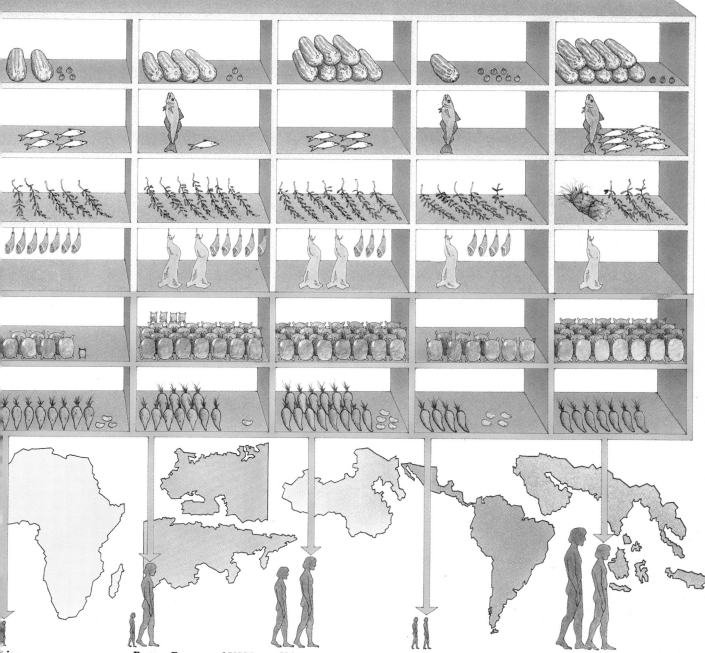

rica
e only region to have wn steadily hungrier ce 1970 – with 11% of world's population ing to survive on 7% of staple crop production.

Eastern Europe and USSR
A larder that would comfortably support its population, if all cereals were consumed by humans. Yet it depends on massive grain imports.

China
No mean achievement that this nation can grow enough food on 7% of the world's arable land to feed 22% of the world's population.

Latin America
This continent barely manages to feed itself, having a low production of cereals and root crops. Much of its arable land is under-utilized.

Asia
Despite a high rate of food production, the sheer size of the population of this region has stretched the land beyond its limits.

THE LAND CRISIS

With every day that goes by, as our numbers and expectations rise, we demand still more from our natural-resource base. In such a situation, it would be wise for us to redouble our sense of caring for the fragile planet that supports our material welfare. Quite the contrary, however. During the present decade, we may well degrade more forests, over-graze more grasslands, lose more land through urban development, and erode more topsoil than during the two decades 1960-80. Unless we change our ways, we could inflict greater ravages on the Earth's ecosystem during the remainder of this century than during the whole of this century up to the present. Far from using our Earth well, we are using it up – for all the world (so to speak) as if we had a spare planet parked out there in space.

The threat of erosion

Few resource problems are so important, while so little publicized, as the disappearance of our soil. Each year, many billion of tonnes are being washed away into the sea or carried away with the wind.

There is no known way that we can replace our soil. If we wait upon natural processes, we shall wait for centuries, if not millennia. The disappearance of our soil threatens to undermine our agriculture, our very means of supporting ourselves. Yet because it is such a cryptic and "silent" problem, few of our leaders give it a fraction of the attention it deserves. It is hard to whip up public opinion about the issue. Europe, the continent least affected by erosion, is estimated to be losing close to one billion tonnes a year, while Asia, the worst affected, could be losing around 25 billion tonnes. The US loses well over one billion tonnes a year (net of natural replacement) from its grainlands – equivalent to more than 300,000 hectares of crop-growing potential.

A similar sad tale can be told around the world, especially in the humid tropics with their thunderstorms. Violent downpours rip the topsoil from denuded hillsides, carving great gulleys in the landscape, while windstorms ravage semi-arid lands planted to crops. Ethiopia, though less than one-sixth the size of the US, is reputed to be losing at least as much topsoil each year. Half of all countries, and half of all arable lands, are suffering the problem at unacceptable levels. If soil erosion is allowed to continue unchecked, we shall find that all of the new land which we hope to bring under the plough by the year 2000 – some 200 million hectares (assuming present new cultivation rates increase

The disappearing soil

If we are to sustain productivity, we must protect our soil. Soil degradation has many causes, but those which actively overtax the land are largely attributed to erosion and over-grazing.

Erosion in the US

One-third of US croplands, well over 50 million ha, is now undergoing a marked decline in long-term productivity because of soil erosion (see map). Were this depletion to continue for another 50 years, it would cut the US grain harvest by between 50 and 75 million tonnes (about half what the US exported in 1980), thus affecting millions of people around the world who depend on American food surpluses.

Why does the US not do more to stem the crisis? The miserable experience of the US Dust Bowl of the 1930s, when 40 million ha of arable land on the Great Plains were severely damaged, must surely have taught a costly lesson. But as long as our economic institutions continue to encourage overproduction at the cost of the future environment, the finger of blame can hardly be pointed at US farmers. They calculate that, at a time of fluctuating crop prices, they have insufficient incentive to allocate time and money to any activity that will mean less than record harvests.

The map, right, shows the cumulative effects of erosion in the US.

Global land loss

Each year about 11 million ha of our arable lands are lost through erosion, desertification, toxification and cropland conversion to non-agricultural uses. If this trend is allowed to continue unchecked, by the year 2000 we shall lose 275 million ha, or 18%, of our arable lands. By 2025, the same amount again could disappear. And this does not take into account the 7 million ha of grasslands which are lost each year through desertification.

Severe – more than 75% topsoil lost

Moderate – 25-7... topsoil l...

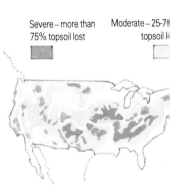

Farmer and son in the face of a dust storm. Oklahoma, 1936

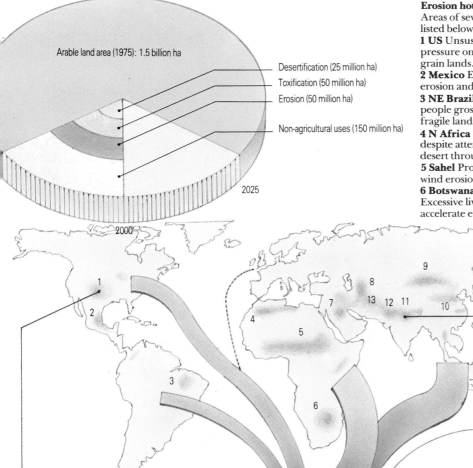

Arable land area (1975): 1.5 billion ha

Desertification (25 million ha)
Toxification (50 million ha)
Erosion (50 million ha)
Non-agricultural uses (150 million ha)

2025
2000

Erosion hotspots
Areas of severe erosion are listed below.
1 US Unsustainable pressure on soils in the grain lands.
2 Mexico Experiencing erosion and droughts.
3 NE Brazil 40 million people grossly over-load fragile lands.
4 N Africa Much erosion, despite attempts to halt the desert through tree belts.
5 Sahel Probably the worst wind erosion area on Earth.
6 Botswana – Namibia Excessive livestock herds accelerate erosion.

7 Middle East Erosion, a problem for centuries, now spreading faster than ever.
8 Central Asia Again, too many livestock, too little careful management.
9 Mongolia Growing numbers of people and growing herds over-burden the environment.
10 Yangtse China is reported to lose 5 billion tonnes of fine "loess" soil annually.
11 Himalayan foothills The worst erosion hotspot (see below).
12 Baluchistan Traditional stock-raising and large herds do the damage.
13 Rajasthan Droughts are becoming a permanent phenomenon.
14 Australia Long droughts, sometimes aggravated by excessive numbers of stock.

Causes of erosion
Human activity causes natural erosion rates to increase many times over. We cultivate steep slopes without adequate terracing, practise inexpert irrigation, and allow livestock to over-graze grasslands. We also over-work the soil until its robust structure turns to dust. Worst of all, we eliminate tree cover, whether forests, shelterbelts, or hedgerows.

The soil washed and blown off our farmlands makes its way eventually into the ocean (a little into lakes). In effect, it is funnelled into a vast "dump" – never to return. The process erodes away a crucial basis of our civilization. The width of the arrows on the map indicates the approximate percentage of global soil loss through water erosion for each continent.

Soil timescales
Formation of 2.5 cm of topsoil can take anything from 100 to 2,500 years, depending on the soil type. Unfortunately, reversing this process is all too quick – we can destroy 2.5 cm of soil in as little as 10 years.

Annual soil loss: 75 billion tonnes

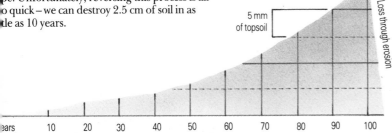

5 mm of topsoil

Loss through erosion

Years   10   20   30   40   50   60   70   80   90   100

New island in the Bay of Bengal
Around one-quarter of a million tonnes of topsoil are washed off the deforested mountain slopes of Nepal each year, and a further sizeable amount from the Himalayan foothills in India's sector of the Ganges catchment zone. As a result, a gigantic shallow is building up in the Bay of Bengal, covering some 5 million ha. When this shallow breaks the surface of the sea, it will be claimed either by India as New Moore Island, or by Bangladesh as South Talpatty. Nepal, the country which contributes most to the phenomenon, is not even being consulted.

several times) – will do no more than offset productivity lost through erosion.

The decline of the tropical forest

Each year, 12 million hectares of forests (an area almost the size of England) are being eliminated from the face of the Earth. Almost all this deforestation occurs in the moist forests and open woodlands of the tropics. We are also witnessing the degradation of at least a further 10 million hectares of forest a year, again mainly in the tropics, especially the humid tropics. (A degraded forest is one which has been grossly disrupted, leaving behind an impoverished travesty of true forest.)

So pervasive is the depletion of tropical forests, and so rapid is the depletion rate, that these superb exemplars of nature may disappear by the year 2050, except possibly for certain sectors of western Amazonia and the Zaire basin, and a few isolated relics in the form of parks and reserves.

Part of the problem is that more people everywhere require more wood. If present trends in wood consumption continue, by the year 2000 we could be consuming four billion tonnes a year. In order to satisfy this growing demand, the commercial logger looks increasingly to tropical forests as timber sources that have been relatively little exploited to date. The amount of tropical forest that is heavily logged each year (light logging, carefully conducted, can be acceptable) amounts to about 4.5 million hectares a year.

Eventually, after decades if not centuries, a heavily logged forest ecosystem can restore itself. But it generally does not get the chance. The main damage done by loggers is unwitting. They lay down a network of timber-haulage tracks, allowing land-hungry people to penetrate deep into forest heartlands that have hitherto remained closed to them. Traditional slash-and-burn agriculture, which had previously represented a sustainable use of the

The shrinking forest

The demand for agricultural land, whether planned or unplanned, is the chief cause of the depletion of tropical forests. Unplanned agriculture, i.e. "spontaneous settlement" by slash-and-burn cultivators, is much more difficult to quantify than planned agriculture (for cash crop plantations, cattle ranches, and organized smallholder cultivation). The bottom graph demonstrates the rising demand for agricultural land in the tropics. In 1950, just over 100 million ha of forest had been cleared; by 1975, this figure had more than doubled to cope with the needs of expanding populations. By 2025 this figure could rise to 700 million ha.

The rate at which the world's tropical forests are disappearing is shown in the central graph. During the period 1950-75, at least 120 million ha of closed moist forest were destroyed, mostly from S and SE Asia. By the end of the century another 270 million ha could be eliminated. If we dare to look ahead to 2025, we stand to lose another 300 million ha at least.

Wood consumption: industrial vs fuelwood

The log and fuelwood symbols, right, show world consumption of wood for the period 1950-2025. In 1950, consumption of industrial wood exceeded that of fuelwood, but by 1975, the balance had tipped in favour of fuelwood, reflecting the demands of growing Third World populations. In fact, in 1975, there was a severe deficit in supply of fuelwood, shown here by dotted symbols. These shortfalls in supply have serious repercussions: Third World peoples use cattle dung and crop residues as fuel rather than fertilizer, resulting in a current loss of grain production equivalent to an estimated 20 million tonnes a year.

By the year 2000, when our overall consumption of wood is likely to increase by one-third, the share accounted for by fuel needs could well decline way below half, due to inadequate supplies.

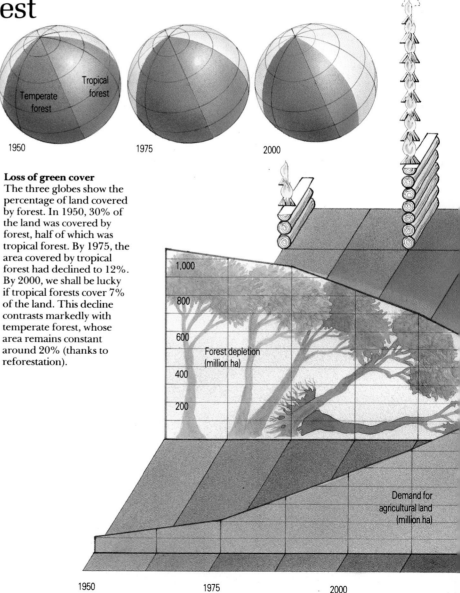

Wood consumption
Each symbol represents 200 million cu m of wood

Deficit in fuelwood supply

Fuelwood consumption

Industrial consumption

Loss of green cover
The three globes show the percentage of land covered by forest. In 1950, 30% of the land was covered by forest, half of which was tropical forest. By 1975, the area covered by tropical forest had declined to 12%. By 2000, we shall be lucky if tropical forests cover 7% of the land. This decline contrasts markedly with temperate forest, whose area remains constant around 20% (thanks to reforestation).

Temperate forest

Tropical forest

1950

1975

2000

1,000

800

600

Forest depletion (million ha)

400

200

Demand for agricultural land (million ha)

1950

1975

2000

forest (at low population densities), now poses the most serious threat. Small-scale cultivators, numbering around 250 million people, cause final elimination of at least five million hectares a year, and gross degradation of another 10 million hectares. Being denied scope for subsistence agriculture elsewhere, these farming communities see little alternative to their lifestyle, even though they realize that it is harmful to their own prospects and those of much larger communities further afield.

A similar sentiment applies to fuelwood gatherers, who, unless supplied with village woodlots and "tree farms" on suitable scale, see little option but to continue with their present course of disruptive and destructive action. Fuelwood gathering depletes some two million hectares of tropical moist forest each year, and at least twice as much open woodland and scrub forest.

Not so hard placed is the cattle rancher, who sets light to at least 2.5 million hectares of forest in Central America and Amazonia each year, mainly to raise beef for lucrative export markets in the developed world. Ranchers could double their output on existing pastures if they were to run their operations more efficiently. But economic incentives and other government inducements, even support from international aid agencies, encourage them to ranch extensively rather than intensively. When pastureland soils lose their residual fertility within half-a-dozen years and weeds over-run the holding, the rancher simply moves on to another patch of forest, and repeats the process.

In several senses, we all play a part in the decline of tropical forests. We seek specialist hardwoods like meranti, mahogany, teak, and ebony at unrealistically low prices, and we demand cheap beef from formerly forested pasturelands. True, some members of the global community are more culpable than others. But hardly anyone can claim that his or her hand is not, in some indirect way or another, on

ontiers of attack
e red zones mark the
as of forest undergoing
id depletion. Few areas
ve inaccessible parts of
stern Amazonia and
ch of the Zaire basin)
immune.

the chain-saw and machete at work in tropical forests. Moreover, we shall all eventually suffer if tropical forests continue to disappear.

The effects of forest clearance

"Man has gone to the Moon but he does not know yet how to make a flame tree or a birdsong. Let us keep our dear countries free from irreversible mistakes which would lead us in the future to long for these same birds and trees."
PRESIDENT HOUPHOUET-BOIGNY OF THE IVORY COAST, A COUNTRY WHICH HAS LOST 66% OF ITS FORESTS AND WOODLANDS IN THE LAST 25 YEARS.

When forest cover in a watershed is lost, the repercussions are far-reaching. The forests' sponge effect is lost, and the release of rainfall becomes erratic. Farmers in the valleylands of southern Asia are particularly vulnerable: rivers such as the Ganges, the Brahmaputra, the Irrawady, the Salween, and the Mekong no longer supply regular amounts of irrigation water – which causes the Green Revolution (see pp 60-1) to be less revolutionary than hoped.

City-dwellers suffer too. In the hinterland of Panama City and of Manila, capital of the Philippines, deforestation has caused so much injury to watershed functions that water supplies are threatened, bringing on a risk of contaminated water and pandemics. In Ecuador, Kenya, and Thailand, cities experience "brown-outs" caused by loss of hill forest: washed-off sediment leads to silting up of hydroelectric dams.

Clearance of tropical forests could also have severely adverse effects on the world's climate. In Amazonia, more than half of all moisture circulating through the region's ecosystem remains within the forest: rainwater is absorbed by plants, before being "breathed out" into the atmosphere. Were a large part of the forest to disappear, the remainder would become less able (however well protected) to retain so much moisture – and the effects could extend further, even drying out the climate for crops in southern Brazil.

Still more important, tropical forests help to stabilize the world's climate by absorbing much solar radiation: they simply "soak up" the sunshine. When forests are cleared, the "shininess" of the planet's land surface increases, radiating more of the sun's energy back into space (the "albedo" effect). An increase in albedo could lead to disruptions of convection patterns, wind currents, and rainfall in lands far beyond the tropics.

Although tropical forests do not significantly affect Earth's oxygen balance, they do play an important part in the carbon dioxide budget. When forests are burned, they release considerable quantities of carbon into the skies. The build-up of carbon dioxide in the atmosphere looks as if it is triggering a "greenhouse effect", bringing on drier climates for some, especially Americans (pp 116-7). What if the great grain belt of North America starts to become

Destroying the protector

As long as forest cover remains intact, rivers run clear and clean, and they run regularly throughout the year. When the forest disappears, the downstream effect is a regime of floods followed by droughts. Washed-off sediment not only causes river beds to silt up, but it also chokes hydropower dams and suffocates coastal fisheries.

Flooding in the Ganges Plain, as in Bangladesh above, provides a graphic example of the effects of deforestation. As the foothill forests are cleared for agriculture, the 500 million people in the valleys grow ever-more vulnerable to flooding. During the 1978 monsoon, India suffered losses of $2 billion, and hundreds of people were drowned.

Forest watershed removed, topsoil washed down

Flood plain

Silted-up river

...splaced forest peoples

...ere are several million people still following ...ditional lifestyles within tropical forests. ...nerally disregarded by the outside world, the ...st that we often hear about these peoples is ...en they shoot arrows at bulldozers. As ...ently as the early 1970s, the Tasaday tribe ...s discovered in a Philippines forest cut off by ...5-km strip from the outside world and ...rsuing a Neolithic lifestyle in isolation. ...So fast are these groups being squeezed out of ...istence, that in Brazilian Amazonia, which ...tured 230 native groups with an estimated 2 ...llion people only 500 years ago, there are now ...ly half as many such groups, with a total below ...,000 persons. The Kayapos, for example, ...ve been massacred in their thousands by ...gal settlers, and have been forcibly ...nsferred from their homelands. The ...otograph above shows the Megkronotis ...dians (of the Kayapos) trudging through the ...es of a forest they refuse to abandon.

...ouring the land for fuel

...cording to UN estimates, more than 100 ...llion people experience acute shortages of ...elwood. Many rural families now devote as ...ch time to finding fuelwood as to any other ...ivity (p. 114). As fallen wood becomes scarce, ...agers lop branches, fell trees, even uproot ...mps. Removing residues robs soil of ...trients, while clearing shrubs hastens erosion, ...ving a barren landscape.

unbuckled, with less food not only for North Americans, but for dozens of countries that import grain from North America?

The advance of the desert

In several drier parts of the world, deserts are increasing at an alarming rate. In those few areas where the process is natural, we call it desertization. But where the desert encroaches through human hand, we term it desertification – an ugly word for an ugly process.

In fact, it is less than accurate to assert that the desert is advancing or encroaching. Rather a strip of additional desert is "tacked on" to the original desert. Lands far away from the edge of true deserts are also being degraded to a desert-like condition. Except over a long period of time, deserts rarely expand through climatic compulsion.

Altogether, one-third of the planet's land surface is semi-arid or arid. These drylands support some 700 million people, of whom almost one in ten lives in an area that is being impoverished through de-vegetation, soil erosion, and dune formation. Each year some 12 million hectares deteriorate to a point where they are agriculturally worthless. Of these, 40 percent are rainfed croplands that lose their topsoil and nutrient stocks; and the rest are rangelands, which, through over-grazing, suffer erosion and a shift in vegetation from nutritious grasses to weeds that even a goat will spurn. Were these lands to continue to support agriculture, their output could be worth at least $20 billion a year.

By contrast with the cost of desertification, the expense of rehabilitating the degraded lands, and of halting the spread of deserts, need be no more than $2.5 billion a year. Yet the funds made available so far amount to less than a quarter of that sum.

Why don't governments, in both developing and developed worlds, invest the necessary funds, on the grounds that it makes economic common sense? A main reason lies with the lowly status of the people affected: they are "marginalized" people in two senses, in that they live in marginal lands, and that they are marginal to the politico-economic structures of their countries. Almost all of them are subsistence peasants, people with little political clout. National leaders know that they represent no threat to the system if their needs are ignored.

The only time that governments see cause to funnel sizeable sums of money into drylands is when trouble of a different order erupts. In the Horn of Africa, around the late 1960s, landless peasants in both Ethiopia and Somalia started heading toward the semi-barren lands of the Ogaden. When the two sides challenged each other for living space, a border war broke out. Normally this patch of scrub would have been ignored by the outside world. But because it lies so close to the tanker lanes from the Gulf, the superpowers have poured vast funds into the zone, in the form of military hardware. These funds would have been more than enough to

The encroaching desert

North and Central Amer
Stock-raising imposes a heavy burden on drylan areas.

The world has five major desert zones (hyper-arid lands), which lie in two belts on either side of the Equator. Desertification does not occur in these natural deserts, but in the arid and semi-arid lands.

There are four main causes of desertification, each of which is made more acute by excessive human numbers: over-cultivation, deforestation, over-grazing, and poor irrigation. Marginal lands are cleared and ploughed in despairing farming attempts; trees and woody plants are slashed for fuel; livestock over-grazes and flattens vegetation; and improper irrigation sterilizes the earth with salts and alkalis.

South America
Pressure of human numbers allied to rudimentary agric are degrading mar lands. One area in Atacama Desert ha recorded rain.

Total land area 1

Risk of desertification

— Moderate
— High
— Very high
— Hyper-arid zone

Creeping outwards
Of the Earth's ice-free land area (outer circle), over one-third is already affected or likely to be affected by desertification. The inner core of 6% represents extreme desert. Spreading out from this are the areas at very high, high, and moderate risk – 3%, 12%, and 13% of our land base respectively.

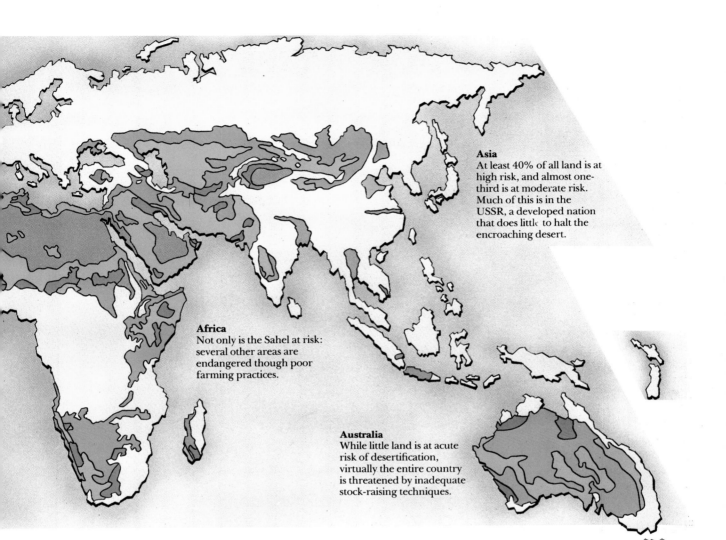

Asia
At least 40% of all land is at high risk, and almost one-third is at moderate risk. Much of this is in the USSR, a developed nation that does little to halt the encroaching desert.

Africa
Not only is the Sahel at risk: several other areas are endangered though poor farming practices.

Australia
While little land is at acute risk of desertification, virtually the entire country is threatened by inadequate stock-raising techniques.

The Sahel disaster

...ertification was brought to the world's ...ntion by the Sahel disaster of the early ...0s. The ostensible cause of the débâcle lay ...the drought that overtook the semi-arid ...e dwellers of the Sahel. But the main ...blem lay further in the past. For the ...vious two decades, the region enjoyed ...er-than-average rainfall. Consequently, ...n cash crop cultivation in lands further ...th (p. 51) started to expand along with the ...igenous populations, throngs of pastoralists ...cultivators moved north, toward the fringe ...he Sahara. Lands that had not been dug for ...turies were cultivated, and livestock were ...wded on to smaller areas of pasture. (The ...otograph, right, shows the effects of over-...zing in Niger.) Sadly, these migrant peoples ...w, from their tribal traditions, that the ...ster phase would probably be transitory, ...ch made the drought all the more terrible ...en it finally struck – at least 100,000 people ...millions of animals died.

...he crisis still persists right along the Sahel. ...man activities continue to reduce the ...ductivity of lands that speedily degrade ...der stress. During the period 1950-75, the ...ert in Sudan pushed its frontier further ...th by 100 km.

rehabilitate the degraded lands in the two countries – and to halt desertification along much of the entire Saharan frontier.

Our hungry world

There are two forms of malnutrition in our world. While tens of millions of people in the developing countries literally starve to death each year, health statistics from the developed countries reveal a growth in the incidence of illness caused by over-eating. An average developing-world person enjoys only about two-thirds as many calories as an average developed-world person, only half as much protein, and only one-fifth as much animal protein. When we count in all the grain fed to livestock, many a

developed-world citizen accounts for three times as much food as his or her counterpart in the developing world.

Thus the scandal of the waist-line: expanding excessively among the rich, and shrinking excessively among the poor. Even a domestic cat in Europe or North America receives more meat each day than many a person in the developing world.

According to FAO and the World Bank, almost 500 million people (more than one in ten on the planet) regularly consume less than the "minimum critical diet" necessary to stay healthy and maintain body weight, even without much physical activity. More than two-thirds of these unfortunates live in Asia, most of the rest in Africa and Latin America.

Hunger and glut

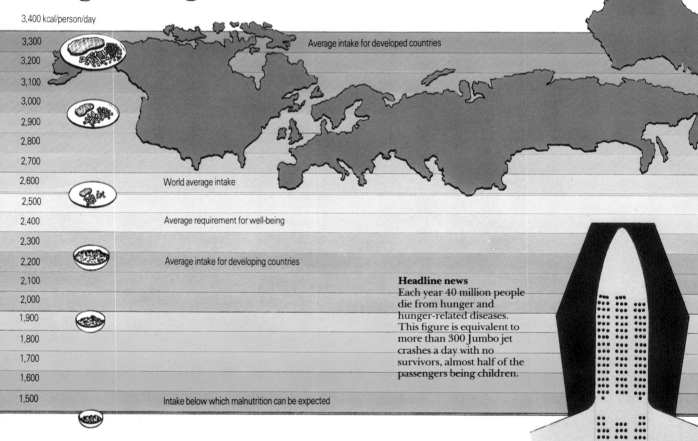

3,400 kcal/person/day

3,300	
3,200	Average intake for developed countries
3,100	
3,000	
2,900	
2,800	
2,700	
2,600	World average intake
2,500	
2,400	Average requirement for well-being
2,300	
2,200	Average intake for developing countries
2,100	
2,000	
1,900	
1,800	
1,700	
1,600	
1,500	Intake below which malnutrition can be expected

Headline news
Each year 40 million people die from hunger and hunger-related diseases. This figure is equivalent to more than 300 Jumbo jet crashes a day with no survivors, almost half of the passengers being children.

The geography of hunger is one of the starkest indicators of the North-South divide. As the world map, above, confirms, the average diet in the North provides a good deal more than the essential average daily intake of calories. The average diet in the South, by contrast, not only falls below the world average calorific intake, but often also falls below the minimum intake required for survival, let alone health. Malnutrition is the concealed cause of many diseases, particularly among children. With their pot bellies and sunken eyes, they quickly become vulnerable to infection. Perhaps worst of all, diarrhoeal diseases drain from a child's stomach whatever nutriment it has been able to ingest – reinforcing basic malnutrition.

Each year, 15 million babies and young children die – a statistic that would be shocking if it were only 15,000. According to James Grant, head of UNICEF, we could save many of these children at an overall cost of $5 each, through programmes promoting immunization, breast-feeding, rehydration therapy (which counteracts diarrhoea) and improved child care generally.

In the North, malnutrition takes the form of over-consumption of sugars, fats, and animal products, resulting in obesity, heart disease, and diabetes. In the US alone, at least one-third of those aged over 40 can be classified as obese. In 1982, the UK spent '235 million on slimming aids – compared to just '50 million donated to private aid agencies like OXFAM.

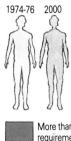

1974-76 2000

Numbers
undernourished
Each figure
represents
5 million people.

More than 100% of
requirement

85-99% of requirement

Less than 85% of
requirement

The hunger gap
The average daily calorific
requirement for well-being
is estimated to be around
2,400 calories (for
developed and developing
countries). Developed
world citizens receive some
40% above this figure,
while the average Third
World person subsists on
10% less.

The map shows the
geography of world
hunger. It gives the
percentage of nutritional
requirements received in
selected countries.

In sub-Saharan Africa, the average amount of food available per head has actually declined since 1970. By fortunate contrast, the situation has apparently improved somewhat in Asia and Latin America.

But the innocent-seeming qualification "apparently" conceals a catch. The sharp disparity of hunger and glut occurs not only among countries, i.e. between Northerners and Southerners. It occurs *within* many countries of the Third World, where the top one-fifth of the population may be 10 to 20 times more affluent than the bottom one-fifth. In Kenya and the Ivory Coast, Brazil and Mexico, Iraq and the Philippines, the privileged gorge themselves alongside the starving. In all these countries, the national statistics for average diets may suggest that things are not so bad; but in Kenya alone, 40 percent of the rural population suffer a deficit of 640 calories a day. Clearly, we must examine the overall statistics more carefully if we are to hear the protests of those who eat less in one day than a typical British person consumes by lunchtime (about 1,500 calories) – and tries to do many hours of hard labour off it.

Go to a global food conference, and you will see that many political leaders from the Third World (like their colleagues from the rich world) are, frankly, fat – and their lives will be shortened just as

surely as will those of the hungry multitudes whom they earnestly discuss. Perhaps attendance at a global food conference should be made conditional upon a suitably trim figure?

By contrast, we find in a few countries, notably China and Sri Lanka, that while the average per-capita consumption of calories is low, hardly anybody starves. The food available is more equitably shared among the community.

The absurdity of hunger and glut within many developing countries is aggravated by excessive consumption in the North. So prodigal is an average American in the use of food, that one-quarter of it is never eaten; it rots in the supermarket or fridge, or is thrown away off the plate.

The consequences of hunger extend beyond physical suffering and misery. It reduces capacity to work, and increases susceptibility to disease. Among children, insufficient protein can retard development, physically and mentally.

Some may protest that the poor countries should grow more food for themselves. Well, so they should – and they would feel encouraged to do so if they did not allocate so much land to cash crops for export. As a first look at some solutions – how we can *manage* our affairs to the advantage of all – it is fitting that the cash-crop factor be examined.

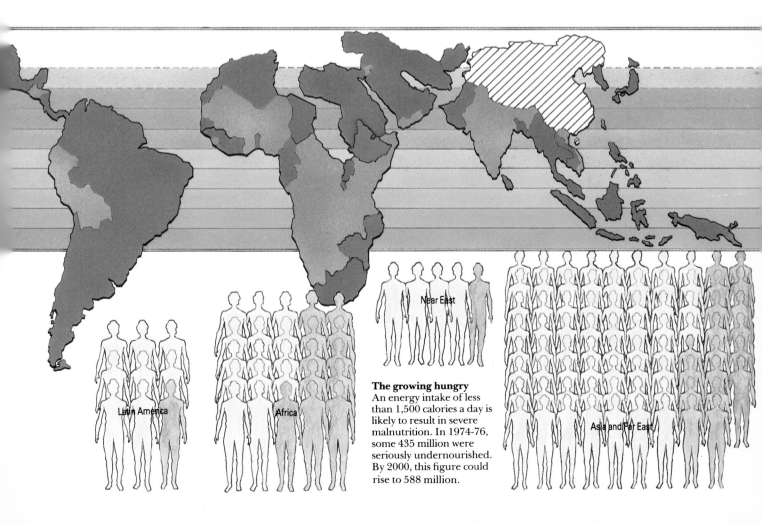

Near East

The growing hungry
An energy intake of less than 1,500 calories a day is likely to result in severe malnutrition. In 1974-76, some 435 million were seriously undernourished. By 2000, this figure could rise to 588 million.

Latin America

Africa

Asia and Far East

MANAGING THE LAND

The cash-crop factor

We live in a hungry world, faced with a deepening land crisis. The costly "escape" strategy of bringing ever more land under the plough will only worsen this crisis, and still barely feed our growing numbers if we carry on as now.

The solution lies not in how much land we have, but how we use it. Let us look at some specific sectors, asking ourselves why we allow things to go wrong, and what we should do to set them right.

Cash crops trade: bonds or bondage?

Cash crops can be either boon or bane for developing countries. In some instances, they supply much impetus to the development process, by bringing in crucial foreign-exchange earnings which lubricate emergent economies. But all too often, because the land could be better employed in growing food for hungry local people rather than non-essential commodities for foreigners, they tend to slow down the development process.

It is difficult for developing economies to break free from the cash crop bind. For most Third World nations, "going it alone" would be impossible: their domestic market is too small, their resource base too narrow. Unless they can trade in the world marketplace, they cannot purchase the tools and technology they need for development. And those countries that have no mineral resources of their own must find the means to earn foreign exchange as best they can. Even if they prefer not to follow a Western model of development, those developing countries that suffer increasing poverty and a deteriorating resource base need hard cash simply to purchase a more critical export from the developed world – grain.

Where does the answer lie? First, the developing nations must get their priorities right. In too many Third World countries, agriculture is subordinated to urban development and industrialization. A selective cash-crop strategy can avoid heavy dependence on a single export commodity, and place more emphasis on efficient food production, a better share-out of farmlands, and fairer distribution of income. Secondly, international agencies can change their approach to aid and development within the agricultural sector. Although some Third World countries have inherited colonial cash-crop links, and others have entered the vicious cash-crop circle by accident, all too many have been led there, even pushed there, by misconceived aid programmes. Not enough of these countries' leaders have the

The major grain exporters
Grain produced in the North is distributed worldwide. More than 100 countries depend on these grain shipments.

North American imports

Western European exports

North American exports

Latin American exports

Latin American imports

Cash crops generate funds for the producer countries through their export value in the world marketplace. Broadly speaking, they fall into two categories: essential food crops, such as cereals and legumes, which are mainly produced in the North and traded all over the world; and less essential crops, such as coffee, cotton, and tobacco, which are predominantly produced in the South for export to the North (reflecting colonial trading links). The map shows trade flows of ten major cash crops (based on 1980 import and export values). Some of the less essential crops command relatively high prices on world markets – for much of the time; and they generate more money than the land could produce through growing staple foods – for much of the time.

But the catch lies in the phrase "for much of the time". Commodity prices are fickle: when consumer demand soars, prices are good – whereupon many farmers are persuaded to go into the cash-crop business, switching from growing food to growing non-essential items. When the global economy turns down again, prices crash, and the farmer is left caught between a rock and a hard place.

Wheat
Coarse grains
Sugar
Soyabeans
Coffee
Cotton
Rice
Cocoa
Tobacco
Natural rubber

What commodities can buy

In 1975, 1 tonne of coffee bought around 290 barrels of oil, yet in 1983 it could purchase only one-third as many; and the crop's capacity to service interest payments for international loans plunged by over 60%. Similarly cocoa and sugar, less valuable commodities, have declined in purchasing power by one-half and five-sixths respectively.

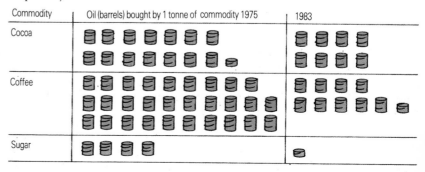

Commodity	Oil (barrels) bought by 1 tonne of commodity 1975	1983
Cocoa		
Coffee		
Sugar		

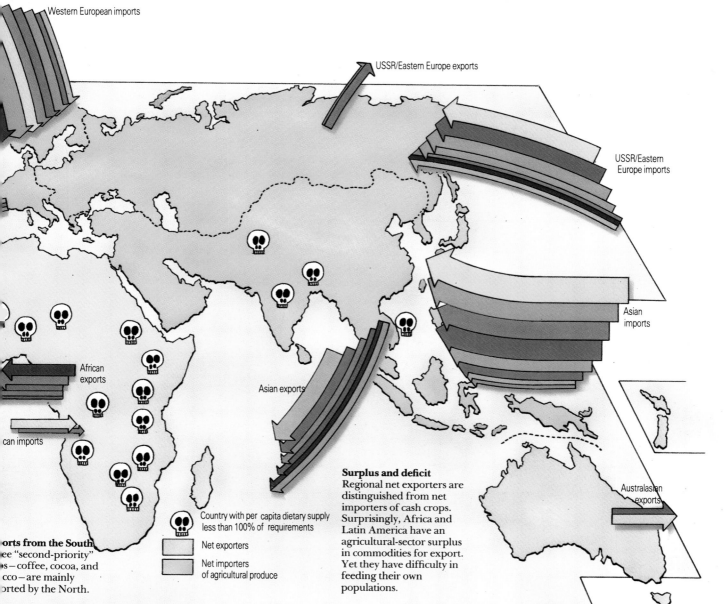

Western European imports

USSR/Eastern Europe exports

USSR/Eastern
Europe imports

Asian
imports

African
exports

Asian exports

can imports

Surplus and deficit
Regional net exporters are
distinguished from net
importers of cash crops.
Surprisingly, Africa and
Latin America have an
agricultural-sector surplus
in commodities for export.
Yet they have difficulty in
feeding their own
populations.

Australasian
exports

Country with per capita dietary supply
less than 100% of requirements

Net exporters

Net importers
of agricultural produce

orts from the South
ee "second-priority"
s—coffee, cocoa, and
cco—are mainly
rted by the North.

nuts in the Sahel
ing their period of colonialism and two
equent decades of independence, the Sahel
tries have not given enough priority to
ving food for local people. Instead, their
hasis has been on export crops such as
n and peanuts. In Niger alone, the amount
nd given over to peanut cultivation has
ed from 142,000 ha in 1954 to 432,000 ha in
3, causing a large reduction in fallow land.
sequently nomadic pastoralists, who
itionally used this land for grazing in the dry
on, moved north to previously unsettled
with poor carrying capacity. (Land carrying
city is a measure of how many people the
climate can permanently support when the
is planted with staple crops.) Population
sures and inadequate farming practices
since combined to turn moderate-to-poor
land into poor land, and poor land into
ss land (see pp 46-7).
hus at a time of famine in the Sahel, bumper
-crop exports have been recorded. And as
eal value of cash crops falls, the people who
ate what was grown on their own lands rely
asingly on imported food crops from the
h. The photograph, right, shows food aid
g distributed in the Sahel.

inclination, let alone the means, to reject aid that deflects their development strategies from their most urgent priority of feeding their peoples.

A streamlined food supply

As international trade expands and the world's economy grows more integrated, so the food of rich-world citizens tends to reach them from a "global farm" via a "global supermarket". At most major food stores in the West, consumers purchase products from all over the world. Similarly, millions of Third World people, together with large numbers of Soviet citizens, consume grain from North America, Australia, and Argentina. True, only one-tenth of all food grown enters international trade. But we can note a similar integrative pattern within individual countries, too, as agriculture gives way to "agribusiness".

There is much to be said for a commercial system that enables us to enjoy abundant and diversified products from remote croplands and to benefit from those farmers who produce most food cheapest. We now produce sufficient food to feed the whole of Earth's human population, a feat that would have been impossible only 100 years ago.

That we manage to feed such multitudes is due in part to giant enterprises that dominate our food system. These enterprises handle not only the sale of food; they often control the growing, processing, and distribution. A sound achievement, as long as it means a streamlined operation, with more, better, and cheaper food at the end of the line.

There lies the snag. We face a situation in which the mega-corporations are coming to wield virtual monopoly power over key sectors of the food trade. And their desire for more control over our food-

The global supermarket

Large-scale Western farmer
Many of these farmers rely on big corporations not only for processing and marketing their produce but also for supplying seeds and fertilizers. Their farms are huge, highly mechanized operations, geared to extract maximum immediate – though not necessarily sustainable – yields.

Seeds

The modern world agricultural system ever more resembles a giant supermarket, where large agribusiness corporations control the supply of seeds and fertilizer, the marketing of produce, and the shaping of consumer tastes. Thus they increasingly influence what is grown, and where; what is eaten, and by whom.

Coffee – where the money goes

Coffee is big business for the Third World. In 1980, it was worth almost $12 billion in export earnings, second only to petroleum. But this sum is only a fraction of the coffee trade's total value. The rest goes to shippers, brokers, processors, wholesalers, and retailers – virtually all located in the developed world.

Most coffee drunk is soluble coffee, and it is in the processing of beans into powder that the greatest profit margin lies. Yet coffee-growing nations of the Third World export only 4% of their coffee in processed form. This is because of the concentrated power of a few giant corporations, backed by protectionist governments, who are able to dictate terms of trade to producer nations. When Brazil started to market its own coffee powder in the US several years ago, it was threatened with an end to all coffee-trade agreements, even a cut-back on US aid. In the face of this hostile reaction, Brazil backed down.

20% to retailers

25% to processors and wholesalers

28% to traders, brokers, and shippers

19% to coffee-producing countries

8% to grower

Third World farmer
Caught up in the global food economy, many sm[...] Third World farmers are induced to cultivate exp[...] crops. This results in less good land being availab[...] for food crops. The agribusiness package (above) is often beyond their means.

producing systems is expanding even further. Since 1970, a few giant petro-corporations have quietly taken over more than 400 small seed businesses; businesses that hitherto produced seeds with vast variety to suit diverse environments, tastes, and price ranges. By controlling the production of seeds, a petro-corporation can breed crops that need extra-large dollops of synthetic fertilizer, pesticides, and other petroleum-based additives, regardless of more desirable trends for future agriculture (viz. away from reliance on fossil-fuel inputs). What happens when the oil wells run dry? The corporation answers that it will tackle those problems as they arise, but meanwhile it is a private profit-making concern, not a public charity.

Probably even more insidious in its ultimately detrimental impact on agriculture is the support provided by giant corporations to the "farmers'

lobby" in developed nations. The Common Agricultural Policy of the EEC causes governments to pay out $14 billion a year to encourage farmers to produce butter mountains and milk lakes. Similarly, American farmers are subsidized to the tune of around $40 billion a year. One "solution" proposed for these grotesque surpluses is to turn the milk lakes into powdered milk, and feed it back to the cows that gave the milk in the first place! By contrast, the World Bank estimates that the sum required to supply Third World subsistence farmers with the means to lift themselves out of self-reinforcing poverty is only $8 billion a year.

The global supermarket, dominated in part by giant corporations, is potentially a powerful medium that could serve us all. But much refinement on the part of governments, consumer organizations, and the like, is required if it is to serve the

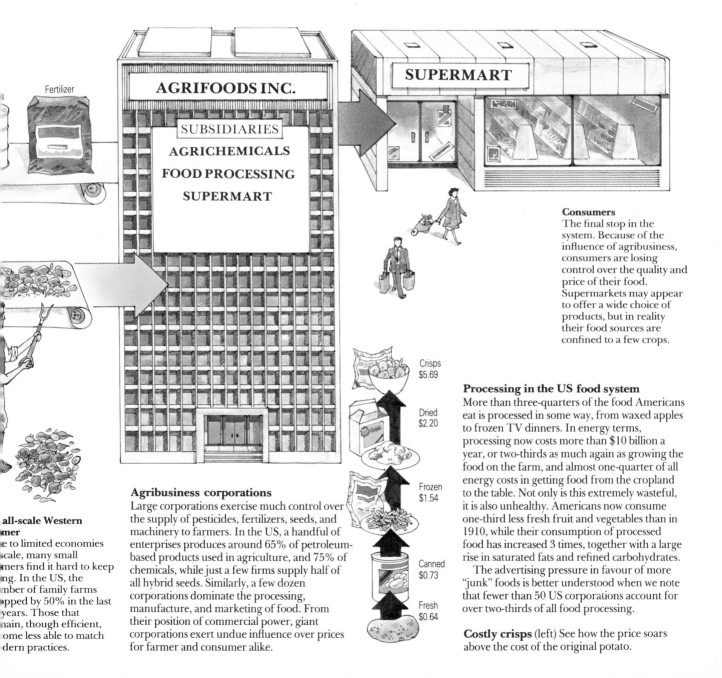

Fertilizer

AGRIFOODS INC.

SUBSIDIARIES

AGRICHEMICALS

FOOD PROCESSING

SUPERMART

SUPERMART

Crisps
$5.69

Dried
$2.20

Frozen
$1.54

Canned
$0.73

Fresh
$0.64

Consumers
The final stop in the system. Because of the influence of agribusiness, consumers are losing control over the quality and price of their food. Supermarkets may appear to offer a wide choice of products, but in reality their food sources are confined to a few crops.

Agribusiness corporations
Large corporations exercise much control over the supply of pesticides, fertilizers, seeds, and machinery to farmers. In the US, a handful of enterprises produces around 65% of petroleum-based products used in agriculture, and 75% of chemicals, while just a few firms supply half of all hybrid seeds. Similarly, a few dozen corporations dominate the processing, manufacture, and marketing of food. From their position of commercial power, giant corporations exert undue influence over prices for farmer and consumer alike.

Processing in the US food system
More than three-quarters of the food Americans eat is processed in some way, from waxed apples to frozen TV dinners. In energy terms, processing now costs more than $10 billion a year, or two-thirds as much again as growing the food on the farm, and almost one-quarter of all energy costs in getting food from the cropland to the table. Not only is this extremely wasteful, it is also unhealthy. Americans now consume one-third less fresh fruit and vegetables than in 1910, while their consumption of processed food has increased 3 times, together with a large rise in saturated fats and refined carbohydrates.

The advertising pressure in favour of more "junk" foods is better understood when we note that fewer than 50 US corporations account for over two-thirds of all food processing.

Costly crisps (left) See how the price soars above the cost of the original potato.

all-scale Western
mer
e to limited economies
scale, many small
mers find it hard to keep
ng. In the US, the
nber of family farms
pped by 50% in the last
years. Those that
nain, though efficient,
ome less able to match
dern practices.

best needs of customer and stockholder alike. Recently, the giant Nestle corporation was persuaded to promote its babies' powdered milk as the next-best alternative rather than as a substitute for mother's milk. This step forward was achieved mainly through citizen activists, proving that we *can* manage our affairs better if we – enough of us – insist that our voices be heard.

The forest cash crop

More people everywhere want more wood. We presently consume about three billion tonnes per year, more than half of it as fuel. By the year 2000 our demand could well increase to four billion tonnes, and it could easily soar to six billion before the middle of the next century.

In the developed world, a large amount of wood is used for paper: almost 200 million tonnes of pulp a year, compared with the developing nations' consumption of around 25 million. Developing nations have powerful incentives to develop their own sources of pulp, as they import virtually all their supplies at a cost that nearly wipes out their earnings from hardwood exports. As literacy increases, so the demand for paper increases: Brazil's consumption doubled during the 1960s, almost doubled again during the 1970s, and will increase by half as much again by the 1990s.

As for industrial timber, Northerners increasingly seek specialist hardwoods, notably those from the tropics, for constructional and semi-luxury purposes (see right). By contrast, timber in the South is used mostly for essential purposes. At least one billion Southerners can be described as living in the Wood Age. Yet because prices for wood are determined internationally, and thus tend to be set by consumption in the North, Southerners find themselves squeezed out of the marketplace. When Northerners have to pay a little more for stylish veneer or a newspaper, there may be complaints about inflation, but the upshot does not generally affect living standards. For a person in the South, an increase in price often means doing without.

These imbalances are aggravated by the forestry policies of several developed nations. Japan, for example, fears for its economic security in world wood markets. Hence it adopts a "siege strategy" by building up its own forests stocks and growing more wood than it cuts, while depending heavily on foreign sources of timber. Within the context of Japan's own needs, this approach makes sense. But within a global setting, it illustrates the "tragedy of the commons" – and will ultimately paint Japan itself into an ever-tighter corner.

What can we do to improve the global wood situation? Plenty. But we need to act as a community of nations for the benefit of all humankind. Adequate funding should be provided for the establishment of commercial fuelwood plantations in the tropics, where the year-round steamy-warm climates are ideal for generating timber – thus increasing

Harvesting the forest

Forest products represent one of our most valuable categories of cash crops. As such, they are widely traded around the world, albeit with unequal patterns between the developed and developing worlds. This trade is likely to expand, especially in so far as two of the main consuming regions, Japan and Western Europe (outside Scandinavia), intend to continue to import huge volumes, even though they could grow more wood at home. (Britain, for example, which imports nine-tenths of its wood needs, could reduce its demand by planting more trees on under-utilized land in Scotland.)

Demand for paper alone in the developed world is forecast to increase by a factor of 2.75 during the period 1975-2000, while developing nations, with their expanding populations, are likely to increase their consumption at least three-fold. The average Northerner consumes more than 150 kg of paper a year, compared with the Southerner's consumption of 5 kg.

The developed world also demands specialist hardwoods for numerous construction purposes, as well as for various luxury items such as parquet floors, fine furniture, decorative panelling, and weekend yachts. In Switzerland, whose forests are extensive and under-utilized, abachi wood is imported from the Ivory Coast to make super-fine coffins.

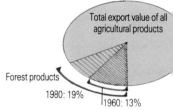

Plywood and other boards 1
Softwoods 37
Pulpwood and paper 29%
Hardwoods 21%

Trade in forest products
Unprocessed hard- and softwoods account for just over half of world trade. Pulp and paper make up about a third.

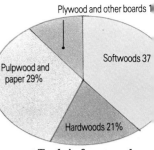

Total export value of all agricultural products
Forest products
1980: 19%
1960: 13%

A valuable export
In 1960, forest products accounted for 13% of all agricultural exports. By 1980 the real-value share had increased to 19%.

Product demand in the North ..
Northerners use huge amounts of wood for constructing houses, office buildings, railway sleepers, pit props, and the like. They also consume a great deal of paper products (notably packaging materials), as well as luxury hardwood items.

.. and South
Southerners likewise consume much wood, but mostly for fuel. Almost all houses in the Third World use wood, but not as high-grade construction material, rather as simple building poles. As for paper products, the average Southerner consumes all too little – to the detriment of education and communications.

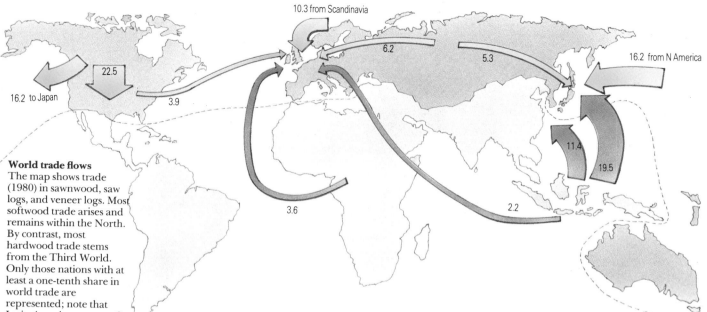

10.3 from Scandinavia

22.5

16.2 to Japan

3.9

6.2

5.3

16.2 from N America

11.4

19.5

3.6

2.2

World trade flows
The map shows trade (1980) in sawnwood, saw logs, and veneer logs. Most softwood trade arises and remains within the North. By contrast, most hardwood trade stems from the Third World. Only those nations with at least a one-tenth share in world trade are represented; note that Latin America accounts for less than 2% (all values are in millions of cubic metres).

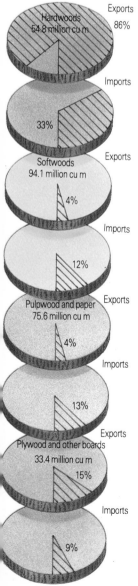

Exports
Hardwoods 54.8 million cu m
86%

Imports
33%

Exports
Softwoods 94.1 million cu m
4%

Imports
12%

Exports
Pulpwood and paper 75.6 million cu m
4%

Imports
13%

Exports
Plywood and other boards 33.4 million cu m
15%

Imports
9%

Imports and exports
The developing world figures only marginally in global trade of forest products, except for its massive exports of hardwood. (It appears to play a fair part in imports of hardwood, but this is all from other Third World nations.) Despite its need for wood, the developing world's share of global trade is projected to rise only a little by 2000.

Hatched area shows the proportion of trade by developing countres

A source of revenue
When large numbers of huge logs are taken from a Southeast Asia forest (top right), at least half of the remaining trees are injured beyond recovery. Yet the logger does not care, as long as there is enough forest to last for the next few years. Governments could be much tougher in enforcing less harmful harvesting techniques, but the need for hard cash often means that they fail to see their forests as sources of future revenue. Fortunately a partial breakthrough is on the way, in the form of increased wood processing: the veneer sheet (bottom right) earns several times more foreign exchange than a raw log, thus relieving pressure to exploit every forest tract.

wood stocks and relieving pressure on virgin forest. In addition, developed nations should review their own forestry policies, with a view to producing more home-grown wood (including hardwood) and encouraging greater recycling of paper (see pp 56-7). There is no doubt about the Earth's capacity to supply us with sufficient wood: the question lies with our commitment.

Planting tomorrow's trees

In the North, we can safely say that we know a good deal about how to manage forests. In the forests of the South, by contrast, we have scarcely made a start. Ironically, much of the problem lies with the streamlined techniques developed in the North. Many mechanized logging operations in the tropics are wasteful and destructive: often 75% of the surrounding canopy is damaged during one operation to extract a few commercially valuable species. Unlike temperate forests, tropical forests are unable to withstand such disruption because of their ecological complexity. In fact, tropical and temperate forests are so dissimilar that it would probably be better if we did not use the same word "forest" to describe them.

The main advance in the North in recent years has been in genetic engineering. Trees grown from tissue culture can quickly reforest large areas of denuded land. Also, geneticists are learning how to isolate the genes that make a tree species grow straight and tall, or produce wood with high tensile strength – whereupon they can replicate such prize characteristics in identical trees in large numbers.

But in the South, because of the critical role played by tropical forests (see pp 30-1, 44-5), it is better to establish "tree farms" on lands already deforested than to harvest the natural forest. A plantation of eucalyptus or pine can generate ten times as much sustainable harvest as can a patch of virgin forest. But a plantation costs at least $1,000 per hectare to establish, let alone to maintain; and the present rate of tree planting is not even one-tenth of the rate at which natural forests are being logged and degraded.

Fuelwood plantations are also urgently required to relieve pressure on natural forests. We need more trees around farms and in village woodlots, at least five times as many in the Third World as a whole right now, and between 20 and 50 times as many in certain African states. The difficulties, however, are not financial. Community forestry relies on the involvement of local people. If everybody's views are sought from the start, hopefully everybody will plant trees and tend them, and everybody will ensure that the harvesting system produces a regular supply of fuelwood.

Similar community efforts are needed to rehabilitate denuded watersheds in the South. In China, South Korea, and parts of India, there has been much success, due to the close coordination of planners and villagers.

Forests of the future

Tropical and temperate forests are so different in their biological makeup, that they need two fundamentally different approaches to their management. Temperate forests are actually expanding slightly, due to reforestation in the North. Densely settled zones such as southern West Germany are one-quarter covered with forests (but see p. 118). Much land, however, is still under-utilized: Scotland, for example, could accommodate much more tree cover.

Recycling paper
Developed countries could reduce their demand for paperpulp by at least one-quarter, simply through greater recycling. During World War II, most Northern countries recovered as much as half of their paper.

Forest management in the South
In most developing countries, forestry departments are understaffed and underfunded. Foresters see their main duty as keeping people out of forests, rather than helping them to establish woodlots, fuelwood plantations, and other village forestry projects. Fortunately, international agencies such as the World Bank are now taking the preservation of tropical forests seriously, and are promoting forestry as an important aspect of rural development. Although the Bank has no effective system for ensuring that ecological considerations are introduced at the outset of all projects, it can choose to withdraw aid if the project proves to be environmentally unsound. Recently, the Bank withdrew support for a Colombian cattle-ranching project after surveys showed the forest soils to be incapable of supporting large-scale development.

Paper products

Waste-paper coll

Paper manufacture

Pulping facto

Replanting watersheds
Nations are realizing the value of restoring tree cover on upland watersheds – a measure that benefits virtually everyone in the community. Although implemented on far too limited a scale as yet, this is an encouraging step forward.

Community forestry
Supported by international development agencies, many countries are encouraging their people to become actively involved in establishing fuelwood plantations. In Gujarat, India, schoolchildren may soon be raising as many tree seedlings as the government.

oning trees
uglas firs, American
amores, and several
er species may soon
out like mushrooms,
anks to recent advances
genetic engineering.
ey will grow straighter
d produce denser wood.
odern forestry should
ogress even more by the
ar 2000.

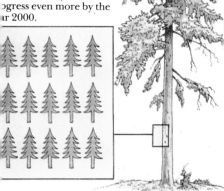

sustainable land-use system
trategy with much potential is agroforestry
own above), which amounts to growing trees
d food crops alongside each other. Forest land
d marginal land, normally rated unsuitable
crops, can be utilized for the production of
d. Certain tree species, notably the
uminous ones, fix atmospheric nitrogen in
soil, thereby helping to rehabilitate degraded
estlands.

e Chipko movement
1974, the women of Reni in northern India
k simple but effective action to stop tree
ing. They threatened to hug the trees if the
berjacks attempted to fell them. The
nen's protest (known as the Chipko
vement) saved 12,000 sq km of sensitive
ershed. The photograph, right, exemplifies
fierce concerns felt by many local people for
r forests.

The forests of West Germany
Covering a third of the country, these forests
occupy an important place in the national
psyche. According to Chancellor Kohl, they are
"of inestimable importance for the water cycle,
for our climate, for our health, for our
recreation, and for the identity of the German
landscape."

Slowly we are beginning to appreciate the manifold benefits tropical forests have to offer over and above temperate forests: benefits that will become available to us only when we manage the forests selectively and with understanding. We are also now recognizing their vital ecological role, especially in conserving soil, regulating the flow of water, generating rainfall, and moderating the climate.

Preventing erosion and desertification

The loss of soil and the spread of deserts is by no means confined to the developing world. A large share of the 275 million hectares of arable land that we are destined to lose by the year 2000 (see p. 40) will be in the developed world.

There are many ways to tackle the problem. We can establish shelterbelts of trees, practise better livestock husbandry, and plant resilient grass cover. We can use a more caring agriculture, in good lands as well as poor ones. But the single best approach is to halt the drift of too many farmers into areas where they should not be. In essence, the problem lies with the people who are rendered landless, pushed to the fringes of their national societies – and with vulnerable lands which are simply not suited to agriculture. In short, we must keep marginal people out of marginal lands.

The key to this approach lies in the enhanced use of our good agricultural land. Put another way, we must try to produce three-quarters of the extra food we shall need in the future, not from virgin territories, but from *existing* farmlands.

There is no doubt that we can do it, as demonstrated by some notable instances. If more farmers in Java practised the intensive and sustainable agriculture that has been standard in neighbouring Bali (which features as many people per unit area as Java, often more), much of Java's devastated land

Terracing

Especially susceptible to erosion are hilly areas wi~~th~~ fertile soils, notably volca~~nic~~ zones with their intensive~~ly~~ cultivated hill slopes. The answer is to construct terraces as exemplified b~~y~~ the 2,000-year-old rice paddies of the northern Philippines.

Managing the soil

The landscape above has been compressed in terms of scale to show the changes in land use as one moves from good agricultural land (left) to desert (right). The techniques suited to each category include soil-conserving practices and intensive use in high-potential lands; reduction of overload on arable lands to prevent topsoil loss; a sustainable mix of crops and livestock on intermediate farmlands; protection of the vulnerable dry lands and mountainous areas; and finally, attempts to halt desertification, and to rehabilitate other marginal lands.

Good land: intensified use

The best way to safeguard poor land is to make full use of the good land. The principal strategy is multiple use, growing crops in rapid rotation, and interplanting several crops at a time. The process is obviously enhanced by irrigation, despite its cost. Organic farming uses crop residues and other forms of mulch as "green manure". A few "garden farm" agro-ecosystems employ several dozen crops on just a couple of hectares, fostering renewable use of land.

Medium-value land

Moderately dry lands can be cultivated for cr~~ops~~ that withstand long rainless spells, e.g. millet, sorghum, amaranth, certain beans, and fast-maturing maize. But to safeguard against erosion, the farmer should employ a series of additional crops that restore soil fertility, suc~~h as~~ cowpea and groundnut, and allow for regula~~r~~ fallow periods.

could be rejuvenated into a garden isle like Bali. Similarly, other parts of Southeast Asia could be more productive if people were encouraged to follow the agricultural systems of the Chinese (see pp 62-3). In Amazonia, if newcomers adopted the traditional crop-growing strategies of long-established peasants in humid Latin America, the fertile floodplains of the Amazon, with their yearly enrichment of alluvial silt, could support millions of small-scale farmers in perpetuity. Only a very small fraction of the rainforests need be utilized to produce a flourishing agricultural civilization rivalling those of historic times in the Ganges and Mekong floodplains.

But if established croplands are to produce twice as much food, this will often mean a basic shift in agricultural strategies. The Green Revolution (pp 60-1) will need to be complemented by a Gene Revolution (pp 66-7). Much better use must be

made of scarce water through, for example, trickle-drip irrigation (pp 32 and 133). Priority should be given to growing food for local communities, with less emphasis on seductive diversions such as cash crops for export—a factor exemplified by the experience of the Sahel (see pp 46 and 51). Of course, this will not appeal to people with a stake in the status quo, such as the local elites who profit from the export trade. These are the people who, during the Sahel disaster, were responsible for maldistribution of $6 billion of foreign aid in the late 1970s. Only one percent went to forestry programmes such as desert-halting shelterbelts, and only three or four percent went to traditional grain-growing agriculture.

In many other lands that are not yet so unfortunate as the Sahel but are heading in a similar direction, there is need for a basic switch in development planning if there is to be more

Hardy animals
Disease-resistant varieties of cattle and sheep that can survive drought and subsist off little forage are best suited to marginal lands. While they do not generate massive amounts of meat and milk, they cause less harm to the environment than do more exotic breeds.

Aerodynamic windbreaks
In Rajasthan, rows of trees are planted along tracks and roads in order to reduce wind erosion. Tall trees are planted nearest the road, smaller trees in the second row, and small shrubs are planted nearest the fields. The aerodynamic design lifts the wind away from the fields without harmful eddies.

Favoured trees
Many trees and shrubs are available in the wild to help us resist desertification. *Prosopis* species are not only highly resistant to drought: their pods are rich in protein and make good livestock fodder. The *Casuarina* tree grows fast in sand and, being a tall upright tree, it makes a first-rate windbreak. *Leucaena* trees grow very swiftly, are fine for fuelwood and, because they fix their own nitrogen, help to restore soil fertility.

Livestock lands
Dry savannahs and grasslands easily suffer through over-large herds of cattle, sheep, and goats. Plainly the aim must be to reduce excess numbers, though in many areas, persuading the herdkeeper to sell off part of the holding can be difficult. Livestock is often the chief means of storing wealth in Third World countries. A backup strategy lies in rotational grazing, which gives over-worked pastures time to recover. Devegetated lands can be improved by planting legume grasses, such as clover and alfalfa, which help to restore soil fertility.

Established desert
Natural desert is irreversible. It is in the borderlands of deserts that we need to apply caring agricultural techniques to stop lands which have been rendered agriculturally worthless from being "tacked on" to natural desert. Shrubs and bushes serve as barriers to hold back dunes; some woody plants, such as guayule and jojoba, produce rubber and liquid wax. Other anti-desert plants include various types of brushwood and hardy trees.

efficient use of existing croplands. There must be a redirection of emphasis from industry and manufacturing to agriculture, from favouring the top ten percent (the entrepreneurs who will be the "locomotives" of economic growth) to favouring the bottom 40 percent, the poorest of the poor. While this runs counter to much conventional wisdom concerning development, it runs parallel to the main thrust of World Bank policies since the late 1970s.

A costly revolution

The Green Revolution is one of the most remarkable advances ever seen in agriculture. In the developed world it started to work its wonders during the 1940s, leading to record crops in North America and Western Europe from the 1950s onwards. In the developing world there was a time lag, but from the early 1960s, exceptional productivity became the norm in several parts of tropical Asia and Latin America. India, for example, produced only around 50 million tonnes of cereals and related food crops per year in the early 1950s; since then, the Green Revolution has taken off, pushing the total up, over two decades, to an extraordinary 108 million tonnes in 1970. Food available annually to an average Indian citizen increased from 141 to 197 kilograms, while net imports of food were more than halved.

But there is a price attached to this success story. The Green Revolution consists principally of planting so-called "high-yield" varieties of rice, wheat, and maize, varieties which produce bumper harvests, and in some cases mature faster, so that the farmer can grow two or even three crops in a year. But they are not so much high-yield as high-response varieties. They do their job only when they receive stacks of fertilizer, pesticides, irrigation water, and other additives, together with good

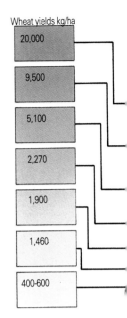

Wheat yields kg/ha
20,000
9,500
5,100
2,270
1,900
1,460
400-600

Green revolution?

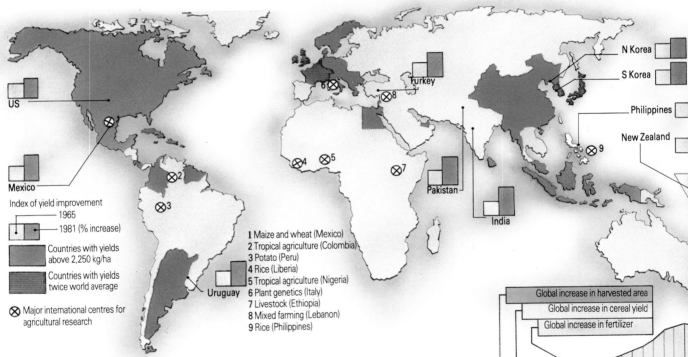

Index of yield improvement
1965
1981 (% increase)

Countries with yields above 2,250 kg/ha

Countries with yields twice world average

⊗ Major international centres for agricultural research

US
Mexico
Uruguay

1 Maize and wheat (Mexico)
2 Tropical agriculture (Colombia)
3 Potato (Peru)
4 Rice (Liberia)
5 Tropical agriculture (Nigeria)
6 Plant genetics (Italy)
7 Livestock (Ethiopia)
8 Mixed farming (Lebanon)
9 Rice (Philippines)

Turkey
Pakistan
India

N Korea
S Korea
Philippines
New Zealand

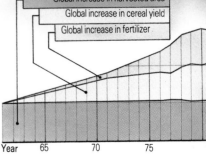

Global increase in harvested area
Global increase in cereal yield
Global increase in fertilizer
Year   65   70   75

As a result of the Green Revolution, a good number of countries have expanded their output of cereal crops in exceptional fashion – notably of rice, wheat, and maize, the three leading cereals. If we take a global average cereal yield of 2,250 kg/ha (1981), we find that substantial numbers of nations now achieve harvests well over this, some of them double. These include such populous developing countries as Mexico, Egypt, Indonesia, and China. In the developed world, which had a head start, we find that France, the UK, the Netherlands, Japan, and the US have established one record after another. But average cereal yields conceal the most dramatic success stories of the Green Revolution (see country indicators on map): India has doubled its wheat yield in 15 years; in the Philippines,

rice yield has risen by 75%; and locally, many farmers are achieving even greater increases. In 1965, the area planted with high-yielding grains in the Third World was only 60,000 ha, a total that expanded to over 50 million ha by the late 1970s. More than half of all wheat lands in India and Pakistan now feature Green Revolution varieties, and in the Philippines, half the area planted to rice. As a measure of the benefits in Asia alone, the increased output totalled at least 15 million tonnes in 1976, roughly double the harvest in 1971, with an economic value of at least $1.5 billion. Meanwhile, research into the new crops and agricultural techniques continues, though grossly underfunded. The map shows the location of some of the major international research centres for agriculture in the Third World.

Inputs and outputs
Using a base-line value of 100 for the early 1960s, we find that the global yield of cereals topped 200% in the late 1970s. The linkage with fertilizer is clear: a value of 285% for the late 1970s (the area harvested increased by 6% over the same period). Since then, yield has tended to level off. The Green Revolution has only given us a breathing space.

farming techniques. Fertilizer from fossil fuels, a key component of the package, was cheap during the Revolution's early years. But after OPEC imposed its first price jump in 1973, costs have soared. The situation has been aggravated by increasing demand. High-yield varieties need 70-90 kilograms of nitrogen per hectare, whereas the average amount available in most developing countries is only about 25 kilograms. If India's farmers were to apply fertilizer at the same rate as Dutch farmers, their needs would amount to one-third of global consumption.

Equally to the point, there has recently been a levelling off of increases in global grain yield. The problem lies with the "fertiliser response ratio", i.e. the return, in increased yields, produced by using additional fertilizer. Worldwide, this response ratio is decreasing, as the biological limits of the new hybrid strains are reached.

There have also been adverse economic and social repercussions. The high-yield varieties tend to be planted by those farmers who can afford the expensive additives. The bigger harvests generate greater incomes, which can then be invested in extra land. Slowly but steadily, the rich farmers broaden the gap between themselves and the poor farmers.

In short, the Green Revolution has achieved some remarkable breakthroughs, but it has many drawbacks and is plainly running out of steam. What of the future? The challenges are sizeable: after doubling our food supplies between 1950 and 1980, we must try to increase them by at least another half by the year 2000. And before we can hope to reach ecological accord with our One-Earth home, we shall need to expand our harvest by more than three times the present output. As "the Father of the Green Revolution", Norman Borlaug, has put it, the Green Revolution has merely given us a few years of

Theoretical maximum

Highest achieved

Highest average
(major wheat producers)

Developed- country
average

Global average

Developing-country
average

Traditional- varieties
average

Cornucopia
The performance of high-yield crops depends on climate and technology. The best average yield for wheat is more than double the world average – but only slightly over half of the highest achieved yield, a quarter of the theoretical maximum. The Green Revolution has a good way to go yet.

Before

**What the Green
Revolution promised
Muda
1.** To increase Malaysia's
self-sufficiency in rice
2. To increase farmers'
incomes, with fair shares
for all.

Before and after in Muda
A multi-faceted landscape with a pluralist society (above) has been transformed into a homogenized landscape dominated by larger holdings (below). The endless resort to slash-and-burn farming in Malaysia's forests.

After

Promise and reality: Muda River
However capable the Green Revolution has proven to be in agronomic terms, its economic and social success has been mixed at best. In northern Malaysia, the Muda River area reveals what can go wrong.

A $90-million dam allowed irrigated paddies to produce two crops of high-yield rice a year, instead of the traditional rice. By the early 1970s, output had almost tripled. Before the project, the area (which accounted for 30% of Malaysia's rice-growing land) supplied 30% of the country's rice; this rapidly rose to 50%. Previously Malaysia had been only half self-sufficient in rice; by 1974, it was 90%. But whereas average incomes for all categories of farmers increased, the wealthier categories enjoyed a boost of 150%, while poorer farmers experienced only a 50% advance. The gap between the rich farmer and the impoverished peasant increased from 900 Malaysian dollars per month to 2,350.

Worse still, the harvests failed to expand after 1974, due to the "plateauing" effect: the more fertilizer farmers applied to their crops, the more their returns diminished, until yields finally levelled off. In this second stage, real incomes fell for all farmers, but especially for the poor who, by 1979, dropped below pre-Revolution levels. Moreover, the richer farmers, finding themselves with disposable income, started to buy up land from the poorer farmers, causing the bottom sector of the community to take up tenant farming, or to be pressurized off the land altogether.

"To those that have shall be given …": the gap between the well-to-do and the absolutely impoverished increases *within* the Third World, as well as between the Third World and the developed world. This regrettable pattern has been repeated in virtually all countries of the Green Revolution, with the signal exceptions of egalitarian societies such as China and Sri Lanka.

grace in which to sort out larger problems, notably the runaway growth of population and the grossly inequitable distribution of land and food.

We need fresh strategies. We must adapt our present powerful agricultural models (pp 62-5), and devise another revolutionary advance in agriculture to complement the Green Revolution. Fortunately we possess the makings of just such an advance (pp 66-7). It is not so much a case of "Can we?". Rather it is a case of "Shall we?".

A model for the developing world

Where India's record is patchy, China's is remarkable. Before the Communist Revolution in 1949, several million people starved each year. Soil erosion was widespread, rivers regularly burst their banks, and droughts brought about by human activity were common. Today China has more than twice as many people, almost all of whom are adequately fed (virtually none is over-fed), soil cover is being restored and fertility enhanced, rivers serve the people instead of swamping them, and much of eastern China looks like a garden landscape. Rice yields are twice as high as India's, due primarily to more irrigation, which in turn allows for increased multiple cropping—a factor which compensates for the fact that China has only half as much arable land per person as India.

The Chinese model

China has largely succeeded in eliminating malnutrition—no mean feat in a country that supports one in five of humankind. The Chinese not only produce massive amounts of food, but—equally to be acclaimed—they ensure it is fairly shared among all. Furthermore, they are leaders in "ecological agriculture", with emphasis on wasting nothing. They recycle much of their crop residues and by-products, and also their general garbage and waste (not surprising, when we remember that the Chinese have long had to learn how to make do with limited natural resources).

The largest irrigation network in the world, built at a cost of much human sweat, enables China to grow more than one-third of the world's rice, almost as much as the next five together, viz. India, Indonesia, Bangladesh, Japan, and Thailand. Farming methods do not rely on heavy machinery, so that hundreds of millions of peasants are usefully employed on the land. Abundant human labour further allows several crops to be grown in one field in alternate rows, with symbiotic benefit all round (e.g. beans, as legumes, supply "free" nitrogen fertilizer to wheat plants). Labour-intensive pest control permits crop spraying only against particular outbreaks—a strategy that is far more cost-effective and environmentally benign than regular broadscale spraying.

A self-sufficient commune

In a 90,000-person commune in the Pearl River delta, a single production team, comprising 89 families, seeks to operate a harmoniously functioning agro-ecosystem. The unit combines crop growing, stock husbandry, fish raising, and renewable energy into a single integrated system. Each team generates virtually all its own food, fertilizer, and energy, while exporting a surplus of food to nearby towns. Little is left to waste: banana leaves and sugarcane fibre, for example, serve as fish food and as fuel for bio-gas stoves; large bio-digester devices break down plant material provided by fast-growing plants such as water hyacinths and Napier grass.

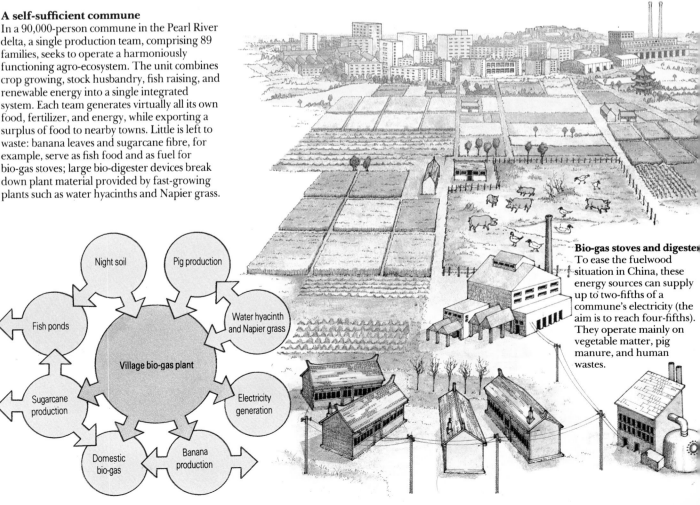

Bio-gas stoves and digester
To ease the fuelwood situation in China, these energy sources can supply up to two-fifths of a commune's electricity (the aim is to reach four-fifths). They operate mainly on vegetable matter, pig manure, and human wastes.

Night soil

Pig production

Fish ponds

Water hyacinth and Napier grass

Village bio-gas plant

Sugarcane production

Electricity generation

Domestic bio-gas

Banana production

To this impressive extent, China's agriculture may serve as a model for other developing countries. True, success depends in part on China's political orientation. But much also depends simply on agricultural skills, regardless of ideology. However often China's leaders may assert that their approach is not for export, and that each country must work out its salvation according to its resources, many a developing country could learn a lot from China.

They could learn about, for instance, organic farming, with its emphasis on recycling of farm wastes for inexpensive fertilizer; about biological controls to keep down pests and weeds; about China's emphasis on human labour rather than costly machinery; about choosing crop varieties that suit local conditions; about soil conservation measures, notably terracing; about use of energy in forms other than fossil fuel, e.g. the methane gas produced by seven million bio-gas digesters; about care for the forests, which support agriculture through their watershed services and supply fuel (thus relieving pressure on valuable cattle dung); and about innovative aquaculture, enabling the Chinese to produce 10 times more animal protein from one unit area of fish pond than the same unit of land given over to livestock.

Nor is this all. China's agriculture and industry are increasingly integrated and decentralized, so

...egration between countryside and city
...avoid the dichotomies that afflict many ...rd World economies, the Chinese try to ...en the distinction between farmer and ...ory worker. Many communes feature light ...ustries, e.g. manufacture of cement and farm ...s. Conversely, most cities feature a spread of ...n plots. This integrated approach allows ...ons and communities to achieve a high ...ree of self-reliance.

...farming
...Chinese have developed aquaculture, or ...farming", into a fine art – as it deserves to ...nsidering that it permits a conversion-...ency ratio (turning feed into animal ...in) far higher than is available through ...stic stock. China produces 2 million tonnes ...shwater fish a year, out of a global total of 6 ...n tonnes. In a typical pond, silver carp and ...ad carp occupy the upper and middle ..., feeding respectively off water plants, ...cane leaves and cut grass, and off plankton ...lgae; while dace occupy the lower layer, ...g off scum. The mini-ecosystem is ...ned with public waste, while the resultant ...e supplies fertilizer for farm crops. ...ugh this approach, a pond yields an ...ge of almost 4.5 tonnes of fish per hectare ...ar, for a protein-production rate 5 times ...than the best crop alternative.

A garden landscape
The visitor to China is struck by the "garden landscapes" of eastern China, where the majority of the population lives. Almost everywhere, farm plots appear carefully tended, with intensive use made of every last square metre of land. The two paintings above from Hu county depict an autumn harvest scene and an orchard that was once a barren hill. These peasant paintings are among the first such works of art to be released to the West.

there is less conflict between city and countryside. Of course China's leaders can simply impose their balanced strategy on their citizenry. But the community tends to be spared the dead hand of the urban elite that blights the development prospects of many Third World countries.

The Western agricultural model

American farmers are extraordinarily productive. Amounting to only about two in 100 of the US populace, they not only feed their fellow citizens, but provide more than half of all agricultural products on international markets. Feeding people is the country's biggest business, with food sales now topping $300 billion a year. American farmers produce 15 percent of the world's wheat, 21 percent of oats, 36 percent of sorghum, and 46 percent of maize on only 11 percent of the world's croplands.

For decades, the world has benefited from America's food surpluses. But the prospect of further unfaltering success is an illusion. While industrial agriculture is extraordinarily productive, it can also be extraordinarily destructive—in a slow, quiet manner, which means that the situation could become critical even before it appears serious.

What are the costs of this advanced form of agriculture? The first and heaviest toll must surely be in soil loss. An astonishing 80 million hectares of US croplands, an area almost twice the size of California, have been rendered unproductive, if not ruined outright. The nation has lost at least one-third of its best topsoils, and erosion rates are now worse than ever, as much as five billion tonnes per year (pp 40-1).

Secondly, the prodigal application of synthetic fertilizers (an average of 125 kilograms per hectare per year) and pesticides is responsible for over half of all US water pollution. The annual cost of this pollution is fast approaching $1 billion. Thirdly, the spread of irrigation, which accounts for over 80 percent of US water use, is steadily depleting the country's groundwater stocks. (The natural rate of replenishment of these supplies is very slow—see pp 108-9). Finally, transport costs incurred in the distribution of food now amount to $5 billion a year, almost as much as growing it on the farm.

Not surprisingly, the industrialization of agriculture in the US has turned many farms into sizeable commercial enterprises. Since 1950 there has been a steady trend toward large holdings, until now there are only half as many farmers. Due to the escalating costs of fertilizer, pesticides, fuel, and land itself, farmers have run themselves deeply into debt, from $40 billion in 1970 to almost $215 billion in 1983, the average debt approaching $70,000. Hence farmers feel obliged to reap ever-larger harvests each year, in apparent indifference to the environmental costs.

American agriculture of the past three decades epitomizes the successes, and the failures, of industrial farming worldwide. The model has been much

Agriculture in the balance

Each year, there are more mouths to feed—about 80 million more. That we have largely managed to feed them so far is an extraordinary tribute to the success of agriculture. Grain production rose from 623 million tonnes in 1950 to 1,447 million in 1983. Much of this massive increase arises from Western-type "high-tech" solutions, using oil-based fertilizers and new hybrids planted in huge monocultures. America's dominance is ever-greater: it now provides 90% of net grain exports. But the 30-year success story conceals a major loss of momentum. Since 1973, overall output has merely kept pace with population; regionally there has been failure to do so, notably in Africa, where local shortages are endemic. Food security is faltering, with growing malnutrition, even famine. In 1983, global grain production per capita fell sharply, partly due to drought: are the scales tipping towards failure?

Each sack represents 50 million tonnes of grain

Eating oil
Since 1950, population growth has reduced grain lands per head by a third, but per capita fertilizer use has risen five-fold. Grain production per capita rose steadily until the 1973 oil crisis, then levelled off. In 1983, it actually fell.

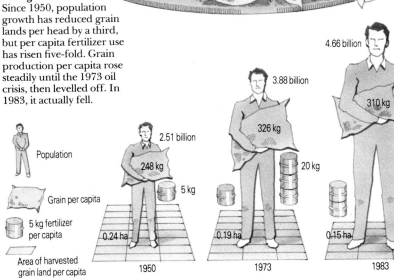

Population

Grain per capita

5 kg fertilizer per capita

Area of harvested grain land per capita

2.51 billion
248 kg
5 kg
0.24 ha
1950

3.88 billion
326 kg
20 kg
0.19 ha
1973

4.66 billion
310 kg
0.15 ha
1983

The costs of advanced agriculture
Many of today's farmers practise a form of "deficit financing". To meet urgent needs, from food to interest on loans, they are depleting our future land base, destroying our wild and cultivated genetic heritage, using up fossil energy and groundwater supplies, and applying toxic chemicals to the land. We lose nearly half our crops to resistant pests and bad storage, produce "milk lakes" we cannot dispose of, and use vital land to grow feed for livestock, to support unhealthy meat-rich diets. Meanwhile, poorer countries experience falling food sufficiency, inadequate research facilities, and growing social inequality.

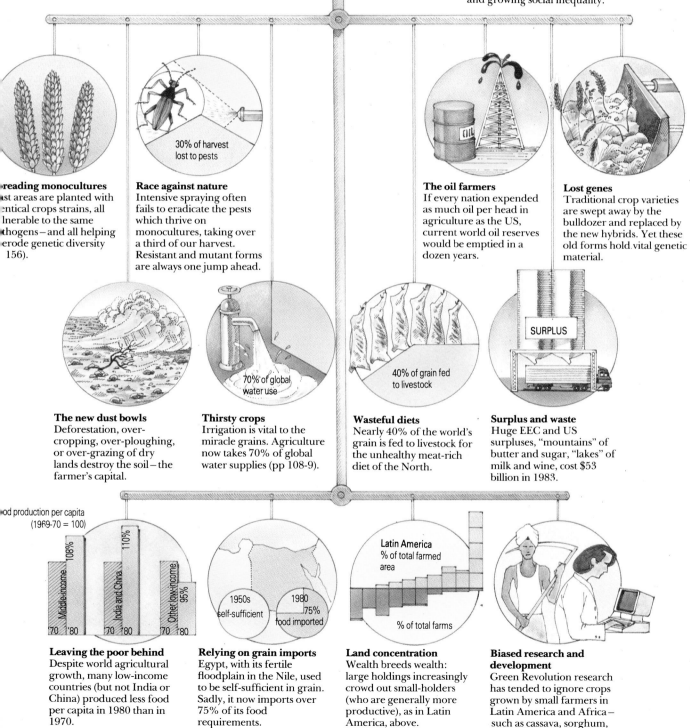

Failure

30% of harvest lost to pests

reading monocultures
st areas are planted with entical crops strains, all lnerable to the same thogens – and all helping erode genetic diversity 156).

Race against nature
Intensive spraying often fails to eradicate the pests which thrive on monocultures, taking over a third of our harvest. Resistant and mutant forms are always one jump ahead.

The oil farmers
If every nation expended as much oil per head in agriculture as the US, current world oil reserves would be emptied in a dozen years.

Lost genes
Traditional crop varieties are swept away by the bulldozer and replaced by the new hybrids. Yet these old forms hold vital genetic material.

70% of global water use

40% of grain fed to livestock

SURPLUS

The new dust bowls
Deforestation, over-cropping, over-ploughing, or over-grazing of dry lands destroy the soil – the farmer's capital.

Thirsty crops
Irrigation is vital to the miracle grains. Agriculture now takes 70% of global water supplies (pp 108-9).

Wasteful diets
Nearly 40% of the world's grain is fed to livestock for the unhealthy meat-rich diet of the North.

Surplus and waste
Huge EEC and US surpluses, "mountains" of butter and sugar, "lakes" of milk and wine, cost $53 billion in 1983.

od production per capita (1969-70 = 100)

Middle-income 108%
'70 '80
India and China 110%
'70 '80
Other low-income 95%
'70 '80

1950s self-sufficient

1980 75% food imported

Latin America % of total farmed area

% of total farms

Leaving the poor behind
Despite world agricultural growth, many low-income countries (but not India or China) produced less food per capita in 1980 than in 1970.

Relying on grain imports
Egypt, with its fertile floodplain in the Nile, used to be self-sufficient in grain. Sadly, it now imports over 75% of its food requirements.

Land concentration
Wealth breeds wealth: large holdings increasingly crowd out small-holders (who are generally more productive), as in Latin America, above.

Biased research and development
Green Revolution research has tended to ignore crops grown by small farmers in Latin America and Africa – such as cassava, sorghum, and millet.

copied and adapted, and applied widely in Green Revolution areas. The success is self-evident, and seductive. But the sting in the tail is now increasingly evident to Americans, who are slowly preparing to embark on a wholly new strategy.

The new agricultural revolution

We need a new revolution in agriculture, both scientific and political. Fortunately the germ of the scientific one already exists. But the political will and means to apply it are yet half-formed.

Hitherto our approach has been to "bend" the environment to suit our crops. Now, thanks to plant breeders and genetic engineers, we can bend the plants instead – manipulating crops to flourish in harmony with their environments, rather than in spite of them. Instead of pouring in fertilizer, water, weedkillers, and pesticides, we can grow plants that fend for themselves – desert-dwellers like jojoba, new arid-land staples like the morama bean or buffalo gourd, crops tolerant of extreme temperatures; even strains of wheat, barley, and tomatoes that permit seawater irrigation.

We already make use of legumes which produce their own fertilizer via the symbiotic nitrogen-fixing bacteria in their roots. By the turn of the century, we may manage to transfer this capacity to other plants, whereupon farmers need not fear the rising cost of synthetic nitrogen. Crop breeders are also exploiting disease resistance in wild species to

More research
Increased funding and ne[w] research centres are badly needed, especially in low-income areas, to develop locally adapted strains and cultivation techniques relevant to small and large scale farmers.

Towards a new agriculture

Ecology has shaped integrated pest management, water-conserving irrigation methods, new organic fertilizers, and new uses of crop residues and green mulches to protect land and improve energy efficiency. Conservation tillage prevents soil loss; now employed on 40 million ha in the US, and increasing rapidly, it has even greater value in tropical areas. Future crops will be self-sufficient and high-yielding, tailored to their setting. But research support is slim – a mere 3% of global science expenditure. (In the US, gene conservation, vital to the future, draws less funds now than in the '70s.) The farms of the future will need more research and greater protection of genetic resources (pp 164-5).

Managing pests
Integrated pest control has been enormously successful in trials. It aims not to wipe out pests, but to keep them at tolerable levels, by applying a range of "natural" restraints – mixed planting; clearing pest reservoirs such as stagnant pools; introducing natural predators; laying bait; releasing sterile pest males; even using hormones to interfere with maturation.

Yeheb

Conservation tillage
Minimum-till farming is energy-efficient and protects the soil. Crop residues and stubble left on the land retain nutrients and prevent erosion. Next year's crop is sown in shallow, restricted furrows, or drilled in without turning the soil.

Plants with a future
Food plants adapted to harsh lands are offering us new solutions.
The Somalian Yeheb bush
This arid-land native has nutritious peanut-sized seeds, and could be a staple crop of the deserts.
The hairy wild potato To keep aphids at bay, this wild plant mimics the alarm scent of aphids. These pest-deterrent devices could one day be bred into crops.

Hairy potato

Food first in the South
If the new agriculture is to lift the South on its wings, it must be truly revolutionary. A sharp turnround is called for, from over-emphasis on industry to farming, from export cash crops to domestic supply, and from commercial landholder to small farmer. To achieve food sufficiency, small farmers must be backed by regional co-operation, for however willing and productive they may be, they need a package of facilities to succeed. These include: credit and better prices; improved marketing, transport and advisory services; appropriate research; an[d] security of tenure and access to good land. The best example of "food first" is China, now feeding 22% of the world's population on 7% [of] the world's arable land.

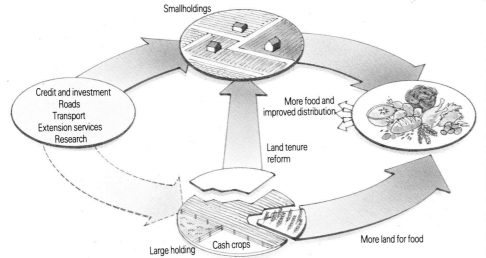

Smallholdings

Credit and investment
Roads
Transport
Extension services
Research

More food and improved distribution

Land tenure reform

Large holding   Cash crops   More land for food

develop crops with built-in defences. Genetic adaptations which enable plants to photosynthesize more efficiently and to grow more rapidly are also being selected for in new crop varieties.

These breakthroughs are the centre-pieces of the forthcoming Gene Revolution, a quantum change greater than either the Green Revolution or the previous Agricultural Revolution, several centuries ago. To succeed, it will require greater emphasis on research than ever before, and a set of new economic strategies to take agriculture out of the "Cinderella" status. But most of all, it will require political changes, a revolution so profound that every individual will be affected. For as long as rich-world citizens, by their high meat diets,

continue to support the inequitable meat/grain connection, land will be over-worked, and people will go hungry. And as long as certain developing nations emphasize industry, urbanization, and export cash crops at the expense of food sufficiency and the small farmer, the same applies.

Given proper backup, the small farmers (who today make up over half of the world's one billion poor) can feed themselves, as many countries, such as China and Sri Lanka, have shown. Given the right advice, rich citizens can improve their diets, as Norway has successfully proved (see below). Given our new scientific understanding, the land can supply a sustainable harvest to feed us. It is merely a matter of getting our priorities right.

Mixed cropping
Interplanting and crop rotation maintain soil balance, reduce pest invasions, and by providing green cover below row plants prevent evaporation and erosion. Legumes, which fix nitrogen, restore fertility if planted between maize or permanent crops.

Gene banks
Preserving crop diversity in cold storage (pp 164-5) and running local seed libraries allow farmers a choice of solutions to cultivation problems.

Greenhouses
Cultivation under glass or in huge plastic tunnels can provide valuable cash crops from lands otherwise unsuited to farming, but is energy intensive. Israel farms the desert in this way to earn export cash, and so import staples.

Spirulina A tiny protein-rich alga that flourishes in the brackish lakes of arid lands is harvested in Mexico and Chad.

Pommelo This large citrus offers a high food value.
The winged bean Almost unknown 10 years ago, this bean promises to become the soyabean of the tropics. Every part of the plant is edible and, being a legume, it fixes nitrogen too.

Winged bean

Pommelo

Trickle-drip techniques
Irrigation controlled via pierced pipes both saves water and reduces the salt build-up due to evaporation.

Less grain to cattle

More grain for people

Low-meat diet

More fallow land

Organic fertilizer

Meat last in the North
The obvious medicine for the soil sickness of developed agriculture is, at first glance, unpalatable: increased fallow periods, and total idling of worst-eroded lands. How then to feed the grain-hungry world? The answer to this dilemma is surprising. An average US citizen today consumes about 800 kg of grain a year, nearly all indirectly as meat—an increase, since 1960, of about 160 kg which is nearly the *total* amount consumed by a better-fed African. Merely by reverting to diets of 20 years ago, rich-world citizens could improve their health, release large amounts of grain, and free some land. The Norwegian government pioneered this approach, with farm incentives and public education. Even individually, many rich-world people are turning to a more meat-free diet, and herein lies much hope for the world.

OCEAN

Introduced by the Rainbow Warrior crew
the Greenpeace vessel

The porpoise, a lactating female, must have put up a terrific struggle before she drowned. Her body was entangled in five layers of monofilament net, of the type which Japanese fishermen stretch across hundreds of miles of ocean at a time. In our travels, we have also stumbled across "ghost nets"–vast, torn fragments of net which have broken loose to drift with the waves, ensnaring unthinkable numbers of ocean creatures.

We have stepped up our campaign against Japan's vast fishing fleets, which are systematically "vacuum-cleaning" the Pacific and North Atlantic. But the over-harvesting of its living resources is only one of the critical threats to the world ocean. Others include serious industrial and oil pollution; the dumping of nuclear and toxic wastes; the sea-bed disturbance caused by deep-sea mining; and the destruction of rich coastal ecosystems, from saltmarsh to mangroves and coral reef. Eventually, with new national and international laws, many such activities will be branded as ecological crimes; but the legislative machinery often grinds exceedingly slowly. Sometimes non-violent direct action by concerned groups is the only way to focus public attention on an issue–and so accelerate the political process.

Our first major vessel, used in many confrontations with whalers, polluters and dumpers, was named *Rainbow Warrior*, after an ancient North American Indian legend. This predicted that "when the Earth is sick and the animals disappear, the Warriors of the Rainbow will come to protect the wildlife and to heal the Earth". They would come from all races, creeds, and colours, putting their faith in deeds, not words.

The daunting task of converting the old, rusting trawler was undertaken by volunteers from all round the world. But the real test came when the crews of our inflatable slammed through the waves off Iceland, interposing themselves as a human barrier between harpooners and their quarry. Later campaigns focused on such issues as dumping of acid and radioactive wastes.

The most exciting thing about these campaigns is the way they have mobilized public support. When *Sirius*, another Greenpeace vessel, sailed on a protest mission to Nordenham, West Germany, to highlight the dumping of titanium dioxide waste in the German Bight, she was accompanied by 54 fishing boats–and carried letters of support from the British, Dutch, and French Fishing Federations. The factory owners were so taken aback that they undertook to reduce dumping at sea, and to increase recycling.

Actions, unfortunately, often speak louder than words. But the words and images which follow in this section explain why our protest is so urgent. We can no longer use the world ocean as a dustbin. We must view it as a living ecosystem, a vital and integral part of our planet's workings. It will prove a critical testing ground for our emerging planet management skills.

THE OCEAN POTENTIAL

Our planet should not be called Earth but Ocean – at least seven-tenths is covered with seas.

We know little about this water planet. Although the oceans are just as diverse as the land, and interwoven with human history, we tend to see them as barriers, as alien spaces. In reality, however, ocean ecosystems are continuous – or rather, a single ecosystem, a world ocean with land masses as the true barriers, though gradients of temperature and salinity separate the oceans into a multiple series of discrete regions.

It takes a "leap of the imagination" to perceive the integral role of the ocean in our planet's workings. The interdependent circulatory systems of ocean and atmosphere determine climatic flows right around the globe. At the same time, the great accumulations of seawater, almost entirely placid beneath the surface, exert a major stabilizing influence on climate: their very bulk produces a "flywheel" effect, a powerful buffer for what would otherwise be drastic fluctuations in our weather. The oceans also serve as a great reservoir of

Warm currents
1 Irminger
2 Norway
3 Gulf Stream
4 North Equatorial
5 Equatorial Counter Current
6 South Equatorial
7 Brazil
8 Kuroshio
9 Alaska
10 Agulhas
11 East Australian

The world ocean

The ocean is a single, dynamic medium, its waters constantly on the move under the influence of the sun's heat (which provides the initial thrust), the Earth's rotation, and solar and lunar tides. The major currents, great "travelators" of the ocean, deliver huge masses of water over long distances, providing a continuous interchange between warm equatorial water and cold water from the poles. The consequences for climate, marine ecosystems, and human fisheries are vital. The warm Gulf Stream, for instance, surging along faster than any ship, transports 55 million cu m per second – 50 times more water than all the world's rivers. Without it, the "temperate" lands of northwestern Europe would be more like the sub-Arctic. The Peru current and the Benguela of southwest Africa produce marine bonanzas as they bring in nutrient-rich waters dragged to the surface by offshore winds – a superabundance of plankton, fish, and seabirds. The map shows the major warm and cold surface currents, and the densities of human populations – a great proportion of them living in coastal zones.

The sea-floor's wealth
The dramatic ridges and trenches of the ocean abyss express its history, for the sea floor is in motion. Just as the continental "plates" drift on a hot, partially molten underlayer, so the ocean bed, too, is made up of moving plates. The great mid-oceanic ridges mark where plates are separating: the molten underlayer pushes up through the rift to form ridge material, while the sea floor spreads steadily away from the ridge axis. At the ocean margins, deep trenches occur as the oceanic and continental plates collide and one is drawn down under the other. Understanding sea-floor plate interactions helps scientists predict the locations of valuable minerals for future exploitation.

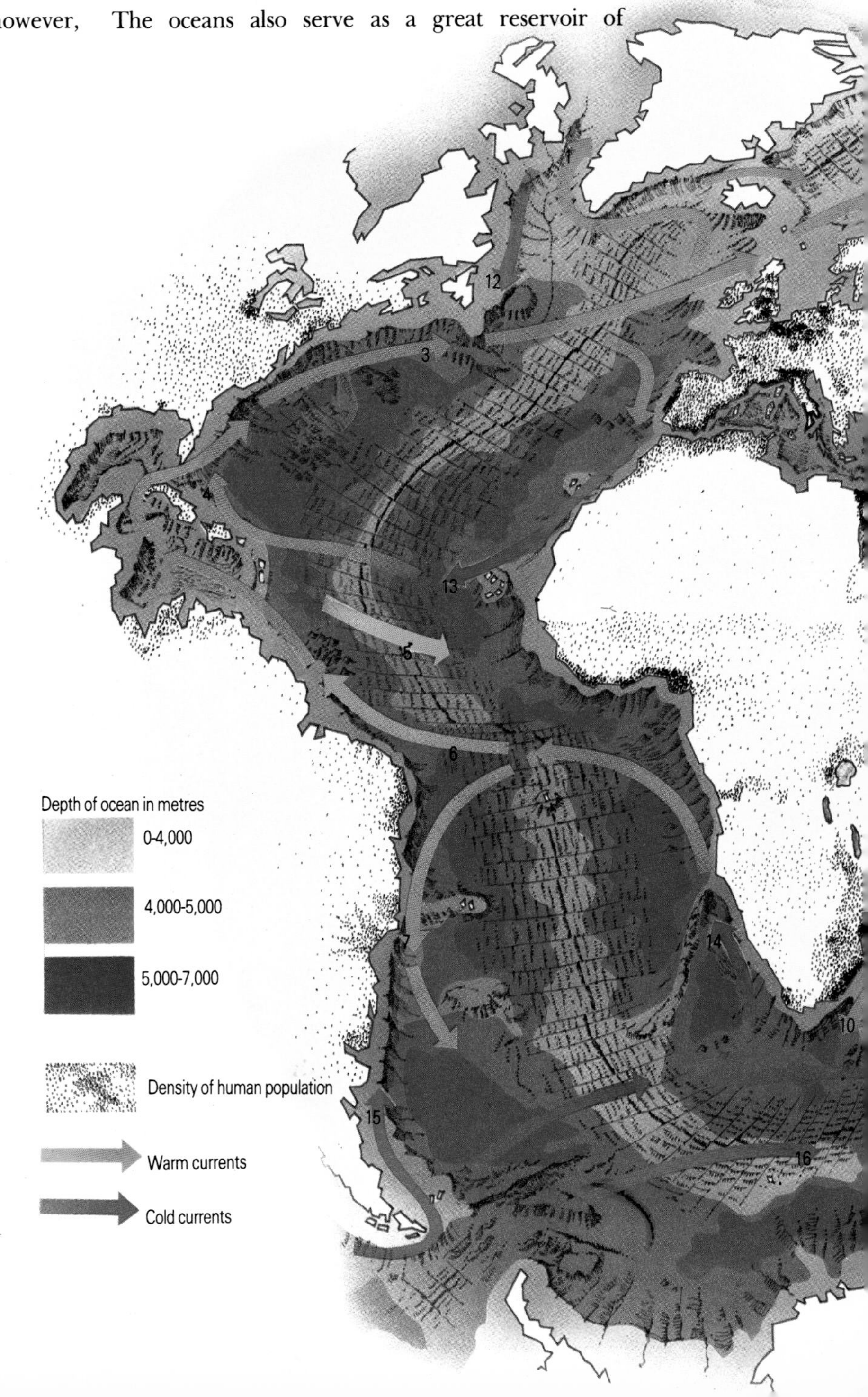

Depth of ocean in metres

0-4,000

4,000-5,000

5,000-7,000

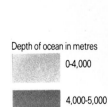

Density of human population

Warm currents

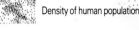

Cold currents

dissolved gases which helps to regulate the composition of the air we breathe.

The oceans give no more of a liquid covering to the globe than a film of moisture on a football, yet their depth and grandeur are remarkable – Mount Everest could be readily lost in the Mariana Trench. Underwater landscapes are extraordinarily varied, with spectacular geologic features. Along the edges of land masses are barely sloping continental shelves, accounting for about eight percent of the ocean's expanse. Fed by sediments washed off the land, these shelves are often very fertile, and support abundant fisheries. Twice as extensive are the continental slopes, with gradients 4-10 times steeper, reaching down as far as 500 metres. Eventually these drop away to 3,000 metres or

more, until they meet the "foothills" of the abyssal floor. This vast plain, sometimes with scarcely a pimple in thousands of kilometres, elsewhere scarred and rugged like terrestrial "badlands", is broken at the centre by mighty ridges, stretching the length and breadth of the four great oceans. Matching them in scale are giant canyons and long, narrow trenches, located along continental margins and associated with island arcs, the deepest plunging 11,000 metres below the surface.

Little known, and apparently remote, the ocean is a remarkably rich "resource realm" of the planet. With a better understanding, we might learn to draw sustainable benefit from its fisheries, minerals, and energy, and from its services as a gigantic weather machine. The ocean ecosphere constitutes a

d currents
Labrador
Canary
Benguela
Falkland
West Wind Drift
West Australian
Oyashio
Californian
Peru (Humboldt)

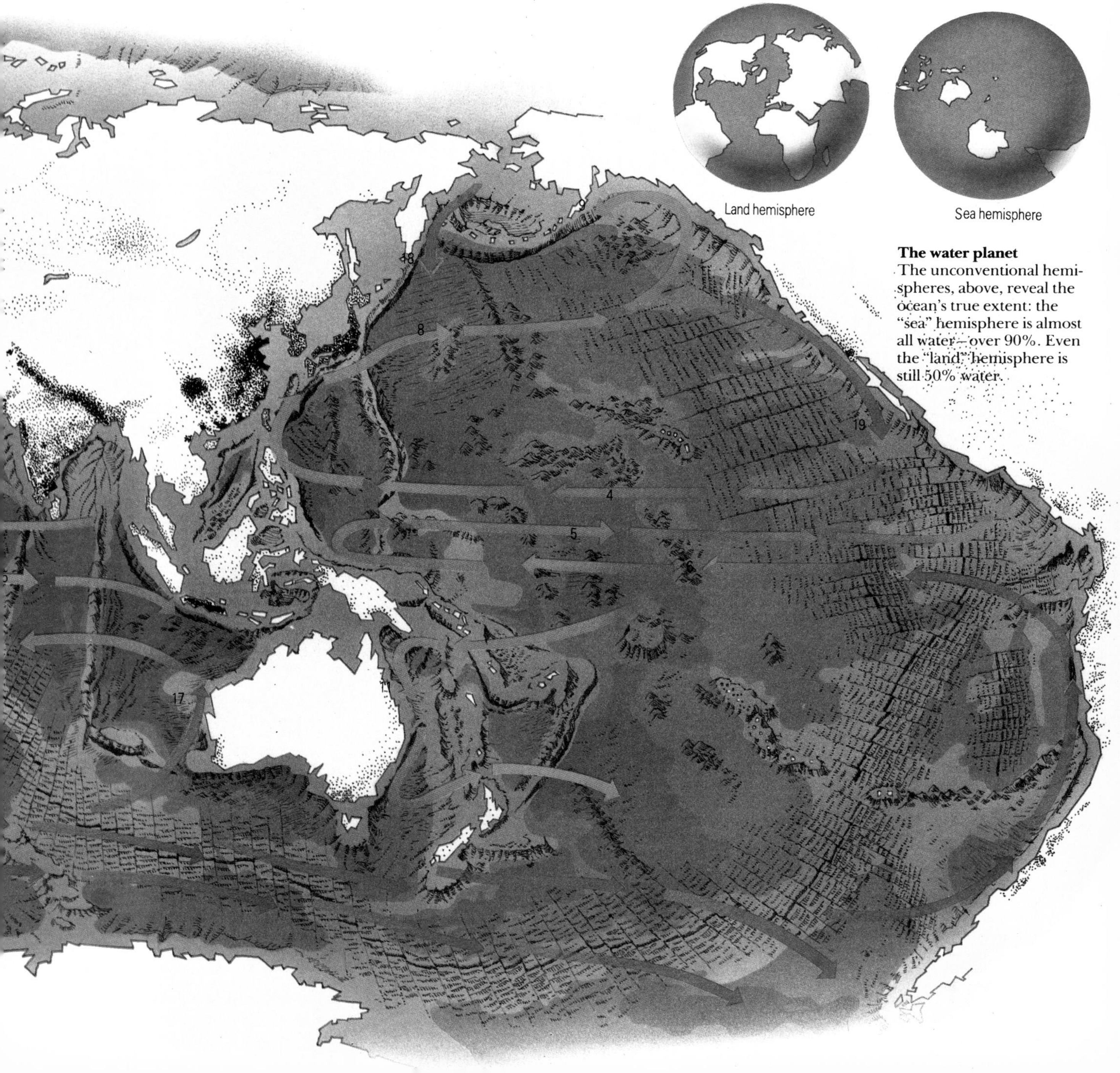

Land hemisphere

Sea hemisphere

The water planet
The unconventional hemispheres, above, reveal the ocean's true extent: the "sea" hemisphere is almost all water – over 90%. Even the "land" hemisphere is still 50% water.

magnificent frontier of scientific research – as exciting to many scientists as our exploration of the Sea of Storms on the waterless surface of the Moon.

The living ocean

The ocean is where life began. More than three-and-a-half billion years ago there evolved simple single-celled algae and bacteria very similar to those that form the basis of life in today's oceans. Collectively known as phytoplankton, from the Greek words meaning "drifting plants", this microflora exploits the energy of the sun and nutrients in the water to manufacture complex molecules of living tissue. Being dependent on sunlight, phytoplankton flourish in a thin layer at the surface of the ocean, a biosphere that extends downwards for 100 metres at most.

Diverse communities of animal "grazers" feed off these rich blooms, especially the diminutive zooplankton – many of them, like the phytoplankton, single-celled creatures. Especially numerous are the radiolarians, whose exquisite silica skeletons are important constituents of deep-sea oozes. Other larger zooplankton include flatworms, small jellyfish, swimming crabs, and various shrimps.

These two categories of plankton are so abundant that they are estimated to generate, respectively, 16 billion and 1.6 billion tonnes of carbon (the basic material of living tissue) each year. Feeding off the plankton is an array of larger creatures, with an annual productivity of around 160 million tonnes. These species, especially the prolific herring family, supply us with two-fifths of our fish. By contrast, fish that eat other fish, such as members of the cod family, generate only about 16 million tonnes of carbon a year, and supply us with about one-eighth of the fish we eat.

Just as on land, life is unevenly distributed in the oceans – the marine world has its equivalents of deserts and rainforests. In certain sectors the sea floor is covered with extensive sand stretches, which, while no more lifeless than the Sahara, are distinctly impoverished compared with the rest of the ocean. At the other extreme, "rainforests" flourish – particularly in coastal wetlands, estuaries, and reefs in upwelling zones. The Great Barrier Reef of north-eastern Australia, for instance, harbours more than 3,000 animal species.

Finally, there is the deep ocean – pitch-dark and near freezing, yet far from lifeless. Our preliminary probings of this remote realm reveal more than 2,000 species of fish, and at least as many invertebrates, many of them grotesque and primitive in form – the result of adaptations to an unpromising environment. But plainly they are altogether unprimitive, in that they subsist, indeed flourish, in such conditions.

The ocean is three-dimensional, and its plant wealth is not "fixed" – phytoplankton drift far and wide. Here, then, is an ecosphere fundamentally different from that on land, yet one so fertile that it

The living ocean

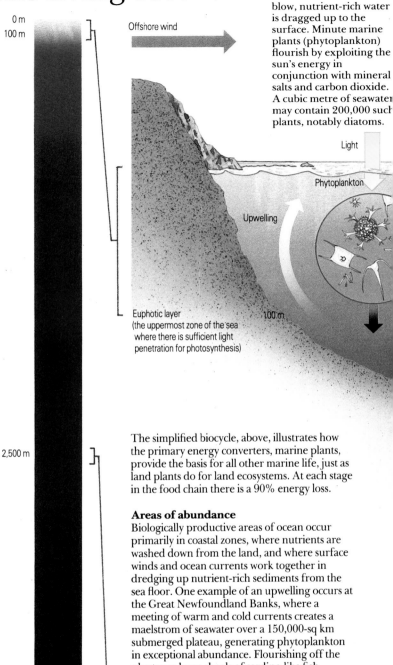

0 m
100 m

Offshore wind

Light

Phytoplankton

Upwelling

2,500 m

Euphotic layer
(the uppermost zone of the sea
where there is sufficient light
penetration for photosynthesis)

100 m

5,000 m

1 Where offshore winds blow, nutrient-rich water is dragged up to the surface. Minute marine plants (phytoplankton) flourish by exploiting the sun's energy in conjunction with mineral salts and carbon dioxide. A cubic metre of seawater may contain 200,000 such plants, notably diatoms.

The simplified biocycle, above, illustrates how the primary energy converters, marine plants, provide the basis for all other marine life, just as land plants do for land ecosystems. At each stage in the food chain there is a 90% energy loss.

Areas of abundance

Biologically productive areas of ocean occur primarily in coastal zones, where nutrients are washed down from the land, and where surface winds and ocean currents work together in dredging up nutrient-rich sediments from the sea floor. One example of an upwelling occurs at the Great Newfoundland Banks, where a meeting of warm and cold currents creates a maelstrom of seawater over a 150,000-sq km submerged plateau, generating phytoplankton in exceptional abundance. Flourishing off the plants are huge shoals of sardine-like fish, capelin, which in turn support many millions of cod, plus gannets, kittiwakes, and razorbills, also seals and humpbacked whales. Regrettably, this fishery has been grossly over-harvested by the ultimate predator, humankind (see pp 82-3).

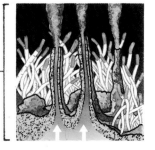

Sulphur-based life-forms
In 1977 a new deep-sea ecosystem was discovered. Like land animals around waterhole, strange-looking worms, clams, and blind white crabs cluster around hot vents in the ocean floor dependent on bacteria with the unique capacity to metabolize hydrogen sulphide.

Zooplankton includes a
great diversity of marine
life-forms, some feeding
on phytoplankton, some
preying on each other.
Especially numerous are
arrow worms, sea
gooseberries, and
copepods. Added to these
are free-swimming larvae
of shore- and bottom-
dwellers such as worms,
crabs, and echinoderms.

3 The "small fry"
zooplankton in turn are
consumed by squid,
jellyfish, and shoaling fish
such as herring and
anchovies. Baleen whales
too exist on a zooplankton
diet, mainly copepods and
krill. The basking shark,
one of the world's largest
fishes, also sustains itself on
a largely plankton diet.

4 Next in the chain,
feeding on the smaller
shoaling fish, are medium-
sized predators such as
tuna. These bulky, fast-
swimming fish are in turn
eaten by marlin and sharks.
Similarly, most seal species
feed on small fish while
themselves serving as prey
to larger creatures—
leopard seals and sharks.

Antarctic Convergence

The band of the Southern Ocean between 50°
and 60°S is known as the Antarctic Convergence.
Counter-rotating currents of cold and sub-
Antarctic water travelling northwards (the East
and West Wind Drifts) here pass under and
interact with subtropical water moving south.
The resulting turbulence drives nutrient-rich
water to the surface, making the area highly
productive, with great swarms of a crustacean
known as krill forming the staple food for
penguins, seals, squid, and whales.

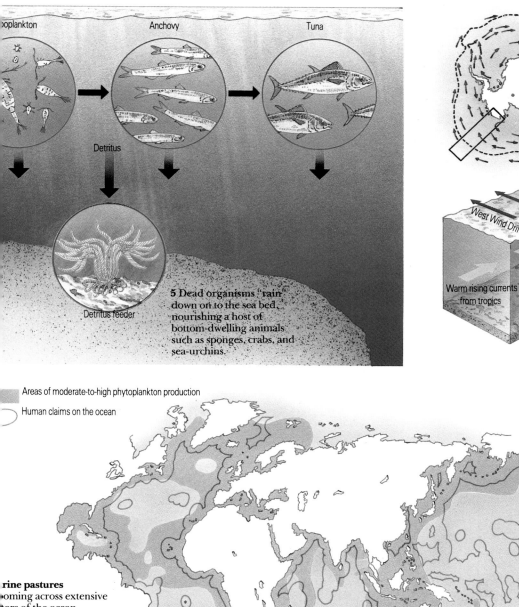

Zooplankton   Anchovy   Tuna

Detritus

Detritus feeder

5 Dead organisms "rain"
down on to the sea bed,
nourishing a host of
bottom-dwelling animals
such as sponges, crabs, and
sea-urchins.

East Wind Drift

Convergence

West Wind Drift

Cold sinking
currents from
Antarctica

Warm rising currents
from tropics

Areas of moderate-to-high phytoplankton production

Human claims on the ocean

Marine pastures

Booming across extensive
sectors of the ocean,
phytoplankton form
"fields" that sustain a
wealth of animal life. The
areas of greatest plankton
abundance are found
where the ocean is rich in
mineral salts. As the map
shows, a high proportion of
these productive zones are
covered by various marine
claims of nations, which
take in 40% of the seas.

supports around half of the planet's biomass. At present, we harvest less than 0.04 percent of marine production. Plainly, we could make much better use of the abundance of the living ocean.

Shores, reefs, and islands

The narrow coastal fringes of the world's ocean are at once its most productive and most vulnerable zones. Their shallow waters, saturated with sunlight and richly supplied with nutrients, provide the basis of most of our fisheries. Coastal and island ecosystems also serve as a great meeting ground between land and sea; large numbers of people live here, whether in traditional fishing communities or in cities. Many human activities exploit the wealth of these ocean borderlands.

The vital margins

Coastal ecosystems represent an extremely valuable resource – one that is increasingly threatened by human interests (pp 86-7). Their rich life depends on high levels of primary production – generation of the vegetable matter which provides the "base energy" of all food chains. Phytoplankton and sea plants are the primary producers of the oceans, their abundance and growth rates varying among ecological zones. The pie-chart (below) shows the proportional areas of open ocean, continental shelf, and coastal sectors, while the columns compare their primary productivity per unit area, illustrating dramatically the concentration of marine wealth in the ocean margins. Algal beds, reefs, and estuaries are more than 16 to 18 times as productive as the open ocean, mangroves well over 20 times.

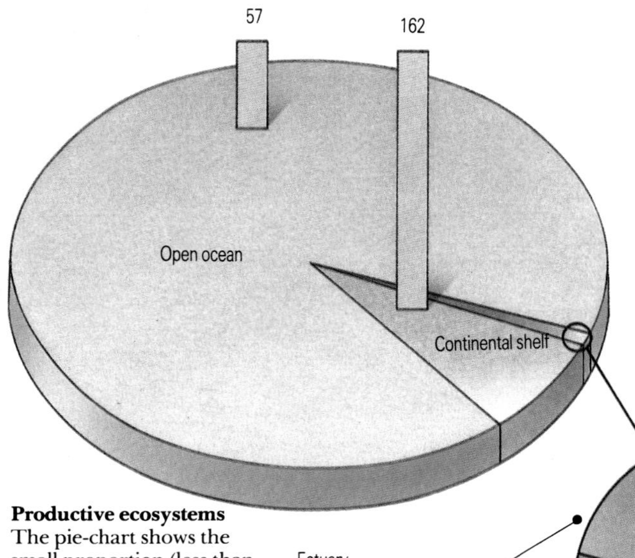

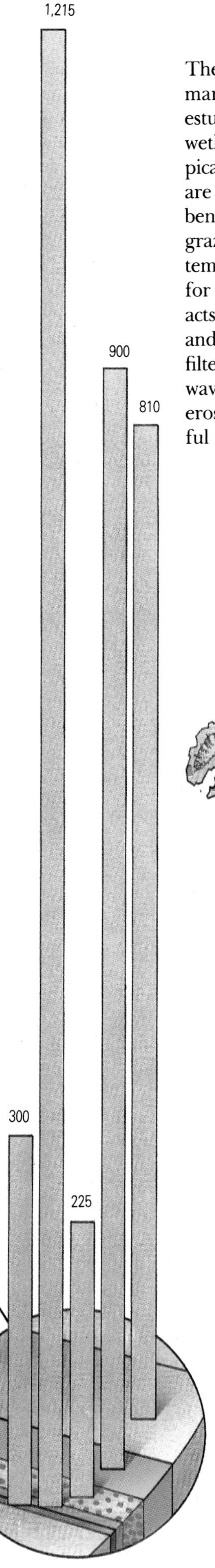

Productive ecosystems
The pie-chart shows the small proportion (less than 1%) occupied by coastal ecosystems. The columns show the "mean net primary productivity" of upwelling areas and coastal ecosystems in grams of carbon/cu m/year.

Open ocean

Continental shelf

57   162

300   225   810   900   1,215

Estuary

Algal bed and coral reef

Upwelling

Mangrove

Saltmarsh

The four vital ecosystems for humankind and f marine life-forms are saltmarshes, mangrove estuaries, and coral reefs. Saltmarshes are tid wetlands of temperate zones, mangroves the tr pical equivalent; their predominant offshore plan are seagrasses, true flowering plants that bloo beneath the sea. Seagrass meadows of the tropics a grazed by sea turtles, dugongs, and manatees; in t temperate zones they form rich winter food reserv for ducks and geese. In both zones the vegetatic acts as a nutrient trap for shellfish such as shrimp and for many finfish. In addition, the plants serve filter out pollution, to mitigate the beating of stor waves and powerful currents, and to preve erosion of the coastline. Estuaries, with their plen ful supplies of fertile silt washed down from rive

Mangrove wealth
Mangroves fringe more than half of all tropica shores, and harbour huge quantities of fish an shellfish, notably prawns and oysters. Mangro fish have been farmed in Indonesia since the 15th century. Today the most important speci is milkfish, raised in over 35,000 ha of culture ponds. Also reared are mullet, groupers, snappers, and sea perch. The simplest form o prawn culture involves netting mature prawn (right) as they leave mangroves for offshore spawning grounds. Between mangroves and land we sometimes find useful wetlands. Alor the Malay Peninsula, for instance, grows the Nypa swamp palm, which supplies local peop with fruit, sugar, vinegar, alcohol, and fibre.

cover twice the area of saltmarshes and mangroves. These river embayments or "tidal ponds", where seawater and freshwater communities intermingle, are very productive and feature vast numbers of annelid worms, crustaceans, and molluscs. Whenever we sit down to a dish of crabs, oysters, mussels, or prawns, we can thank the extreme productivity of estuaries. Further, they serve as nurseries for ocean fish such as silverside, anchovy, menhaden, and catfish. In one of the finest fishing areas in the world, the continental shelf of the eastern US, at least three-quarters of fished species spend a portion of their life cycles in estuaries.

Most diverse of all ecosystems are tropical coral reefs. They may also be the world's oldest ecosystems, in so far as they appear to be the only ones that have survived intact since the emergence of life. They feature more plant and animal phyla (major categories of life) than any other ecosystem; in their limited expanse coral reefs support one-third of all fish species. They also reveal more mutual-benefit relationships, or symbioses, between organisms than any other community. The more we learn about these successful and enduring symbioses, the better we shall know how to regulate relationships between plants and animals on land.

Other coastal ecosystems supply us with a host of products for our material welfare. Rocky shores feature algae of many shapes and sizes; seaweeds alone supply alginate compounds that contribute to literally hundreds of end-products, such as plastics, waxes, polishes, deodorants, soaps, detergents,

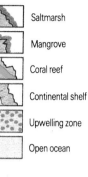

Saltmarsh

Mangrove

Coral reef

Continental shelf

Upwelling zone

Open ocean

Coral pharmacopoeias
A coral reef is an arena of intense competition for food and space – as this swarming Red Sea community demonstrates. To safeguard their space, reef organisms generate chemicals also useful to humans, e.g. histamines, hormones, and antibiotics.

Offshore harvest
Coastal waters attract a rich complement of wildlife, from seabirds to marine mammals, feeding from the same shoals that support human fisheries. Off Patagonia, above, kelp gulls and dusky dolphins provide a "marker" to the sea's harvest.

shampoos, cosmetics, paints, dyes, lubricants, food stabilizers and emulsifiers.

Filling our nets

We have fished rich offshore waters since earliest times, allowing upwelling ocean currents and seasonal migrations of the shoals to bring the wealth of the sea to our nets. Even today, despite mechanized deep-sea fleets and tightened territorial limits, the global shoal remains a renewable resource which nations must share, because neither the fish, nor the ocean ecosystems on which our catch depends, recognize human boundaries.

In 1950 we harvested 21 million tonnes of fish from the seas. Thereafter we expanded our catch at the extraordinary rate of 6-7 percent a year, a rate surpassing even the "miracle grains" of the Green Revolution (see pp 60-1). By the early 1970s, the catch soared to over 70 million tonnes, but it has failed to rise much further, due to massive mismanagement (pp 82-3).

Certain fishery experts believe that our potential catch could eventually expand to 100 million tonnes a year. To achieve this level, we would have to adopt fishing strategies to generate a more sustainable yield. But what do we mean by that key phrase, "sustainable yield"? Theoretically it refers to the *optimum* annual catch that can be derived indefinitely from species we now harvest, without causing a stock failure. Fishery biologists tell us that when we start to exploit an untouched stock, the surplus fish respond by reproducing more abundantly due to an apparent food surplus. Yet the same biologists also tell us that in many cases they do not know how many fish were there in the first place. By contrast with our inadequate biological skills, our technological skills advance in leaps and bounds, enabling fleets to scoop up entire stocks with only a fraction of the effort needed 20 years ago. These problems are compounded by money markets, which demand that exploiters recoup their investments and seize their profits within just a few years, regardless of how long the fishery resource may take to bounce back. Result: our view of what might be a sustainable yield can be at least 10 times different from Nature's.

We harvest five main groups of marine species. Northerners' menus are largely made up of demersal fish (primarily bottom-dwellers) including cod, haddock, skate, sole, and plaice. The catch of these is rather more than 20 million tonnes a year. Pelagic fish (surface-dwellers), including herring, mackerel, capelin, and anchovy (used mainly for fishmeal), together with high-value species such as tuna and salmon, supply more than 30 million tonnes a year. Way behind these two front-runners are crustaceans, such as lobsters, shrimps, and other shellfish, providing about 2.5 million tonnes. Last come cephalopods, including the octopus and squid families, which yield about 1 million tonnes. As for marine mammals, notably whales, their potential

The global shoal

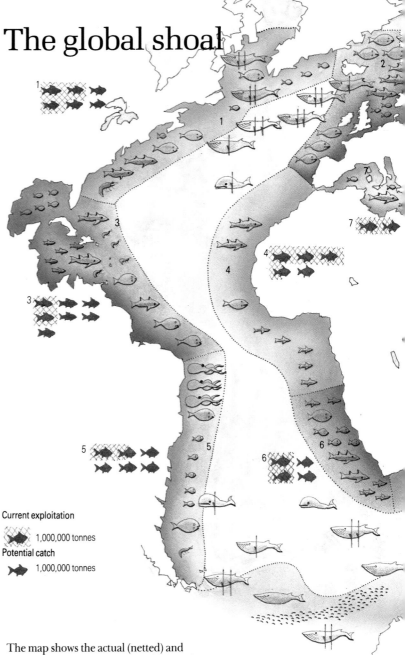

Current exploitation

🐟 1,000,000 tonnes

Potential catch

🐟 1,000,000 tonnes

The map shows the actual (netted) and potentially sustainable catches of fish and shellfish (1979-80) by fishing region, as well as the distribution and exploitation levels of whale stocks. As the netted symbols show, several of the northern areas are already fished to the limit of their sustainable potential, or even beyond it. The map also shows, for each fishing region, a breakdown of the potential catch into fish (demersal and pelagic), crustaceans, and cephalopods. Of the overall potential, 40% lies in the northern hemisphere, and 60% in the southern – the proportions of the actual catch being at present roughly the other way round. The Southern Ocean also offers vast swarms of tiny shrimp-like krill, with a theoretical potential catch of around 50 million tonnes a year, from which we take less than 1 million now. While seafood amounts to only 2% of our diets, it is much more important in terms of animal protein, a crucial element in our food. The seas provide 14% of our animal protein direct to the table and, in the case of developed-world citizens, a good deal more as fishmeal fed to livestock and as fertilizer.

Catch in tonnes

Demersal fish

🐟 1,000,000   🐟 100,000

Pelagic fish

🐟 1,000,000   🐟 100,000

Crustaceans

🦐 1,000,000   🦐 100,000

Cephalopods

🦑 100,000

⬚ Krill concentrations

Percentage exploitation of whale stocks

Sperm whales   Baleen whales

🐋 over 75%   🐋

🐋 25-75%   🐋

🐋 less than 25%   🐋

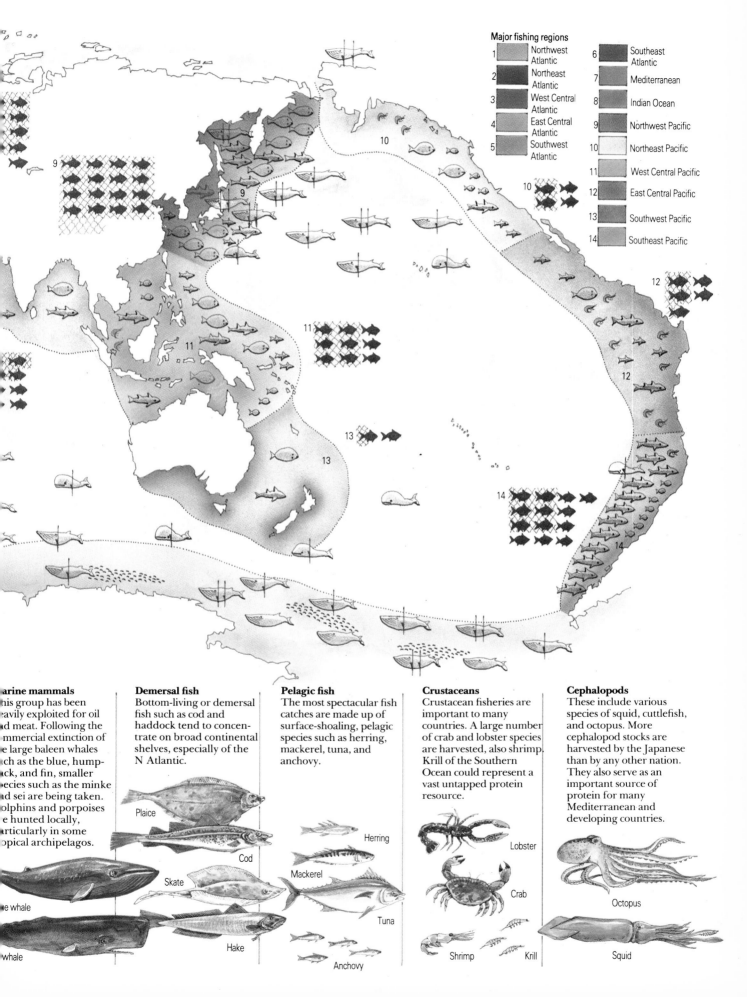

Major fishing regions

1 Northwest Atlantic
2 Northeast Atlantic
3 West Central Atlantic
4 East Central Atlantic
5 Southwest Atlantic
6 Southeast Atlantic
7 Mediterranean
8 Indian Ocean
9 Northwest Pacific
10 Northeast Pacific
11 West Central Pacific
12 East Central Pacific
13 Southwest Pacific
14 Southeast Pacific

arine mammals
his group has been
eavily exploited for oil
d meat. Following the
mmercial extinction of
e large baleen whales
ch as the blue, hump-
ck, and fin, smaller
ecies such as the minke
d sei are being taken.
olphins and porpoises
e hunted locally,
rticularly in some
opical archipelagos.

e whale

whale

Demersal fish
Bottom-living or demersal
fish such as cod and
haddock tend to concen-
trate on broad continental
shelves, especially of the
N Atlantic.

Plaice

Cod

Skate

Hake

Pelagic fish
The most spectacular fish
catches are made up of
surface-shoaling, pelagic
species such as herring,
mackerel, tuna, and
anchovy.

Herring

Mackerel

Tuna

Anchovy

Crustaceans
Crustacean fisheries are
important to many
countries. A large number
of crab and lobster species
are harvested, also shrimp.
Krill of the Southern
Ocean could represent a
vast untapped protein
resource.

Lobster

Crab

Shrimp

Krill

Cephalopods
These include various
species of squid, cuttlefish,
and octopus. More
cephalopod stocks are
harvested by the Japanese
than by any other nation.
They also serve as an
important source of
protein for many
Mediterranean and
developing countries.

Octopus

Squid

has been squandered, and is now tailing away to the merest fraction of what it might have been with rational management.

The new technological revolution

Ocean technology is an infant phenomenon as yet. But by the end of the century it could be supplying us with sizeable flows of critical minerals and energy. The "us", however, probably comprises very few nations – those with the funds and expertise to gain a head start in the nascent industry.

The wealth of the oceans is beyond doubt. Continental shelves harbour nearly half of the Earth's oil and gas resources, while seawater itself contains over 70 elements, some very important. One cubic kilometre of seawater holds about 230 million tonnes of salt; it also contains around a million tonnes of magnesium and 65,000 tonnes of bromine. We have extracted salt by evaporation for more than 4,000 years; today we also extract magnesium and bromine by chemical processes.

Not yet harvested but much more important are manganese nodules on the sea floor. These potato-shaped objects have a high metal content, primarily

manganese (25-30 percent), but also nickel (1.3 percent), copper (1.1 percent), cobalt (0.25 percent), plus molybdenum and vanadium – all valuable in steel alloys. Although most manganese deposits are spread thinly over large areas, often at great depths, certain concentrations could in the future support commercial operations.

More accessible are deposits of silver, copper, and zinc in Red Sea muds, worth $7 billion. Still more readily available is uranium in seawater – over 4 billion tonnes of it, much more than on land. Japan, with a strong commitment to nuclear energy and no domestic stocks of uranium, eventually aims to extract 1,000 tonnes a year.

As for ocean energy, tidal, wave, and thermal projects all have potential, and functional proto-types of all three are in operation.

Much of the ocean's mineral wealth lies beyond national jurisdictions of any sort, and should count as part of the common heritage of humankind (see pp 96-7). The global community already shares certain technologies, both between nations and through international consortia (the oil industry is an obvious example). Yet there will still be winners

France

Ocean technology

Dredging
Used to mine many materials, from sand and gravel to diamonds, dredgers also help to keep shipping lanes open. Technology is increasing the depth of operation from the present average of 30 m.

Wave energy
The Lanchester Clam is one of a variety of UK designs to extract energy from waves. Early commercial application is unlikely unless energy prices increase hugely.

Spiral wave power
The Dam Atoll is a conceptual design from the US, with potential applications from cleaning up oil spills and reducing wave erosion to desalination and power generation (1-2 megawatts).

CONDEEP® concrete gravity platform
These massive floating structures store thousand of tonnes of crude oil in enclosed submarine concrete tanks. At work i the North Sea is the Stratford B platform, the heaviest object ever move by humans, with a displacement weight of over 900,000 tonnes. It c operate at the edge of th continental shelf at dept of over 140 m.

The frontier of the marine technology revolution is steadily being pushed deeper into the oceans in the search for critical resources, despite the obstacles of safety, cost-effectiveness, and territorial rights. The illustration demonstrates a range of present ocean technology from inshore to deep water, the coastal and continental shelf operations being the most established. Dredging, for instance, is a big-business operation, mining sand, gravel, and shell deposits for cement for the construction industry. An estimated 500 billion tonnes of gravel alone lie on the Atlantic shelf of North America. The oil and gas industries were pioneers in exploiting coastal mineral deposits, beginning off California in 1891. They moved into deep-water oil technology in the 1960s,

boosting development in the 1970s as the cost of land-based crude oil and natural gas soared. The guyed (deep-ocean) tower shown here could operate down to 300 m; another rig system, known as the "tension leg platform", could operate down to 500 m. Beyond this depth, platforms become unstable, so technologists may opt for moving the whole production plant to the sea bed instead. The scheme illustrated aims to house an entire production facility in 5 interlocking concrete chambers on the sea bed, down to 1,000 m. Deepest of all are deposits of manganese nodules: while these are not mined so far, potential recovery areas at depths of 4,000-5,000 m are being explored with underwater TV systems and other techniques.

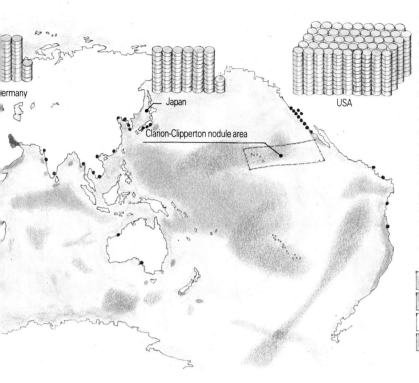

Ocean wealth and investment

A comparison of annual dollar investment in ocean technology clearly reveals the handful of nations leading the field (left). The map also indicates major reserves of mineral-rich nodules and sediments, active seawater extraction plants, and areas with OTEC potential. In many countries investment has slowed due to soaring costs and uncertain profits. But Japan has doubled its expenditure since 1980, concentrating on uranium extraction, nodule mining, and OTEC. Current sea-bed investigations by other countries include a US survey of polymetallic sulphides along the rift zone off Oregon (the only known large deposit lying within the proposed US exclusive economic zone), and the French exploration of manganese nodule deposits lying in their economic zone off Tahiti.

- Main areas of manganese nodules
- Metal-rich sediments
- Mineral extraction plants from seawater
- Offshore phosphorite deposits
- OTEC potential (areas with temperature gradients of 22° C or more)
- Annual investment 1980 (each coin $20 million)

Ocean Thermal Energy Conversion (OTEC)

OTEC exploits the temperature difference between the warm surface and cool bottom layers in tropical seas to provide power. The process works like a giant refrigerator in reverse, evaporating and condensing a working fluid to drive a turbine that produces electricity.

Manganese nodule mining

The recovery of mineral-rich nodules from depths as great as 5,000 m has proved feasible in pilot tests, but is extremely costly. Commercial operation will depend on metal prices rising substantially; it also awaits a satisfactory resolution of present sea-bed ownership disputes by the United Nations Conference on the Law of the Sea (UNCLOS).

...yed tower

...is anchored structure is ...e of a new generation of ...ep-water oil platforms. ...ock 480 platform, for ...ample, in the Gulf of ...exico will be placed at a ...pth of 300 m and pinned ...the sea floor by a spoke-...e array of cables, each ...re than 900 m long.

Deep-sea oil production

Designed to extract oil at depths where platform recovery is uneconomic, these structures will be gas- or nuclear-powered.

and losers in the race for ocean wealth: most nations simply lack the technology.

The ends of the Earth

Remote and ice-bound, the polar environments used to be among the least disturbed on Earth. But things are changing: now that their natural riches are recognized, the familiar tug-of-war between protection of unique ecosystems and exploitation of critical assets dominates their future.

We tend to think of the two polar zones as being similar. Yet they are quite different. The Arctic is essentially an enclosed sea, the smallest of the oceans, as well as the only one to be almost entirely landlocked. The Antarctic, by contrast, comprises a vast open ocean surrounding an ice-covered land mass twice the size of Western Europe.

One-third of the Arctic is underlaid with continental shelves from surrounding territories; it supports some of our richest fishing grounds, now accounting for roughly one-tenth of the global catch. A single haul of the net can bring in 100 tonnes of fish. In Antarctica, by contrast, much of the sea is overlain with ice shelves. The region contains nine-tenths of all ice on the planet, the ice cap averaging 2,300 metres deep, compared with a few dozen metres at the North Pole. Some nations, notably the water-poor and oil-rich countries of the Middle East, have even considered towing outsize bergs from Antarctica.

The polar zones are not the lifeless deserts we might expect. The Arctic fringes break out into spectacular blooms each summer, supporting large numbers of herbivores, from lemmings to reindeer and caribou. The territories north of the Arctic Circle also support two million humans, including over 800,000 aboriginal peoples.

The Antarctic continent has only two flowering plant species (plus a number of mosses and lichens), no native vertebrates, and (alone among continents) no long-standing human settlements. Yet the surrounding ocean, one of the most productive zones on Earth, generates massive summer outbursts of marine phytoplankton, fostered by exceptionally rich nutrient-bearing upwellings. These support vast populations of krill, which provide the food base for eight species of whales and the main support of 40 bird species, from penguins (90 percent of the bird biomass) to albatrosses.

The mineral resources of the Arctic are known to be vast. Already reserves are being exploited, especially by the USSR. As for Antarctica, there may be great oil deposits lying under the narrow continental shelf, but there is no conclusive evidence that these reserves exist.

So, for all their potential, Antarctica's resources – perhaps the last great untouched reservoir – should be considered as "frozen stakes" until a management policy (p. 94) is negotiated. Will we have the economic, political, and environmental wisdom to get it right?

Polar zones

Main areas of distribution of:

- Cod
- Alaska pollack
- Capelin
- Fur seal
- Harp and hooded seals
- Coal field
- Mining
- Oil and gas production
- Major ice drifts

Arctic resources
The Arctic, with its extensive continental shelf over which shoaling fish congregate, contains some of the richest fisheries.
Fish Over half the catch consists of cod, haddock, and Pacific pollack. Capelin is the main pelagic fish taken on the Atlantic side.
Seals About 30,000 fur seals, mostly sub-adult males, are taken from the Pribilof islands each year, while 180,000 harp and 130,000 hooded seals, mainly suckling pups, are taken from the North Atlantic area by Canadians, Norwegians, and Russians. Early in 1983, the EEC, the main importer of skins, announced a ban on trade in skins of the youngest pups of harps ("whitecoats") and hooded seals ("bluebacks"). This has led to a decline in the Canadian/ Norwegian kill in the NW Atlantic.
Minerals Almost two-thirds of the USSR's gas reserves lie within the Arctic Circle. There are also important deposits of nickel, copper, platinum, apatite, tin, diamonds, gold, and coal. Canada believes that recoverable oil deposits in the Arctic could far exceed all its other reserves, while Alaska's present output of oil, already 20% of US production, could prove to be only 1% of potential reserves.

Antarctic resources

Commercial fishing in the Southern Ocean has yet to prove profitable: while there is a wealth of plankton, the waters are deep with no broad continental shelf (unlike the Arctic).

Fish Of the 100 or so fish species of the region, only a few, such as the Antarctic cod toothfish and Patagonian hake, have been extensively trawled. The main operators are the USSR, Poland, and East Germany.

Whales Despite a ban by the International Whaling Commission on catching the blue, fin, humpback, and right whales, pirate whalers still operate. The Japanese and Russians are the only nations that still take unprotected species – the sei, minke, and killer whales. The Japanese use whales for meat and pet food, while the Russians, who used to concentrate on sperm whales until a ban in 1981, export minke whale meat to Japan and use it as animal feed.

Minerals A wide range of mineral ores have been found in Antarctica, the stocks that most warrant early investigation being deposits of coal in the Transantarctic mountains and Amery Ice Shelf, and of iron ore in the Prince Charles Mountains. The most promising resource is offshore oil around the narrow continental shelf: estimates suggest 50 billion barrels, or 15% of Middle East reserves.

Main areas of distribution of:

- Antarctic cod
- Toothfish
- Krill concentration
- Krill distribution
- Coal-bearing area
- Potential oil and gas areas
- Mineral occurrences

rill

ssive swarms of krill are eady being harvested – 1980-81, approximately 0,000 tonnes were taken om the Southern Ocean. the height of the season, 0 tonnes per day can be en by the powerful ssian and Japanese wlers with their fine-shed nets. The krill is ocessed or used as feed.

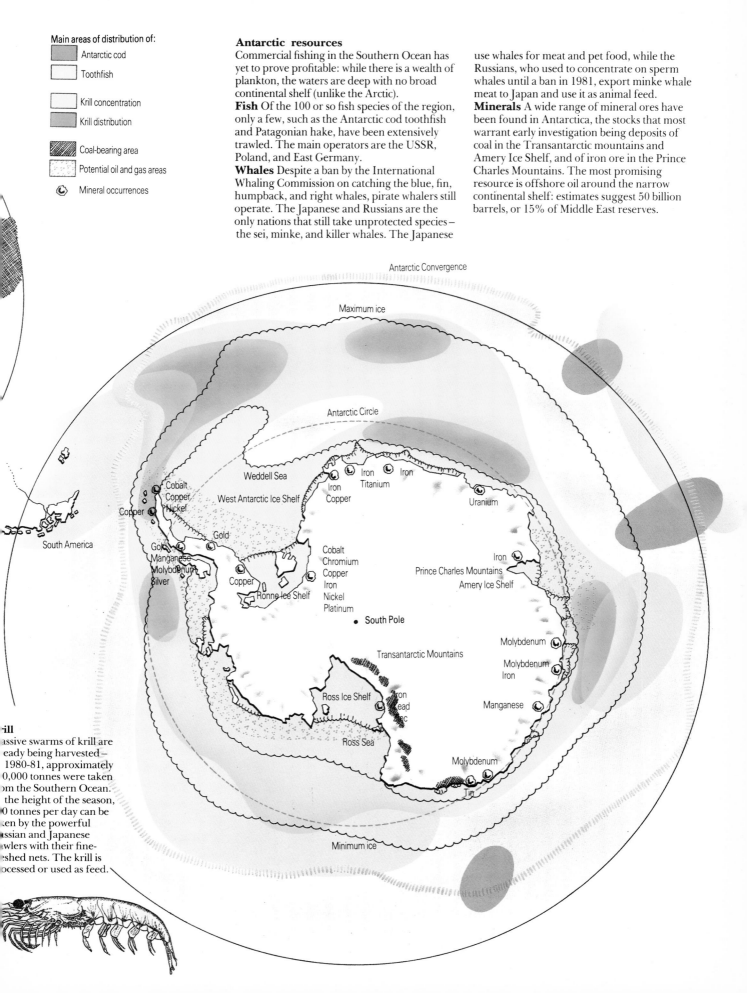

THE OCEAN CRISIS

The ocean offers abundant resources to sustain us. But through ignorance and misunderstanding we are placing this wealth in jeopardy—causing gross impoverishment of many fisheries, near extinction for most large whales, widespread pollution of fish-rich waters, and degradation and disruption of many coastal habitats.

Declining fish stocks

Why has the steady increase in catch between 1950 and 1970, averaging 7 percent per year, failed to continue? Today, we struggle to maintain much growth at all, and even this conceals big changes in the catch composition, which now depends heavily on small fish for processing into meal. As a result, the food value per tonne has also declined.

The sad truth is that over-fishing is destroying our harvests. While the 1950s witnessed a few fishing failures, the 1960s and '70s have seen more and more traditional fisheries collapse, some quite spectacularly, with a general reduction in stocks.

Part of the problem lies with technology. Large, long-distance fleets employ techniques such as purse-seining, using fine nets to "vacuum" the sea. Part lies with our ignorance of marine ecosystems. The main cause, however, has been expanding demand for fish and fish products (for feed and fertilizer) from Northerners.

As Western Europeans and North Americans eat more meat, they create a booming demand for animal-feed supplements, including fishmeal. About a third of the global fish catch now goes into meal and oil, mostly to feed the hungry North. Meanwhile the Third World watches its already meagre share of the catch dwindle still further.

Other Northerners simply want more fish. Japan, for instance, relies on the oceans for 60 percent of its animal-protein supply (compared with a global average of 15 percent). Hence its famous "fish and rice" diet. The USSR, too, has increasingly looked to the seas for its high-quality protein; today a Soviet citizen eats twice as much fish as an American. Their approach to the potentially renewable riches of the sea is epitomized by what they have done to the great whales (pp 88-9).

They are not alone, however. In the North Atlantic, Americans and Western Europeans have contributed to a 40 percent decline in stocks of herring, a 90 percent decline in halibut, and similar depletions of haddock, cod, and several other prime species—in fact 27 out of 30 fisheries. Worse still,

The empty nets

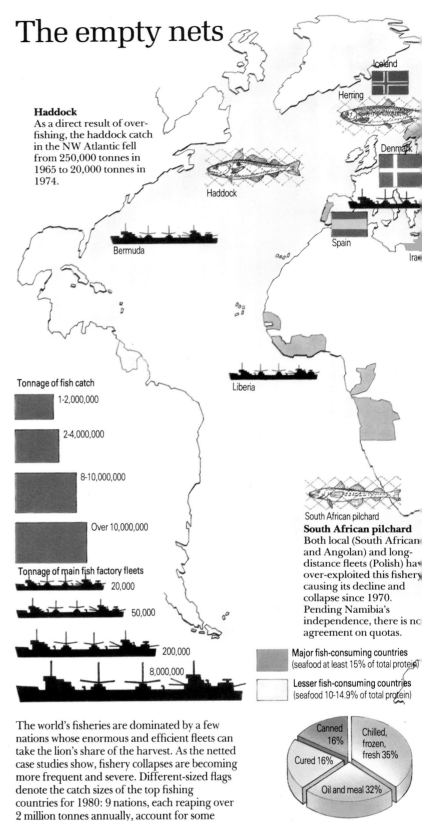

Haddock
As a direct result of over-fishing, the haddock catch in the NW Atlantic fell from 250,000 tonnes in 1965 to 20,000 tonnes in 1974.

Haddock

Bermuda

Tonnage of fish catch

1-2,000,000

2-4,000,000

8-10,000,000

Over 10,000,000

Tonnage of main fish factory fleets

20,000

50,000

200,000

8,000,000

Iceland

Herring

Denmark

Spain

Ira

Liberia

South African pilchard

South African pilchard
Both local (South African and Angolan) and long-distance fleets (Polish) have over-exploited this fishery causing its decline and collapse since 1970. Pending Namibia's independence, there is no agreement on quotas.

Major fish-consuming countries
(seafood at least 15% of total protein)

Lesser fish-consuming countries
(seafood 10-14.9% of total protein)

Canned 16%

Chilled, frozen, fresh 35%

Cured 16%

Oil and meal 32%

How we use the catch
Of the total marine catch, nearly a third is used for feed and fertilizer. Rough 16% is cured (salted, smoked), 16% is canned, and 35% is either chilled, frozen, or consumed fresh The pie-chart shows the marine catch for 1980.

The world's fisheries are dominated by a few nations whose enormous and efficient fleets can take the lion's share of the harvest. As the netted case studies show, fishery collapses are becoming more frequent and severe. Different-sized flags denote the catch sizes of the top fishing countries for 1980: 9 nations, each reaping over 2 million tonnes annually, account for some 58% of the global total, with Japan heading the list at 10.2 million tonnes, followed by the USSR at 8.7 million tonnes. A further 9 countries each take over 1 million tonnes. Ship symbols denote national tonnage of industrial-scale fishing fleets (the issue is complicated by the use of flags of convenience, notably by Japan). The major fish-consuming nations are indicated according to their level of dependence on fish protein in their diets.

h Sea herring
...strialized fishing in the ...1960s and '70s caused ...line in stock from 4 ...n tonnes to less than 1 ...n tonnes.

USSR

Alaska pollack
The biggest single-species fishery in the world since the anchoveta collapse, pollack are taken mainly by Japan (38%) and the USSR (51%). From a mere 150,000 tonnes in 1950, the catch peaked at over 5 million tonnes in 1975-76. Since then it has barely touched 4 million tonnes.

Canada

...and

Germany

N Korea

Alaska pollack

Japan

USA

China

S Korea

California sardine

India

Thailand

Philippines

Chub mackerel

Mexico

Chub mackerel
This species is fished in wide areas of the Atlantic and Pacific, especially by Japan. The Japanese catch in the NW Pacific has declined as a result of over-fishing from 1.6 million tonnes in 1978 to 0.7 million tonnes in 1982.

California sardine
In the 1930s, annual catches of sardine exceeded 500,000 tonnes, providing prosperity to fishing peoples of Monterey – immortalized in Steinbeck's *Cannery Row*. By the 1950s over-fishing resulted in stock collapse, with only a moderate recovery in the late 1970s.

Panama

Anchovy

Peru

Indonesia

Ocean shrimp
...fleets operating in ...inshore waters are ...g up the valuable ...depriving ...al fishing peoples ...livelihood. The ...is aggravated by ...ursery areas and ...ollution.

The anchoveta crisis
When the global catch went into sharp decline in 1972, it was primarily due to a slump in the enormously productive anchoveta fishery off Peru. The problem lay both with over-fishing and with the El Niño current, a mass of warm water that intruded upon the cool and nutrient-rich Peru current underpinning the fishery. The graph illustrates the sudden decline in catch with the arrival of El Niño from 1972 onwards (see pp 130-1).

Chile

Indian mackerel
In the Gulf of Thailand, the change from traditional fishing to modern types of trawl in the 1960s initially produced an increase in catches of Indian mackerel and other species. But despite ever-more intensive fishing, catches have declined from 1977.

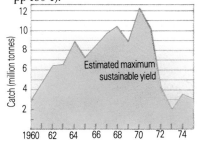

Estimated maximum sustainable yield

Catch (million tonnes)

12 10 8 6 4 2

1960 62 64 66 68 70 72 74

echanized fishing vs local fisheries
...echnological advance in fishing has brought its ...oblems – most evident in the waters off Third ...orld countries. Indiscriminate fishing by long-...stance foreign fleets is now on the decline, due ...high fuel costs and territorial agreements. But ...suse of aid offered to establish national ...heries, intended to help local communities, ...s resulted in the same over-exploitation – ...pleting the fish stocks and depriving the ...orer coastal peoples of their livelihood.
...The confrontation between capital-intensive ...heries and coastal fishing peoples affects 6.5 ...llion people in India and 20-25 million people ...roughout SE Asia. When representatives of ...astal fishing villages put their case at the 1978 ...O Asian Small Fishermen's Workshop in ...ngkok, they protested about the priority ...en to large-scale, capital-intensive fishing, the

pollution caused by industry, and the resulting poverty of small fishing communities.

Factory fishing off West Africa
Africa's coasts feature some prolific fisheries. Each year they provide 3 million tonnes of fish, of which 80% comes from a relatively short upwelling sector along the western seaboard from the Strait of Gibraltar to the Zaire river. Industrial fishing fleets have exploited this zone with sophisticated catching gear and cold-storage facilities – long-distance equipment characteristic of advanced nations rather than of local African enterprises. One such giant vessel, serviced by as many as 15 catcher ships, can in one day take about 1,000 tonnes and process the whole lot into fishmeal.
In the mid-1960s, West Africans watched half

their catch being taken away by developed nations. By the mid-1970s, the 22 African nations concerned had increased their catch substantially – but witnessed their share decline to one-third of all fish taken, the bulk being accounted for by the USSR, Spain, France, Poland, Japan, and 14 developed nations.
One tonne of fishmeal fed to livestock in Europe produces less than half a tonne of pork or poultry, far less again if used as fertilizer to grow animal-feed grains. Were the West African fish resources to be used for direct human consumption by the 140 million people of West Africa, they would represent an additional 12 kg of animal protein per person per year – a 50% increase for many people.

these northern nations, after misusing and over-using their local fisheries, have been venturing further afield to abuse fisheries off western Africa and elsewhere in the tropical developing world.

Sources of marine pollution

The seas are a sump. They continuously absorb vast quantities of silt and minerals washed down from the land. Now, however, we are asking them to accept growing amounts of human-generated materials as well, from sewage sludge, industrial effluent, and agricultural run-off, all with their chemical contaminants, to radioactive wastes.

The oceans can do a good job for us as a gigantic "waste treatment works". The question is, how much waste can they safely handle? That is to say, what sorts of waste are they fitted to absorb, where can they best accommodate it, how long will they take to degrade it through natural processes – and what level of adverse consequences are we prepared to accept?

These critical factors are not receiving nearly enough attention. Each year we dump hundreds of new chemicals into the seas, to go with the thousands already there, and with next to no idea of their potential impact. Human-made toxic substances are being detected in deep ocean trenches, even as far as Antarctica. This phenomenon is the result of global circulatory systems, processes of which we have hardly any understanding.

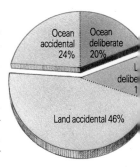

Polluting the oceans

The oceans receive the brunt of human waste, be it by deliberate dumping or by natural run-off from the land. At least 83% of all marine pollution derives from land-based activities. The illustration below shows a major conveyor of these pollutants, a river flanked by both agricultural land and industry, a scene that reflects much of the industrialized North. As the river becomes polluted, a high percentage of waste is flushed downstream and deposited in the biologically productive estuarine waters and coastal zones. Here, the poisons enter marine food chains, building up their concentrations in higher species. This process of bioamplification was sharply illustrated in Japan in the early 1950s by Minamata disease – methyl mercury poisoning due to eating tuna with heavy concentrations of mercury in their tissues (the wastes originated from a coastal factory). By 1975, there were 3,500 known victims.

The New York Bight
Dumping of waste is primarily responsible for the pollution of the New York Bight, and is causing severe health problems. The pie-charts give the proportion of waste elements that end up in the estuary or bight either directly from the land or by the barging of spoils – sewage sludge and toxic industrial waste.

To estuary

Direct to bight

To bight via dumping

Discharge (tonnes per day)

Carbon 2,600

Oil and grease 870

Nitrogen 520

Iron 230

Copper 13.8

Lead 12.7

Mercury 0.3

PCBs 0.014

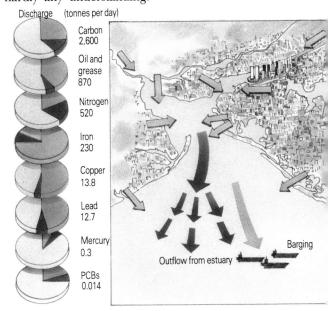
Outflow from estuary

Barging

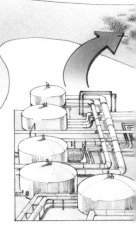

Agricultural run-off
Pesticides and herbicides, not readily bio-degradable, are persistent pollutants. As they pass through marine food chains, their effect is concentrated. Nitrates from fertilizers over-enrich water, causing algal growth and eventual deoxygenation.

Urban centres
Municipal drainage systems pour out domestic and industrial sewage, contaminated with toxic chemicals, heavy metals, oil, and organic nutrients. Construction sites release enormous amounts of sediment into rivers.

Industry
Much of the complex mix that goes into industrial waste ends up in the sea. Included in this mélange are partially bio-degradable food wastes, heavy metals, and persistent pesticides. It often takes a human casualty to alert us to the source of the pollution.

Nuclear reactors
Radioactive waste is discharged into coastal waters from nuclear reprocessing plants such as those at Sellafield (UK) and La Hague (France). Both plants have been implicated in sickness and deaths of local people.

Oil refineries
Oil terminals tend to be sited along coasts, often built on valuable saltmars or near productive estuaries. Accidental oil le and seepage from refineries contribute som 200,000 tonnes of oil annually to ocean pollutio

il in the ocean ecosystem
ome 6 million tonnes of oil
ter the ocean each year
many routes: from the
mosphere, the land, by
tural seepage from the
a bed, and from oil
oduction and transport
sea. The pie-chart shows
e proportional input of
l into the ocean from
rious sources. By far the
rgest amount – some 2
illion tonnes – enters by
n-off from the land,
pecially from cities.

Chemical run-off caused by humans into the oceans is much greater than Nature's contribution – mercury two-and-a-half times the natural rate, manganese four times, zinc, copper, and lead about 12 times, antimony 30 times, and phosphorus 80 times. As for oil, human-caused pollution – often by wanton carelessness, or even deliberate discharge – accounts for four-fifths or more of the total volume entering the seas – some 6 million tonnes a year. We hear much about oil-killed birds and other marine creatures. Fortunately they generally recover their numbers within a few years. The worst damage is more insidious: certain components of oil are toxic, others are carcinogenic, and they tend to persist for extended periods of time.

Heavy metals such as mercury, lead, cadmium, and arsenic, and chemicals such as DDT and PCBs must rank high on the list of harmful pollutants. We have learned to our cost of the effects of mercury through the Minamata episode in Japan (see below, left) and more recent deaths in Indonesia; and we have discovered too late the impact of DDT and PCBs, through reproductive failures among birds of prey and other wildlife.

The most significant factor of all is that at least 85 percent of ocean pollution arises from human activities on land, rather than at sea, and that 90 percent of these pollutants remain in coastal waters – by far the most biologically productive sector of the oceans. The wanton destruction that is

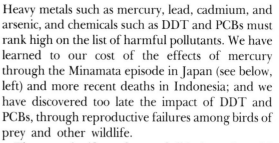

Polluted areas

Main oil-tanker routes

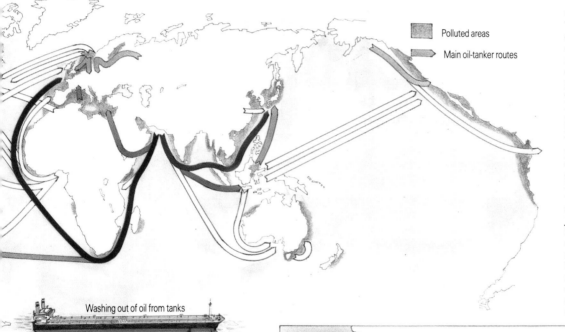

Washing out of oil from tanks

age dumping

Nuclear dumping

Global marine pollution
The global circulation of ocean currents and the continuity of marine life means that no part of the ocean is exempt from pollution: the classic example is the discovery of DDT in the fat of Antarctic penguins, thousands of kilometres from source. The map (left) illustrates pollution hotspots – coastal areas close to industrial conurbations such as the North Sea, and regions with high populations such as the sea off Rio de Janeiro, Brazil and the Java Sea, Indonesia. The map also shows oil-tanker routes, the heaviest traffic being from the Middle East to Europe. Most tanker accidents occur along congested routes, close to the coast.

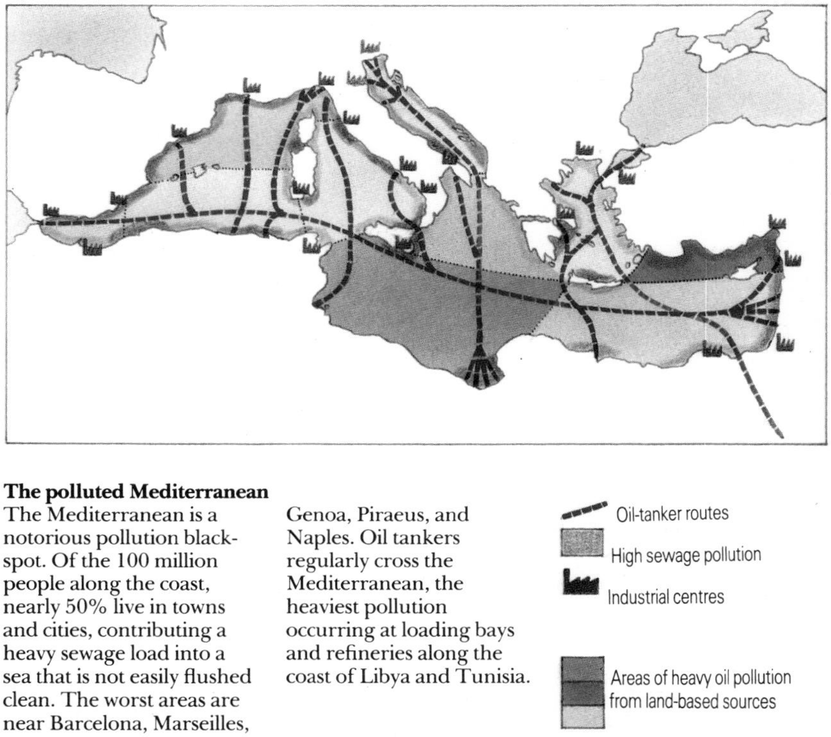

a-borne pollution
l spills receive much media coverage but
present only a fraction of sea-based ocean
llution. Much more extensive is the deliberate
mping of waste in the open ocean beyond
rritorial limits. Similarly, the dumping of
wage sludge – organic, industrial, and human
fuse – is potentially dangerous due to the mass
bacteria and viruses contained in the sludge.
he dumping of radioactive waste, which began
far back as 1949 and has continued
ermittently ever since, is an even graver
reat. Until 1970 the US and other countries
mped radioactive waste in deep-water drums
d storage tanks which have subsequently
oved leaky.

The polluted Mediterranean
The Mediterranean is a notorious pollution black-spot. Of the 100 million people along the coast, nearly 50% live in towns and cities, contributing a heavy sewage load into a sea that is not easily flushed clean. The worst areas are near Barcelona, Marseilles,

Genoa, Piraeus, and Naples. Oil tankers regularly cross the Mediterranean, the heaviest pollution occurring at loading bays and refineries along the coast of Libya and Tunisia.

- - - Oil-tanker routes

High sewage pollution

Industrial centres

Areas of heavy oil pollution from land-based sources

occurring in these vital zones will have serious consequences, not only for human welfare, but for the entire marine realm.

Our vulnerable coastline

"The lasting benefits that society derives from wetlands often far exceeds the immediate advantage their owners might get from draining or filling them. Their destruction shifts economic and environmental costs to other citizens ... who have no voice in the decision to alter them."

PRESIDENT CARTER'S ENVIRONMENTAL MESSAGE OF 1977

The destruction of marine habitats is most serious in coastal zones. Saltmarshes, estuaries, mangroves, and coral reefs, all areas of great beauty and vital to our welfare, are especially vulnerable to human disruption and degradation.

Coastal cities often look to nearby wetlands as a cheap way to dispose of rubbish, from industrial refuse to household garbage. Equally damaging is the dredging of offshore sand and gravel that destroys fish-spawning grounds. Along US coasts, dredging, together with filling operations, has eliminated more than 20,000 square kilometres of valuable wetlands.

Just as important and especially susceptible are estuaries, "crossroads" between land and ocean ecosystems, and hence locations of much human activity. So productive are estuaries in terms of fish life, that they are estimated to generate almost 80 million tonnes of fish a year, or more than our entire annual catch from the seas. Yet many of these prime habitats are being degraded at a rate that eliminates entire communities of fish. Of 80,000 square kilometres of US estuarine waters, one-third is now closed to shellfishing because of habitat disruption. Overall the destruction of offshore habitats costs the country more than $80 million a year through loss of commercial fisheries alone.

Another prime cause of habitat loss lies with eutrophication brought on by sewage sludge and fertilizer run-off. The added phosphates and nitrates cause a "bloom" of marine algae; as they die and decompose, they use up much of the available oxygen, choking out other life (except the bacteria that produce hydrogen sulphide by breaking down sulphates in their search for oxygen). Sewage decay also uses up oxygen, leading to the death of entire marine communities. Off New York and New Jersey, 9 million tonnes of sewage are dumped on to the continental shelf each year, impoverishing 12,000 square kilometres of ocean habitat and destroying whole populations of fish.

In the tropics, similar pressures are destroying both mangroves and coral reefs. In the Philippines, for example, 44,000 square kilometres of coral reefs supply one-tenth of the commercial fish catch, while extensive mangroves support exports of oysters, mussels, clams, and cockles. Both harvests are declining due to severe habitat degradation. Despite the designation of reserves for mangroves and reefs,

Destruction of habitat

Almost two-thirds of the human population live in one-third of the world's land adjacent to coasts. Of the ten largest metropolitan areas, seven (accounting for some 50 million people) border estuarine regions – New York, Tokyo, London, Shanghai, Buenos Aires, Osaka, and Los Angeles. In several cases these conurbations have all but obliterated the original coastal wetlands – biologically productive areas which are also important as pollution filters and as natural buffers between land and sea. The US, for example, is rich in estuaries. Those along the Atlantic and Gulf coasts are especially important as a fishery and shellfish resource. As many as 95-98% of commercial fishery species of these regions spend their early life feeding in the rich, warm, and sheltered estuarine waters. But for how long can they sustain their productivity, in the face of a proliferation of industrial complexes which are not only sited on wetlands, but spill their wastes into the fertile waters?

Just as worrying, if often less dramatic than pollution, are the effects of dredging and other forms of land management. The sludge dredged from the waterways of south Louisiana, as shown in the photograph below, forms a "levee", or continuous raised spoil bank, which effectively impounds many marshes. Natural drainage channels are either interrupted or cut – leading to widespread habitat destruction.

Chesapeake Bay
Chesapeake Bay on the U Atlantic coast is one of the world's most productive ecosystems and has long provided oysters, crabs, and fish in abundance. Bu today the Bay is becoming depleted, due to the effec of industrial pollution and agricultural fertilizers.

The Mississippi Delta
Louisiana's 1.2 million ha of saltmarshes account for some 40% of US coastal wetlands – a fraction of their original extent. Apart from natural erosion, the discovery of oil in 1901 led to construction of a vast network of waterways (below). This activity, together with land drainage, has adversely affected the wetlands, notably the shrimp nursery areas and menhaden fisheries of the Gulf of Mexico.

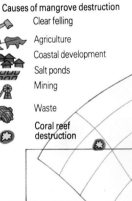

Causes of mangrove destruction
- Clear felling
- Agriculture
- Coastal development
- Salt ponds
- Mining
- Waste
- Coral reef destruction

Deforestation
Large tracts of mangrove SE Asia have been cut to provide woodchips, especially for the Japanes Sabah, for example, has lost over 122,000 ha of mangroves (40% of the total mangrove area).

Conversion to agriculture and aquaculture

In Asia and Africa, pressure on arable land has led to clearance of mangroves for agricultural land (e.g. rice cultivation in W Africa). Impoundment of mangroves for aquaculture is a more traditional activity; over 1 million ha of mangroves have been cleared for fish farming in the Indo-Pacific zone. The natural values of mangroves are seldom taken into account before converting these coastal ecosystems into agricultural or aquacultural "factories".

Salt pond construction

A classic example of conflicting resource needs in coastal zones lies with the clearance of mangroves for salt/brine evaporation ponds, as in NW India, W Africa, and Malaysia.

Waste disposal

Garbage and solid waste are often dumped in mangroves, while sewage effluents and hazardous chemicals contribute to their poisoning.

Mining

Mine waste can cause smothering of mangrove roots. In northern Puerto Rico, for example, mining for sand and an airport development have led to the destruction of a large tract of mangrove.

Coastal development

The clearance of mangroves for domestic and industrial development is a major problem, particularly in high-income countries. In southern Queensland, Australia, large tracts of mangrove have been destroyed for housing and canals. Similarly, much of the mangroves on the estuary of the Singapore river have been lost to housing and industry.

Mangrove forest destruction

Throughout the tropics, pressure from fast-growing populations is jeopardizing mangrove ecosystems. In Bangladesh, for example, where only 12% of the coast still features mangroves, 30% of the population (over 30 million people) depend on these shoreline forests for their livelihood. The map pinpoints areas of widescale mangrove loss, keyed to the most damaging factors involved – the most serious being felling for coastal development. The photograph, above, shows mangroves killed by oil spillage.

The assault on coral reefs and lagoons

The widescale destruction of coral reefs is a tragedy for humans and marine realm alike – coral reefs shelter island waters, harbour enormous numbers of species, and could one day provide us with a pharmacopoeia of new drugs (pp 74-5). Dredging and the removal of coral for construction is one factor; terrestrial erosion is another, often resulting in the smothering of reefs (Kanehoe Bay, Hawaii, is a classic case). Equally destructive is pollution caused by sewage, industrial waste, thermal and desalination effluents, and oil. Other factors include tourism, with collection of corals, shells, and puffer fish for the souvenir trade; mining and blasting; oil and gas production; over-fishing; even nuclear testing – all contribute to the death of reefs. The most complete and widespread destruction of coral reefs is now conducted by the US military. Diego Garcia in the Indian Ocean, once the fertile home of 2,000 people, is now virtually completely covered in concrete, its biological productivity destroyed.

the pressure of rising human numbers and demand for resources are eradicating these irreplaceable ecosystems at an alarming rate.

The tragedy of the commons

"Whales have become newly symbolic of real values in a world environment of which man is newly aware. Whales live in families, they play in the moonlight, they talk to one another, and they care for one another in distress. They are awesome and mysterious. In their cold, wet, and forbidding world they are complete and successful. They deserve to be saved, not as potential meatballs, but as a source of encouragement to mankind."

VICTOR SCHEFFER, AMERICAN WHALE EXPERT

The ocean has given rise to all manner of unhappy conflicts, from disputes over resources to depletion of marine species, whether seen as competitors or as prey. This is not so much due to the aggressive nature of fishing peoples and others "who go down to the seas in ships". Rather the problem lies with the nature of the marine realm as a "commons environment".

Apart from coastal zones, all people enjoy open access to the ocean, for them to exploit as they see fit. Each individual or nation has viewed the resources as free for the taking; each has sought to outdo the rest. This self-defeating process is compounded as the competition for a diminishing resource grows more severe, until all too often, the exploiters drive the resource to extinction.

The tragic futility of this outcome is symbolized by the record of the great whales. A whale swimming in the ocean belongs to nobody; when it is killed, it becomes the private property of the whaler, and the profit accrues to the whaler alone. As the

Whose ocean?

Conflict is the theme song of the oceans – a commons environment where uncontrolled exploitation and competition for resources makes the original inhabitants inevitably the losers. Of these, none has suffered more heavily than the great whales.

A non-sustainable harvest

The first whale species to attract unwanted human attention was the right whale – so dubbed because it was the "right" one to pursue – easy to catch and a rich source of oil and whalebone. The Victorian desire to cut a fine figure led to a huge demand for whalebone corsets, and the right whale was ultimately driven almost to extinction. Another early victim was the Western grey whale, hunted for oil, meat, and blubber. These disasters were only the beginning of the story. In this century, with improved technology, soaring demand for whale products, and no common management strategy, we have over-hunted species after species. As each stock fails, we turn our attention to the next.

Since 1900, whaling has focused on the Antarctic, where the whales congregate in summer to feed. The first Antarctic whale to be hunted commercially was the humpback: around 7,000 a year were taken in the 1900s. Once humpback stocks dropped, the blue whale, our largest living mammal, became the target; again, about 7,000 a year were harvested in the 1930s. Next in line was the fin whale – but now, more efficient catcher boats produced a massive rise in exploitation levels. Over 26,000 fin whales were taken in 1940 – the peak catch for this species. After the fin, the sei whale became the main quarry, with a peak catch of 20,000 in 1965. Finally, the whaling industry switched to the smaller minke whale, of which 8,000 were taken in 1970.

In 1946 the International Whaling Commission was established to regulate "the orderly development of the whaling industry". Until recently the IWC was an abject failure in regulating whale numbers, as quotas lacked a sound scientific base, and even then they were often ignored. By the late 1970s, as world concern for whales mounted and more non-whaling countries joined the IWC, stricter limits were applied. A date of 1985/6 has been set by the IWC for the cessation of all commercial whaling, but Japan and the USSR have lodged objections to that decision, which is therefore not binding on them. But, even if they ignore the moratorium, they are doing far less whaling and are not taking endangered stocks.

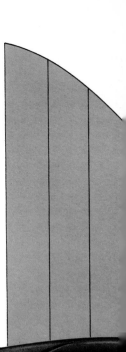

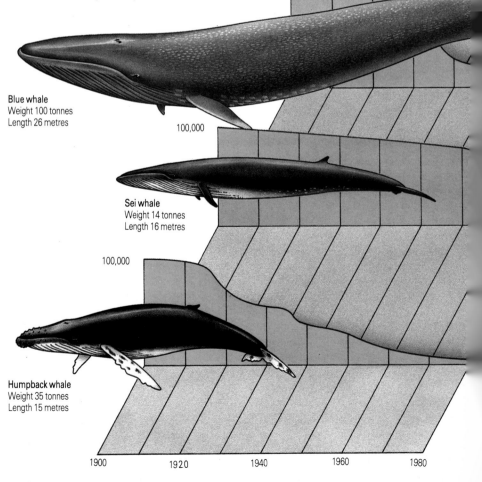

400,000

200,000

Blue whale
Weight 100 tonnes
Length 26 metres

100,000

Sei whale
Weight 14 tonnes
Length 16 metres

100,000

Humpback whale
Weight 35 tonnes
Length 15 metres

1900   1920   1940   1960   1980

Defeat of the giants
One after another, the
Antarctic populations of
the great whales have
plummeted. Hunting of
these species is no longer
viable, their future unsure.
Because of slow maturation
and calving rates, it will
take many years for the
populations to recover, if at
all. The population curves,
left, are based on estimates
of Southern Ocean
populations for 1900-80.

Fin whale
Weight 40 tonnes
Length 22 metres

hunting intensifies, whalers have to spend extra effort in finding their next target. Worse still, all people (including the whalers) face an aggravated risk of a whale species going extinct. Concern for the whales, and the whaling industry, has already led to massive restrictions, though often too late. A moratorium has been voted but certain countries choose not to honour it. Until effective protection is agreed (as now seems likely within the next few years), the individual whaler's main concern will be to grab another whale. Little merit is seen in personally sacrificing one's own whaling prospects.

Not only advancing technology, but sky-high interest rates on capital, encourage whaling entrepreneurs to try to recover their investment, plus profits, as soon as possible – often in as little as half a decade. This short-term economic pressure militates against any long-term sustainable harvest of a

resource with such a lengthy self-renewal period. A whale population may grow by only 5 percent a year – a rate that is way below a typical rate of discount on capital investment.

The present-day ocean crisis can be likened to the parable of the "grazing commons" in medieval England. Traditionally, herdkeepers grazed their cattle on common pasture. One area might be used by 10 herdkeepers each with one cow. If one keeper brought along an extra cow, this would result in slightly less grazing per cow, although for the enterprising keeper, the loss would be offset by receiving two shares of the grazing. If, however, all the other keepers followed suit, they would all soon find themselves poorer and poorer. Thus the tragedy of the commons: while each user works out a plan that appears rational, the collective result is that the commons are wrecked.

The troubled oceans
Competition for ocean space and resources takes many forms. The map below highlights typical incidences of several kinds: territorial disputes, resource disputes, and conflicts between human fishing and the needs of marine mammals. As competition for fish stocks intensifies, territorial disputes between fishing nations become commonplace. The Cod Wars between Iceland and Britain in the 1960s and '70s were a dramatic example, receiving much media coverage. Britain eventually had to back down, in the face of Iceland's adoption of the Exclusive Economic Zone (EEZ) – a principle which Britain itself was soon to reinforce.

A rather different confrontation arises when a marine resource serves several needs. In the North Atlantic, capelin is taken for use as

fishmeal, but is also eaten by cod – itself a valuable food fish.

Conflict between humans and marine mammals has always been intense. Apart from the hunt for whales, regular culls to safeguard the interest of local fisheries are common, from grey seals in the Orkney islands to dolphins off Japan. Accidental netting (incidental take) of small marine mammals, especially dolphins and porpoises, destroys enormous numbers of these animals. In the 1950s and '60s, hundreds of thousands of dolphins were killed each year in tuna nets in the Pacific. This fishery has since modified its techniques, and dolphin mortality has been reduced. But the slaughter continues – for example, tens of thousands of Dall's porpoise are taken each year in salmon gill nets.

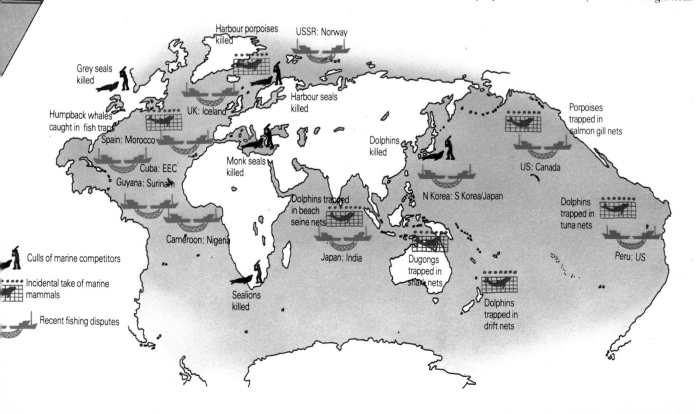

MANAGING THE OCEAN

Despite much research, we lack the understanding to exploit marine resources in a sustainable manner. The ocean is beset with crises, ecological and political. And although attempts at management have a long history, there are relatively few success stories. Fortunately, there are signs of a new approach. Fisheries planning is becoming more precise, and fresh moves are underway to control pollution and protect marine environments. A series of conventions and treaties are coming into force,

and the concept of common heritage is still alive, if less robust than was initially hoped, in the new Law of the Sea.

A new fishing strategy

How shall we do a better job of taking a sustainable harvest from the sea? Hitherto we have employed an approach resembling that of hunter-gatherers toward agriculture; we have exploited wild creatures in a wild manner, with predictable results.

We can take a huge step forward right away by applying measures we have long known to be valid and yet persistently ignored to our cost. We can agree on realistic catch quotas, for instance, based on a true understanding of the population dynamics of fisheries, and enforce them strictly. We can impose moratoria on fishing stocks, before they crash, rather than too late as with the Peruvian anchovy and North Sea herring. We can set minimum net-mesh sizes (or caught fish sizes) to

Fishery commissions and advisory bodies
1 Regional Fisheries Advisory Commission for SW Atlantic (CARPAS)
2 Fishery Committee for the EC Atlantic (CECAF)
3 General Fisheries Council for the Mediterranean (GFCM)
4 Indian Ocean Fishery Commission (IOFC)
5 Indo-Pacific Fishery Commission (IPFC)
6 WC Atlantic Fishery Commission (WECAFC)
7 International Baltic Sea Fishery Commission (IBSFC)
8 NW Atlantic Fishery Organization (NAFO)
9 International Commission for the SE Atlantic Fisheries Commission (ICSEAF)
10 International N Pacific Fisheries Commission (INPFC)

Harvesting the sea

With ever-rising demand for the ocean's living protein, and increasing depletion of fisheries and marine mammals, we can no longer afford to ignore ecosystem interactions in our fishing policies. Despite a welter of fishery bodies, quotas for both fish and mammals have generally been too high, reflecting political compromise rather than scientific advice, and protection has been ineffectual. In the future we shall need more realistic quotas and tougher enforcement, while fishery management will increasingly involve choices – where to tap a food chain, which species to harvest and how much, and which to protect. The effects of human intervention are already apparent in some ecosystems as shown below. Before we interfere even more seriously, as in the Antarctic, we must study the consequences.

Fishery management
Since the 1930s there has been a proliferation of fishery commissions and advisory bodies dealing with fishing areas and quotas of fish and mammal species. Some work in a consultative capacity, others set quotas and have their own back-up research programmes. The North Pacific Fur Seal Commission was the first of these bodies to be established in 1911. Within the new Exclusive Economic Zones (EEZs), coastal states rather than fishery commissions have had more direct control over quotas and catches.

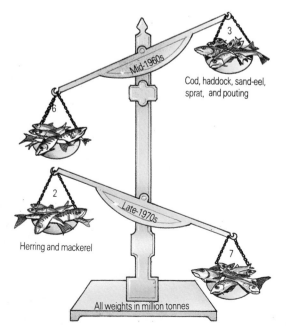

Shifting the balance
Since the mid-1960s, the North Sea harvest has remained level. But the nets are no longer filled with mackerel and herring, once so abundant. Instead we haul in a mixture of smaller species, with some cod and haddock. True, our fishing patterns have changed. But human exploitation has apparently shifted the balance of North Sea ecosystems too. Out of a fairly constant fishing stock, herring and mackerel once comprised two-thirds, but now make up less than one-third; while pout, sand-eels, sprats, and larger gadoids have multiplied, perhaps because their larval forms are less likely to be preyed upon since depletion of the herring and mackerel.

Cod, haddock, sand-eel, sprat, and pouting

Herring and mackerel

All weights in million tonnes

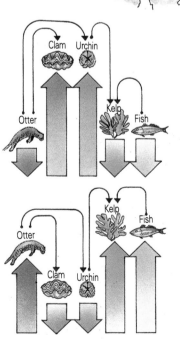

Otter vs clam
Protection of the Californian sea otter in 1972 was welcomed by conservationists, but ha some unforeseen consequences. The upp diagram shows the pre protection ratio of the otter to other coastal species, the lower one t situation today. An inc in sea otters has been matched by a decrease clams and sea-urchins, which the otter feeds. Reduction of sea-urchi has resulted in vigorou growth of kelp (seawee which in turn provides shelter for fish. Traditi clam gathering and harvesting of sea-urchi once provided income the coastal towns. Thes have now been partial replaced by tourism.

allow immature fish to live and grow—a basic piece of common sense. We can institute laws to protect ocean communities, and cease to persecute the dolphins, seals, and other marine predators or to entrap them carelessly in our nets.

Probably the two most important measures we can take, however, are to reduce our pressure on ocean resources overall, and adopt a fundamentally modified strategy for fishing. Thus far we have tended to concentrate on individual fish species, invoking a concept of maximum sustainable yield. For the future, we must take account of ecological interactions within an ocean community, and apply a multi-species management strategy.

In the Antarctic Ocean, for example, we find many species of whale and seal, together with vast colonies of seabirds, all supported by abundant stocks of krill. Whereas there used to be 100,000 blue whales, they have now been reduced to just a few thousand; and all other krill-feeding whale

species, with the exception of the minke, have been grossly depleted. As a result, their consumption of krill has been reduced from about 190 million tonnes a year to only about 60 million tonnes. So far as we can tell, this has released a large amount of krill for the seabirds and seals.

These feeding links have major significance for our plans to harvest krill. Would the deficit, if we create one, hit the seabirds and seals, which are under no threat—or would it fall on the whale species, at least six of which are struggling to move away from the brink of extinction?

Human hunters have long posed a threat to marine mammals. Not only whales, but turtles, dolphins, manatees, dugongs, Californian sea otters, sealions, certain seals, and polar bears have suffered widespread loss. Most of the 100-plus species need some form of protection. But safeguard measures are not enough, unless we also take account of prey stocks, many of which are increasingly harvested for

Krill—the vital link

Antarctic waters are among the most productive in the world, the main link in the food chain being small shrimp-like krill. During the summer they feed on phyto- and zooplankton, growing from about 45 mm to 150 mm. Summer swarms of krill have been estimated at 650 million tonnes, a huge amount of living matter for only one species.

anging demands on krill

ior to their exploitation,
e great whales consumed
arge proportion of the
nual crop of krill which
o supported abundant
bird and seal colonies.
ce the great whales'
cline, seals and seabirds
ve been the major krill
sumers. Human
eries take only 1.15% of
total krill stock (1982).
ure human demand
st be taken into account
ver the baleen whales
to recover.

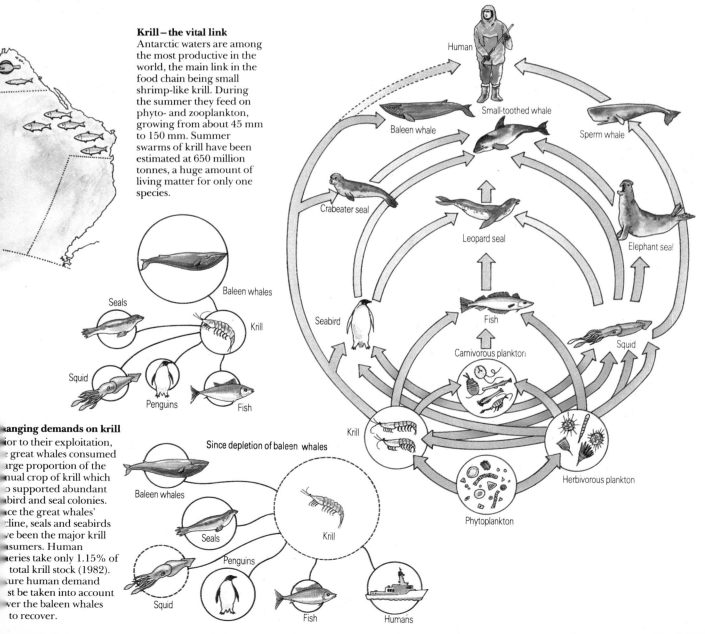

Since depletion of baleen whales

human consumption. An ecosystem-level approach will not only help the disappearing mammals; it will support the long-term welfare of the whole ocean community, including humankind.

Pollution control

The ocean offers vast scope for us to dispose of waste; but it requires vast care. Common sense demands that we should control pollution at source, and clean up its past legacy. Under the International Convention for the Prevention of Pollution from Ships (known as MARPOL), strict limits are now set on the amounts of oil that ships can discharge. In certain sensitive zones, such as the Baltic and Mediterranean Seas and the Persian Gulf, oil discharge is prohibited altogether. What is more, oil cargoes can be "fingerprinted" through additives, and the culprits of pollution identified. As a result, the amount of oil released at sea has been considerably reduced, even though we have more and larger oil-bearing ships.

MARPOL is also tackling controls for discharge and dumping of wastes. In dealing with pollution problems which cross regional boundaries, the international convention, backed by agencies like the International Maritime Organisation, is a useful tool. There is support from technology too: better ways to incinerate waste at sea, better means to disperse sewage sludge, and better techniques to keep toxic contaminants out of chemical effluents.

Matching the international approach are important conventions dealing with specific areas. The Bonn Agreement of 1969 focused on the control of oil pollution in the North Sea—a heavily polluted and congested shipping area. The agreement safeguards vulnerable coastal areas from oil spillage, with member countries co-operating in any clean-up operations. The comprehensive Helsinki Convention (1974) has been the first to cover not only seaborne pollution, but the more serious issue of land-based pollution too. This convention highlights the need for an overall strategy at a regional level, and has served as a prototype for the United Nations Environmental Programme (UNEP).

To its credit, UNEP has picked up this environmental football, and has run far and fast with it. Begun in 1974, its Regional Seas Programme is now thoroughly under way, supported by 26 international organizations and 120 nations. Ten regional clean-up efforts are being implemented, based on the model of the first such initiative, the extraordinarily successful Mediterranean Plan. The Programme supplies a unique international forum where numerous disparate parties—for example, Israel and Libya, Iran and Iraq, the US and Cuba—sit down together to resolve common problems through common solutions.

This brave strategy represents a quantum leap in "environmental diplomacy". The problems of ocean pollution have seemed intractable precisely because they have been international problems. The

Clean-up for the ocean

Spearheading the clean-up of the oceans is the regional approach exemplified in UNEP's Regional Seas Programme, backed by international conventions and improved technology. Since the 1975 Mediterranean Action Plan, UNEP has launched on average one plan a year, with programmes well underway in Kuwait and the Caribbean. Long-term success, however, depends on finance. UNEP provides only the seed money – $8 million, for example, in the first 5 years of the Mediterranean Plan. The main funds must be raised by the countries concerned. In 1981, both the Kuwait and the Mediterranean plans suffered shortage of funds, even though these are the richest areas.

Baltic Sea: region cov
Helsinki Convention (1

North Sea: region covered by
Bonn Agreement (1969)

Caribbean Region

Incineration at sea
Purpose-built incineration tankers offer an alternative to dumping. At 1,350°C, toxic polychlorinated biphenyls (PCBs) break down to hydrochloric acid and water.

Mediterranean Regic

Red S
of Ad

West and Central
African Region

Coverage of UNEP Regional Seas Programme

Countries that have ratified MARPOL protocol (Oct 1983)

Countries with oil-disposal facilities

South-West Atlantic Region

MARPOL

In 1973 MARPOL was formulated to control all forms of pollution from ships. It sets minimum distances from land for the discharge of treated and untreated sewage, garbage, and toxic waste. Oil pollution provisions oblige ships over 400 tonnes to carry tanks for the retention of oil residues, and ports handling oil to have proper disposal facilities. The Convention also prohibits the discharge of toxic waste in the Bal and the Black Sea, and discharge of oil in the Baltic, Black Sea, Mediterranean, Persian Gulf, and Red Sea. In 1 MARPOL was ratified b 25 states.

Treated garbage	Treated sewage	Shipping over 400 tonnes	Some toxic waste	Untreated garbage	Untreated sewage	Oil dischar

3 4   12   nautical miles   50

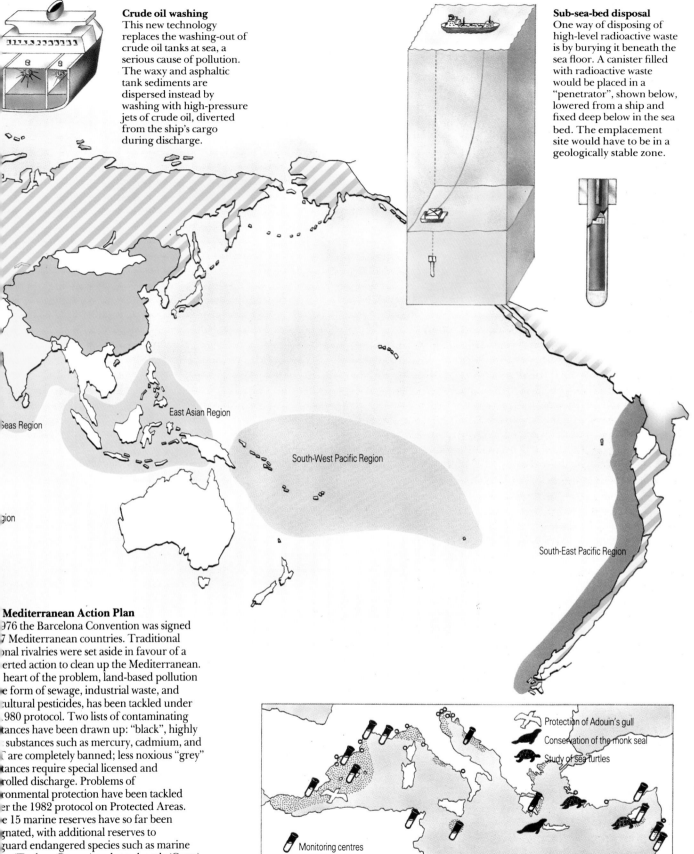

Crude oil washing
This new technology replaces the washing-out of crude oil tanks at sea, a serious cause of pollution. The waxy and asphaltic tank sediments are dispersed instead by washing with high-pressure jets of crude oil, diverted from the ship's cargo during discharge.

Sub-sea-bed disposal
One way of disposing of high-level radioactive waste is by burying it beneath the sea floor. A canister filled with radioactive waste would be placed in a "penetrator", shown below, lowered from a ship and fixed deep below in the sea bed. The emplacement site would have to be in a geologically stable zone.

Seas Region

East Asian Region

South-West Pacific Region

gion

South-East Pacific Region

Mediterranean Action Plan
976 the Barcelona Convention was signed
7 Mediterranean countries. Traditional
nal rivalries were set aside in favour of a
erted action to clean up the Mediterranean.
heart of the problem, land-based pollution
e form of sewage, industrial waste, and
cultural pesticides, has been tackled under
980 protocol. Two lists of contaminating
tances have been drawn up: "black", highly
substances such as mercury, cadmium, and
are completely banned; less noxious "grey"
tances require special licensed and
rolled discharge. Problems of
ronmental protection have been tackled
er the 1982 protocol on Protected Areas.
e 15 marine reserves have so far been
gnated, with additional reserves to
guard endangered species such as marine
es (Turkey, Cyprus) and monk seals (Crete).
g-term monitoring of pollution is carried
y over 80 marine laboratories, including an
ombating Centre established in Malta in
5 to co-ordinate communication and
ning in the Mediterranean.

Protection of Adouin's gull
Conservation of the monk seal
Study of sea turtles

Monitoring centres

Study area of coastal pollutants

IUCN/WWF conservation projects

Regional Seas Programme demonstrates that the community of nations can prove itself equal to some unusually difficult challenges.

The Antarctic heritage

Antarctica, a common heritage of all humanity if ever there was one, remains under the aegis of the Antarctic Treaty powers. A mere 16 nations (1984), seven of whom have territorial stakes in the continent, hold sole decision-making rights over all activities in the region. True, the Treaty has proved a successful experiment in international co-operation. Such antagonistic nations as the US, the USSR, the UK, and Argentina have agreed to keep one-tenth of the Earth's land surface demilitarized,

nuclear-free, and devoted to research. But membership is absurdly small, and the parties meet in secrecy. Hence the charge that they form an exclusive "club" dominated by developed nations – an association of the world's largest real-estate operators, a last stand of colonialism, and a political anachronism. Understandably, other groups, especially Third World nations, want a say in the future of Antarctica, and a share in its potential wealth.

Conservationists promote the idea of a world park, to safeguard this unique and largely undisturbed ecosystem in pristine purity. But nations with an eye to its abundant mineral and living resources are highly unlikely to countenance these being declared "off limits" in perpetuity. A more realistic

	Antarctic Treaty Limit
	CCAMLR limit
UK●	Research stations
	Potential island Exclu Economic Zones (EE
	Antarctic Convergenc
	Krill distribution
	Krill concentration

Managing Antarctica

Explorers laid the first claims to Antarctica in the early part of this century, and by 1943 the continent was staked out by 7 nations, viz. Argentina, Australia, Chile, France, New Zealand, Norway, and the UK. It was another 30 years before an approach to international management was formulated in the Antarctic Treaty, signed by the claimants and 5 additional nations. Despite territorial disputes, the Treaty powers have since 1959 managed the Antarctic as an area devoted to peaceful purposes. Research is co-ordinated by the Scientific Committee on Antarctic Research (SCAR); protective measures include the Convention on the Conservation of Antarctic Seals (1978) and the more far-reaching 1982 Convention on the Conservation of Antarctic Marine Living Resources (CCAMLR), designed to manage the krill resource. The map shows the scope of the Treaty and CCAMLR, and the potential effect of the Exclusive Economic Zones (EEZs) off sub-Antarctic islands.

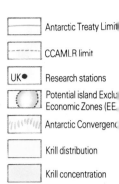

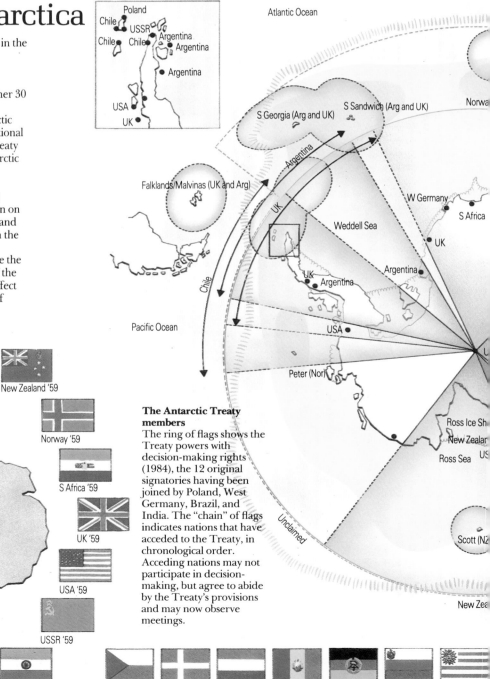

The Antarctic Treaty members
The ring of flags shows the Treaty powers with decision-making rights (1984), the 12 original signatories having been joined by Poland, West Germany, Brazil, and India. The "chain" of flags indicates nations that have acceded to the Treaty, in chronological order. Acceding nations may not participate in decision-making, but agree to abide by the Treaty's provisions and may now observe meetings.

France '59   Japan '59   New Zealand '59

Chile '59   Norway '59

Belgium '59   S Africa '59

Australia '59   UK '59

Argentina '59   USA '59

Poland '77   USSR '59

W Germany '79   Brazil '83   India '83

Czech '62   Denmark '65   Neth '67   Romania '71   E Germany '74   Bulgaria '78   Uruguay '80

CCAMLR

The Convention on the Conservation of Antarctic Marine Living Resources came into force in April 1982. CCAMLR is primarily concerned with controlling Antarctic fisheries, particularly krill, to ensure that catch levels neither jeopardize krill populations nor impede the recovery of the great whales. Despite this new "ecosystem" approach, conservationists maintain that CCAMLR's powers are inadequate.

goal, proposed by non-aligned countries, is a global regime, perhaps modelled on the UNCLOS International Seabed Authority (p. 96), through which the community of nations could participate in such exploitation as is agreed. Yet this approach is definitely unacceptable to the Treaty claimants, who claim legal rights and have a better understanding of the area. They have also made major investments as pioneers of the region.

A third option is some form of joint regulation by Treaty powers: it is most likely that this would be based on a system of "jurisdictional ambiguity". Sovereignty issues would be left open, with a tacit understanding that they remain unresolved. Regrettably, such an approach does not reflect the interests of non-Treaty states — and might give short shrift to environmental interests.

The perplexing problems of Antarctica are not amenable to any one solution, acceptable all round. Pending a long-term management strategy, we need some immediate measures: a freeze at present levels of fishing of krill; a sanctuary for whales and seals throughout the region; an Environmental Protection Administration, with parks and reserves of suitably large size; and an accelerated programme of research. Finally and above all, we need the participation of many more nations and national governmental organizations. As long as the bulk of nation states feel themselves to be disenfranchised from one of the planet's greatest assets, there is

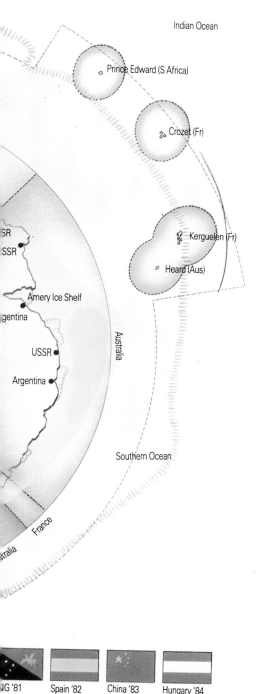

Indian Ocean

Prince Edward (S Africa)

Crozet (Fr)

Kerguelen (Fr)

Heard (Aus)

Antarctica

USSR

Amery Ice Shelf

Argentina

USSR

Argentina

Australia

France

Southern Ocean

1 billion barrels of oil

North Sea

Alaska

Antarctica's hidden wealth

The first indirect evidence of Antarctica's huge oil potential came in 1972, when drilling on the continental shelf of the Ross Sea discovered traces of the gases methane and ethane. Despite the fact that no oil has yet been struck, some estimates put reserves at around 50 billion barrels (bb), equivalent to exploitable stocks of around 15 bb. Compared with proven oil reserves elsewhere, this is a considerable store. Discovery of mineral wealth has introduced a new urgency to Antarctic politics — the territorial claims of Treaty parties, previously of notional value, now have real economic significance.

Comparison of oil reserves

A US government report (1976) estimated Antarctica's recoverable oil reserves at 15 bb, compared with around 58 bb in Saudi Arabia, almost 20 bb in the British sector of the North Sea, and 8 bb in Alaska. For all its promise, however, the difficulties of extraction are immense: the inhospitable climate and geographical isolation of Antarctica are formidable obstacles, even to modern technology.

Global regime

Even before the Treaty, developing countries were pressing for a global regime for Antarctica. A proposal in the 1950s by India was withdrawn after opposition from future Treaty nations; but the matter has been repeatedly raised. In 1982-3, Malaysia asked the General Assembly to put Antarctica on the agenda. To counter criticism, the Treaty powers have responded by inviting acceding states to observe their meetings, and agreeing to release more of their internal documents.

PNG '81   Spain '82   China '83   Hungary '84

unlikely to be an enduring resolution to the challenge of its management.

From high seas to managed seas

Laws work pretty well for over 40 percent of the oceans. For the rest—the waters beyond either the Exclusive Economic Zones (EEZs) or the continental shelves—the law of the jungle reigns, at least for those countries that are not party to the Law of the Sea Convention.

How have we reached this situation? Nations used to exercise exclusive control only over their "territorial sea", being a narrow coastal zone about three nautical miles wide (roughly the sector that could be covered by cannon fire from land). All the rest were subject to the doctrine of the "freedom of the high seas". This tradition persisted, with minor amendments such as an extension of the territorial sea to 12 miles (and occasionally to 200 miles), until the 1960s, when it became plain that advancing technology was allowing certain nations to take an undue share of the ocean's wealth.

In the 1960s, a philosophy was enunciated that the ocean (or at the very least its deep sea beds) should become a common heritage of humankind, to be managed by an international body such as the United Nations. This "universalist" spirit stimulated the convening of the Third Law of the Sea Conference (UNCLOS), which eventually ran from 1973 to 1982. The aim was to develop a single all-embracing treaty, covering all issues, including fisheries, navigation, continental shelves, the deep sea bed, scientific research, and pollution of the marine environment. The result was to be a "package deal" that would establish a world order for whatever uses were to be made of the oceans.

Alas for high hopes. The 150-plus participating nations have failed to agree on anything near a comprehensive treaty backed by international law and enforced by marine tribunals. The concept of a common heritage needing international management now survives only for the deep sea bed. Worse still, while 134 participating nations have signed the final document with its 320 articles, a number of others have declined, including the US, the UK, and West Germany. Without these leading sea-bed mining and maritime nations, the Treaty will remain a broken-backed affair. In any case, of the many nations that appear to accept the Treaty in principle, only a few have ratified it.

But not all is lost. We still have a large number of international treaties dealing with separate marine issues. The International Maritime Organisation, for example, does a fair job with navigation and the control of pollution from ships, while UNEP's Regional Seas Programme has made a sound start on the clean-up of specific areas.

UNCLOS has enabled us to progress a long way beyond the hopelessly confused situation of the 1960s. Moreover, it is inspiring us to draw upon a large body of customary laws and established

The laws of the sea

Our view of the legal status of the ocean is turning full circle. Once it was a boundless, two-dimensional expanse, belonging to no-one. Now we perceive it as a finite, three-dimensional resource, which should belong to all. Over the centuries, this traditional "freedom of the seas" has been gradually encroached on by national claims, fishing agreements, and a growing body of customary and international laws. In the last 50 years, however, a new principle has emerged to dominate conference tables. Like a beacon, the idea of "common heritage" steered the long deliberations of UNCLOS III. They fell short of the goal, but still achieved a new "written constitution" for the ocean.

Mare Liberum 1609
The Dutchman, Grotius, first proclaimed the "freedom of the seas" in keeping with the exploratory spirit of the age. Territorial waters we limited to about 3 nautica miles from land.

19th century agreements
In 1839 Belgium ignored an Anglo-French Oyster Beds treaty, demonstrating the need for multilateral support. The first international convention on the Policing of the North Sea Fisheries beyond Territorial Waters was signed in 1882.

Regulating exploitation
In 1893, the US tried to control exploitation of fur seals, but an international tribunal ruled this illegal. The Convention on North Pacific Fur Seals (1911) was the first international agreement on stock regulation.

The League of Nations Conference 1930
The first major international conference on the law of the sea raised two issues destined to dominate conferences for 50 years: territorial sea limits and "common heritage". An enlightened delegate, Snr Suarez, proposed that living ocean resources should be viewed as a common patrimony.

Fishery commi 1930s and 40s
Commissions se regulate fisheri politically ineffe unable to imple scientific advice and NW Atlant Commissions, f did not cover al fishing the area such bodies wer appreciate the i of quotas.

The Achilles heel

The UNCLOS III Convention is presented to the world nations as an "all or nothing" package, a feature which is proving to be the "Achilles heel" of the new Law of the Sea. When a country like the US strongly objects to one UNCLOS recommendation, such as an international regime for the sea beds, it is obliged to reject the entire treaty. Though many states have now signed the treaty, most will spend a long time deliberating before ratifying—it needs 60 ratifications, but as yet has only 9. Because full implementation of the Law of the Sea treaty is a long way off, a number of states press for interim measures, and some of these contradict the spirit of the new constitution. The US, Belgium, West Germany, Italy, France, the UK, Japan, and the USSR have enacted unilateral legislation to enable national licensing of sea-bed mining, though this directly conflicts with the UNCLOS recommendation for international development of sea-bed resources.

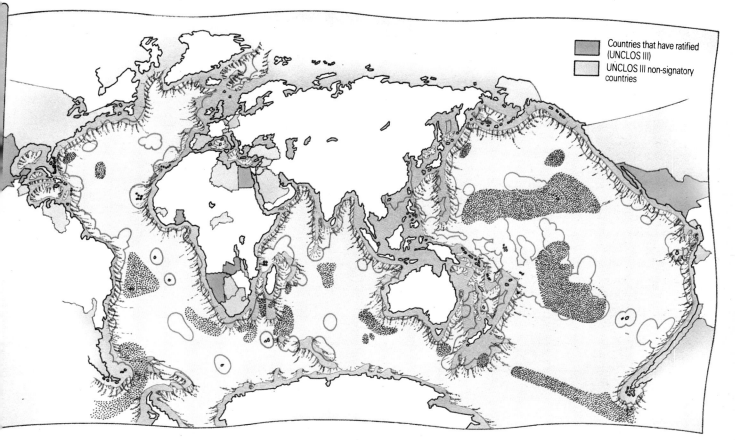

Legend:
- Countries that have ratified (UNCLOS III)
- UNCLOS III non-signatory countries
- Continental shelf
- Open ocean
- EEZ
- Extensive manganese nodule deposits

President Truman's Unilateral Proclamation 1945

The discovery of oil and gas in the continental shelves sparked off a race between coastal states to extend their territorial limits. The front-runner was the US, led by President Truman. Chile and Peru followed in 1947, each claiming over 200 nautical miles.

UNCLOS I and II

With just four conventions, the First and Second UN Conferences on the Law of the Sea tried to provide a comprehensive formula for managing the world ocean. But the conferences fell far short of their aim.

N Conference on e Sea 1973-82

nising start rationalized ocean nent, UNCLOS he first time, unites of the Sea into ten constitution". visions for EEZs ew responsibility l states to manage e environment. of navigation and nrough nal straits are ed. But the ity to regard the whole has been common resources are o the deep sea

Common heritage

In 1967, Ambassador Pardo, the Maltese representative to the UN, declared the resources of the deep sea beds to be the "common heritage of mankind". This echoed the 1930 proposal by Snr Suarez, except that it was now backed up with political muscle. Between UNCLOS I and 1973, the number of UN member states had doubled to over 140. Most of the new voters were developing nations.

UNCLOS III

So far (1984), 9 states or entities have signed and ratified the UNCLOS treaty, and 35 have rejected it. Between these extremes lie 125 of the 134 states which are signatories to UNCLOS, but not yet legally bound by it.

UNCLOS III places over 40% of the ocean under the jurisdiction of coastal states, defined in 4 zones of increasing size: (1) Territorial Sea (12 nautical miles from land), (2) Contiguous Zone (24 miles), (3) Extended Economic Zone (200 miles more), and (4) Continental Shelf. The Territorial Sea guarantees sovereign rights; the Contiguous Zone, control for limited purposes; and the EEZ, functional rights over economic activity, scientific research, and environmental preservation. The Continental Shelf is potentially the most extensive "national area" of the sea bed: states may explore and exploit it without infringing the legal status of water and air above.

The traditional "freedom of the seas" remains for 60% of the ocean. But 42% of this, the deep sea beds area, is designated the "common heritage of mankind", and will be controlled by an International Seabed Authority, (ISA).

This proposal split the Law of the Sea Conference. The developed nations were reluctant to share their technological expertise in ocean mining with the developing nations, but the latter are determined not to lose out on what could be an important future resource – manganese nodules.

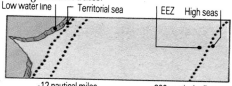

Low water line — Territorial sea — EEZ — High seas
12 nautical miles   200 nautical miles

treaties. It serves to reinforce many existing conventions and organizations. Finally, it provides a starting point from which we can develop new rules, regulations, and practices. We are much better off with UNCLOS than without it.

A testing ground for planet management

The state of the world ocean is a sensitive litmus test of our developing skills in planet management. Focus down almost anywhere in the 360 million square kilometres of the world ocean and you will find some sign of humanity's presence and impact, however slight. Move in close to the major centres of population, and the symptoms are all too apparent.

Year by year, our influence becomes more pervasive. New technologies enable us to reach ever further into the ocean, while industrial pollutants highlight its complexity as a resource by turning up thousands of kilometres from human habitation. As we come to grips with the multiple dimensions of the ocean ecosystem, it is increasingly clear that, while it may sometimes prove more robust than ecosystems on land, our errors in ocean management can be even harder to remedy.

Clearly, we need an agreed strategy for managing our ocean resources, and for developing them as appropriate. The new Law of the Sea Convention reserves three-fifths of the ocean as a common resource, where the traditional freedoms of the seas still apply. It also recognizes the wealth of the ocean floor, accounting for 42 percent of Earth's surface, as a common planetary inheritance of all humankind. Simultaneously it places two-fifths of the ocean under the control of individual nations, together with the relevant sea-bed resources. This may fly in the face of common-heritage values, but it is true that national ownership rights can promote a sense of responsibility.

There are also real dangers in this approach, however. The ocean cannot readily be sliced up like some gigantic pie: it is a continuous ecosystem and many of its components, like the major currents, flow to the horizons with sublime indifference to human politics. Better, say some scientists, to view the ocean as a whole.

The ocean, in short, is an indivisible resource, whereas the nation state tends to be a divisive force at a global level. However well it performs as a management tool to serve local needs, the nation state, virtually by definition, is incapable of matching up to the collective needs of the community of nations, let alone to the broader needs and interests of present and future generations.

How, then, can we re-establish a concept of the ocean as the common heritage of humankind, to be administered as a necessarily shared resource? How can governments be persuaded to approach joint problems in a spirit of joint endeavour? We cannot refuse the challenge. For, without doubt, the world ocean will be a critical proving-ground if we are to succeed in our new role as planet caretakers.

Future ocean

The migratory routes of the Arctic tern, humpback whale, and the Pacific salmon highlight the way marine life links far-flung corners of the world ocean. The map, right, also shows some early building blocks for ocean management. Intense shipping activity in the English Channel, for example, has resulted in traffic-management schemes designed to cut shipping losses and pollution. Nation states which are at odds ideologically have come together to work on management schemes for the Caribbean and for such vulnerable, enclosed seas as the Baltic and Mediterranean. Pressures on the world ocean will grow as we seek to harness both its renewable and non-renewable resources, from mackerel to manganese nodules. Some marine ecosystems, like the Great Barrier Reef, can be designated as international conservation areas. Others, like the Antarctic Ocean, will demand new, multi-species management strategies if they are to produce a sustainable yield.

Cleaning up the Caribbean

The Caribbean may not yet be as polluted as some other semi-enclosed seas, but the prevailing east-to-west currents trap pollutants against the coasts. The Mississippi River injects pollution from US industries, cities, and farms. Pesticide residues wash down from banana, cotton, and sugar plantations. Industry in Puerto Rico and Trinidad discharges effluent direct into the sea, while only 10% of the sewage produced in the region is treated. There are clear implications for Caribbean tourism and fisheries. While the Caribbean Action Plan, focusing on 66 environment and development projects, has been slow to take off, the threat to the Caribbean has induced 27 nations, many with divergent political views, to adopt new treaties to protect and develop the marine environment.

Tern migratory route

Humback whale migratory route

Atlantic salmon

Pacific salmon

Arctic Ocean

Pacific Oce

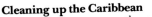

Warm surface water

Cold bottom water

Ocean energy
The world ocean will be a major source of renewable energy, whether in the form of algal biomass, currents, tides, waves or the thermal energy exploited by OTEC technology, left. With all these activities, as with the exploitation of manganese nodules (in the Pacific) and metalliferous muds (in the Red Sea), or with offshore oil production, environmental impact assessment will be a key management tool.

Policing the sea-lanes

In the first six months of 1979, there were six ship-to-ship collisions in the area of the Dover Strait, an accident rate unequalled since 1969 – and despite wider use of highly sophisticated navigational aids, both on ships and on shore. Worldwide in 1980, a total of 387 ships was lost, and in 1979, 465. Traffic-management schemes have been introduced in accident black-spots like the English Channel (see radar picture, right). The growing size of oil tankers has compounded the pollution threat. Equally troublesome are smaller releases of oil, which may be tracked back to source in future by chemical "fingerprinting" of oil prior to shipment. The world ocean, in short, needs a formidable policing effort.

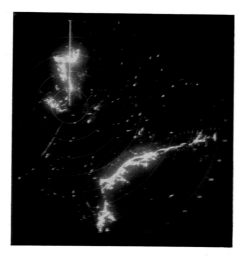

Multi-species management

The sustainable development of the world ocean's living resources depends on enormous inputs of scientific information, as in the case of the Antarctic fisheries (see pp 80-1 and 90-1). The productivity of Antarctic waters is extraordinary, with the standing stock of the shrimp-like krill *Euphasia superba* estimated at some 650 million tonnes. "Super swarms" of krill may be several kilometres across and contain several million tonnes. But many other species also depend on this resource, necessitating multi-species management. Over-exploiting krill could push some newly protected whale stocks towards "incidental" extinction. Elsewhere, as a sign of shifting priorities, whale-watching is a major growth industry, even out-earning the hunting of whales.

The Great Barrier Reef

In 1980, Australia presented the world with an unusual gift: a protected area of 11,800 sq km of coral reefs, islands, and surrounding waters, the first section of the Great Barrier Reef to be set aside as a marine park. The Great Barrier Reef extends 2,000 km along Australia's northeast coast and covers 207,000 sq km. The reef supports some 400 species of coral and an estimated 1,500 fish species. Much of the reef has been under pressure for some time, starting with phosphate mining and turtle-meat industries, and followed by sea-bed mining, oil drilling, and tourism. Deforestation and intensive farming on the mainland also impact on the reef, but the embryonic marine park is a portent of better things to come.

ic Ocean

Indian Ocean

ELEMENTS

Introduced by James E. Lovelock

Originator of the Gaia hypothesis

To my mind, the outstanding spin-off from space research is not new technology, but that for the first time we have been able to look at Earth from the outside – and have been stimulated to ask new questions.

Having worked on the Martian atmosphere, looking for signs of life, I later switched back to Earth and concentrated on the nature of our own atmosphere. This work resulted in the Gaia hypothesis, which suggests that the entire range of living matter on Earth, from whales to viruses, can be regarded as a single entity, capable of manipulating its environment to suit its needs.

It was a long way from devising plausible life-detection experiments to the hypothesis that Earth's atmosphere, and the cycling of elements within it, is actively maintained and regulated by the biosphere. But we found that the chemistry of the atmosphere violates the rules of steady state chemistry. Disequilibria of the scale that we observed (p. 13) suggest that the atmosphere is not merely a biological product, as oxygen often is, but more probably a biological construction – like a cat's fur, or a bird's feathers; an extension of a living system, designed to maintain a chosen environment.

We defined Gaia as a complex entity involving the Earth's biosphere, atmosphere, oceans, and soil, the totality constituting a "feedback" or "cybernetic" system which seeks an optimal physical and chemical environment for life on this planet. Gaia remains a hypothesis, but much evidence suggests that many elements of this system act as the hypothesis predicts.

Meanwhile, the human species, aided by the industries at its command, has significantly altered some of the planet's major chemical cycles. We have increased the carbon cycle by 20 percent, the nitrogen cycle by 50 percent, and the sulphur cycle by over 100 percent. We have increased the flow of toxins into air, water, and food chains. We have reduced the planet's green cover, while our factory outpourings reach the upper atmosphere, and far into the oceans. And as our numbers grow, so will these perturbations.

If the biosphere does control the atmosphere, the control system is unlikely to be easily disturbed. Nevertheless, we shall have to tread warily to avoid the cybernetic disasters of runaway positive feedback or of sustained oscillation between two or more undesirable states. We could wake one morning to find that we have landed ourselves with the lifelong task of planetary maintenance engineering. Then, at last, we should be riding in that strange contraption, "Spaceship Earth".

I hope and believe that we shall achieve a sensible and economic technology which is more in harmony with Gaia. We are more likely to achieve this goal by retaining and modifying technology than by a reactionary "back to nature" campaign. A high level of technology is by no means always energy-dependent. Think of the bicycle, the hang glider, modern sailing craft, or a mini-computer performing in minutes human-years of calculation, yet using less electricity than a light-bulb. The elemental resources of Gaia – energy, water, air, and climate – are so abundant and self-renewing as to make us potential millionaires. And potentially, at least, we have the intelligence to learn how to work with Gaia, rather than undermining her.

James E Lovelock.

THE ELEMENTAL POTENTIAL

We all know that energy supplies us with heat and light. It carries us about. It makes our machines function. Indeed, it sustains our entire economic system. So much is obvious. But energy also fuels our lifestyles in less apparent ways. It not only cooks our food, it grows it. Without massive energy subsidies, in the form of fertilizers and pesticides, our agriculture would be much less productive. When we sit down to a meal, we are, in effect, eating oil and coal.

By exploiting the planet's fossil fuels, which represent the biologically stored solar energy of millennia, we have been able to build up and power an industrial civilization which is radically different, both in nature and scale, from earlier civilizations. A single tonne of oil generates energy equivalent to the energy output of 660 horses over 24 hours.

But this new energy wealth is not shared equitably: an average American consumes 330 times as much energy as the average Ethiopian. Without enough, affordable energy, the world's developing nations will find that critical development programmes are still-born. Given the constraints on fossil fuels and the problems associated with nuclear power (see p. 124), there has been growing interest in harnessing the largest nuclear reactor in our solar system: the sun.

The sun radiates more energy into space than 200,000 million million of our largest existing commercial nuclear reactors – although the Earth receives only one part in a billion of this vast output. Even so, our annual solar energy budget is roughly equivalent to 500,000 billion barrels of oil, or to perhaps a million times the world's proven oil reserves in the late 1970s. At any given moment, incoming solar energy striking the Earth's atmosphere is equivalent to some 40,000 one-bar electric fires burning constantly for every man, woman, and child of the Earth's human population.

By the early 1980s, however, all the world's solar collectors were yielding energy equivalent to a mere 0.01 percent of the total annual oil consumption. Exploitation of the energy trapped by plants (biomass energy) was much more significant, supplying at least 15 percent of the world's energy budget. The potential of biomass is, as yet, hardly tapped, but many possibilities exist for its future exploitation (see pp 128-9).

No-one doubts that the non-renewable energy sources, predominantly the fossil fuels and nuclear power, will continue to make a solid contribution to

The global powerhouse

The sun's energy is the mainspring of all life on Earth. Without it the oceans would freeze. Temperatures on the planet's surface would drop almost to absolute zero (-273œC). Solar energy drives the great geophysical and geochemical cycles that sustain life, among them the water cycle, the oxygen cycle, the carbon cycle, and the climate. The sun provides our food, by photosynthesis, and most of our fuel. Fossil fuels are simply stored solar energy – the product of photosynthesis millions of years in the past. Over 99% of the energy flow in and out of the Earth's surface results from solar radiation. Heat from the Earth's core and the gravitational forces of sun and moon supply the rest. Solar radiation striking the Earth is equivalent to all the energy from 173 million large power stations going full blast all day, every day. But 30% of this energy is reflected away back into space. Most of the rest either warms the air, sea, and land (47%) – or fuels evaporation and the water cycle (23%).

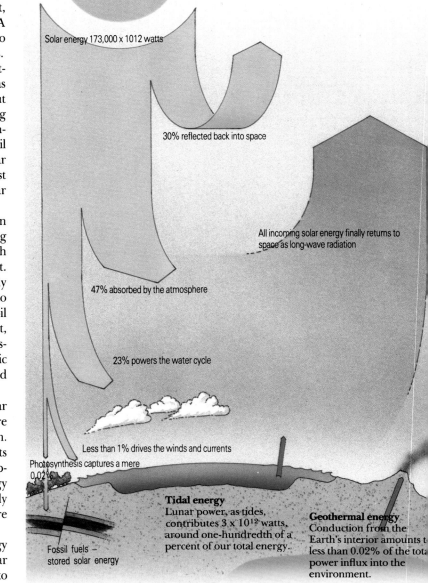

Solar energy 173,000 x 1012 watts

30% reflected back into space

All incoming solar energy finally returns to space as long-wave radiation

47% absorbed by the atmosphere

23% powers the water cycle

Less than 1% drives the winds and currents

Photosynthesis captures a mere 0.02%

Tidal energy
Lunar power, as tides, contributes 3×10^{12} watts, around one-hundredth of a percent of our total energy.

Geothermal energy
Conduction from the Earth's interior amounts t less than 0.02% of the tota power influx into the environment.

Fossil fuels – stored solar energy

The human energy budget

Prior to the Industrial Revolution, the sun was the only source of energy widely available to humankind. It provided food for muscles – a fit person generates in a day's work the equivalent of a single-bar electric fire used for an hour. Wood has been used since prehistory. Sails to use sun-created wind were first raised 5,000 years ago, windmills 2,000 years later, and water-wheels, which use water raised by the sun, 2,000 years after that. Coal came into general use just 300 years ago, and oil and gas only in the last 100 years. Not until the 20th century did non-solar energy arrive in the forms of geothermal and nuclear power. The natural flows of energy that have been used for millenia are known as *renewable* sources. The amount of energy fossil fuels can supply is ultimately limited by geology. These are known as *non-renewable* sources. The pie-chart, below, shows the current contribution of each energy source and how this might change by the year 2000. As global energy demand grows and non-renewable sources begin to run out, so attention is turning back to the renewables.

Non-renewables

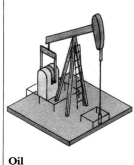

Oil
Oil is the world's largest energy source. But the time when this will no longer be so is already in sight. We are not going to run out of oil, but must switch from a growing to a declining supply. Since 1979 world consumption of oil has fallen by 14%. It is likely to fall another 15% by 2000.

Coal
Coal is the most plentiful fossil fuel. Just three countries, China, the USSR, and the US, own 57% of the world's reserves. Coal use is growing by some 3% per year – a rate that will intensify the problems of acid rain and carbon dioxide.

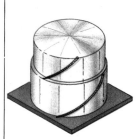

Natural gas
Natural gas accounts for 18% of the world's current annual energy budget. This share is likely to increase as gas replaces oil in a number of uses, although increasing volumes of gas will need to be extracted from remote areas. Because of its uneven distribution and difficulties of transporting it, gas is likely to remain of use to only a few nations.

newables

Biomass
Biomass energy is plant or animal matter that can be converted into fuel. Nearly half the world's population rely on biomass, mostly in the form of wood – which is the principal fuel for 80% of people in developing countries.

2000 1980 World energy supplies

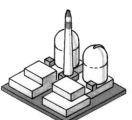

Nuclear power
Nuclear power, once hailed as the answer to all the world's energy problems, now supplies 2% of total energy demand. There are currently 282 plants operating in 25 countries. Perhaps another 100 plants may be working by the end of the century, but sharply rising costs and the loss of public confidence will restrict future growth.

Hydropower
Falling water generates 5% of the world's electricity, about 5% of total energy demand. Although the most mature of the renewable technologies (over 30% of the developed world's hydro potential is harnessed), it is still underexploited.

Solar
Some 60 million solar-powered calculators were sold in 1983. The sun already contributes significantly to the energy needs of buildings through the walls and windows, but because this energy is free it is not counted in official statistics. Recent years have seen a massive increase in investment in technologies to make use of the sun's energy.

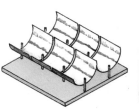

Power from the sea
Ocean power comes in four main forms: wave power, tidal power, current power, and ocean thermal energy conversion – which exploits temperature differences between the surface and depths. The ultimate energy potential is massive, but only a small fraction is likely to be harnessed.

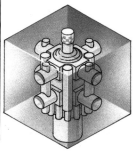

Geothermal
The Earth's temperature rises 1°C every 30 m down, more in geologically active areas. Geothermal power makes use of this heat, either directly as hot water or to produce electricity. There are over 130 geothermal power plants currently producing electricity.

Wind
Winds are caused by uneven heating of the Earth's surface. The power of the wind is proportional to the cube of windspeed, so doubling the speed increases the power 8 times. Windmills can be used either to generate electricity or to do mechanical work.

our energy needs. But we shall also need to develop many of the more promising renewable energy options shown here if we are to ensure that the world has enough energy to take us through the 21st century.

Energy-rich, energy-poor

The grossly unequal endowments of non-renewable and renewable energy inherited by virtue of geology, biological history, or geographical location mean that there can be no single energy solution for the problems which have emerged since the first oil shock engineered by the Organization of Petroleum

Exporting Countries (OPEC). Coal cannot be *the* alternative to oil, any more than nuclear fission or renewable energy can.

Those who have rehearsed the transition away from oil, in whichever direction, have found that many of the glib formulas which surfaced after the OPEC breakthrough simply do not work. Big may not always be best, but small is certainly not uniformly beautiful. The growing recognition that the only way forward is to consider all potential sources of energy, together with all the component needs which go to make up the total energy picture, has led some countries to focus more on what

Energy units key
Energy (measured in joules and tonnes of oil equivalent) is the capacity to do work. Power (measured in watts) is the rate of energy delivery. 1 joule is work done when 1 kg is lifted up 1 m. 1 GJ = 1 billion joules. 1 watt is 1 joule/second. 1 kilowatt-hour is 1,000 watts per hour. 1 mtoe (million tonnes of oil equivalent) generates 4 billion kilowatt-hours of electricity.

The energy store

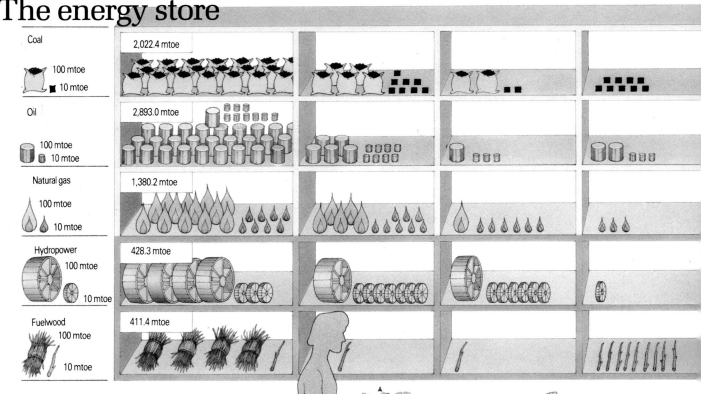

Geology is not fair. The available energy resources are not evenly distributed. Rather, they tend to be concentrated in a few places. The developed world, with only a quarter of the world's population, owns two-thirds of the world's fossil fuel resources. And it consumes a lot more, too. The US, with just 6% of the population, uses 30% of all energy produced – a stark contrast to India whose 20% of global population use only 2% of the energy. Production of coal, oil, and gas in eight regions are shown on the top three shelves; the two renewables, hydropower and wood (bottom two shelves), are shown in terms of consumption only. (Fuelwood is rarely traded, so official data tend to underestimate the true position.) The regional maps, right, show the location of fossil fuel resources. Areas such as Africa, India, and Latin America, with few fossil fuel reserves, must rely on fuelwood and expensive oil imports. The height of each figure reflects regional per capita energy consumption. The adjacent pie-charts compare energy sources for eight different users.

N America, Oceania, Japan
This region has the highest per capita consumption, using twice as much as W Europe and 17 times that of S Asia. But, while the US has huge reserves, Japan must import more than 80% of its needs.

Western Europe
Even though W Europe has reduced its oil dependence since 1973, oil is still the main source of energy. North Sea reserves are unable to meet demands – W Europe imports more than half its supplies.

Africa
Apart from Libyan and Nigerian oil and South African coal, Africa is ill-supplied with fossil fuels. Biomass supplies 80% of the energy needs of an African villager. Often wood is burnt inefficiently.

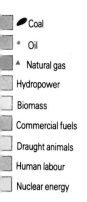

Coal
Oil
Natural gas
Hydropower
Biomass
Commercial fuels
Draught animals
Human labour
Nuclear energy

energy they are likely to need – and on the whole range of sources which might help meet that need.

Increased energy efficiency will help close the gap between supply and demand, but many countries will continue to show striking mismatches between energy they consume, let alone need, and energy they produce – or can potentially produce. Many developed nations owe their prosperity to domestic fossil fuel stocks which they are close to exhausting, if they have not already done so. Thanks to world trade, however, developed nations, with only one-quarter of the global population, continue to consume four-fifths of the global energy budget.

The leading fossil fuel, meanwhile, is still oil, which accounts for 45 percent of commercial energy worldwide – although its contribution could fall to 35 percent (of a larger total energy budget) by the year 2000. Thereafter, its contribution could tail away as it comes to be used more as a chemical feedstock than as a fuel. Natural gas could last almost as long as oil. Coal, by contrast, is available in abundance. Total world reserves are estimated to be 250 times the amount we consume each year. But environmental problems, notably acid rain and carbon dioxide (see pp 116-9), will ensure that any transition back to coal is far from easy.

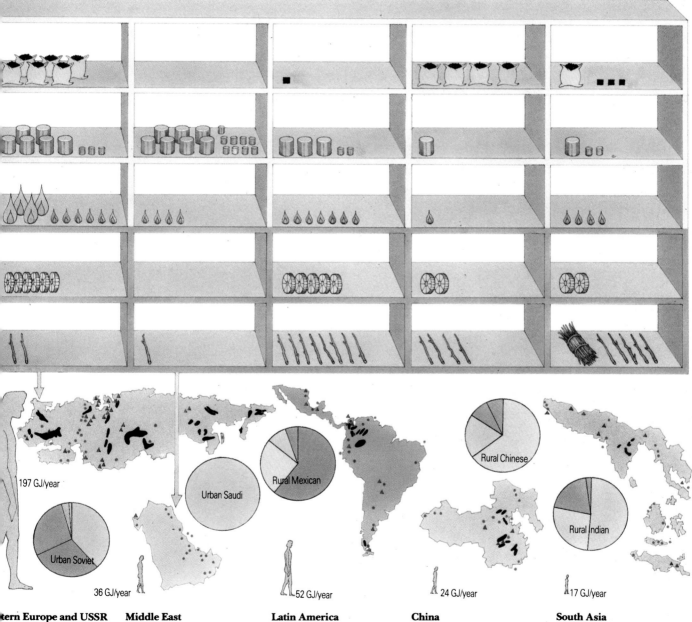

197 GJ/year

Urban Soviet

36 GJ/year

Urban Saudi

52 GJ/year

Rural Mexican

24 GJ/year

Rural Chinese

Rural Indian

17 GJ/year

tern Europe and USSR
e USSR is rich in energy
its resources are by no
ns fully explored. The
ld's largest oil
ducer, it has recently
un to export large
ntities of natural gas. Its
se continues to grow.

Middle East
Over half the world's
known reserves of oil are
located in the Middle East.
Producing 16% of the
world's energy, it consumes
only 2% – although
demand is likely to grow.

Latin America
Although poorly provided
with reserves, Latin
America is a net exporter
of energy, thanks mainly to
the Mexican and
Venezuelan oilfields.
Fuelwood shortages can be
acute in some countries.

China
China is the world's second
largest producer of coal.
But so large is its
population that its per
capita consumption is still
low. Animal and human
power provide nearly a
third of the energy used.

South Asia
This energy-poor region
contains 6 out of the 10
bottom countries in terms
of energy consumption per
capita. Almost all the
energy used is directed to
the production and
cooking of food.

Among the renewables, biomass and hydropower make the most significant contributions to the world energy budget. As with food and water, we have enough energy in total – but supply and distribution are out of phase with developing demand.

Our changing climate

Climate is an expression of the great interacting realms of atmosphere, land, and ocean. A region may enjoy a climate of hot dry summers and cold dry winters, with intervening seasons of warm moist conditions. Or it may suffer a climate of warm damp summers and mild wet winters, with nothing much better – as viewed by some people at least – in between. By contrast, weather is what we experience day by day, in the form of cloudy or blue skies, rain and humidity, wind and the like. So whereas weather can change from hour to hour and week to week, climate represents an average pattern over years, decades, and centuries.

Over lengthy periods, moreover, climate can change. A long-term shift of only 1°C is enough to trigger profound shifts, as witness the phenomenon of the Little Ice Age in Western Europe, which peaked in the late 17th century. A drop of 4°C is enough to bring on a full ice age, with swift results for the planetary habitat: at the onset of the last glaciation almost 11,000 years ago, advancing ice sheets eliminated huge forests of the northern hemisphere in just a century. As for more recent

The maritime effect
The winds, the Earth's rotation, and the placem of the continents cause t great ocean currents. Because they move huge masses of water, sometim cold, sometimes warm, from region to region, th also influence the climate Thus the UK, which is warmed by the North Atlantic Drift originatin off Florida, has a milder climate than Labrador, which is on the same latitude, but is cooled by current from the Arctic Ocean.

The climate asset

Five major factors shape climate: the sun's energy, the atmosphere, the Earth's shape and position in space, its rotation, and the oceans. Because the Earth is a sphere, air is warmed more at the Equator than at the poles. As the warm, moist air rises, it flows polewards, cooling and drying as it goes. On reaching latitude 30° it begins to sink, warm up, and flow back towards the Equator. These vertical flows of air on either side of the Equator, called "Hadley cells", are responsible for the belts of desert and arid land found around the Tropics of Cancer and Capricorn. Air, as wind, flows from areas of high pressure, associated with higher temperatures, towards areas of low pressure. The energy of the Earth's rotation, the "Coriolis force", bends the winds to give the characteristic patterns shown on the map, right. The diagram, below, illustrates the vegetational impact of rainfall and temperature. Where cold polar winds meet the warm westerlies of the mid-latitudes, the changeable weather typical of temperate regions is found. The movement of large masses of ocean water also influences climate since small differences in temperature absorb, or release, enormous quantities of heat. The map shows the seven main climatic types, the size of the circles indicating annual mean precipitation.

Latitude and temperature
The subsolar point, where the sun appears directly overhead, varies with the seasons between 23°N and 23°S. Here the sun's rays are perpendicular to the Earth's surface. With increasing latitudes, less sunshine is intercepted and average temperatures fall.

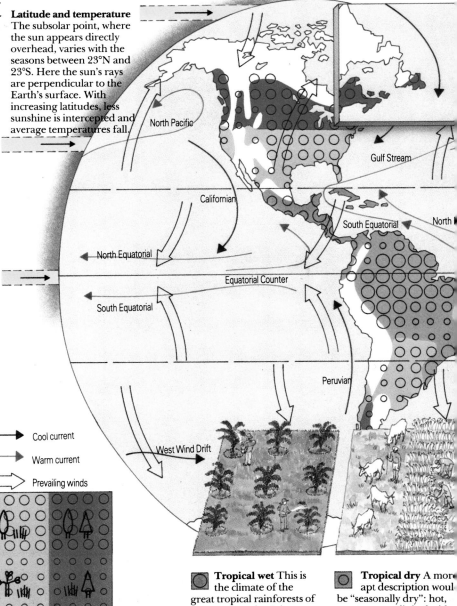

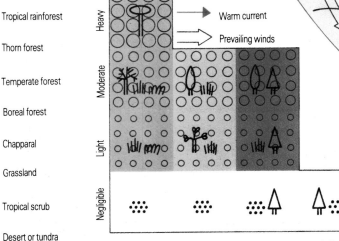

Tropical wet This is the climate of the great tropical rainforests of the Amazon, the Zaire Basin, and SE Asia. Rainfall exceeds 240 cm a year, mean temperature exceeds 24°C. Rainforests are highly productive areas.

Tropical dry A more apt description would be "seasonally dry": hot, wet summers linked with warm, dry winters. Food crops include millet, maize groundnuts, and beans. Some areas are only suitable for grazing.

...nge, what we now assume is "normal" is actually ...e of the warmest phases of the past 1,000 years. ...is warm phase should, instead, be regarded as ...proaching an extreme for sustained "good ...ather". In the northern-hemisphere land areas ...ween 1881 and 1983, the warmest year was ...81 – while three of the winters since 1978 rank ...ong the six warmest.

...Climatic change, in short, is the norm. The one ...ng that we can be sure about with regard to ...ure climate is that it will feature deep-seated ...fts, even if we leave climate to get on with its own ...ural course – without disrupting it by, for exam-...e, contributing to carbon dioxide build-up in the ...nosphere (see p. 116).

All this has major implications for our capacity to keep producing food. Throughout the world, climate is a critical factor in agriculture. During the late 1960s, the Sahel drought brought disaster to entire nations. In 1972, another drought inflicted such damage on the Soviet wheat crop that it helped to quadruple world prices within two years. In 1974, a delayed monsoon in India wrought havoc for millions of people. In 1975, pulses of cold air ravaged Brazil's coffee crop, causing inflationary upheavals in coffee prices around the world.

Conversely, of course, a stable climate, or rather a climate with slow and predictable changes, can be a tremendous asset. Just as much as energy or water, climate represents an "elemental" dimension to our

How land shapes climate
The rain-shadow effect of coastal mountains is well known. Warm, moist winds rise on the windward side of mountains. As they rise they expand and cool, causing the water vapour they carry to condense and fall as rain. The dry, cool air descends on the other side of the mountains. As it does so it is compressed and warmed. The resultant dry, warm wind creates a markedly different climate and vegetation, as in California's Sierra Nevada.

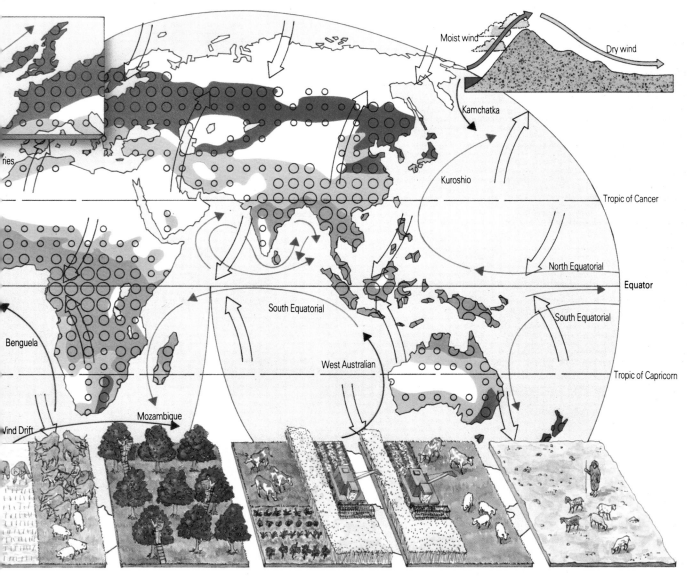

Warm humid The ...climate of ...eastern US and much ...ina is warm and ...d. It is a ideally suited ...ltiple cropping – the ...temperatures and ...ar rainfall enable ...to be grown all year ...d.

Warm dry The long, dry summers and mild, wet winters of the Mediterranean fostered Western civilization. With irrigation, many crops can be grown. But it can be an unforgiving climate if badly managed.

Cool humid The dominant role of north Europe had its foundations in the cool, humid climate. The constraints on agriculture are the low levels of sunlight, the cold winters, and short-term summer dryness.

Cool dry The great grasslands of the world, the Steppes of Russia, the Plains and Prairies of N America, the Pampas of S America, are cool and dry. These are the lands of corn and cattle. Rainfall is low and irregular in summer.

Desert or mountains Mountainous regions, with poor soil cover and low temperatures, are unsuited for most crops. High temperatures, low rainfall, and scant vegetation also make deserts unsuitable. Nomads roam here.

Earth that can basically enrich our lives. Provided we have time to adapt to long-term fluctuations of climate, we can surely hope to cope with a future of ever-changing climate.

The liquid of life

Water, water everywhere – but it is astonishing how little of it is directly usable. Only a small fraction of is fresh, and 99.5 percent of this freshwater is "locked up" in ice caps and glaciers. And of that tiny fraction of available freshwater, only 3 percent occurs in the atmosphere, rivers, and lakes, the rest being held in underground aquifers.

Even so, the "usable hydrosphere" contains more water than we are likely to need in the foreseeable future. The problem, as is so often the case with natural resources, is that water is not evenly distributed around the globe. Many people spend their time fighting floods, others go thirsty.

Perhaps more than we care to recognize, our lifestyles depend on the availability of freshwater. If, for whatever reason, our taps were to run dry, our household routines would collapse, our health would be at risk, factories would grind to a halt, and agriculture would be in dire straits. The entire fabric of our societies could begin to unravel. We may take freshwater for granted, in short, but we do so at our peril.

Certain sectors of our economies are particularly thirsty, with agricultural irrigation among the top consumers. The demand for water for irrigation in developing countries is likely to account for 30 percent of the growth in water consumption by the year 1990. Overall, however, there is enough usable freshwater to meet the domestic, industrial, and irrigation needs of at least twice the current world population.

Although the sun evaporates almost half a billion cubic kilometres of water from the seas each year, we should think of usable water as that proportion of evaporated water which ends up on land – and runs off into rivers and lakes. Here we are talking of less than 40,000 cubic kilometres of water, or less than one-tenth of the total originally evaporated from the seas.

This figure, furthermore, is only a year-round average, taking no account of seasonal and other fluctuations. The average low-water flow for inhabited continents is only about one-third of the total figure, with the remainder of the water disappearing in the form of floods before we can harness it.

So the "stable runoff" available for use is more like 14,000 cubic kilometres. This is still a phenomenal amount of water. Of course, as we become more "advanced", so we use ever-increasing amounts of water: whereas the absolute minimum a person needs for domestic use is 5 litres a day, with a more realistic figure around 15 litres, a developed world citizen consumes well over 100. When we add in industry, this total can jump to 500 litres, especially in northern cities. Nonetheless, improving

The freshwater reservoir

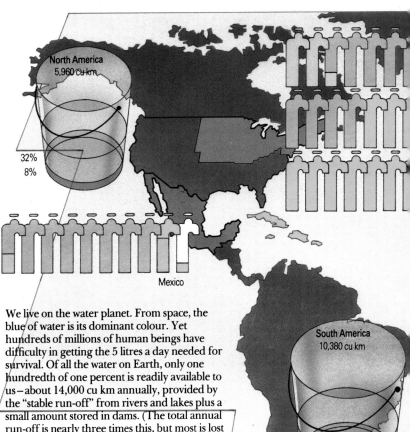

We live on the water planet. From space, the blue of water is its dominant colour. Yet hundreds of millions of human beings have difficulty in getting the 5 litres a day needed for survival. Of all the water on Earth, only one hundredth of one percent is readily available to us – about 14,000 cu km annually, provided by the "stable run-off" from rivers and lakes plus a small amount stored in dams. (The total annual run-off is nearly three times this, but most is lost in floods or held in swamps and soil.) Even so, this supply would support many times our present population, if it could all be exploited. But both the water and the world's peoples are unevenly distributed. Each bucket, right, shows the total run-off in a region, the height of water indicating the usable proportion. Together with population size, this determines the water available per capita, shown by the colour gradings on the map. Regions in the low and very low categories will experience more severe water shortages as populations increase (p 132-3). The water taps show how this per capita supply is used in selected countries – the lion's share in the US, for example, goes to industry, whereas in India, which uses only a quarter as much, it goes to agriculture.

All volumes in cukm

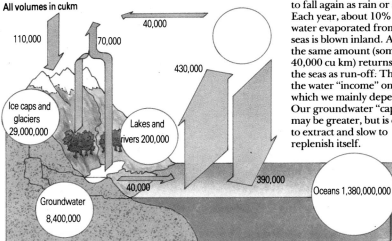

The water cycle

Over 97% of all water on Earth is salty. Under 3% is fresh, most of which is locked away in the ice-cap. The atmosphere, rivers, lakes, and underground stores hold less than 1%. The water cycle, driven by the sun, lifts purified water from the land and oceans to fall again as rain or snow. Each year, about 10% of water evaporated from the seas is blown inland. About the same amount (some 40,000 cu km) returns to the seas as run-off. This is the water "income" on which we mainly depend. Our groundwater "capital" may be greater, but is costly to extract and slow to replenish itself.

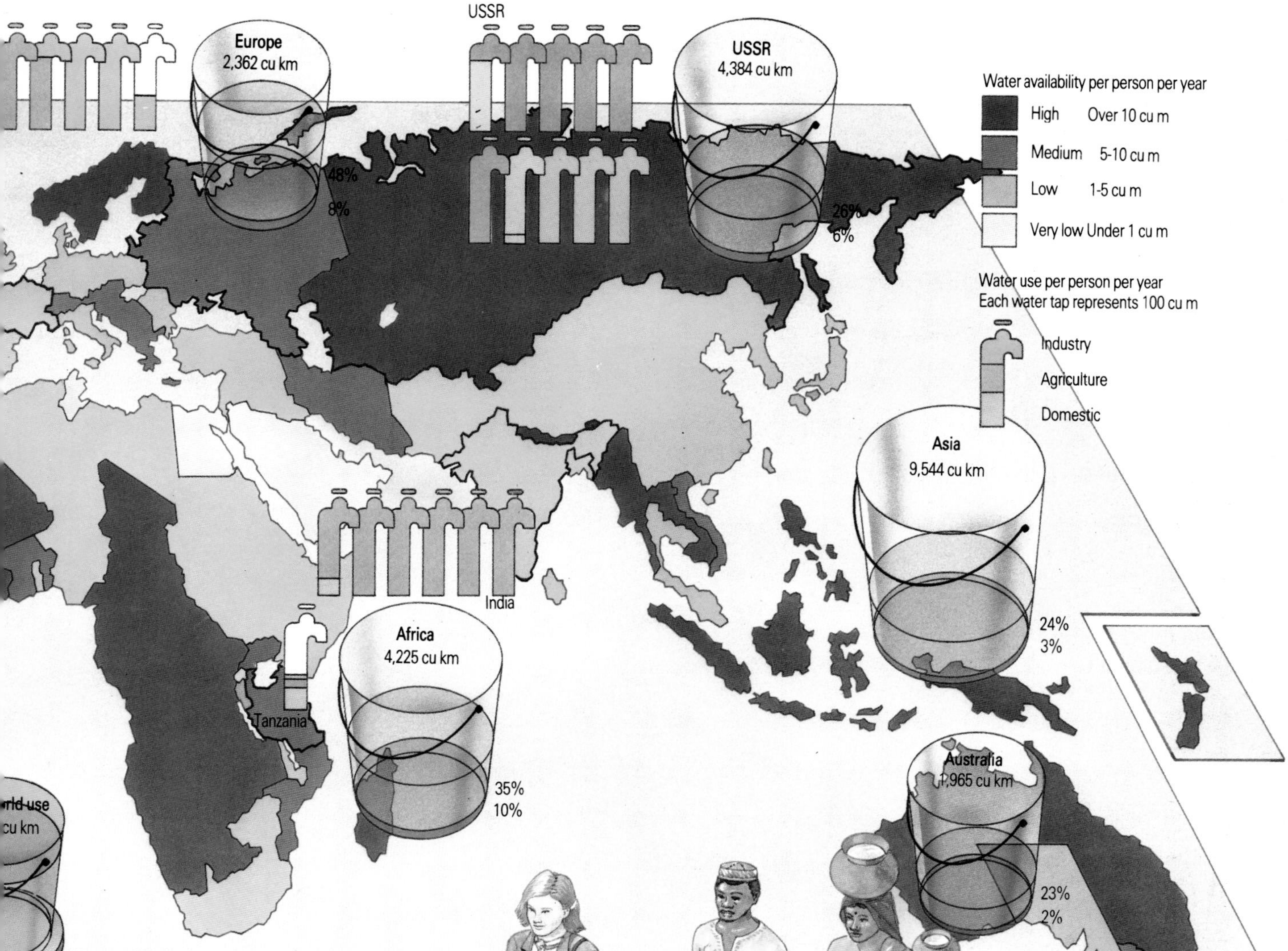
Europe
2,362 cu km
48%
8%
USSR
USSR
4,384 cu km
26%
6%
Water availability per person per year
High Over 10 cu m
Medium 5-10 cu m
Low 1-5 cu m
Very low Under 1 cu m
Water use per person per year
Each water tap represents 100 cu m
Industry
Agriculture
Domestic
Asia
9,544 cu km
24%
3%
India
Africa
4,225 cu km
Tanzania
35%
10%
Australia
1,965 cu km
23%
2%
rld use
cu km

Uses of water
To sustain a reasonable quality of life requires about 80 litres of water per person per day. But average consumption ranges from 5.4 litres per day in Madagascar (barely enough to survive) to 500 litres per day in the US. World water use now amounts to some 3,000 cu km a year. Irrigation accounts for 73%, industry for 22%, and 5% is for domestic use. Up to 90% of the water used domestically and by industry may be returned to rivers and re-used, but some 75% of the water supplied for irrigation is lost.

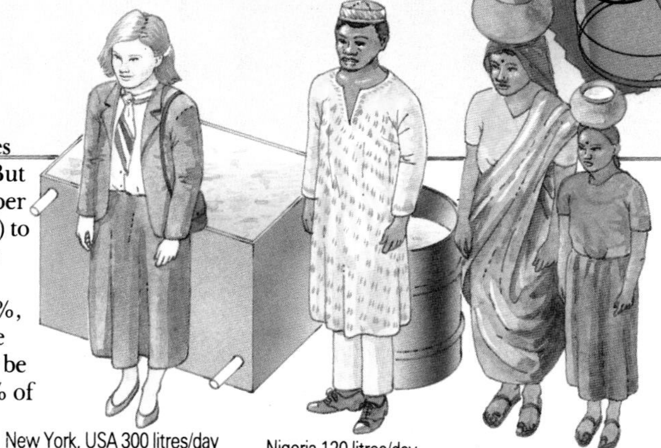
New York, USA 300 litres/day
Nigeria 120 litres/day
India 25 litres/day

UK-Bangladesh comparison
The amount of water used for domestic purposes varies enormously. The pie-charts, below, compare the daily domestic water use of a British city dweller (175 litres of mains-supplied water) with that of a Bangladeshi rural villager (45 litres from a tubewell).

trial use
ut cheap supplies of industry would to a halt. Water is s a coolant, a solvent, hing applications, or dilution of ion. As shown below, nount of water d for different cts varies greatly. roduction of plastics icularly thirsty.

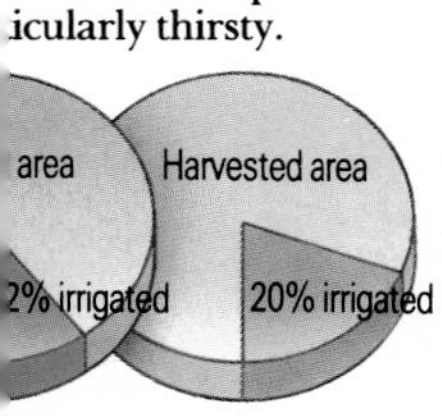
area
Harvested area
2% irrigated
20% irrigated

Irrigation
Irrigation is vital for agriculture. 12% of the world's cultivated land is irrigated. But, since irrigated land is often cropped more than once a year, the contribution to the world's harvests by irrigated land is much greater than 12%. It may contribute as much as 20% of the global harvest.

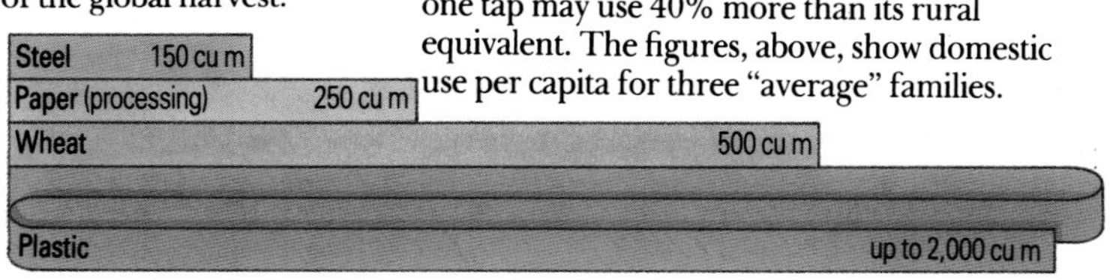
Steel 150 cu m
Paper (processing) 250 cu m
Wheat 500 cu m
Plastic up to 2,000 cu m

Domestic usage
Water consumption reflects not only how much is available per head, but also how difficult it is to fetch or how expensive to buy. In countries with piped water, consumption is much higher than in developing countries, where a 2-km walk to find water is not unusual. One cubic metre (1,000 litres) of poor-quality water in the Third World may cost $20, against 10 cents for the same volume of high-quality water in a rich country. An urban Third World household with one tap may use 40% more than its rural equivalent. The figures, above, show domestic use per capita for three "average" families.

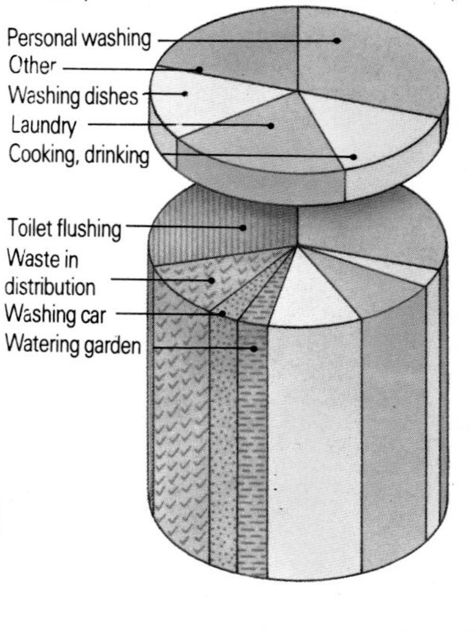
Personal washing
Other
Washing dishes
Laundry
Cooking, drinking
Toilet flushing
Waste in distribution
Washing car
Watering garden

water catchment, storage, supply, use, and recycling techniques should enable us to stretch our global water resource almost indefinitely – provided that we start soon.

Mining our mineral wealth

The planet's mineral wealth has been tapped since pre-history, its surface dotted with the workings and spoil-heaps of earlier mining activities. Where once we picked shallow excavations with antlers and other crude tools, today we use dynamite and massive machines to extract the minerals which underpin almost every aspect of our lives.

Fortunately, we still have sufficient stocks of most minerals to last us well beyond the year 2000. The "mineral showdowns" which were predicted in the wake of the first OPEC oil crisis now seem a rather more distant prospect – although the potential for such showdowns undoubtedly exists.

Industry depends heavily on some 80 minerals, including a number which, like aluminium and iron, are in relatively plentiful supply. True, a few countries will soon exhaust their domestic supplies of such materials, but there is enough elsewhere to go round, without the risk of cartelized cutbacks on production and supply.

A small number of minerals, however, qualify as strategic commodities. That is, they are critically important to industry, while being in relatively short supply. Chromium, for example, does more than put a shine on bumpers: it also contributes to irreplaceable alloys used in tool steel and in jet engines. Manganese is essential for high-grade steels. Platinum is used for catalytic converters, which are at the heart of many auto-emission control systems, and for advanced communications equipment. Cobalt is crucial for high-strength, high-temperature alloys used in aerospace.

The US, the EEC, and Japan import most of their supplies of these key commodities, primarily from politically volatile regions of central and southern Africa. Fortunately, however, new sources are becoming available as new discoveries are made – although some of these potential sources will be expensive to exploit.

Overall, three-quarters of the 80 materials are abundant enough to meet all our anticipated needs, or, where they are not, ready substitutes exist. But at least 18 minerals represent a rather thornier problem, even when greater recovery and recycling are taken into account: for example, lead, sulphur, tin, tungsten, and zinc.

Inevitably, the major mineral consumers will face rising prices for some key materials. Supply restrictions are less likely, however, since producer countries in the Third World are generally dependent on steady exports for foreign exchange. Zambia, for example, relies on minerals for over half its national income. Meanwhile, countries like the US have stockpiled enough reserves of the more critical minerals to last them for many years.

The mineral reserve

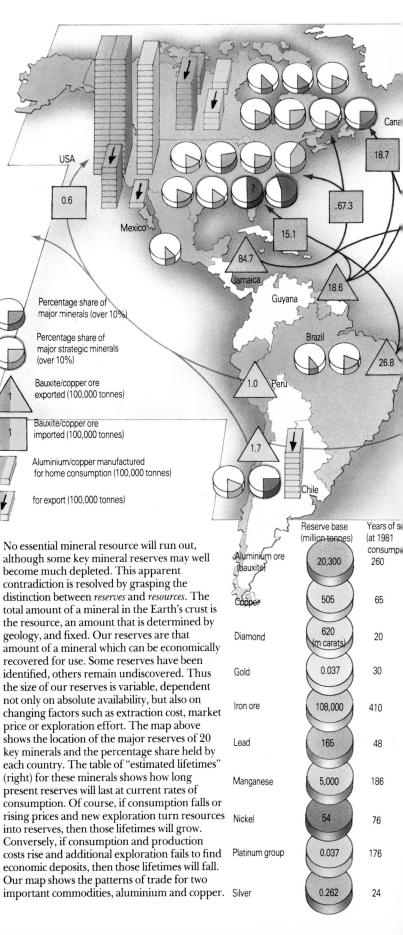

Percentage share of major minerals (over 10%)

Percentage share of major strategic minerals (over 10%)

Bauxite/copper ore exported (100,000 tonnes)

Bauxite/copper ore imported (100,000 tonnes)

Aluminium/copper manufactured for home consumption (100,000 tonnes)

for export (100,000 tonnes)

No essential mineral resource will run out, although some key mineral reserves may well become much depleted. This apparent contradiction is resolved by grasping the distinction between *reserves* and *resources*. The total amount of a mineral in the Earth's crust is the resource, an amount that is determined by geology, and fixed. Our reserves are that amount of a mineral which can be economically recovered for use. Some reserves have been identified, others remain undiscovered. Thus the size of our reserves is variable, dependent not only on absolute availability, but also on changing factors such as extraction cost, market price or exploration effort. The map above shows the location of the major reserves of 20 key minerals and the percentage share held by each country. The table of "estimated lifetimes" (right) for these minerals shows how long present mineral reserves will last at current rates of consumption. Of course, if consumption falls or rising prices and new exploration turn resources into reserves, then those lifetimes will grow. Conversely, if consumption and production costs rise and additional exploration fails to find economic deposits, then those lifetimes will fall. Our map shows the patterns of trade for two important commodities, aluminium and copper.

	Reserve base (million tonnes)	Years of supply (at 1981 consumption)
Aluminium ore (bauxite)	20,300	260
Copper	505	65
Diamond	620 (m carats)	20
Gold	0.037	30
Iron ore	108,000	410
Lead	165	48
Manganese	5,000	186
Nickel	54	76
Platinum group	0.037	176
Silver	0.262	24

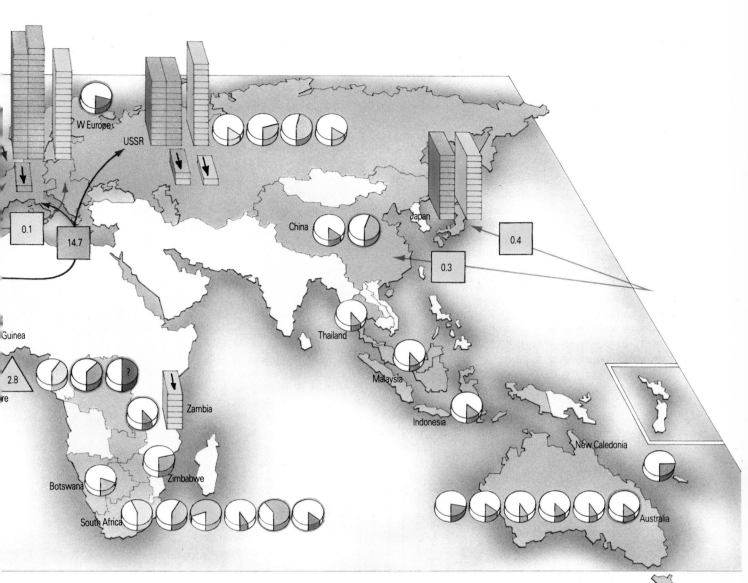

W Europe

USSR

0.1

14.7

Guinea

2.8

China

Japan

0.4

0.3

Thailand

Malaysia

Indonesia

New Caledonia

Zambia

Botswana

Zimbabwe

South Africa

Australia

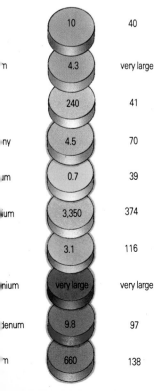

10	40
4.3	very large
240	41
4.5	70
0.7	39
3,350	374
3.1	116
very large	very large
9.8	97
660	138

Stockpiling
Minerals are an integral part of diplomacy. Each country tries to ensure access to those minerals which affect its vital national interests, especially defence. Strategically important minerals are vulnerable to interruptions of supply, often for political reasons. Lacking indigenous supplies, many Western countries have been building up stockpiles of such minerals as manganese, chromium, cobalt, and platinum. One unintended effect of stockpiles is to even out the sharp fluctuations in mineral prices. Substitution and recycling can also be strategic options, boosting supply.

American stockpiles
The US has stockpiled over half a tonne of bauxite (the ore from which aluminium is made) for each American citizen. As the world's largest consumer of strategic minerals, the US is particularly vulnerable to interruptions to its supplies, importing 100% of its titanium, 97% of its manganese, and over 90% of its chromium, largely from developing countries.

Recycling
Almost half the iron needed for steel-making now comes from scrap and nearly a third of the aluminium. Recycling can bring major energy savings. For example, the energy required to produce one tonne of secondary aluminium from scrap is only 5% of the energy used to extract and process primary metal from ore. Scrap is now a vital source of supply for metals.

Substitution
Metals that are easy to substitute include antimony, cadmium, selenium, tellurium, and tin. Tin has been losing out to glass, plastics, steel, and aluminium in the can-making and packaging industries: aluminium now accounts for over 90% of all US drinks cans. But substitution is no panacea: platinum is an unrivalled catalyst and stainless steel depends on chromium.

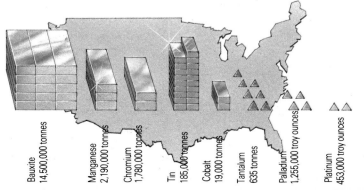

Bauxite 14,500,000 tonnes
Manganese 2,190,000 tonnes
Chromium 1,780,000 tonnes
Tin 185,000 tonnes
Cobalt 19,000 tonnes
Tantalum 635 tonnes
Palladium 1,255,000 troy ounces
Platinum 453,000 troy ounces

THE ELEMENTS CRISIS

The world awoke in the 1970s to a new crisis: the elements crisis. Some elements were seen to be in increasingly short supply, while other elements, in the form of pollution, had been turning up in the wrong places—and causing havoc in the process. But nothing woke up more people to the new realities than the first oil shock of 1973-4.

Oil—the end of an era?

Until 1973, the world's oil consumers forgot—if, indeed, they ever knew—that they were spending energy capital accumulated over many millions of years. They forgot that they were exploiting Nature's literally "unrepeatable offer". OPEC had its own reasons for shocking its clients out of their complacency, but in doing so it did the world a long-term service.

The oil-consuming nations were spurred to look for new sources of oil and to promote increased energy efficiency throughout their economies. Even so, the impact of rising oil prices was dramatic. West Germany, for example, managed to cut its oil imports between 1973 and 1980, but its total energy import bill rose from DM 8 billion in 1972, through DM 31 billion in 1978 to DM 75 billion in 1981. A current account surplus of DM 18.5 billion in 1978 was converted into a deficit of nearly DM 30 billion by 1980, with the Bundesbank attributing more than half of this swing to rising energy prices.

The best indicator of West Germany's success in dealing with its energy problems is the changing relationship between its energy consumption and its gross national product (GNP). From 1973 to 1980, West Germany's primary energy consumption increased by only 3.1 percent, while its GNP grew, in real terms, by 17.5 percent. Japan's GNP grew by 35 percent over the same period, its energy use by only 15 percent.

The most pronounced effects of the energy crisis, however, were to be found in developing countries— where commodity exports were buying ever-less oil. In 1975, for example, a tonne of copper bought 115 barrels of oil, whereas by 1981 it bought only 57. In other words, 101 percent more copper was needed in 1981 than in 1975 to purchase a barrel of oil!

Some countries, like Britain, Norway, and the US, have found massive new oil resources. Others have begun to explore the potential of unconventional oil sources, such as oil shale and tar sands. Venezuela has massive deposits of heavy oils, while both South and North America are rich in oil shale deposits.

The oil crisis

Many experts now estimate the world's ultimately recoverable resources of oil at about 300 billion tonnes. About 70 billion tonnes have already been extracted and current reserves total some 90 billion tonnes. The remaining 140 billion tonnes are the resources—estimated to be available, but not yet discovered. It is important to remember the distinction between *reserves*, whose magnitude is much more accurately known, and *resources*, whose magnitude can only be estimated after further exploration.

The Permian basin of west Texas, perhaps the most thoroughly explored sedimentary basin in the world, illustrates the problem. Although experts agree that reserves in this area are some 1 billion tonnes, estimates of the amount of oil in undiscovered fields, the resources, range from 50 million to 1 billion tonnes. Furthermore, all these estimates are based on recovering between 30 and 40% of the oil actually present. As oil prices rise and technology advances, it becomes possible to recover more of the available oil. How much oil there is for use is thus a function not only of the absolute amount present, but also of its price and the level of technology.

The availability of oil is also a function of politics since the resources are very unevenly distributed. About 30% of the world's remaining resources are in the Middle East, about 25% in the Communist countries, and about 20% in North and South America (about half each). The map summarizes the world oil situation in 1982, showing how much oil each region has produced, the size of its reserves, and the lifetime of those reserves at current consumption and price levels. The arrows plot the trade in oil between nations, not detailed shipping movements.

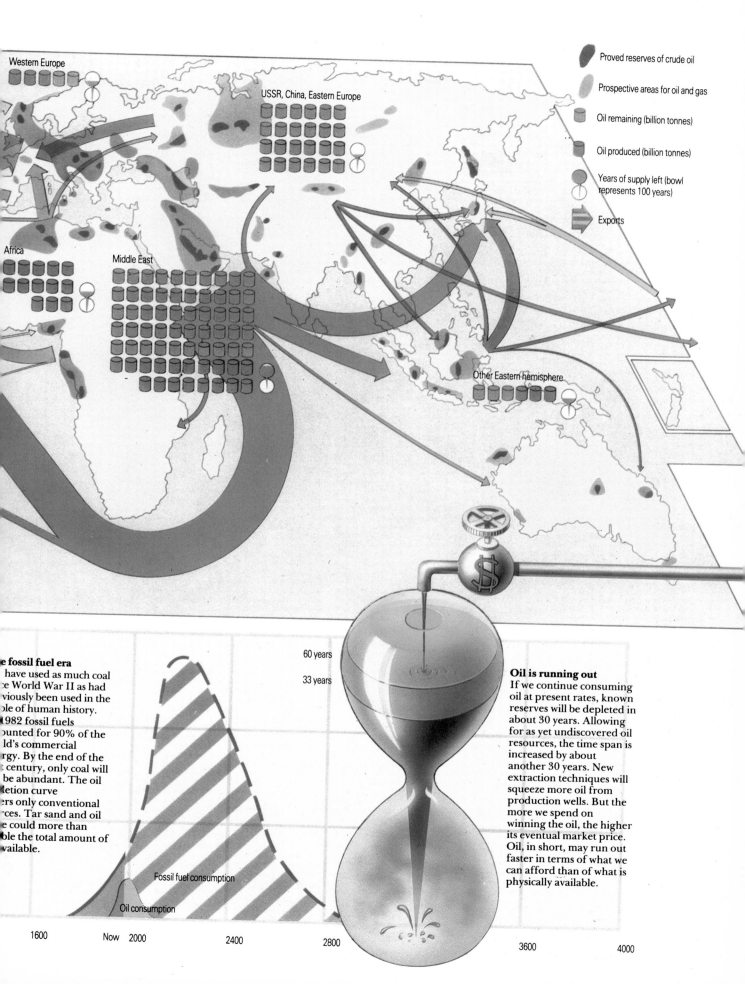

Proved reserves of crude oil

Prospective areas for oil and gas

Oil remaining (billion tonnes)

Oil produced (billion tonnes)

Years of supply left (bowl represents 100 years)

Exports

Western Europe

USSR, China, Eastern Europe

Africa

Middle East

Other Eastern hemisphere

e fossil fuel era

have used as much coal
e World War II as had
viously been used in the
ble of human history.
1982 fossil fuels
unted for 90% of the
ld's commercial
rgy. By the end of the
t century, only coal will
be abundant. The oil
letion curve
rs only conventional
rces. Tar sand and oil
e could more than
ble the total amount of
vailable.

60 years

33 years

Fossil fuel consumption

Oil consumption

1600   Now 2000   2400   2800   3600   4000

Oil is running out

If we continue consuming
oil at present rates, known
reserves will be depleted in
about 30 years. Allowing
for as yet undiscovered oil
resources, the time span is
increased by about
another 30 years. New
extraction techniques will
squeeze more oil from
production wells. But the
more we spend on
winning the oil, the higher
its eventual market price.
Oil, in short, may run out
faster in terms of what we
can afford than of what is
physically available.

Many projects have foundered, however, as the world recession and growing energy efficiency have caused a temporary oil surplus and falling prices. But the energy scene has shifted for good: never again will oil be the cheap resource it once was.

The other energy crisis

At least two billion people, or the majority of people in the Third World, rely on wood as fuel to cook their food. Many of them are overcutting available trees. For the poorest third of humankind, the real energy crisis is fuelwood – and it was so long before OPEC appeared on our horizons. Fuelwood dominates daily life, as increasing amounts of time and labour are spent in finding it and carrying it home. If it has to be bought, the price can account for two-fifths of a family's cash income. And the problem is growing worse.

Half of all wood cut worldwide each year is used as fuel for cooking and heating, at least four-fifths of it in the Third World. A minimum of 1.5 billion people encounter daily difficulty in finding enough fuelwood, even though they average only about 3 kilograms a day, little more than a few sticks. They cut trees faster than the timber stock replenishes itself. Moreover, their growing numbers and the increasing human densities spread the problem further afield. As a result, a potentially sustainable wood-gathering activity becomes destructive and, ultimately, unsustainable. The fuelwood issue, in fact, is a classic instance of how impoverished people in the Third World can find themselves obliged to destroy tomorrow's livelihood in order to secure today's essentials. They do not do it out of ignorance. They do it out of tragic compulsion.

Worse still, at least 125 million people simply cannot lay hands on sufficient fuelwood to meet even their minimal needs. For many families, it now costs as much to heat the supper bowl as to fill it. An uncooked supper is not only untasty, it brings health problems, since it is likely to contain parasites that gnaw at the human gut.

For many Third World people, then, the energy crisis does not devolve into a debate on how to limit the electricity consumed in a gadget-oriented home. It strikes directly at the struggle to keep body and soul together.

We have already seen (pp 42-5) how deforestation brings a tide of troubles in its wake. In the case of fuelwood deficits, there are some added woes. Millions of families seek substitutes in materials such as cattle dung. In Asia and Africa alone, at least 400 million tonnes of dung are burned as fuel each year. If applied to fields, this dung could help produce 20 million tonnes of grain – enough food to sustain tens of millions of people.

Unless we can devise a response to this great and growing energy problem, we can expect that within just another four decades the number of people overcutting an already thin fuelwood resource will more than double, while the number facing acute

The fuelwood crisis

Of the 2 billion people who rely on wood as the primary energy source, some 70% do not have access to secure supplies. By the year 2000, some 2.7 billion people, half the population of the developing world, will find their minimum fuel needs insecure or unmet. The map below indicates the severity of the crisis in developing countries (except China). It is worst in the arid

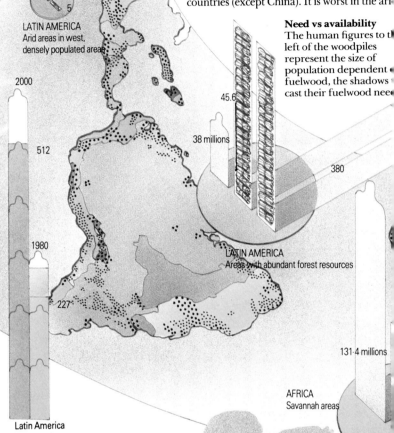

16 millions

14

5

LATIN AMERICA
Arid areas in west, densely populated areas

2000

512

1980

227

Latin America

45.6

38 millions

380

LATIN AMERICA
Areas with abundant forest resources

131.4 millions

AFRICA
Savannah areas

Need vs availability
The human figures to the left of the woodpiles represent the size of population dependent on fuelwood, the shadows cast their fuelwood need

Populations facing shortages
The numbers of people facing shortages are shown in columns for 4 regions. Each figure in a column represents 100 million people – those in orange (1980) and red (2000) face acute scarcity or deficit, those in yellow are depleting their resources faster than they are replenished.

A vicious spiral
Virtually all of the trees within a radius of 70 km of Ouagadougou in the Sahel have been consumed for fuelwood. Scarcity occurs most in the ecologically fragile drylands and highlands where loss of tree cover leads to flooding, soil erosion, and the silting up of river beds or dams. The search for alternative fuels leads to the burning of dung that would otherwise have been returned to the soil. This reduces crop yields, forcing farmers to clear more forest to maintain food supplies. This, in turn, reduces the availability of fuelwood and results in another twist down the vicious spiral illustrated on the right.

and semi-arid areas of Africa, the populous areas of southern Asia, and the arid and mountainous regions of Latin America. Fuelwood collection here can take 100-300 days of work each year – or as much as one-quarter of an urban family's income.

(in millions cu m). The woodpiles denote fuelwood availability – their shadows reveal a stark imbalance in many areas when measured against need.

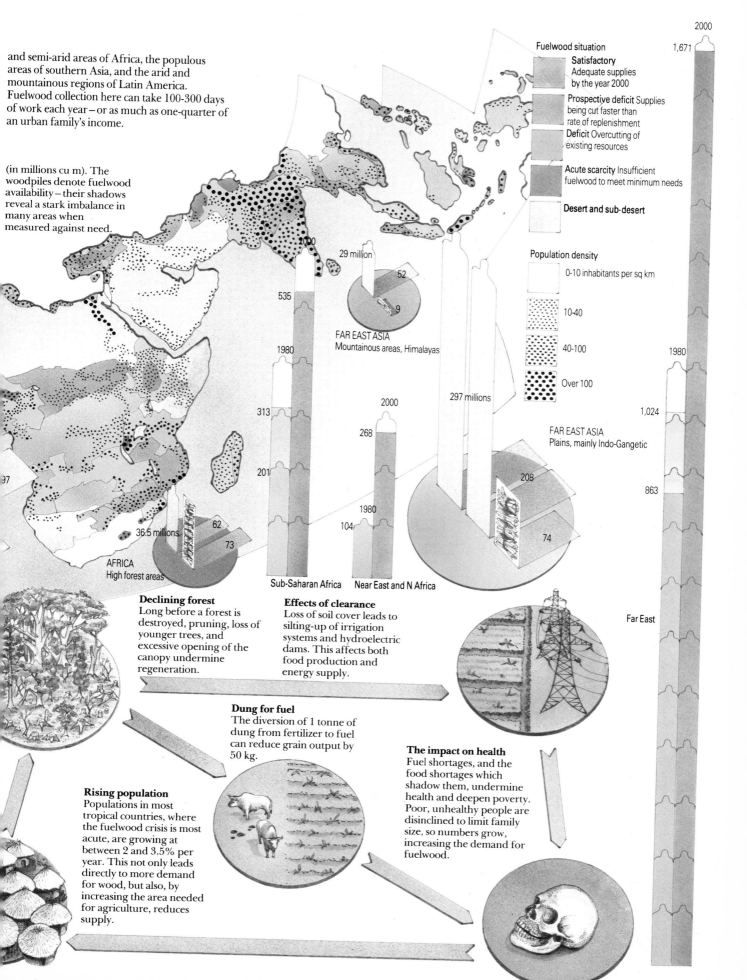

Fuelwood situation

Satisfactory Adequate supplies by the year 2000

Prospective deficit Supplies being cut faster than rate of replenishment

Deficit Overcutting of existing resources

Acute scarcity Insufficient fuelwood to meet minimum needs

Desert and sub-desert

Population density

0-10 inhabitants per sq km

10-40

40-100

Over 100

2000
1,671

1980
1,024

863

Far East

FAR EAST ASIA
Mountainous areas, Himalayas

29 million
52
9

535

1980
313

201

535

2000
268

1980
104

297 millions

FAR EAST ASIA
Plains, mainly Indo-Gangetic

208

74

36.5 millions
62
73

AFRICA
High forest areas

Sub-Saharan Africa

Near East and N Africa

Declining forest
Long before a forest is destroyed, pruning, loss of younger trees, and excessive opening of the canopy undermine regeneration.

Effects of clearance
Loss of soil cover leads to silting-up of irrigation systems and hydroelectric dams. This affects both food production and energy supply.

Dung for fuel
The diversion of 1 tonne of dung from fertilizer to fuel can reduce grain output by 50 kg.

The impact on health
Fuel shortages, and the food shortages which shadow them, undermine health and deepen poverty. Poor, unhealthy people are disinclined to limit family size, so numbers grow, increasing the demand for fuelwood.

Rising population
Populations in most tropical countries, where the fuelwood crisis is most acute, are growing at between 2 and 3.5% per year. This not only leads directly to more demand for wood, but also, by increasing the area needed for agriculture, reduces supply.

shortages could exceed one billion. The environmental and human implications of these shortages will be tremendous. And the longer the damage continues, the harder it will be to find a viable long-term solution.

The build-up of carbon dioxide

Carbon dioxide is what puts fizz into soft drinks. It is also one of the most important gases in the atmosphere, even though it amounts to a mere 0.03 percent. When the sun's energy strikes the Earth's atmosphere, much of it bounces back into space. But some is absorbed by carbon dioxide, warming the surface of our globe through what is commonly referred to as a "greenhouse effect".

Carbon dioxide is now increasing, slowly but steadily. When we started to burn fossil fuels on a large scale with the onset of the Industrial Revolution, we caused a great deal of "locked up" carbon to be released; and this trend is now being aggravated by our burning of tropical forests. Whereas the level of carbon dioxide in 1850 amounted to 265 parts per million, it has now grown to 340 parts, and unchecked it could well reach 600 by the year 2050. The result is a steady warming of our planet, projected to rise to a mean 3°C above normal within the lifetimes of our children. While there will be little change at the Equator, the poles may well become 7°C warmer, with all that ultimately implies for the ice caps.

The greenhouse effect

Incoming radiation
Of the incoming short-wave solar radiation, only 24% hits the Earth's surface directly – 3% of which is promptly reflected back into space. The rest of the incoming short-wave radiation gets caught up in the Earth's atmosphere, where it is either scattered back to space (25%), deflected to the surface (26%), or simply absorbed (25%).

Total outflow of energy
3 + 25 + 67 + 5 = 100

Incoming solar radiation

25%

100%

3%

Outgoing terrestrial radiation

67%

5%

25%

2060 600 ppm
1980 340 ppm
1850 265 ppm

Carbon dioxide levels in the atmosphere have increased by about 30% from 1850 to 1980 – and are projected to leap a further 75% by 2060.

24%

26%

Carbon dioxide plays a key role in determining the Earth's climate. It lets through virtually all the incoming short-wave solar energy, but traps and retains much of the long-wave energy that the Earth radiates out towards space. The net effect is to keep the Earth's surface at a higher temperature than if carbon dioxide were not present in the atmosphere. This is popularly known as "the greenhouse effect" (although, strictly speaking, a greenhouse keeps warm by a rather different mechanism).

The concentration of carbon dioxide in the atmosphere is increasing. Since 1850 it has increased by almost 30%, due primarily to combustion of fossil fuels. We are now burning close to 5 billion tonnes of fossil fuels a year, releasing several times as much carbon dioxide by weight into the atmosphere. If fossil fuel consumption continues to rise (and we add in the impact of forest burning in the tropics), by 2060 carbon dioxide levels could reach 600 parts per million (ppm).

Outgoing radiation
The Earth, being cooler than the sun, emits its energy in longer wavelengths (infra-red radiation). Because the atmosphere is largely opaque to these wavelengths, they bounce back and forth between the surface and atmosphere. So the equivalent of 109% of incoming solar radiation is absorbed – and 67% is re-radiated into space.

Energy absorbed by atmosphere
25 + 109 + 29 = 163
Energy re-radiated from atmosphere
96 + 67 = 163

96%

109%

29%

Absorbed at surface
24 + 26 – 3 = 47

Lost from surface
114 + 29 – 96 = 47

114%

Latent and sens

Latent heat (24%) and sensible heat (5%) are two significant flows of energy which are also absorbed b the atmosphere.

Elsewhere, rainfall patterns will be disrupted. Some areas will become wetter, others drier. Much of the North American grain belt could suffer permanent drought. A 1°C increase in temperature plus a 10 percent decrease in rainfall could reduce the wheat crop by one-fifth – with consequences not only for North Americans, but for the 100-plus countries that now benefit from the US grain surplus. The USSR, by contrast, could merely push its main grain-growing area northwards into warmed-up Siberia, with its suitable soils.

While a warmer world will be able to grow more food overall, some nations will be winners and others losers. The changes in economic muscle could prove profound, as long as humankind insists on running its affairs in nation-state packages. Further down the line, the polar ice caps could eventually melt, causing sea levels to rise by 5-7 metres. Much of the Netherlands would be flooded, together with half of Florida and huge sectors of other low-lying areas such as Bengal.

The phenomenon of increasing carbon dioxide amounts to a global experiment that we are imposing on our climate, with unprecedented capacity to disrupt our lives and those of future generations. Unfortunately, there are no easy solutions. Even a 300 percent tax on fossil fuels, to cut global consumption, might delay a doubling of atmospheric carbon dioxide by only a decade or two. It is clear, however, that we need to accelerate the

Global impacts

Assuming that atmospheric carbon dioxide more than doubles its pre-1900 concentration by 2060, what will be the global impact of such a change? Most experts agree that an increase in global temperature of a mean 3°C is more than likely – or an increase of 1°C at the Equator, around 3°C in temperate latitudes, and as much as 7°C at the poles. Accompanying these temperature changes would be changes in moisture patterns which could quickly affect agricultural productivity, and eventually sea levels around the world.

The map below shows possible soil moisture patterns on a warmer Earth, superimposed on present-day grain-growing regions. The political implications of such changes could be far-reaching: the US grain belt could suffer a significant decline in yields, while countries of the arid Middle East might find themselves with

a food resource to restore their economies after their oil wells run dry.

Flooding in Florida

Not just Florida, but low-lying land areas all over the world could eventually find themselves sinking beneath the waves. An increase of much above 5°C would cause the Arctic ice pack to disappear completely during the summer, while, at the other pole, the West Antarctic Ice Sheet could break way from its "moorings" and disintegrate within just a few centuries. Sea levels could rise by 5-7 m, affecting 40% of Florida's population. Presumably the US could afford to "move its cities inland" – but what about the two-fifths of the world's population who also live in coastal areas and have few funds – let alone space – to cater for such mass migrations inland?

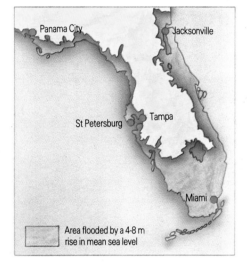

Area flooded by a 4-8 m rise in mean sea level

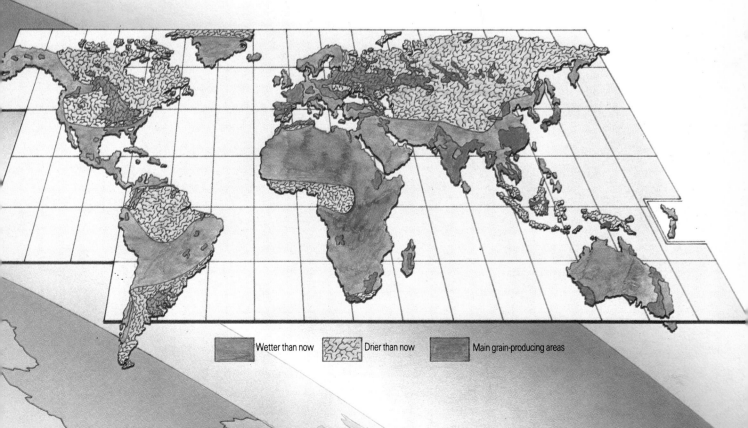

Wetter than now | Drier than now | Main grain-producing areas

transition to energy-efficient societies, drawing on energy sources which do not contribute to carbon dioxide build-up. We must also urgently reverse the process of deforestation, since forests act as prime "sinks" of carbon.

Atmospheric pollution

Air pollution has been tackled with some success in the developed countries. Smoke and sulphur pollution has been cut markedly, although auto pollution remains a problem in many urban areas. Simultaneously, however, several countries of Europe and North America experience growing problems with acid rain – whether they cause such problems or suffer from them. And the cities of the Third World, from Bombay to Mexico City, are experiencing air pollution, whether from domestic, industrial or vehicular sources.

Acid rain is now the most controversial form of air pollution in the developed world. Factories spew forth sulphur oxides and nitrogen oxides, which dissolve in rain before returning to earth as sulphuric and nitric acids. In parts of Pennsylvania, the result is a corrosive solvent 1,000 times as acidic as natural rain. Equally to the point, the pollutants are dispersed through the atmosphere until they descend far removed from their point of origin, often in another country.

To date, this phenomenon hits worst at northeastern Canada, parts of the US, central Europe, and Scandinavia – though Australia and Brazil are noticing early signs of this silent scourge. Thousands of lakes are now lifeless, unable to support fish of many sorts. In West Germany, the Black Forest is losing one-third of its trees, and many scientists attribute this trend to a combination of acid rain and other forms of air pollution. Damage to the West German timber industry is estimated at $800 million per year (plus $600 million to agriculture through loss of soil fertility). West Germans believe that at least half of the acid rain deposited on their forests comes from outside their country.

Preliminary projections suggest that damage could become ten times as severe by the end of the century if not checked. But certain political leaders are reluctant to take action until there is more conclusive evidence. Moreover, since the pollution often takes little notice of national frontiers, a solution depends on international agreement – a scarce commodity in environmental affairs. Yet a basic dilemma with acid rain – as with many environmental problems – is that the onslaught apparently arrives so fast and its workings are so complex that we cannot afford to wait until we can formulate a 100% correct answer.

What about cars? The exhaust-caused smogs of Los Angeles and Tokyo are starting to fade. Regrettably, they are being replicated by photochemical palls over Melbourne, Ankara, and Mexico City. Cars are also the source of well over half the 450,000 tonnes of lead that are ejected as fine

The invisible threat

Acidification ranks among the most serious threats to the environment in the northern hemisphere. Heavily industrialized areas pump some 90 million tonnes of sulphur dioxide into the air each year. Hardest hit are southern Sweden, Norway, parts of central Europe, and the eastern part of North America. Some 18,000 lakes in Sweden alone are now so acidified that fish stocks have been severely reduced. In Bavaria and other areas of central Europe, whole forests are dying. The map shows areas that are particularly sensitive to acid rain, typically with thin, rocky topsoils.

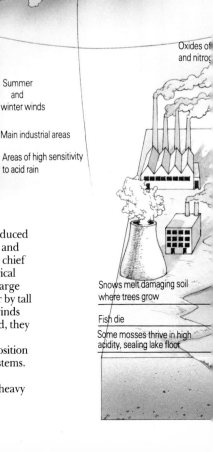

Acid winds from the US
More than half of the 12 million tonnes of acid deposited on eastern Canada each year originate in the US.

Oxides of [...]
and nitrog[...]

⇦ Summer and winter winds

● ● ● Main industrial areas

▬ Areas of high sensitivity to acid rain

Snows melt damaging soil where trees grow

Fish die

Some mosses thrive in high acidity, sealing lake floor

How acid rain is formed

Acid rain, including sleet and snow, is produced primarily by the release of sulphur oxides and nitrogen oxides into the atmosphere. The chief sources of such emissions tend to be electrical generating plants, industrial boilers, and large smelters. Gases that are vented into the air by tall smokestacks get caught up in prevailing winds where, in the course of transport over land, they are transformed into dilute solutions of sulphuric acid and nitric acids. Their deposition as acid rain can have dire effects on ecosystems. Acidified water leaches important plant nutrients out of the ground and activates heavy metals such as cadmium and mercury, contaminating water supplies.

Lead emissions from cars

Each year 450,000 tonnes of lead are released into the air by humans, compared with 3,500 tonnes from natural sources. Lead from vehicle exhaust represents more than half of this pollution. Lead is added to petrol to improve its combustion properties, and is released to the air as fine particles. The illustration (below right) demonstrates the various pathways by which lead finds its way to children living in areas of high traffic density.

Third World worst

Alerted to the dangers of lead, pressure groups in the North have successfully campaigned for the reduction of lead in petrol. Many Third World countries, however, still have intolerably high levels of lead in the atmosphere because oil companies persist in selling heavily leaded petrol. A Motor Gasoline Quality Survey in 1983 revealed that levels of lead in petrol in the Third World are almost consistently double those in the developed world.

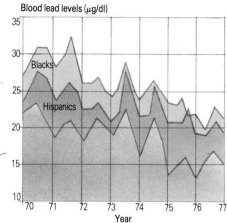

Blood lead levels (μg/dl)

Blacks

Hispanics

Leaded petrol sales

Year

The maximum lead intake

for an average 70-kg human is about 6 μg/kg body weight/day. Children absorb lead more easily, so a maximum for them would be 1.2 μg/kg/day. There is a strong correlation, left, between leaded petrol sales and blood lead in New York children.

Air 54% (direct inhalation 5%, deposited on food 22%, deposited on fingers 27%)

Average daily lead intake per urban 2-year-old child 45 μg

Water 7%

Food 39%

Smog in Los Angeles

Air pollution comes in guises other than acid rain. Photochemical smog, of the kind formed in the Los Angeles basin, has had a dramatic impact on the ecosystems of southern California, causing extensive damage to forests as well as posing a serious health hazard. The smog is composed of a number of chemicals, notably ozone and peroxyacetyl nitrate (PAN), both of which are extremely harmful to plants. These substances are formed by the action of strong sunlight on a mixture of nitrogen oxides and hydrocarbons exhausted to the air by vehicles, combustion, and industrial processes.

The geographical features of Los Angeles serve to promote the formation of such smogs. Wind patterns and the surrounding mountains create conditions for the formation of temperature inversions, trapping air pollution close to the ground. Controls designed to reduce emissions from vehicles and other sources have been introduced in a successful attempt to combat the smog.

id exports

e UK is heavily pendent on coal power neration and will remain because of its large coal erves. It contributes re acid rain to Norway an Norway itself, and is e largest external source Swedish air pollution.

des combine with water to ome acid rain

Acid snow at high altitudes

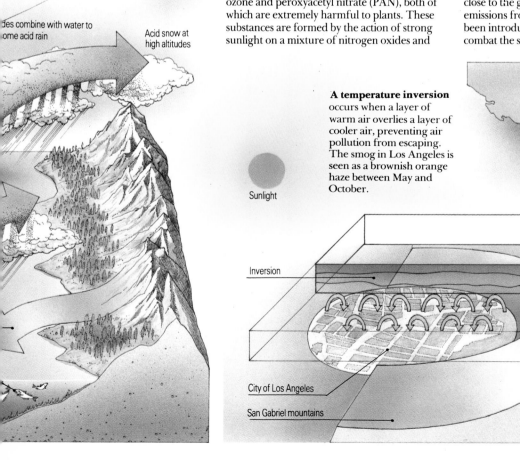

A temperature inversion occurs when a layer of warm air overlies a layer of cooler air, preventing air pollution from escaping. The smog in Los Angeles is seen as a brownish orange haze between May and October.

Sunlight

Inversion

City of Los Angeles

San Gabriel mountains

particles into our skies each year. Equally serious, there is now a build-up of charcoal-caused smoke over Third World cities such as Lagos, Jakarta, and Calcutta – the poor person's smog.

Death from polluted water

Water, a supposed fount of life, kills at least 25 million people in developing nations each year, three-fifths of them being children. Of the world's leading diseases, roughly half depend on water for their impact: they either breed in or are spread by water. All too often, there is not enough water in Third World communities for basic domestic needs, so it tends to be used time and again. It ends up as thoroughly dirty water, an ideal habitat for pathogens and carriers of disease.

Well over half of all citizens in developing countries, China excepted, do not have access to plentiful clean water supplies. Worse, three out of four enjoy no acceptable form of sanitation. In cities, the situation is better: only one-quarter lacks clean water and under half sanitation. But in rural areas, deprivation is the norm: seven-tenths (1.3 billion people) and almost nine-tenths (1.7 billion) respectively. In practical terms, lack of drinking water means no supply within several hundred metres; lack of sanitation means no bucket latrine or pit privy, let alone sewerage system. So ponds and rivers are the main sources of drinking water – and the main sites for impromptu toilets. While the number of hospital beds per 1,000 people is often thought of as a sound criterion of health services, a far better measure is the number of household taps and serviceable toilets.

Despite some efforts to help the situation, they have not nearly kept up with population growth. So year by year there are more multitudes of people without access to a basic element of human welfare, safe water. In developed nations, by contrast, at least 98 percent of citizens have ready access to clean water, as much as they want.

The cost to human health in the Third World is enormous. In one way or another, water is implicated in trachoma blindness (500 million sufferers), malaria (350 million), schistosomiasis (250 million), and elephantiasis (250 million), plus typhoid, cholera, infectious hepatitis, leprosy, yellow fever, and probably worst of all, diarrhoea. Every hour more than 1,000 children die from diarrhoeal diseases: if this scourge could be eliminated, we would see an end to much of the malnutrition that afflicts the Third World, and that fosters many other diseases. In Africa alone, one million children succumb to malaria each year.

In addition to water-related deaths, many times more sufferers are left grossly debilitated, hardly able to do a decent day's work. In India, water-borne diseases claim 73 million work-days each year, while costs through medical treatment and lost production amount to almost $1 billion.

There are still further costs. If inadequate or

Water that kills

The map shows the regional distribution of populations without reasonable access to safe water. In more than half of the developing countries, less than 50% of the population has a source of potable water or facilities for sewage disposal.

Percentage of population with access to safe water

- 0-40
- 41-80
- 81-100
- No data

The provision of clean, adequate supplies of water and the safe disposal of human waste represent one of the most urgent problems facing the developing world today. In the absence of such facilities, rivers, lakes, and ponds serve both as a source of "clean" water for human settlements and as a sink for all their wastes. Drinking water is often drawn from places where bathing and laundering are being done, and the same water source is frequently used as a public toilet.

Dirty water is believed to be the principal transmission agent for at least 80% of the diseases which afflict the Third World. Of these, diarrhoea is the most serious: almost 50% of deaths in the Third World involve children under the age of 5 suffering from some form of this disease. The five main types of water-related diseases are classified, right, with specific examples alongside.

Dangerous waterholes
The rural poor, who lack access to standpipes, have little choice but to collect their water from rivers, streams, ponds, mud holes or wells. Millions of women and children often spend 6 hours a day walking long distances to bring home a few litres of dirty water.

North

Safe water 93%

Adequate sanitation 90%

Safe water and sanitation – for whom?
In the North, 9 out of 10 people have ample clean, piped water and mains sanitation. In the South, only 2 out of 5 people have easy access to safe water, and 1 in 4 to proper sanitation. Rural people in the Third World fare worst of all. During the decade 1970-80, the numbers of rural people without clean water increased by 67 million to 1.15 billion, while those without proper sanitation rose by 300 million to almost 1.4 billion. Numbers lacking sanitation in Third World cities doubled during the period 1975-80.

South

43%

25%

Water (% of population without clean water)

	1970	1975	1980
Rural	86%	78%	71%
Urban	33%	23%	25%
Rural	89%	85%	87%
Urban	29%	25%	47%

Sanitation (% of population without proper facilities,

"The number of water taps per 1,000 persons is a better indication of health than the number of hospital beds."
WORLD HEALTH ORGANISATION

Infections
millions per year   1,000   100   Deaths
thousands per year   1,000   100   10

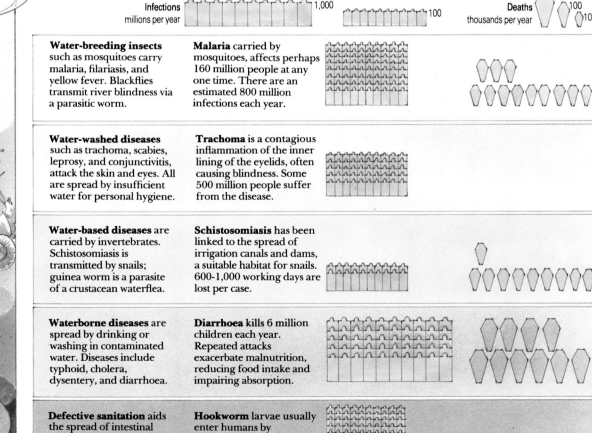

Water-breeding insects such as mosquitoes carry malaria, filariasis, and yellow fever. Blackflies transmit river blindness via a parasitic worm.

Malaria carried by mosquitoes, affects perhaps 160 million people at any one time. There are an estimated 800 million infections each year.

Water-washed diseases such as trachoma, scabies, leprosy, and conjunctivitis, attack the skin and eyes. All are spread by insufficient water for personal hygiene.

Trachoma is a contagious inflammation of the inner lining of the eyelids, often causing blindness. Some 500 million people suffer from the disease.

Water-based diseases are carried by invertebrates. Schistosomiasis is transmitted by snails; guinea worm is a parasite of a crustacean waterflea.

Schistosomiasis has been linked to the spread of irrigation canals and dams, a suitable habitat for snails. 600-1,000 working days are lost per case.

Waterborne diseases are spread by drinking or washing in contaminated water. Diseases include typhoid, cholera, dysentery, and diarrhoea.

Diarrhoea kills 6 million children each year. Repeated attacks exacerbate malnutrition, reducing food intake and impairing absorption.

Defective sanitation aids the spread of intestinal worms. Eggs are excreted in human faeces. The infection cycle begins on swallowing the eggs.

Hookworm larvae usually enter humans by burrowing through the soles of the feet. Heavy infestations can cause death in children.

unsafe water causes child deaths on a vast scale, so child deaths stimulate birth rates, which in turn serve to perpetuate the population explosion.

Hazardous chemicals – a growing problem

Slowly but steadily, we are poisoning our environments. After doing a good job on cutting back the traditional pollutants, notably visible contaminants such as smoke, we are fostering an insidious spread of toxic chemicals and metals in quantities that are very hard to detect. Some of these pollutants are deadlier than anything we have had to face to date. DDT, dieldrin, and other pesticides are suspected of causing cancer and birth defects, among other problems. Polychlorinated biphenyls (PCBs) consti-

tute a family of chemicals with over 200 types, and are used in plastics, electrical insulators, and hydraulic fluids; they are unusually toxic and persistent, affecting the vital organs. Heavy metals, such as mercury, lead, cadmium, chromium, and nickel, are believed to cause cancer, plus disorders of the lungs, heart, kidneys, and the central nervous system.

Yet we generate vast amounts of these materials. In the US, industry spews forth at least 250 million tonnes of noxious waste each year, or about one tonne per citizen. Worse, much is disposed of in a manner that does not meet basic standards of environmental safety. Until recently, the main mode of disposal has involved simple dumping in landfill tips, at least 1,000 of which are health hazards.

Widening circle of poison

Our planetary environment is a closed system. Persistent materials pumped into the air, dumped in rivers and seas, or hidden from view in landfills do not simply melt away. The waste by-products of our industrial processes are a growing threat – sometimes an international threat. The developed world regularly exports to the Third World hundreds of millions of kilograms of potentially lethal chemicals – chemicals classified as too dangerous for use in their country of origin. The irony is that these same chemicals (especially pesticides) return to the developed world on bananas, coffee beans, tomatoes, and other food stuffs imported from the developing nations. In 1981 the US revoked export restrictions on these substances on the grounds that US exports were being put at a "competitive disadvantage".

Metallic and non-metallic pollutants

Since the 1930s, when arsenic was the only metal known to be a carcinogen, beryllium, cadmium, cobalt, chromium, iron, lead, nickel, selenium, titanium, and zinc have been added to the list. PCBs, which are totally synthetic and have no natural counterparts, have now been classified as carcinogens. Once PCBs enter the environment, a process of bio-amplification occurs. Samples taken in the North Sea indicate a PCB concentration of 0.000002 parts per million (ppm) in sea water, but 160 ppm in marine mammals. Cancer-forming chemicals, including PCBs, are found in the tissues of 99% of all Americans. In 1982, the National Cancer Institute disclosed that Americans have a 31% chance of contracting cancer before the age of 74, much of the sources being environmental.

Chemical time-bombs

Abandoned hazardous waste dumps can be chemical time-bombs. In 1978 the community of Love Canal, New York, was itself abandoned when an unusual number of cancers and birth defects came to light. The Hooker Chemical Company had used the site from the late 1940s to dump dioxin, lindane, and mirex. It had taken just 30 years for these chemicals to work their way to the surface. Often such materials contaminate underground water.

Exporting the problem

Faced with growing public concern and ever-tightening environmental controls, some waste-disposal companies have tried to solve their problems by shipping the wastes to the Third World for disposal. A worrying export industry.

Bogotá – river of death

Only about one-quarter of Colombia's population has access to pollution-free water; along the banks of the Bogotá River this figure is almost nil. Colombia's largest industrial complex and over 5 million people use the Bogotá as an open sewer. Tocaima, a small town totally dependent on the river for domestic and agricultural water supply, has the country's highest infant mortality rate; between 1974 and 1979 the rate increased by nearly 70%, while cases of gastro enteritis and diarrhoea increased by one-third. Tocaima is not alone in suffering ill-health.

1967

Toxic waste

Contamination of water supplies

As for advanced nations, they manufacture 70,000 different chemicals, most of which have not been thoroughly tested to assess their long-term effects on humans. Certain pollutants, especially pesticides and PCBs, accumulate in fatty tissues of organisms. As they pass up food chains – from, say, microscopic creatures in water bodies, to plants, then to eaters of plants, finally to eaters of plant-eaters such as humans – they become concentrated. This process of bio-amplification can magnify their effective dosage by 10-100 times at each stage. As a result, their eventual concentration can increase a million times by the time they reach humans.

Nor do the advanced nations retain these hazardous chemicals for their own use. Of the US output of pesticides, worth $8 billion per year, two-fifths is exported, chiefly to developing countries where safety regulations are not well developed. Of these US exports, one-quarter is made up of chemicals whose use is severely restricted or banned at home. Thus arises a widening "circle of poison".

Ironically, much of the Third World produce treated with developed-world pesticides is grown for developed-world markets. Almost half the coffee imported by the US from Latin America contains chemical residues, while beef shipments are sometimes stopped because they harbour several times more DDT (used as a spray against cattle diseases) than is permitted by US domestic regulations. Similarly, West Germany has rejected contaminated

% growth in synthetics
production of organic
micals grew from 4.75
lion tonnes in 1967 to
million tonnes in 1977 –
increase of 67%.

1977

Pesticides

Perfect produce?
Extreme importance is attached by Northerners to the appearance of imported food. Some 20% of all agrochemicals used only serve to improve the look of vegetables and fruit.

DDT
One of the best-documented examples of how a substance can enter the food chain and become concentrated is DDT. Wholesale use of DDT has resulted in pollution of rivers, and the absorption of tiny amounts by small fish. Instead of being excreted, DDT tends to lodge in the fatty tissues of living organisms. As small fish are eaten by big fish, which, in turn, are eaten by birds (and people), so the ratio of DDT to body weight increases. Although DDT was prohibited for use within the US as long ago as 1972, the US still manufactures over 18 million kg a year for export, largely to the Third World. Ignorance in the Third World of the dangers involved with the use of pesticides such as DDT is a major problem. A sample of rural workers in Central America shows that they have 11 times as much DDT in their bodies as the average American citizen.

Body blows
Heavy metal pollutants are responsible for wide-ranging damage to vital organs. Mercury and lead attack the central nervous system (1), nickel and beryllium damage the lungs (2), antimony can lead to heart disease (3), and cadmium causes kidney damage (4).

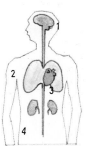

Third World toxics
Chemical companies in the North often sell products to less regulated markets in the South. They also build new factories there, to escape environmental controls. By 1975, El Salvador produced 20% of the world's total output of the pesticide parathion.

Chemical-resistant pests
Indiscriminate pesticide use has produced new strains of pest which are resistant to the commonly used sprays. To counter this, even higher doses are used, further endangering human health and wildlife – and accelerating resistance.

Pesticide poisonings
In 1981, OXFAM stated that there were 750,000 cases of accidental pesticide poisoning a year. Third World countries, accounting for less than 15% of world pesticide consumption, suffered 50% of poisonings and 75% of the resulting deaths.

tobacco grown in Thailand, while Scandinavian countries have refused fruit and vegetables from Africa. The issue of hazardous chemicals amounts to one of our greatest environmental challenges.

Nuclear energy – a failed promise?

The vision of cheap nuclear electricity may have evaporated, but many protagonists still believe that nuclear power provides the main hope of the abundant energy they see as critical for future social stability. As oil supplies diminish, they argue, an expanding nuclear industry will help prevent the need to make forced changes in our lifestyles – and provide a means for the worldwide improvement of living standards. There are risks, they accept, but

these must be traded off against potential benefits. During the '60s and '70s, energy utilities in the US, UK, Japan, France, the USSR, and other countries committed huge financial and scientific resources to their nuclear development programmes. By 1981, more than 250 reactors in 22 countries supplied 8 percent of the world's electricity.

But optimistic predictions to the effect that nuclear power would provide 50 percent of the world's electricity by the year 2000 now look hopelessly unrealistic. Outside the Comecon countries, which still have ambitious nuclear programmes, the world's nuclear power industry looks as though it is driving itself into a cul-de-sac. The industry could probably live with the disapproval of

The nuclear dilemma

The nuclear industry is sick. Far from providing a cheap and plentiful supply of energy that would satisfy world demand for the foreseeable future, it has provided us with an expensive energy source fraught with intractable technical problems and unacceptable environmental risks. Long-lived radioactive wastes cast a shadow which reaches across the generations.

A nuclear dead-end?

In 1970 energy planners were forecasting that over 200 nuclear power stations would be operating in Western Europe by 1985. By 1983, the forecasts for 1985 had dropped to 73. This same pattern has been repeated across the world, with a fall from nearly 600 to under 200. Nuclear power, for all the promises of its early enthusiasts, has run into a cul-de-sac. Falling energy demand, rising real costs, and public concern have all played their part in bringing about this state of affairs. Many billions of dollars have been wasted, particularly in the US, on projects that have been abandoned before completion. Electricity companies are discovering that it is cheaper and easier to encourage people to use energy more efficiently, and so reduce demand, than it is to build new capacity to meet growing demand. Weapons proliferation is another danger. Even more alarming, this material could fall into the hands of terrorists. The nuclear era may turn out to be unexpectedly short-lived.

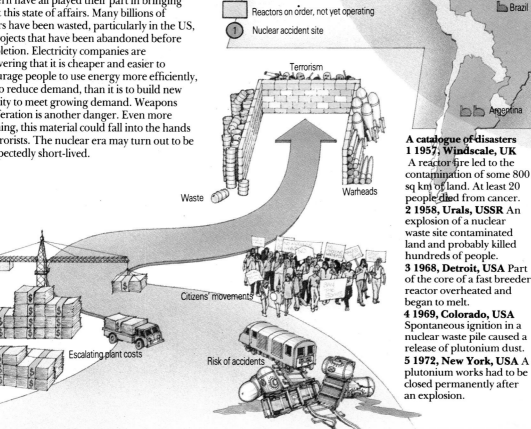

10 operating reactors
1 operating reactor
Cancelled orders
31-50% electricity generated by nuclear power
11-30%
0-10%
% unavailable
Reactors on order, not yet operating
① Nuclear accident site

Canada
USA
Mexico
Puerto Rico
Brazil
Argentina

Terrorism
Waste
Warheads
Citizens' movements
Escalating plant costs
Risk of accidents

A catalogue of disasters
1 1957, Windscale, UK
A reactor fire led to the contamination of some 800 sq km of land. At least 20 people died from cancer.
2 1958, Urals, USSR An explosion of a nuclear waste site contaminated land and probably killed hundreds of people.
3 1968, Detroit, USA Part of the core of a fast breeder reactor overheated and began to melt.
4 1969, Colorado, USA Spontaneous ignition in a nuclear waste pile caused a release of plutonium dust.
5 1972, New York, USA A plutonium works had to be closed permanently after an explosion.

6 1975, Browns Ferry,
A workman started a fire with a candle that knocke out five emergency syste and nearly destroyed the reactor.
7 1976 Windscale, UK month after its discovery leak of radioactive water reported. The size of the leak: 2 million litres.
8 1979 Harrisburg, USA Operator error led to the world's most serious core accident yet, destroying a $1 billion reactor.
9 1981 Windscale, UK Release of iodine 131 int Cumbrian countryside. Local milk supplies contaminated.

environmentalists, but now its most serious problem is in the field of economics. Massive cost over-runs, with US plants proving 5-10 times more expensive than had been projected, have resulted in the largest municipal bond default in US history and have pushed many utilities to the brink of bankruptcy. Inflation and high interest rates have combined with tightening regulations to undermine the economics of nuclear power schemes. Nuclear construction programmes have virtually ground to a halt in the US, with 100 plants cancelled and no new ones ordered since 1977.

But those countries which have declared nuclear moratoria have not typically done so because of economic problems. Sweden's reactors were among

the safest and most efficient in the world. The real problems were social and political: people simply do not believe that we can control the wider impacts of nuclear technology. Growing concerns about the environmental risks involved, about the inability of industry to dispose safely of long-lived radioactive wastes, and about the proliferation of nuclear weaponry, have all helped derail nuclear power.

But, although the industry is down, it certainly is not out. Despite the well-publicized risks involved, some countries, China included, still want to press ahead with nuclear power. The nuclear industry is not going to disappear, but it is increasingly seen as a particularly high-risk option – not as the energy panacea originally promised.

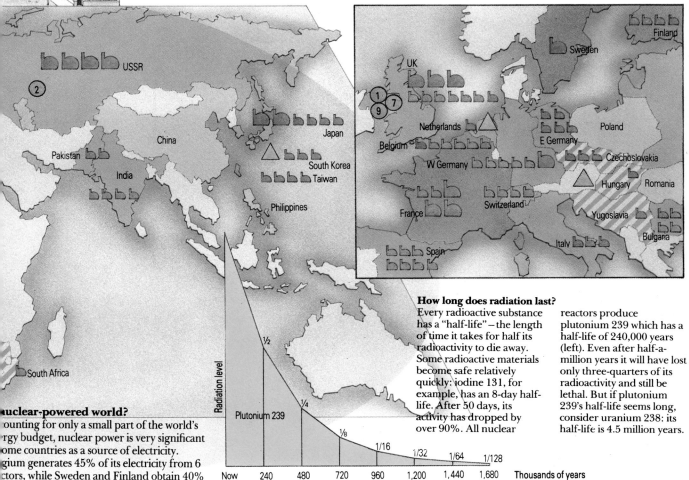

How long does radiation last?
Every radioactive substance has a "half-life" – the length of time it takes for half its radioactivity to die away. Some radioactive materials become safe relatively quickly: iodine 131, for example, has an 8-day half-life. After 50 days, its activity has dropped by over 90%. All nuclear reactors produce plutonium 239 which has a half-life of 240,000 years (left). Even after half-a-million years it will have lost only three-quarters of its radioactivity and still be lethal. But if plutonium 239's half-life seems long, consider uranium 238: its half-life is 4.5 million years.

nuclear-powered world?
ounting for only a small part of the world's rgy budget, nuclear power is very significant ome countries as a source of electricity. gium generates 45% of its electricity from 6 ctors, while Sweden and Finland obtain 40% heir electricity from nuclear power. French lear plants supply 48% of the country's tricity, compared to 13% in the US. Some ly industrializing countries, especially wan and South Korea, have ambitious grammes, and China plans to expand its lear capacity. The high capital cost (all of ch would have to be in foreign exchange) the small size of their electricity grids are or obstacles for any Third World country ting to go nuclear. Indeed, so unlikely is lear power to be of benefit in such countries akistan or Iraq, that the desire to acquire lear-weapon-making capability seems the plausible explanation for nuclear elopments.

Dealing with waste
Twenty-seven years after the first commercial nuclear reactor began operating, there is still no acceptable solution to the problem of radioactive waste. Used fuel rods can be recycled to recover uranium and plutonium. But this process still leaves highly radioactive wastes to be disposed of. It is possible to store this waste in glass or turn it into synthetic rock, but there is still considerable scientific argument over the effectiveness of these processes. Other radioactive wastes include the tailings from uranium mining and nuclear power stations that have been "mothballed" or shut down.

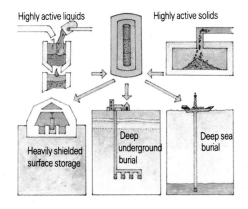

MANAGING THE ELEMENTS

Beset as we are with crises of Earth's elements, we can take heart from some solid efforts to get to grips with some of them. We are using oil much more efficiently. For those people who rarely see a drop of oil, relying instead on fuelwood, there is hope that more trees may eventually be planted than are chopped down. Political leaders scarcely thought about water ten years ago, yet we now have a UN Water and Sanitation Decade. Our skies have been cleansed of many pollutants. And, in a rare show of accord, the world's governments are putting together a convention to safeguard the ozone layer.

Managing energy in the North
Using exciting technologies, strongly promoted by government incentives, we could, by the year 2000, cut energy consumption by one-quarter and fossil-fuel consumption by almost one-half from our 1980 levels. Increasing contributions from renewable energy sources and from energy-efficiency programmes will speed the transition. As a result, there will be much less pollution, such as acid rain, and there will be a slowing in carbon dioxide build-up in the atmosphere.

At the same time, our economies could continue to expand apace. For the first 30 years after World War II, economic growth seemed inextricably linked to growth in energy consumption. Yet since the rise of OPEC, economic growth in Western Europe and Japan has been twice as fast as energy growth, in the US three times as fast. In part, this has been due to a decline in oil consumption, ranging from 14 percent in the US to 20 percent in West Germany. In part too, it has been due to energy savings: our economies have become one-fifth more efficient in energy use, and conservation has contributed several times more to meeting our energy needs than all new sources combined.

In Japan, household appliances – refrigerators, air conditioners and other electricity-hungry devices – use at least 50 percent less energy than in the mid-1970s. Airlines have cut the fuel used per passenger kilometre by almost one-third, while the "gas-guzzlers" on American roads are being made much more efficient than was dreamed of only ten years back. American buildings consume one-third of the nation's energy for heating, cooling, and lighting, yet the 100 million buildings that will be in place by the year 2000 (two-fifths more than in 1980) need use only half as much energy if they are made more efficient through insulation and

An energy-efficient future?

Current patterns of energy use cannot be sustained. Oil and gas will become too scarce and expensive for all but the most essential uses. Coal will suffer a similar fate within a few more centuries. Non-conventional hydrocarbon sources, like oil shale, represent the modern-day equivalent of squeezing blood out of a stone. And nuclear power is a long way from fulfilling its early promise. Our key objective now must be to increase the efficiency of all forms of energy use, to squeeze more work from each watt. Energy conservation is often much cheaper than generating an equivalent amount of energy to that saved. Since the early 1970s, the Western nations have boosted their energy efficiency by 20% – and further improvements are ahead.

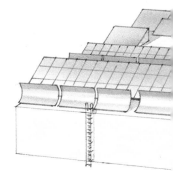

Waste heat warms facto
Fuel-efficient factories w
turn out energy-efficien
products. Highly insulat
they will use heat pumps
and combined heat and
power systems.

The fuel misers
The energy efficiency of tomorrow's average house and car will be dramatically better than for their 1960 counterparts.

Solar panels, installed on the roof, can significantly cut fuel bills for heat and electricity – particularly when coupled with new heat storage and distribution systems.

Insulation is now built into most new houses, both in roof-space and cavity walls. Coupled with double-glazing, such methods significantly cut the energy needed to keep a northern house comfortable from the current requirement of 12-20 kilowatts to an efficient and cost-effective 5 kilowatts.

Building in intelligence can help improve the efficiency of all energy-consuming systems, whether they be entire houses (with thermostats controlling temperatures) or individual items of domestic equipment. By using advanced microelectronics, it will soon be possible for the electricity-supply utility to keep energy-consuming equipment in each household constantly informed of the present price of electricity being supplied.

Improved car design has already turned yesterday's gas guzzlers into today's lighter, sleeker vehicles. But the fuel consumption of even the latest cars could be halved with the use of more plastics in bodywork, more ceramic components in the engine, and microprocessor-based fuel-management systems.

1960s house

Heat loss
Before the oil crises of th
'70s, few gave much
thought to heat lost from
uninsulated, single-glaze
houses. And coal fires we
less efficient than central
heating.

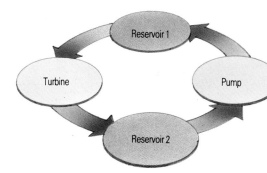

Pumped storage
Electricity has to be
consumed as it is produce
Power stations, to run
efficiently, must run at a
reasonably constant
output – but demand
fluctuates wildly. Pumped
storage schemes, left, help
by using surplus power to
pump water uphill –
releasing it, through
turbines, at peak times.

Pinpointing heat loss
The image on the right shows heat loss from an industrial complex. Aerial infra-red photography helps energy managers pinpoint where they can spend their conservation budgets to the best effect. White, yellow, and red areas show points of greatest heat loss.

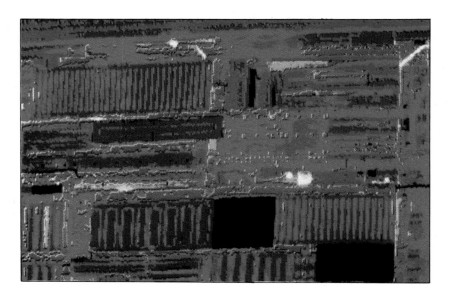

use

ation

Electronic intelligence

Double glazing

Improved car design

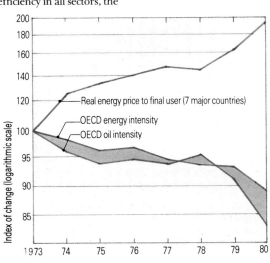

Uncoupling growth from energy

The plight of California's high-tech Silicon Valley, where more and more drivers wait in ever-longer traffic jams and innumerable hectares disappear under new roads and parking lots, illustrates a basic problem: the private car is an unduly wasteful transport technology, both in terms of energy and environmental resources. Mass transit systems, even the humble bicycle, outstrip the car in the sustainability stakes. By stressing energy efficiency in all sectors, the industrial nations have relaxed the relationship between growth in their economies and growth in energy demand. As energy prices have soared (below), the energy intensity of our activities (calculated by dividing total primary energy demand by real GDP) has fallen – with the oil shocks of 1973 and 1979 accelerating the downward trend.

Real energy price to final user (7 major countries)
OECD energy intensity
OECD oil intensity

Index of change (logarithmic scale)

1973 74 75 76 77 78 79 80

weather-proofing. Energy conservation in the US is already an industry worth $10 billion a year: as early as 1990, it could achieve the equivalent of eliminating all oil imports.

Supplying energy to the South

Developing countries, with international aid, have recently begun to face up to the fuelwood crisis. But, if we are to meet the challenge, we must plant trees five times faster in the Third World as a whole, and in the worst-off areas, such as those of West Africa, between 15 and 50 times as fast.

Not that the task is so simple as raising money – although development agencies, led by the World Bank, are finally getting round to the job. Local people need to be helped to confront the challenge in ways *they* think are relevant. Too often the approach has been a "top down" affair, with urban bureaucrats trying to impose their plans on rural communities. Result: the planted trees are not cared for – or are poached. So at least as important as money is a "grass roots" spirit, that mobilizes the initiative of local people.

Fortunately, an expanded strategy along these lines is under way, known as "community forestry". It looks at village woodlots not only as sources of fuelwood, but as safeguards for topsoil, as windbreaks to protect crops, and as sources of food.

At the same time, we could do much through the simple expedient of improved cooking stoves that

Managing energy in the South

Managing energy policy in the developing countries of the South is, in many ways, much more complex than managing it in the industrialized North. Northern energy strategies are chiefly determined by price competition between four main fuels (electricity, oil, coal, and gas) supplied by large, often monopolistic, public or private suppliers. An extensive infrastructure provides each consumer with a range of options for meeting their energy needs. In the South, the biomass fuels, dung, wood, and charcoal, join the fuel mix in the poorer countries, playing a far larger role than fossil fuels or electricity. Often, there is no market at all in the primary fuel and where there is a market it is local or regional. The penetration of electricity is typically small and confined to major cities. Fossil fuels, at world market prices, are rarely cheap enough for anything but the most essential uses.

Reforestation in South Korea
Since wood is the primary fuel in the South, successful reforestation programmes are a key to future energy security. Both China and South Korea, operating in vastly different economic contexts, have mounted successful programmes, the South Korean programme in particular illustrating many of the lessons that must be learnt. Nearly 70% of Korea is now covered in trees, half of them young, and some 40,000 ha a year have been planted since 1976. Up until 1973, however, Korea's efforts at reforestation failed. Later, a new approach was tried, combining strong government support – it paid 65% of the costs – with intensive local participation. Village committees with locally elected leaders selected the best sites for planting and offered villagers a chance to share in the profits from the scheme. Grass-roots involvement is an essential condition for effective reforestation.

Fuelwood plantations
A plantation of fast-growing trees, such as *Leucaena*, can yield up to 50 tonnes of wood per hectare each year. They are especially useful for meeting urban fuelwood needs but are expensive to set up.

Village woodlots
Village woodlots are part of a new approach to reforestation known as "social" or "community" forestry. Trees planted on village or private land produce wood and other products for village, rather than commercial, use. Foresters educate and advise, but the villagers manage.

Fuel from sugarcane
One-quarter of the cars now sold in Brazil run on pure ethanol produced from the fermentation of sugarcane – the rest run on a 20% ethanol blend. Each tonne of cane produces 70 litres of ethanol. Finding an indigenous liquid fuel for transport is a pressing Southern energy problem.

erate more heat while burning less wood. Most ves deliver less than 20 percent of potential heat, ny only 5 percent (a developed-world stove is 70 cent efficient). An improved-design stove can cut t losses by almost half, while costing a mere $10. t getting enough built at a low-enough cost, and ting them used by people with deep-rooted king traditions, is not proving easy.

Other forms of biomass are available besides od. Most developing nations are in the tropics, ere plants generally thrive. Sugarcane, cassava, l maize contain enough sugar or starch to erate ethanol through fermentation, while fast-wing water weeds and algae produce methane. zil, Zimbabwe, and the Philippines already

obtain much of their liquid fuel from biomass—and a "petroleum plantation" will never run dry.

Of course, the sun's energy can be tapped through other means, such as photovoltaic cells and solar pumps. Regrettably, however, these may well remain too costly for the poor. Alternative technologies range from established items such as hydropower and geothermal energy, to innovative devices such as high-tech windmills and tidal power. Some of these look promising, others less so. But there are plenty of options to help developing countries through their energy squeeze—provided the investment and the technology can be made available from the North. The recent rate of oil-field discovery has been nine times greater in the South than

Mini-hydropower schemes

ina has built some 000 small-scale hydro ts since 1968. Between m they produce over 00 megawatts of ctricity, the equivalent of nuclear power stations. all-scale hydro projects relatively cheap and pler to construct than ger systems, relying on a n, penstock, turbine, l generator. Since ctricity is generated close he point of use, they do require massive extra estment in a grid to ribute the energy duced. They are ideal powering rural ustries and supplying ools and hospitals.

Windmills

In developing countries, small efficient windmills offer a potential energy source for pumping water to irrigate land and supply livestock. Even with moderate winds, wind power can pump water more cheaply than diesel or bullock power. However, the technical skills to service windmills are rarely abundant in the South and the initial capital cost is often high.

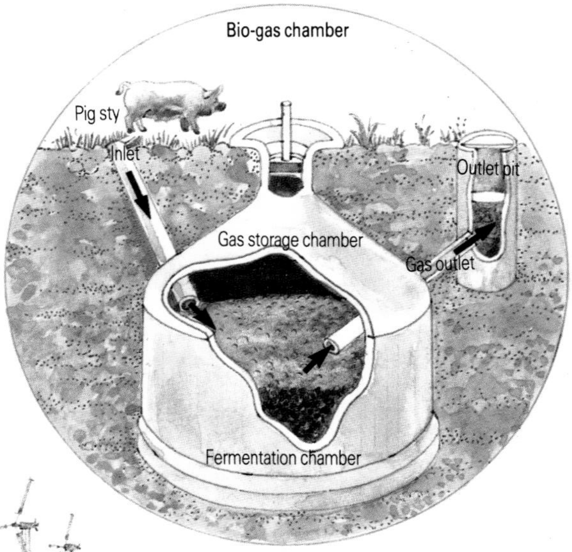

Bio-gas chamber
Pig sty
Inlet
Outlet pit
Gas storage chamber
Gas outlet
Fermentation chamber

More efficient stoves

Half the world's people cook with wood—millions of them over the open "three-stone" fire that is both dirty and dangerous. Laboratory tests suggest that more efficient stoves could save up to 70% of the wood used in an open fire. But too many programmes to provide efficient stoves fail. Bringing a stove from the laboratory into widespread use is a very complex process. To succeed, the needs and wishes of the intended users must be considered at every stage.

Bio-gas

Bio-gas plants, used in 46 developing countries, are an integrated technology, providing both fuel and fertilizer. The fermentation of animal dung, human excreta, or crop residues in an airtight container yields a methane-rich gas. This can be used to heat stoves, light lamps, run machinery, or produce electricity. The residue left by bio-gas production can be used as a fertilizer or as a component in animal feed. Sewage systems built to collect human wastes for bio-gas production also help to improve hygiene.

elsewhere. In an interdependent world, it makes economic and political sense for the North – which uses and wastes most energy – to ensure that the Third World has the technology needed to harness its energy resources on a sustainable basis.

Understanding climatic change

Climate is a fragile resource, susceptible to all manner of human intrusions. True, certain Gaian principles help Earth to look after its own. Increased carbon dioxide levels in the atmosphere stimulate plant growth through enhanced photosynthesis, so carbon dioxide will foster a fertilization effect. But the compensatory capacity of Gaia is all too limited for the immediate future.

The climate factor

At any time, it is likely that at least one region is suffering a major climatic extreme. Certain years are, however, exceptional: 1982-3 was notable for its unusual and extreme weather patterns. The blows fell hardest on the less developed countries in the South, with widespread disruption of agriculture. One aid agency, OXFAM, estimated that the economic effects would take at least 5 years to work their way through. A possible cause: El Niño, a warm current and associated low pressure system originating in the central Pacific.

Weather and climate prediction

Television viewers across Europe and North America receive sophisticated satellite pictures of developing weather patterns on their screens. In the US, a country of volatile climatic extremes, these pictures can help avert disaster by identifying the probable path of a destructive blizzard or hurricane. Climatology, however, has lagged far behind day-to-day weather prediction. Using computer models we can look only 5 days ahead with any accuracy, due to the unstable nature of the atmosphere. Different models are used in climatic change experiments. These take into account the normally slowly changing variations in ocean temperature which, because of their vast heat-retaining property, hold one of the keys to climatic change. The present aim of the World Climate Programme is to improve the monitoring of small temperature and pressure anomalies which can suddenly build up and dominate the weather pattern of whole continents – as witness the impact of El Niño on global climate.

Weather modification

Modifying weather by technological means began in the 1940s when seeding clouds with dry ice or silver iodide was thought to cause rain. Seeding is also used to dissipate cold fog, suppress hail, and deflect hurricanes. Its success is uncertain and repercussions on neighbouring regions are poorly understood. In arid regions, vegetation is planted to extract groundwater and boost humidity. The effects of altering the climate intentionally are as yet insignificant compared with the climatic impact of deforestation, carbon dioxide build-up, and particulate air pollution.

Our climate impinges on many resources, notably agriculture, energy, and water. As our food supplies become more limited and more vulnerable, we must take ever-greater account of climate, and learn how to use it to best advantage.

First of all, we must work to enhance our foresight capacity. The phenomenon of El Niño, for example, a warm, southward-flowing current of the east-central Pacific, seems to occur unusually strongly about once a decade. If only we could anticipate its next arrival, we could take steps to counter the massive climate dislocations it brings in its wake. In 1982-83, when El Niño was a whole 7°C warmer than usual, it altered weather patterns across three-quarters of the globe, causing floods

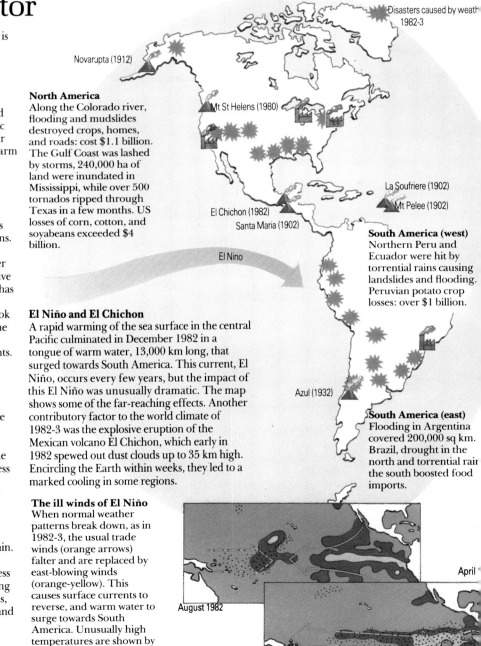

Volcanic eruptions since 18[ ] affecting climate

Major industrial conurbatio[ ]

Disasters caused by weath[ ] 1982-3

Novarupta (1912)

Mt St Helens (1980)

La Soufriere (1902)
Mt Pelee (1902)

El Chichon (1982)
Santa Maria (1902)

Azul (1932)

El Nino

North America
Along the Colorado river, flooding and mudslides destroyed crops, homes, and roads: cost $1.1 billion. The Gulf Coast was lashed by storms, 240,000 ha of land were inundated in Mississippi, while over 500 tornados ripped through Texas in a few months. US losses of corn, cotton, and soyabeans exceeded $4 billion.

South America (west)
Northern Peru and Ecuador were hit by torrential rains causing landslides and flooding. Peruvian potato crop losses: over $1 billion.

South America (east)
Flooding in Argentina covered 200,000 sq km. Brazil, drought in the north and torrential rain[ ] the south boosted food imports.

El Niño and El Chichon
A rapid warming of the sea surface in the central Pacific culminated in December 1982 in a tongue of warm water, 13,000 km long, that surged towards South America. This current, El Niño, occurs every few years, but the impact of this El Niño was unusually dramatic. The map shows some of the far-reaching effects. Another contributory factor to the world climate of 1982-3 was the explosive eruption of the Mexican volcano El Chichon, which early in 1982 spewed out dust clouds up to 35 km high. Encircling the Earth within weeks, they led to a marked cooling in some regions.

The ill winds of El Niño
When normal weather patterns break down, as in 1982-3, the usual trade winds (orange arrows) falter and are replaced by east-blowing winds (orange-yellow). This causes surface currents to reverse, and warm water to surge towards South America. Unusually high temperatures are shown by shades of dark to light green (lighter is warmer); dots indicate heavy rain.

August 1982

April [ ]

along western coasts of both South and North America, and droughts in southern Africa, southern Asia, and Australia, causing damage costed at $8 billion. If we could tackle the El Niño phenomenon in a more systematic fashion, both through greater forecasting capacity (better monitoring and analysis) and through anticipatory agriculture (drought-resistant crops), we could do much to relieve its worst depredations.

We also need to improve our understanding of the effects of broadscale vegetation changes, such as tropical deforestation. As it is, governments act with all too little knowledge. In Amazonia, it now appears that steady elimination of the forest cover could affect the rainfall regime in southern Brazil several

hundred kilometres to the south – the site of Brazil's main agricultural lands. In a broader context still, tropical deforestation could, through an increase in "albedo" or the "shininess" of the Earth's surface, influence rainfall as far away as the temperate zones, including America's grain belt.

Let us close with a semi-success story. We are protected from deadly radiation from the sun by a thin layer of ozone in the upper stratosphere. This critical shield can be damaged by chlorofluoromethanes, released by aerosols, refrigerators, and air conditioners. Were the ozone layer to become unduly depleted, humans would become more prone to skin cancer among other ailments, and certain grain crops could become less productive.

> *"As food supplies become more limited and more vulnerable, the need to take climate into account becomes increasingly important – and the responsibility that society must accept for future climate change becomes greater."*
> M KELLY AND J PALUTIKOF
> MARXISM TODAY MARCH 1982

rope
rall an exceptionally
d, wet spring was
owed by a summer of
ught, punctuated by
nder and hailstorms
wrecked many crops.

USSR
1972 and 1975 saw significant shortfalls in the Soviet grain harvest due to irregular climate patterns.

China
Drought in the North disrupted spring- and summer-sown crops. In the south, storms and typhoons caused more crop damage. In Tibet, drought affected 60% of arable land.

Bezymianni (1956)
Ksudach (1907)

India and Bangladesh
Severe flooding affected NW India. In Bangladesh, torrential rains affected 70,000 people.

Philippines
Typhoon Vera alone caused damage worth $9 million, leaving 500,000 homeless and hundreds of people dead.

Africa
Drought hit southern Africa with both crops and livestock severely hit. South Africa, normally an exporter of maize, had to import 1.5 million tonnes. Particularly affected were the bantu "homelands", where 75% of livestock (45,000 animals) were slaughtered. In the Sahel, drought was especially severe in Mauritania, Senegal, and Chad.

Krakatoa (1883)
Agung (1963)

Indonesia
Drought brought famine and cholera. Water had to be transported to over 650 Javan towns.

Tarawera (1886)

Australia and Polynesia
Eastern Australia suffered the worst drought in living memory. Cost: $2.5 billion. Cyclones left 25,000 Tahitians homeless. More than 30,000 Fijians on emergency rations.

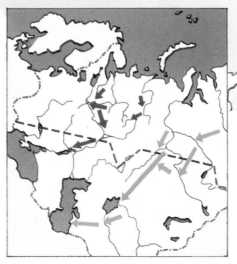

→ European variant
→ Siberian variant
- - Boundary
between water-surplus and water-deficit regions

ving rivers – climatic consequences
iculture in southern European Russia and tral Asia is heavily dependent on irrigation emes which have already depleted local water plies. To alleviate this shortage, the USSR is sidering the diversion of major rivers that into the Arctic Ocean. This, the largest rt to reallocate one of the Earth's main urces, is a magnificent concept. But, ough the project would be tackled gradually every stage monitored, the diversion of up 0% of the water entering the Arctic Ocean ld influence ice cover, ocean salinity, and l and global climate patterns.

Soviet river diversion
Two immense schemes are planned. The European scheme will result in the transfer of up to 20 cu km of water per year (10 times the flow of water of the river Thames) from the Baltic river basins via the rivers Volga and Dnepr. The Siberian scheme aims to extract even more water from the Ob and Yenisey.

Fortunately the US has offered a lead by banning its use of the culprit materials, and the UN is now on the way to formulating an ozone convention for the entire community of nations.

Our growing demand for water

Water is an infinitely renewable resource. By the end of the century, we shall need between two and three times as much as in 1980. Through careful management, everybody can enjoy enough and to spare – though if we carry on as we do now, another 15 years could find some 30 nations in deep trouble.

Fortunately, however, we have plenty of options. The thirstiest sector, irrigation, accounts for 70 percent of all water use, producing 30 percent of our food from 15 percent of our croplands – and the irrigated expanse is projected to more than double by the year 2000. Irrigation is usually only 30 percent efficient, even in the US. But in California and Israel, farmers make three times better use of scarce water, through "trickle-drip" irrigation. This technique applies small amounts of water direct to the parts of the plant that need it most. This results in much more food being grown with only half as much water, and with reduced risk of salinization. Only about 5,000 sq km of cropland now receive the benefits of this Blue Revolution, or less than half of one percent of all irrigated lands. Plainly there is much scope for the future.

More perplexing yet equally urgent, is the political dimension. Of 200 major rivers, almost three-quarters are shared by two countries, and the rest by three or more. Already there are disputes between India and Bangladesh over the Ganges, and Brazil and Argentina over La Plata, among at least a dozen such conflicts – and we can expect there will be many more instances, unless we can rise to the challenge in a co-operative spirit.

A river basin represents a natural unit for management of a resource that recognizes no national boundaries. Fortunately we can draw on "blueprint experience" of success stories such as those of the Danube and Nile. In the case of the Nile, Sudan and Egypt work together to extract maximum benefit from a river that, despite its length, is small by its year-round volume. Despite some adverse repercussions of the Aswan Dam, Egypt sustains its agriculture and emergent industries through virtually 100 percent use of the Nile's river flow.

If irrigation agriculture now takes the largest share of water supplies, industry accounts for the fastest-growing share, while domestic demand is likewise soaring – an intersectoral source of conflict. The case of Israel is instructive, a country that already exploits 95 percent of its water resources, and that seeks to make more efficient use through recycling. A full one-fifth of water used by industry and households is recovered, mainly for irrigation. In 1962, the final amount of water used solely to generate $100 of manufactured goods was 20 cubic

Managing water

Projected global water demand is unlikely to exceed potential global supply for a long time, but its importance increases each year as agriculture and industry impose ever greater demands. By the year 2000, at least 30 countries will experience scarcity. Water management is the only way to boost both the quantity and quality of our long-term water resource. There are two central activities in water management: (1) the boosting of supply by investment in dams and other measures for controlling the water cycle; and (2), demand management, which ensures that water is targeted where it is needed.

Multiple uses of water
The damming of rivers can help satisfy a number of needs at once: it helps control flooding, provides the potential for generating hydropower, and stores water for a variety of uses, including irrigation. The resulting reservoirs represent a multi-purpose resource – with potential for aquaculture and leisure activities.

Aswan: the unexpected impacts
Egypt's Aswan Dam has brought the country obvious rewards, largely in the form of hydropower which meets half its electricity needs. It also brought freedom from seasonal flooding – but at considerable cost. Over 100 million tonnes of silt, clay, and sand, which once fertilized downstream fields during periods of flooding, are now silting up Lake Nasser, forcing increased imports of fertilizers. This lock-up of silt also hit downstream industries, starving Cairo brick-makers of a vital raw material, while the offshore sardine fisheries, which depended on the flow of nutrients from the Nile, were early casualties. The Nile Delta itself is in retreat. The Nile sediments that built the Delta were composed of 40% silt, 30% fine sand, and 30% clay. Simultaneously, problems of soil salinity and waterlogging have been accentuated. An FAO study concluded that 35% of Egypt's cultivated surface is afflicted by salinity and nearly 90% by waterlogging. To crown all of this, the water-based parasitic disease schistosomiasis (p. 121) has exploded among people living around Lake Nasser and along the new irrigation canals. Thorough impact studies could have lessened many such problems.

Computerized monitoring
The growing use of computers, now increasingly tied into satellite-based monitoring systems, provides nearly instantaneous information on pollution or flood hazards.

Drip-feed irrigation
Centre-pivot irrigation systems can bring desert areas into cultivation – but are expensive to build and often "quarry" supplies of underground water, which is water "capital" accumulated over many thousands of years. Drip-feed irrigation systems help conserve scarce water resources, but have other benefits too. They remove the threat of parasitic disease spread by irrigation canals, and reduce soil salinization – which claims over 1 million ha a year.

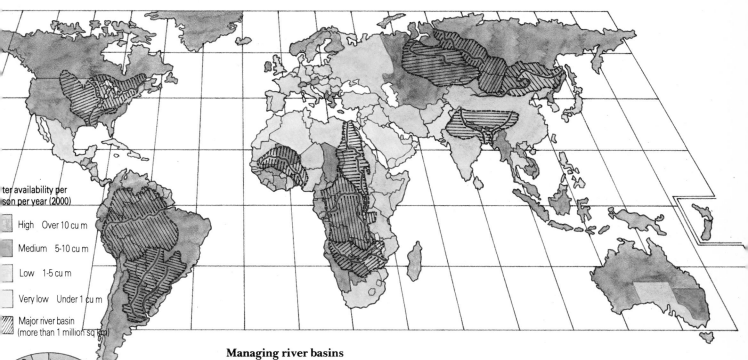

ter availability per
son per year (2000)

High   Over 10 cu m

Medium   5-10 cu m

Low   1-5 cu m

Very low   Under 1 cu m

Major river basin
(more than 1 million sq km)

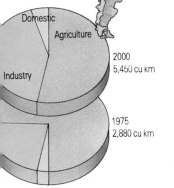

Domestic

Agriculture

Industry

2000
5,450 cu km

1975
2,880 cu km

Managing river basins

Population growth alone will double water demand in at least half the countries of the world by the end of the century. The map shows the projected per capita water availability for the year 2000. These pressures will aggravate disputes over river basins and other resources. River basins – the tracts of country drained by rivers and their tributaries – need to be treated as single units. Activities in one part of a basin can have far-reaching impacts. Thus it is vital that studies are carried out so that developers are fully aware of the repercussions of a particular project or activity. The river basin, like most natural resources, is often a shared resource and must be managed as a shared concern. This can be problematic when, as shown on the map, river basins cross political boundaries. With 148 of the 200 first-order river basins shared by two countries, the potential for conflict is enormous. On the other hand, the potential for collaboration is also there – and must be exploited.

ater demand trends

the year 2000, agriculture will still consume
e largest share (54%) of the world's water. But
e pie-charts, above, indicate that industrial
mand will be taking a much larger share of
e total water resource by the end of the
ntury – although we should remember that
dustry does not generally "consume" water in
e way that agriculture does.

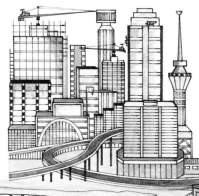

Urban plumbing
Leaking urban supply systems must be replaced. Water-using equipment can be redesigned to use water efficiently. Water treatment ensures water returned to the cycle is of a suitable quality.

Getting into hot water
Up to 80% of industrial water demand is for cooling. The bulk of this water can be returned to the cycle, but devastates river life if it is too warm. A new alternative involves using the hot water to boost the productivity of greenhouses or fishponds.

metres, in 1975 only a little over one-third as much, the difference being made up by re-use within industry and by transfer to agriculture.

The UN Water Decade
The International Drinking Water Supply and Sanitation Decade, 1981-90, encapsulates an impulse that we should take pride in – an effort to supply some of the most basic facilities to more than one billion people in the Third World. Ten years ago the very idea would have been laughable, not simply because of its grandiose scope but because few political leaders bothered with the issue. Yet the community of nations got together in 1978 to talk about taps and latrines, and to devise a plan to supply them on a grand scale.

The aim of the Decade
To bring about a real improvement in health through an integrated approach to sanitation and water management.

The cost has been estimated at $30-60 billion a ye one-third to come from development agencies the rest from Third World governments th selves. This works out at $80 million a day, to compared with $250 million that we spend cigarettes worldwide. So far as funding g however, the plan is turning out to be an insp hope, rather than a realistic goal.

But that is far from the whole story. The eff has spurred some Third World governments to t a close look at needs and options, and to draw their own plans. As a result, they are finding t health programmes based on new hospitals in c divert attention from real priorities such as cl water for every grass hut in rural areas – the z where most people live and where facilities are m

Clean water for all

The scope of the UN's Water and Sanitation Decade objectives is massive. The World Health Organization (the body co-ordinating the Decade) calculates that for complete success during the years 1981 to 1990, 1.8 billion additional people in the Third World will need to have access to clean water, and an additional 2.4 billion access to sanitation (these figures allow for projected population growth during the period). It is already clear that full implementation is a remote possibility. But this does not mean that the Decade will be a failure. More realistic targets set by participating individual countries are being reported to the WHO (see map, right). By 1983, from a sample of 71 developing countries, 26 had set Decade targets and 39 had partially set them. Actual plans had been drawn up by 18 countries and a further 32 countries were preparing them. The momentum of the Decade does now seem to be gathering speed. Actual expenditure on clean water and sanitation projects in 1982 was about $10 billion, but for the Decade to have any lasting impact, available funds must also be channelled into a variety of related areas (as indicated below).

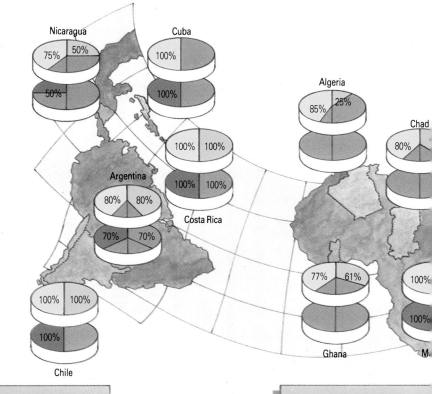

Funds
Secure and reliable funding is vital for the huge investments required by the Decade. This means a combination of local funds and those derived from central governments, overseas donors and banks. Between a third and a fifth of the investment will come from external sources.

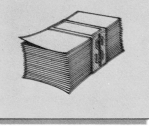

Policy
The policy aims to: "foster complementary water supply and sanitation projects; focus on under-served populations; generate replicable and self-sustaining programmes; develop socially relevant and affordable systems; and link supply and sanitation with other improvements."

Education
The supply of clean water and sanitation must be linked to environmental health education programmes.

Grass roots
Special attention must be paid to training people at the village level. Trainees should be selected from within the communities.

Local funding
Funds to be made available to provide care and health education at a local level, avoiding over-centralized facilities.

lacking. In other words, they will get a better return on each scarce "health dollar" if they invest it in preventive medicine, primarily in the form of plentiful supplies of clean water.

Equally important, water supplies may fail to serve as a magic elixir of health for all if they are not matched with grass-roots education in environmental hygiene. Equally important again, the best way to supply those many millions of taps and toilets is not to rely on water engineers alone, but to mobilize huge armies of village helpers in the form of health auxiliaries and other kinds of "barefoot doctors", i.e. basic-skills persons who penetrate to every last corner of the Third World – and who understand local people through their own local experience. In short, the medicine-oriented spirit of many public health officials should give way to a people-oriented approach (see also pp 194-5).

Thus the question to be asked about the Water Decade is not only "How shall we undertake this visionary effort?" Rather we should add "Why has it not been done before – what priorities have been mixed up?" In this sense, it is no great tragedy that funds have not been forthcoming. Perforce many Third World governments are adopting scaled-down plans, with emphasis on self-reliance by communities – precisely the factor without which those funds might not have achieved much.

So the splendid scheme is not a failure. In many countries, it has prompted an overhaul of health activities from top to bottom. As a measure of what can be done with limited means, the nation that is a

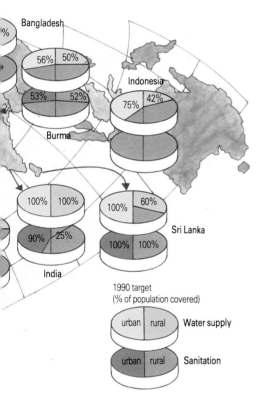

Bangladesh
56% 50%
53% 52%
Burma
Indonesia
75% 42%
100% 100%
100% 60%
90% 25%
100% 100%
Sri Lanka
India

1990 target
(% of population covered)
urban | rural Water supply
urban | rural Sanitation

Better health
Clean water supplies, improved sanitation, and relevant hygiene education produce a significant improvement in health.

Child mortality
Clean water could save many of the 8 million children who die each year of diarrhoeal diseases.

Stable population
Reduction in child mortality leads to more effective central planning and resource allocation, and a fall in birth rate.

Malawi – getting it right
Malawi, one of the poorest communities, is the only Third World country likely to achieve the objective of clean water for its entire population. Their target date is the year 2000. Two major factors have contributed to Malawi's success: village-based self-help schemes and the choice of appropriate technologies. For a large water project, a committee is formed involving local villagers and government officials, who provide technical support. The community which is to benefit from the project provides the labour and local organization. Prior to 1977, the government favoured borewells. These, however, were expensive to sink and required constant maintenance. Where sufficient ground water was available, gravity-piped water schemes were found to be a more suitable alternative. Malawi is still in the process of looking for the perfect pump and so far more than 200 designs have been tested.

leader in the field is Malawi, one of the poorest communities of all, with a GNP per head of $200 – but with the right priorities.

Towards a conserver society

While reviewing energy, water, and other elements, we have seen how we need to make better use of our resources. We have enough and to spare, provided we are less profligate in our ways. Fortunately, there is massive scope for us to improve. The challenge lies not so much with "technical fixes", but with our approach to our world around us. Hitherto we have engaged in something of a Wild West economy, supposing that there are always pastures new beyond the horizon. Now we know there are no new horizons to explore and exploit: our planet is a closed ecosystem, and we are running up against the boundaries of our biosphere. So a more appropriate image is Earth as a spaceship, where most materials have to be recycled. For us, "moving on" will be a case of leaving behind the throwaway society, and advancing to a conserver society.

To qualify as citizens of a conserver society, we must shift entrenched attitudes and thinking. We need to recognize that there is rarely such a thing as "waste": rather there are materials that sometimes end up in the wrong place.

The transition has already begun. The European steel industry re-uses scrap metal with energy savings as high as 50%; in the case of copper, 90%; and of aluminium, 95%. Recycling a glass container saves only 8%; but in parts of the US, a citizen buying a bottle of soda or beer now pays a deposit against return of the empty bottle. If all drinks containers in the US were to be re-used, the annual savings would amount to 0.5 million tonnes of glass – plus almost 50 million barrels of oil used in production processes. In Japan, OPEC spurred an increase in recycling of raw materials from 16% to 48% in just five years ("this year's Toyota is last year's Ford"). In Norway, the price of a new car now includes a disposal-cost item of about $100, redeemable when the junked car is turned in at an approved receiving centre. Major new businesses are emerging to exploit waste chemicals and oil. The thrifty Chinese claim they re-use 2.5 million tonnes of scrap iron each year, and at least one million tonnes of waste paper.

All this recycling also helps with the problem of waste disposal. An average American generates about one tonne of waste each year. To get rid of this garbage, the US uses almost 15,000 landfills and other sites – an area of some 200,000 hectares.

In the main, the conserver society depends on the commitment of individuals. But they can be inspired by government incentives and penalties – which should apply at least as strongly to industry and other commercial interests. Governments can also foster the anti-waste campaign by initiatives to eliminate "concealed waste", even by helping to make planned obsolescence obsolete.

Waste into wealth

Every living organism uses energy to process raw materials and, in doing so, it often produces some form of waste. In natural systems, such wastes are soon exploited by other organisms, in a perpetual cycle of re-use. Human communities process materials on a grand scale, using enormous quantities of energy and other resources in doing so. We also produce mountains of waste, the bulk of which passes through the system just once. The case studies, far right, illustrate the current situation for some materials which are recycled, at least in part. In many Third World countries, fortunately, a high proportion of many waste materials is re-used. But there is a darker side to the picture: on the outskirts of Cairo, for example, tens of thousands of people sort through the city's waste in conditions of indescribable squalor, while in India scrap collectors are killed or maimed during their hunt for spent cartridge cases on army-firing ranges. Some developing countries are trying to work out ways in which they can improve the working conditions of their recyclers. As for the developed countries, although the "throwaway society" still flourishes, new recycling industries are emerging, generating new employment and boosting energy efficiency.

Sorting waste for re-use

The key to material recovery and recyling is separation, whether performed by "rubbish sifters" (*zabbaleen*) or by the latest automatic sorting equipment. Japan, which now recycles about 10% of its municipal waste, provides many examples. Ueda City pays an entrepreneur a portion of the money saved when s/he recycles wastes which would otherwise have been landfilled. Residents sort the material into combustible and non-combustible fractions. Glass is removed by hand, ferrous metal by magnet.

Jobs from junk

Derelict cars, battered and rusting, can be recycled, but the increasing use of "unitary construction" means that they cannot easily be separated. Now such organizations as the Intermediate Technology Development Group (UK) are devising methods for recovering the scrap in cars profitably. In developing countries, oxy-acetylene torches are often too expensive, so simple, robust cutting methods are being developed. The "entry" cost: a one-week training course and tools costing no more than $60 per person.

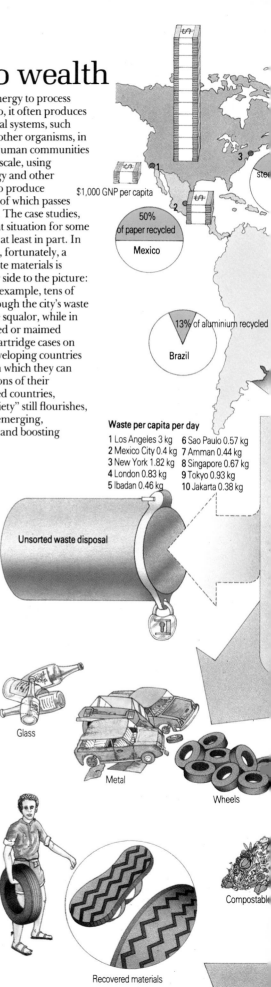

$1,000 GNP per capita

50% of paper recycled
Mexico

13% of aluminium recycled
Brazil

Waste per capita per day

1 Los Angeles 3 kg	6 Sao Paulo 0.57 kg
2 Mexico City 0.4 kg	7 Amman 0.44 kg
3 New York 1.82 kg	8 Singapore 0.67 kg
4 London 0.83 kg	9 Tokyo 0.93 kg
5 Ibadan 0.46 kg	10 Jakarta 0.38 kg

Unsorted waste disposal

Glass

Metal

Wheels

Compostable

Recovered materials

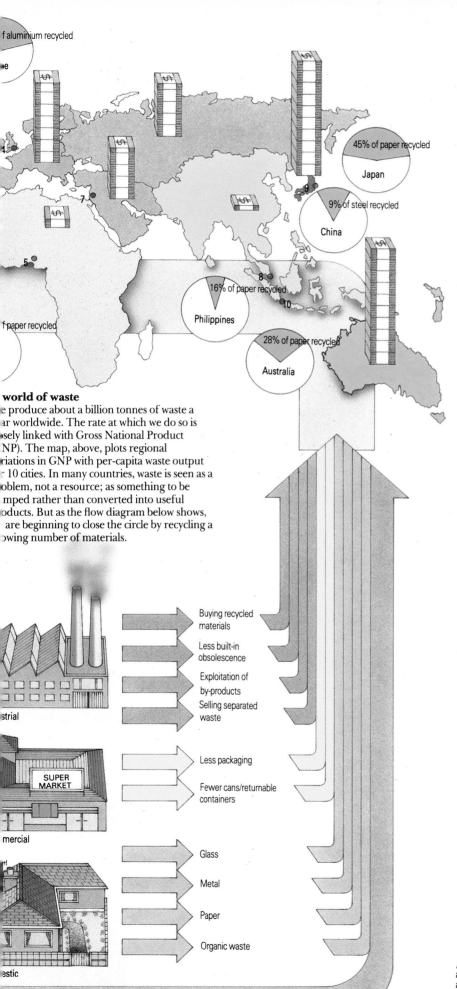

aluminium recycled

45% of paper recycled

Japan

9% of steel recycled

China

16% of paper recycled

Philippines

28% of paper recycled

Australia

paper recycled

world of waste

e produce about a billion tonnes of waste a
ar worldwide. The rate at which we do so is
sely linked with Gross National Product
NP). The map, above, plots regional
riations in GNP with per-capita waste output
r 10 cities. In many countries, waste is seen as a
oblem, not a resource; as something to be
mped rather than converted into useful
oducts. But as the flow diagram below shows,
are beginning to close the circle by recycling a
owing number of materials.

Buying recycled
materials

Less built-in
obsolescence

Exploitation of
by-products

Selling separated
waste

strial

SUPER
MARKET

Less packaging

Fewer cans/returnable
containers

mercial

Glass

Metal

Paper

Organic waste

estic

Recycling iron

The world steel industry uses scrap for about
45% of its iron requirements, with some
countries reaching 60-75%. The world recession
has hit the scrap industry hard, but new
technologies are increasing the demand for
scrap. The most buoyant sector of the US steel
industry, for example, uses the "minimill",
which is based on electric-arc furnaces and the
use of scrap. The US dominates the world
ferrous scrap market.

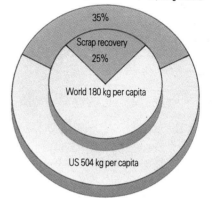

Annual steel consumption and scrap recycling 1980-2

35%

Scrap recovery

25%

World 180 kg per capita

US 504 kg per capita

Recycling paper

Only 25% of the world's paper is currently
recycled, although there is no good technical or
economic reason why this recycling rate should
not be doubled by the year 2000. Recycling half
of the world's paper consumption would meet
almost 75% of new paper demand – and would
release 8 million ha of forest from paper
production. Fibre-rich countries, such as Canada
and Sweden, are not in the front-rank of paper
recyclers. Recycling rates are much higher in
such fibre-poor countries as Japan (45%),
Mexico (50%), and the Netherlands (43%).

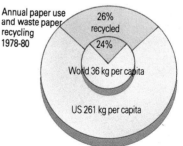

Annual paper use
and waste paper
recycling
1978-80

26%
recycled

24%

World 36 kg per capita

US 261 kg per capita

Recycling aluminium

Throw away an aluminium soft-drink container
and you throw away the energy equivalent of
half a can of gasoline. It is estimated that 80% of
all aluminium used could be recycled, but less
than 30% of world production comes from scrap.
In 1980, aluminium scrap moving across
national boundaries totalled 800,000 tonnes
(representing over 5% of world production), a
trade valued at $600 million. Over half the
aluminium cans used in the US are now
recycled, and even more dramatic results will be
possible as deposits are charged on cans.

Annual
aluminium use
and recycling
1981

Scrap recovery

32%

28%

World 3 kg per capita

US 25 kg per capita

EVOLUTION

Introduced by Paul Ehrlich

Professor of Population Studies, Stanford University

The human population has reached almost five billion people by, in essence, "burning its capital"–destroying and dispersing a one-time bonanza of fossil fuels, minerals, deep soils, water, and biological diversity. It is the loss of biological diversity that may prove the most serious; certainly it is the most irreversible. *Homo sapiens* depends on the genetic variety present in the many millions of species and billions of their populations for a huge range of services, many of them absolutely essential to the support of civilization.

We are causing some loss of genetic diversity directly, by wiping out or severely over-harvesting certain species and populations, from rhinoceroses, elephants, spotted cats, and whales to orchids and cacti. But the major danger comes indirectly, from habitat destruction. Humanity is paving over, ploughing under, chopping down, damming, poisoning, and otherwise ruining habitats at a truly horrifying rate. It is primarily this that threatens the mountain gorilla, the California condor, and a host of lesser known organisms. The destruction of tropical forests alone could easily reduce the organic diversity of our planet by 50 percent in the next few decades.

Attempts are being made to arrest the decay of Earth's organic diversity: the Convention on International Trade in Endangered Species has delayed the extermination of some prominent species and, at least on paper, a world system of "Biosphere Reserves" is being organized. But our efforts may be too little and too late. It is one thing to draw lines on maps around areas of tropical forest and declare them protected, quite another to find the will and resources to preserve them in perpetuity.

Even today, too much attention is focused on the preservation of *species*, whereas the loss of genetic diversity *within* species is probably a more immediate and vital issue. The biochemical make-up of plants, for instance, is notoriously variable geographically–and plant chemicals have provided a great many of society's medicines and industrial products. By the time species are recognized as endangered, their utility to human beings is often greatly compromised: populations are too small to be significant in ecosystems, gene pools are too depleted to permit successful domestication, and useful characteristics are lost.

What *should* be done is clear. In developed nations, disturbance of any more land should be forbidden, and creation of exotic monocultures, be they golf courses, wheat fields, or tree plantations, restrained everywhere. Priority should be given to making the already huge areas occupied by humanity more hospitable to other organisms, and above all, to arresting the steady flux of poisons into the air and water, especially acid rain. Programmes to protect and re-establish relatively natural ecosystems are doomed to failure while poisons remain unchecked.

The problem is vastly more serious in the less developed nations, where raw population pressure and poverty make the continued destruction of natural systems seem inevitable. Poor nations, like poor people, must look always to their immediate needs. It is only by finding ways to help them provide for those needs that the rich nations can support conservation in the poor nations, and thus (in the long run) save themselves–for human survival is intertwined with the survival of genetic diversity, and thus with the fate of every natural system.

THE EVOLUTIONARY POTENTIAL

The first flickerings of life emerged 3.6 billion years ago, shortly after the planet coalesced from a swirling mass of gases into solid state. From a primeval impulse of DNA, the "building block" of life, there has evolved a steadily expanding stream of life-forms, swelling to a flood as species have become ever-more numerous and diverse. The creative flow has been far from constant, however. It got off to a slow start, and as recently as the late Permian era 225 million years ago, there were no more than 350,000 species or so – mostly marine creatures. But thereafter the spread of life on to land led to an outburst of creativity that has ultimately produced many millions of species.

Not that the prehistoric parade has merely grown larger. Certain categories have emerged to dominate from time to time, then have been relegated to the sidelines. Our modern world is sometimes considered as primarily a world of mammals. But mammals, which constitute only one in a thousand of today's community, are relative newcomers. They did not reach prominence until the end of a reptilian era that lasted for 160 million years.

The evolutionary process has culminated in today's array of life, a vast resource of material on which natural selection can work to generate still more abundant and complex manifestations of life. Our present life pool represents but a small part of the potential panoply of life that will steadily develop if *Homo sapiens*, a newly dominant species, allows the process to persist with the creative capacity that has been at work virtually since the beginning of life.

Peering into the dim past, then, we can discern a procession of ever-changing life-forms, new ones appearing as old ones fade from the scene. The average duration of a species has been only about five million years, which means that of the half billion or so species that have ever lived, at least 98 percent have disappeared.

As we gaze on the life pool of today, let us reflect that it does not amount to a mere conglomeration of species that go their separate ways. They depend on each other for multiple services. Plants, for example, supply more than food for plant eaters. They also help to maintain the mix of gases in our atmosphere – oxygen, nitrogen, carbon dioxide, and so forth – that support all forms of life. Even the lowliest manifestations of life, bacteria, serve to recycle nutrients that keep plants going. In short, the life pool is much more than the sum of its parts.

The life pool

All life is one. This is not a cliché, but a biological reality. Over 3.6 billion years, a teeming variety of life-forms has evolved, yet in every living cell there are common features of nucleic acids that encode inheritance, and adenosine triphosphate that provides energy. In every living organism, hormones and similar compounds carry vital chemical messages. In turn, organisms are linked together in intricate ecosystems. What happens to one can affect all: our present biosphere has evolved only after photosynthesis in early algae and plants began to release essential oxygen into the atmosphere. Evolution produces vast diversity, yet it links all living forms in a single process.

We, as members of the species *Homo sapiens*, are the first life-forms to be able to modify the evolutionary process, yet we do so largely in ignorance and by accident. We take small account of the intricate food chains that maintain both species and ecological harmony, or of the rich store of genetic information that species represent. Indeed, scientists have classified not more than 10% of the planet's organisms (see below).

The biosystem is a library of survival strategies; it makes up an entire literature, a language, and a tradition, every unique part of which may bear upon any other. Built up over billions of years of selection and extinction, it is not to be tampered with lightly.

Lampre*
Sea squirts
Echinoderms

Insects

Centipedes
Millipedes

Crustaceans

Spiders:
scorpions

Segmented worms

Squid: octopus

Bivalves: molluscs

Single-shell
molluscs

Brachiopods

Flat worms

Jellyfish: corals

Spong

Si
an

Undiscovered species
3-8 million
(mostly invertebrates)

Known species
c.1.7 million

A census of species
Science has identified 1.5 million species of animals and 300,000 of plants. But millions of others remain unclassified – even mammal species, such as bats. Each year too, 20 new species of reptiles are found. Exploration is adding continuously to the numbers classified.

Invertebrates
1,400,000
(insects 1,000,000)

Vertebrates 4

Vascular plants
250,000

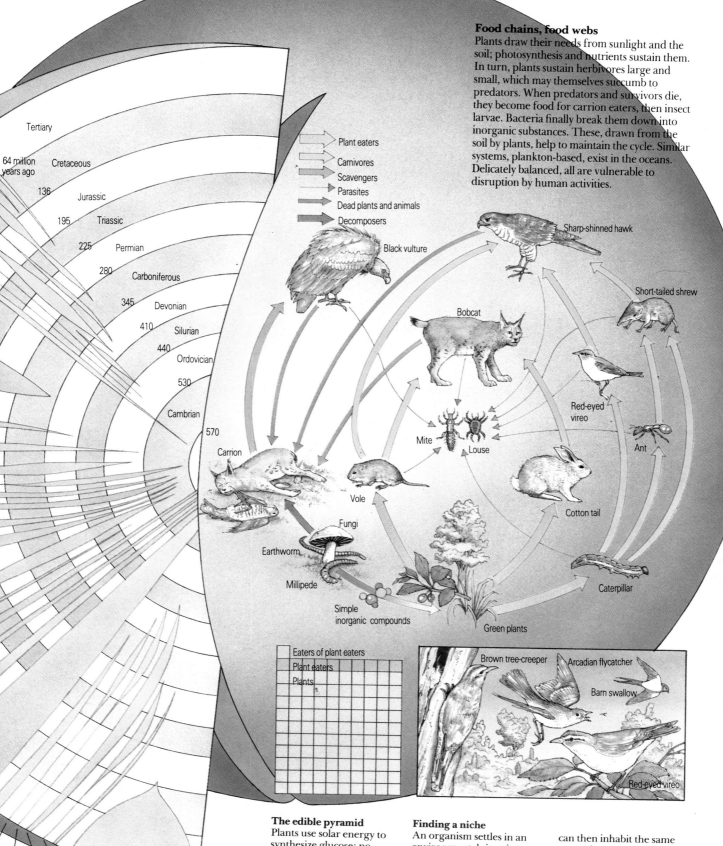

Tertiary

64 million
years ago

Cretaceous

136

Jurassic

195

Triassic

225

Permian

280

Carboniferous

345

Devonian

410

Silurian

440

Ordovician

530

Cambrian

570

Plant eaters
Carnivores
Scavengers
Parasites
Dead plants and animals
Decomposers

Black vulture

Sharp-shinned hawk

Short-tailed shrew

Bobcat

Red-eyed
vireo

Mite

Louse

Ant

Carrion

Vole

Cotton tail

Fungi

Earthworm

Millipede

Caterpillar

Simple
inorganic compounds

Green plants

Eaters of plant eaters
Plant eaters
Plants

Brown tree-creeper

Arcadian flycatcher

Barn swallow

Red-eyed vireo

Cycads

Conifers

Flowering plants

b mosses

Ferns

Food chains, food webs

Plants draw their needs from sunlight and the
soil; photosynthesis and nutrients sustain them.
In turn, plants sustain herbivores large and
small, which may themselves succumb to
predators. When predators and survivors die,
they become food for carrion eaters, then insect
larvae. Bacteria finally break them down into
inorganic substances. These, drawn from the
soil by plants, help to maintain the cycle. Similar
systems, plankton-based, exist in the oceans.
Delicately balanced, all are vulnerable to
disruption by human activities.

The edible pyramid

Plants use solar energy to
synthesize glucose: no
animal can do this. Plants
provide 10 of the amino
acids essential to animal
survival. Without
photosynthesis, the life we
know could not exist. All
over the planet, on land
and sea, plants act as the
base of every food chain.

Finding a niche

An organism settles in an
environmental situation, or
ecological niche, which suits
its particular adaptations.
Modified over time, these
adaptations confirm it in its
niche: new species are
formed by divergence from
previous norms. Many
individuals, all pursuing
their own survival strategy,
can then inhabit the same
general environment. Thus
birds in one tree may not
seek the same food; or – by
catching insects on the
leaves, under the bark, or
on the wing – they may seek
the same food, but in
different ways.

It is a single unifying phenomenon of our planet Earth – the only planet known to feature the genetic code of life, DNA.

The natural habitat

Our blue planet, the only planet known to support any spark of life, supports it in extraordinary abundance and variety. From the tallest mountain peak to the deepest ocean trench, from rainless desert to dripping rainforest, there is scarcely a corner of the Earth's surface which does not reveal some variation on life's theme. Indeed, the diversity of our evolutionary resource defies imagination.

Clearly, this evolutionary resource is anything but uniform. Life's most basic impulses send it racing down endlessly branching paths. Wherever we go, we encounter environmental variety. Each woodland, each stretch of open savannah, each wetland or montane ecosystem, has its own distinctive communities of plants and animals. But life has evolved clear strategies to meet such environmental challenges – and we see the results in recognizable associations such as the "spruce-moose" biome of North America's boreal forests.

Moreover, just as environments change, so life strategies are themselves in constant flux, developing ever-new variations on the vital theme. The key factors which help shape the patterns of life, and particularly vegetation patterns, include temperature and rainfall, together with two closely connected factors – latitude and altitude.

Once we know how hot or wet an environment is, or how cold and dry, and provided we know its location, we can make a fair guess about what forms of plant life are likely to predominate. Of course, other factors, such as soil type and topography, can also have an important influence. But, as a general rule, we know that at the Equator we shall find year-round warmth and moisture, and we shall expect to encounter evergreen rainforest.

As we move towards the tropics, rainfall becomes more seasonal, and we expect to see deciduous trees able to counter periodic drought. As the average rainfall decreases, we encounter increasingly open woodland, giving way to bush and then grassy plains. Finally, after moving through various forms of scrub, we find continental deserts. Other kinds of desert are found in unlikely places. The coastal deserts of Chile and Namibia, for example, are formed where cold offshore currents cool the air and prevent it rising high enough to produce rain.

Moving out from the tropics towards the poles, we find these vegetation patterns echoed by different forest formations and different types of grassland. The conditions are colder and winter becomes a force to be reckoned with. We encounter communities which are less fecund and varied than their tropical counterparts. Here, life strategies branch out from distinctive adaptations in response to seasonal change: caribou migrate to less harsh areas, birds head for distant horizons, while bears

Life strategies

Combinations of warmth and rainfall generate diverse life strategies. To portray these life strategies, biologists use an idealized or super-continent (right). It balloons to the north, reflecting the great land masses of Eurasia and North America. It tapers towards the Equator, and extends like a tear-drop into the southern hemisphere, to represent the shape of southern Africa and South America.

Compare this super-continent with a real-world map. We can see that if Central America were to bulge out along the Tropic of Cancer, instead of almost dwindling away, we would have another vast desert corresponding to the Sahara; and if Africa bulged out along the Equator, we could expect a rainforest of Amazonian proportions.

Life strategies are broadly classified into large domains, known as biomes. These biomes reflect basic bio-communities which have evolved mainly in response to local variations in climate and topography.

Freshwater ecosystems

From river-source to sea, many kinds of life strategies are invoked here. When the river is narrow and its current fast, plants cannot survive and most fish cannot thrive. When the river bed is less steep, plants root in the mud which lies in sheltered spots near the river banks. The current is still fast, but fish like trout or minnow can breed here. Further downstream, where the banks slope more gently, the water is turbid, and the bed is full of sand and gravel, bream flourish. Finally, in the more salty and muddy estuarine region, flounder and smelt predominate, while salmon pass through on their spawning and feeding migrations.

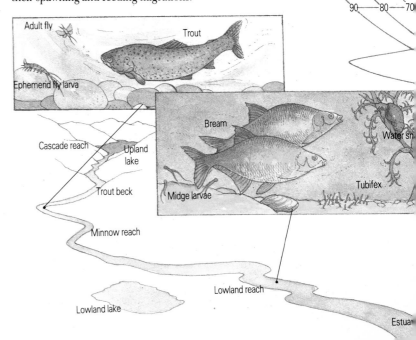

Boreal forest
The boreal forest, accounting for 11% of the super-continent, fringes the northern sub-polar regions. Moose browse on spruce and birch, falling prey in turn to the timber wolf.

Temperate forest
Growing as tall as their boreal counterparts, the trees of the temperate forest cover 9% of the super-continent. They comprise a mixture of deciduous and coniferous trees, and shelter a bewildering array of insects, birds, and animals.

Savannah
Herbivores in their millions, such as the wildebeest and zebra, are found on open savannah, which covers another 11% of the super-continent—their predators include the lion, cheetah, and hyena.

Desert
Deserts cover almost one-quarter of the land surface (semi-desert 13%, hot desert 8%, and cold and coastal deserts, 2%). The cacti, roadrunner, and chuckwalla lizard, above, are found in the hot deserts of North America.

Tropical forest
Nearly a fifth of the super-continent is covered by tropical forests. Tropical deciduous forest covers 6%, while rainforests account for 13%. Rainforests follow the most vital life strategies, utilizing the abundant warmth and rainfall.

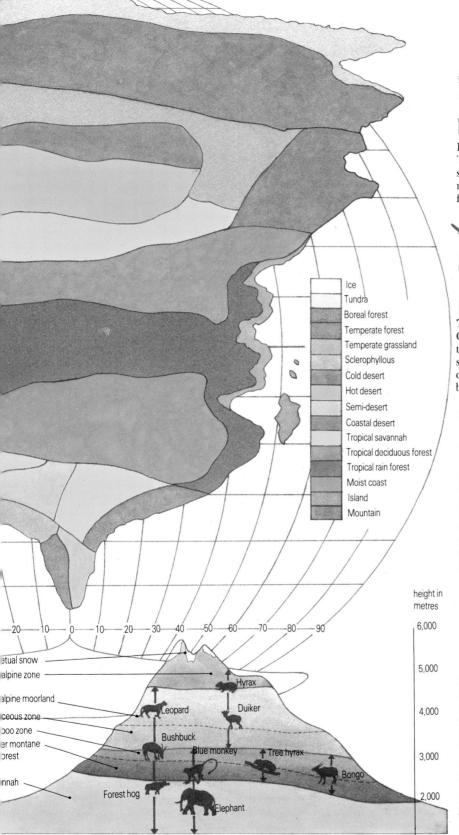

Ice
Tundra
Boreal forest
Temperate forest
Temperate grassland
Sclerophyllous
Cold desert
Hot desert
Semi-desert
Coastal desert
Tropical savannah
Tropical deciduous forest
Tropical rain forest
Moist coast
Island
Mountain

height in metres

-20 -10 0 10 20 30 40 50 60 70 80 90

6,000

5,000

4,000

3,000

2,000

perpetual snow
alpine zone
alpine moorland
ericaceous zone
bamboo zone
upper montane
forest
savannah

Hyrax
Duiker
Leopard
Bushbuck
Blue monkey
Tree hyrax
Bongo
Forest hog
Elephant

Montane ecosystem
In the montane ecosystems of Africa, there is a complex succession of vegetation zones between the savannah, at the lowest level, and the permanent snowfields which cap such mountains as Mount Kenya, Mount

Kilimanjaro, and the Mountains of the Moon. Moving up through the haunts of the elephant, forest hog, blue monkey, and bushbuck, we find far fewer animals as the snow comes closer.

and squirrels go underground. In some areas of the world we can move through a bewildering succession of life strategies within a surprisingly short distance, for example, as we climb through a montane ecosystem.

Shaping our food base

Until 10,000 years ago, our ancestors had little effect on the plants and animals around them. Then came a quantum leap with more profound implications than any during the previous one million years, both for humankind and for a growing spectrum of once wild species. Often accidentally, our ancestors found ways to domesticate a few animals and plants, entering into an evolutionary partnership with selected species. No other living creature has accomplished this much control over the evolutionary process, and it has been an advance to alter the face of the Earth.

The first essential step occurred when our ancestors concentrated on those forms of wild grasses – cereals – that promised to yield most food. They planted varieties with larger grains, with shorter growing seasons, and with other attributes that would serve their needs. They began to apply selection pressures that hitherto had remained the domain of "natural" evolution. Before long, they had developed types of wheat, for example, whose seed heads did not "shatter" and drop their seeds to the ground when ripe: these early breeders preferred to keep the seeds for their own use. This meant that without human help, wheat plants could no longer propagate themselves.

A similar pattern was repeated with the animals, such as sheep and cattle. Selected for their docility among other traits, domesticated strains must soon have lost their capacity to survive on their own. Not only tamed by humans, but weighed down with flesh or milk, today's cattle breeds would be hard put to survive in the wild.

As one domestication followed another, our ancestors assembled a group of species that supplied them with a growing range of benefits. From these early successes in domestication, there evolved the phenomenon of full-scale agriculture. Today, a considerable proportion of the Earth's surface is devoted to staple crops or to huge herds of livestock. As a result of this "globalization" of basic food sources, a growing proportion of the world's population feeds from a common bowl.

Curiously enough, our ancestors contented themselves with just a handful of domesticates. Although hunter-gatherers had exploited hundreds of plants and dozens of animals, these early agriculturalists confined their attentions mainly to a total of less than 50 species. These basic food sources still meet our needs today. Thirty crops supply 95 percent of our nutrition, and a mere eight, led by wheat, maize, and rice, provide three-quarters of our diets. Our meat and milk come from a still smaller range of species. Thus we practise an agriculture that is, in

Partners in evolution

Homo sapiens has derived great benefit from a special partnership with Earth's plant and animal species. Intensive farming of a minority of species has released a large proportion of humankind for work other than food-growing, and thousand-fold increases in population have become possible.

Purposeful crossbreeding to produce improved varieties is a modern development. Previously, agriculturalists would select the more productive species and leave evolution to work its own advances by natural crossbreeding. As a result, the earliest domestications occurred in the areas of greatest diversity shown on the world map, right, where the probability of "crosses" leading to improved varieties was greatest. The areas are not rigidly defined; some species were being domesticated at the same time though in different places.

Animal farm

As with crop plants, humankind has evolved a special partnership with animals: a small number of highly efficient animals provides all our needs. Dairy cows can yield up to 4,800 litres per lactation with current farming methods. They are fed high-energy concentrates by computer-controlled feeders. The price of this efficient production is the near-total dependence of such animals on their keepers.

No
Tu

Meso Americ
Maize
Tomato
Cassava
Sweet potato
Turkey

Areas of origin:
domestic plants and

Maize: dispersal

Travelling partners
Our most valued and adaptable crops have travelled with us in early migrations, invasions, explorations, and to colonial settlements. Som have spread to the far corners of the Earth. Others, such as coffee, no dominate lands far from their point of origin. The map shows the peregrinations of corn and wheat

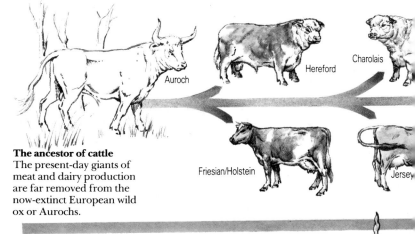

The ancestor of cattle
The present-day giants of meat and dairy production are far removed from the now-extinct European wild ox or Aurochs.

Auroch   Hereford   Charolais

Friesian/Holstein   Jersey

The corn story

Originally allowed to grow in fields of primitive corn because it enhanced the yield, the wild Mexican grass Teosinte became the ancestor of modern corn. The diagrams, right, which are based on modern breeding experiments, reveal how the hard outer casing of the Teosinte "spike" is gradually made softer. Eventually, we arrive at the giant modern variety (far right), drawn to scale – its kernel fruit totally exposed. Without human intervention to remove and plant its kernels, modern corn would become extinct in a few generations: the seedlings would be so densely clustered that they would compete among themselves for water, soil, and nutrients, and fail to reach reproductive size.

Teosinte

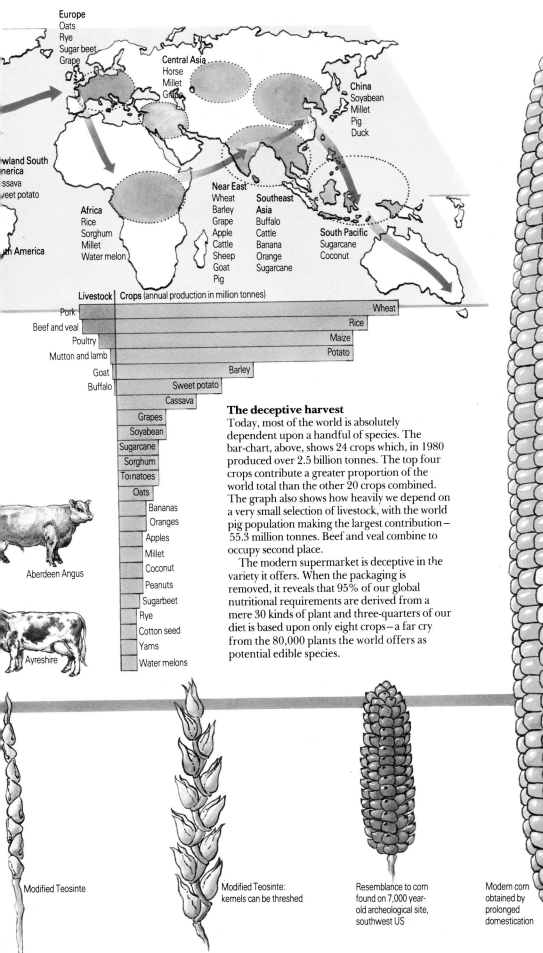

Europe
Oats
Rye
Sugar beet
Grape

Central Asia
Horse
Millet
Grape

China
Soyabean
Millet
Pig
Duck

Lowland South America
Cassava
Sweet potato

South America

Africa
Rice
Sorghum
Millet
Water melon

Near East
Wheat
Barley
Grape
Apple
Cattle
Sheep
Goat
Pig

Southeast Asia
Buffalo
Cattle
Banana
Orange
Sugarcane

South Pacific
Sugarcane
Coconut

Livestock | Crops (annual production in million tonnes)

Pork
Beef and veal
Poultry
Mutton and lamb
Goat
Buffalo

Wheat
Rice
Maize
Potato
Barley
Sweet potato
Cassava
Grapes
Soyabean
Sugarcane
Sorghum
Tomatoes
Oats
Bananas
Oranges
Apples
Millet
Coconut
Peanuts
Sugarbeet
Rye
Cotton seed
Yams
Water melons

Aberdeen Angus

Ayreshire

The deceptive harvest

Today, most of the world is absolutely dependent upon a handful of species. The bar-chart, above, shows 24 crops which, in 1980 produced over 2.5 billion tonnes. The top four crops contribute a greater proportion of the world total than the other 20 crops combined. The graph also shows how heavily we depend on a very small selection of livestock, with the world pig population making the largest contribution – 55.3 million tonnes. Beef and veal combine to occupy second place.

The modern supermarket is deceptive in the variety it offers. When the packaging is removed, it reveals that 95% of our global nutritional requirements are derived from a mere 30 kinds of plant and three-quarters of our diet is based upon only eight crops – a far cry from the 80,000 plants the world offers as potential edible species.

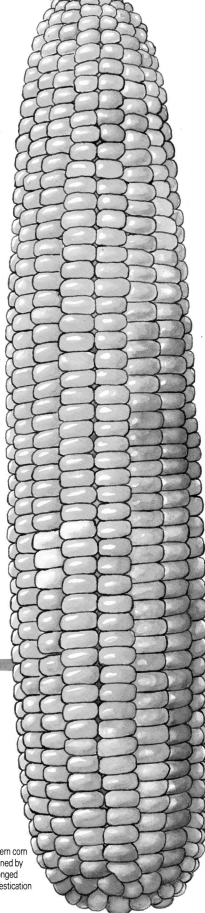

Modified Teosinte

Modified Teosinte: kernels can be threshed

Resemblance to corn found on 7,000 year-old archeological site, southwest US

Modern corn obtained by prolonged domestication

terms of its array of sources, not much more than a Neolithic agriculture. What prospects could lie ahead of us if we were to develop more of these evolutionary partnerships, realizing more of the potential of our genetic resources?

Tapping diversity

Diversity is the hallmark of life on Earth, whether we compare different species, races, and populations within a species, or different individuals within a population. Just as the innumerable species that make up the life stream are bewilderingly diverse to the eye, so even outwardly identical organisms prove to be astonishingly diverse if we concentrate our gaze on the level of the gene.

One individual organism may have thousands of genes, each gene influencing some inherited trait such as height, weight, rate of growth, or resistance to disease. Even if the individuals within a species are counted in millions or billions, such statistics shrink in scale when compared with the total number of potential genetic permutations those individuals could produce. And it is this diversity, passed on by genes, which holds the key to a species' ability to adapt so readily in response to environmental pressures. Naturally, only a tiny fraction of this genetic potential is ever expressed, since most organisms die before they can reproduce. Even so, this genetic potential is one of our world's most valuable resources.

Jojoba
Long considered a des[...] weed, jojoba produces [...] wax which retails to Ja[...] for $3,000 a barrel as [...] substitute for sperm w[...] oil. As jojoba plantatio[...] come "on stream", the [...] should fall steeply.

The genetic resource

Our genetic resources represent an extraordinarily well-stocked library. Each species can be seen as a single book on one of an unknown number of shelves, each page a slice of its gene pool.

So far, we have made surprisingly little use of this library, concentrating on a few volumes of immediate interest. Yet even these few volumes have provided us with uncounted benefits, some of which are described here.

Tragically, this vast, valuable, and irreplaceable gene library is being vandalized. Complete volumes, indeed entire shelves, are being lost in bouts of habitat destruction, and key sections of the library are now in danger of being gutted. We are losing genetic information and materials whose value we can only guess at.

We must conserve and exploit this unique genetic resource. Once its value is fully recognized, its beneficiaries will be more likely to secure its future.

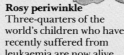

Rosy periwinkle
Three-quarters of the world's children who have recently suffered from leukaemia are now alive due to properties discovered in the rosy periwinkle plant.

Tilapia
Tilapia fish may soon usurp carp as the choice of the world's fish farms. The East African tilapia fish, with 164 species in Lake Malawi alone, converts food to flesh faster than most other fish and is increasingly used in aquaculture projects.

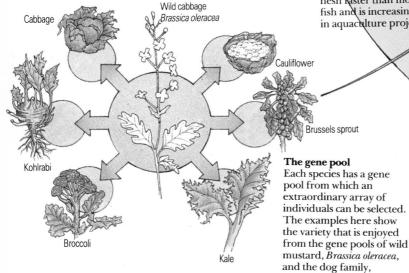

Wild cabbage
Brassica oleracea

Cabbage

Cauliflower

Brussels sprout

Kohlrabi

Broccoli

Kale

The gene pool
Each species has a gene pool from which an extraordinary array of individuals can be selected. The examples here show the variety that is enjoyed from the gene pools of wild mustard, *Brassica oleracea*, and the dog family, Canidae. If all but pedigree greyhounds disappeared from the Earth, we could say that "the dog" had been conserved – but imagine the loss of genetic variety.

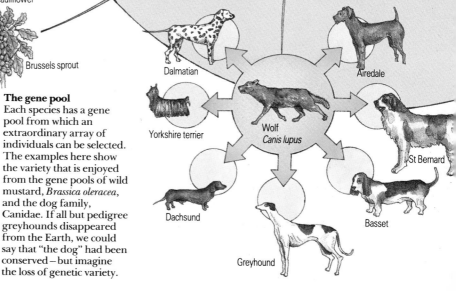

Dalmatian

Airedale

Yorkshire terrier

Wolf
Canis lupus

St Bernard

Dachsund

Basset

Greyhound

ayule

ayule, another wild
ub, grows in areas with
t rainfall and produces
tural rubber. The
ub's genetic diversity is
reme, thus an
eptionally important
urce.

Every day, and almost always unconsciously, we use products whose very availability and usefulness reflect that genetic wealth. Our staple food crops achieve marvels of productivity every year, not simply because we have developed new fertilizers and pesticides, but because of genetic improvements achieved by the world's crop breeders.

Similar advances, with similar roots, are achieved every day in medicine. Every time we buy a drug or other pharmaceutical, there is almost a 50:50 chance that we can thank the genetic resources of a wild species for its efficacy. The value of medicinal products derived from such sources now approaches $40 billion every year. For example, if you had leukaemia as a child in 1960, or if you were suffering from Hodgkin's disease or a number of other cancers, you had a one-in-five chance of long-term survival. Today, thanks to two drugs developed from the rosy periwinkle, a tropical forest plant, you would have a four-in-five chance.

Similarly, industry processes and packages this genetic wealth. Every time we polish the furniture, pull on our jogging shoes, or hit a golf ball, walk across a carpet or ride high in a jet, we can thank genetic resources that in one way or another contribute to such products.

But while today's benefits are astonishing enough, they represent the tip of an iceberg. So far, scientists have taken only a preliminary look at some 10 percent of the 250,000 plant species, a considerable

Molluscs

Molluscs are first-rate pollution monitors. Other marine organisms may prove useful for viral research.

Sharks

any species of shark are proving valuable for research into liver ailments and certain cancers.

Value of the wild

Every hour of every day, a growing number of plants and animals unwittingly underpin and improve the quality of our lives. A single gene from Ethiopia protects California's barley crop, worth $150 million a year, against yellow dwarf disease. Aspirin, probably the world's most widely used drug, has been developed from a chemical blueprint supplied by willow bark.

There are many other examples. The widely used contraceptive pill stems from the discovery of diosgenin in wild Mexican yams. Yet we are destroying this wealth as fast as it is being discovered. The pollution of the Great Lakes of Africa, for example, which contain as many as 400 tilapia fish species, could destroy this wild gene pool and reduce our chances of breeding superior fish. Similarly, despite their value to haemophilia research, the ungainly Florida manatee has been reduced in number to a mere 850. Perhaps worst of all, is the certain knowledge that we are destroying species even before their full value has been estimated.

madillos

e only animal known to
tract leprosy, the
nadillo helps to prepare
ccine for all sufferers.

Manatees

The Florida manatee has slow-clotting blood. This characteristic has led to new insights in the area of haemophilia research.

netic engineering

nlocking the potential of our genetic
urces, genetic engineers could have an
act greater than that of atomic scientists. The
gene-manipulation techniques, now
oming available, could accelerate breeding
grammes—and achieve genetic combinations
ch would scarcely be possible in nature.
or the moment, as the examples, right, show,
penefit from accelerated plant-breeding
grammes. But the use of tissue culture and
e-transfer techniques promises to launch a
era. If, in the future, we could transfer the
ogen-fixing ability of the bean to wheat, for
mple, we might be able to dispense with
ly fertilizers. The agricultural biotechnology
ustry could be worth $100 billion a year by
late 1990s—but genetic engineers could
mately be left with much less raw genetic
erial to work with if the world's wild gene
ls are depleted.

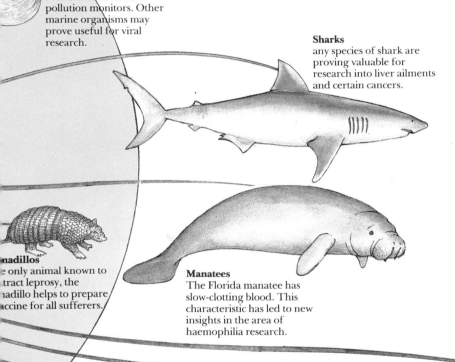

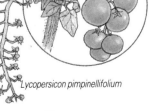

Lycopersicon pimpinellifolium

Helianthus petiolaris

Manihot glasiovii

Tomato

Without the resistance to Fusarium wilt provided by the wild Peruvian tomato, many of today's most successful commercial tomato varieties would not have remained viable.

Sunflower

The symbol of a healthy diet, the sunflower now ranks as one of the world's most important oil crops. Sunflower breeders have drawn heavily on the gene pool of the wild sunflower, *Helianthus petiolaris*.

Cassava

The yield of this vital food crop has been boosted experimentally by as much as 18 times since disease-resistance traits were transferred from its wild cousin, *Manihot glasiovii*.

number of which have already proved to be of enormous economic importance. And we have scarcely begun to investigate the potential of the animal kingdom.

Librarians of the rainforest

How are we to unlock the secrets of the wild? How can we best penetrate the ancient "library" that is the genetic resource?

The people of Surinam say: "Na boesi, ingi sabe ala sani" – "In the jungle, the Indian knows everything." It is here, amongst the populations of traditional and vanishing cultures, that one important answer lies. Traditional cultures are the "librarians" of our "gene library" and each holds a stack of index cards carefully drawn up after thousands of years of patient trial and error.

There are other ways to "unlock the wild". We can try random screening of plants, for example, as done in the US. But this ultimately entails thousands of screening tests, much time, and a great deal of money. A better option is to search through the literature of traditional cultures. Or we can carry out studies of unpublished ethnobotanical data, which, combined with spot tests, often lead us to species worthy of further research.

But best of all is for ethnobotanists to concentrate on fieldwork. One study of Amazonian rainforests by two US scientists has led to the identification of more than 1,000 plants which have potential economic benefits. The project was dedicated to examining traditional uses of forest plants by native dwellers of the rainforests. The research revealed that at least six plants were used as contraceptives by

Keys to the wild

As we become increasingly remote from natural environments, and from the resources they contain, so we become ever-more dependent on the knowledge and skills of those live in close harmony with their immediate environment. Many of our foods and pharmaceuticals were first investigated because of their use by indigenous peoples. Instead of bulldozing aside these "human keys" to the wild, we should see them as a vital, intrinsic element of the ecosystems we are trying to conserve.

Even with the extraordinarily sophisticated equipment now available for extracting and analysing animal, microbial, and plant materials, our basic problem is simply knowing where to start. There are many examples of the ways in which traditional societies have helped focus our search for new medicines, new foods, and other products. By respecting and conserving human diversity, we will ensure that we can tap the hidden wealth in conserved areas.

Heart-stopping poison from Guyana
Indians in a Guyana rainforest have used a special fish poison for centuries which, rather than leaving the fish prey to other fish eaters such as piranhas, drastically changes their behaviour – causing them almost to fly out of water. Dr Conrad Gorinsky has pointed to the possibilities of this drug in heart surgery, since is able to stop the heart without killing the org. The heart can be re-started after surgery. The plant species responsible for this poison was discovered in 1774 by Christophe Fusee Aubl but was wrongly described as having the characteristics of a very close but inactive relative. This type of confusion is not uncommon. To the Indians of Guyana, Aubl *Clibadium sylvestre* (Aubl.) is quite distinct and be identified by its smell and the different bra on its leaves.

the forest's inhabitants. Other discoveries, to name but a few, included a cure for fungal skin infection, a high-protein coconut fruit that could be used for feed and fertilizer, and a seed that could be used to make soap. These are just a few examples. Reports have also been made of the large and tasty fruit of the *Sapotaceae* tree for which, according to early Amazonian explorers, Indians would leap from their canoes and swim eagerly to the shore.

Yet forest peoples, probably the only humans who successfully manage forests on a sustainable basis, are in a state of crisis. These "librarians" look set for dismissal, their library threatened with closure. Experience shows that these cultures, evolved and developed over thousands of years, can disappear at frightening speed. The Kreen-Akore of Brazil, for example, has been almost wiped out within decades.

Many more poorly known South American forest peoples will cease to exist as cultural entities by the end of the century.

One way out of this dilemma is to put the world of the "gene librarians" on a sound economic footing. Already several African and Asian nations have begun to encourage the development of traditional medicine as an important component of their public health care programmes – we now have tribal healers upgraded to "bare-foot" doctors (pp 194-5). Indigenous medicines are relatively cheap, and readily accepted by the local populace. Developing countries often cannot afford to spend millions of dollars on importing medicines. Some countries, such as Thailand and Nepal, have developed their medicinal plants into a means of earning foreign exchange, each exporting medicines worth over $1

Mayapple

Indians, mayapple, and cancer
North American Indians have provided one key to an important wild resource – the mayapple. The vanishing tribes of North American Indians, centuries ago, unlocked the secrets of this remarkable plant species. Used by Penobscot Indians to treat warts and by Cherokees to treat deafness and kill parasitic worms, the secret properties of the mayapple were then passed on to the colonists. Today they are under the microscopic eye of modern chemists. A new drug, VePesid, a semi-synthetic derivative of podophyllotoxin – a natural extract of mayapple – is now being used to treat testicular cancer. It has already had remarkable results and, in some instances, has attained up to 47% recovery rate for treated patients. The mayapple story is not yet over. Following the advice of North American Indians, it has also been successfully used to repel potato beetles. Moreover, the mayapple shows some interesting activity towards important viruses such as Herpes 1, Herpes 2, Influenza A, and measles.

edicine men and toothache-trees
cal experts, like the medicine man shown ove, are being consulted in their hundreds by WF and IUCN in an attempt to collect ormation on the uses of plants by traditional ieties. In Tanzania, one scientist has covered a tree used by local people to cure thache – not only is it a completely new cies, but its genus has not been recorded in rica. In Amazonia, an ethnobotanic team has alogued more than 1,000 plants used by th American rainforest Indians which have nomic potential as food, medicines, or ustrial raw materials. Tubocurarine, for mple, is used as a muscle relaxant. Derived m the pareira plant, it is found wild in the pical forests of southern Brazil, Peru, ombia, and Panama.

million a year. Even in West Germany, a few forests are managed to encourage the growth of purple foxglove, the source of digitalis.

Our daily interactions with Nature

From pets in our homes to bees in our croplands, from greenery in our cities to myriad creatures in the great "out there", we enjoy fellowship with wildlife – wildlife meaning all non-human beings that share our planet. In ways we rarely think about, we benefit from this community of fellow species that play their part in our daily rounds. Often enough too, we return the compliment: many creatures prosper through their association with us.

Take our gardens, for example: 16 million of them in Britain alone. A well established garden may well play host at one time or another to dozens of plant species, hundreds if not thousands of insects, and 60 birds. Who does not feel enriched by the sheer diversity, let alone the colour, of flowers? And who would not feel impoverished if they could no longer wake to the "dawn chorus"? Many of these organisms would likewise find themselves hard pressed without the presence of humans.

Our city trees offer more than just "visual amenity" to urban environments. They do a clean-up job on pollution, especially chemical contaminants such as sulphur dioxide that otherwise damage our buildings and our lungs. In London's leafy Hyde Park, the pollution level is sometimes a good one-quarter less than in built-up areas nearby. The leaves of a one-hectare clump of elm or beech trees can extract 40 tonnes of dirt from the atmosphere, whereupon rain washes it into the ground.

In the countryside, there are even greater throngs of "wild friends". While the average biomass of humans in the US is about 18 kilograms per hectare, protozoa total about 150 kilograms, insects and earthworms 1,000, bacteria 1,700, and fungi 2,500. These organisms help to support an average of 55 tonnes of plants, many of them crop plants. Certain of these so-called lowly forms of life help to convert nitrogen from the atmosphere into fertilizer for plants. Crops worldwide absorb 140 million tonnes of nitrogen each year, 90 million of them provided free by natural sources, or twice as much as farmers apply. The annual value of this biological nitrogen is at least $20 billion.

Of course, there are certain forms that we would prefer to be less prominent. Rats, cockroaches, and weeds prosper through our unwitting support – an undesirable form of fellowship. But these are trifling exceptions in the overall scheme of things. The millions of species that share the Earth's ecosystem with us constitute an integral community whose complexity and richness we are scarcely beginning to grasp. Through their interactions with one another and with us, they maintain the Gaian workings of our planet. Thus they are all of "use" to us, whether directly or indirectly, whether we recognize their contributions or not.

Fellowship with wildlife

Few doubt the pleasure and comfort which domestic pets can afford. But we tend to overlook the indispensable contributions made by wild and semi-wild species. Think of earthworms: they bring 2-63 tonnes of soil to the surface of each hectare of land in their castings, while ants transport another 10 tonnes per hectare. Or think of the wastes we generate: each year, for example, the US sewage system carries away some 160 million tonnes of material, most of which is broken down by micro-organisms. Environmental concern tends to concentrate on rare endangered species and large charismatic animals. But the smaller, often unseen organisms of natural biotas are at least as important to us.

Bumble bee

Honey bee

Unpaid helpers
Without pollination by wild bees, honey bees, and other insects, seed production would be impossible, there would be no fruit, and our harvest of many vegetable would be reduced. In New York State an estimated 8 10^{12} blossoms may be pollinated in a single day – more than half by wild an solitary bees.

Life in the scales
The relative impact that various natural species groups exert on our environment can be judged in part by the weight of their biomass per unit area. In the US, insects, earthworms, protozoa, algae, bacteria, and fungi total about 6,700 kg/ha in biomass – approximately 350 times the average human biomass. Adding the plant biomass to that of animals produces a total of 62,000 kg/ha.

Biological controls
China's Big Sand Commune raises 220,000 ducks to control insect pests in fields of young rice. Ducklings, right, consume about 200 (mostly injurious) insects per hour and cut the use of chemical insecticides from 770,000 kg in 1973 to 6,700 kg in 1975. Imported parasitic insects have saved the Florida citrus industry $35 million a year following an outlay of $35,000.

Town and suburb

We share our houses, villages, and cities with many wildlife species, adapted to the niches we have fostered. House martins nest under eaves and pigeons haunt public spaces (as, in India, do monkeys). True, some animals are a nuisance rather than a benefit – the urban fox, for example – but most of our wild neighbours are either harmless or positively beneficial.

Agricultural land

In agricultural areas, hedgerows can shield croplands from wind, forests can provide protection from flooding, and small predators can keep crop pests at bay. Micro-organisms help break down the pesticides applied to crops, while the vital process of fertilization is aided by invertebrates. A total of 90 US crops, valued at more than $4 billion, are dependent upon insect pollination. Of an estimated 140 million tonnes of nitrogen removed from the soil in crop production, more than 90 million tonnes are made up of biologically fixed nitrogen, representing an annual "free gift" of $20 billion.

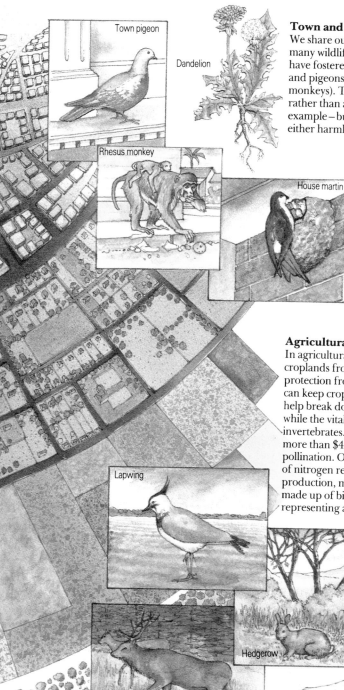

Town pigeon

Dandelion

Rhesus monkey

House martin

Hyena

Lapwing

Hedgerow

Deer

The wilderness

"The good of going into the mountains is that life is reconsidered."

RALPH WALDO EMERSON

Apart from being an increasingly important resource for tourism and recreation, wilderness areas represent the last refuges of untapped diversity. This diversity is found not simply in wild plants and animals, but in the relationship between traditional cultures and their environments. The knowledge developed by such cultures constitutes a set of "keys" to these surviving wild resources (see p. 148).

EVOLUTION IN CRISIS

On the timescale of evolution, our species scarcely registers. But in terms of its impact on the resources of the planet, and on the genetic heritage which is the living foundation of the future, our brief history is all too significant. It is a story of destruction.

Habitat destruction

So far as we know, ours is the only green planet in the universe. Yet we, the latest inhabitants, are depleting this rich heritage at a rate that will grossly impoverish the Earth's green cover in a twinkling of geological time.

We have already seen (pp 42-7) that by the end of this century, we are likely to expand deserts by a full two-thirds, and to eliminate at least one-third of tropical forests. We look set to destroy much of our inheritance of coral reefs, mangroves, estuaries, and wetlands. We shall plough up enormous areas of grassland. Still other areas will be paved over, chopped down, dug up, drained, and poisoned – or will be "developed" until their natural potential is homogenized out of existence. All this we shall do in the name of human welfare.

Unless we achieve a remarkable turn-round in the stewardship of our heritage, the next century will witness a speeding up of the destructive process as human numbers continue to surge and human appetites for raw materials grow keener. Yet who can blame the subsistence farmers who, in order to feed their starving families, knowingly degrade the natural resource base of tomorrow's livelihood? Perhaps more culpable are the super-affluent citizens of the developed nations who, by demanding ever-greater flows of natural resources from all over the world, are just as destructive.

Our great-grandchildren may well look out on a planet that has suffered far greater depletion than during the course of a major glaciation. Were they, by then, to have learned how to live in ecological accord with the Earth's life-support systems, they will surely find that the damage of 150 years of human activity will take millennia to restore.

We are finding that some tropical forests, once removed, do not readily re-establish. When soil cover disappears, together with critical stocks of nutrients, the forest's comeback is pre-empted. Desertification is also irreversible, except at massive cost. Moreover, certain sectors of the biosphere, notably tropical forests, coral reefs, and wetland ecosystems, serve, by virtue of their biotic richness and their ecological complexity, as "powerhouses"

The irreplaceable heritage

Living organisms are the heirs of 3.6 billion years of evolution. Just as the complexities of their inheritance almost defy calculation, so the consequences of our disruption of their networks of biological interdependence cannot readily be analysed or predicted. Yet humanity often seems to regard this heritage with indifference at best. Mismanagement now threatens to destroy entire sectors of the biosphere, inflicting grievous injury on our very life-support systems.

Various pressures bring this about; poverty in one part of the world is matched by excessive consumerism elsewhere. But the outcome tends to be the same – wholesale over-exploitation of humanity's environment. Entire ecosystems are undermined: over-grazing and brush clearance constantly extend the deserts; coastal wetlands, drained for agriculture, spill toxic chemicals instead of nutrients into the sea, while industrial wastes and sewage aggravate their impact; each minute, 20 ha of tropical forest are destroyed, diminishing the habitat of thousands of species; in Europe, intensive cultivation eliminates woodlands and hedgerows, together with their myriad organisms.

The balances and linkages that are the very process of life on Earth thus come under threat. What if they finally unravel?

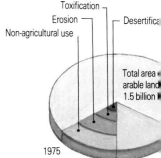

The disappearing soil
We stand to lose 18% of the world's arable land by the year 2000. Salinization alone may cost us 2.75 million ha – equal to the food supply for over 9 million people (see also pp 40-1).

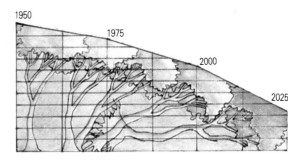

The shrinking forest
One-fifth of Brazil's forests have gone; Thailand, almost two-fifths forested only 10 years ago, is likely to have nothing left but relict fragments within another 10 years. The graph shows the decline in area of closed tropical forest (see also pp 42-3).

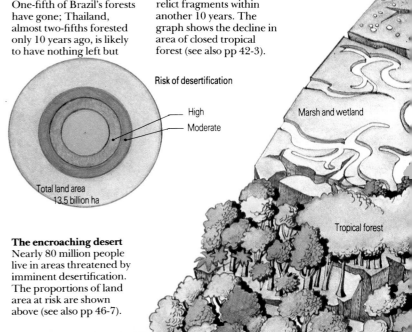

The encroaching desert
Nearly 80 million people live in areas threatened by imminent desertification. The proportions of land area at risk are shown above (see also pp 46-7).

s of UK habitats	%
...land meadows	95
...land heath	50-60
...ient lowland woodlands	30-50
...land wetlands (fens)	50
...gerows	25
...and heaths and grasslands	30

...itain's vanishing countryside
...ery year, 4,000 small farms in Britain are
...en over by larger units. The environmental
...ults are clear. Every year 3,200 km of
...dgerow and almost 75,000 ha of heathland
...appear, with all the plants and animals they
...pport. In just over 40 years, 224,000 km of
...dgerows have been torn out, and half the
...g-established deciduous woodlands
...stroyed. Over 80% of the flower-rich lowland
...adows have been ploughed up or built over.
...ready more than 300 plant species are
...icially listed as endangered.

Threatened Cape flora
The Cape's floristic
kingdom covering 1.8
million ha is one of the 6
most significant
concentrations of flora on
Earth. In this region occur
68% of the 2,373 South
African plants under
severe threat.

Acid rain in Scandinavia
In a lake with a pH of 5.5
(lower figures on the pH
scale indicate greater
acidity), most fish perish;
with a pH of 4, the whole
lake ecosystem can die. Ten
thousand lakes in Sweden
are now practically lifeless
(see pp 118-9).

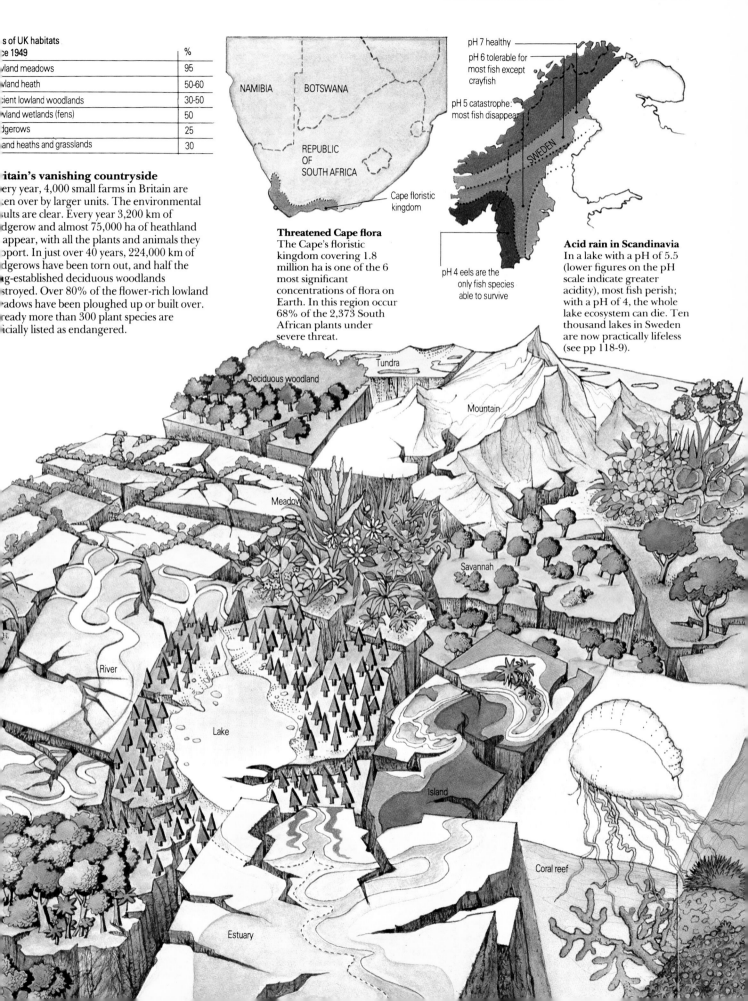

of evolution. By destroying these salient sectors of the biosphere, we are impoverishing the future course of evolution.

Loss of species

Well over 90 percent of all species that have ever lived have disappeared. They have become extinct through natural processes, often being superseded by "better" or "fitter" species. After humankind first appeared on the scene and learnt to hunt animals for food, commerce, and sport, often disrupting natural environments in the process, the extinction rate started to soar, until eventually it reached about one species a year in the early 20th century.

Today, when natural environments are being degraded and destroyed on every side, the extinction rate has surely reached one species a day, and some biologists argue that it is higher still. By the end of the century, it is estimated, we could lose one million species. By the middle of the 21st century, perhaps a quarter of all species may be lost.

In its scale and compressed time span, this process of extinction will represent a greater biological débâcle than anything experienced since life began. It will massively exceed the "great dying" of the dinosaurs and their kin, together with associated organisms, 65 million years ago, when a sizeable share of Earth's species disappeared.

We know that there are about 45,000 species of vertebrates on Earth, and about 250,000 species of higher plants, with somewhere around 100,000 species of lower plants. The great bulk of the 5-10 million species currently thought to exist are invertebrates, of which insects comprise almost 80 percent. And it is among the invertebrates, particularly among the insects, that the major extinctions are now occurring.

When conservationists used to say that we were losing one species a year, they were referring almost exclusively to mammals and birds, which in total account for only about 13,000 species. Botanists have compiled a reasonably detailed account of the plants currently threatened with extinction. They have come up with a total of 25,000 species. Further they believe that, as a rough rule of thumb, there are between 20 and 40 animal species for every one plant species, dependent on those plants for their survival. So for every plant that disappears, many more animal species may eventually disappear.

We know that of the plant species, about one in ten can be categorized as threatened, and the same sort of proportion holds for mammals and birds. It also apparently holds for other vertebrates, such as fish, reptiles, and amphibians. If we extrapolate this proportion to the invertebrates, we have good reason to suspect that somewhere between 500,000 and one million species are under threat right now.

Ironically, the reduced stock of species which survives this wave of extinctions is likely to include an unusually high number of opportunistic species, able to move into ecological niches vacated by

The destruction of diversity

We are in the early phase of what looks likely to be an unprecedented era of extinctions. Extinction has always been a way of life on Earth, but the present wave of extinctions caused by human pressures and exploitation are calculated to be running at up to 400 times the natural rate. Indeed, the rate of species loss is so great that it threatens to disrupt evolution itself.

If large-scale habitat disruption and destruction continue to accelerate, we run a real risk that the diminished stock of species will not represent an adequate resource base on which natural selection can work to rebuild the rich panoply of life. So far as we can discern from the fossil record, the "bounce back" period could well extend over several million years. The process of species formation will clearly continue, even accelerate in places, but it will be outrun by extinction. We should be worried about the loss of diversity for its own sake and because it threatens existing and potential future resources. But the implications of the headlong destruction of species for the future course of evolution are more worrying still. "Death is one thing", as Drs Soule and Wilcox neatly put it; "an end to birth is something else".

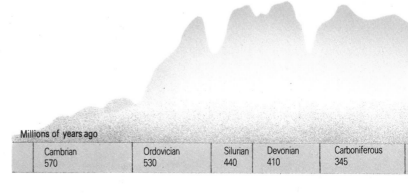

The flame of life

From its first flickerings, an estimated 3.6 billion years ago, the flame of life has burned ever brighter, dying down during the major periods of extinction, but leaping back to even greater heights thereafter. Today the flame of life is threatened by intense human pressures: habitat destruction is gathering pace, while the superpowers are developing weapons which threaten to extinguish all higher life-forms. Even if we manage to avoid nuclear Armageddon, we risk snuffing out an extraordinary number of life-forms.

Millions of years ago				
Cambrian 570	Ordovician 530	Silurian 440	Devonian 410	Carboniferous 345

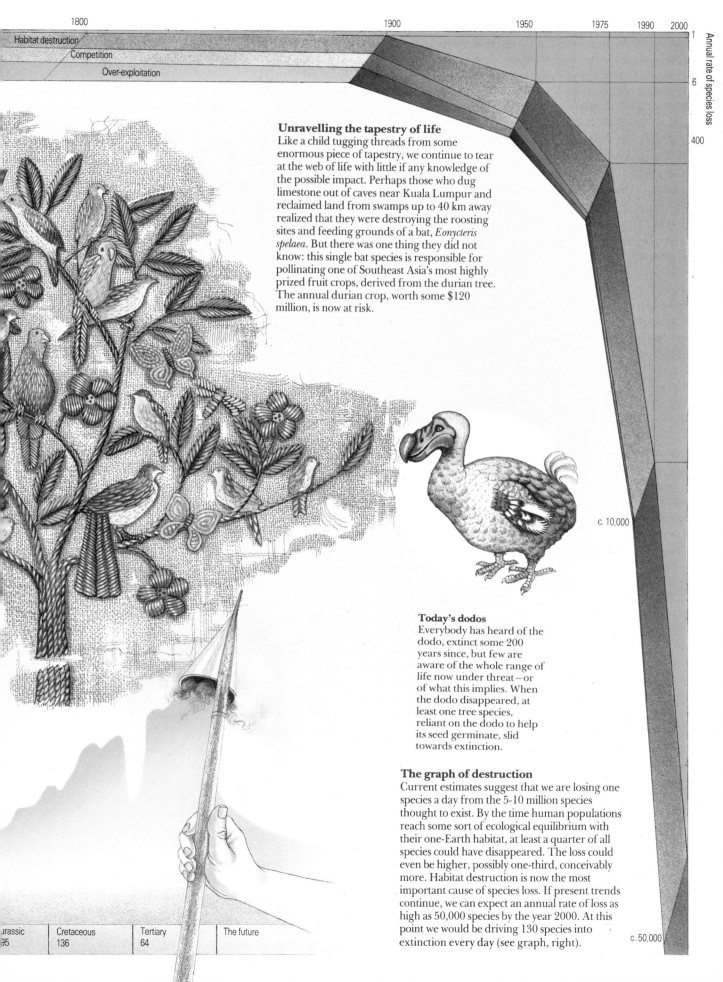

| 1800 | | 1900 | 1950 | 1975 | 1990 | 2000 |

Annual rate of species loss

1

6

400

Habitat destruction

Competition

Over-exploitation

Unravelling the tapestry of life
Like a child tugging threads from some
enormous piece of tapestry, we continue to tear
at the web of life with little if any knowledge of
the possible impact. Perhaps those who dug
limestone out of caves near Kuala Lumpur and
reclaimed land from swamps up to 40 km away
realized that they were destroying the roosting
sites and feeding grounds of a bat, *Eonycteris
spelaea*. But there was one thing they did not
know: this single bat species is responsible for
pollinating one of Southeast Asia's most highly
prized fruit crops, derived from the durian tree.
The annual durian crop, worth some $120
million, is now at risk.

c. 10,000

Today's dodos
Everybody has heard of the
dodo, extinct some 200
years since, but few are
aware of the whole range of
life now under threat – or
of what this implies. When
the dodo disappeared, at
least one tree species,
reliant on the dodo to help
its seed germinate, slid
towards extinction.

The graph of destruction
Current estimates suggest that we are losing one
species a day from the 5-10 million species
thought to exist. By the time human populations
reach some sort of ecological equilibrium with
their one-Earth habitat, at least a quarter of all
species could have disappeared. The loss could
even be higher, possibly one-third, conceivably
more. Habitat destruction is now the most
important cause of species loss. If present trends
continue, we can expect an annual rate of loss as
high as 50,000 species by the year 2000. At this
point we would be driving 130 species into
extinction every day (see graph, right).

c. 50,000

| urassic 95 | Cretaceous 136 | Tertiary 64 | The future |

recently extinct species or to thrive on our rubbish. Previous opportunists have included the house-fly, the rabbit, the rat, and "weedy" plants. We run a risk of creating a pest-dominated world.

A crisis of uniformity

Each mammal, insect, or plant pushed into the abyss of extinction takes with it genes which could have proved very valuable. As species disappear, so do gene pools–and so does the prospect of exploiting those genes to improve our future welfare. Losses through extinction are irreversible, although our ignorance about the economic potential of so many of our genetic resources means we are often totally unaware of what we have lost.

Worse, the erosion of genetic diversity is greater than the statistics on species loss alone would suggest. If a species with one million individuals is reduced to only 10,000 (which may still be enough to ensure the species' survival), it may have lost 90 percent of its races, populations, and other genetic sub-units, with a concomitant loss of half of its genetic diversity. This "concealed" erosion of genetic diversity is generally overlooked, although ultimately it could represent as grave a threat as the loss of the species itself.

More immediately, we are losing wild and semi-domesticated plants whose genes are essential if we are to maintain our major crop plants. Of the estimated 80,000 edible plants, only about 150 have been cultivated on a large scale–and less than 20 provide 90 percent of our food. The more we bend these 20 plants to our needs, the more vulnerable they become–and the more they need infusions of genes from outside their own shrinking gene pools.

There has been a parallel decline in the number of strains of many farm animals. In pursuit of immediate profits, the livestock industry tends to concentrate on a limited number of breeds, with the result that we are heading towards emergency levels of "homogenized breeding". In Europe and the Mediterranean basin, 118 cattle varieties are under threat–and only 30 breeds are holding their own.

The case of the Cornish chicken illustrates the error of allowing older strains to die out. This fast-growing subspecies of the domestic fowl was superseded by new breeds which laid more eggs or tasted better. Then, as the Cornish chicken faded away, breeders decided they needed an infusion of its genes to boost the growth rate of the very chickens which had usurped its place on the farm.

Sometimes, too, a plant or animal can act as a signpost to hidden genetic riches. So it has been with the rosy periwinkle, a Madagascar forest plant which has given us two potent anti-cancer drugs. So rare are the critical alkaloidal chemicals in most forms of the plant, that pharmacologists once had to process 500 tonnes of plant material to extract one kilogram of drug. Now a West Indian variant has been found which contains 10 times more of the alkaloid, enhancing the production process.

Traditional varieties
Small, but well supported, the sack of traditional maize hangs from a thick, multi-stranded rope, representing many plant varieties. Genetic diversity defends this plant population against pest and pathogen.

New varieties
Today's maize dangles from a dangerously thin thread. The bigger the sack, the more readily it could fall: the US harvest almost suffered this fate in 1970 when a maize fungus disease threatened over half of all major maize lands. At the eleventh hour, a "technical fix" was achieved by drafting in a more resistant strain from Mexico, the ancestral home of maize.

Genetic erosion

"The products of agro-technology are displacing the source upon which the technology is based. It is analagous to taking stones from the foundation to repair the roof."

PROFESSOR GARRISON WILKES
UNIVERSITY OF MASSACHUSETTS

Habitat destruction is not the only threat to the process of evolution. Genetic erosion is depleting the gene base of many existing crop plants and farm animals. Productive diversity is replaced by dangerous homogeneity, and future avenues of agricultural development are cut off.

The scale of the potential loss is indicated by the recent history of *Zea diploperennis*, a rare perennial maize discovered in 1978. Found in a few hectares of farmland in the Sierra de Manantlan, Mexico, this hitherto unknown variety was down to some 2,000 plants–and the elimination of its habitat continues. Yet its genes could open up the prospect of perennial maize production and increased resistance to at least four of the seven most important maize diseases, all of which could lead to billion dollar savings.

There are many more examples. Take the Rio Palenque Research Station in Ecuador. In area it amounts to as little as 170 ha, yet it supports 1,025 plant species–the highest recorded concentration of plant diversity on Earth. Regrettably, this last patch of wet forest of coastal Ecuador is being undermined by local people who enter the forest to cut wood for fuel and construction.

1840's Irish potato blight, 2 mil.

1860's Vine diseases crippled E wine industry.

1870-90 Coffee rust robbed Ce valuable export.

1942 Rice crop destroyed, milli Bengalis died.

1946 US oat crop devastated b epidemic.

1950's Wheat stem rust devas

1970 Maize fungus threatened corn hectarage.

Counting human cost
The potential impacts of monoculture collapse ha become ever greater, as increasing numbers of people come to depend c a shrinking number of c varieties. If the world ma crop failed tomorrow, it would do a great deal mc than cut our supplies of food and feed. It would also impinge on many other products to which maize makes a contribution, such as aspirin, penicillin, tyres, plastics–even the "finish on these very pages.

High yield, high risk

Modern plant breeding, with its emphasis on inbred, uniform strains, has fostered a widespread trend towards large-scale monocultures (see pp 60-1). Whereas the traditional farmed landscape (top left) was genetically diverse, the emerging agricultural landscape (below left) is much more uniform. Most inbred strains of crop plant offer short-lived resistance to pathogens and pests. For example, the average lifetime of wheat varieties is only 5-15 years. As a result, plant diseases and pest infestations can sweep through monocultures like a prairie fire.

Number of wheat varieties in Greece

100
80
60
40
20

1930   1940   1950   1960   1970

Loss of diversity

Genetic erosion is affecting even areas of high diversity. Greece has lost 95% of its native wheat varieties in just 40 years (see left).

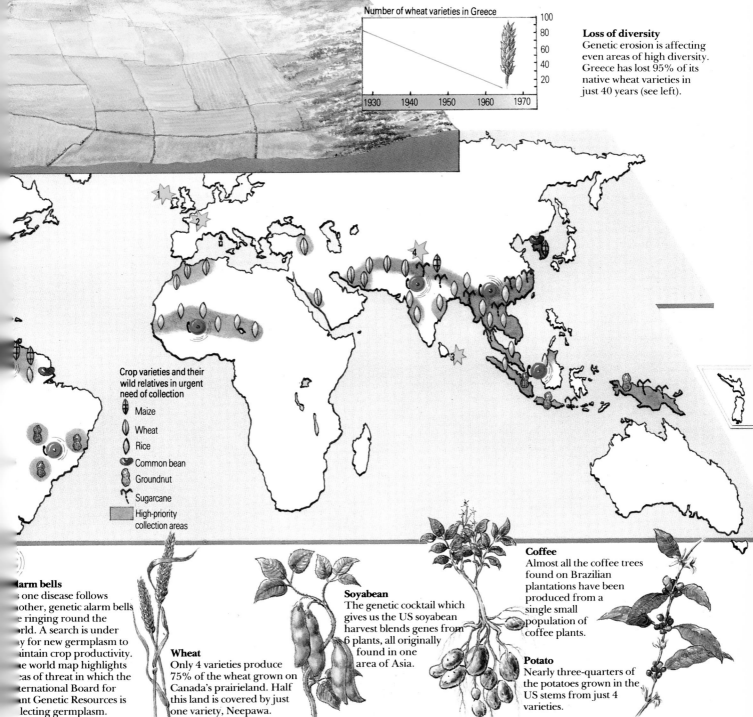

Crop varieties and their wild relatives in urgent need of collection

- Maize
- Wheat
- Rice
- Common bean
- Groundnut
- Sugarcane
- High-priority collection areas

arm bells
s one disease follows
other, genetic alarm bells
e ringing round the
rld. A search is under
y for new germplasm to
intain crop productivity.
e world map highlights
as of threat in which the
ternational Board for
nt Genetic Resources is
lecting germplasm.

Wheat
Only 4 varieties produce 75% of the wheat grown on Canada's prairieland. Half this land is covered by just one variety, Neepawa.

Soyabean
The genetic cocktail which gives us the US soyabean harvest blends genes from 6 plants, all originally found in one area of Asia.

Coffee
Almost all the coffee trees found on Brazilian plantations have been produced from a single small population of coffee plants.

Potato
Nearly three-quarters of the potatoes grown in the US stems from just 4 varieties.

Towards a lonely planet

Human beings, uniquely intelligent, have achieved a self-awareness that both gives them power over and separates them from the life around them. The natural world is seen as theirs to exploit and despoil. The biological and mineral storehouses of the Earth, once thought inexhaustible, are ruthlessly plundered. In the process, the web of interdependence from which humanity itself is derived begins to fall apart. Yet in this rage to prosper lie the seeds of deep despair. As the human species creates around it a constantly growing desolation, it is in danger of finding itself isolated on a desecrated planet. Its only companions will be the cowed species it has domesticated and the rodent survivors, wily and vicious, that have resisted its assault. Racing along our current path of development, we ignore at our peril the warnings sounded by those whose eyes are not blinkered by short-term priorities.

"Man has long lost his ability to foresee and forestall. He will end by destroying the earth."
Albert Schweitzer

"Extinction does not simply mean the loss of one volume from the library of nature. It means the loss of a loose-leaf book whose individual pages, were the species to survive, would remain available in perpetuity for selective transfer and improvement of other species."
Professor Thomas Eisner
Cornell University

"For as long as Man continues to be the ruthless destroyer of lower living beings, he will never know health or peace. For as long as men massacre animals, they will kill each other. Indeed, he who sows the seeds of murder and pain cannot reap joy and love."
Pythagoras

"I owe an allegiance to the planet that has made me possible, and to all the life on that planet, whether friendly or not. I also owe an allegiance to the 3½ billion years of life that made it possible for me to be here, and all the rest of you too. We have a responsibility to the largest population of all, the hundred of billions of people who have not yet been born, who have a right to be, who deserve a world at least as beautiful as ours, whose genes are now in our custody and no one else's."
David R. Brower, Chairman, Friends of the Earth

"Unwittingly for the most part, but right around the world, we are eliminating the panoply of life. We elbow species off the planet, we deny room to entire communities of nature, we domesticate the Earth. With growing energy and ingenuity, we surpass ourselves time and again in our efforts to exert dominion over fowl of the air and fish of the sea.

We do all this in the name of human advancement. Yet instead of making better use of lands we have already to our use, we proclaim our need to expand into every last corner of the Earth. Our response to natural environments has changed little for thousands of years. We dig them up, we chop them down, we burn them, we drain them, we pave them over, we poison them in order to mould them to our image. We homogenize the globe.

Eventually we may achieve our aim, by eliminating every "competitor" for living space on the crowded Earth. When the last creature has been accounted for, we shall have made ourselves masters of all creation. We shall look around, and we shall see nothing but each other. Alone at last."
Norman Myers

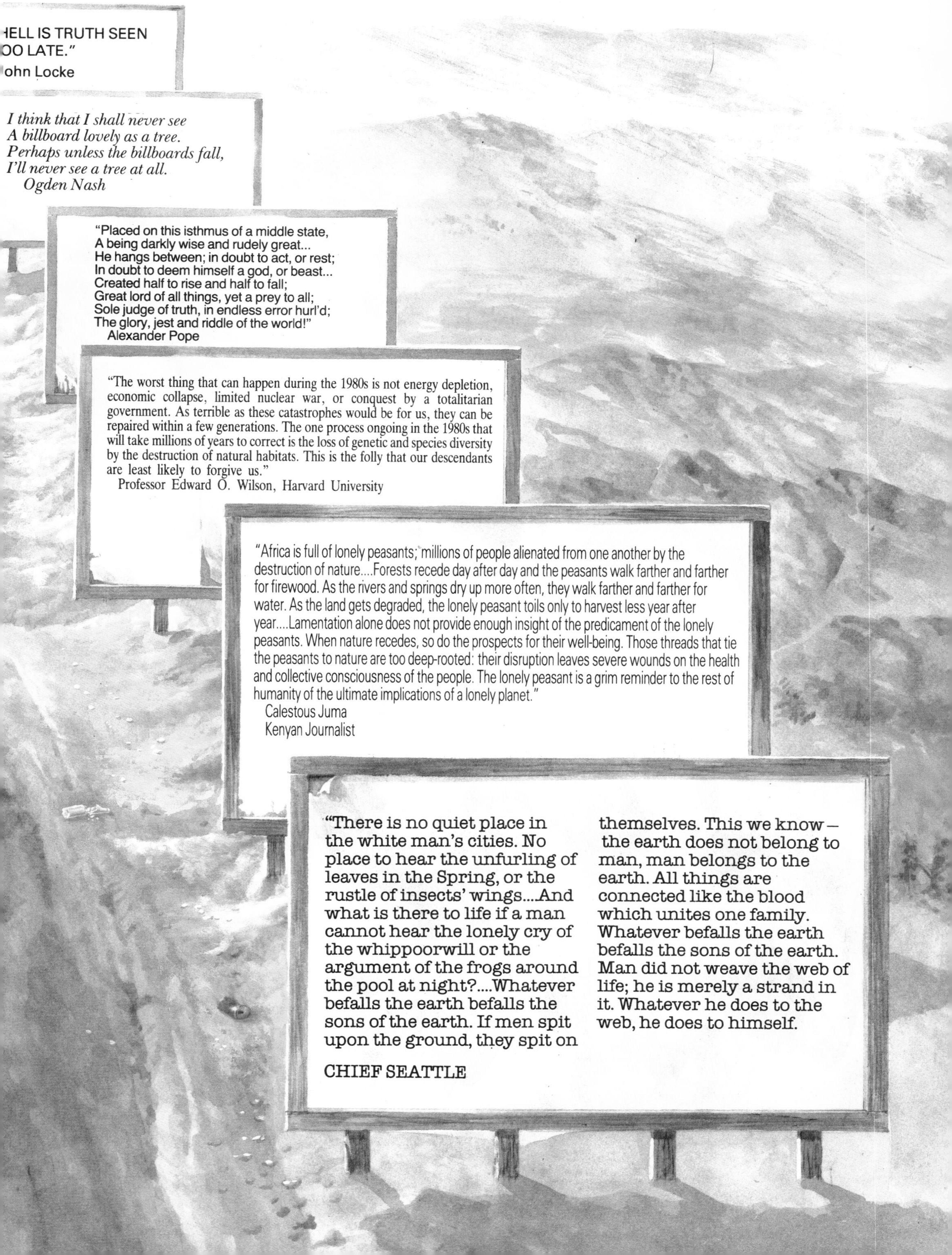

"HELL IS TRUTH SEEN
TOO LATE."
John Locke

*I think that I shall never see
A billboard lovely as a tree.
Perhaps unless the billboards fall,
I'll never see a tree at all.*
   Ogden Nash

"Placed on this isthmus of a middle state,
A being darkly wise and rudely great...
He hangs between; in doubt to act, or rest;
In doubt to deem himself a god, or beast...
Created half to rise and half to fall;
Great lord of all things, yet a prey to all;
Sole judge of truth, in endless error hurl'd;
The glory, jest and riddle of the world!"
   Alexander Pope

"The worst thing that can happen during the 1980s is not energy depletion, economic collapse, limited nuclear war, or conquest by a totalitarian government. As terrible as these catastrophes would be for us, they can be repaired within a few generations. The one process ongoing in the 1980s that will take millions of years to correct is the loss of genetic and species diversity by the destruction of natural habitats. This is the folly that our descendants are least likely to forgive us."
   Professor Edward O. Wilson, Harvard University

"Africa is full of lonely peasants; millions of people alienated from one another by the destruction of nature....Forests recede day after day and the peasants walk farther and farther for firewood. As the rivers and springs dry up more often, they walk farther and farther for water. As the land gets degraded, the lonely peasant toils only to harvest less year after year....Lamentation alone does not provide enough insight of the predicament of the lonely peasants. When nature recedes, so do the prospects for their well-being. Those threads that tie the peasants to nature are too deep-rooted: their disruption leaves severe wounds on the health and collective consciousness of the people. The lonely peasant is a grim reminder to the rest of humanity of the ultimate implications of a lonely planet."
   Calestous Juma
   Kenyan Journalist

"There is no quiet place in the white man's cities. No place to hear the unfurling of leaves in the Spring, or the rustle of insects' wings....And what is there to life if a man cannot hear the lonely cry of the whippoorwill or the argument of the frogs around the pool at night?....Whatever befalls the earth befalls the sons of the earth. If men spit upon the ground, they spit on themselves. This we know — the earth does not belong to man, man belongs to the earth. All things are connected like the blood which unites one family. Whatever befalls the earth befalls the sons of the earth. Man did not weave the web of life; he is merely a strand in it. Whatever he does to the web, he does to himself.

CHIEF SEATTLE

EVOLUTION IN MANAGEMENT

Our ability to disrupt the planet has been well tested. Now, we are challenged by a unique opportunity to turn that same massive ability to the task of large-scale managment of Earth's living resources, on a sustainable basis, combining two imperatives – development and conservation.

Protecting our heritage

To safeguard the world's wildlife and wildlands, we have established a growing number of parks and reserves. Some, such as Tanzania's Serengeti and Australia's Great Barrier Reef, have been set up to protect wildlife and its habitats. Others, such as Yosemite in the US and Nepal's Mount Everest Park, seek to protect spectacular scenery.

The protected-areas movement emerged just over 100 years ago, with the establishment of the Yellowstone National Park in the US. But it has only really taken off during the last 25 years, as country after country has recognized the need to safeguard pristine nature before it is too late. We still urgently require more protected areas: our present network is less than one-third of our overall needs.

Conserving the wild

Only a very small percentage of the world's land surface has been set aside to protect wild species and their genetic resources. Worse, the parks and reserves which we do have are far from representative of major types of ecosystems. Almost half the total conserved area can be found in North America, in the boreal forest and semi-frozen areas of Greenland and Arctic Canada. Of nearly 200 biogeographical provinces in the world, one in eight is not represented by a single park or reserve – and a similar number are represented by only one or two protected areas. Among the most poorly protected biogeographical provinces are tropical moist forests, grasslands, and Mediterranean-type zones. We are a long way from achieving the extensive, strategically sited network of protected areas which we need. Some of the most important gaps are highlighted here.

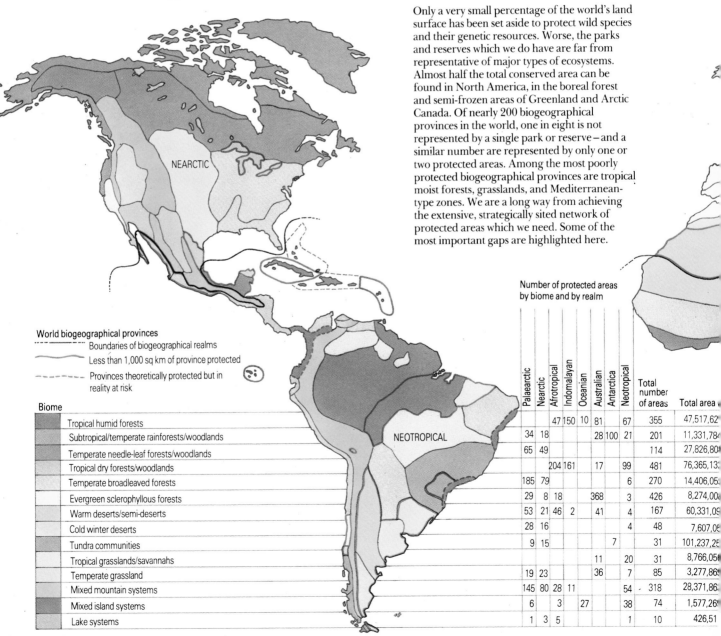

World biogeographical provinces

- - - - Boundaries of biogeographical realms
‿‿‿‿ Less than 1,000 sq km of province protected
- - - Provinces theoretically protected but in reality at risk

Number of protected areas by biome and by realm

Biome	Palaearctic	Nearctic	Afrotropical	Indomalayan	Oceanian	Australian	Antarctica	Neotropical	Total number of areas	Total area
Tropical humid forests			47	150	10	81		67	355	47,517,52
Subtropical/temperate rainforests/woodlands	34	18				28	100	21	201	11,331,784
Temperate needle-leaf forests/woodlands	65	49							114	27,826,80
Tropical dry forests/woodlands			204	161		17		99	481	76,365,13
Temperate broadleaved forests	185	79						6	270	14,406,05
Evergreen sclerophyllous forests	29	8	18			368		3	426	8,274,00
Warm deserts/semi-deserts	53	21	46	2		41		4	167	60,331,09
Cold winter deserts	28	16						4	48	7,607,05
Tundra communities	9	15					7		31	101,237,25
Tropical grasslands/savannahs						11		20	31	8,766,05
Temperate grassland	19	23				36		7	85	3,277,86
Mixed mountain systems	145	80	28	11				54	318	28,371,86
Mixed island systems	6		3		27			38	74	1,577,26
Lake systems	1	3	5					1	10	426,51

NEARCTIC

NEOTROPICAL

anwhile, just as natural landscapes are being dified, so the protected-areas movement is adapt- to the growing pressures. The traditional, purist roach has been to establish reserves from which forms of human exploitation are banned. reasingly, however, conservationists recognize t it will become ever-more difficult to declare re tracts of land "off limits" to human use and elopment. We know what we want to protect ks *from*: now we must devote more thought to at we are protecting them *for*. If existing parks to survive, let alone be joined by new protected as, they must be seen to be meeting the real ds of people—not just the esoteric interests of ure enthusiasts. This is all the more urgent in the rd World, where there is the greatest need to

achieve a comprehensive parks system—and where there is the greatest pressure on existing protected areas from land-hungry farmers.

Fortunately, it is possible to demonstrate that parks do indeed serve the cause of development. In northern Sulawesi, for example, a rainforest park has been set up which will mean that Indonesia will forfeit revenues from uncut timber. But the government is backing the initiative on the grounds that it will protect a rainfall-catchment zone which is critical for several million rice-paddy farmers in the valley bottomlands below. In several African parks, where dams have been built to supply water for the wildlife, local people raise fish for market. Elsewhere, dry-season grazing for livestock may be permitted, or some subsistence hunting tolerated.

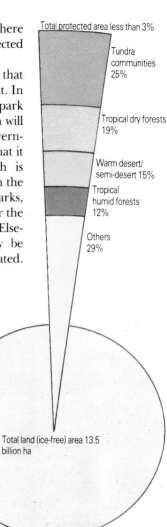

Total protected area less than 3%

Tundra communities 25%

Tropical dry forests 19%

Warm desert/ semi-desert 15%

Tropical humid forests 12%

Others 29%

Total land (ice-free) area 13.5 billion ha

Thin end of the wedge
The precariously thin wedge of protected land, above, is disproportionately rich in tundra, warm desert, and tropical dry forest reserves—and dangerously short of such key biomes as tropical grasslands, evergreen sclerophyllous forests, and mixed island systems.

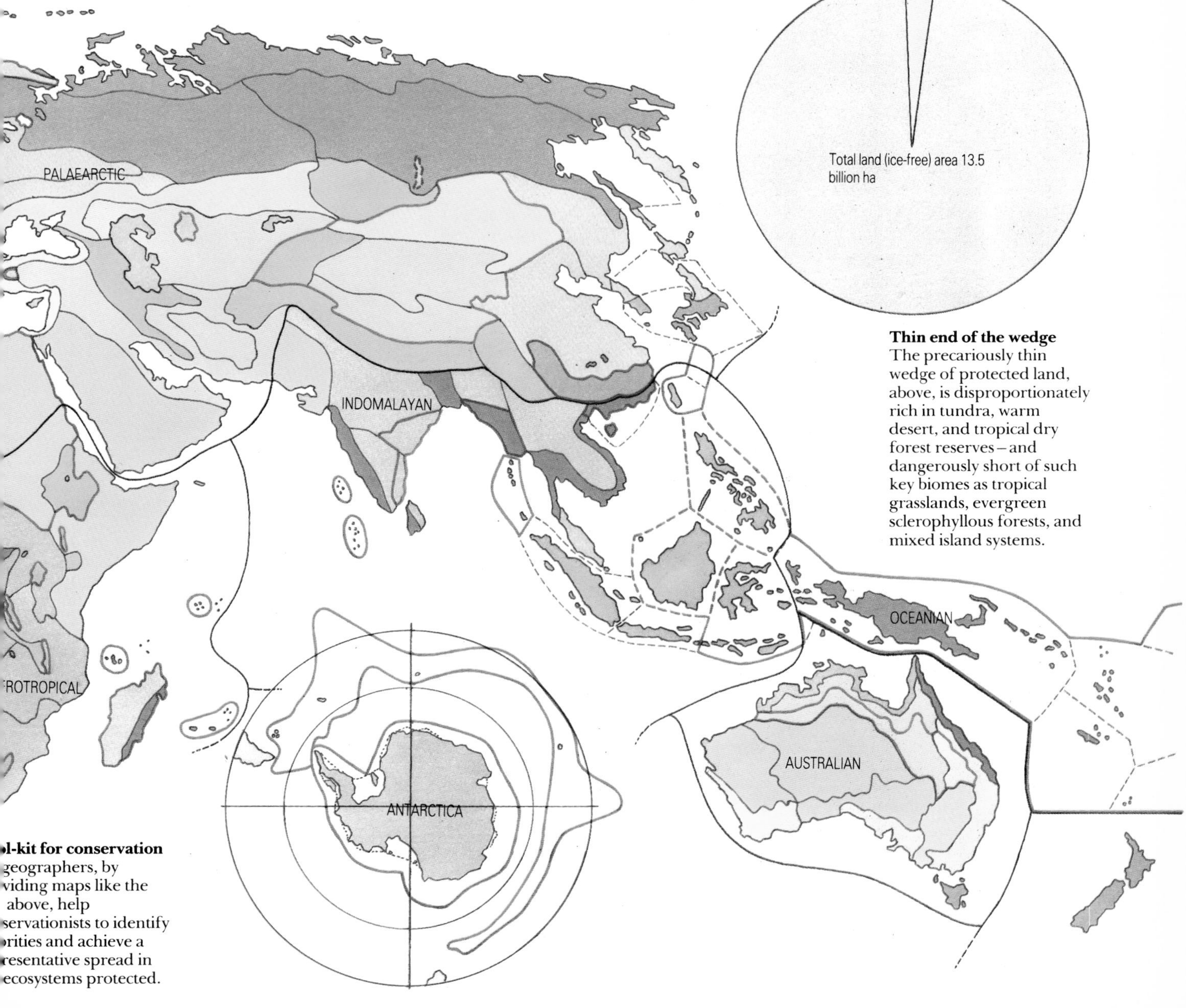

PALAEARCTIC

INDOMALAYAN

OCEANIAN

ROTROPICAL

ANTARCTICA

AUSTRALIAN

l-kit for conservation
geographers, by viding maps like the above, help servationists to identify rities and achieve a resentative spread in ecosystems protected.

In all the instances cited, local people do not clamour for the park to be abolished. Rather, they support its survival.

Options for sustainable management

The world's wildlife represents a multi-faceted resource. It is an aesthetic, even spiritual and recreational resource. It has always been a source of food. And it provides furs and a wide spectrum of other materials. Wildlife can therefore be seen as a vast reservoir of products, both actual and potential, all of which can contribute directly to our welfare.

Yet we are in the process of crowding out this essential resource. As human communities occupy and exploit natural environments on every side, so wildlife habitats disappear. Unless wild creatures can stake a competitive claim to their sectors of the planet, they will surely be squeezed out of many a stronghold. Fortunately, they can make a solid case in the marketplace.

Throughout history, we have hunted wild creatures for food, hides, and other products. Not always in appropriate manner: there is a regrettably long list of species that have been over-hunted, some of them to extinction, as witness the sad stories of the sea cow, the bison, and the passenger pigeon. Equally to the point, however, we have learned to take a sustainable harvest from a similarly long list of species, notably the deer of North America, which yield an ever-larger crop year by year.

In many instances, this harvest generates a rationale for long-term conservation. Through haphazard hunting, the saiga antelope in the USSR was reduced to remnant numbers earlier this century, until a carefully controlled system of exploitation supplied the incentive to rebuild the animal's stocks. Today, the saiga antelope flourishes in its millions, an achievement which supplies a model for the rebuilding of many other threatened species around the world.

Take the capybara. The largest rodent on Earth, weighing as much as 40 kilograms, the capybara lives in the savannahs of Venezuela and Colombia. For decades, the animal has been losing ground to cattle. Now it has been revealed that the capybara, with the high fertility that characterizes rodents (a female produces three dozen offspring in her lifetime, by contrast with less than 10 for a cow), can supply abundant and tasty meat. A number of pioneering projects now capture about 50,000 capybaras each year, yielding more meat per unit area than does a cattle herd. By safeguarding the capybara's habitat, moreover, with its critical wetland sectors, ranchers help the survival of caimans, turtles, and wildfowl, among other depleted species.

Similar innovative schemes are under way to supply incentives for the conservation of crocodiles in Thailand, oryx in Kenya, vicuna in Peru, and even butterflies in Papua New Guinea. Many of these projects channel revenues into the pockets of local people as well as large-scale entrepreneurs,

Harvesting wildlife

Animals need not be domesticated to benefit human economies. They can be harvested in the wild: from the beginning, humans have hunted, fished, or trapped. Wider possibilities for profit from the wild are, however, now being pursued, giving a new dimension, a new energy, to conservation initiatives. They bring with them, nevertheless, perils of their own.

The harvesting of the wild demands a clear understanding of the ecosystems in which we plan to intervene. The dynamic balance of wild species, both with each other and with their environment, can be readily upset. The arrival of human predators affects animals already hunting in the area. New economic dependencies may be created, emphasizing profit at the expense of sensitive management. Yet the advantages are many, and not only in the economic sphere. For example, areas too poor for normal farming often provide sound ranges for game herds. Failing species can be introduced into new habitats or even re-introduced into old ones. In short, conservation and profit can go hand-in-hand.

Wildlife pays its way
Farming wild species has proved successful in much of the fur trade, while in Papua New Guinea and Zimbabwe, crocodiles are farmed for meat and skin. Culling or cropping game reserve herds can assist park income and species health. In selected areas, it is proving practicable to ranch animals previously hunted. The controlled farming of seaborne wildlife may soon be widespread. The central diagram reflects a new approach to the wild base on rational management rather than arbitrary exploitation.

☐ Fur and skin farming
☐ Ranching
☐ Game reserves
☐ The wild
☐ Ocean

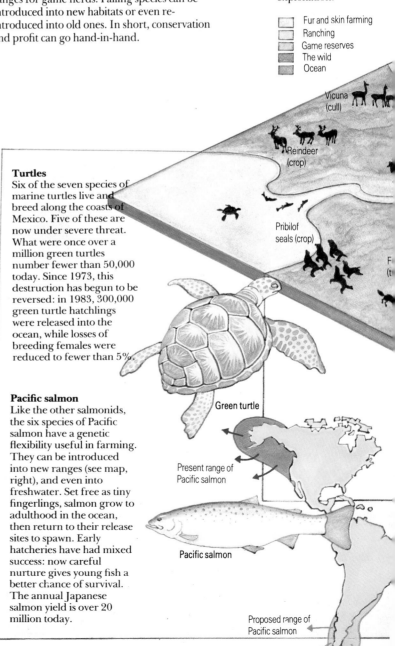

Turtles
Six of the seven species of marine turtles live and breed along the coasts of Mexico. Five of these are now under severe threat. What were once over a million green turtles number fewer than 50,000 today. Since 1973, this destruction has begun to be reversed: in 1983, 300,000 green turtle hatchlings were released into the ocean, while losses of breeding females were reduced to fewer than 5%.

Pacific salmon
Like the other salmonids, the six species of Pacific salmon have a genetic flexibility useful in farming. They can be introduced into new ranges (see map, right), and even into freshwater. Set free as tiny fingerlings, salmon grow to adulthood in the ocean, then return to their release sites to spawn. Early hatcheries have had mixed success: now careful nurture gives young fish a better chance of survival. The annual Japanese salmon yield is over 20 million today.

Vicuna (cull)

Reindeer (crop)

Pribilof seals (crop)

Green turtle

Present range of Pacific salmon

Pacific salmon

Proposed range of Pacific salmon

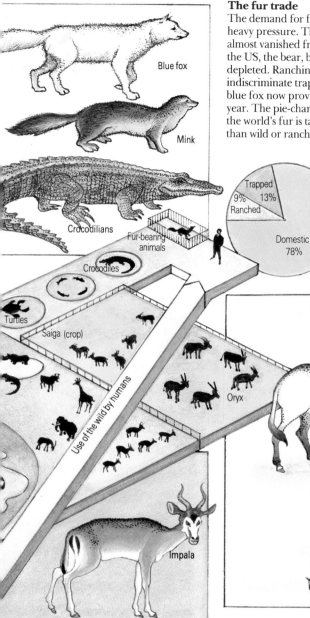

Blue fox

Mink

Crocodilians

Fur-bearing animals

Crocodiles

Turtles

Saiga (crop)

Use of the wild by humans

Impala

The fur trade

The demand for fur has put many species under heavy pressure. The chinchilla and ocelot have almost vanished from parts of Latin America. In the US, the bear, bobcat, and lynx are also depleted. Ranching provides an alternative to indiscriminate trapping. Ranched mink and blue fox now provide millions of pelts every year. The pie-chart, below, shows that most of the world's fur is taken from domestic rather than wild or ranched animals.

World fur harvest
(total 303 million animals killed annually for fur): methods of acquisition

Trapped 13%
Ranched 9%
Domestic 78%

Overkill

Over-hunted species can soon face extinction. Yemenis value rhinoceros-horn dagger handles. Yemeni horn imports in 1966-77 represented a yearly kill of 2,580 rhinos. In Italy, up to 400 million migratory birds, some protected further north, are killed annually. American poachers even pursue the protected bald eagle by helicopter. The graph, below, shows the dramatic decline of the black rhino in Kenya – a decline repeated in many African countries.

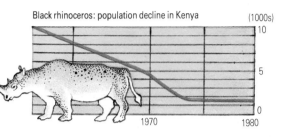

Black rhinoceros: population decline in Kenya   (1000s)
10
5
0
1970   1980

Ranching

Wild animals enclosed for farming often develop serious ailments. Ranching can avoid this problem. Wild species are often immune from diseases that afflict the domesticated. Ranched in East Africa, the oryx needs only 5% of the water cattle do, matures more quickly, has more calves and, in semi-arid conditions, is thus more profitable. With 31% of the world's surface area covered with arid or semi-arid land, ranching of wild creatures has obvious potential.

Oryx

Oryx

Saiga

Vicuna

Cropping

Cropping limits wild herds in crowded reserves. Meat and hides can then increase income: a Ugandan national park has met half its costs by cropping hippopotamus. Wide variations in population estimates for the Peruvian vicuna, however, nearly led to disastrous slaughter.

...lling

...ctive culling, weeding out the weak and least ...ductive individuals, can increase the ...nomic yield of a wild herd. It can also have ...xpected results. The population of ...lebeest and zebra, culled in Kruger National ...k from 1965 to 1972, dropped by 50% in the ...ars that followed. Culling clearly demands ...iled knowledge of population structures.

...r seals

...ng over-hunted, only 3 ...he 9 species of fur seal ...now harvested. By ...09, the northern fur seal ...d been reduced to ...6,000 individuals. ...eaties in 1911 limited the ... and now populations ...estimated to be around

2 million. New methods of culling, introduced in 1956, were meant to create a smaller, more productive herd. This attempt to secure a maximum sustainable yield failed, largely due to lack of information.

Northern fur seals

thus enhancing the image of wildlife in the eyes of rural communities, who are often in a position to make or break the cause of wildlife.

Conserving the unknown

The best way to preserve threatened gene pools is to protect the relevant habitats, by designating them as national parks or game reserves. A second option involves protecting the gene pools off-site, whether in botanical gardens, zoos, or gene banks. This second approach offers many apparent advantages, but it also suffers from some critical drawbacks.

Almost all our present gene banks are off-site, including seed and germplasm storage facilities, clonal plantations, seed orchards, and rare-breeds farms. Such facilities will play an increasingly important role, but their contribution will be limited by a number of key factors. First, there is the sheer size of the task. The diversity of the wild genetic resource is so great that it seems highly unlikely that off-site gene banks could ever save more than a fraction of the total resource.

More importantly, the seeds of some crop species and their wild relatives cannot be dried prior to storage, because they are killed in the process. Gene banks, for example, cannot preserve many seed plants. This applies especially to most vegetatively propagated plants, such as potato, cassava, members of the orchid family, and tree species such as apples and pears that do not breed true from seeds. Many tropical plant species, such as the cacao tree, can be conserved outside the wild only with the greatest difficulty. Some wild species also prove much more difficult to maintain and regenerate than their domesticated relatives, including a number of peanut and sunflower species. Other species, such as barley, beans, and maize, sustain genetic damage during long-term storage.

In addition, the entire stock of a gene bank can be destroyed by a prolonged power cut or by human negligence. Worst of all, a plant's evolution is effectively frozen while it enjoys the refrigerated safety of the gene bank. Outside, evolution goes on – and the protected plant may emerge to find that its wild pathogens and pests have evolved new forms of attack to which it is now unduly vulnerable.

So off-site gene banks can only provide part of the answer to genetic erosion. Ultimately, the only viable long-term approach must involve safeguarding gene pools in the wild. But even today, very few on-site conservation areas coincide with the most valuable concentrations of genetic resources – the so-called "Vavilov centres". Even if we can get such "gene parks" set up in the right places, other solutions are needed to protect the traditional crop varieties which are still cultivated by small-scale farmers throughout the Third World.

One idea which has been proposed to boost on-site conservation of such primitive strains is a tax on corporations selling genetically improved seed. Global sales of the seed industry now exceed $10

Preserving the genetic resourc

There are three main options for the preservation of genetic diversity. We can protect it *on site*, by conserving the entire ecosystem in which it naturally occurs. If this is not possible, we can store part of the organism, such as its seed or semen, *off site*, in some form of gene bank. Or we can keep whole organisms *off site* – in an aquarium, botanical garden, culture collection, plantation, or zoo. Most progress has been made with off-site conservation of crop genetic resources, through an international network of "base collections" covering more than 20 of the world's most important crops. But many species do not take kindly to life in botanical gardens, zoos, or the refrigerated world of the gene bank. So, while all three options have a vital role to play, the first must be our priority.

Gene banks
The seeds of many plant species, especially those with small, dry seeds, can often be stored in a dormant state for long periods at a humidity level of 5% and at a temperature of -20°C. A small gene bank can protect many thousands of species.

Botanical gardens
The world's botanical gardens play a vital role, but they have a problem of storage capacity. The Royal Botanic Garden at Kew, England, receives around 2,000 accessions of seeds each year, yet its total holding of about 25,000 species has scarcely changed over 40 years. As new material arrives, older specimens are discarded.

Zoos
Zoos have recorded a strin of successes with their captive breeding of some threatened species (see left). But there is a rule of thumb that a vertebrate stock of less than 50 individuals is liable to carr the seeds of its own destruction, with harmful genes accumulating rapid in inbred populations. An many species refuse to breed at all in captivity.

Rare-breeds centres
At least 20 breeds of British farm animal have become extinct during the 20th century. To counter this trend, rare-breeds survival centres have been set up, serving as living museums. They provide an opportunity for the general public to underwrite genetic conservation, by paying to see breeds on which their own future may well depend.

On-site protection

The focus of on-site protection programmes tends to be on species of popular appeal, and on species under threat; on unique ecosystems; on ecosystems which are representative of a particular type of habitat; or on some combination of all these approaches. The key objective is to protect as much genetic diversity as possible.

On-site gene banks score over off-site gene banks for a number of reasons, not least because the evolution of species in on-site reserves can continue uninterrupted, providing the breeder with a dynamic reservoir of genes that confer resistance to pests or pathogens.

On-site reserves also serve as living laboratories, allowing the breeder to study a species' ecology. This can throw up valuable information which might otherwise be overlooked; several crucial characteristics of wild tomatoes have surfaced in this way, including their tolerance of saline soils, high temperatures, and humidities, and their resistance to insects and disease.

Land races and wild genes

Among the most threatened gene pools are those of "land races", a term covering primitive traditional plant cultivars and animal breeds. With most wild species, extinction tends to be a fairly gradual process, but land races, developed by local farmers, often enjoy only very limited distribution and can be lost in a single episode of habitat destruction.

Wild gene pools are now increasingly recognized as vital resources for future plant and animal breeding. Variety, in genetic terms at least, is more than the spice of life – it is the key to future survival.

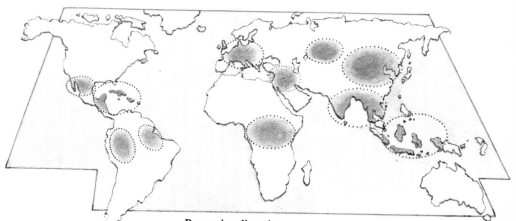

Preserving diversity

The theories of Nikolay Vavilov are at the heart of many conservation programmes. He suggested that the centre of origin of a cultivated plant is to be found in the region where its wild cousins show maximum adaptiveness. The "Vavilov Centres" are prime targets for conservation. The map shows these centres in modified form.

The gene library

At present, international seed companies can borrow and benefit from the gene libraries of the world (many in developing countries) at virtually no charge. As the wild resource becomes more valuable, a strong case develops for making the end-user pay a "lending fee" for "books borrowed". Putting a value on the wild resource in this way will give developing countries a clear economic incentive to preserve the wild habitats.

billion a year, so that even a one percent tax on sales would generate $100 million a year. The revenues could be used to subsidize peasant farmers, enabling them to maintain some of their traditional varieties alongside higher-yield varieties.

Legislating for life

There are three obvious ways to put wildlife conservation on a legal footing. The first is to establish laws for individual species, such as the vicuna, or for a small group of species, such as marine mammals. The second is to establish a treaty for a region, as in the case of the Convention on Conservation of European Wildlife and Natural Habitats. The third is to establish a treaty of worldwide scope, such as the Convention on Wetlands of International Importance. Of these three, the first is easiest to establish, while the third tends to have the most significant impact.

When more than one nation is involved, negotiations become complex and enforcement can be a problem. Since many species occur in several countries at once (the cheetah, for example, is found in 20-odd African countries) or migrate from one country to another, it is often essential that several nations make common cause together.

The most recent breakthrough is CITES – the Convention on International Trade in Endangered Species. This treaty has been adopted by over 80 nations. It tackles the widespread, illicit trade in threatened species, whether they be tropical fish bound for the world's aquaria or spotted-cat skins destined for wealthy shoulders. The legitimate trade is worth billions of dollars a year, and while the illicit trade has been cut back by CITES, it remains big business. Back-sliding nations such as Japan still import huge quantities of tortoiseshell, crocodile skins, musk, and other wildlife products – despite the fact that they have signed CITES.

Meanwhile, wildlife continues to disappear faster than ever. The problem is not so much the poacher or other law-breaker, with rifle or trap in hand: instead, it is the settler, the subsistence farmer, persons without any malign intent towards wildlife. But they use tools such as the axe or plough, which are ultimately far more destructive. Clearly, we need a global treaty which builds on the undoubted successes of CITES, a treaty which protects critical habitats. A Convention, perhaps, on the Protection of Endangered Species – to be known as COPES?

The idea would be that each nation should accept responsibility for all species within its borders. In return, a nation would be able to apply for support from the community of nations to enable it to do a better job. Many developing nations harbour enormous concentrations of species – Panama, for example, may contain as many species as the entire US – but they lack the financial and scientific resources to protect them properly.

Wherever species may be found, they are part of everyone's heritage – so we should all share the cost

Laws and conventions

International law, based on treaties and conventions, was not used to protect wildlife until less than a century ago. The first wildlife treaties were largely concerned with economically important species – and with eliminating species viewed as pests. Two years before the first European wildlife treaty was signed, in 1902, a Convention was concluded which aimed to protect African game for trophy hunters and ivory traders – and which called for the destruction of such "noxious" pests as crocodiles, lions, leopards, hyenas, poisonous snakes, and birds of prey. Since then, there has been a growing spate of treaties and conventions, the most important of which is almost certainly CITES – the Convention on International Trade in Endangered Species. Enforcement is a continuing weakness, with countries like Japan signing CITES, and then proceeding to turn a blind eye to illicit dealing in wildlife products.

Live trade
1 Terrestrial orchids
2 Rare cacti
3 Rare macaws
4 Chimpanzees
5 Coral fish

Wildlife products
6 American ginseng – medicine
7 Hawksbill turtle – shell
8 Spotted cats – fur trade
9 Lizards – skins
10 Rhinoceros horn – ornament
11 Elephant – ivory
12 Pangolin – luxury leather
13 Kangaroo – meat, skins

Hyacinth macaw
The largest of all macaws, this rare parrot is protected in Brazil but smuggled into Bolivia, where documents for its export can be obtained.

CITES
Signed by over 80 countries since 1973, CITES prohibits international commercial trade in the rarest 600 or so species of animals and plants and requires licences from the country of origin for exports of about another 200 groups. CITES has clamped down on the trade in many endangered species – try, for example, to buy a tiger-skin coat in London, Paris, or New York. But wildlife is big business and illegal trade continues. A single orchid or Amazonian parrot can fetch $5,000. A fur coat made from South American ocelots can sell for $40,000 in Germany. Rhino horns are worth their weight in gold. The world map, above, shows nations that are legally bound to enforce CITES and some examples of illegal trade which continue to undermine the impact of the Convention.

Protecting the range
Rigorously protected in its Indian wintering grounds, the Siberian crane is sliding relentlessly towards extinction because it is unprotected on its migratory route through Pakistan and Afghanistan. If it is to survive, its entire range must be included in an international treaty.

Walruses and polar bears
The killing of whales, polar bears, and about a dozen species of seal is regulated. Some, like the walrus, have few natural enemies other than humankind.

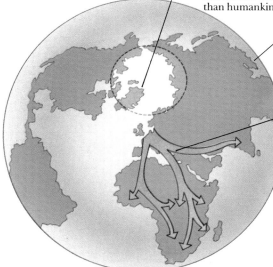

Fisheries
With over 50 fisheries treaties "in force", the drastic depletion of many fish stocks demonstrates how miserably most of these treaties have fared.

Crossing political boundaries
The lack of conventions covering migratory birds in Africa, Asia, and Europe is particularly worrying. Hundreds of species use the Palearctic migratory route between Europe and Africa. Migratory routes require international protection.

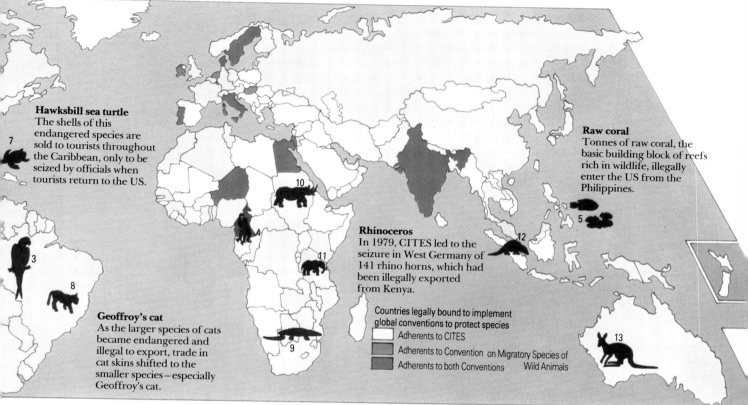

Hawksbill sea turtle
The shells of this endangered species are sold to tourists throughout the Caribbean, only to be seized by officials when tourists return to the US.

Raw coral
Tonnes of raw coral, the basic building block of reefs rich in wildlife, illegally enter the US from the Philippines.

Geoffroy's cat
As the larger species of cats became endangered and illegal to export, trade in cat skins shifted to the smaller species – especially Geoffroy's cat.

Rhinoceros
In 1979, CITES led to the seizure in West Germany of 141 rhino horns, which had been illegally exported from Kenya.

Countries legally bound to implement global conventions to protect species
Adherents to CITES
Adherents to Convention on Migratory Species of Wild Animals
Adherents to both Conventions

Protecting migratory species
There are six bilateral treaties currently in force to protect migratory birds. Four of these involve the US, based on agreements with Canada, Japan, Mexico, and the USSR. The other two involve Japan, which has agreements with Australia and the USSR. Migratory species are covered by the global Convention on Migratory Species of Wild Animals. This Convention came into force in November 1983 but as yet has been signed by only 15 countries (see map, above).

Protecting the world heritage
Unique, because it is so far the only treaty to offer a financial incentive to countries to protect outstanding wildlife habitats, the Convention Concerning the Protection of the World Cultural and Natural Heritage aims to protect natural and human-made features such as the Serengeti and the Pyramids, the Galapagos Islands and the Taj Mahal, which are so outstanding that they are part of everyone's heritage. Support grants come from governments, also from the World Wildlife Fund (for ratifying nations, see map, below).

Protecting wetlands
The Convention on Wetlands of International Importance Especially as Waterfowl Habitat has been signed by 34 countries (see below) – and 279 wetland sites, covering nearly 19 million ha, have been included in the Convention's List of Wetlands of International Importance. This Convention was one of four signed in the 1970s which are neither limited to a few species nor to geographical regions. The other three are CITES, the World Heritage Convention, and the Convention on the Conservation of Migratory Species of Wild Animals.

Countries legally bound to implement global conventions for protection of habitats
Adherents to Convention Concerning Protection of the World Cultural and National Heritage
Adherents to Convention on Wetlands of International Importance Especially As Waterfowl Habitats
Adherents to both Conventions

of their protection. To date there is no adequate mechanism allowing the richer nations to help others on a suitable scale.

Strategies for a sustainable future

We have a fairly good idea of how we should set about protecting our heritage of wildlife and genetic resources. The key will be to establish many more parks and reserves—perhaps covering as much as 10 percent of some regions of the world. But what, meanwhile, happens to the other 90 percent? If we allow these areas to be "developed out of existence", we shall undermine a sizeable proportion of our renewable resource base. And the protected areas will almost certainly be swamped by tides of humanity seeking new resources.

So we must expand our vision beyond the traditional concerns of conservation. We must pay increasing attention to the entire biosphere and to the many life-support systems which we have tended to take for granted, even as we make ever-growing demands upon them. In short, we need a strategy for a new conservation that embraces all life on Earth.

Happily, we now have some excellent ideas, summed up in the term *eco-development*. This term refers to development which takes into account the ultimate health of our planetary ecosystem. The basics of this new approach have been spelled out in a pioneering assessment and manifesto, the World Conservation Strategy (WCS).

Conservation and development, the strategy suggests, are two sides of the same coin: conservation cannot succeed without sustainable development, and development cannot be sustained without conservation. Brave words—but how can we convert them into action? One way is to bring the Strategy to the attention of political leaders. Next, every government should prepare its own National Conservation Strategy. Over 30 nations are preparing such strategies, planning the best overall use of their natural resources for the indefinite future. Simultaneously, international agencies, such as the UN and the World Bank, are becoming more aware of conservation needs and opportunities.

We have made considerable progress to date, developing new techniques such as environmental impact assessment (EIA) to ensure that development projects do not undermine their own chances of success by ignoring critical environmental factors.

Even more important, environmental values have to be incorporated at the policy level, from which particular project proposals flow. There is little point in trying to expand rice production through irrigated areas of Southeast Asia without safeguarding forested watersheds that supply regular amounts of water for year-round cultivation.

National Conservation Strategies are under way in developing countries like Nepal and Zambia. Developed countries too are carrying out similar exercises. We are starting in the right direction.

National Conservation Strategies in action
Conservation strategies are being prepared to suit the needs of different countries. In New Zealand and Uganda, priority is given to monitoring fish stocks and regulating levels of exploitation. In Zambia the NCS looks to minimize the adverse effects of mining, while in Nepal, fuelwood and soil erosion are high on the list. The NCS for Nepal aims to put environmental planning on a permanent footing. At government level, this involves creating new committees and commissions (see right).

Towards a new conservation

A revolutionary new document, the World Conservation Strategy, was launched in March 1980. Backed by the combined forces of IUCN, WWF, UNEP, FAO, and UNESCO, and cross-checked by 400 scientists, the Strategy presents a single, integrated approach to global problems.

It rests on three important propositions. First, species and populations, whether plant or animal, must be helped to retain their capacity for self-renewal. Second, the basic life-support systems of the planet, including climate, the water cycle, and soils, must be conserved intact if life is to continue. And third, genetic diversity is a major key to our future—so it too must be maintained.

The world applauded the Strategy when it first appeared, but little more than 30 countries (see world map) have translated the global strategy into national action.

The potential contribution of national strategies is considerable, as the case of Nepal, right, demonstrates. Although many countries already have national frameworks for tackling environmental problems, a strategy built around the WCS can add a vital new dimension—improving co-ordination and co-operation at both national and international levels.

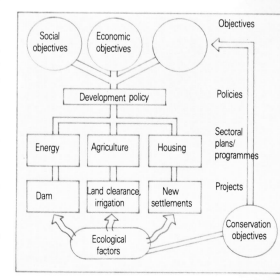

Integrating conservation
Most attempts to assess the environmental impacts of development have focused on specific projects, whereas many critical decisions are taken higher up the decision chain, left. Conservation objectives must be integrated with other main objectives in formulating national policies, before they crystallize into projects and programmes. When ecological factors are considered only at the bottom of the chain, their influence is limited, at best. If integrated at the top level of decision-making, they can have a highly positive influence.

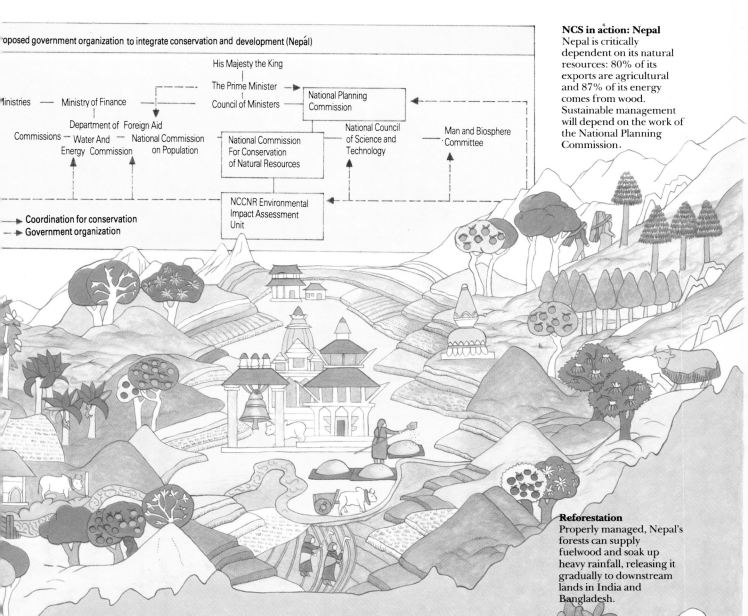

Proposed government organization to integrate conservation and development (Nepal)

His Majesty the King

The Prime Minister

Council of Ministers

Ministries — Ministry of Finance

Department of Foreign Aid

Commissions — Water And National Commission
Energy Commission on Population

National Planning Commission

National Commission For Conservation of Natural Resources

National Council of Science and Technology

Man and Biosphere Committee

NCCNR Environmental Impact Assessment Unit

➤ Coordination for conservation
➤ Government organization

NCS in action: Nepal
Nepal is critically dependent on its natural resources: 80% of its exports are agricultural and 87% of its energy comes from wood. Sustainable management will depend on the work of the National Planning Commission.

Reforestation
Properly managed, Nepal's forests can supply fuelwood and soak up heavy rainfall, releasing it gradually to downstream lands in India and Bangladesh.

Hydroelectric power
Nepal hopes to tap a potential 83,000 megawatts of electric power, while protecting valuable valley farmland by careful siting of dams.

New technology
Improved suspension and pneumatic tyres can increase the carrying capacity of a bullock cart from 750 to 2,500 kg.

tional Park pays its way
pal's Royal Chitwan tional Park protects no, tiger, and gharial. Its tch-grass slows down er-bank erosion and plies a large harvest to al villages.

an and the Biosphere – MAB
ESCO's Man and the Biosphere gramme, launched well over 10 years ago, gan by promoting "in-situ" long-term servation of the world's representative systems, with their component plants, mals, and micro-organisms. The Programme arted from traditional conservation cepts, emphasizing the need for scientific earch and constant monitoring of the ironment. Over the years, the Programme evolved to reflect the pervasive influence of mankind in the biosphere – and our constant ponsibility for its continuing evolution.

HUMANKIND

Introduced by Tarzie Vittachi

Assistant Secretary General of UNICEF

Shortly before she died, Cambridge economist Joan Robinson wrote to a friend: "I have spent most of my life in prescription. I wish I had spent more time on description". This was a pithy diagnosis of the problems which have dogged the development process over the last three decades. We have been too ready to prescribe instant remedies for the ailments of the poor, too conceited to spend time uncovering and articulating the reality of poverty – what the poor themselves perceive as their capabilities, needs, and aspirations.

So the first development decade concentrated on top-down, or "trickle down", approaches, focusing on massive infrastructure projects such as highways and high-dams. The second development decade, derided by Tom Mboya, then Kenyan Minister of Development, as the "dollar a year" development decade, was largely spent in analysing what when wrong with the first.

The third development decade began by acknowledging the failure of the top-down approach; instead, it emphasized bottom-up development – omitting to recognize that life is rarely a question of either/or, but of both/and. New "softer" approaches, based on primary health care and "basic needs", were legitimized when the World Bank devoted its 1980 report to human development, a major shift from its early focus on economic or material targets.

As destitution and malnutrition proliferated, vociferous demands were made for fairer shares for the South and the poor, and a "New International Economic Order" (NIEO) became the central target for the development set. Half-way through the third development decade, however, the NIEO has been wrecked on the rocks of conservatism and monetarism in the Western world. The rich socialist states are unlikely to change their line that underdevelopment is a legacy of past imperialism – and that the West is responsible for bailing the South out. And the brief flash of hope that OPEC, flush with petro-dollars, would invest heavily in the Third World has turned out to be a mirage.

Development theories have, at best, been only partially successful: the number of people living in absolute poverty is rapidly scaling up to a billion. Central planning and implementation of development programmes have only worked where there are powerful governments of left or right, unencumbered by opposition. Development in more open societies has often failed because it has been based on the notion that supply creates demand. A prime example was birth control: contraceptives were supplied in rainbow colours, but there were fewer takers than hoped for.

The "demand" approach by contrast, seeks to reveal and activate latent demand for development. People know what they need – health, food, clean water, shelter, education, transport, and a better life. But generations of deprivation have persuaded them that their plight is their ineluctable fate.

Fate is what happens to one, destiny what should happen. Our strategy must be to demonstrate that the line of fate can be moved towards the line of destiny if people would work on their own potential. The communications process, instead of being a one-way channel carrying prescriptions from the centre to the village, must also be able to carry messages from the village to the centre – this is what Joan Robinson meant by "description".

Varindra Tarzie Vittachi

THE HUMAN POTENTIAL

The Chinese proclaim that, "of all things, people are the most precious". And so they are. When one person is joined by a second, their joint capacity is not simply doubled: they can inspire one another, laugh together, and love each other. When all the peoples of the planet are considered together, they represent a capacity for labour, knowledge, creativity, conscious understanding, and happiness that cannot be measured. But, however the Chinese may delight in people as the finest manifestations of life's forces on Earth, they certainly do not believe that more must be better.

In fact, no other community matches the Chinese in their efforts to limit their numbers – on the grounds that more Chinese would result in poorer Chinese. The quality of human life is quite distinct from its quantity. There are five million Danes, for example, and over 730 million Indians – yet it would be grotesque to suppose that Indians are 150 times better off than Danes.

The size of a country's or region's population can, of course, increase its political influence – but this relationship is far from automatic (the control of wealth is far more significant). In 1900, 17 percent of the world's total population lived in Europe, whereas by the year 2000, only about 8 percent will do so. The developing world, which today is home to 75 percent of the global population, could account for 90 percent within 50 years. The weight of numbers may well effect a shift in focus towards the South.

In the South, the population is predominantly young, putting pressure on child health and education services. In the industrialized North, the size of the over-60s sector has social and economic implications which worry many governments. As longevity increases, nation after nation will be affected by the "grey wave", and we will have to develop new ways to care for the world's senior citizens. They represent a valuable reservoir of skills and experience.

In the light of social and economic advance, and technological change, the potential of the young people should be even greater. The percentage of young people in education has never been larger. The level of education, training, and creative enthusiasm in a population can powerfully influence the extent to which the potential of the human resource is released and harnessed. Some developing countries, notably China, have achieved near-miracles in improving the education, health, and life expectancy of their citizens, giving a

People potential

The greatest natural resource on the planet is the human race itself. And, in a world in need of ever-increasing care and protection, the full potential of every individual has never been more in demand. Releasing such potential is rarely easy, rarely comfortable, but the scale of the challenge we now face makes it essential. There is no shortage of urgent tasks, all of which are well within our capacity – providing we can mobilize the necessary political will, and physical energies, amplified through appropriate technologies. But lack of basic needs such as food, water, fuel, and shelter, plus social neglect, and often sheer prejudice, continue to obscure many elements of the human resource: one of the most blatant examples has been the failure to capitalize on the abilities of women; another is the neglect of the young and unemployed. We have the human resources we need, if only we are prepared to give them a chance.

Biceps and brains
The power and ability of people is not amenable to measurement. In theory, the 2.6 billion people aged 15-64 could till the world's cultivable land in 3 days. But such muscle power, roughly equal to 2 billion kilowatts of energy per hour, pales beside creative and inventive power – the great art of the world, for instance, or the creation of artificial intelligence.

China
Considering the enormity of the problems they have faced, successive Chinese governments have made real progress in developing people potential. The 1982 census reported a total population of 1.02 billion, and China's GNP is relatively low, at $290 per person. Yet adult literacy is now 66%, a vast improvement on the pre-1949 picture. A comprehensive health service has boosted life expectancy to 64 years. And the recently recognized private sector is boosting employment. The darker side is that personal liberty has been curtailed.

100%
90%
80%
70%

Global provisions

Attempting to express in global terms the numbers of people, out of 4.7 billion, whose basic needs are fulfilled is probably one of the ultimate exercises in statistical frustration. But however rough the measures, the revelations of recent global surveys are overwhelming – both in numbers of those who *are* literate, and in good health, and in areas of massive neglect. On the sunlit face of life, there is an abundance of human energy; in the shadows, a lost resource of millions trapped in the struggle to survive.

1 Nourishment 450 million people are starving or (the majority) ill-fed.

2 Infant mortality 19 children per 1,000 die before age 1 in the North; in the South 93 per 1,000.

3 Primary-school enrolment A huge increase since 1950 has achieved 73.9% enrolment.

4 Literacy The proportions of adult literacy are less than half for women, and about two-thirds for men.

5 Housing About three-quarters of world housing has been classified as substandard. Sanitation is the most serious problem.

6 Social protection National expenditure on social welfare ranges from practically nil to over half a nation's budget.

7 Civil liberties and political freedom The Freedom House index, one of the least subjective measures of human freedoms, gives the North an average of 80%; but the South, with many dictatorships, has an average of only 20%.

8 Employment At least a third of the world's workforce is unemployed or underemployed.

9 Longevity National averages vary from less than 40 to well over 70 years.

years
years

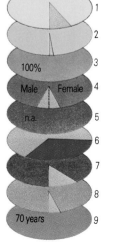

Costa Rica

ta Rica

...etimes described as the "Switzerland of ...n America", this tiny country represents an ...s of peace (its army was abolished more than ...ears ago) in an area of intense political ...ion and military conflicts. The 2.2 million ...a Ricans enjoy a high quality of life: in 1980, ...P was $1,730 per person, and life ...ectancy, at 70, is the second highest in Latin ...erica. The country's literacy rate, at 90%, is ...nd only to Cuba. But national debt ($3.3 ...on in 1982) threatens to undermine its ...omic stability.

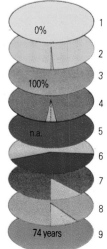

Denmark

Denmark appears to be doing more to develop the potential of its people than almost any other industrial country. With a population of a little over 5 million, at a density of 80 people per square kilometre, it has achieved a 99% literacy rate, an average life expectancy of 75 years, a stable population, and a remarkable degree of economic self-sufficiency. Denmark's income distribution is the best in Europe and, in aid to the Third World, Denmark is the fourth highest donor (taken as a percentage of GNP) among the developed nations.

powerful boost to their capacity to contribute to their societies. The real challenge is to enable all people, old and young, to realize more of their potential. Freeing our human resources from the difficulties that prevent their participation represents our best hope of making the transition in good order and in good time.

The working potential

In early days, "work" and "activity" meant much the same thing – learning or teaching, preparing food or hunting for it, growing up or growing old, were all of equal importance. But in "advanced" societies, there has long been a dominant popular equation linking work to jobs, jobs to money, and money to human worth. This is fast becoming questionable in the North – and was never entirely relevant in the South. Two key factors are contributing to the shift of values: the growth of the workforce, and the changing nature of work.

We can already enumerate the workforce of the year 2000, because its numbers are now among us: there is only a 15-year lag before the average newborn child becomes a new worker. The greatest increases will be in the South, adding some 780 million extra potential workers to the 1980 figure of 1.25 billion. The implication is that 30-40 million new jobs will need to be created each year.

As for the changing nature of work, the industrialized nations of the North have already under-

The world at work

Human skill and energy represent a resource which is potentially renewable in perpetuity. But tremendous shifts are now taking place in the way these skills and energy are used. Some 300 years ago it took over 90 percent of the world's labour force working on farms to feed a much smaller population, whereas today the proportion of population working on the land in many developed countries has fallen to below 10 percent, in some cases considerably less. Major changes in the structure and technological base of industries, fuelled partly by the information revolution and partly by market changes (pp 206-7), have created labour surpluses in many regions, coupled with shortages of certain skills.

Labour force estimates
The histograms, below left and right, show male and female workforces, in millions, for seven regions of the world. This is the economically active population – that is, all those above a specific age (15 in most countries) who have worked for profit or who have sought work.
Developed countries
These show an increasing proportion of women in the workforce, notably in E Europe and USSR. A relatively small overall growth is projected.

Services 100%

United States
The shift from traditional land-based employment is nowhere clearer than in the US. Agricultural work has shrunk dramatically (see triangle). Waged work has reached 90%. White-collar jobs are increasing, blue-collar ones falling.

West Germany
Europe's strongest industrial nation has a high proportion of waged work, of which 12.8% counts as "professional and technical" work. Like the US, the recent trends in employment are moving towards the services sector.

Hungary
Few Communist countries release full data for ILO surveys, but most have a high waged sector and low unemployment. Hungary's workforce shows a marked shift from the land into industry. Over 40% of the workforce is female.

Wage labour trends
The International Labour Office (ILO) work categories reveal massive self-employment in the South, and dominant waged work in the North. (The categories, however, are not always readily comparable between nations.)

◻ Waged
◻ Self-employed
◼ Other

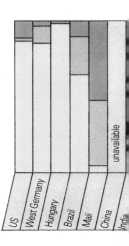

e a massive transformation. There are freely
ered contracts and increasing employee protec-
. The welfare state cushions the workforce to
e extent from the impact of recession and
mployment. In the OECD region, services such
nance and business, wholesale and retail trades,
government employment now offer more jobs
traditional industries.

he premium set on waged employment by
ens of developed countries stems from the
timacy it bestows in society. A job not only
vides money, but psychological rewards. Nearly
ercent of the workforce relies on waged work.
traditional rural societies, by contrast, whole
ilies invest their labour in a great deal of unpaid
work, which escapes definition by conventional
statistics. Of the measured workforce, agriculture
still claims 70 percent in low-income countries, and
45 percent in middle-income countries. Formal
employment is supported by a huge informal sector,
giving as much as 60 percent of employment in the
biggest cities.

Work patterns are likely to change radically in the
future. The key characteristic of many new technologies is that they amplify the productivity of
workers, whether they work predominantly with
their biceps or brains. Some believe that the result in
developed economies will be widespread deskilling
of workers, others that the future lies with retrain-
ing, job-sharing, and self-employment. For the

Developing countries The
burgeoning pool of labour
in the Third World
represents both a daunting
challenge for policy makers
and an enormous potential
resource. Few countries
have made sustained
efforts to draw the un- and
underemployed into the
economy, but there have
been highly successful job-
creation programmes in
countries like China. In
South Korea, too, resource
regeneration programmes
have boosted employment.

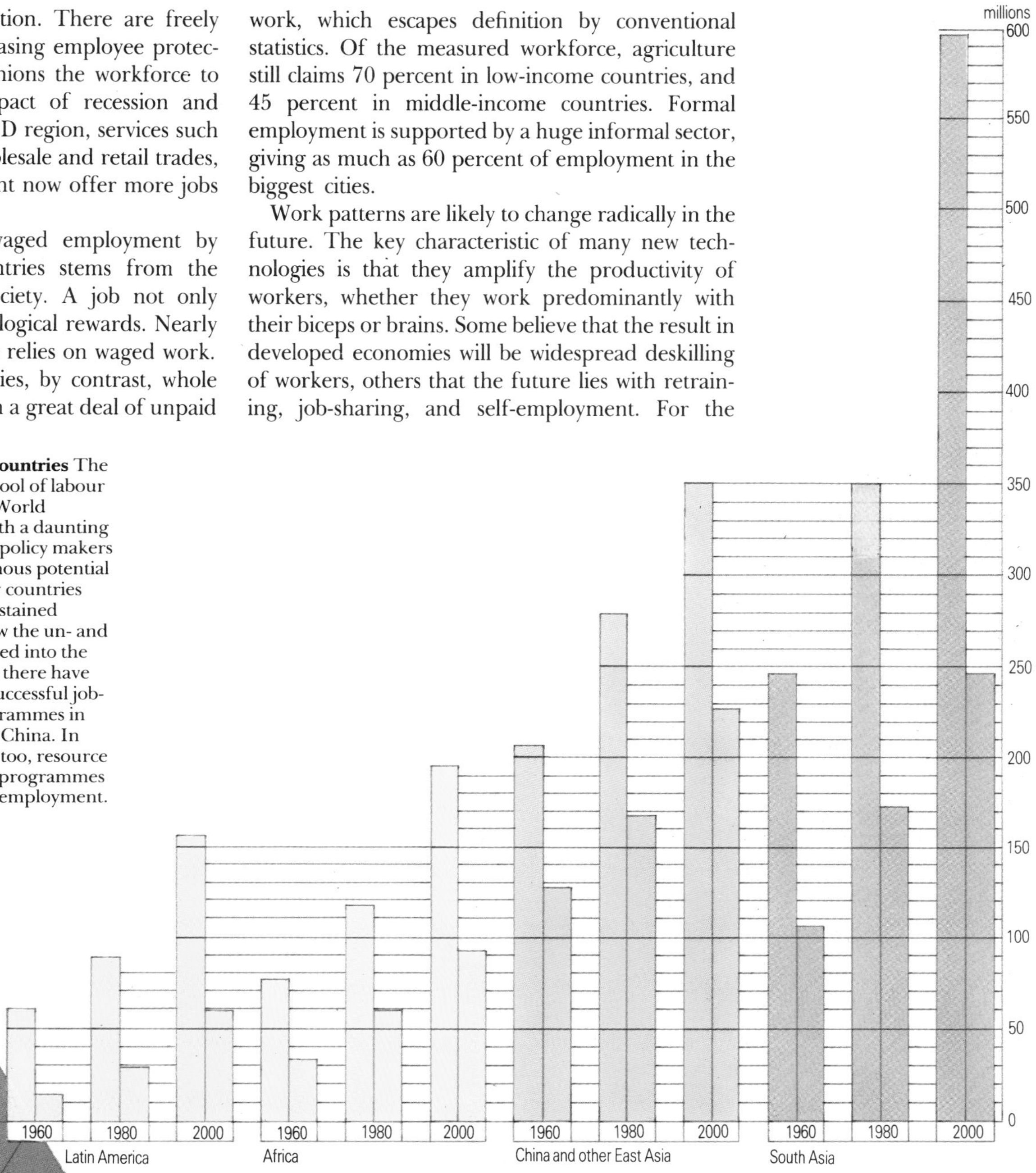

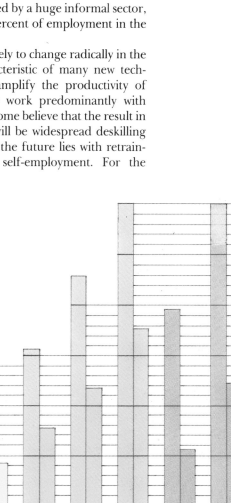

millions
600
550
500
450
400
350
300
250
200
150
100
50
0

1960   1980   2000   1960   1980   2000   1960   1980   2000   1960   1980   2000
Latin America   Africa   China and other East Asia   South Asia

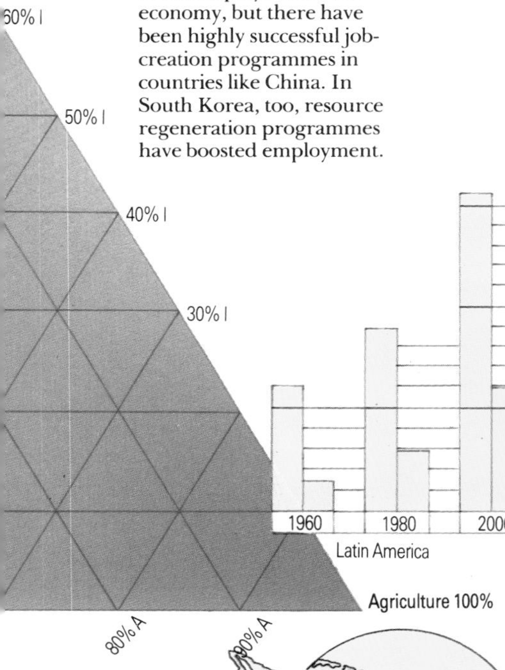

Agriculture 100%

80% A   100% A

**our distribution
ngle**
 seven countries whose
ur distribution trends
0-80) are plotted in the
ram above mostly
or world trends in the
main areas of work.
ws pointing down
agricultural work
ing, with employment
dustry and services
easing. Many Southern
tries still have large
cultural workforces.
or shifts, as in Brazil
Hungary, reflect
rnment economic
grammes. Chinese data
available only for 1980.

Brazil
Brazil's economic transition
has ridden on the back of
rapid industrial growth.
Surveys show a parallel rise
in those with professional
skills. There is also a
thriving black-market
sector (in part due to loss of
agricultural work).

Mali
Mali's low unemployment
and huge self-employment
match a high farm-
ownership ratio. The
workforce focuses on bare
subsistence: upgrading the
farming economy could
release resources for other
developments.

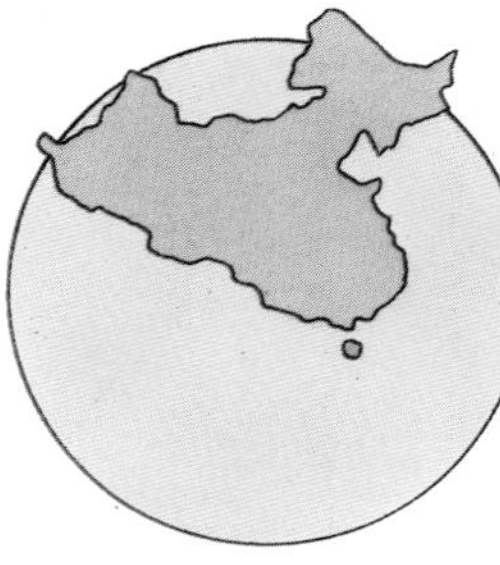

China
Of the huge Chinese
population, some 1.02
billion in 1982, at least 85%
are peasants. They own
their land communally, but
are encouraged to show
private initiative. As China
industrializes, the peasant
force will shrink.

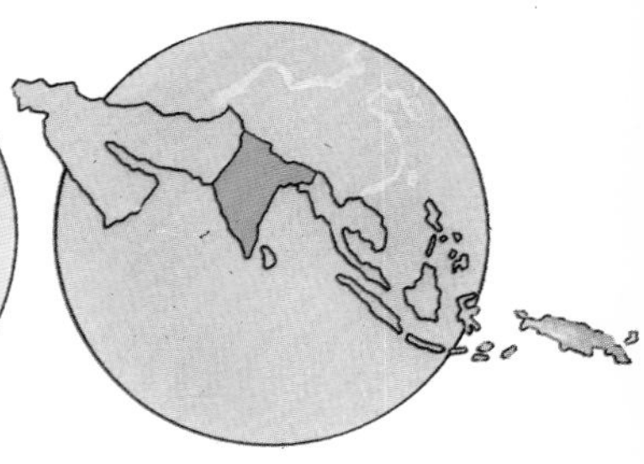

India
With the world's second
largest population, India
ranks as the ninth largest
economy. The workforce is
predominantly self-
employed. Population
growth could swell the
labour force to 385 million
by 2000.

present, problems in the South are different. Here the need is to ensure that people have not only jobs, but adequate income. It is easy to forget, however, that many newly independent countries have already come very far, demonstrating that populations previously restricted to unskilled labour can produce, within a few decades, the professional and other skilled workers they need.

Knowledge versus wisdom

The human race can be justly proud of its science and learning. In the few centuries since Galileo deduced our position in the heavens, the ingenuity, imagination, and perseverance of our species have led to the detailed exploration of our vast solar system. As one quantum leap in understanding has followed another, new technologies have emerged in their wake, enabling us to deal far more effectively with the tasks we undertake. Like the proverbial lilypads multiplying on a pond, knowledge breeds knowledge at an exponential rate, carrying science forward even faster.

Recent times have witnessed an unprecedented spread of knowledge throughout the human population. The advent of machine printing sparked the information revolution, creating a base for mass education. Press, radio, and television have successively reached ever larger audiences. Today, almost one-fifth of the world's 4.7 billion people is participating in some form of education. Annual book production now totals 726,000 titles: one person reading a book a day would take nearly 2,000 years to read one year's supply!

Formal educational systems and school enrolment are, fortunately, growing faster than the school-age population; the number of children in primary and secondary education has almost tripled in 20 years, reaching 394 million in 1980. There remains, however, a huge challenge in developing countries, where many children do not have a school to attend.

But learning and knowledge is not necessarily wisdom. In acquiring new knowledge, traditional communities have been overwhelmed, losing some of the perceptions which previously sustained them. Some of our new skills run counter to all conventional wisdom: several nations now have the power to vaporize atomically large regions of the planet.

While science is pre-eminent, it is increasingly remote from the humanities. Indeed, the development of systematic thought has long since progressed beyond the stage where one person, like Aristotle, could be at the frontiers of knowledge in Mathematics, Science, Philosophy, Art, and Politics.

Western civilization has almost relinquished the holistic approach to learning, understanding, and acting. The "systems theories", which attempt a unified overview, also tend towards specialization. Yet the keys to re-integration are beginning to emerge. Many now seek guidance from traditional societies on how to re-establish a balance between humankind and its environment. Our species is still

Homo sapiens

Every species other than *Homo sapiens* adapts its form and behaviour to the pressures of its environment. *Homo sapiens*, on the contrary, has achieved the remarkable feat of being able to adapt the environment instead, overcoming many natural limitations, through the development of technologies and cultures. While this has brought myriad benefits, the spiralling growth of knowledge has been possible only through a high degree of specialization (top right). We need to develop a new holism, appropriate for our advanced societies in the Gaian ecosystem.

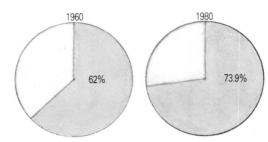

Primary-school enrolment

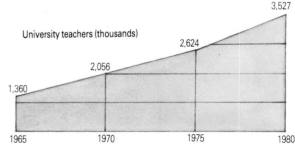

University teachers (thousands)

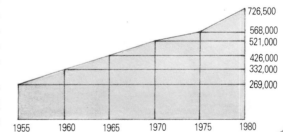

Brought to book
The world output of books has expanded rapidly to reach nearly three-quarters of a million titles in 1980. In regional production, the North is highest.

The global school
The '60s and early '70s were the great boom year in education: by 1980, 70 of the developing countri primary-age children wer in school, and 32% of secondary-age children. the North, 94% of primary-age children wer in school and 84% of secondary-age children.

Adult education explosie
The late '60s saw the glob total of tertiary-level teachers surge from 1.36 2.06 million – a growth ra of 8.6% a year. This slow to 5.5% in the '70s. From lower base, the developin country total grew by 9.3 a year, compared to 4% i the North. Today the wo total tops 3.5 million.

The information explosion
The output of new knowledge is growing side side with economic and social development, i not with wisdom. Recent growth is being fun by research and development budgets now topping $150 billion, a major proportion goir on military research and development. New technologies are being developed in order to store, index, and analyse the explosion of dat

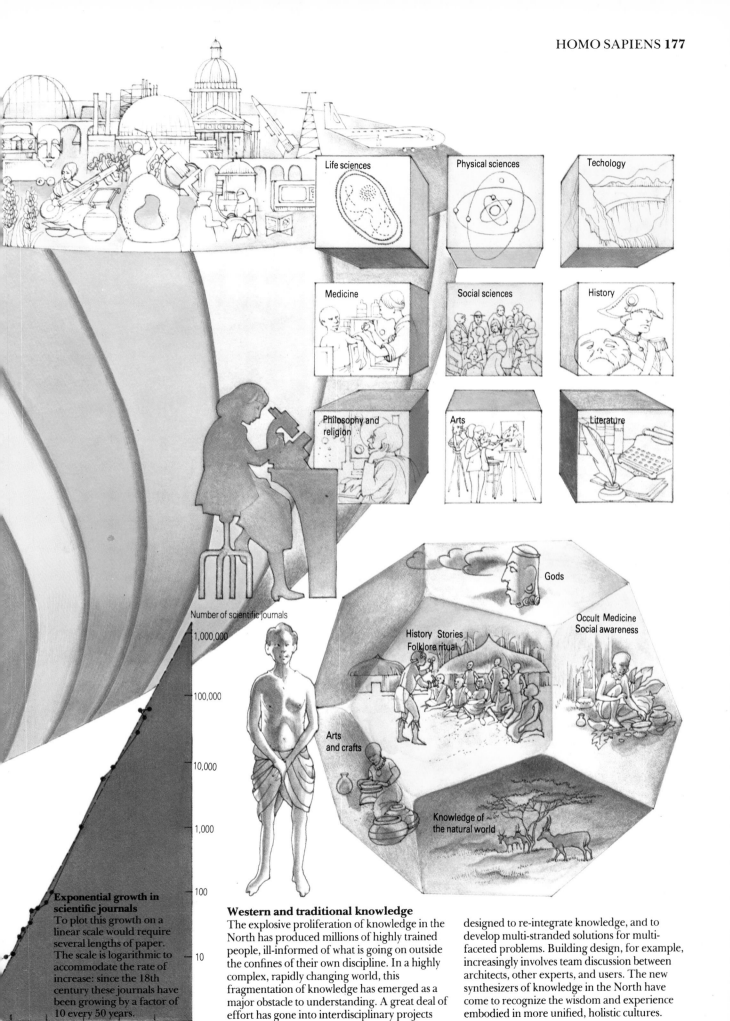

Life sciences

Physical sciences

Techology

Medicine

Social sciences

History

Philosophy and religion

Arts

Literature

Gods

History Stories Folklore ritual

Occult Medicine Social awareness

Arts and crafts

Knowledge of the natural world

Number of scientific journals

1,000,000

100,000

10,000

1,000

100

10

Exponential growth in scientific journals
To plot this growth on a linear scale would require several lengths of paper. The scale is logarithmic to accommodate the rate of increase: since the 18th century these journals have been growing by a factor of 10 every 50 years.

1800   1900   2000

Western and traditional knowledge
The explosive proliferation of knowledge in the North has produced millions of highly trained people, ill-informed of what is going on outside the confines of their own discipline. In a highly complex, rapidly changing world, this fragmentation of knowledge has emerged as a major obstacle to understanding. A great deal of effort has gone into interdisciplinary projects

designed to re-integrate knowledge, and to develop multi-stranded solutions for multi-faceted problems. Building design, for example, increasingly involves team discussion between architects, other experts, and users. The new synthesizers of knowledge in the North have come to recognize the wisdom and experience embodied in more unified, holistic cultures.

in the adolescent phase, learning more facts than it knows what to do with. But the global challenges we now face are beginning to provoke new levels of understanding, of wisdom, which are vitally needed if we are to manage our inheritance properly.

Human identity

Catchphrases are often an attempt to encapsulate or pin down particular human predicaments. Two current catchphrases, "sense of identity" and "crisis of conscience", are particularly common. They may be too simple, but they reflect contemporary uncertainties and the quest undertaken by growing numbers of people to re-establish their confidence in themselves as human beings. This quest is particularly intense in the more affluent regions.

In its most basic form, identity can be established in short order. Most of us live within some civic structure, making use of a range of services – and we can readily be located through the records that the suppliers of these services hold. Our sense of place and space is shaped by family and the local environment. But in a polyglot world, where cultures collide, cross-fertilize, and divide, language and custom are also key tools in upholding one's developing sense of identity.

Cases where individuals have developed multiple identities, for whatever reason, are simply extreme examples of a natural process which happens to us all. As in the weaving of a tapestry, the weft of experience is overlaid upon the warp of territory and of social relationship. The sense of belonging, which is such a key element in building up our sense of identity, can be experienced at a number of levels simultaneously: at the level of the family, of the local community, of the ethnic group, or of the nation state. At an even more fundamental level, we may believe that we are all God's children, that we are among the Chosen, or even that we are part of the Gaian system.

There is also an intimate link between economic activity and sense of identity: fruitful work enhances self-esteem. The advent of automation and of depersonalizing technology has created a situation where many workers are alienated from the product of their labours. It is ironic, too, that many people, both in the developed world and, increasingly, in the developing countries, shore up their diminishing self-esteem with the material trappings of so-called success – "gadgets" which have been designed for obsolescence.

If we accept this form of self-aggrandisement as the key to identity and sense of individual worth, it might seem that the squatter or shanty dweller, for example, is one of the dispossessed. Strikingly, quite the opposite may be true. Many shanty towns in developing countries represent an intense affirmation of self and identity, of the spirit of enterprise, and of confidence in the inner resources of human beings – although expressed at a different level from more "sophisticated" Westerners.

A sense of identity

Who am I? Why am I here? What will happen to me? Questions such as these, and the answers given in reply, help shape our sense of identity. This sense of identity is one of our most critical resources, anchoring us in an ever-changing world – and giving us a base from which we can help shape events, even as they shape us.

If we think of the human brain, that infinitely adaptable organ, as so much computer hardware, then we can picture the world's languages, religions, and ideologies as competing software – designed to programme socially each new generation.

Our sense of identity reflects the varying influence of many programmes and programmers, some complementary, some in conflict. And new influences are constantly emerging which challenge – and may reshape – our view of ourselves and of our world. The world maps, below, illustrate some of the genetic and cultural influences which make us what we are – or believe ourselves to be.

Mappable elements of race, religion, and language would, however, be misleading if it were not stressed that few areas are homogeneous in any of these respects. They present a surface picture with little scope for detail; least of all can they accurately portray the group or individual perceptions of identity, loyalties, and beliefs.

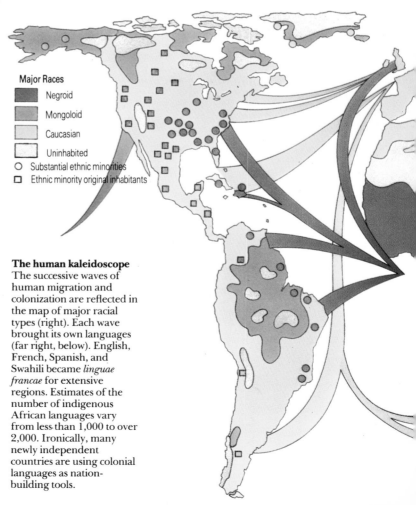

Christianity   Islam   Hinduism

Major Races
- ■ Negroid
- ▨ Mongoloid
- ▧ Caucasian
- □ Uninhabited
- ○ Substantial ethnic minorities
- □ Ethnic minority original inhabitants

The human kaleidoscope
The successive waves of human migration and colonization are reflected in the map of major racial types (right). Each wave brought its own languages (far right, below). English, French, Spanish, and Swahili became *linguae francae* for extensive regions. Estimates of the number of indigenous African languages vary from less than 1,000 to over 2,000. Ironically, many newly independent countries are using colonial languages as nation-building tools.

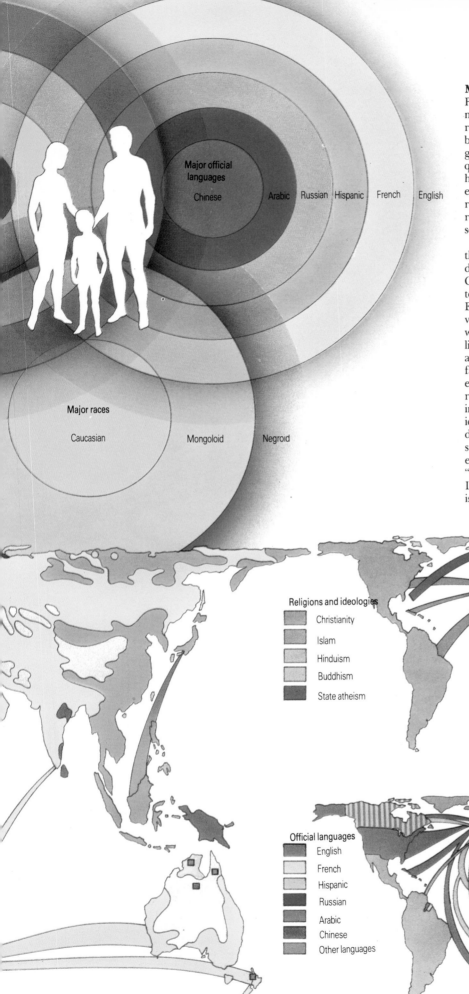

Major official languages

Chinese · Arabic · Russian · Hispanic · French · English

Major races

Caucasian · Mongoloid · Negroid

Multiple identities

Plotted as colours on maps, below, the world's major racial groupings, official languages, and religions and ideologies look as stable as national borders. But, like such borders, their geographical extent can expand or shrink very quickly. Our individual sense of identity, however, can be reshaped even faster by external events and pressures – be it a resurgence of religious fundamentalism, a revolution, or the spreading shock waves of some new sub-culture.

The power of religion has been illustrated by the resurgence of Islam in the Middle East. And, despite the influence of state atheism, most Communist countries still contain regions loyal to traditional religions. In parts of Eastern Europe, the Catholic faith has become the vehicle of national consciousness. The major world religions and ideologies are plotted below, linking vast territories. But many other factors also shape the bedrock of identity, including family, community, the sense of place, education, employment, and national or regional allegiances. As our societies grow increasingly complex, so we develop "multiple identities" – or what might be more properly described as multi-faceted identities. In one study of ethnic groups in London, UK, for example, many subjects had several overlapping "loyalties" such as English, Black English, West Indian, and Londoner. The sense of belonging is never a simple matter.

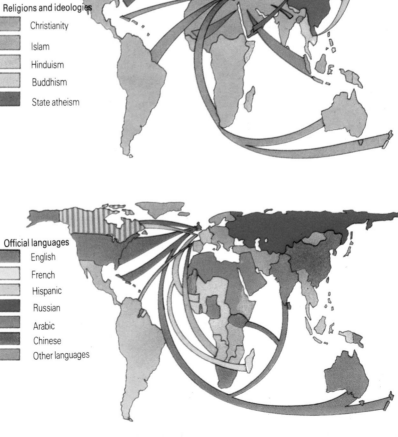

Religions and ideologies
- Christianity
- Islam
- Hinduism
- Buddhism
- State atheism

Official languages
- English
- French
- Hispanic
- Russian
- Arabic
- Chinese
- Other languages

CRISIS: THE INABILITY TO PARTICIPATE

Statistics on those excluded from the benefits of global society can be numbing. During the past year, hunger has claimed some 40 million lives; worklessness, disease, refugee problems, poverty, and social neglect have marred hundreds of millions more, the numbers growing every day. The tragedy of this waste of human potential is that so much of it could be avoided, with fairly minor adjustments to our budgets, although large ones to our "priorities". What cannot be avoided, however, is the disastrous consequences for humanity of our runaway numbers, in some regions outstripping all efforts to increase provision.

Population growth

Despite huge increases in global food output since the 1950s, per capita grain production in the '80s has not topped the mid-'70s level because of world population growth. In 1983, it actually fell, due to a sudden drought hitting already overtaxed lands, causing widespread famine. Tragically, this scenario is likely to be repeated. In the past 33 years, human numbers have doubled, and they may rise by almost as much again over the next 16-20 years. The existing inequities of supply and the geographic mismatch between people and resources are seriously exacerbated by current population growth rates–generally highest in the poorer countries.

A key factor in the growth of human numbers is a population's age profile. A greater proportion of young people gives a greater potential for future growth in numbers. Some 45 percent of Africans, 40 percent of Latin Americans, and 37 percent of Asians are under 15 years old–a series of potential population time bombs.

Apparently small annual growth rates can add up to potentially devastating increases in population. A 3 percent annual growth rate leads to a doubling of population every 23 years–even a 2 percent rise implies a doubling every 35 years. Demographers have plotted an "S" curve for *Homo sapiens* showing Africa still in the rapid growth phase, with three other regions slowing down, but still doubling their populations in 35-40 years, at present growth rates.

The human species is unique in having developed artificial means to limit reproduction. Yet many nations fail to use this capability. Often people are forced into desperate measures: the global number of abortions, for example, is estimated to be at least 130,000 *a day*. All too often, a combination of poverty, very high child mortality, and lack of social

The numbers game

In a world with a finite capacity to support life, our seemingly infinite capacity for reproduction remains our central problem. In the last 100 years, world population increased from about 1.5 billion to 4.7 billion. UN estimates project a world population in excess of 6 billion by the year 2000–and anywhere between 8 billion and 15 billion before world population stabilizes in the early 22nd century.

How alarming are these figures? Assuming traditional farming methods are improved in the South, only the Middle East would be incapable of feeding its population in the year 2000. If all available land is used, together with an increase in fertilizer use, and surpluses are shipped across frontiers, most regions could support more than their current populations.

But a more realistic breakdown of the demand-and-supply picture, country by country, indicates a major crisis ahead. By the year 2000, 1.7 billion people are projected to be living in countries that cannot support their existing populations. Thirty of these countries will be in Africa, 14 in Central America, 6 in Asia, and 15 in the Middle East. If governments reject the possibility of controlling population growth, their struggle against famine, disease, and high infant mortality will be even harder.

The populations switchback

Many populations of wild animals explode and collapse regularly. Stability requires a finely tuned balance between numbers born and numbers dying (see below). The large "S" curve diagram, right, shows the current positions of human populations in several regions. Although an obvious route to stability is to reduce the birth rate, this does not achieve an immediate balance. A nation with a "youthful profile" to its population clearly contains many potential parents. China's two-child family policy could not prevent its present population of 1.025 billion from growing to 1.8 billion prior to zero growth. So China is trying to establish the one-child family plan in an attempt to keep its eventual total to 1.2 billion.

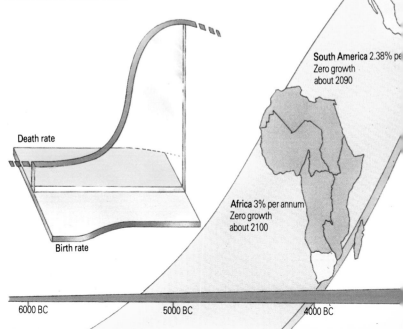

Population density
Over 300
Over 140
Over 100
Over 50
Over 2(
Ov

Infant mortality by region
Over 100 per 1,000
Over 50 per 1,000
Under 50 per 1,000

So
So
2.1
Ze
ab

South America 2.38% pe
Zero growth
about 2090

Africa 3% per annum
Zero growth
about 2100

Death rate

Birth rate

6000 BC   5000 BC   4000 BC

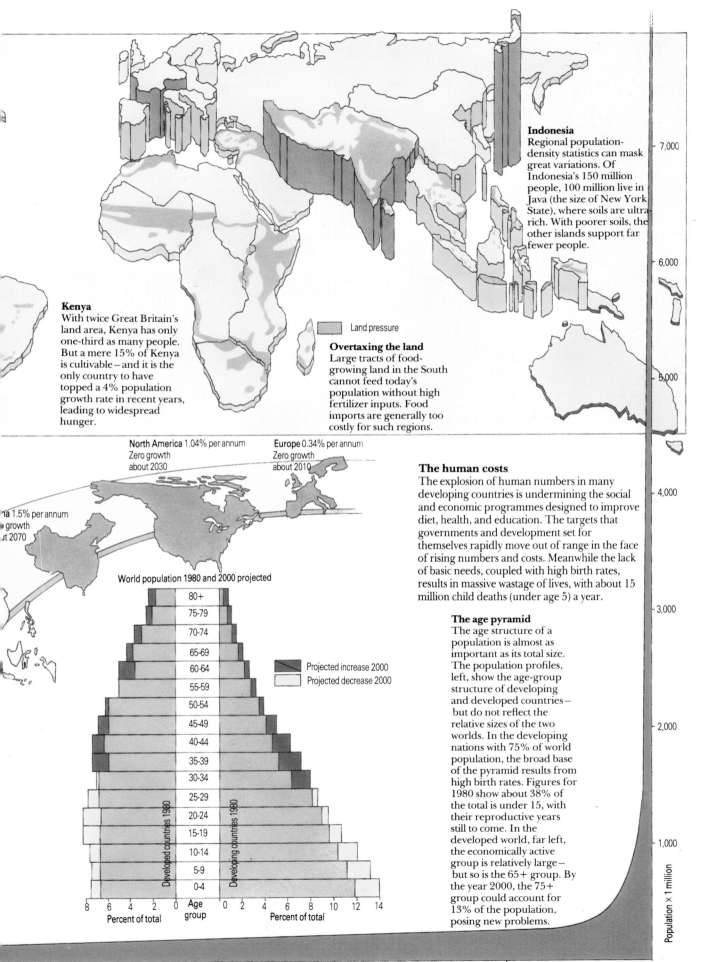

Indonesia
Regional population-density statistics can mask great variations. Of Indonesia's 150 million people, 100 million live in Java (the size of New York State), where soils are ultra-rich. With poorer soils, the other islands support far fewer people.

Kenya
With twice Great Britain's land area, Kenya has only one-third as many people. But a mere 15% of Kenya is cultivable – and it is the only country to have topped a 4% population growth rate in recent years, leading to widespread hunger.

Land pressure

Overtaxing the land
Large tracts of food-growing land in the South cannot feed today's population without high fertilizer inputs. Food imports are generally too costly for such regions.

North America 1.04% per annum
Zero growth
about 2030

Europe 0.34% per annum
Zero growth
about 2010

na 1.5% per annum
growth
ut 2070

World population 1980 and 2000 projected

Projected increase 2000
Projected decrease 2000

Developed countries 1980
Developing countries 1980

80+
75-79
70-74
65-69
60-64
55-59
50-54
45-49
40-44
35-39
30-34
25-29
20-24
15-19
10-14
5-9
0-4

Age group

8 6 4 2 0
Percent of total

0 2 4 6 8 10 12 14
Percent of total

The human costs
The explosion of human numbers in many developing countries is undermining the social and economic programmes designed to improve diet, health, and education. The targets that governments and development set for themselves rapidly move out of range in the face of rising numbers and costs. Meanwhile the lack of basic needs, coupled with high birth rates, results in massive wastage of lives, with about 15 million child deaths (under age 5) a year.

The age pyramid
The age structure of a population is almost as important as its total size. The population profiles, left, show the age-group structure of developing and developed countries – but do not reflect the relative sizes of the two worlds. In the developing nations with 75% of world population, the broad base of the pyramid results from high birth rates. Figures for 1980 show about 38% of the total is under 15, with their reproductive years still to come. In the developed world, far left, the economically active group is relatively large – but so is the 65+ group. By the year 2000, the 75+ group could account for 13% of the population, posing new problems.

7,000
6,000
5,000
4,000
3,000
2,000
1,000

Population × 1 million

2000 BC   1000 BC   AD 1   1000   2000

provision of every type convinces parents that they need more children – to ensure that enough survive the rigours of childhood to help work for the household income and to care for their parents in old age. And so the cycle of deprivation and environmental degradation continues.

The employment crisis

Jobs have recently been disappearing in the North at a rate unequalled since the Great Depression, while in the South a grossly inadequate supply of jobs is being severely aggravated by rapid population growth. Politicians in the North wrestle with the social and economic implications of mass unemployment; they now admit that their original goal of full employment is becoming unattainable. While the impact of the work famine differs between regions of the world, it is universally perceived as one of the most pressing of today's crises.

Figures for the OECD countries show that unemployment has recently been growing fast: between 1960 and 1973, the unemployment rate ranged between 4 and 7 percent in North America and between 2 and 3 percent for Western Europe, but by 1982 it had risen to 10 percent in the US and a 9 percent average for all industrialized countries. The figures for the Comecon countries show full employment, but conceal underemployment.

In the developing countries the problem is not only lack of an effective waged employment sector,

People of working age
(1 figure represents c. 50 m
Employed

Unemployed or underemp

Others

Children entering the
workforce 1985-2005

GNP per capita by country

Over $10,000

Over $7,000

Over $4,000

Over $1,700

Under $1,700

The work famine

In both North and South the problems of un- and underemployment (unproductive work for little reward) are growing. The ILO's workforce figures cover only 64% of the working-age population in the South. The "others", family labourers for example, added to the ranks of un- and underemployed, outnumber the employees. Worse still, those who will reach working age between 1985 and 2005 threaten to overwhelm opportunities for adequate work.

Northern unemployment

In the North, unemployment has grown from 6% in 1975 to nearly 10% in 1984. Economic trends and technological change render many skilled workers obsolete, and trap the untrained and unskilled – especially young people – in a vicious circle of inexperience and rejection. The resulting sense of frustration and inadequacy may last throughout a person's life.

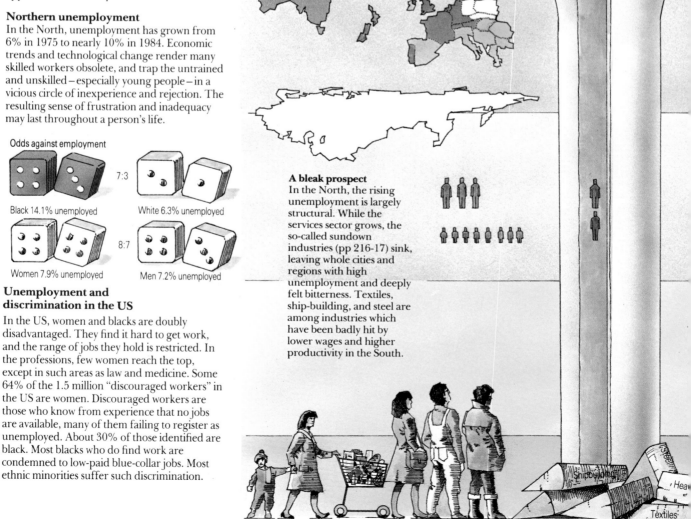

Odds against employment

7:3

Black 14.1% unemployed — White 6.3% unemployed

8:7

Women 7.9% unemployed — Men 7.2% unemployed

North 80% of working-age population in workforce

A bleak prospect
In the North, the rising unemployment is largely structural. While the services sector grows, the so-called sundown industries (pp 216-17) sink, leaving whole cities and regions with high unemployment and deeply felt bitterness. Textiles, ship-building, and steel are among industries which have been badly hit by lower wages and higher productivity in the South.

Unemployment and discrimination in the US

In the US, women and blacks are doubly disadvantaged. They find it hard to get work, and the range of jobs they hold is restricted. In the professions, few women reach the top, except in such areas as law and medicine. Some 64% of the 1.5 million "discouraged workers" in the US are women. Discouraged workers are those who know from experience that no jobs are available, many of them failing to register as unemployed. About 30% of those identified are black. Most blacks who do find work are condemned to low-paid blue-collar jobs. Most ethnic minorities suffer such discrimination.

but extremely low incomes generally. Eight out of ten people depend on working the land: of the world's one billion absolute poor, half are small farmers and about a fifth are landless peasants searching for work.

Poor rewards are all the worse since workers are a proportionately small part of the population. The under-15 age group accounts for over 30 percent of the total population. Then there are the "others", adults outside the workforce who may be unpaid family labourers or unregistered unemployed people. While 100 workers in the North support an average of 50 dependants, in the South the workers are swamped: in Africa 100 workers support 92 dependants. Millions more join the job market every year. There is a relentless quest for work which encourages a pattern of discrimination .

Women, the young, and racial minorities are particularly disadvantaged, both in the North and the South. In the US, the number of "discouraged workers", those who have given up the hunt for work in despair, is now estimated at 1.5 million. In the South, women suffer exploitation in the unpaid family-labour system, while those who have succeeded in finding a paid job tend to be the first to be hit by recession and upgrading of technology.

But those who suffer most are often the migrants and minorities. The lure of jobs encourages migration from rural, undeveloped areas to urban, industrialized areas – where the streets are seldom

Underemployment in the South
In the South, the most pressing crisis is one of huge underemployment as well as unemployment. Without unemployment benefits and social security, the poor must work if they are to survive at all. But survival often depends on a job with little substance to it apart from low pay and long hours – unprotected by work legislation of any sort. About 60% of workers in the South are self-employed. Government intervention and overseas aid often focus on inappropriate high-technology, capital-intensive projects. They also concentrate on boosting production of cash crops and goods, rather than providing the work which the poor need to buy food and goods. Many respond by moving to the cities.

The "invisible" workforce
The statistics on the male and female workforce in the South suggest that women are less than half the total. In fact, their work is officially invisible, like that of children. Women in the South suffer a "double burden" of duties, bearing domestic responsibilities and acting as unpaid family labourers in the fields (pp 192-3). A 15- to 18-hour day is not uncommon. Where productivity is lowest, children are also engaged in work, in conditions which may well retard their development. Over 98% of almost 100 million child labourers worldwide are found in the South. In Thailand, for example, about 3.5 million aged 11-16 years are in the labour force. Many are at work far younger. In the dry season, poor peasants in the northeast region are often forced to sell their children to child traders. Most go as factory hands and domestic servants, others as child prostitutes.

South hit by North
Employment in the South is hit both by accumulation of wealth by the few and by Northern protectionism. The EEC's agricultural strategy, for example, undermines the sugar industry in the Caribbean. And much Northern investment has gone into job-destroying technology.

uth 64% of working-age population in workforce

Traditional industries

Sugar

Agriculture

Jute

paved with gold. In Western Europe, the post-war economic boom attracted more than 15 million immigrants and "guest workers", who are often treated as scapegoats during a recession.

Crisis in health
Ill-health incapacitates an enormous proportion of the world's 4.7 billion people. As bald statistics are often unintelligible, consider some major world diseases in terms of populations of known size: the equivalent of the entire population of non-Communist Europe partly blind with trachoma; the entire population of Iran sightless with river blindness; everyone in Japan, Malaysia, and the Philippines sweating and shivering with malaria; and all

Americans urinating blood because of bilharzia. These equivalents show only part of the grotesque extent of world sickness.

Despite the fact that 800 million people in the South have no access to medical services, we spend 20 percent more each year on war than on health. A tragedy – or a crime against humanity?

The microbe, meanwhile, continues to display extraordinary ingenuity in outwitting medical science; new health threats are constantly emerging. This century has seen epidemics resulting from lifestyles in the North: coronary heart disease; the cancers; industrial disease; nervous and mental health problems; and the growing toll in road accidents, alcoholism, and drug-addiction deaths.

Sickness and stress

Worldwide, the bulk of health expenditure still goes on curing illnesses rather than on tackling their root causes. High-technology medicine consumes vast budgets. By contrast, primary health care, community schemes, and preventive medicine are often drastically underfunded. And despite major publicity campaigns, the public at large is often ignorant of the links between illness and, for example, diet or cigarette or alcohol consumption.

Ill-health in the North
In the industrialized North, most of the pressing health problems have sprung from the very conditions generally considered to be the hallmarks of progress. The population profile (right) shows a growing proportion of older people, many of them suffering from neglect as well as ill-health; the shaded areas show morbidity. Most seriously, there are the "new deaths": cancers and cardiovascular disease promoted by modern environments and lifestyles. There is also a growing array of minor illnesses, many readily preventable.

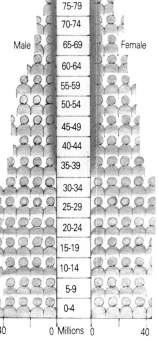

The new outcasts
Increased longevity has created new outcasts in the North – elderly people living alone or in nursing homes and hospitals. This problem will get significantly worse, as the populations of developed countries age. A US survey estimated that between 20 and 40% of elderly people in nursing homes and hospitals could live in the community if only adequate home care was provided. A recent study, right, of the percentage of people aged 60+ living with more than 4 people in a developed country (green) and a developing one (brown) highlights growing isolation in the North.

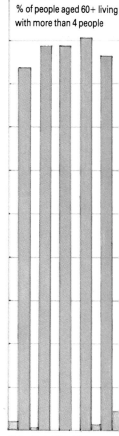

% of people aged 60+ living with more than 4 people

60-4 65-9 70-4 75-9 80-4

240   200   160

The new deaths
Circulatory-system diseases accounted for more than 50% of deaths in 10 developed countries, and for more than 40% in 13 others. About 20% of all deaths were due to cancer, a third of these involving the respiratory system. Smoking is associated with 80% of premature deaths.

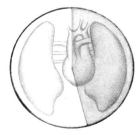

Minds under stress
Spending on tranquillizers in the North matches total public health expenditure in the world's 67 poorest countries. Many drugs used for stress-related illness are addictive. Worldwide, there are over 40 million mentally ill people. More than 1 million Europeans are in mental homes.

Ivory tower medicine
The bulk of health budgets in the North, in some cases as much as two-thirds, goes to "disease palaces" – which only cure about 10-20% of diseases. The emphasis on hospitals and high technology has often locked up resources which might otherwise have been used to prevent illness.

Global health care
The total health budget in the North is 10 times greater than that in the South, even though the developing countries' population is larger and in far greater need. In the South (right), health care often centres on towns and most people lack access to basic services.

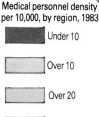

Medical personnel density per 10,000, by region, 1983

Under 10
Over 10
Over 20
Over 50

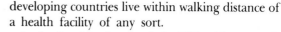

this from want 1945-83

Deaths from war 1945-83

eath tolls
nce 1945, there have
en 20 times as many
aths from neglect,
cluding lack of food,
safe water, and poor
nitation, as from wars (1
ull = 10 million deaths).

The developing countries have a double burden to bear. The central battleground for them remains infectious disease, but they also have to provide the infrastructure for health care. Even simple, readily countered threats, such as the micro-organisms that cause diarrhoeal diseases, kill millions of children in the South.

Malnutrition is perhaps the cruellest affliction, with children, young girls, and pregnant and lactating women most at risk. Vitamin-A deficiency, for example, causes some 200,000 infants to go blind every year. It can be tackled – in Bangladesh and Indonesia, the distribution of vitamins to children at risk costs less than 20 cents per child per year. But less than 15 percent of the people in

developing countries live within walking distance of a health facility of any sort.

In the South, a short period of ill-health can push a family into a deepening spiral of poverty, forcing it to sell land, animals, or other possessions which, with high interest rates, it will never be able to buy back. With all these existing problems, the South can ill-afford to import the lifestyle-related diseases of the North. But lung cancer, for example, is now as common among smokers in the South as among their Northern counterparts.

Around the world, too, there is the rising spectre of infirm old age. Even in the North, where the average age of populations is highest, far too little is being done to help the aged cope with such chronic

Immunizable diseases
According to UNICEF, only 20% of the world's children are protected against the major immunizable diseases, despite the proliferation of immunization campaigns. The six major killers (measles, whooping cough, polio, TB, tetanus, and diphtheria) account for 5 million deaths a year, disabling a further 5 million. Effective vaccination depends on cold storage for unstable vaccines and on boosters.

Sickness in the South
High overall mortality, and very high infant mortality, are the bitter reality in many developing countries. In the first step on the population pyramid, left, 1 in 6 children die; disability and illness then affect a further third of the population. Among the causes are the lack of health workers, the lack of information about health, the lack of immunization and essential drugs, and poor sanitation. Poverty and malnutrition, the most intractable problems of all, are endemic. Moderate to severe malnutrition affects 1 in 5 Latin Americans, 1 in 3 Africans and Asians. There is a complex interplay between all of these killers that frustrates single-minded solutions: poor sanitation causes diarrhoea, which aggravates malnutrition, sapping energy and earning-capacity. UNICEF estimates that approximately one-third of child admissions to hospital in the South are caused by diarrhoea. Several hundred million people suffer from waterborne diseases for which no vaccine exists, notably schistosomiasis (bilharzia) and onchocerciasis (river blindness). Tackling water hazards (pp 120-1, 134-5) has proved a herculean task, aggravated by mis-spending. The Philippines government, for example, has just spent $50 million on a heart surgery unit which will benefit a few hundred people at most.

The child killers
While an average of 19 out of every 1,000 infants (age 0-12 months) die in the North, almost 100 die in the South – national figures run up to 210. Of all infant deaths between 1975 and 1980, the South suffered 97%. Causes: diarrhoea, malnutrition, and infectious disease.

Diarrhoea
The deadliest killer of small children in the South is diarrhoea; attacks amount to 1 billion a year. In one South American survey, malnutrition associated with diarrhoea caused 57% of deaths. The best cure, ORT (p.195), is cheap and simple, but fails without education for its use.

Imported drugs
Private spending on health in developing countries outstrips government spending 3 to 4 times, and at least a third of this money goes on useless or harmful drugs. Companies are notoriously slow to remove "contra-indicated" drugs from the Third World market.

health problems as rheumatism and arthritis, while growing numbers of old people are simply sidelined into institutions.

Barriers against progress

Today, there are 825 million illiterate people, 800 million of them in developing countries. The predicament of ill-health and lack of education cannot be examined in isolation. A global map of ill-health would coincide with maps of malnutrition, poverty, and illiteracy. The illiterate person is not only unable to read or write, but he, or more usually she, is also poor, hungry, and highly vulnerable to disease and exploitation.

Many of the newly independent nations have made great progress in promoting literacy. But the apparent fall in global percentage illiteracy rates is deceptive: the number of people without adequate functional literacy is still increasing. Africa, where the greatest recent advances have been made, reports a 74 percent illiteracy rate, Asia 47 percent, and Latin America 24 percent.

When we focus on sheer numbers, we begin to see the gap between the people and the provisions. Between 1960 and 1980, the number of illiterate men grew by 20 million and the number of illiterate women by 74 million. Financial constraints dictate priorities. The South has only 11.6 percent of the world's education budget. Since the early 1970s there has been an alarming plunge in educational expenditure (as a percentage of GNP), particularly among developing countries. Venezuela's spending fell from 22.9 to 8.2 percent between 1970 and 1980. Many African countries have dropped beneath the 10 percent line. Over 70 percent of primary-age children in the South were enrolled in school in 1980, but at least 120 million children did not have a school to attend.

Behind the global school-enrolment figures lies a second chasm. Of every 100 children entering primary education in the South, 24 drop out in the first year, eight more after two years and seven more after three years. Illness, the need to work, and high costs play havoc with the attendance rates. So only 61 out of the original 100 complete four years of primary education. And those who fail to learn basic skills by the end of normal school age have little chance of acquiring them as adults.

It is ironic that many developing nations still model their higher education systems along Western lines. The arts are often treated as the art of the European élite, while medical training fosters the expensive, high-technology, essentially curative health care of the North. It is no coincidence that the predominant language in education is often the legacy of the former colonialists, perpetuating the idea of foreign intellectual superiority.

Success in higher education can aggravate problems higher up the scale. In Tanzania, for example, when 1.4 million Tanzanians passed the adult literacy test, further education could offer only

The literacy chasm

Lost cultures
The history of the dominant European cultures is also a history of the destruction of countless tribal and other diversified cultures. Education can be one of the most powerful tools of suppression.

School enrolment by country

Primary and secondary < 50%
Primary > 50%; secondary < 50%
Primary and secondary > 50%
Primary > 50%; secondary > 75%

In the modern nation state, governed by written statutes and fuelled by forms and letters among other written materials, literacy is an increasingly critical skill. Illiterate, you will not get a good job, indeed you may not get a job at all. Illiterate, you are very unlikely to know your statutory rights, and unlikelier still to be able to enforce them. In some countries, you can vote only if you are literate. Illiterate, you may fall victim to any unscrupulous official or confidence trickster. All too often, the most deprived communities, the rural villages and the urban slums, benefit least from national spending on education.

Newsprint distribution

North 81%

South 19%

South 28%

Radio distribution

North 72%

South 26

The media chasm
The North/South literacy chasm is mirrored by unequal access to media resources. The North has most of the newsprint, radios and TVs. The North also dominates markets for news (p.214). Limited access to radio and TV is a major handicap in developing countries, where there are high proportions of illiterate adults who could benefit from the latest media-based education programmes. Such programmes can also help preserve vanishing cultures, particulary those based on rich oral traditions.

Television distribution

North 7

The bias in higher learning

Since the 1960s, higher education in the North and South has expanded rapidly, but the subjects studied, and the students, still largely reflect a narrow social stratum. Many institutions in the South have been built on Western models. Low-income countries can scarcely afford the luxury of disciplines not directly related to their economic well-being. As for students, 80% of higher-education students in one Asian country come from the richest 20% of society.

Textbook colonialism

School children in Africa and Asia once studied Wordsworth or Baudelaire. Though newly independent states introduce new curricula, they often lack suitable teaching materials. The North still holds the largest educational publishers.

Aborigine education

At the white man's school, what are our children taught?
Are they told of the battles our people fought,
Are they told of how our people died?
Are they told why our people cried?
Australia's true history is never read,
But the blackman keeps it in his head.

ABORIGINAL POEM FROM BUNJI, DECEMBER 1971

That might be said of many minorities. Textbooks and teachers have often put forward a negative, misleading picture of minority cultures.

Schooling in Muslim countries

The numbers of girls and women enrolled in schools and universities in the Middle East has risen dramatically since the 1950s (when, in some rural villages, sending girls to school amounted to a crime). But female literacy remains very low – worst in Saudi Arabia where female literacy is a little over 0%.

The world's illiterates

Despite the success of many literacy programmes, and although fewer than 30% of adults throughout the world are illiterate, the total number of illiterates has grown by 80 million since 1970. Illiteracy is very much more common among women than men, as the pie-charts show, with the problem showing up in its most extreme form in Africa (see diagram, left). In Latin America, which has made great progress since the 1950s, male/female literacy ratios stand at 76%/70%. In Asia, the ratio is 56%/34%, and in Africa, 35%/15%.

African literacy

Africa: female literacy

Illiterate   Literate

Africa: male literacy

Illiterate   Literate

1 million

World literacy

Female literacy 54%

Male literacy 67%

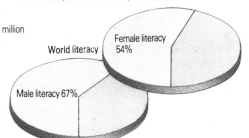

3,400 places. The expectations of those who have succeeded in education are inevitably very high; opportunities for suitable work are very low.

Exile and persecution

The very word *refugee* rings alarm bells; it evokes a sense of immediate crisis, and never more so than today when, according to the most conservative estimates, there are between 10 and 15 million refugees worldwide. Half of them are children, who may never know their country, and young people of school age. Four-fifths of them have fled disasters in the South. There is an urgent need for concerted government action worldwide.

A refugee, in the blunt definition of the UN Convention of 1951 and the Protocol of 1967, is a person who cannot return to his or her own country because of a "well-founded fear of persecution for reasons of race, religion, nationality, political association or social grouping". The majority of refugees have been created not by natural disasters, but by political instabilities, including the 160 or so undeclared wars waged since 1945.

The latest statistics of the UN High Commission for Refugees (UNHCR) include over three million Afghan refugees, now the largest national refugee group in the world. The Palestinians come second: since the creation of the state of Israel, close to two million refugees have been created, counting only those in families still needing UN assistance. But many refugees elude the statistics altogether. Of the Boat People from Vietnam, for example, only those who got through were counted. Guatemalan refugees are not included in the official statistics. It is estimated that some 500,000 Salvadoreans and 100,000 Haitians are in the US illegally, the former having fled civil war, the latter the ramshackle economy and repression.

Some of the countries now hosting considerable numbers of refugees are among those least able to afford such an increased burden. Africa is probably the worst-affected continent, hosting roughly a third of the world's refugee population. Approximately one in every hundred Africans is a refugee. There are entire ghettoes of refugees in some cities. Certain governments are adopting restrictive regulations or changing their reception policies.

Quite apart from the political exiles and refugees, there are countless social and economic outcasts within countries, including many "internal" refugees – migrants in search of hope. Some are worse off than "official" refugees. Members of the Baha'i religion in Iran have been subject to harassment, persecution, imprisonment, and execution since 1979. Many immigrant workers in Europe suffer less savage, but real discrimination. In tens of countries across the world, ethnic minorities are in danger of being crushed out of existence. The effect of persecution can strengthen a group's identity – but far more often it consigns the victim to deprivation, isolation, and even extinction.

Outcasts and refugees

There is mounting international concern that the number of refugees worldwide has soared since the 1960s. In addition millions more people do not or cannot escape the oppressions that haunt their lives, and some may be even worse off than the exiles. They may be severely persecuted for their race, religion, politics, or nationality, and it may not be within the power of any relief organization to assist them. Or they may depend on one of numerous charitable organizations, who are desperately short of funds. But not all the unwanted are behind bars or in the world's human "reserves". Every country has its "second-class" citizens – people who suffer and are disadvantaged because they are old, sick, homeless, jobless, or because their skin is a different colour.

Refugees 1983
Estimates of refugee intake
by country

Over 1,000,000
Over 500,000
Over 100,000
Over 50,000
Over 10,000
Under 1,000
Direction of exodus
Areas of war and civil conflict
Famine threats: area c. 1983
UNHCR estimates, excluding
Palestinian refugees under
the mandate of a separate
UN agency

The world's refugees

In many regions, the number of refugees is rising like a floodtide, despite the increasingly desperate efforts of the UNHCR. To those torn from their homes and, often, from their families, whether by political, social, or religious oppression, the UNHCR has to add victims of natural disasters, such as famine.

Over 80% of the 10-15 million refugees are from the South. The resulting problems can overwhelm poorer host countries, precipitating economic and ecological disaster. In the worst cases, people unable to return home and unable (or unwilling) to resettle can spend years in semi-permanent camps, losing their sense of identity and purpose.

The disappearing tribes

Some Latin American Indians are still treated almost as wild animals, or worse. They are "protected" in mean reserves, or they are pushed out far into marginal lands. Even there they may be harassed by new settlers or come into conflict with government or commercial interests. The Yanomame Indians, for instance, now live in the dense forest of the Guyana Shield in Brazil and Venezuela (left), but are threatened by the intrusion one of Brazil's new highways, the Perimetral Norte, which will cut through previously impenetrable Amazonian terrain. Their small world, their distinctive culture, and their ancient history are likely to become fodder for bulldozers.

Asia

Refugee camps in Indonesia, the Philippines, and Hong Kong are the only home for several million Asian refugees. Wars and oppression in Indo China have caused immense human suffering. A peak figure of 202,000 Vietnamese Boat People arrived in other countries in 1979, braving the elements and the pirates who have killed, raped, or robbed untold numbers. As many as 250,000 are thought to have drowned.

Africa

In the late 1970s, Africa overtook Asia as the wellhead of refugees. The estimate today is about 5 million refugees. Liberation wars in the Horn of Africa and Chad caused mass displacement. In 1980, Somalia had 1 refugee for every 5 original inhabitants. The Sudan is now under growing pressure, while conflicts in Angola, Namibia, and Zimbabwe are producing floods of displaced people.

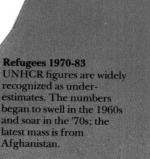

Refugees 1970-83

UNHCR figures are widely recognized as under-estimates. The numbers began to swell in the 1960s and soar in the '70s; the latest mass is from Afghanistan.

Refugees 1970-83

1970 71 72 73 74 75 76 77 78 79 80 81 82 83

MANAGING OURSELVES

" 'Well, in *our* country' said Alice . . . 'you'd generally get to somewhere else – if you ran very fast for a long time, as we've been doing.' 'A slow sort of country!' said the Queen. 'Now, *here*, you see, it takes all the running you can do to keep in the same place. If you want to get somewhere else, you must run at least twice as fast as that!' " These words by Lewis Carroll aptly express the plight of many Third World countries in the development race – they have to "run twice as fast" to make any headway. They are handicapped by their rising numbers, by wars, by sickness, and by legacies of inequity. Removing the handicaps is an urgent task, for each nation and for the global community. Fortunately, development is showing signs of moving out into entire communities, to help the women, the poor, the illiterate, the workless, and the rejected minorities to reach the starting line.

What changes birth rate

Family planning

Services

Better health

Employment

Later marriages

Education
Improved women's status

More equal incomes

Managing numbers

Ninety-five percent of the world's population lives in countries with family planning services of some description, but, according to the International Planned Parenthood Federation (IPPF), some 400 million couples of reproductive age in developing countries are not practising contraception.

The forces working against the lowering of fertility rates are deeply rooted in cultural, social, and economic conditions that have prevailed for generations. It is no coincidence that fertility rates are highest in developing countries, where economic deprivation is endemic, and lowest in affluent educated societies with good social provision. The desire for large families is the result of many factors, among them high infant mortality, labour-intensive means of subsistence, and the need for support in old age.

Some aspects of the development process, such as improved health, better education, and increased employment opportunities for women, work together with family planning to cut fertility rates. A good measure of national well-being is the Physical Quality of Life Index (PQLI). Birth rates generally vary in inverse proportion to PQLI ratings, though both may be affected by deeper cultural factors.

Physical Quality of Life Index
The PQLI is a useful measure of human progress. Calculated by employing three indices – child mortality, literacy, and life expectancy – it gives equal weight to each factor. Although there is some correlation between high income and high PQLI, there can be significant variations. Sri Lanka, for example, has a low per capita income but a high PQLI. The generally inverse correlation between birth rate and PQLI is shown below.

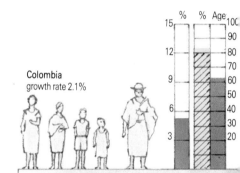

Colombia
growth rate 2.1%

Colombia
With an infant mortality rate less than half India's, Colombia has achieved a dramatic demographic transition – from a 3.2% annual rate of population growth to a current rate of 2% (projected to drop to about 1.7% around 1990). The government's multi-faceted social policy has increased life expectancy, while infant deaths have dropped to 56 per 1,000 live births.

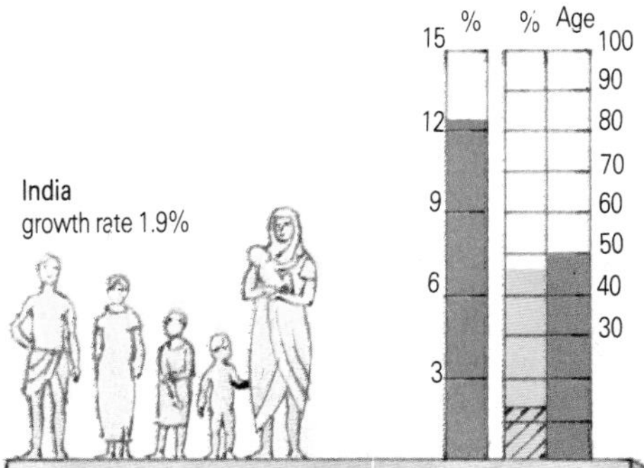

India
growth rate 1.9%

India
India's population has exploded, reaching some 730 million in 1983. Average infant mortality and illiteracy are still high, but the state of Kerala has succeeded in lowering child deaths by improving health services and working conditions.

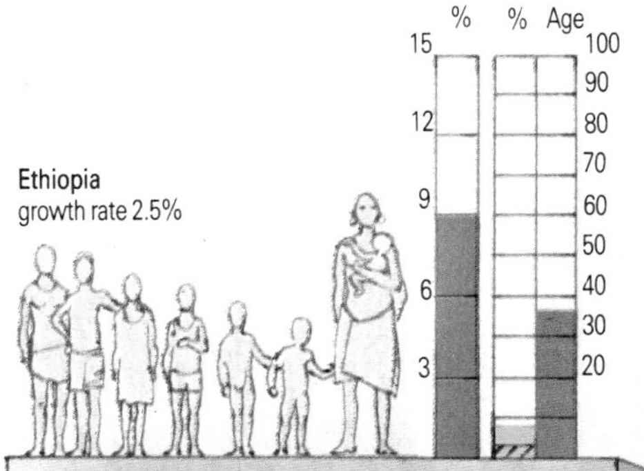

Ethiopia
growth rate 2.5%

Ethiopia
Less than 1.5% of all Ethiopian couples use any form of contraception – and government support for birth control is very recent. The revolution of 1974 has led to a new emphasis on primary health, which will help family planning.

Target: 8 billion
Worldwide family planning services could save over 130,000 abortions per day, and countless unwanted births. They could also bring down the ultimate global population from 10 billion in 2100 (UN median) to less than 8 billion (still double the 1980 population). There would be 2.4 billion fewer people to provide with food, water, health, and shelter.

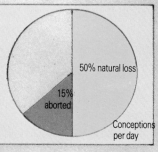

50% natural loss

15% aborted

Conceptions per day

Population management

Population trends are not easy to influence and manage. In a sense, governments face a "chicken and egg" situation – birth control is most effective in a context of improved health care and rising employment and incomes. But it is often lack of birth control that makes these factors so difficult to achieve. However, experience confirms that best results are obtained when modernization, including improved status and education for women, runs in tandem with effective family planning.

Family planning has been making major inroads over the last decade, with countries such as China and India making major cuts in their population growth rates. More recently, Peru, Senegal, and Ethiopia have been taking an interest, as population growth is increasingly seen as a major obstacle to their development.

The costs have often been substantial, the results mixed. In Kerala, India, family planning has been assisted by good health services, the strong economic status of women, high literacy, and excellent communications. Indonesia has introduced effective family planning to the poor of East Java and Bali, thanks to government support for village services. Other successes have been scored in Cuba, Costa Rica, Hong Kong, South Korea, Mauritius, and Taiwan. Family planning has been less successful in

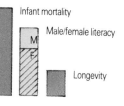

Infant mortality

Male/female literacy

Longevity

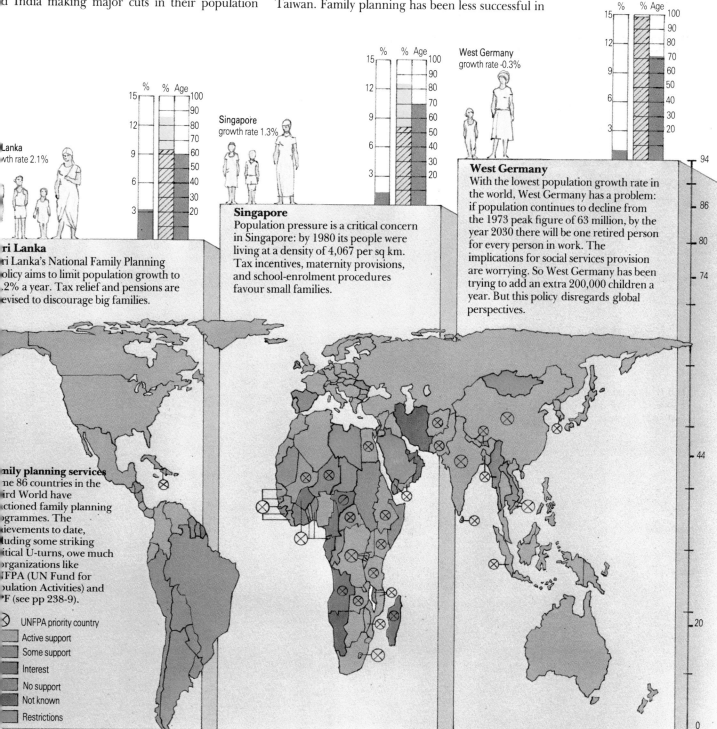

Sri Lanka
growth rate 2.1%

Sri Lanka
Sri Lanka's National Family Planning policy aims to limit population growth to 1.2% a year. Tax relief and pensions are devised to discourage big families.

Singapore
growth rate 1.3%

Singapore
Population pressure is a critical concern in Singapore: by 1980 its people were living at a density of 4,067 per sq km. Tax incentives, maternity provisions, and school-enrolment procedures favour small families.

West Germany
growth rate -0.3%

West Germany
With the lowest population growth rate in the world, West Germany has a problem: if population continues to decline from the 1973 peak figure of 63 million, by the year 2030 there will be one retired person for every person in work. The implications for social services provision are worrying. So West Germany has been trying to add an extra 200,000 children a year. But this policy disregards global perspectives.

Family planning services
Some 86 countries in the Third World have sanctioned family planning programmes. The achievements to date, including some striking political U-turns, owe much to organizations like UNFPA (UN Fund for Population Activities) and IPPF (see pp 238-9).

⊗ UNFPA priority country

Active support

Some support

Interest

No support

Not known

Restrictions

Muslim countries such as Pakistan, underscoring the importance of cultural traditions. Sub-Saharan Africa has been least successful, because of cultural factors and very weak health care.

Equality for women?

The statistics on the contributions which women make to society, and on the share of society's assets they actually own, tell a devastating story. It is a story that dispels cosy notions about a woman's place in the world. No longer can men claim to be the sole providers and bearers of responsibility: a worldwide scan shows that it is women, the often ignored "other half", who sustain families, looking after their health and providing food and care. They also make enormous contributions to domestic and national income.

Think about women today, especially in developing countries, and it is difficult to avoid thinking about oppression. Yet their contribution is remarkable: in Africa as a whole, they do 60 percent of all agricultural work, 50 percent of all animal husbandry, and all the food processing. In Tanzania, women work an average of 2,600 hours a year in agriculture, while the men put in only about 1,800 hours. Most of this work, however, goes unrecognized: women account for less than a third of the official workforce in the South.

In the North, by contrast, one of the most significant socio-economic trends in the post-war period has been the entry of women into the ranks of official workers. Almost 40 percent of the workforce in the US, UK, and Japan today is female. But the unpaid, "invisible" work done by women at home is still substantial: in the US, it is estimated at 40 percent of Gross Domestic Product.

In waged work, discrimination hits women in both North and South, with a strong tendency for them to be regarded as cheap labour. The problem is twin-headed: women often end up in the worst-paid jobs or, where they break out of stereotypical female work, are paid less for comparable work. Female workers are paid 25 percent less than male workers in the UK, 40 percent less in the US.

Illiteracy is a key factor inhibiting women in the South. Two out of three women are illiterate, a far higher proportion than for men. The literacy chasm is closely linked to other indicators of deprivation such as poverty and malnutrition, and it is promoted by segregation of the sexes.

Even today, only a small fraction of women are actively engaged in politics, but the voice of women is increasingly heard. And it is, more and more, a voice in defence of peace, conservation, and humanitarian values. The contemporary women's movement comprises hundreds of international organizations and thousands of pressure groups. It can be described as the most global social movement of the 1970s and 1980s. Self-help groups are legion. Peace campaigners like the Greenham Common Women, UK, and the tree-huggers of the Chipko Andolan

The voice of women

Despite the growing impact of women's movements, it is still an indisputable fact that women are under-represented at all levels of decision-making. No nation on Earth has a 50:50 balance of the sexes in its legislature – and there are still countries where universal suffrage is denied. Even after 50 years of suffrage in some countries, women have achieved less than 10% national representation.

The high proportion of women in further education in many parts of the world underscores this waste of national resources. A few countries, like Sweden and Cuba, encourage equal sharing of home responsibilities to facilitate power-sharing at the top. Few other nations are tackling this grass-roots inequality. But women's contribution in the workforce is helping to open new doors to power. In such countries as Egypt and Jordan, for example, the growing impact of working women has triggered new laws designed to improve their position.

Getting men to share political power and the breadwinner role can be a major hurdle in male-oriented cultures, but women are making inroads by taking the initiative both in the the work sector and in political movements, demonstrating and working for their equality.

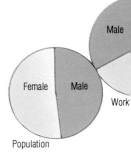

Equal work, equal pay?
The imbalances between female work-hours, income, and ownership (above) have been revealed by a survey made by the UN Decade for Women. This is despite rising numbers at work. Equal-pay laws need to be enforced rigorously and extended. Another key target must be the sharing household work.

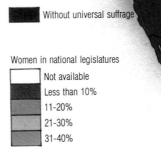

Without universal suffrage

Women in national legislatures
- Not available
- Less than 10%
- 11-20%
- 21-30%
- 31-40%

Women in the legislature
No activist would be satisfied with the rate of progress shown here (right). Some states still deny women the vote, others are reluctant to share power between the sexes, but there has been an enormous swing towards equality since 1945 – when only 31 countries allowed women to vote. The voice of women is strongest in Scandinavia and in some Communist states, where equal participation is positively promoted. Some developing countries, like Egypt, reserve seats for women in their legislatures. A complete picture of women's political status is not yet possible, since many governments have not released such data. Figures here include those published by the 1980 World Conference for Women. They generally show participation at national rather than "ministerial" levels, where, even in Communist countries, there are far fewer women than men.

Zambian woman's workday
1 Walking to field
2 Ploughing, planting
3 Collecting firewood
4 Pounding grain or legumes
5 Fetching water
6 Lighting fire, cooking
7 Serving food, eating
8 Cleaning and washing

Female

Male

Ownership

Male

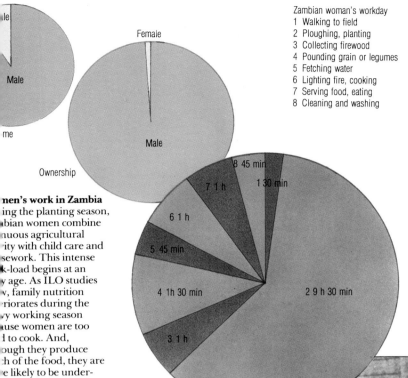

8 45 min
1 30 min
7 1 h
6 1 h
5 45 min
4 1h 30 min
3 1 h
2 9 h 30 min

men's work in Zambia
ing the planting season,
bian women combine
nuous agricultural
rity with child care and
sework. This intense
k-load begins at an
y age. As ILO studies
v, family nutrition
riorates during the
vy working season
use women are too
d to cook. And,
ough they produce
h of the food, they are
e likely to be under-
rished than are men.

The Self-employed Woman's Association
Founded in Gujarat, India, in 1972, this co-
operative provides new hope and horizons for
some of the country's poorest women. At least
12,000 women have taken part in SEWA – all
benefiting from special credit schemes, training
programmes, welfare facilities, and negotiated
minimum earnings. Members of SEWA range
from weavers to vegetable sellers, but their aims
are constant: economic and social uplift.

Women's protest movements
Demonstrations against
tyranny and the threat of
war have been increasingly
forceful. In Chile (above)
and Argentina, the
mothers of "the
disappeared" protest their
loss despite reprisal threats.
At Greenham Common in
the UK (right), women
have kept non-violent
permanent vigil since
September 1981 to demon-
strate their opposition to
the installation of Cruise
missiles – despite continual
harassment. No-one
pretends that women have
a monopoly in peace
protests, but peace has
become a unifying theme in
women's movements
worldwide.

en in the Muslim world
e orthodox Muslim
s still bar women from
ng. But the rising
ber of women moving
the workforce,
icularly in the non-oil
s, has begun to modify
0-year-old customs.

Despite the unhappy
example of Iran, such
countries as Jordan, Iraq,
and Egypt have forged
ahead with government-
backed programmes
designed to attract more
women into the workforce.

movement in India (p. 57) are part of an upsurge of activity which has found international expression in the UN Decade for Women, 1975-85.

Global health care

Physiological causes are by no means the only roots of ill-health. Indeed, the problem of finding management solutions to massive world ill-health is enormously complex. Problems do not hinge only on primary health, vaccines, clean drinking water, and sanitation. They include political decisions on the relative priorities of health and defence; the state of the world economy and the prospects for employment; decent low-cost housing; and the

status of women and the entire stratum of underprivileged people.

Freedom from the threat of war is one of the key social objectives of the World Health Organization (WHO) in Europe. It also hopes to achieve equity both between and within the 33 nations of Europe, and to ensure that health services do not favour the few at the expense of the majority.

A critical element in ending global inequality is primary health care, based on a close alliance between local communities and their health workers. Strengthening this sector alleviates the distress of isolation and ignorance, and it promotes prevention through early recognition of problems – an

Health for all

In both North and South, there is a new awareness of the far-reaching advantages of primary health care. Community services critically depend on popular support, and emphasize the preventive role of medicine.

Health care for the North

Community programmes are a fairly recent phenomenon in the North. In the US, Neighbourhood Health Centres reduce infant deaths in particular and hospital admissions in general. In Karelia, Finland, a voluntary campaign promotes healthy lifestyles, lowering the incidence of heart disease. The scope for improvement through motivation is enormous. Self-help groups like Alcoholics Anonymous have come to play an essential role.

Prevention is the key

Provided that there is a safe environment, food for balanced diets, clean water, and reasonable access to housing, work, and education, the ultimate success of preventive medicine is in people's own hands. There has been enormous media support for health-promoting lifestyles in the US, and this trend is increasingly seen in Europe. Information on the risks involved in eating fatty foods, sugar, and salt has influenced dietary habits. Cigarette smoking is declining in the North, reducing the incidence of illnesses.

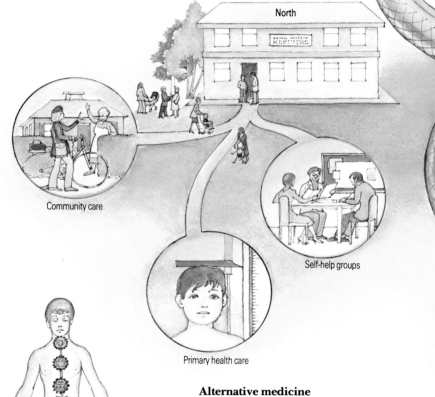

North

Community care

Self-help groups

Primary health care

Alternative medicine

Western medicine is beginning to accept both the traditional practices and the medicines of the East. Doctors in the North have mostly lost the art of treating the whole person, although many are now rediscovering the effectiveness of a comprehensive approach to health and sickness. Clinical studies have shown that many traditional medicines and therapies can be highly effective. Homeopathy, acupuncture, and Eastern exercises, such as yoga, are gaining widespread recognition.

A healthier Norway

Norway's concern to improve national health has led to a major campaign to achieve better diets – promoted through health education and community programmes. The results include major cuts in deaths from heart disease (a drop of 45-50% was recorded in Oslo), a general decline in teenager tooth decay (fillings were cut by 60% between 1970 and 1979), and benefits in terms of the incidence of some cancers. The campaign has also achieved a rapid increase in breast-feeding.

Heart disease in Oslo 1972-77

Control group

Illness 5.7%

Death 33%

Intervention group

Illness 3%

Death 16%

Percent of mothers breast-feeding at 8 months in Oslo

%
90
80
70
60
50
40
30
20
10
0

1950   60   70   80 84

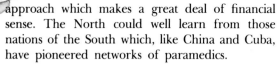

approach which makes a great deal of financial sense. The North could well learn from those nations of the South which, like China and Cuba, have pioneered networks of paramedics.

The battle to achieve health in developing nations is being fought across a far larger field. There is an acute need for adequate sanitation and safe drinking water. Family planning services are not available to many people, while funds for medical training, essential drugs, and health-care technology are very short. Some key approaches, such as vaccination and oral rehydration therapy, have proved enormously cost-effective, but they still need extensive services and political support.

The challenge facing most governments in the South demands new priorities, with city-centred, doctor-oriented administrations converted into extensive networks for community care. Primary health care can cost relatively little. Many resources are often already in existence since traditional healers and midwives can usually be trained in hygiene and primary medicine.

But ultimately, the drive for health comes from people, not simply from governments. Public participation is often the key to success – in planning community services, lobbying for environmental reform, in the introduction of clean water, and preventive campaigns. Health is a function not only

Regional hospitals
The decentralization of health care and hospital services is essential in the developing countries. The provision of regional hospitals helps to bridge the gap between rural and urban health levels.

South

Doctor

Immunization
The expanded WHO Programme of Immunization launched in 1977 sparked 130 separate campaigns. These use volunteers and heavy media promotion, with substantial progress reported by many nations.

Family planning
Experience in many countries has confirmed that professionally run family planning services can improve the health of mothers and children. Better spacing between births cuts infant deaths and allows for longer breast-feeding. Growth monitoring has proved an extremely effective means of preventive child care.

An adequate diet
The world can easily afford to feed its 450 million ill-fed people. For the cost of a few modern fighter aircraft, millions can be fed. And vitamin and protein supplements which combat serious illness cost under 20 cents per child per year.

Barefoot doctors
Official health services in the South have begun to exploit the reservoir of skills found among traditional healers and midwives. China has 15-20 times more homeopathic doctors than it has conventionally trained doctors. In Africa, there is one traditional healer for every 500 people, compared to one doctor for every 40,000.

Health for all in the South
Several developing countries have made enormous strides in community health, increasing life expectancy, banishing endemic diseases such as smallpox, and reducing child mortality. Oral rehydration therapy (ORT) – giving patients a simple mixture of sugar and salts in water – is a major cure for diarrhoea. The benefits of primary health-care schemes have included improvements in educational performance and worker productivity. China spends about $4 per person per year, which is broadly comparable with health expenditure in many developing countries, but has achieved major successes by giving top priority to primary health care and to birth control measures. Other successes have been reported in Colombia, Cuba, S Korea, Sri Lanka, and Tanzania. Key targets include increased breast-feeding, major immunization programmes, and safe water.

sanitation

safe water

Paramedic

Village health care
One of the most fundamental elements in any Primary Health Care (PHC) strategy is the involvement of the community. This is the key to mobilizing the human, material, and financial resources. There have been notable successes in campaigns in Africa and South America, but they depend on the sustained backing of national health authorities. WHO research has shown that a trained local health worker, equipped with only 15-20 drugs, can effectively treat the majority of common illnesses. Community PHC depends on a multi-stranded approach, from drugs to the provision of sanitation and decent housing.

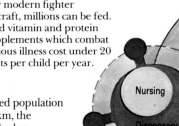

Primary health-care unit

Nursing

Dispensary

Regional hospital

16-km radius

60- to 80-km radius

health revolution in Sudan
» provide health care to a scattered population vering an area of 2.5 million sq km, the danese government has established an ective network of health-care units. The units, ich are linked to a dispensary, usually cover a ius of about 16 km and serve an average of 00 people. These units are backed up by velling health-care workers serving distant or madic communities. In 1970, Sudan had out 0.60 medical staff per 10,000 people – w it has 1.15 per 10,000.

of medical care, but of the overall integrated development of society. The central objectives of health promotion and health-care programmes should be to improve health, eliminate poverty and inequality, spread education, and enable the poor and underprivileged groups to assert themselves.

Community tools and access to ideas

A growing number of communities are watching angrily as their economic life-blood flows away. In the North, structural change is ripping the economic heart out of entire regions which depend for their livelihood on the sundown industries. In the South, the powerful undertow exerted by the exploding cities is undermining rural communities by draining away their young people.

What can be done? Are these community deaths as inevitable as they seem? Sometimes they are: sometimes communities have established themselves on a single, precarious resource, on a narrow economic base peculiar to a particular location, and are therefore left out on a limb when their economic monoculture collapses. But, as often as not, communities find that there are other ways of making a living, of rebuilding a viable community.

Dealing with outright disaster, like a flood or major factory accident, is often easier for a community than coping with a long drawn-out process of decline, yet there are many examples of communities which have gone against the flow of economic decay, refusing to give way to despair; with totally inadequate resources, they have managed to pull themselves up by communal will. Policy makers and planners need to recognize, and support, all these regenerative activities.

In the North, old industrial buildings have been converted into thriving community workshops. Urban "greening" projects have harnessed the enthusiasm, energy, and skills of local residents – which are the real "tools for community". In the UK, for example, towns like Rochdale have started to upgrade derelict areas to attract new industrial employment. Cities and towns across Europe and North America have transformed derelict land and building sites into parks and community gardens, boosting the sense of community both during construction and use.

In the South, the provision of local employment, often based on co-operatives and the use of various forms of appropriate technology, has helped build local economies better able to counter the call of the city. In Sri Lanka, the co-operative movement Sarvodaya Shramadana, which means "the awakening of all through the sharing of time, thought, and labour", draws on "gifts of labour" from villagers and volunteers to help poor Sri Lankans.

And, in both North and South, a growing number of schools have turned themselves into community centres, offering adult education, tutorial help for students undertaking distance learning, parents' groups, and adult literacy support schemes.

Tools and ideas

Unemployment and underemployment are undermining the economic base of an alarming number of communities in both North and South. Technological change, the fluctuating world economy, and the exploding world population are all contributing factors. To turn the tide of people surging into the cities in search of work and better facilities, it is essential that rural and small-town economies should be stimulated, and educational and health care services decentralized.

Community participation has proved to be a vital ingredient in the planning and implementation of public and private-sector development programmes. Given the tools and other resources, communities have pushed through their own programmes. The Naam movement in Upper Volta (pp 240-1) is a prime example, and there are now thousands of other communities which are pulling together.

Communities in school
Education has to keep pace with changes in work and technology. Schools and colleges are vital tools for communities adapting to new needs, and are also major employers in their own right. In both North and South, good rural schools, used as a resource by all the community, can help stem the flow of people to crowded cities.

Co-operative membership 1981-2
International Co-operative Alliance
membership 366,764,185

35% consumer societies
5% housing
2% workers
4% miscellaneous
1% fisheries
18% agricultural
35% credit, thrift, and saving

Working ideas
Improved methods and low-cost technologies can revitalize existing work and help create new industry. Groups like International Technology Development (ITDG) promote proven systems (like fish farming) and appropriate tools to be used where expensive technology is often irrelevant. Information is vital. One Indian scheme, SITE, used a satellite to broadcast developmental programmes (pp 224-5).

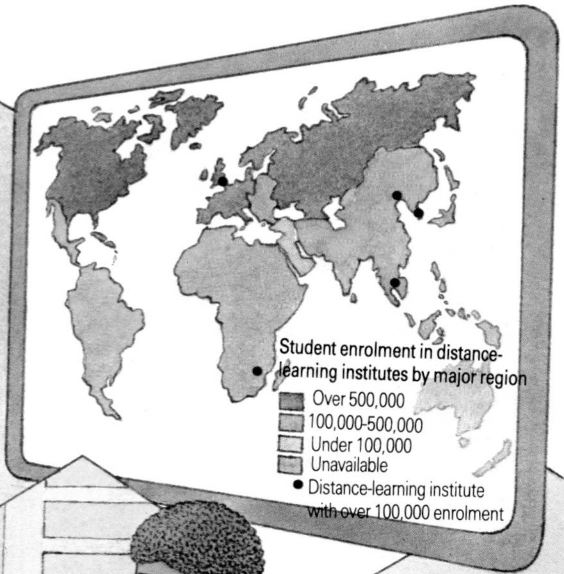

Distance learning

Students learning at home through correspondence, radio, TV, or telephone can help overcome problems of access to education. China and the USSR reach millions this way, while S American governments have pushed up literacy rates.

Student enrolment in distance-learning institutes by major region

- Over 500,000
- 100,000-500,000
- Under 100,000
- Unavailable
- ● Distance-learning institute with over 100,000 enrolment

Community co-operatives

Worker participation and profit-sharing schemes can both boost productivity and encourage innovation. There have been many ventures throughout Asia, including SEWA (pp 192-3) and, in Sri Lanka, Sarvodaya Shramadana – which has mobilized as many as 3,000 villages for communal road-building, farming, and local industry schemes. The ICA membership (left), covers multitudinous schemes.

Children's TV and radio

The mass-communication media have done much to build up the "global village". A successful television programme like *Sesame Street* can spark off hundreds of editions worldwide, and help children to understand the polycultural world.

Rural regeneration

Most developing countries that are committed to tackling rural poverty have implemented land reforms, notably China, Cuba, South Korea, and Taiwan. Such land distribution promotes employment and rural development. Where there is surplus labour, large-scale regeneration schemes prove highly productive. Examples include reafforestation schemes in India and in South Korea (pp 56-7).

New uses in old buildings

Whole cities and towns in the North are blighted by industrial decay. Small workshop schemes, such as those created by British Steel in Clydeside, Scotland, in 1979, have proved fruitful. British Steel (BSC) provided credit and business advice to former employees setting up new firms and co-operatives in obsolete buildings. The "greening" movement is also promoting community gardens and parks in cities.

Where they have done so, they have helped people adapt to change, giving them access to a range of tools for community-building, and to the ideas and information they need to launch new ventures.

Preserving cultural diversity

You can travel around the world without ever leaving New York, according to New Yorkers. The city has acted as a gateway to the US for successive tides of immigrants and refugees – all of whom were somehow supposed to emerge from the American melting pot as homogenized Americans. But New York's ethnic geography tells a different story. It has developed a patchwork of ethnic neighbourhoods, in which cultural diversity has proved highly resistant to the "American way". Similarly, it is becoming clear that there are limits to how far the global melting pot can proceed. While we may move towards common global objectives, we should retain our distinctive cultural bases.

The worldwide acceleration in cultural exchange, via mass media and tourism, has led to exciting cross-fertilization, but has also proved socially threatening. Many countries have come to fear the impact of other cultures, particularly the US "Coke culture". For some, particularly those countries with

A polycultural world?

Cultural diversity is a fact of life, a fact whose significance we are all too inclined to overlook. Every day, in a thousand different ways, we benefit from the intercultural exchange which is such a dominant feature of our times. Both in North and South, culture-shapers such as artists and musicians draw heavily on the traditional cultures of Africa, the Americas, and Asia. Western medicine absorbs new techniques, such as acupuncture, from countries whose medical practice had previously been derided. The diffusion of Eastern philosophies to the West has helped to promote holistic thinking. And, while we continue to push marginal tribal peoples to (and beyond) the brink of extinction, there is growing concern about their plight and awakening interest in their unique human experience and cultures.

Within the dominant culture, too, there is a resurgence of regional identity, and of diverse political and religious groups, lifestyles, and tastes. As we develop a one-world sense of identity, there are, fortunately, signs that the end-result will not be an homogenized human monoculture. Instead, while peoples like Canada's Inuit, New Zealand's Maoris, and South Africa's blacks fight to preserve and rebuild their cultural sense of identity, there is a new awareness even in the most dominant cultures that any future global community will have polycultural roots.

burgeoning modern cities, "culture shock" is proving to be a devastating phenomenon.

Side by side with the wave of homogenizing modernization is arising a new and acute awareness of the importance of diverse identities. Around the world, many groups of minorities have begun to re-assert themselves, and to demand the right to recognition and equality. The US Indians are asserting "Red Power", demanding the restoration of tribal lands. Canadian Indians have scored some notable successes in their struggle to get adequate compensation for loss of tribal lands. New Zealand's Maoris voice their firm belief in the value of their culture, as opposed to that of the "Pakeha" who have ruled them for two centuries.

But the recognition of minorities' rights must proceed faster. Too much lip service is paid to the special rights of indigenous people to ancestral lands—"rights" which are still tossed aside when they clash with economic interests. If such people are to enjoy real legal protection, then the momentum has to come from society as a whole—and above all from government action. Brazilians must decide to protect the Amerindians, New Zealanders to protect the Maoris, and Indians to protect the adivasis—India's original inhabitants.

CIVILIZATION

Introduced by Alvin Toffler

Author of Future Shock and The Third Wave

A new civilization is forming. So profoundly revolutionary is this new civilization that it challenges all our old assumptions. Old ways of thinking, old formulations, dogmas, and ideologies, no matter how cherished or how useful in the past, no longer fit the facts. The world that is fast emerging from the clash of new values and technologies, new geopolitical relationships, new life styles and modes of communication, demands wholly new ideas and analogies, classifications and concepts. We cannot cram the embryonic world of tomorrow into yesterday's conventional cubbyholes.

The dawn of this new civilization is the single most explosive fact of our lifetimes. It is an event as profound as that First Wave of change unleashed 10,000 years ago by the invention of agriculture, or the earthshaking Second Wave of change touched off by the Industrial Revolution. We are the children of the next transformation, the Third Wave. Humanity faces a quantum leap forward. It faces the deepest social upheaval and creative re-structuring of all time. Without clearly recognizing it, we are engaged in building a remarkable new civilization from the ground up.

Every civilization operates in and on the biosphere, and reflects or alters the mix of population and resources. Every civilization has a characteristic techno-sphere—an energy base linked to a production system which is in turn linked to a distribution system. Every civilization has a socio-sphere consisting of interrelated social institutions. Every civilization has an info-sphere—channels of communication through which necessary information flows. Every civilization has its own power-sphere. And every civilization has a set of characteristic relationships with the outside world—exploitative, symbiotic, militant, or pacific. Encouragingly, the embryonic Third Wave civilization we find is not only coherent and workable in ecological and economic terms, but—if we put our minds to it—could be made more decent and democratic than our own.

In no way is this to suggest inevitability. The period of transition will be marked by extreme social disruption, by wild economic swings, sectional clashes, secession attempts, technological upsets, political turbulence, violence, wars, and threats of war. In a climate of disintegrating Second Wave institutions and values, authoritarian demagogues and movements will seek, and possibly attain, power. No intelligent person can be smug about the outcome. The clash of two civilizations presents titanic dangers.

Yet the odds lie not with destruction but with ultimate survival. Ultimately we see a civilization founded once more on self-sustaining, renewable rather than exhaustible energy sources. The most basic raw material for Third Wave civilization, one that can never be exhausted, is information—including imagination. No one knows in detail what the future holds or what will work best in a Third Wave society. For this reason we should think not of a single massive reorganization or of a single revolutionary, cataclysmic change imposed from the top, but of thousands of conscious, decentralized experiments that permit us to test new models of political decision-making and new forms of development.

Excerpts from *The Third Wave* by Alvin Toffler, 1980.

THE POWER OF CIVILIZATION

For more than 5,000 years, this planet has witnessed the rise and fall of successive civilizations. Each has spread its technology, culture, and beliefs widely; each has declined when its resource base, or its administration, or both, became overstretched, vulnerable to external attack or internal disintegration. The powerhouse behind all these cultures has been the phenomenon of the city–the centre of civilization, reflecting both the best and worst of human aspirations.

We have been building cities ever since we learned to drain and effectively use the fertile river valleys of Egypt, Mesopotamia, and China. The resultant agricultural surplus allowed a division of labour, and the leisure to think and organize which underpin urban civilization. Over the ages, our towns and cities, often sited strategically on trading junctions, have served as cultural and racial melting pots. At their best, they have poured forth the wealth of art, literature, architecture, scientific discovery, and social, political and ethical concepts which are humankind's legacy to the future.

But the sheer pressure of human numbers in cities has always created huge problems. Poverty, as well as wealth, is concentrated; crime as well as justice; disease as well as medicine. Today, many Third World cities are ringed by vast shanty towns encompassing much human wretchedness. Some, like Calcutta and Lagos, have become administrative nightmares; everywhere, space is at a premium.

The burgeoning Third World cities demonstrate another high cost of urban civilization: cities are in essence parasitical, having an insatiable appetite for food, energy, raw materials, and human labour. The economy of early cities was linked directly to the productivity of the surrounding countryside; later, colonialism and trade links helped to support their growing populations. Modern cities, by contrast, are nodes on a web of long-range communications, dependent on local, regional and global markets for their supplies.

Until the Industrial Revolution, only one person in five lived in a settlement of over 10,000 people. In the past 100 years, however, there has been a massive influx to the cities, first in the North, latterly in the developing nations. On present trends, the cities of the Third World will swell to house over half its population by the year 2000, compared to one-third now.

What potential will the mega-cities of the South have as centres of the newly emerging 21st-century

The world city

When people congregate in cities, they can specialize to a much greater extent than in rural areas. This specialization becomes more diverse as cities grow until, as with the modern city, the functions of its inhabitants are as different, yet as interdependent, as those of individual cells in the human body.

When cities were relatively isolated, each developed a distinct culture: some became famous for their religious sites, others for their universities, public buildings, textiles, glass, or other artefacts. But today, worldwide cultural diversity is being eroded by mass markets and media. The middle classes in the big cities around the world often wear the same clothes, listen to the same pop-music and watch the same television programmes. We are seeing the emergence of a global "city culture".

The major conurbations are increasingly linked by transport and telecommunications, creating a single "world city" with increasing functional specialization of its individual members. Although separated geographically, they are combined in action: London, Zurich, and Tokyo operate as linked financial centres and the UN, based in New York, has specialized agencies in Paris, Nairobi, and Rome.

Financial control
While economic and political power once coincided, tele-communications have relaxed the link: New York, Rio de Janeiro, and Frankfurt are financial (but not political) capitals.

Literature
It is impossible to imagine world literature without Joyce's Dublin, Dicken's London, or Sartre's Paris. Most social, intellectual and spiritual currents which fuel literature still concentrate in the cities.

The changing city
Cities first developed some 4 to 5,000 years ago when a combination of agricultural and technological developments boosted productivity to the point where urban economies could support a range of specialist workers. Early cities were walled for defence – and within these walls craft industry flourished, sustained by the peasantry of the hinterland.

As cities outgrew the productive diversity of the surrounding areas, trade developed in importance, remaining the principal engine of city growth until the Industrial Revolution. It brought the need for banking and other commercial services, and with them, a wealthy and powerful merchant class. With the fall of the Roman Empire, urban life dwindled until the resurgence of European trade in the 11th and 12th centuries. In the 18th century, the mechanization of agriculture and industry released labour from the land and created a growing demand for it in factory cities. Railways and later the internal combustion engine helped reshape cities, the spreading suburbs and expanding new towns draining population from inner city areas. Now another wave of change, based on new technologies, is beginning to shift the world's cities into what has been dubbed the "post-industrial society".

Architecture
Many cities still bear the imprint of Rome's 1,000-year domination of European civilization. The 20th-century counterpart New York, with its trendsetting skyscrapers.

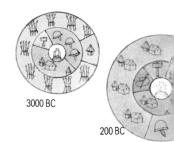

3000 BC

200 BC

The "chained" cities
The circles (above) represent stages of development of an idealized city, the chains their growing dependence on trade. Key factors are the financial, industrial and defence sectors.

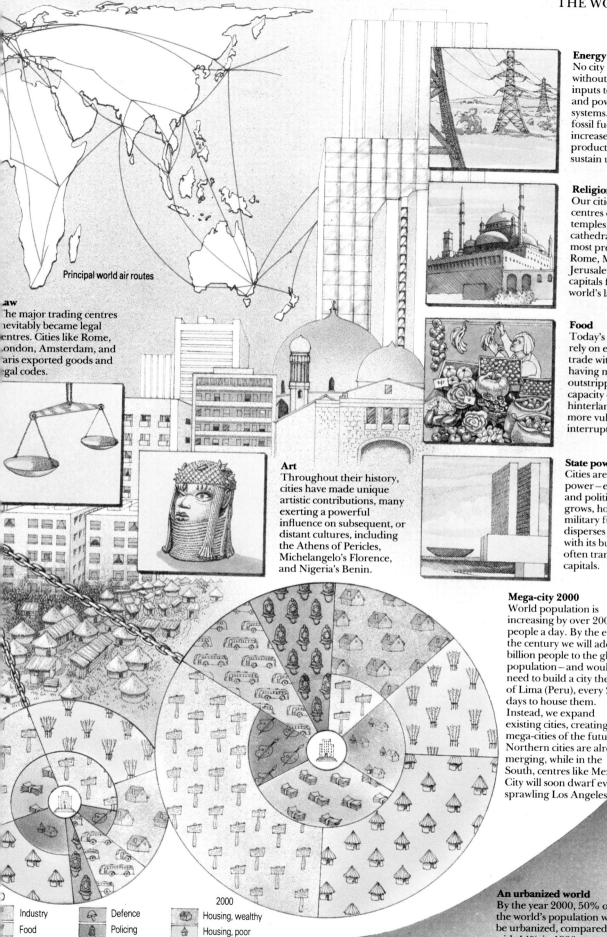

Principal world air routes

Energy
No city could survive without massive energy inputs to drive machines and power transport systems. The harnessing of fossil fuels allowed the increases in agricultural productivity needed to sustain urban growth.

Religion
Our cities have always been centres of worship – their temples, mosques and cathedrals are among our most precious buildings. Rome, Mecca, and Jerusalem are religious capitals for three of the world's largest faiths.

Food
Today's cities have come to rely on ever-increasing trade with remote regions, having mostly long since outstripped the productive capacity of their original hinterlands; and they are more vulnerable to interruptions of supply.

Law
The major trading centres inevitably became legal centres. Cities like Rome, London, Amsterdam, and Paris exported goods and legal codes.

State power
Cities are great centres of power – economic, military and political. As commerce grows, however, the military function usually disperses and State power, with its bureaucracy, is often transferred to new capitals.

Art
Throughout their history, cities have made unique artistic contributions, many exerting a powerful influence on subsequent, or distant cultures, including the Athens of Pericles, Michelangelo's Florence, and Nigeria's Benin.

Mega-city 2000
World population is increasing by over 200,000 people a day. By the end of the century we will add 2 billion people to the global population – and would need to build a city the size of Lima (Peru), every 20 days to house them. Instead, we expand existing cities, creating the mega-cities of the future. Northern cities are already merging, while in the South, centres like Mexico City will soon dwarf even sprawling Los Angeles.

An urbanized world
By the year 2000, 50% of the world's population will be urbanized, compared with 14% in 1900.

Industry	Defence	Housing, wealthy
Food	Policing	Housing, poor
Transport	Finance	Housing, wealthy
Administration	Culture	and poor

2000

1800 1825 1850 1875 1900 1925 1950 1975 2000

50%
40%
30%
20%
10%

civilization? Will they retain their central role? The upsurge of communications and new information technologies makes it increasingly possible for city functions to be decentralized. It also opens the door to integration of urban and rural sectors in a one-world economic network.

The global factory

No civilization in history has held such technological power in its grasp as does our present generation. And none has allocated to science such a commanding, almost mystical role as the provider of health, wealth, power, freedom, and happiness. But, while technology and mass production have brought enormous rewards, the global factory has proved a double-edged weapon in our battle to improve the human condition.

The world production system has undergone a rapid, increasingly radical change since the optimistic post-war era – a boom period which was fuelled by cheap energy and sustained by the belief that surging growth in the North would boost standards of living in the South.

The outpourings of the global factory spawned the affluent, throwaway society – wasteful, pressurized, dominating the global imagination with its seductive imagery of gleaming automobiles and shining cities. But it also produced cures for major epidemic diseases, doubled food production, and provided mass mobility, communications, and mass media which effectively shrank the planet into a "global village".

The key technologies of the 1950s and 1960s were based on steel, chemicals, and oil. The bulldozer, tractor, and chainsaw, together with fertilizers and pesticides, revolutionized agriculture. New drugs and surgical techniques transformed medicine. Wave after wave of durable goods, from refrigerators to radios, poured off faster, automated production lines.

And then, during the early 1970s, a series of convulsions ran through the global economic system. Soaring oil prices, depleted natural resources, widespread pollution and health hazards, an escalating and ever-more sophisticated arms race, and worsening world poverty and hunger, dealt hammer blows to our faith in technology.

Government backing for technology and private investment in research are still rising on an unprecedented scale. However, over 97 percent of the world's research and development budget is spent in the North and global production has become astonishingly concentrated: in 1980, the top ten nations accounted for 83 percent of world production – and just three nations (the US, Japan, and West Germany) accounted for around 50 percent. An unquantified but large proportion is in the hands of the transnational corporations, whose power has been escalating since 1945.

More positively, new technologies have emerged which, while they trigger some deep anxieties, do

The world factory

The engine that drives the global factory is commerce, fuelled by research, energy, and innovative ideas. Riding on successive waves of social and technological change, the factory is constantly adjusting to fluctuations in demand, partly created by advertising, and to changes in labour productivity and relations sparked by new technologies. If it seems to promise happiness to many, it also provides power to the few. Both research and production are concentrated in just a few countries of the North; much is in the hands of international megacorporations. This concentration of power often makes it near impossible to develop equitable alternatives to the approaches and technologies promoted by the major industrial nations. But the present order is beginning to alter in the face of profound social and technological changes: we are seeing the birth of a radically different form of global factory.

Technology – for whose benefit?

Fears of mass unemployment and an emerging technocracy beyond the control of ordinary citizens may simply express natural hostility to a new social structure. The new technologies actually provide the possibility of greater diversity and freedom of work and more consumer control.

However, over $35 billion, plus half a million scientists and engineers, were used to feed the military "albatross" in 1979 alone, an investment which contributes little to economic and social advancement. The US and the USSR now devote half their R & D budgets to military research, which may well be a factor in their recent decline in economic competitiveness.

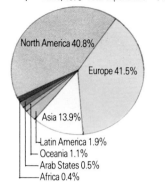

Distribution of research and development expenditure, 1978 Total expenditure = $12

North America 40.8%
Europe 41.5%
Asia 13.9%
Latin America 1.9%
Oceania 1.1%
Arab States 0.5%
Africa 0.4%

The manufacturing base
A major impetus for technological innovation humanity's constant desi for a greater variety of goods. Growth of the service sector depends o strong manufacturing ba to provide a large range machines and equipmen Thus manufacturing operations are a key constituent of the world technological resource. These constitute continuous flow goods, such as chemicals and ste and batch items, which make up the great mass consumer goods, such as cars and clothes.

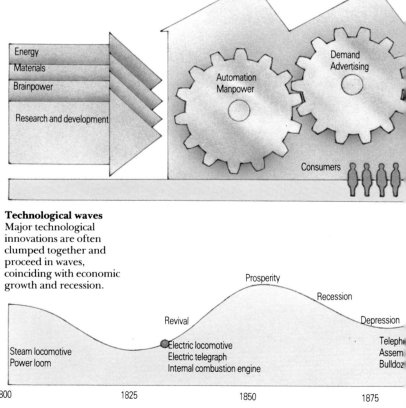

Energy
Materials
Brainpower
Research and development

Automation
Manpower

Demand
Advertising

Consumers

Technological waves
Major technological innovations are often clumped together and proceed in waves, coinciding with economic growth and recession.

Prosperity
Revival
Recession
Depression

Steam locomotive
Power loom

Electric locomotive
Electric telegraph
Internal combustion engine

Teleph
Assem
Bulldoz

1800   1825   1850   1875

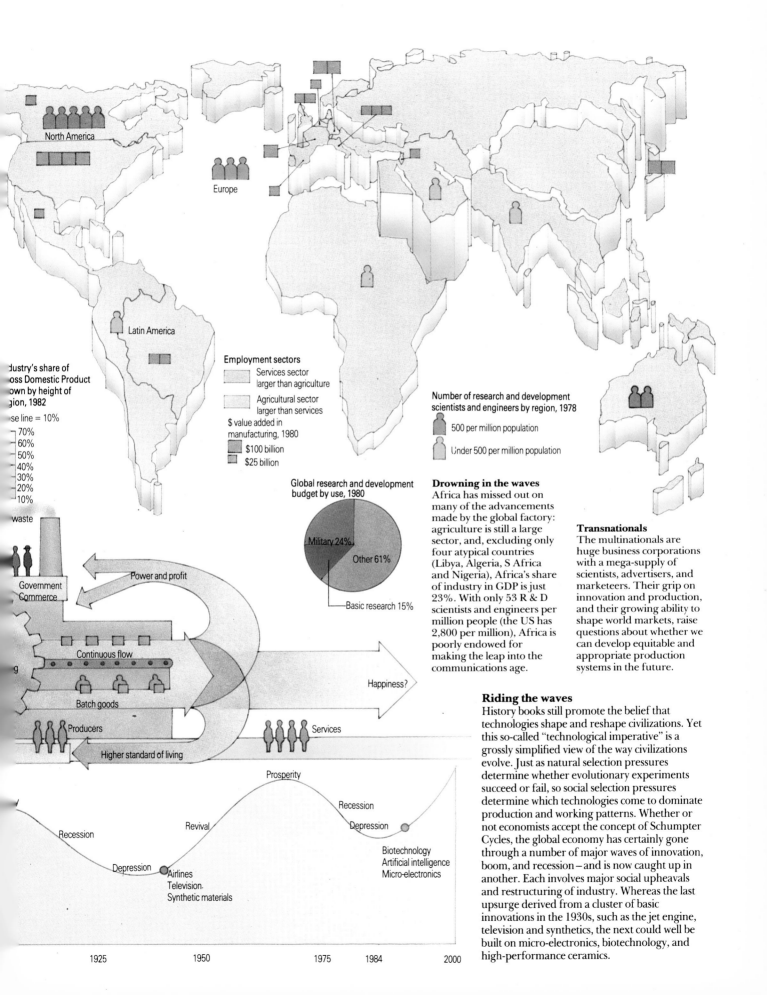

North America

Europe

Latin America

Industry's share of
Gross Domestic Product
shown by height of
region, 1982

Base line = 10%

- 70%
- 60%
- 50%
- 40%
- 30%
- 20%
- 10%

Employment sectors

Services sector
larger than agriculture

Agricultural sector
larger than services

$ value added in
manufacturing, 1980

$100 billion

$25 billion

**Number of research and development
scientists and engineers by region, 1978**

500 per million population

Under 500 per million population

waste

Government
Commerce

Power and profit

Continuous flow

Batch goods

Producers

Higher standard of living

Happiness?

Services

**Global research and development
budget by use, 1980**

Military 24%

Other 61%

Basic research 15%

Drowning in the waves
Africa has missed out on
many of the advancements
made by the global factory:
agriculture is still a large
sector, and, excluding only
four atypical countries
(Libya, Algeria, S Africa
and Nigeria), Africa's share
of industry in GDP is just
23%. With only 53 R & D
scientists and engineers per
million people (the US has
2,800 per million), Africa is
poorly endowed for
making the leap into the
communications age.

Transnationals
The multinationals are
huge business corporations
with a mega-supply of
scientists, advertisers, and
marketeers. Their grip on
innovation and production,
and their growing ability to
shape world markets, raise
questions about whether we
can develop equitable and
appropriate production
systems in the future.

Riding the waves
History books still promote the belief that
technologies shape and reshape civilizations. Yet
this so-called "technological imperative" is a
grossly simplified view of the way civilizations
evolve. Just as natural selection pressures
determine whether evolutionary experiments
succeed or fail, so social selection pressures
determine which technologies come to dominate
production and working patterns. Whether or
not economists accept the concept of Schumpter
Cycles, the global economy has certainly gone
through a number of major waves of innovation,
boom, and recession – and is now caught up in
another. Each involves major social upheavals
and restructuring of industry. Whereas the last
upsurge derived from a cluster of basic
innovations in the 1930s, such as the jet engine,
television and synthetics, the next could well be
built on micro-electronics, biotechnology, and
high-performance ceramics.

Prosperity

Recession

Revival

Recession

Depression

Biotechnology
Artificial intelligence
Micro-electronics

Recession

Depression

Airlines
Television
Synthetic materials

1925   1950   1975 1984 2000

appear to offer new hope for the developing nations. Micro-electronics, information technology, new materials, and biotechnology are just some of the locally adaptable, low-energy, low-pollution technologies which may provide means for many parts of the South to boost their productivity.

The communications resource

The world is witnessing a communications revolution – a "third wave" of human advance transforming society just as dramatically as did the Industrial Revolution (the "second wave") and the Agricultural Revolution (the "first wave") several thousand years earlier. The interaction of several recent high-technology developments – space satellites, micro-electronics, optic fibres, laser beams, and the computer – is hugely magnifying our ability to store and analyse data, and to communicate and disseminate information, with major consequences for the nature of civilization.

In terms of communications, the world has shrunk rapidly. Today the contents of a dozen volumes of Encyclopaedia Britannica can be transmitted across the world in seconds. There has also been a shift from broadcasting to "narrowcasting". For example, the US cable television network offers people a choice of a hundred or more channels catering to every possible taste and viewpoint; the channels can be two-way, allowing viewers to communicate directly with those planning the service.

Satellites amplify the coverage and flexibility of both television and telephone communications. Indonesia's successful linking of its 3,000 islands by radio and telephone via satellite would not have been practicable by more conventional means. The use of satellites has an enormous potential for serving human needs: in weather forecasting, planning more efficient land use, and the detection and management of the Earth's natural resources. Remote-sensing satellites, like the US's Landsat, can map minerals, forests, and other resources using infra-red frequencies, and also provide early information on cyclones, crop yields, hazards such as blights, and other dangers from acid rain to pollution. Theoretically this should improve planning and enable governments to arrive at better policy decisions.

Computer and telecommunication links are also producing a mounting flood of data transactions. Data flows include financial information of every kind – commodity and share prices, currency rates, debt and credit ratings – as well as market supply-and-demand trends, and "sensitive" product and technology information. Governments and businesses have vested interests in controlling information banks, and have a dangerous tendency to resist releasing information.

Of even greater concern is the unequal ownership of communications, both the technology and its information sources. Northern governments and multinational companies own the majority of the

The power of communications

The store of human knowledge has never been higher, nor our ability to communicate it greater. In today's world, split between the affluent North and the developing South, the new communications technologies have huge potential for solving problems – both for decentralizing facilities that have always tied people to towns and cities, for instance, and for speeding up development in the poorer countries of the world. They can also operate at many levels and can be tailored to suit widely varied needs. With literacy rates low in the South, broadcasting, for example, can represent a lifeline to vital information and participation, boosting educational programmes to rural communitites who were formerly without access.

Language and new technology
For most of human history, languages have diverged and multiplied as human groups have dispersed and developed different identities. The mass media has tended to standardize and to strengthen the official languages (pp 178-9). However, we can now support language diversity, through cable TV and local radio stations.

The geostationary orbit
To avoid Earth stations having to track a satellite as it orbits, the satellite's speed can be matched exactly to that of the rotating planet. Such a satellite can send signals to half the globe, but its focus is usually limited to a smaller "footprint."

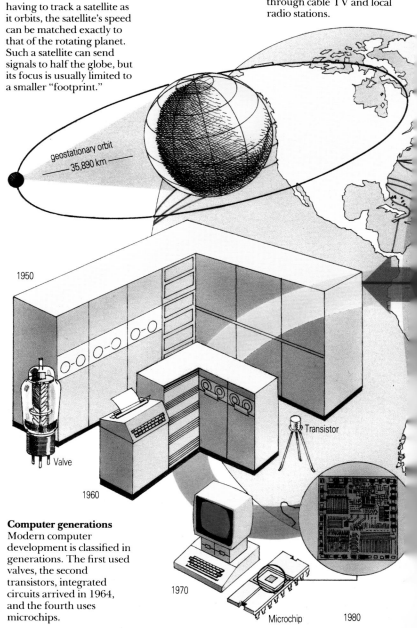

geostationary orbit
—— 35,890 km ——

1950

Transistor

Valve

1960

Microchip   1980

1970

Computer generations
Modern computer development is classified in generations. The first used valves, the second transistors, integrated circuits arrived in 1964, and the fourth uses microchips.

Telegraph vs telephone
The first practicable electric telegraph system was invented in 1837. The telephone, born in 1876, proved far more revolutionary for the general public; it allowed, for the first time, two-way direct communications over distance, even between continents, without coding.

Radio
The earliest regular radio broadcast began in 1922. Radio soon proved to be an instrument of social modernization, and has had a massive impact on the Third World, due to its relative cheapness and ability to reach vast audiences of both literate and illiterate people. The majority of radio services are still state-controlled, but the US service is mostly commercial.

arly telecommunication
he first long-distance mmunication required e message to be coded to a set of symbols. rican village drummers n communicate over long stances at the speed of und. Beacon messages re followed by liograph, early flag stems by semaphore.

The printing revolution
Mechanized printing magnified our ability to reach more and more people. Now the 19th-century steam-powered presses have been superseded by cheaper type-setting, printing, and copying techniques which have resulted in an explosive growth of publications (pp 176-7).

bmarine cables
1980 a single submarine le (below) could carry 00 telephone calls.

Television
TV broadcasting, begun in 1936, has combined the potential of cinema's audio-visual impact and radio's accessibility, to reform people's perceptions of the world. But only 14% of TV sets are in the South, with 75% of world population.

Path of geostationary orbit

Satellite power
The first artificial satellite was Sputnik 1, launched in 1957. More than 14,000 have since gone into orbit, but most have burnt up on re-entry. Out of the 290 still functioning, the US has 180, the USSR 100.

he information revolution
he first computers, built in the 1950s, cost ormous sums, and filled several rooms. Now llions of private users have desk-top mputers, while commerce, banking, and dustry have been revolutionized by advanced ormation systems and international ecommunications. Whereas in 1979 there was average of 14 million international nsactions *daily* between data users in Western rope, the number is projected to rise to

around 120 million by 1987. The emerging fifth generation of computers, with "artificial intelligence", represents another quantum leap in our ability to telecommunicate.

Computers are revolutionizing personal life too – from schooling and working at home to "armchair" banking, holiday booking, and shopping. The advent of word processors, two-way broadcast, and TV computer links, together with the rapid take-up of computer skills by the

younger generation, has produced a fast-changing society fuelled by easy access to information and technology. The consequences are still unknown – George Orwell's fear of "Big Brother" control may be applicable to the international economy, manipulated by Northern governments and megacorporations. But mass access makes the breakdown of information monopolies a more likely outcome in the richer nations.

new hardware, and exploit its power, reinforcing their monopoly of global expertise. Many people in the South do not have access to a television (or indeed a radio), let alone a personal computer. Few countries can afford satellite technology. This inequitable sharing of potential benefits is greatly reducing opportunities for development.

Changing trade flows

The huge stepping-up of activity on the global "trading floor" since World War II has profoundly influenced the emerging world economy. By the early 1980s, world output of goods and services exceeded 12 trillion dollars, of which about a fifth was destined for international markets. Trade has been increasing faster than production, and nations exchanging goods and services are ever more interdependent: suppliers in one part of the world rely on buyers in another, and consumers enjoy a growing choice of foreign products.

As the market has expanded, the production of goods has increasingly split up around the world – components and raw materials from one country are shipped overseas for assembly or processing, then returned to their origin, or re-exported to a third nation. It is mainly labour-intensive processes that are shifting Southwards however; technology-based and more profitable industries remain in the North. This "assembly line" approach has been fuelled by the emergence of the multinational corporations, and of newly industrialized countries (NICs) like South Korea or Brazil, where low wage-rates attract Western-based investment. These "new Japans", elbowing their way on to the trading floor, are challenging older industrial countries.

Multinationals have long been involved in production of Third World primary commodities, from minerals to tea, coffee, rubber, palm oil, and bananas. But the growth of their involvement in manufacturing, with subsidiaries around the world taking a sizeable share of global production and trade, is a more modern phenomenon. Of the 100 biggest economic entities on Earth, about half are countries – the other half megacompanies.

These trends are a matter of bitter controversy. Some argue that rapid expansion of trade has been the engine of economic growth, and that market specialization encourages efficiency, so that all prosper. Others are more hostile to the whole trend to interdependence. They hold that the benefits have gone overwhelmingly to rich nations, and that specialization simply means Third World countries stay locked into low-wage, low-technology functions, while the rich countries and multinationals maintain their dominance.

This debate has influenced decisions by the developing countries on whether or not to link their economies to the world market. To follow the process of export orientation means gearing production to satisfying overseas demand, while importing goods needed at home. The alternative,

The world market

The traders in the world market do not bargain on an equal footing; there are huge disparities in their share of trade, and the value of goods they exported. A large part of the trade flows are directed by the megacorporations, mainly based in the rich North, which dominate the market. Snapping at its heels, however, are newly industrialized Third World nations. The OPEC group (Organization of Petroleum Exporting Countries) exploits their high-earning commodity, oil – a temporary bonanza. But the majority of developing nations still export low-value primary products. Often unable to buy the North's manufacturing exports, their share of world trade is small – only 3% for non-OPEC Africa. If the rapid growth of the world market is to provide prosperity for all, much depends on restructuring the trading flow, to make room for the "new Japans", and to increase the earnings of the poor majority.

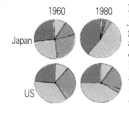

Market leaders: Japan, US
Japan's manufacturing growth has surpassed all non-Communist countries. The US is the leading industrial nation, also accounting for one-fifth of world agricultural exports.

Structure of merchandise imports
- Food ⎤
- Fuel ⎬ Primary commodities
- Other ⎦
- Machinery and transport equipment
- Other manufacturers

Structure of merchandise exports
- Fuels, metals and minerals ⎤ Primary commodities
- Other ⎦
- Textiles and clothing
- Machinery and transport equipment
- Other manufactures

Rich industrial countries

Value of exports, 1982
$1,200 billion

On the face of it, the rich industrial countries have the cards stacked in their favour. They account for 65% of all export earnings, have benefited greatly from the boom in manufacturing value, and are able to import raw materials at a price advantage. But the older sundown industries such as steel, are facing very tough competition from cheaper Third World products. Recession, higher oil prices, and weakening markets in the poorer nations are all a threat to the viability of Northern consumer goods production and heavy industries.

OPEC

Value of exports 1982
$225 billion

Share of world oil production

1973 — 56%
1978 — 76%
1982 — 33%

Most oil nations are major net exporters, but have little industry. After the 1973 Arab-Israeli war, OPEC's share of world oil production rose to 76% (by 1978); overall, prices rose ten-fold. Disruptions to trade were major. Today, OPEC earns 12% of world export income, almost half the Third World total, from a single, non-renewable resource.

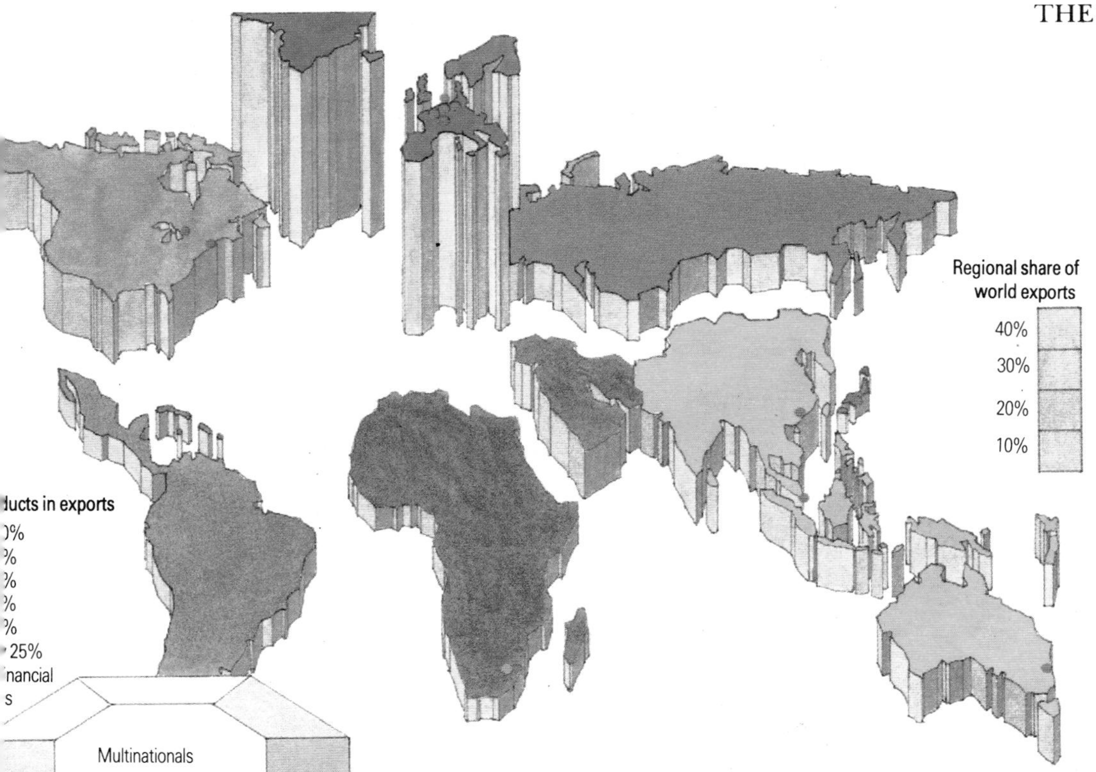

The exporting world
Indicating each region's share of world export earnings by height, as on the map (left), immediately reveals the dominance of the older industrial nations. Europe (41%) and North America (14%) account for over half; tiny Japan (7%) for more than either Africa (5%) or Latin America (6%). The newly oil-rich Middle East earns about 11% of the total, while Asia, USSR, and E Europe take only 18%. Many of these, however, are not principally market-oriented economies. Worst off are countries exporting primary commodities – the extent of their dependence is shown by shading.

Regional share of
world exports
40%
30%
20%
10%

Single commodity traders
One commodity, coffee, remains Ethiopia's principal export. The agricultural sector is inefficient, and economic reform is frustrated by political instability. In contrast, Jamaica's exports, once primarily sugarcane and bauxite, have changed due to US investment and local alumina processing.

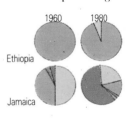

1960   1980

Ethiopia

Jamaica

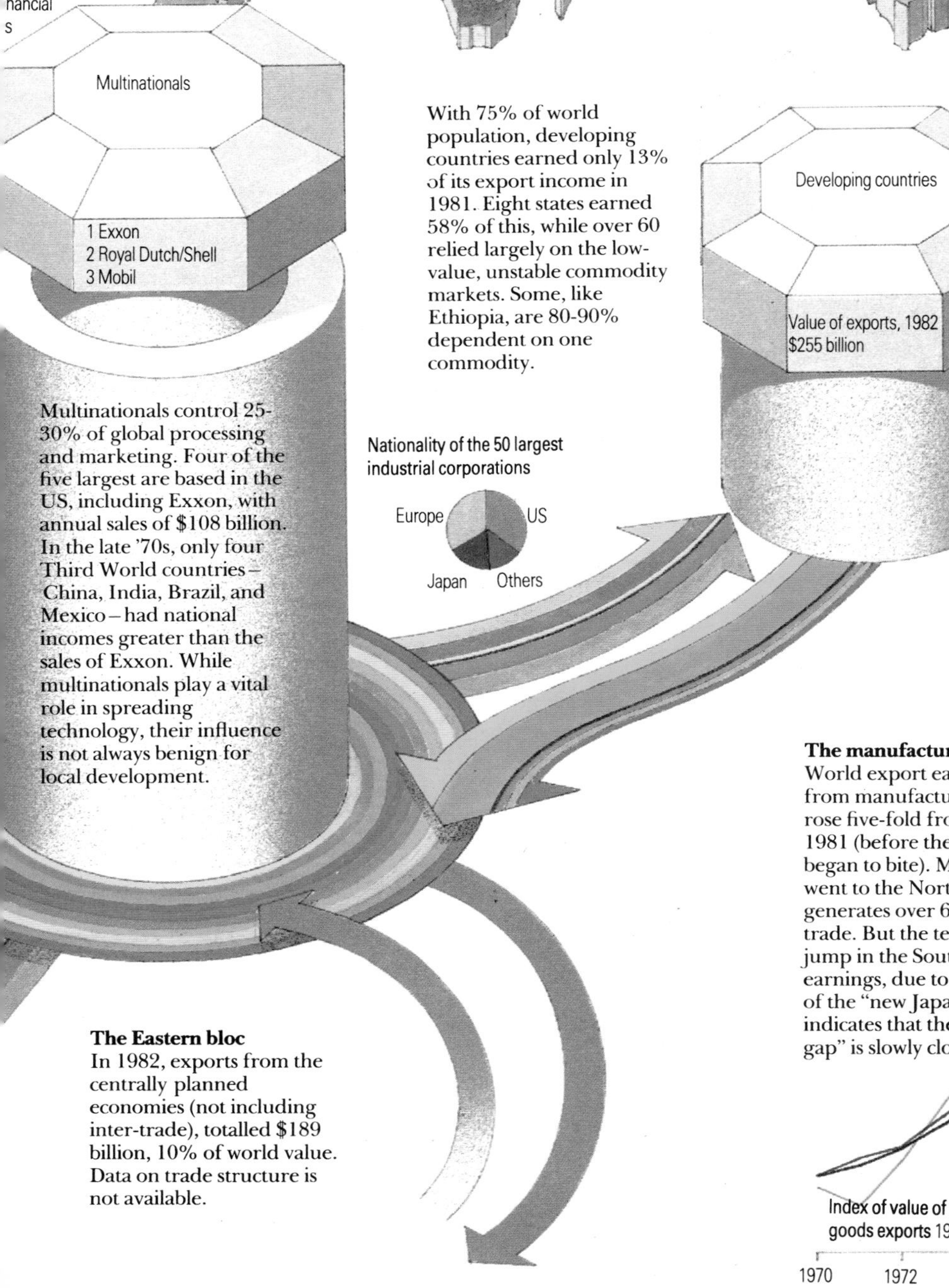

ducts in exports
)%
%
%
%
25%
nancial
s

Multinationals

1 Exxon
2 Royal Dutch/Shell
3 Mobil

With 75% of world population, developing countries earned only 13% of its export income in 1981. Eight states earned 58% of this, while over 60 relied largely on the low-value, unstable commodity markets. Some, like Ethiopia, are 80-90% dependent on one commodity.

Developing countries

Value of exports, 1982
$255 billion

Multinationals control 25-30% of global processing and marketing. Four of the five largest are based in the US, including Exxon, with annual sales of $108 billion. In the late '70s, only four Third World countries – China, India, Brazil, and Mexico – had national incomes greater than the sales of Exxon. While multinationals play a vital role in spreading technology, their influence is not always benign for local development.

Nationality of the 50 largest
industrial corporations

Europe   US
Japan   Others

The manufacturing boom
World export earnings from manufactured goods rose five-fold from 1970 to 1981 (before the recession began to bite). Most of this went to the North, which generates over 60% of the trade. But the ten-fold jump in the South's earnings, due to the growth of the "new Japans", indicates that the "export gap" is slowly closing.

The Eastern bloc
In 1982, exports from the centrally planned economies (not including inter-trade), totalled $189 billion, 10% of world value. Data on trade structure is not available.

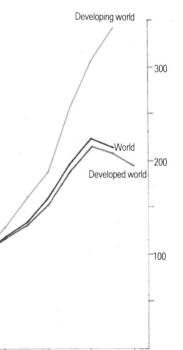

Developing world
300
World
200
Developed world
100

Index of value of manufactured
goods exports 1975=100

1970   1972   1974   1976   1978   1980   1982

import substitution, means self-sufficiency through gearing production to domestic needs. Of the countries that are trying self-sufficiency, a few manage above-average economic growth, despite the attendant problems. Some export-oriented nations prosper; but their dependence on fluctuating markets and prices, especially those of raw commodities, makes their prospects uncertain.

Assets and earning power

The wealth of the planet is enormous. Even our human share of it—including the monumental assets of civilization—is considerable. What we have made of this resource, however, is clearly a very different matter.

Today, the First World, with under a fifth of the world's population, enjoys two-thirds of world income. Conversely, the 75 percent who live in the Third World have only 20 percent. The balance goes to the Eastern bloc (the Second World).

These stark indicators of world inequality do not tell us much about relative affluence and poverty, or about potential. Income, usually referring to Gross National Product (GNP), is the conventional yardstick for assessing a nation's prosperity. We need to know too about national *wealth*, whether in the form of railways, factories, major rivers, soil and unexploited natural resources, or workforce skills and the health and education of a nation's children.

This kind of wealth is, like the proverbial talents, a stock of assets that can be increased or depleted, from which income can be derived. In this sense, a poor country in the South, such as Zaire, with vast but unexploited natural resources, is potentially very rich. By contrast, high-income Japan is rich through the ingenuity of its people, plus their capacity and enthusiasm for hard work.

A high GNP tends to bring power and influence. GNP determines a nation's shareholdings in the International Monetary Fund (IMF), for example, and the size of its shareholdings in turn determines its votes and borrowing rights. The rich countries do not borrow much. But they do decide policy, and so ensure that the international economic system functions in the way that they prescribe.

Exploitable natural wealth can provide counter-bargaining power however—witness the disruption to global economic patterns caused by OPEC's oil bonanza, or the emerging value of genetic resources in the South (pp 156-7).

But the problem for poorer countries is that, whatever their resources, their development costs money. They must either save the little income they earn, or they must borrow. During the 1970s, banks were the major source of capital, largely because of vast, virtually unspendable sums of petro-dollars that were deposited in banks—which then went looking for credit-worthy customers in the South. But now, bank lending has almost dried up as world recession and high interest rates have turned the resulting debts into almost unsupportable burdens.

The world's wealth

No nation's wealth is independent of world power structures and priorities. Income is increasingly dependent on market factors, and development on world rankings for aid, credit-worthiness, or investment. Since the 1944 Bretton Woods agreement on the World Bank and the IMF, the flow of wealth across the world and the ground rules for who gets what, on what terms, have been controlled by a group of largely Northern-based institutions comprising the financial community. Properly managed, international wealth flows *can* help poorer nations realize their potential. Wealth however, tends to flow towards wealth rather than where it is most needed.

Credit and investment

A nation's ability to raise credit or attract multinational investment is more often a measure of its strength than its need. The sources of credit are private banks, plus two major sister institutions: the World Bank, which provides investment capital, and the IMF, which concentrates on short-term balance-of-payments assistance for countries in difficulty.

Credit-worthiness hinges not only on performance indicators (some countries like Singapore and Brazil have brought good returns through their rapid economic growth), but also on political stability and "preferred" economic policies. A handful of rich, industrialized nations control the voting rights at the IMF (p.231).

Wealth vs income

For individuals, as for nations, income and wealth do not necessarily go together. The table below compares the situations of an Amazonian smallholder, with 50 ha of land and four cows, with that of a young, salaried European, making down-payments on an apartment.

	Small farmer Latin America	European professional
Wealth ($)	8,000	6,000
Annual income ($)		
cash	780	18,000
kind	460	—
Total income ($)	1,240	18,000

Technology and aid

Access to technology and skills for development costs money. Increasingly, developing countries rely on commercial enterprise or aid – multilateral funds from agencies like UNICEF, or bilateral agreements between countries. Aid rose to $28 billion a year in 1982, and investment in the South by multinationals to $11 billion. Though inadequate, these sums do help—at a price. Large corporations sometimes harmfully exploit local economies; bilateral agreements can lock recipient countries into buying unwanted goods and services.

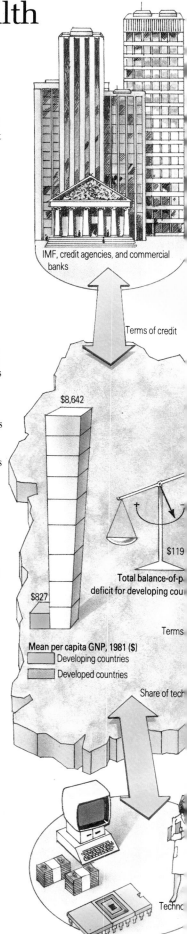

IMF, credit agencies, and commercial banks

Terms of credit

$8,642

$827

$119

Total balance-of-p deficit for developing cou

Terms

Mean per capita GNP, 1981 ($)
Developing countries
Developed countries

Share of tech

Techno

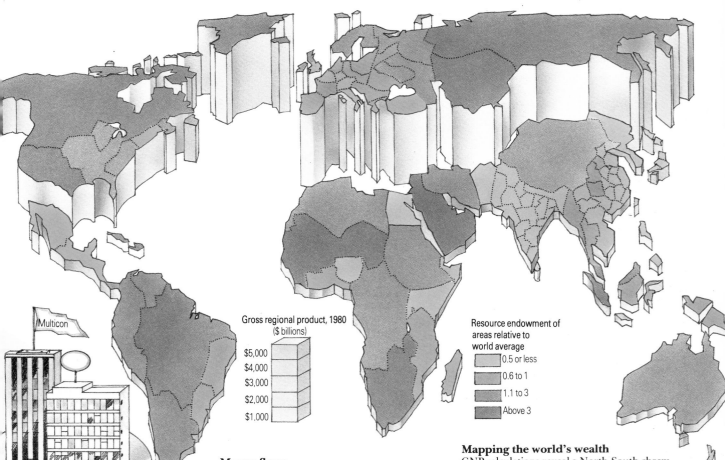

Multicon

Multinationals

Gross regional product, 1980
($ billions)

$5,000
$4,000
$3,000
$2,000
$1,000

Resource endowment of
areas relative to
world average

	0.5 or less
	0.6 to 1
	1.1 to 3
	Above 3

Money flows

As nations trade in goods, money flows through
the system – towards high-value exports. The
oil-price rises of the '70s caused a huge flow
away from the West towards OPEC. In the
South, chronic current-account deficits, partly
caused by low export earnings, have been
exacerbated by the exchange system (below). To
help poorer nations afford imports, banks and
other institutions lend them money, earning
interest in return. Trouble starts when the trade
deficit is such that interest payments cannot be
met, let alone capital repayments.

Mapping the world's wealth

GNP calculations reveal a North-South chasm
(above). However, natural resources, another
type of wealth, present a different picture.
Estimated according to four major factors – the
biological productivity of land, non-fuel
minerals, fossil fuels, and the sheer extent of
territory (assessed by 1970s values) – resources
appear to be richly distributed. The map also
indicates equal-population areas. Resources
often remain frozen assets, however: although
in some cases it may be uneconomic to exploit
them, lack of *capacity* to do so is more often the
limiting factor.

Goods

ade in goods

ation's terms of trade, i.e. the profitability of
mport/export equation, affects both its cash
w and its balance of payments. North-South
de consists primarily of manufactured goods
wing from North to South, and raw materials
m South to North. The terms of trade for
commodities have declined seriously
npared to oil or manufactured goods, to the
advantage of the poor. Exports earn less
le imports cost more. Result: massive deficits
d sharp cutbacks on imports.

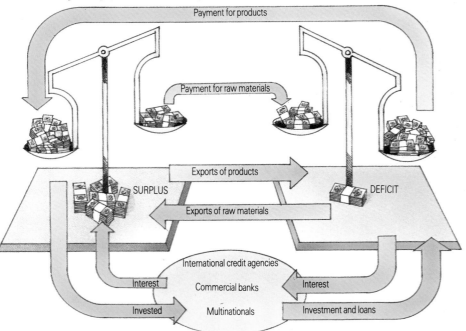

Payment for products

Payment for raw materials

SURPLUS

Exports of products

DEFICIT

Exports of raw materials

International credit agencies

Interest   Commercial banks   Interest

Invested   Multinationals   Investment and loans

CRISIS: THE DIVIDED WORLD

Despite three decades of growth and development planning, the numbers of absolute poor have steadily increased. With present growth rates, Brazil, a leader of Third World development, would take 362 years to close its income gap with the rich world; Mauritania, one of the poorer nations, would need 3,224 years – if such equality were ever possible. The gap between rich and poor threatens the very roots of our global civilization.

Cities in crisis

Cities in the developing world are exploding under the pressure of their populations. Their surging growth is similar to that of the 19th-century industrializing North, but on a massive scale. Every day an estimated 75,000 poor people, hoping for work, stream in from rural areas to overwhelm city services and administrations. The majority of the newcomers head for the *barrios*, *favelas*, and shanty towns – made from corrugated iron, plastic sheets, and packing cases – which now ring the outskirts of most cities. Such squatter settlements house some 75 percent of the entire population of Ibadan (Nigeria), and about 67 percent in Calcutta.

Many millions live in the most degrading and menacing environment. In 1980, about 177 million people in developing-world cities did not have safe drinking water and 331 million were without adequate sanitation. Widespread diarrhoea, dysentery, and typhoid are inevitable. Food and fuel are scarce, and accidents common.

With known unemployment frequently between 20 and 30 percent, the urban poor are trapped in a vicious circle. Those lucky enough to have a job suffer long hours, low wages, exposure to chemicals and dust, excess noise, and dangerous machinery.

Administrations stretched beyond capacity by the swelling slumland have developed harsh policies. The most draconian are straight eviction for those on illegally occupied land, and bulldozing of settlements. Many city governments also refuse to extend basic services and infrastructure, fearing that any such improvements will attract more newcomers.

Even the most workless and derelict post-industrial cities of the North do not compare with such misery; but life is also bleak. Instead of outer-city growth, Northern cities are afflicted by inner-city decay. As industries decline, and the rich move out to suburbs, those least able to move – the old, the ethnic minorities, and the poorly educated – are left behind. This results in declining revenues for local

Chaos in the cities

Most major Third World cities are really two cities: the inner city of the rich elite, which mimics the forms and lifestyles of the affluent North, and the largely self-built outer city of the poor. Urban incomes in the South average three times rural incomes, and modern services such as doctors, teachers, sanitation, clean water, and electricity are at least within reach. Thus the city acts as a "honeypot" for the rural poor; appalling though conditions are, they can be much better than in the countryside. Unable to afford ready-built housing, immigrants have no choice but to swell the shanty towns, where populations are now growing at four times the overall city growth rate. Many are already unmanageable. In Cairo, for instance, a water and sanitation system built to service a population of 2 million is collapsing under the burden of 11 million people.

Proportions of urban population

By the end of the century, just over half the world's population will be living in urban areas. Two-thirds of them are likely to be in cities of 100,000 or more inhabitants, and over 20% in cities with more than a million people.

Populations of cities and agglomerations (with over 5 million people)

Over 30 million
25-30 million
20-25 million
15-20 million
10-15 million
5 million and over

Cities with population o[f] by 1980
Change in population by
Projected change in pop[ulation] to 2000

Urbanized world population 2000 75%

Urbanized world pop[ulation] 1980 50%

The older Northern conurbations, by contrast, are often struggling through a long, drawn-out, post-industrial crisis. Instead of a massive influx of the poor, they have suffered instead from an exodus of the rich. Lacking new inputs, the city structure – buildings, sewers, and roads – has increasingly fallen into disrepair. Instead of overcrowding, hunger, lack of water, and poor sanitation, the streets of Harlem (New York), Watts (Los Angeles) or Toxteth (Liverpool) offer loneliness, drug-addiction, and violence. Some city halls face bankruptcy, their falling revenues unable to meet the upkeep of the decaying physical and social fabric around them – notably New York, and Liverpool, UK.

Unemployment, homelessness, and tension between social and racial groups are exacerbated by economic recession and competition for scarce jobs. The elderly, in particular, are vulnerable – to neglect, to isolation, and to the mounting petty crime which outstrips police control. A UK study showed the British housing stock in need of over $35 billion of repairs – at present rates of funding, one estimate suggested that renovation might take 400 years.

Northern city degradation

The Northern post-industrial society no longer needs to concentrate employment and resources in the inner cities. Chicago, for instance, lost 212,000 jobs from 1969 to 1979, its suburbs gaining 220,000. The work remaining is mainly administrative and "white-collar", but the wealthier citizens who hold these positions are moving to the suburbs. In Hartford, Connecticut, suburbanites hold 90% of all jobs paying $15,000 or more. The same tale could be told in much of Europe.

Many inner cities have become "reservations" for the worst-off members of society, unable to provide the economic development to move people up the income ladder. Bootle (right), near Liverpool, typifies this urban decay.

Mega-cities

In 1920 the world's urban population amounted to 360 million; by the end of the century it will be nearly 3 billion. Only seven cities had a population larger than 5 million in 1950; by 2000 there will be 57 such mega-cities, 42 of them in the Third World. Twenty-five cities are likely to have a population greater than 10 million, and all but three of these will be in the South. Mexico City, with over 30 million people, will be the largest.

Bangkok squatters

Klong Toey is a community in the metropolitan district of Krung Thep Maha Nakhon, better known as Bangkok. More than 30,000 people live as squatters in houses they have built themselves over a swamp. Most of the inhabitants are recent migrants from Thailand's rural areas. An average of 6 people live in each dwelling, often as many as 4 to a room. Only 3 in 100 people have direct access to a water supply, most people draw water from the river or buy it. Lack of sewage connection or rubbish disposal (both virtually non-existent) is a constant threat to health. A third of the school-age children cannot attend school. Klong Toey is well-off compared to many other Southern urban communities.

authorities, which respond by cutting services. The growth of crime that often accompanies this pattern encourages more of the wealthier people to leave the city, concentrating poverty into ever-deeper pockets Slums lie side by side with affluence even in cities like New York, which have moved well into the modern communications age.

Communications in crisis

Information is power, more valuable than oil, more precious than gold. And most of it is created, stored, and distributed in the rich countries. A few Western nations are the arbiters of taste and cultural values throughout much of the world. Their news media

have something close to a monopoly in interpretation, judging of news value, and dissemination of ideas. Even stories about the South, published in the South, will often have passed through a Western filter. At the same time, government censorship in the Third World (sometimes in the belief that this will help nation-building, but more often to preserve personal power) has created a thirst for foreign newspapers, magazines, films, television, and radio programmes – thus perpetuating the West's values and its economic interests.

The Western monopoly could be further strengthened by technology. Take satellites: the smaller, cheaper types of satellite, currently using the lower

Monopolies in media control

The first public perception of the huge power of Information Technology (IT) came through George Orwell's novel *Nineteen eighty-four*. Orwell foresaw state control, thought control, and total invasion of privacy through mass media and censorship. The picture today, though less extreme, is disturbing. The mass media are in the control of state authorities and a few transnational companies. Censorship is widespread, particularly in one-party states and the dictatorships of the South. Almost everywhere, privacy is invaded through computerization of personal files.

The IT revolution is strongly centred in the North, and it proceeds apace, far faster than regulations to prevent its abuse. With few exceptions, the South is outside the network. And the Third World lacks many of the benefits of basic communications: 9 out of 100 people have a radio; 1 in 30 has a daily newspaper; and 1 in 500 a TV.

Broadcast "invasion"
US commercial TV has a huge export market. Neighbouring Canada, in a 1970s survey, imported nearly half of its TV shows. The Canadian authorities complain that their people are swamped by US culture. The same process of "invasion" applies between the US and Europe, US and Mexico, and within Europe.

Global press control
The press plays a critical role in forming public opinion. But 90% of foreign news published in the world's newspapers comes from just four Western news agencies – Reuters, UPI, AP, and AFP (right). About a quarter of their output is concerned with the Third World.

Telephone tapping
Modern society is highly vulnerable to disruption and invasion of privacy. During struggles with Solidarity in Gdansk, the Polish government was able to cut internal and external telecommunication. Even in the UK the government was taken to the European Court of Human Rights in 1983 after the exposure of a secret telephone-tapping centre.

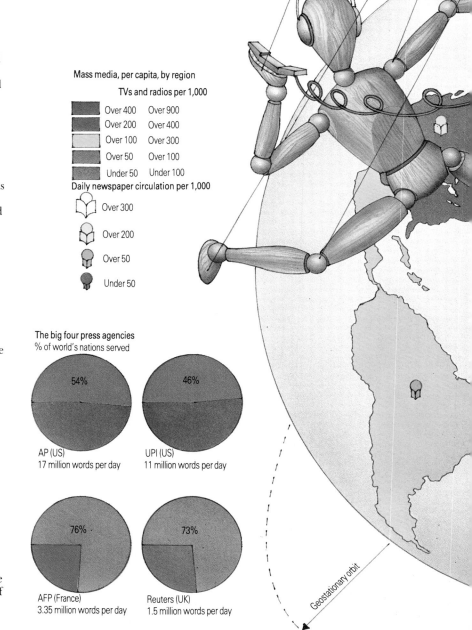

Mass media, per capita, by region

TVs and radios per 1,000

Over 400	Over 900
Over 200	Over 400
Over 100	Over 300
Over 50	Over 100
Under 50	Under 100

Daily newspaper circulation per 1,000

Over 300

Over 200

Over 50

Under 50

The big four press agencies
% of world's nations served

54%
AP (US)
17 million words per day

46%
UPI (US)
11 million words per day

76%
AFP (France)
3.35 million words per day

73%
Reuters (UK)
1.5 million words per day

Governments

Geostationary orbit

Multinational companies

frequency bands, are potentially of most benefit to developing countries. But their use is mainly controlled by the technologically advanced countries "in the interests of efficiency". The North can already gather more information about the South – its mineral potential, its crop yields, its untapped water resources – than these countries know about themselves. For example, a commodity speculator in New York is more likely to know about a coffe tree blight in Brazil before a Brazilian farmer is informed. The commercial, and to a lesser extent, the military advantage that this gives to the North is considerable. The Third World cannot afford to let the First World increase its stranglehold.

Similar questions arise in relation to cross-border data flows between computers. Critical information about a country's markets and companies can be collected and transmitted abroad, without ever being available to the country of origin, undermining national control. Even Canada has had to devise a bank by-law to prevent its banks from sending data to the US for processing. Brazil has already prevented local subsidiaries of Western multinationals from linking their Brazilian customers, via satellite, to overseas data bases. These companies have been asked to replicate their foreign data bases locally. The revolution in data transmission also affects the global financial systems.

Data-processing monopoly
In 1978, Japan, Western Europe, and the US accounted for 83% of the world data-processing industry. This monopoly effectively stifles the growth of a Third World data-processing industry.

Satellites
▭○▭ 10 functioning satellite payloads
▭●▭ US
▭●▭ USSR
▭●▭ Others: Japan, China, France, Italy, India, UK, European Space Agency

Who pulls the strings?
As long as people have sought power – whether political or economic – they have sought to exercise control over communication channels and information. The greater the extent of mass media, and the more powerful the development of Information Technology (IT), the more people can be manipulated by the controllers.

With mass media, the crudest control is straight censorship. More subtle ways are the licensing of printing presses or newspapers (which is widespread) – and even the restrictive allocation of typewriters, paper, and copying machines (as in Eastern Europe). Government control over radio and TV in nearly all nations has gone far beyond what is actually necessary for state security. Legal controls like the libel laws and secrets acts back up the state's control. People languish in prison because of what they have written, or what they have said. And where the state can manipulate the media without opposition, what is printed or broadcast bears little resemblance to objective truth.

The transnationals have tight control in the production of electronic components, computers, and telecommunications technology. As national economies become more dependent on these technologies, the power of the companies will increase. They are creating an "electronic brain-drain", gathering business from the South.

Satellite control
The North controls most of the geostationary orbit (pp 206-7). The orbit and the radio spectrum are finite resources, and crowding has caused conflict.

Multinationals, using international banks to access their own funds, become their own bankers and send massive sums of money between countries. The banks may be riding "electronic tigers". Computers can be programmed to buy and sell stocks and shares automatically when prices reach predetermined levels, which canon occasion lead to wild swings in the marketplace.

Looming economic crisis

The world market is in deep trouble. As the world economy began to deteriorate in the 1970s, the climate for international trade became steadily bleaker. Growth declined, unemployment in industrialized countries rose, and inflation rose too. Over-production in some industries contrasted with idle factories in others. The price of money rose steadily, thrusting developing countries further into debt, and the exchange rate of key currencies became badly misaligned. Global GNP per capita has not improved since the late 1970s (though some authorities claim that recovery is under way).

Alongside these malfunctions, a new trade protectionism emerged in the West. The transfer of some production processes to low-cost Third World areas and the rise of the "new Japans" now began to appear as a threat to jobs in Europe and North America. Workers and employers started to demand protection and the rationing of imports – often by artificial "agreements" which exporters in Japan and the South were forced to accept.

Protectionism and unstable pricing make trade and production everywhere less efficient. They have a serious additional consequence for the North. If the Third World's earnings are restricted, so too is its spending, and a deflationary bias enters the world economy. According to World Bank estimates, if the industrialized countries increase protection by the equivalent of a 15 percent rise in import taxes, the cost to the GDP of middle-income developing countries would be 3.4 percent. The cost to GDP in the North is put at 3.3 percent.

The developing countries themselves also practise protectionism. Barriers are erected around infant industries (especially those involved in advanced technology) that would otherwise fall in the face of powerful competition from Japan and the West.

The Third World debt problem, which exploded in 1982, has exacerbated the problem. Many countries have been forced to slash imports. In 1983 the seven major debtors in Latin America cut imports to more than 40 percent below 1981 levels. Desperate to earn money to meet debt bills, some also resorted to subsidies to help their exports, fuelling the North's demand for protectionism.

While protectionism afflicts the industrializing nations, declining terms of trade, especially in relation to oil and manufactured imports, damage countries exporting raw materials and foodstuffs (though they too face some trade barriers). World Bank figures show a drop of over 22 percent in the

Market tremors

As Japan and the newly industrializing countries (NICs) clash with the dominant West, major shifts in the market lead to a rash of protectionist barriers – which does no one much good in the long term. World trade slows down, economic distortions grow, and the gap between nations widens. The height of trading stations (right) indicates percentage increases in trade value over 10 years; the dials at the top show the shift in their share of the market. The West, particularly the US, has lost heavily to Japan, OPEC, and the NICs. The remarkable progress of Japan and West Germany may in part be due to their lack of a "military albatross" around their necks – long prohibited from arms expenditure, their non-military industrial growth has soared.

Newly industrialized countries (NICs)

Moving from 7% to 17% of the market in 10 years, the NICs sell goods from textiles to computers. To the first wave of Asian, Latin American and Mediterranean NICs is now added a second, a dozen or so, ranging from Colombia to Sri Lanka. The inability of the market system to accommodate these new Japans is a serious threat. What will happen as their numbers grow, and they challenge high-technology markets?

Development distortion

Export-led growth does not benefit all equally. Lured by Western affluence, many developing nations have neglected fundamental development issues such as agricultural reform, rural development, and health, in favour of prestige projects from airports and hospitals to dams and model farms, and concentrated on cash exports to pay for them. As the market fails, they are now reaping a bitter reward. Some multinationals have been deeply involved in this development distortion, while intermediaries cream off up to a third of the profits. Bilateral aid deals tied to purchasing Northern manufactured goods have often not helped. Even the Green Revolution can exacerbate divisions between rich and poor (pp 60-1). Burdened with debt, or locked in the commodity trap with rising poverty, many nations face a radical rethink of their whole development policies.

DCs

Developed countries (DC

Older industrial nations face severe problems: conflicts in the relationship with successful Japan; strains posed by the NICs and reduced markets in th South. In 10 years, their world share of the market fell from 73% to 48%. Worst hit are the sundown industries, such as textiles cars, and steel. The North will have to plan for adjustments on an unprecedented scale.

NICs

17%
7%

LDCs

1%
1%

Least developed countrie

Despite a 450% increase i trade (largely imports), th poorest nations' overall share of the market is still about 1%. Northern protectionism hurts. So does nearly stagnant worl demand, which reduces income from exports. Rea per-capita income in man African states will probabl be lower in 1990 than it w in 1960.

Japan
14%
7%

OPEC
20%
12%

15%
10%
5%
0%
-5%
-10%
-15%

Trends in world trade volume
(annual percentage change)

1971 72 73 74 75 76 77 78 79 80 81 82

Declining trade
Three decades of market growth ended in the 1970s as the recession spread. Initial recovery was followed by increasing stagnation until, in 1980, "negative growth" set in.

Oil power
In 1973 and again in 1979, OPEC sharply raised oil prices in a bid to boost their purchasing power. Worst hit are poor nations, who cannot afford the oil, nor the dearer Western goods, as costs are passed on. OPEC has since tried, and failed, to use oil power to help the Third World negotiate a new economic order (p. 231).

Barriers to trade
The "new protectionism" against Third World manufactured goods employs many invisible barriers: import quotas, licensing regulations, health restrictions, customs procedures, and petty requirements. Then there are "orderly marketing agreements" and "voluntary" export deals (far from voluntary for the exporters). Subsidies are increasingly used by the North to protect domestic goods, by the South to push their exports. Cartels (producer associations) have multiplied – steel being a recent example. Third World commodity cartels, however, from bananas to coffee, have achieved little. Agricultural protectionism by the EEC, Japan, and the US is costly to South and North alike: a study in the late '70s concluded that a 50% cut in trade barriers affecting 99 commodities would boost Third World export earnings by $3 billion. Northerners can pay 2 to 5 times world prices for food, while dumping their surpluses.

Japan
Old industrialized countries
Newly industrialized countries
Possible future NICs
Those left out
"Non-market" economies

Key to world markets
Change in share of trade to 1981

Share of market economy trade, 1971 Total market value = $606 billion

% increase in trade
100
200
300
400
500
600
700

Imports:
% of 1971-81 trade increase

Exports:
% of 1971-81 trade increase

 financial confidence

cession

Dumping grounds
One of the most unpleasant facets of the world market is its tendency to push poorer nations into ever-more vulnerable positions. Negative terms of trade affect more than 60 commodity-dependent nations, who have to run ever faster to keep up, and find development planning difficult. Surpluses transferred from the North do not help: they can destabilize market prices and create problems in food sufficiency. Pesticides, inferior goods, and drugs – unwanted or banned – also go to the South, again, with heavy multinational involvement. The Bangladesh Ministry of Health banned 1,700 "useless or dangerous" drugs in 1982, most of them produced by eight multinationals. Bangladesh blamed damage to their economy on failure to control multinational imports, transfer of technology, and restrictive practices.

The commodities trap
Julius Nyerere of Tanzania once remarked: "In 1965 I could buy a tractor by selling 17.25 tonnes of sisal. By 1974, I needed 57% more. Now the sisal price has fallen again but the tractor price has risen still further". The graph below shows the changing value of primary commodities and oil, relative to manufactured goods.

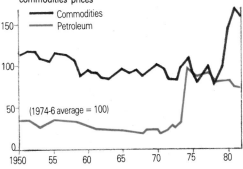

Weighted index of commodities' prices

Commodities
Petroleum

150

100

50

(1974-6 average = 100)

0
1950 55 60 65 70 75 80

purchasing power of exports for poorer African nations between 1973 and 1982. This decline is losing exporters billions of dollars, and is a major factor behind the crisis of development they now face. The prospect for Africa in the coming years is grim. Worldwide growth has not been shared, and recession is now driving the poor to extremity.

North and South: the divided planet

"At the end of three decades of international action devoted to development the result, by 1985, is likely to be an increase of $50 per capita in the annual incomes of the poorest group over 1965 incomes, compared with an increase of $3,900 per capita for those of the richest".
SECRETARY-GENERAL, COMMONWEALTH SECRETARIAT

For the last two centuries there has been a widening gap between the rich countries of the North and much of Africa, Asia, and Latin America. By the middle of the last century, the difference in per capita income was about two to one. In this century, the divergence has increased, particularly since the 1950s. Today, GNP per capita in Western Europe, North America, and Japan is, on average, some 40 times greater than in the low-income countries, and five to six times higher than even in the fast-developing countries like Brazil. And this evidence of a divided world conceals ever deeper divisions at levels other than those of national economies.

The source of Northern affluence is much disputed – it is variously attributed to industrialization, to climatic factors and cultural values, and to colonialism, which transferred resources from the South to Europe and the US. Some economists, moreover, assert that the international financial and trading system, designed by the rich countries in pursuit of their own interests, is inherently biased against poor countries.

A few newly industrialized countries in Southeast Asia and Latin America have managed to make substantial progress (though many are now deeply in debt). But for a sizeable sector of humanity, progress is mostly non-existent. Some are even going backward; most will take hundreds of years to close the gap with the North (if its consumerist lifestyle is thought desirable), if they ever can. Almost one in five of humankind fall *below* the income threshold necessary for the most meagre existence. And the overall number of poor is still rising.

Another factor in Southern poverty is gross inequality in income distribution. Latin America exhibits greater inequality than almost any other region, mainly because of the inequitable distribution of land-holdings and political elitism.

Many individual countries have pursued economic growth first and foremost, in the belief that everyone benefits from this in the long run, through a "trickle-down" process – they reject redistribution of wealth as being "anti-growth", despite evidence that the two can go hand in hand. "Trickle down" has advanced the richer sectors of Third World

Haves and have-nots

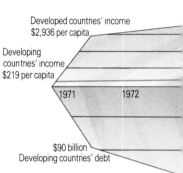

The wedge driving the North and South apart has two components: slightly different growth rates, starting from a considerable GNP gap; and deepening Third World debt, exacerbated by soaring interest rates and falling export earnings. Every 1% rise in US interest rates adds about $4 billion to the debt bill. Latin America owes $340 billion; Brazil, Mexico, Venezuela, and Argentina alone over $260 billion. The "conditionality" factor – stringent economic medicine, aimed at cutting consumption and boosting exports, attached to IMF emergency loans – sometimes worsens the situation of the poorest in the short term. Per capita incomes in Latin America and Africa have fallen dramatically. Falling living standards have caused rioting in several countries, from Morocco to the Dominican Republic, and political instability has increased, with its attendant risk of military repression. In Africa the situation is desperate, because conditions on the continent have been deteriorating that much longer, and the effects of long-term droughts are wreaking havoc.

The technology gap

Development, and hence wealth, demand access to advanced technology – almost all of which originates in the industrialized countries. The transfer of technology to the South via multinational companies is mostly concentrated in a limited number of countries which offer "suitable" economic environments. The rest depend largely on the handouts of aid.

For some nations, lack of access to much-needed technology rules out much hope of competing in the modernized world; even for those who are favoured, lack of control over planning, choice, and management of technology can have equally severe results. Debt-ridden Paraguay and Brazil, for instance, have spent $18 billion on the Itaipu Dam, the world's largest hydroelectric power project – eventually it will produce excess electricity.

Many bilateral aid agencies place their programmes in the hands of Northern experts, who may be insufficiently aware of local needs and can easily perpetuate the receiving country's dependence. One of the saddest examples is that of Egypt's Aswan Dam power scheme (pp 132-3), which has diminished the productivity of agricultural land and fisheries, thus leaving Egypt more dependent on foreign food imports. Capital-intensive Western technology is inappropriate for many developing nations, with their massive labour surplus and their chronic shortage of capital and foreign exchange.

Developed countries' income $2,936 per capita

Developing countries' income $219 per capita

1971   1972

$90 billion Developing countries' debt

Brazil's burden
Brazil is the biggest debtor in the world. By June 1984 it already owed $90 billion. For millions of poverty-stricken Brazilians looking for jobs, in rural areas or crowded into the notorious shanty towns, the nation's economic crisis is a harsh, unremitting reality. Brazil argues that its debt mountain has been imposed by external factors: its huge borrowing in the 1970s was justified by rapid economic growth. But since then it has been dealt a series of body blows; first the OPEC price rise, then the terrifying rise of interest rates, and finally Northern recession and protectionism halting its export boom.

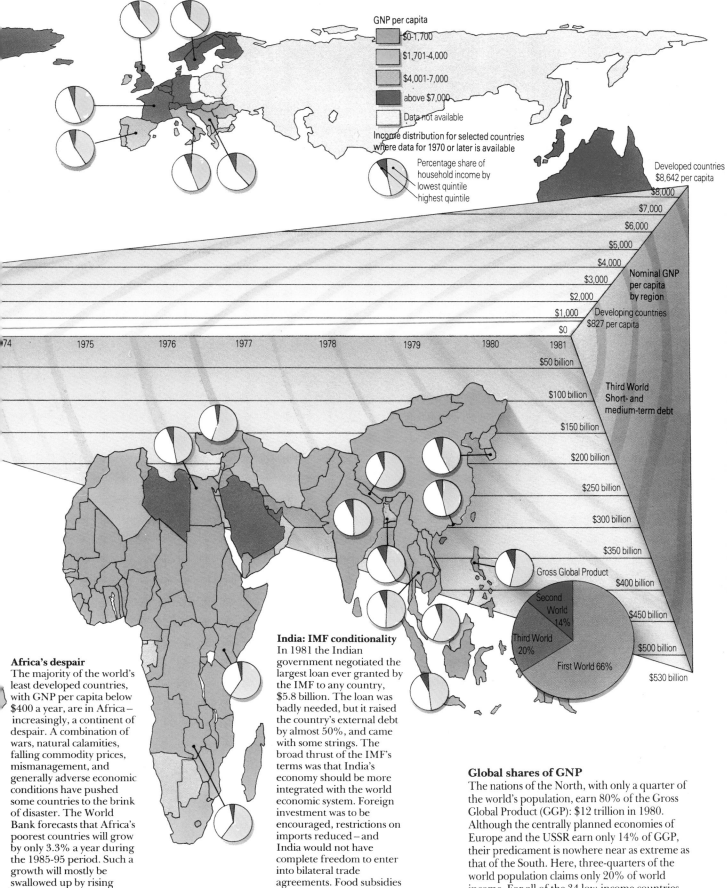

GNP per capita
- $0-1,700
- $1,701-4,000
- $4,001-7,000
- above $7,000
- Data not available

Income distribution for selected countries where data for 1970 or later is available

Percentage share of household income by lowest quintile / highest quintile

Developed countries $8,642 per capita

$8,000
$7,000
$6,000
$5,000
$4,000
$3,000
$2,000
$1,000
$0

Nominal GNP per capita by region

Developing countries $827 per capita

74   1975   1976   1977   1978   1979   1980   1981

$50 billion
$100 billion
$150 billion
$200 billion
$250 billion
$300 billion
$350 billion
$400 billion
$450 billion
$500 billion
$530 billion

Third World Short- and medium-term debt

Gross Global Product

Second World 14%
Third World 20%
First World 66%

Africa's despair
The majority of the world's least developed countries, with GNP per capita below $400 a year, are in Africa – increasingly, a continent of despair. A combination of wars, natural calamities, falling commodity prices, mismanagement, and generally adverse economic conditions have pushed some countries to the brink of disaster. The World Bank forecasts that Africa's poorest countries will grow by only 3.3% a year during the 1985-95 period. Such a growth will mostly be swallowed up by rising population. But if the situation proves any worse, many countries will go backwards faster still.

India: IMF conditionality
In 1981 the Indian government negotiated the largest loan ever granted by the IMF to any country, $5.8 billion. The loan was badly needed, but it raised the country's external debt by almost 50%, and came with some strings. The broad thrust of the IMF's terms was that India's economy should be more integrated with the world economic system. Foreign investment was to be encouraged, restrictions on imports reduced – and India would not have complete freedom to enter into bilateral trade agreements. Food subsidies were cut too. Furious criticism only abated with the 20% reduction of the loan in July 1984.

Global shares of GNP
The nations of the North, with only a quarter of the world's population, earn 80% of the Gross Global Product (GGP): $12 trillion in 1980. Although the centrally planned economies of Europe and the USSR earn only 14% of GGP, their predicament is nowhere near as extreme as that of the South. Here, three-quarters of the world population claims only 20% of world income. For all of the 34 low-income countries (with under $400 GNP per capita), the income gap is widening. More than 2 billion people live in these countries, all of them in Africa and Asia.

society, at the expense of the poorer. The global community, with its emphasis on growth, has fallen into much the same trap. The last straw has been the recession of the early 1980s, causing alarming rates of bankruptcy and unemployment in the North, but having its worst effect in the South. And the privatization of Third World debts, on flexible interest rates, has deepened the international crisis even further.

One billion poor

Absolute poverty has been described by Robert McNamara, a former President of the World Bank, as a "condition of life so characterized by malnutrition, illiteracy, disease, high infant mortality and low life expectancy as to be beneath any reasonable definition of human decency". The engine of growth seems to be forcing more and more people into economic vulnerability. They have been systematically marginalized, their ability to supply their own basic needs unrelentingly reduced.

Of almost one billion absolute poor, 90 percent live in the countryside; more than half are small farmers, and between a fifth and a quarter are landless labourers. Of these, 80 percent live in India, Pakistan, and Bangladesh. Most countries with a high proportion of absolute poor (Bangladesh with 75 percent, for example, or Indonesia with 50 percent) are found contiguously in two "poverty belts". One extends across the middle of Africa, from the Sahara to Lake Malawi. The other, beginning with the two Yemens and Afghanistan, stretches eastwards across South Asia and some East Asian countries.

These nations frequently exist in a fragile tropical environment, upset by the pressure of expanding populations, and afflicted by droughts, floods, soil erosion, and the encroachment of deserts. Not only has their economic performance been inadequate in recent years, but the changing character of national environment may make supporting their present populations impossible.

There is rarely any system of state benefits to ease the plight of the poor. They are most likely to be without the medical facilities to cope with sickness and disability, without schools to raise the levels of literacy, and without a hope of better employment. On top of physical isolation, they also suffer the social isolation of being unwanted; women, in particular, find it impossible to escape their burdens (pp 192-3). Furthermore, the poor household may belong to a socially inferior class, forced by custom to accept the lowest paid and most menial tasks, and physically segregated. Their children will be condemned to the same lowly status.

The pressures of poverty have often caused explosions in the past. In the 1980s, still more people are being driven beyond the limits of endurance. In South America there are new poverty outbursts, such as the looting of hundreds of food shops in Rio de Janeiro, in September 1983.

The poverty bomb

Poverty is self-sustaining and self-generating, a trap that holds about one billion people, nearly a fifth of the world's population. In general, the poor in the North can at least survive, through a safety net of social services (although not all-embracing). Their poverty can be seen as "extreme social deprivation". In the South, however, the term "absolute poverty" is the only one applicable. Even if they survive a malnourished childhood, hundreds of millions will never have the opportunity to realize their full human potential. All the routes out of the trap are firmly shut, because of lack of education, technical aid or credit, employment, sanitation or safe water, access to health services, transport, or communication.

Most Southern governments are unlikely to implement wide-ranging reforms: resources are too scarce (pp 218-19) and they lack political will. So the poor are left with the greatest toll of death and misery – and they are wide open to exploitation by landlords and merchants, petty officials and police, and any employer. Insecurity and powerlessness are their lot.

Power
Franchise may be denied to the homeless and the illiterate. Blacks in South Africa cannot vote. The poor are powerless to represent themselves.

Income
The majority of people in developing countries manage to survive on an income of under $100 per annum – most on less.

Credit
A few reasonable credit schemes have been set up for the urban poor. There is little hope for those in remote regions.

Fuel
Over 2 billion people rely on wood for household fuel – but the supply, for 70% of them, is insecure.

Literacy
There are over 825 mil illiterate adults, mostly the South; the majority women.

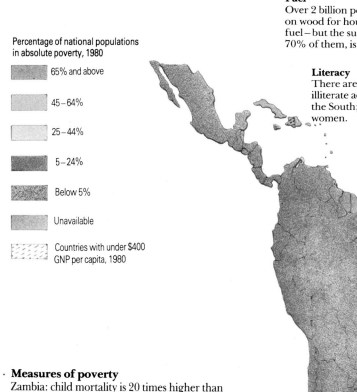

Percentage of national populations in absolute poverty, 1980

- 65% and above
- 45 – 64%
- 25 – 44%
- 5 – 24%
- Below 5%
- Unavailable
- Countries with under $400 GNP per capita, 1980

Measures of poverty
Zambia: child mortality is 20 times higher than in West Germany.
Mali: average life expectancy is 30 years less than in Sweden.
Ethiopia: only one in seven can read. Tanzania: there is only one doctor per 17,500 citizens.
India: average calorie deficiency of 23%.

Housing
In 60 countries, over 40% of houses have no piped water. Some 1.4 billion people do not have access to clean water.

Work
In the registered workforce, 600 million people are un- or underemployed. There are 13 million bonded slaves (trapped by debt) worldwide.

Health care
Over 450 million people are mentally or physically disabled; 800 million cannot get minimal health care. At least 15 million children die every year.

Transport
Poor transport obstructs development.

Food (see below)

The pattern of subsistence
A typically very poor family is likely to live in a hut or rudimentary house. There will be virtually no furniture. There will be no electricity or sanitation or access to safe water. They will probably be subsistence farmers or lowly paid workers. Household chores, such as fetching water, will take many hours. They have little chance of legal redress for any abuses, and little ability to dispute wage levels, crop prices, or interest rates.

The lighted fuse
The poverty bomb (above) has a multi-stranded fuse made up of population growth, political inequity, and environmental misuse.

The mechanics of famine
Some 450 million people are starving or malnourished. There is not necessarily a link between severe malnutrition and a shortage of food. Studies carried out for the ILO suggest that in Ethiopia and Bangladesh in the 1970s it was not so much the famine that caused the poor to starve, but rather the inability of poor people to purchase what was available. Most at risk were the landless, and the unskilled or the semi-skilled. In 1973 in Ethiopia, for example, a localized crop failure resulted in fewer people being required on the land and generally lower demand within the economy. In national terms, food had not decreased.

MANAGING OUR CIVILIZATION

The increasing division of wealth and power in the world is inimical to all our interests. The North needs the South, if only because a large share of its export markets are located there: 42 percent of Japan's and 33 percent of the US's. The South, equally, depends on the North. Interdependence applies not only to our global systems, but also within nations, and between countryside and cities. Lop-sided rural and urban development, with cities monopolizing government attention, has already proved a disastrous recipe. Reliant on each other, our management objectives and resources must be shared universally between nations, and between peoples and their governments.

Coping with city chaos

The management of city problems cannot be separated from wider issues – of income distribution (both between social groups and between nations), the international economy, sustainable develop-ment, and human values. There may well be many innovative schemes to improve life in cities, but they nearly all hinge on economic strength, on cities having the resources, and the will, to pay for their infrastructure and services.

What the poor of Third World shanty towns lack most is a voice in city management, and security of tenure for inhabitants who live in perpetual fear of eviction. Even the poorest settlement is bursting with human energy: provision of cheap materials and tools would enable families to build and improve houses. Above all, safe water and sanitation are critical, plus environmental controls to prevent pollution and uncontrolled dumping of waste.

Much of this can be done only with government backing, and within the framework of national development, since plans must strike a reasonable balance between the interest of the city and the countryside. Holding down food prices in towns, for example, may upset the rural economy; then even greater numbers of rural poor flock to the cities, swelling the shanty towns. Improving city health care, schools, transport, and other services must not be achieved at the expense of the countryside. In some Third World states, rural land reform and agricultural development have helped slow down the stampede to cities, and improved food supply.

Ultimately, much depends on national priorities – whose interests do the governments serve? The question applies just as much in the North, where financial constraints are far less acute. Northern

Urban regeneration

The science-fiction city of the future – Le Corbusier's grand schemes, or Niemeyer's Brasilia – seems ever less likely to replace our decaying Northern cities and sprawling Southern slums. A few new "open field" towns may be built as satellites to our biggest cities to fulfil this dream, like Reston or Columbia in the US; gleaming towers may rise in the South; but neither will house the millions of urban poor. The new urban strategies are aimed at mobilizing local communities and stretching scarce resources to cope with massive problems. Just as it is vital that the North responds to troubles in the South, so must more affluent citizens help the inner or outer city poor.

Liveable cities in the North

The massive slum clearance and building boom of the '60s and '70s are over and reaction has set in. The human costs of uprooting communities, to rehouse them in socially and constructionally disastrous high-rise blocks, are all too evident. Gradual renewal of our decaying city centres is now under way, through re-use of existing structures plus more sensitive new architecture. The renewal is often community-based (as in Watts, Los Angeles), and many small agencies have sprung up to help municipal and private efforts. Nothing, however, can replace major long-term investment by governments, to deal with obsolescence and disrepair.

Community participation

Encouraging a dialogue between city officials and shanty town dwellers can produce more effective initiatives than top-down planning. Redirected, local skills and organization can carry out low-cost schemes on a large scale, as in El Salvador. Establishing local administrative centres helps to focus community spirit, and allows a degree of self-management.

Urban employment

Current thinking aims at providing incentives to employers, through aid and technical advice, and the provision of small workshops. The World Bank now funds many such schemes. The huge informal economy of many of the South's largest cities (between 40% and 60% in Jakarta, Bombay, and Lima, for example) is a major provider of jobs, and at present receives negligible support through government credit. There is a great demand for loans and sites for small businesses, for the establishment of credit union savings – and vocational training to help the urban poor.

Targeting the inner city

Bringing the decaying areas of older cities back to life typically requires a multi-pronged approach, with inputs of private, voluntary, and official funding and effort. Rehabilitation of usable existing housing is matched by small "in-fill" schemes of new homes, harmonizing with existing street architecture; conversion and re-use of obsolete industrial buildings provide space for small workshops and businesses, or for commercial or community centres, from markets to sports halls. Local employment projects and light-industry units help to revitalize the community, which also needs new open spaces, communal facilities, and environmental improvements, from pedestrian or limited car access schemes, to tree planting and gardens. Based on these approaches, the "village in the city" is emerging all over Europe, and in US cities from Philadelphia to San Francisco.

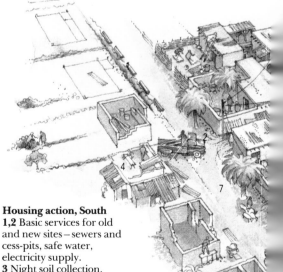

Housing action, South

1,2 Basic services for old and new sites – sewers and cess-pits, safe water, electricity supply.
3 Night soil collection.
4 Self-help house building, aided by long-term loans, and backed by government grants and development agencies.
5 Community centre and local planning office.
6 Old shanty town awaiting basic services.
7 Street uplift – through refuse-collection schemes, street lighting, trees.
8 Improved market area with new well.

Renewing a community

The "gradual renewal" strategy is applied to a Victorian area of a UK city (left). The city government works with housing agencies and co-operatives to repair the most damaged properties. Improvement grants generally help upgrade the area, while community employment and environmental schemes inject new life.

Housing action, North

1 Newly built community centre and day nursery run by local people.
2 Modern infill housing for sale, supported by low-cost home ownership scheme.
3, 4, 5 Renovation – through improvement grants for private owners, or undertaken by non-profit agency, or city government.
6 New extensions for bathrooms and kitchens.
7 Street uplift – speed humps, controlled parking, landscapes.
8 Community art – murals decorating blank walls, painted by community artist and local children.
9 Corner shops retained for local shopping – also for use as Neighbourhood Office of city government.
10 New neighbourhood park with children's playground.
11 Unimproved terrace awaiting action.
12 Small workshop development for locally based employment.
13 Local bus transport.

Home improvements, North

Improvement packages for housing focus on structural repair, economical use of energy via insulation and more hygiene facilities.

World Bank projects

The World Bank has funded improvement schemes worldwide (right). They include shanty town and transport improvements. The Francistown Project in Botswana succeeded in giving 95% of households clean water, roads, and street lighting. Squatters were given legal tenure.

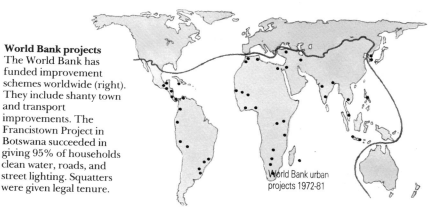

World Bank urban projects 1972-81

Power services, South

Initial electricity servicing should include lighting to major communal areas, road intersections, and small-scale industrial and commercial needs.

Southern city regeneration

Whenever cityward migrations have reached unusual proportions, conventional housing and infrastructure services have been hard-pressed to cope. The many millions of poor people now crowding into Southern slums and squatter settlements cannot afford even the simplest permanent housing schemes (86% of urban populations in Bangladesh, for instance, are below the absolute poverty line). Authorities are being forced to take a different line, tackling only the most basic provision themselves, and letting the settlers do the rest, with minimal aid. Just one of their intractable problems is that of water supply which is often privately owned – and very scarce. The most urgent need, however, is for greater rural investment, to slow the flood to the cities.

In the last decade "sites and services" schemes have concentrated on providing water, sanitation, street foundations, and power, but leaving construction of housing to individual occupants. This policy has evolved into "upgrading" of existing slums and shanties. One project in Lusaka, Zambia, in the '70s, tackled the upgrading and servicing of 31,000 plots, bringing basic needs to about 30% of people.

As in the North, community involvement and leadership are critical. El Salvador, prior to heightened civil unrest in the early '80s, boasted an almost model scheme – a local non-profit making group concentrating on low-cost housing, operating through long-term repayment, appropriate technology, and communal self-help.

But all these efforts must go hand-in-hand with better employment opportunities to generate income. Credit can be provided by quasi-governmental agencies; donor agencies can also play a useful role by helping to provide capital for small-scale industry.

cities too require investment for development, plus grants, loan-credit schemes, and enterprise zones to attract new business.

Strategies for communication

The power of advanced communications technology for assisting development is immense. It has been used to study and control locust damage in Africa; for the better management of rangelands in Kenya; in the study of the humid tropical forests of Peru. It is helping in conservation, the design of road and rail networks, mineral prospecting, and weather forecasting. Apart from land and resource management, satellite technology helps in education and can transmit medical, nutritional and agricultural advice to large numbers of people, often otherwise isolated.

If the communications revolution is to benefit everyone, however, ways must be found of making the technology widely available, ensuring universal access to information, establishing a diversity of information sources, and achieving maximum participation in the transmission of ideas.

Advances in satellite technology help reduce the costs involved. Countries that cannot launch their own satellite may be able to pay others to launch them. They can also rent communications services from the West's Intelsat or the Soviet Intersputnik systems for telephone, telex, data and video transmissions. Regional co-operation is the most effective way that Third World nations can utilize the space potential. Colombia, Mexico, and Brazil have plans to launch their own satellite and provide a telephone and television link with remote rural areas. It is suggested that the UN should create a Centre for Outer Space, which would provide help and services to member states.

To make full use of the information gathered by satellite, developing countries must have the capacity to process and analyse it. In the field of data processing, international rules for the regulation and control of data flows must be devised. These should encourage multinationals to share skills, technology and data with the developing countries. Huge libraries of information made available at the touch of a few keys could help reduce the information gap between South and North; but it is just as important to obtain the appropriate information, and develop the capacity to analyse and apply it.

The communications revolution could break the information monopolies. Sweden has shown the way by extending its Freedom of Information laws to ensure private citizens' access to the data banks of government departments. But many democratic countries, notably the UK, resist such reforms. New information technologies are also creating a far greater diversity in the media: cable television, video cassettes, home computers, and the proliferation of software programmes will provide an immense choice, like books on a library shelf. For the future, the entire role of communications must also change,

The will to communicate

The importance of the free communication of ideas and information cannot be over-emphasized: it is a vital key to the management of our global crises. At present many voices – of minorities and of people outside the communications network – go unheard. It may take a single determined journalist reporting on a crisis – such as the situation in Kampuchea in 1982 – to release massive funds for aid. Or an investigative newspaper reporter to uncover governmental or business corruption, such as the Watergate scandal in 1974.

Getting access to the medium, as well as the message, is particularly important in the South. Developing countries need more satellites to multiply TV broadcasts, and allow telephone communication in remote areas. They must also be able to benefit from the abundance of information collected about Southern resources from Northern satellites.

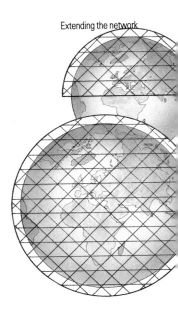

Extending the network

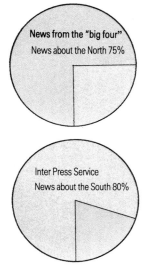

News from the "big four"
News about the North 75%

Inter Press Service
News about the South 80%

Reversing the flow

From a global viewpoint, news coverage and analysis of events in the South are as important to the North as vice versa. One Third World news agency attempting to break the barriers that prevent full North-South information flow is the Inter Press Service (IPS). Started in 1964 by a group of journalists writing about problems in Latin America, it has grown, with the aid of 30% grant from UNESCO, into an organization issuing 100,000 words per day (still a fraction of the amount produced by the big Northern press agencies). IPS now supplies 26 national agencies and 400 publications in 36 countries, including the United Arab Emirates, Austria, Zimbabwe and Mexico. Its editorial and transmitting services are made available to other agencies. However, the service should be superseded by a Third World news agency run by developing countries themselves, without UN grants.

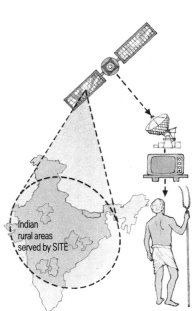

Indian rural areas served by SITE

Satellites for education in India

Broadcasts by satellite reached 24,000 villages in six different states of India in 1975-76. The joint Indian-American Satellite Instructional Television Experiment (SITE) used the ATS-satellite provided by NASA, and demonstrated that India could manufacture and maintain both the required Earth stations and the community receiving sets in far-off villages. The communities, many of whom had never seen TV, showed large gains in knowledge about health and hygiene, family planning and political awareness from the educational and developmental programmes. The experiment also gave experience in designing and producing relevant programmes for widely spread areas with different languages and problems. Satellite TV broadcasts are immensely valuable to developing countries as they can reach rural communities, and cost a third of the price for ground-based programmes.

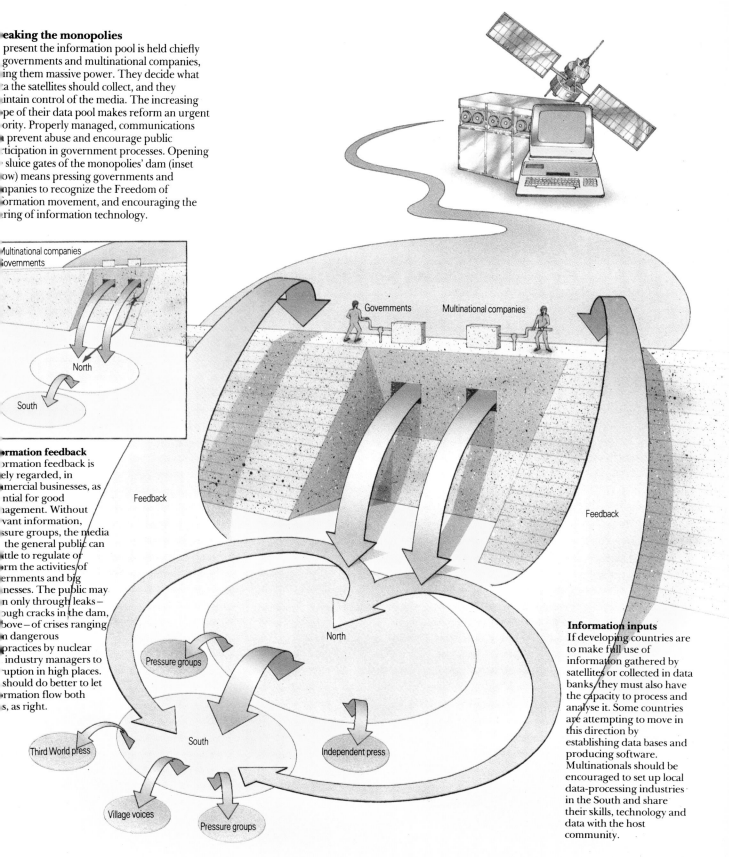

eaking the monopolies

present the information pool is held chiefly governments and multinational companies, ing them massive power. They decide what a the satellites should collect, and they intain control of the media. The increasing pe of their data pool makes reform an urgent ority. Properly managed, communications prevent abuse and encourage public ticipation in government processes. Opening sluice gates of the monopolies' dam (inset ow) means pressing governments and panies to recognize the Freedom of ormation movement, and encouraging the ring of information technology.

Multinational companies

Governments

North

South

rmation feedback

ormation feedback is ely regarded, in mercial businesses, as ntial for good agement. Without vant information, ssure groups, the media the general public can ttle to regulate or rm the activities of ernments and big nesses. The public may n only through leaks – ugh cracks in the dam, bove – of crises ranging n dangerous practices by nuclear industry managers to uption in high places. should do better to let ormation flow both s, as right.

Feedback

Feedback

Governments   Multinational companies

North

Pressure groups

South

Third World press

Village voices

Pressure groups

Independent press

Information inputs

If developing countries are to make full use of information gathered by satellites or collected in data banks, they must also have the capacity to process and analyse it. Some countries are attempting to move in this direction by establishing data bases and producing software. Multinationals should be encouraged to set up local data-processing industries in the South and share their skills, technology and data with the host community.

dependent media

day the advent of citizens' band radio and le TV promotes, in Alvin Toffler's phrase, "demassification of society", discouraging t control, while broadcasting minority views. anaian national unity was noticeably fostered different ethnic groups sharing the various dia in the 1960s.

Village access

At grass-roots level, communications need not now demand high technology. A small 500-watt transmitter powered by two heavy-duty car batteries can broadcast over a range of about 20 km. Such a service provides information of all kinds, and stimulates communications skills. Local newspapers can be launched cheaply too.

Access to Information Technology

Sharing technology regionally offers most independence, while reducing costs. Some Arab states are planning regional telecommunications and the exchange of TV programmes. PADIS, the Pan-African-Documentation and Information System, pools data for the use of African technicians, planners, and others.

from a one-way flow, from North to South, to full dialogue between North and South, so that the current information advantage of the rich societies can be shared with the rest of the world.

Towards new technologies

The technologies developed in the North since the Industrial Revolution may sometimes seem like a Pandoran box of mischief and sorrow, accompanied by a forlorn spirit of human hope. Many of the latest fruits of our civilization fly in the face of conventional wisdom and humanitarian concern – for instance, the latest refinements in missiles of destruction (pp 248-9), destructive nuclear experiments, the increasing use of human embryos in

scientific experiments – all raise alarming questions about science and the needs of humankind. Modern technology may even be seen as a means of magnifying the chasm between the world's élite and the poor majority – enabling Northern governments and companies to exercise "world control".

It is a truism, however, that no technology is intrinsically evil – like information, it depends on who pulls the strings. Undoubtedly, scientific research and development have produced stunning solutions to disease, food production, and problems of communication. The benefits of satellites, for instance, have already been applied to specific communications problems in the South (pp 224-5). The immediate issue is not only the nature of some

Technology transfer

Technology is transmitted in many different ways, through publications, personal exchanges, development aid, or outright piracy. Most, however, is transferred commercially. Far more attention needs to be paid to the usefulness of the technologies transferred to the South, to ensure that they are not, unwittingly, the 20th-century equivalent of the Trojan Horse – bringing unsuspected political, social and environmental problems in their wake. At present the rate of transfer from the North and from transnationals is lamentably slow. We need to find ways to accelerate transfer, build up Southern research and development, nurture new skills, and lift those controls on information that impede the process.

Southern technology impetus

Targeting the South's "technofamine" requires massive input from both North and South. Barely 1% of current Northern research and development (R & D) spending is focused on problems in the South (while 32% is devoted to defence and space research). In order to build up R & D capacity, by the South, for the South, governments and Southern businesses must persuade megacorporations to play a significantly responsible role in North-South relations. Technological aid efforts should be extended, and Southern universities must be strengthened. When curricula reflect specifically Southern needs, they can expand existing schemes for bringing technology to the village (such as India's Peoples' Science movements). However informal the platform, education to help leap the current technology gap is vital.

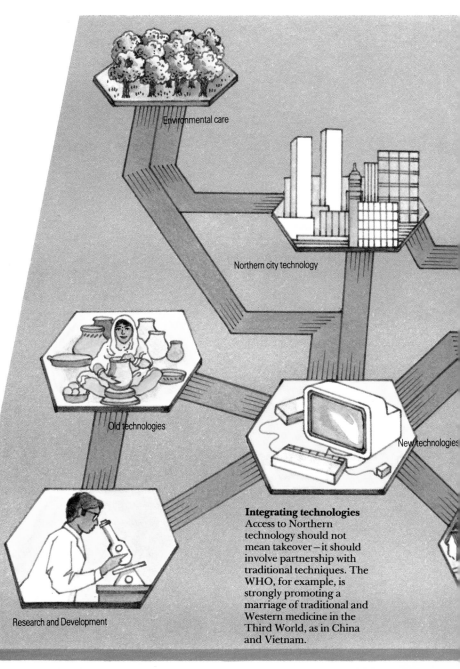

Integrating technologies
Access to Northern technology should not mean takeover – it should involve partnership with traditional techniques. The WHO, for example, is strongly promoting a marriage of traditional and Western medicine in the Third World, as in China and Vietnam.

Environmental care

Northern city technology

Old technologies

New technologies

Research and Development

of our "advances", but the sharing of technological control. As the Brandt Commission concludes, "it can even be argued that their (the developing countries') principal weakness is the lack of access to technology, or command of it".

Many of the technologies currently transferred, including those in the nuclear power and weapons fields, reflect this imbalance, and have proved expensive, almost useless, or positively harmful in the South – despite the myriad efforts of organizations which develop and transfer appropriate technologies. International organizations, however, are taking a growing interest in the social, economic and environmental implications of technology transfer. The ILO, for example, has been conducting a worldwide programme of research on the blending of emerging technologies, such as solar energy, micro-electronics, biotechnology, and new materials, with the traditional technologies of the South. A range of pioneer projects explore technological fusions that could boost productivity and competitiveness, without causing massive unemployment or any other dislocation in the process.

We should be en route for a polytechnical world, with space-age know-how partnering traditional technologies, with high and low technologies operating together, and labour-intensive techniques and automation taking their appropriate places. But all developments must be controlled and conditioned by a planetwide perception of our technologies as

Advances in the North
Having experienced some of the worst ill-effects of industrialization, Northern governments are just beginning to lead the way in environmental protection, pollution control, decentralizing information technologies, and the exploration of renewable energy sources – such as solar, water, and wind power. In a better world, such advances, and certain lessons of the Northern industrial experience, should be transferred to the South.

Transnational transfer
Transnationals should be obliged to share their expertise with the developing countries where, at present, some have a record of excessive profiteering and exploitation. They must help their host nations build up their own technology bases, both in fostering pure research and projects of applied technology.

Aid from multinationals
Recent developments in biotechnology pioneered by North-based companies may help the South tackle environmental degradation and productivity. Cloning of trees to aid reforestation and silviculture is a prime example. Thousands of identical plants can be produced at the same time. High-yielding eucalyptus trees in Brazil and oil palms in Malaysia (producing 20-30% more oil than average) are two excellent examples of such techniques.

Patent release
Patents, protecting new products and plans against direct imitation, are mostly registered in the North. The World Intellectual Property Organization aims to develop model patent laws, tipping the balance back towards the South by limiting the duration of patent cover on some types of product.

Appropriate technology
Northern technology, based on Northern infrastructures, social patterns, and education, is not always immediately relevant to Southern needs – particularly to local productivity and employment. In the 1960s, the late E. F. Schumacher, trying to envisage a more practical aid, came up with the ideal of appropriate technology. Despite criticisms – that the South needs more than recipes for small-scale enterprise – the fruits of appropriate technology have been widely accepted. The Intermediate Technology Development Group (ITDG) helps foster hundreds of schemes, from local power generators to all kinds of low-cost equipment for small-scale use.

NORTH

on control

Agriculture and countryside

Multinationals

Environment

SOUTH

nology

City technology

Agriculture and environment

double-edged swords, constructive or destructive. We need to concentrate on resource efficiency, pollution control, and halting and repairing environmental degradation. We need a Gaian technology that is sustainable, energy-efficient, diverse, non-toxic, peaceful, and people-centred.

Trade and development

Nearly every attempt to redress the world's many interlocking crises is threatened by the current market crisis. Any solution to the growing global economic malaise must involve a recognition of the mutual interdependence of North and South, both in establishing demand and in sharing the means of supplying it. Confusingly, an enormous range of possible approaches to this end are being proposed, three of which merit immediate discussion. They can be summarized as "the market knows best", "the market must change", and "the South must delink its markets from those of the North".

As far as the "marketeers" are concerned, the basic problem is seen to be excessive government interference, which has prevented the proper functioning of the market. Price controls, protectionism, and subsidies have given the wrong signals to entrepreneurs, leading to the erosion of incentives and the misallocation of resources. Marketeers think in terms of a development "continuum", running from the poorest to the wealthiest countries – with the implication that the poorest can pull themselves up by their bootstraps.

In contrast, the "reformers", whose views have been convincingly stated in the two reports of the Brandt Commission, argue that nations do not compete as equals – and that global measures are needed to mobilize the weaker nations. Even if the free market could bring benefits to the poor, the reformers stress that this would take too long.

The "delinkers" are essentially a coalition of those who have been disillusioned by failures to win reforms and those who believe that the international capitalist system, whether reformed or not, is inimical to the interests of the developing countries. Some delinkers would go for a total delinking of the South from the rich economies of the North, while others would prefer to see a greater stimulation of South-South trade and co-operation. Some also believe that this approach would ultimately benefit the North, since, while the Northern share of trade would be proportionately smaller, the global economic "cake" would be bigger.

Until the early 1980s, the reformers probably represented the biggest constituency, although the centre of gravity has shifted towards market-oriented solutions. The prospect of continuing economic problems, with erratic growth rates in the North and protracted debt problems in the South, suggests that the plight of the South could well deteriorate further in the near future.

There is a growing consensus that any attempt to manage the global market in its present state must

Growing interdependence

Some Northerners believe that they can get along without the South. They are dangerously mistaken. The North badly needs the fuel, minerals, and foodstuffs it imports from the South, as well as the cash it earns from exporting goods and skills. Some 40% of North American exports of manufactured goods go to developing countries, 44% of Japan's. If demand falls in the South, the effects are soon felt further North. North and South often like to imagine that they are separate, with complete freedom of movement, yet nothing could be further from the truth. Self-sufficiency may be appropriate in some cases, but at the global level we must recognize growing interdependence.

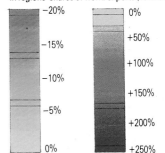
Scales showing percentage change in regions' shares of world exports (1970-82)

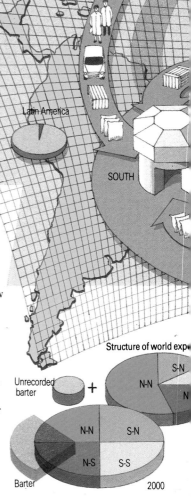

Fairer trading
Tariffs, "invisible" protectionist barriers, subsidies, adverse terms of trade, unstable pricing – all are interlinked. They are both the symptoms and the prime causes of the struggle for shares of a shrinking cake. Dumping, and North/South export/import ties, also act as disincentives to domestic food production. Before the world cake can grow, fairer trading must become a common goal: we must roll back trade barriers, index-link commodity prices to manufactured goods, realign the industrial base – and above all, encourage domestic development and food sufficiency.

Sharing the bigger cake
Present world trade includes a little known sector – barter, which, broadly defined, may now account for over 20% of world trade. Rubber, for instance, is exchanged for cocoa beans, timber for transport equipment, and just about everything for oil. Most of this trade takes place between developing countries, who lack the foreign exchange to employ conventional trade methods. This suggests that emphasizing barter may be one way to stimulate greater South-South trade. However, the very nature of barter agreements makes them difficult to quantify, or plan. The pie-charts (right), compare the present shares of the export "cake" with a possible future division: by increasing South-South and South-North trade and boosting the barter economy, the whole trade flow could be increased.

Redeploying industry

In the words of the Brandt report: "Among the greatest challenges to international economic policy for the rest of this century is the preparation for a new deployment of industrial capacity in the world economy – a shift of historic dimensions."

If the North dismantles its protectionism, it must also cede its sundown industries to the new Japans. Staged labour redeployment and moving capital to more profitable areas will help ease the transitions.

Delinking the South from the North

The traditional market structure established during the colonial period is changing fast – hence the rash of "new protectionism". Some economists, however, argue that the North, in order to maintain its position, must keep the poorer South in a state of "economic servitude" – and will never voluntarily reform the biased market. The only hope for the South, some believe, is a complete "delinking" of its economy from that of the North, and freedom from the stranglehold of international capitalism.

"Economic miracles"

Japan is the most obvious example of explosive economic growth; West Germany, some OPEC nations, and a few new Japans are also contenders. Such "economic miracle" countries invade established markets and cause much disruption. They must also take a growing share of world responsibilities.

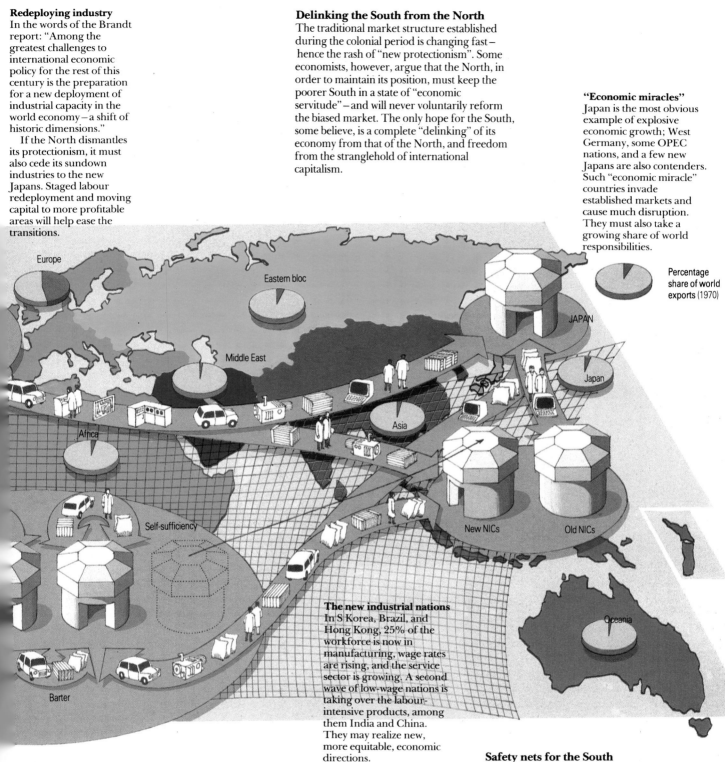

Percentage share of world exports (1970)

The new industrial nations

In S Korea, Brazil, and Hong Kong, 25% of the workforce is now in manufacturing, wage rates are rising, and the service sector is growing. A second wave of low-wage nations is taking over the labour-intensive products, among them India and China. They may realize new, more equitable, economic directions.

Self-reliance and South-South trade

Despite recent increases, South-South trade remains at a lower level than common sense would dictate. In 1980, it accounted for 30% of developing countries' total imports and 25% of their exports. Among the reasons: prejudice against so-called "second-best" products made by other developing countries; and poor transport and communications links – the roads built by colonial powers lead to coastal ports, rather than to neighbouring nations. Worse, many developing nations tend to produce competing, rather than complementary, products, while the rich markets of the North seem to offer a better return. On the whole, regional groupings – such as ECOWAS in West Africa and Andean in South America – have proved disappointing. A system of generalized tariff preferences would help compensate for Northern trade barriers. A new "South" bank is also proposed, to offer buyers extended credit, and so help boost trade. Coupled with increasing technical co-operation between developing countries, such measures could help foster Southern self-reliance and expertise.

Safety nets for the South

There have been many international commodity agreements, but they have done little to stabilize prices. Arranging compensation for developing countries' lost export earnings, when prices fall, is one approach which has been tried by the Lomé trade/aid convention (p. 231). A more ambitious scheme might provide a safety net for all poorer countries, offering a guaranteed minimum income. A Common Fund for the South is also mooted: producers and consumers of the 18 top commodities exported by low-income countries could contribute to a central financing facility, buying up surpluses, and so maintain prices at an agreed stable level.

take a somewhat pragmatic approach – combining market solutions, Brandt-style reforms, and greater co-operation between developing countries. Success will increasingly depend on a willingness to dispense with economic dogma and experiment with alternative management approaches, learning from failures and building on success stories.

Managing the world's wealth

"No society can surely be flourishing and happy, of which the far greater part of the members are poor and miserable."
ADAM SMITH, THE WEALTH OF NATIONS

The stark contrast between the world's haves and have-nots, together with the short-fused "poverty bomb" (pp 220-1), are symptoms of a number of interlocking, mutually reinforcing crises which have already proved largely immune to a wide range of management solutions. The key question: how can we begin to close the gap between the rich countries of the North and the poor countries of the South?

In the 1960s, the emphasis was on rapid growth, in the belief that the benefits would "trickle down" to the poor. By the early 1970s, however, it was clear that this would achieve too little, too late. A seminal speech in 1973 by Robert McNamara, then President of the World Bank, signalled a switch to "growth with redistribution". The new objective was to ensure that the poor shared directly in the benefits of development through land reform, improved access to credit facilities, and projects providing jobs and adequate incomes to the landless and unskilled.

A key element in this new approach was the focusing of assistance on education, health care, and training programmes for the poor. Other concepts which emerged included the "basic needs" approach and, later, integrated rural development – but they were all overtaken by the world depression of the early 1980s. As one poor country after another ran into debt and balance-of-payments problems, so they were forced to cut social programmes, real wages, and imports, switching resources instead to their exporting sectors.

Clearly, if there is to be any hope of reducing world poverty, a massive effort is required across a very broad front. It must involve reforms at the international level, in trade and financial systems, coupled with far-reaching policies promoting income-distribution and a full-scale attack on poverty at the most localized level.

The international economic system must be redesigned to provide poorer nations with a fair return on their exports and the finance to invest in the sustainable development of their national resources, and programmes to abate poverty. Voting power within the International Monetary Fund needs to reflect more fairly the interests of both North and South, to allow discussion and reform of loan conditions, – and the fund needs to be greatly increased. In an interdependent world, we cannot afford to "let the Devil take the hindmost".

Closing the gap

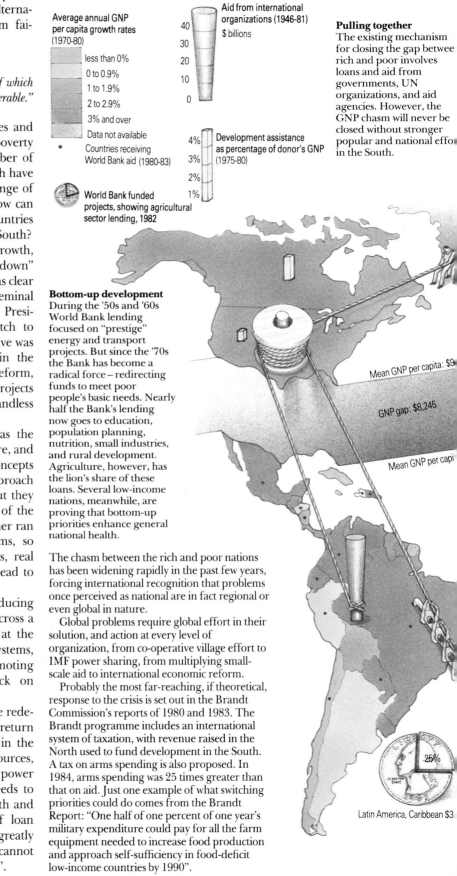

Average annual GNP per capita growth rates (1970-80)

- less than 0%
- 0 to 0.9%
- 1 to 1.9%
- 2 to 2.9%
- 3% and over
- Data not available
- Countries receiving World Bank aid (1980-83)

World Bank funded projects, showing agricultural sector lending, 1982

Aid from international organizations (1946-81) $ billions
40
30
20
10
0

Development assistance as percentage of donor's GNP (1975-80)
4%
3%
2%
1%

Pulling together
The existing mechanism for closing the gap between rich and poor involves loans and aid from governments, UN organizations, and aid agencies. However, the GNP chasm will never be closed without stronger popular and national effort in the South.

Mean GNP per capita: $9

GNP gap: $8,245

Mean GNP per capita

Bottom-up development
During the '50s and '60s World Bank lending focused on "prestige" energy and transport projects. But since the '70s the Bank has become a radical force – redirecting funds to meet poor people's basic needs. Nearly half the Bank's lending now goes to education, population planning, nutrition, small industries, and rural development. Agriculture, however, has the lion's share of these loans. Several low-income nations, meanwhile, are proving that bottom-up priorities enhance general national health.

The chasm between the rich and poor nations has been widening rapidly in the past few years, forcing international recognition that problems once perceived as national are in fact regional or even global in nature.

Global problems require global effort in their solution, and action at every level of organization, from co-operative village effort to IMF power sharing, from multiplying small-scale aid to international economic reform.

Probably the most far-reaching, if theoretical, response to the crisis is set out in the Brandt Commission's reports of 1980 and 1983. The Brandt programme includes an international system of taxation, with revenue raised in the North used to fund development in the South. A tax on arms spending is also proposed. In 1984, arms spending was 25 times greater than that on aid. Just one example of what switching priorities could do comes from the Brandt Report: "One half of one percent of one year's military expenditure could pay for all the farm equipment needed to increase food production and approach self-sufficiency in food-deficit low-income countries by 1990".

25%

Latin America, Caribbean $3

A New International Economic Order

Through the 1970s and early 1980s, international organizations came up with a variety of blueprints for the future, spearheaded by the call for the New International Economic Order (NIEO). The NIEO comprises the ideal of international redistribution, provisions for basic needs and services, and the sustainable management of our natural resource base. It was adopted by the UN General Assembly in 1974, and by the Group of 77 (which includes 122 developing countries) in 1976; details include a fairer deal on commodity prices, a massive increase in Third World manufacturing, and a call for the financial resources necessary to effect the transition. In effect, the NIEO would be an international welfare state. But since the recession the North, with few exceptions, has rejected nearly all the Third World's proposals.

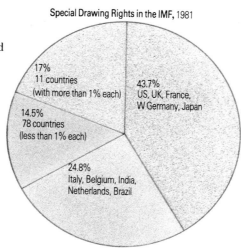

Special Drawing Rights in the IMF, 1981

17% 11 countries (with more than 1% each)

14.5% 78 countries (less than 1% each)

24.8% Italy, Belgium, India, Netherlands, Brazil

43.7% US, UK, France, W Germany, Japan

Reforming the IMF

Member nations of the IMF contribute to the Fund on the basis of their GNP, which also determines their "special drawing rights" (SDRs), left, and their *voting power*. Since the rich North dominates policy, bitter controversies have arisen. Third World borrowers complain that the "medicine" applied to their economies now reflects Northern monetarism and market-oriented interests – instead of development strategy. Shortage of foreign exchange, plus "conditionality", have spurred a Third World preference for private financial assistance. Whatever we make of the IMF's policies, it is plain that they should be arrived at by a fairer voting structure. Otherwise, the South's proposals to form their own Third World financing arrangements may become reality – dividing the world even further.

The Lomé negotiations

Through the Lomé Conventions, 1975-80 and 1980-85, 64 countries from Africa, the Caribbean, and the Pacific (ACP) have special trade/aid links with the richer countries of the EEC. Lomé's objectives were to increase trade through reduced tariffs; the Stabex system aimed to stabilize export earnings; and the European Development Fund gives aid for specific projects. The first Convention was seen as a major step towards the NIEO. But aid funds have proved very low, and the ACP countries have been alarmed by the conditions set. World recession has resulted in a significant fallback from the original ideals.

18%
Europe, Middle East, N Africa $2.38 billion

23%
E Asia and Pacific $2.72 billion

30%
W Africa $1.1 billion

28%
E Africa $0.7 billion

34%
S Asia $3.12 billion

Targeting poverty

Direct action is top priority. Departments of the UN have specific projects – such as WHO's Expanded Programme of Immunization, which aims to immunize all children against the six major immunizable diseases by 1990 (pp 194-5), and the UN Water Decade, whose target is safe water for all by 1990 (pp 134-5). Charities drumming up aid for areas hit by war and famine are making an impact. But they all need more funds. Adjustments in government priorities, with health, education, employment, and food regarded as universal rights, may prove the best long-term solution.

"Sweat equity"

Raising the level of the rural poor is an essential prerequisite of any real achievement. Small farmers and village industries are only too willing to offer muscle power or "sweat equity", and apply new ideas – but they need fair terms and appropriate advice.

Defusing the debt bomb

The South must be able to finance development without the imposition of crippling terms. Even limited long-term concessional aid is more desirable than short-term commercial loans where interest rates may fluctuate.

MANAGEMENT

Introduced by William Clark

President of the International Institute for Environment and Development

Although we have far to go in learning how to manage our small, fragile planet and in forming the planet-wide institutions to do so, at least the insights and experience of the last 30 years have shown us the necessity of wise management. We have come to appreciate that there are limits to our exploitation of a finite resource base. We recognize that there are also social limits which are threatened by the enormous divides between wealth and poverty within nations and between nations. Our physical and economic interdependence are established facts.

The basic issue is not a lack of resources. Many detailed scientific studies have shown that the entire planet's population can be adequately housed and fed and provided with a livelihood which allows them to live beyond the fear of poverty. There are even sufficient resources for the six or more billion people who will be here by the end of the century. The issue is how existing resources are managed. The key to the future is the concept of sustainable development.

By sustainable development, I mean the rational use of resources to meet all human basic needs. To be sustainable, development cannot ignore long-term costs for short-term gains. Concern for the environment is not a luxury that only richer nations can afford. If some development project is damaging forests or soil or water or clean air, then it is not true development. So often, it is pursuit of short-term gain in the name of development which not only damages ecosystems but hits hardest at the poor.

Since the world's economy and virtually all its inhabited areas are organized in nation states, only through complementary national strategies can sustainable development be implemented. For half or more of the world's nation states, the priority is to build them more stable and sustainable niches in the world economy; at present, perhaps half the world's nations have economies on the point of bankruptcy or indeed collapse. This is not the foundation on which to build sustainable development, for it cannot provide the basis for addressing the needs of the poor and disadvantaged.

Over the last century or so, most of the richer nations in the North have extended a safety net of basic service provision, health care, and social security to which all citizens have a right. This has greatly decreased poverty and suffering. As increasingly efficient and rapid communications systems effectively shrink the size of our planet, we as a planetary community must extend a comparable safety net to assist those nations which lack the capital and resources to meet their population's basic needs. Many have argued against such an approach, using the same arguments propounded in earlier decades by rich élites who opposed taxes to pay for water supplies, sewage systems, education, health care, and social security. In the short term, no doubt the élite would have been slightly richer without these taxes. But at what cost in the longer term? Just as their wealth depended on a stable national society, so too do the privileged Northerners' wealth depend on a stable planetary society. A small, rich, privileged minority of nations busily defending their wealth is a recipe for planetary disaster.

THE MANAGEMENT POTENTIAL

We live in a world dominated by nations, more than 200 of them, from mini-states to superpowers. And, whether we like it or not, the nation-state system is likely to endure for some time to come. For, however much it may be modified in practice, it remains entrenched as an ideal. Yet the nation state is a relatively recent historical phenomenon.

The very concept is no more than 400 years old, and a mere 40 years ago there were only 50 or so such entities. They originally began to crystallize where groups of people needed to act in defence of common values, or for common economic aims. United by a common language, culture, or religion, they came to acknowledge allegiance to some central authority. The near-explosive growth in the number of nations is illustrated by the fact that while just 51 nations signed the original UN Charter in 1945, the UN now has 158 national members.

As an intensely territorial species, humankind has embraced nationalism with considerable fervour. And, while national self-interest has not infrequently led to new levels of barbarism, the nation state has generally been a more effective tool for the management of human affairs than the smaller units it replaced.

At the international level, the nation state often does a much better job than it is given credit for. No other available management structure rivals it as a basis for collective living. It has proved to be an excellent vehicle not only for trade and commerce, but for communications and a whole host of other transactions among the family of nations.

Like any other family, it suffers from squabbles, rifts, and outright conflict. In the wrong hands, the nation state can be a deadly instrument of divisiveness. But however much national leaders may proclaim their rights of sovereign independence, their rhetoric is very often overtaken by their day-to-day dealings with one another. By virtue of trade flows, monetary patterns, inflation linkages, and myriad other relationships, nations are becoming ever more involved in each other's affairs.

Modern nations face many predicaments that can be tackled effectively only through collaborative effort. These problems range from threats of nuclear war and terrorism, through energy and food-supply issues, to environmental problems such as acid rain and carbon dioxide build-up.

In short, nations are increasingly inclined to swap certain aspects of independence for the benefits of interdependence. As we seek to engage in this new

The family of nations

"The people of the world respect a nation that can see beyond its own image".
PRESIDENT JOHN F. KENNEDY

Edgar Mitchell, the sixth man to stand on the moon, described the experience of seeing our distant Earth as "instant global consciousness". But global consciousness need not imply that we must have a single, global government. Indeed, the larger the management units in which we group ourselves, the greater is the stress placed on decision-making. Instead, global consciousness must be enacted at many levels of society and coordinated through national governments. The global flag is already in spirit being hoisted up an international flag-pole by many national (and transnational) human groups. It is expressed through the world peace movement, the proliferation of non-governmental organizations, and the recent increase in media coverage of world issues. The global flag is supported by many smaller flags which represent increased participation in government, legal and constitutional reform, and increased spending on social welfare at home and abroad (in the form of foreign aid). These are the new priorities of the modern nations. Foreign aid, for example, becomes vital in order to improve the stability of the global community, which in turn serves national interests. Indeed, expenditure in this direction is a better guarantee of "security" than expenditure on military defence. Real security will grow out of the firm ground of global economic stability.

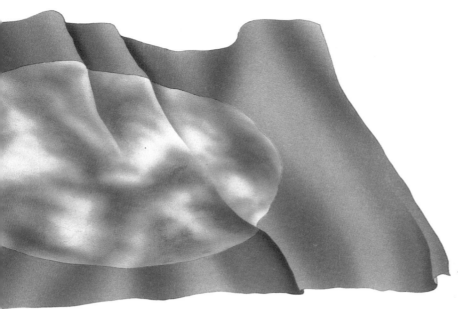

Imperfect tools

Our 200 national governments can be crude management tools. Often they cut into delicate areas of local human interaction or create sparks as they grind up against each other in the regional and global arenas.

Suitably sharpened, national governments could be made far more useful to the way we run our planet. We need only look out of the window and survey the skies to see how climate, as but one ecological process, transcends national borders and demands sensitive co-operative management. Or, we need only listen to grass-roots opinion to realize that national governments need to co-operate with groups at a local level.

When sparks do fly between nations, it is often in the name of "national interest". But what does national interest mean? Increasingly, it coincides with global interest in tackling international problems – ocean and atmosphere management, for example, or the global threat of nuclear war.

Proliferation of nations

- Countries independent before 1815
- Countries independent 1815-1900
- Countries independent 1900-45
- Countries independent 1945-60
- Countries independent since 1960

Challenges to the nation state

Nations are a relatively recent phenomenon (see map, above), often with a short and questionable pedigree. New national boundaries in Africa, for example, have created artificial divisions which separate ethnic communities, divide tribal lands, and attempt to enclose in one net groups with sharply divergent interests. In developing countries, instability, factions, and civil wars are endemic symptoms of adolescent nationhood. In developed countries, the upsurge of social change, education, and disenchantment with central control has created internal pressures on the nation system. Meanwhile, the enormous growth in recent decades of commercial megacorporations, transnational pressure groups, and international agencies has encroached on national identity. Yet the state plays an increasingly vital role in world affairs as a conduit between local, regional, and global levels of interest and power.

order, we will often find that there is no better instrument of management (as opposed to policy-making) than the nation state. If it did not exist, we might find ourselves having to invent something rather like it.

International and regional organizations
Despite the upsurge in the number of nations and in nationalist sentiment during the past four decades, there has been a simultaneous growth in internationalism. We now have a plethora of organizations whose sole purpose is to take care of our international needs.

Indeed, we can take heart from this growing web of international bodies, reflecting as they do the increasing interdependence of nations. No nation can afford to go totally its own way, not even the superpowers. Disputes between and within nations often depend for their outcome on world opinion – a fact of which national governments are all too well aware. Good public relations may win more battles than effective firepower.

Just as what Washington decides impinges upon London, Tokyo, Jakarta, and Rio de Janeiro, so the way that Riyadh acts affects Zurich, Nairobi, Moscow, and New York. This fast-growing interdependence of the community of nations is one of the most striking revolutions of our time. Far from feeling daunted by the increasing complexity of the global community, we should view it as a remarkably diverse resource to meet our ever more complex needs, with its individual pieces more important than the whole.

True, the two major attempts to establish an international order have stemmed from periods of acute crisis. World War I produced the League of Nations, World War II the United Nations. Today we face an even greater challenge: we need to produce a dramatically more capable system for collective endeavour *ahead* of any future crisis.

The omens are by no means all bad. Despite outbursts of hostility, the community of nations displays no small capacity for co-operation. Virtually every nation willingly operates within a network of international relationships. Already we have an array of regional bodies, from the Rhine River Commission to the Organization of American States (OAS), the Association of Southeast Asian Nations (ASEAN), the Organization of African Unity (OAU), and the Arab League. We have broader-scale consultative bodies, such as the Organization for Economic Co-operation and Development (OECD), and more cohesive groupings which begin to override national sovereignty, like NATO and OPEC. We have North-South organizations like the Commonwealth. And, at the global level, we have the United Nations, with some 30 specialized agencies: a system of near-universal membership for near-universal concerns.

Some of the elements of the one-Earth, one-people society are there. The question is how can we

Reluctant internationalists

The world is walking a tightrope: it needs a safety net. We risk not just war but serious environmental collapse, so long as we continue to view the major "organs" of the biosphere in terms of national self-interest. We have established safety nets before: the League of Nations, for example, emerged from the unparalleled bloodshed of World War I, the United Nations from World War II. But we cannot afford to wait for the nuclear convulsions of a possible World War III to put an improved safety net in place.

We already have many strands of co-operation from which this net can be woven. A central strand must be the UN, together with its myriad specialized agencies. Another possible strand is made up of the many geopolitical organizations which have emerged since 1945, including the EEC, OAU, OPEC, Comecon, and ASEAN, which need to be set into the new planetary pattern.

Every day, fine threads of global activity help pull us together, from international collaboration in space to the posting of an airmail letter. But our new safety net is far from complete – and in many areas already looks frayed. New strands must be added soon: we are a long way out on the tightrope.

Fragile nets
Safety nets of the past have relied too heavily on fragile strands of political and diplomatic accords. The Congress system, fashioned by diplomats in Vienna in the wake of the Napoleonic Wars, held together an unsteady peace until 1914, when it was torn asunder. The League of Nations introduced some harder-wearing strands based on functional relationships, but the central strands were still predominantly political and diplomatic. This safety net was shredded by World War II. The third major attempt has focused much more on functional relationships, such as those tied together within such UN agencies as FAO, UNESCO, UNEP, and WHO. These strands help hold the half-completed net in place.

United Nations

If we unravel the UN system, there are seven key strands: the General Assembly; its Secretariat; the Trusteeship Council; the International Council of Justice; the Economic and Social Council; the Security Council; and the other UN organizations. While the system remains effectively impotent in the security field, it has developed a new role of preventive diplomacy and peace-keeping unforeseen by its founding members. Above all, the UN has facilitated the process of decolonization and health improvements, and eased the crushing burdens of many newly independent countries.

Regional success stories

The Regional Seas Programme, launched by the United Nations Environment Programme (UNEP) in 1974, is promoting regional management of 11 regional seas (see pp 92-3). The UNEP programme has achieved some key breakthroughs. In the Mediterranean it has coaxed political agreement out of such arch-rivals as Israel and Syria, Greece and Turkey. The Caribbean programme unites 28 states behind the single cause of cleaning up their regional marine environment. Regionalism is not only a vital management strategy, it can also act as a bridge between nations at opposing ends of the political spectrum.

North and South

The UN is but one strand in the global safety net. There are also North-South bodies like the Commonwealth. Its Heads of Governments' meetings bring together large numbers of states of diverse political, economic, and cultural complexions. The Commonwealth, to paraphrase its Secretary General, cannot negotiate for the world, but it can help the world to negotiate.

Supra-national groupings

Although their task has never been easy, a growing number of supra-national groupings have emerged – including the EEC and OPEC.

The legal thread

Like knots in a net, laws anchor the elements of the developing global management network. As well as the body of international law on human rights and national relations, we now have a growing list of global conventions covering environmental issues: the oceans, the trade in wildlife products, and the world's wetlands, for example. But national support is far from sufficient. The Third Law of the Sea has been ratified by a mere nine nations. And many vital areas, such as tropical rainforests, are hardly covered at all.

Regional political groups

A new family of post-colonial regional organizations has emerged in Africa and Asia, including the OAU, the ASEAN, and the Arab League. These supplement such earlier regional bodies as the Rhine River Commission.

Consultative forums

A number of multinational consultative bodies have also emerged. For developed countries, there is the OECD, the "rich nations' club"; for developing countries, there is the Group of 77.

expand the array and put together the parts of the jigsaw in a way which makes sense in both economic and ecological terms?

Twelve thousand alternatives

Impatient of many of its old hierarchies, the world has made a radical shift in the way it organizes its affairs. There has been an explosive growth in recent decades of small and large pressure groups, advisory agencies, research groups, technology and information specialists, aid charities, "network" associations, and professional bodies – the list seems endless. We now have about 400 significant intergovernmental bodies in the international field, and upwards of 4,000 other bodies, dubbed "non-governmental organizations" (NGOs), with memberships and budgets spanning several countries.

Some NGOs are groups of professionals which set international codes of practice, and some are religious in orientation, but the groups which have really caught the world's imagination are those which have campaigned on specific issues – such as whaling, intermediate technology, Third World aid, and corporate responsibility. They range from development groups like OXFAM and CARE, to conservation-minded groups such as Greenpeace.

All such groups serve as rallying points for common concerns, disseminating information among their members, totalling many millions. They engage in "networking" activities, which allow them to operate as pressure groups, seeking to influence governments and international agencies. Their strength reflects their single-minded devotion to highly focused campaigns, backed up with specialist skills and information.

The impact of such NGOs has been far greater than one might suppose. OXFAM and a number of other NGOs, for example, alerted the world to the Sahel drought disaster. Environmental NGOs mobilized the public concern which resulted in the 1972 Stockholm Conference on the Human Environment. This led to the establishment of UNEP, and they have since followed through with a number of highly effective campaigns. Of course, NGOs lack political power in the everyday sense, but they exert a moral authority which cannot lightly be ignored. Most important of all, they can transcend national boundaries, engendering a spirit of "global constituency" which helps overcome national prejudices and political roadblocks.

Until about 10 years ago, NGOs were largely a developed-world phenomenon. At the Stockholm Conference, all Third World NGOs could have fitted around a single table. Today, individual countries such as Indonesia and Sri Lanka have well over 400 NGOs apiece. Partly in response to their lobbying, over 100 Third World governments have established environmental agencies of some sort.

Indeed, the spread of NGOs throughout the world represents one of the most hopeful portents for the future. They not only act as a conscience and

Voice of the world

The giant bodies of state and transnational industries are powerful but often slow-moving and cumbersome. But the world is beginning to find its voice and give direction to these elephantine structures. Ordinary people talk to each other across political boundaries through non-governmental organizations (NGOs), and ally themselves with other groups to lobby in the corridors of power. A striking symptom of this global "clearing of the throat" is the proliferation of NGOs in the last 30 years, ranging from the Red Cross to anti-Vietnam War protest groups, and current front-runners like Amnesty International, OXFAM, Greenpeace, Friends of the Earth, and World Wildlife Fund. There are now over 12,000 such groups, an embryonic nervous system for our global society, affording a degree of sensitivity unmatched by the nation states and their 2,000 intergovernmental agencies, which are too often tongue-tied by diplomacy.

The rise of the NGOs
The number of international non-government organizations (INGOs) with activities spanning more than three countries, rocketed to 4,77 by 1983 (right). If we add to this total another 1,119 groups which are not fully autonomous, 1,111 which have a more formal structure, 607 religious bodies, and 4,514 internationally oriented NGOs based in a single country, we find a grand total of some 12,130 NGO

1910   1920   1930

Number of INGOs

5,000

4,000

3,000

2,000

1,000

1960   1970   1980   1990

Planned parenthood
Fifty years ago, the dissemination of information about birth control was illegal in the US, and only 30 years ago, the population explosion was not considered to be a problem. Today, by contrast, birth control facilities are available in almost every country – and the majority of the world's governments have their own population programmes. Blazing the trail through this dramatic historical about-face has been the International Planned Parenthood Federation (IPPF), formed in 1952. After major clashes with opponents in government, the medical profession, and the Catholic church, the IPPF gained consultative status with the UN in 1964. The real turning-point came with the 1974 World Population Conference, the first to focus on birth control. Today, the IPPF has 114 member countries and a $55 million budget.

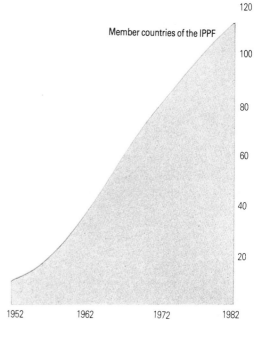

120

Member countries of the IPPF

100

80

60

40

20

1952   1962   1972   1982

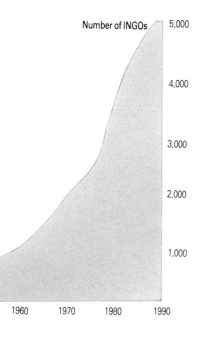

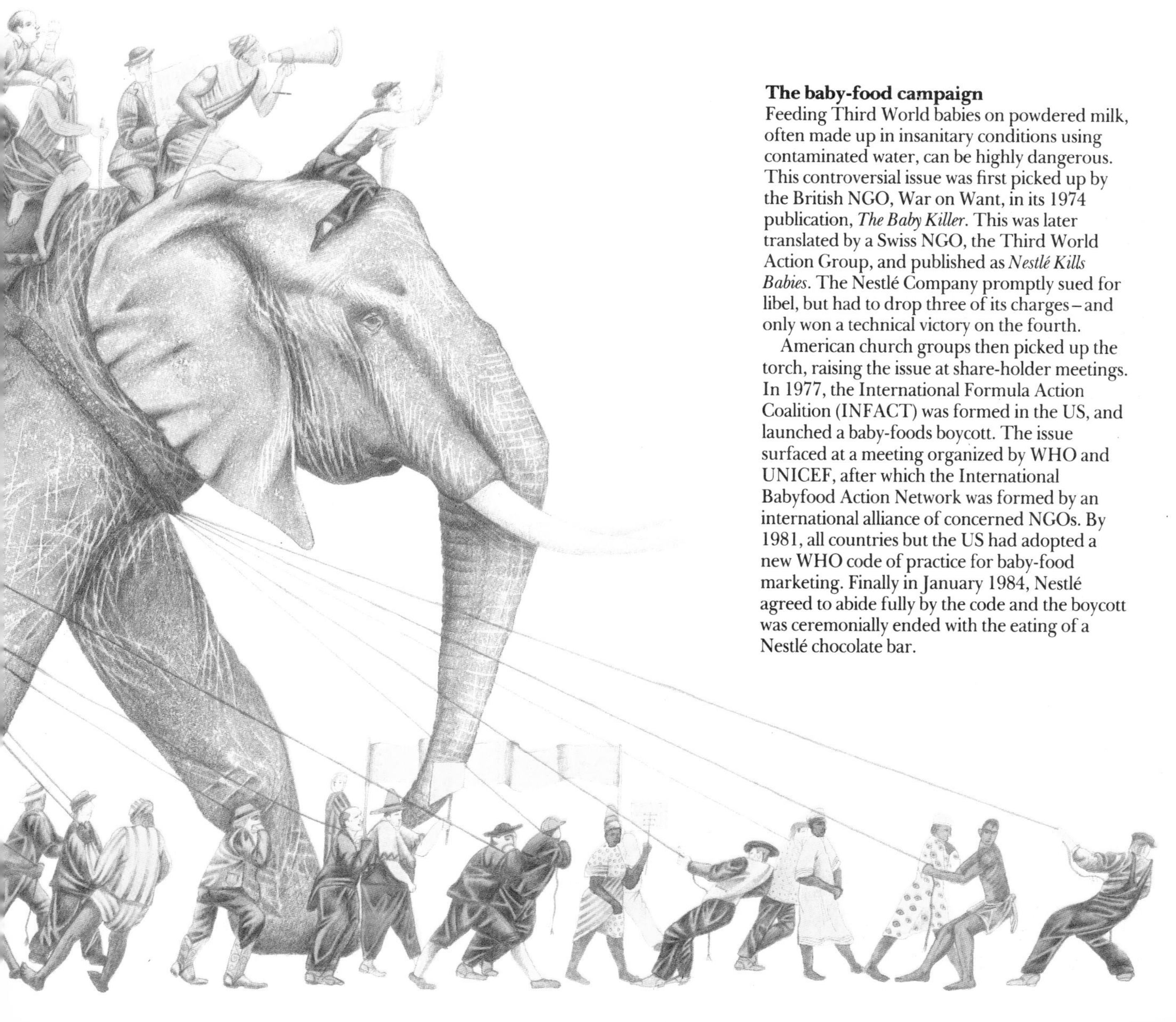

The baby-food campaign
Feeding Third World babies on powdered milk, often made up in insanitary conditions using contaminated water, can be highly dangerous. This controversial issue was first picked up by the British NGO, War on Want, in its 1974 publication, *The Baby Killer*. This was later translated by a Swiss NGO, the Third World Action Group, and published as *Nestlé Kills Babies*. The Nestlé Company promptly sued for libel, but had to drop three of its charges – and only won a technical victory on the fourth.

American church groups then picked up the torch, raising the issue at share-holder meetings. In 1977, the International Formula Action Coalition (INFACT) was formed in the US, and launched a baby-foods boycott. The issue surfaced at a meeting organized by WHO and UNICEF, after which the International Babyfood Action Network was formed by an international alliance of concerned NGOs. By 1981, all countries but the US had adopted a new WHO code of practice for baby-food marketing. Finally in January 1984, Nestlé agreed to abide fully by the code and the boycott was ceremonially ended with the eating of a Nestlé chocolate bar.

spur for the growing array of official agencies that act on behalf of the world community, but are the most visible expression of a growing global citizenry.

Broadening the base of power

Experts propose, people dispose. Without the spontaneous involvement of grass-roots communities, the best-laid plans of development technocrats often come to naught. By contrast, with active participation at "village level", whether it be in a true village, in a more extended farming community, or in an urban setting, modest means can achieve the most surprising results.

Such, at least, has been the experience of communities as far apart as Calcutta, Nairobi, Glasgow,

Watts (in Los Angeles), and the back-country areas of China, Sri Lanka, Costa Rica, and Upper Volta. The traditional approach of "the expert knows best", sometimes called "top-down development", is giving way to a wholly new strategy known as "bottom-up development".

The growing enthusiasm for local self-help, with local people looking to outsiders for financial and practical support rather than for direction, represents one of the more striking advances of recent years. Local people, who have often lived with the problems at issue for decades, even generations, generally know where a problem's roots lie – and can differentiate between symptoms and root causes. Typically, too, they can see ways to solid,

Voice of the village

Why plant a new tree where an established, healthy tree already stands? Traditional communities, whether in villages or major cities, are like the established tree. Their roots are deeply anchored in the history and culture of the locality. Development proposals produced by remote government officials and development agencies often ignore these grass-roots management systems. Instead, they often try to transplant management systems developed in very different local circumstances. Now, as many of those transplants wilt in the heat of reality, there has been renewed interest in building on the base provided by some of the more traditional, local political and management systems. This is in no way a retrograde step – organizations like the UN must listen to what the people most affected say, and know, about the issues. But if this approach is to work, such systems must be given real responsibilities and backed with hard cash.

South Shore banks on the future
When the commercial banks pull out of a declining inner city area in the North, it is generally the last nail in the coffin. Chicago's South Shore community achieved an extraordinary victory when it refused to let the old South Shore National Bank move out. Local people took their case to the government, arguing that they needed the bank to help renew the neighbourhood. Federal regulators denied the bank's request to move, and the bank was bought by the Illinois Neighbourhood Development Corporation. All this was in the early 1970s: today the revitalized bank is serving as a powerhouse for the renewal of South Shore, boosting employment and funding housing.

workable solutions, which build on, rather than swamp, their own culture and experience. That a radical approach of this sort can be made to work is demonstrated by a host of recent initiatives, such as the Chipko and the People's Science movements in India, the Sarvodaya Shramadana or "Gift of Labour" organization in Sri Lanka, the Village Education Resource Centre in Bangladesh, and the Naam programme in Upper Volta.

Some of this creative initiative is fostered by private activist bodies in the developed world, such as the Intermediate Technology Development Group in the UK and similar groups in West Germany, the Netherlands, and the US. The essential element in these recent breakthroughs, however, lies in the willingness and capacity of local people to tackle their own problems.

Nor should we suppose that the "top-down" approach has been confined to the Third World. In both the US and UK, for example, local citizens have taken matters into their own hands. Faced with the decay of the inner cities, of the areas and buildings in which they live, they have responded by setting up tenants' associations and small-scale co-operatives. Initial successes increase the confidence and self-esteem of entire communities, which in turn can lead to a new readiness to take responsibility for local problems. Clearly, political leaders, officialdom, and experts must "grow new ears" that pick up the voice of the village.

Naam brings new confidence

The Naam movement began in the early 1970s in the Yatenga Province of Upper Volta. The immediate cause was a prolonged drought, but the movement's roots are firmly entrenched in the local Mossi culture. The word "Naam" harks back to an old tradition of self-help and village-level co-operation. This was the weapon with which the movement's founder, Bernard Ledea Ouedraogo, aimed to defeat the crisis of confidence which he saw afflicting his people. This crisis had been brought on by years of environmental stress, in combination with a sense of impotence stemming from their dealings with apparently superior outsiders. Today, Mossi culture has been rekindled, and the movement is operating in over 700 village groups. New dams have been built and new trees planted. Grain warehouses have been rebuilt, and villagers can now borrow grain in the difficult weeks before the harvest, repaying the loan in kind once the harvest is complete – saving them from predatory moneylenders.

Chipko protects the roots

When commercial loggers began large-scale felling of trees near to Reni, a village in the northern Indian district of Chamoli, their chainsaws were slicing through the very roots of local society and threatening the livelihoods of local communities. In an astonishing display of courage and determination, the Reni villagers wrapped their arms around the trees, to protect them from felling – sparking off the Chipko Andolan movement (the "movement to hug"). Eventually, following an inquiry, the government declared 12,000 sq km of the sensitive watershed region of the Alakananda basin "off limits" to loggers (see also p.57). Today, the Chipko movement runs many reforestation programmes in other villages where livelihoods are threatened.

CRISIS: THE THREAT OF WAR

Breaking points

"In the global context, true security cannot be achieved by a mounting build-up of weapons (defense in a narrow sense), but only by providing basic conditions for solving non-military problems which threaten them. Our survival depends not only on military balance, but on global cooperation to ensure a sustainable biological environment."
REPORT OF THE BRANDT COMMISSION

We are reaching the ultimate breaking point. If we do not "get our act together" fast, we shall suffer the consequences of management breakdown – confrontation rather than co-operation, conflict rather than harmony, and in the end, war of an intensity that we have not hitherto envisaged. What greater incentive could we possibly have to accomplish planet management?

The crisis of perception

As we over-stress the natural resource base of our planet, we set up strains and tensions that lead to fractures in our societies. Often, these environmental "breaking points" trigger conflicts, both within and between nations.

Human communities depend for their livelihood on a range of basic resources, on living resources such as grasslands, forests, and soils, and on non-living resources such as water, fossil fuels, and minerals. If a community depletes its endowment of resources, and/or is denied fair access to resources elsewhere, its economy is undermined, its political structure becomes destabilized, and its social fabric starts to fray.

Such problems are greatly compounded by the nation-state system which has dangerous limitations when it comes to managing the emerging threats to our planetary life-support systems. National leaders, with honourable exceptions, have been slow to recognize the new sources of conflict: there is, in short, a crisis of perception which could prove the most critical of all. For without the political capacity to adapt to new threats, we face a continuous slide into chronic anarchy and endemic violence – as manageable problems deteriorate into unmanageable conflicts.

To focus on one of many problem areas, consider Central America. Whatever the ostensibly political nature of the upheavals that afflict this troubled region, the central problems can often be traced back to the maldistribution of resources. The grossly inequitable distribution of farmland, for example, applicable to most of the region's countries, means that conflict is perpetuating – and will continue to worsen as long as the problem remains unrecognized by political leaders. Even the 1983 Kissinger Commission, a major effort to come to grips with this inherent regional instability, failed to acknowledge this basic cause of recent upheavals.

This tragic story of misperception is being replicated in several other critical regions of the world,

The problem of security has outgrown the reach of the nation state. No nation or people can be secure when the planet itself is insecure. The vital interests of nations extend to the basic systems of the Earth itself. These are represented on the world map. They include croplands, pasturelands, forests, and fisheries; the great global commons of oceans, atmosphere, climate, and Antarctica; and natural cycles that sustain life. Although we depend on these planetary systems, we seem unable to manage them nationally.

Since 1972, we have had a series of conferences covering planetary problems such as desertification, population, energy, food, and health. None of these problems is solely national or even international; none has anything to do with military strength; rather they are supra-national or global in scope. In each case a World Plan of Action has been adopted – and promptly forgotten by governments immersed in geo-political traditions. Problems of such dimensions, which are everybody's concern, tend to be nobody's business.

Environmental backlash
In the Third World, population pressures on non-renewable resources force more and more people out of rural areas into cities. Greater urbanization generates increasing violence, terrorism and political unrest. Dangerous cracks

Future shocks

Nuclear insecurity, world economic instability, over-population, climatic dislocation, and pollution of air and ocean threaten even the most predictable parts of all our daily lives. And there is more to come. The projected increase of carbon dioxide in the global atmosphere may disrupt agriculture and the world economy (pp 116-17). Increased pressure for migration will swell the Hispanic population of the US, and population growth is likely to push the number of Muslims in the USSR from 43 to 64 million (20% of the Soviet population) by the year 2000 – creating new tensions in the superpowers. North/South conflict will deal other future shocks. These two halves of the world are already locking horns in the battle over genetic resources which could represent a powerful weapon for developing nations. Mexico and Ethiopia, two major germplasm suppliers, among other Third World nations, are finding ways to exploit the dependence of the North on the genetic diversity of the South. If we make no attempt to manage these existing crises, we risk a slide into far deeper conflict.

Breaking point: Ethiopia

Gross degradation of the natural resource base of countries in the Horn of Africa precipitated the downfall of Haile Selassie in 1974, and conflict in the Ogaden desert in the late 1970s. Superpowers were alerted in response to the threatened security of the nearby oil-tanker route.

Ocean conflict

Nations conflict over the common resources of oceans and Antarctica. Already national lines cut across Antarctica (below), while the new EEZs place 40% of the ocean under national control (pp 94-7). The UK and Iceland have come to the edge of hostilities over cod fisheries; 16 similar conflicts can be documented around the world. Meanwhile, North clashes with South over the Third Law of the Sea as developing countries attempt to secure their share of deep sea minerals.

our mismanaged system
appearing in the war
nes, shown above.
vious symptoms of stress
lude drought, pollution,
forestation, and the
ring divergence between
life expectancies of
ople living in the North
d South.

	Mountains
	Rivers, lakes
	Ice caps
	Forest
	Prairie, steppe
	Savannah
	Desert
	Tundra
	Political boundaries
	EEZ

War zones

Drought

Deforestation

● Pollution

◐ Radioactivity leaks
(Windscale UK)

Life expectancy
74-75 years

Life expectancy
40-41 years

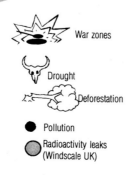

such as Southeast Asia, the Horn of Africa, and the Middle East. Israel's reluctance to share water supplies on the West Bank, water which it regards as vital to the development of its agriculture, probably constitutes a leading factor in determining the future security of the whole Middle East region. Competition for limited resources will spark many more such confrontations, unless we act promptly and imaginatively to defuse these issues before they finally explode.

The "Third World" war

Since World War II ground to its bloody conclusion, not a single war has been legally declared. Yet there have been at least 160 armed conflicts, most of them in the developing countries. Altogether, by 1980, they had lasted 500 years. As the world grows increasingly resource-stressed and politically turbulent, the rate of conflict rises. By the 1950s, the average number of outbreaks was nine a year, whereas today it is 14.

Of the wars in developing countries, at least half have been civil wars of one form or another, many fought over tribal or religious differences. But their real roots often lie in basic resource problems, reflecting the inequities in resource distribution both within and between countries.

Tragically, it is safer to be a soldier in battle than a civilian on the so-called sidelines. Of the estimated 16 million people killed in war since 1945, more than all the soldiers killed in World War II, most have been civilians. War now involves and consumes entire communities: it has become total in a way we have not known before.

Towards a violent planet

Our world is becoming increasingly violent. Superpowers may avoid open confrontation, but engage in "proxy" wars or shuttle men and munitions from square to square on the global "chessboard". Partly as a result, the Third World is in turmoil. There are now over 50 military governments in the developing world, and since 1945 16 million lives have been lost, most of them civilian lives. Over 4 million lives have been lost in the Far East alone.

But war deaths tell only part of the story. Millions more have been injured and maimed. And the world now has well over 10 million refugees, mostly women and children, in flight from conflict and oppression. Many of the world's governments have turned on their own citizens. Many others, too, have turned to terrorism, and defiance of law. The world, in short, is ridden by conflict; a shower of sparks in the nuclear tinder-box.

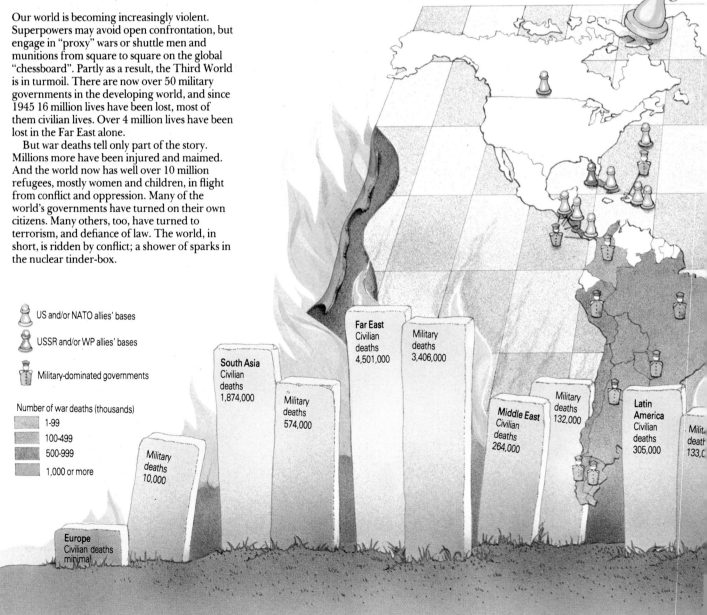

US and/or NATO allies' bases

USSR and/or WP allies' bases

Military-dominated governments

Number of war deaths (thousands)

- 1–99
- 100–499
- 500–999
- 1,000 or more

Europe
Civilian deaths minimal

Military deaths 10,000

South Asia
Civilian deaths 1,874,000

Military deaths 574,000

Far East
Civilian deaths 4,501,000

Military deaths 3,406,000

Middle East
Civilian deaths 264,000

Military deaths 132,000

Latin America
Civilian deaths 305,000

Milit. death 133,0

Yet even though modern wars may be ostensibly local affairs, there tends to be a great deal of superpower involvement. In fact, a growing number of developing-country wars are, or tend to become, "proxy wars", fought by locals on behalf of the big power blocs, and heavily supplied with arms and advisers from outside. Without this foreign support, most of these conflicts would be shorter and less destructive.

Many developing-country politicians are only too willing to serve a surrogate role – or to court outside support by painting their domestic opponents as US- and communist-inspired. Both the US and the USSR have almost three-quarters of a million armed men abroad, with US forces having access to some 360 bases in dozens of countries. Other countries, notably the UK, France, Syria, Libya, South Africa,

Vietnam, and Cuba, have almost half a million military personnel outside their borders.

This expansion of the interests and "reach" of the two principal protagonists and their allies means that a minor dispute in some obscure corner of the Earth, such as El Salvador, can erupt as a major conflict as it engages their geopolitical interests.

Ironically, many of these wars consume resources which, used more wisely, could have addressed the root causes of conflict much more cost-effectively. It is almost always more expensive to go to war than to choose an alternative course if political leaders were to consider the needs of their people rather than the dictates of national or individual prestige. The Gulf War, for instance, is thought to have cost Iran over $100 billion – equal to four years of all government revenues, including oil. As for the UK, it has spent

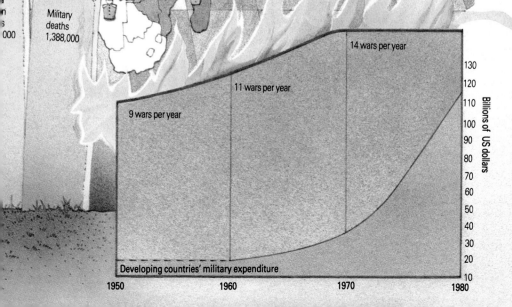

Fuelling the flames
Many small countries are sucked into the vortex of superpower conflict – and serve as conduits for illegal arms distribution. The flames of conflict are further fuelled by arms bought on the open market, with the Middle East currently the biggest customer. Worldwide, the number of countries making their own major weapons systems (tanks, warships, and missiles) has leapt from 5 in 1945 to as many as 50 today.

Military deaths 1,388,000

14 wars per year

11 wars per year

9 wars per year

Billions of US dollars

130
120
110
100
90
80
70
60
50
40
30
20
10

Developing countries' military expenditure

1950   1960   1970   1980

The changing face of war
If war means the active engagement of at least one regular army in organized fighting, with some continuity between armed clashes, then there have been about 160 wars since 1945. Most have been fought in the Third World – 60% have involved attempts to topple the ruling regime. The tempo of wars is increasing. In the 1950s, the average number of wars was 9 a year; today it is 14 (see graph, left). This ominous trend continues as the Third World's military spending soars even higher.

several million pounds for each Falklander during and after the Argentinian invasion of the islands. Extraordinary quantities of resources have, quite literally, gone up in smoke.

The price of "security"
Within the few minutes that it takes the reader to get through this portion of text, governments will devote several million dollars to military activities. Each year, we spend an average of almost $150 per world citizen on the arms race. Add all this up and the total figure reaches $750 billion a year – or 6 percent of global GNP.

Suppose that we could divert a mere 10 percent of the world's military budget into constructive activities. Many of the problems we face on our over-burdened planet could be eliminated.

In 1983 the World Bank spent $13.5 billion – barely one week of arms spending – to assist projects in developing countries. If the Bank's spending power was boosted to the equivalent of one month's spending on the arms race, we could make some real headway against the various challenges which face us. The six largest UN programmes (for development, food, refugees, children, the Palestinian question, and population) spent $2.7 billion in 1982, which is equivalent to barely one-and-a-half days of the arms race. The entire UN system could run for nearly two centuries on only one year's world military spending. Total support from international organizations, including the World Bank and the UN, amounted to $134 billion from 1946 to 1981 – the equivalent of little more than nine weeks of the arms race.

These figures put a fresh complexion on protests by the US, the UK, and other rich nations of the West, that they are less and less able to "afford" assistance to developing countries. The richer they become, the more they lavish on the arms race. Instead of giving the Third World tools for development, they are sold the tools for destruction. As the late Barbara Ward put it, "they ask for bread, and we give them a recoilless rifle." To be fair, the superpowers and their allies often have willing customers in the Third World: indeed, the Third World has increased its share of the world military budget from 9 percent to 16 percent over the past decade (excluding China).

The supreme irony is that, while political leaders around the world beat ploughshares into swords, proclaiming that they will not surrender one square metre of territory to a foreign invader, they allow huge areas of once-fertile lands to wash or blow away each year. They could surely purchase more real security, in the proper, broader sense of that term, if they used the funds to safeguard natural resources of agriculture and forestry for example, on which their country's future depends.

In short, we are at a stage where we need to expand our concepts of security. The misuse of our wealth for militarism is not only an absurd hangover

The cost of militarism

"I think that people want peace so much that one of these days governments had better get out of their way and let them have it."
PRESIDENT EISENHOWER

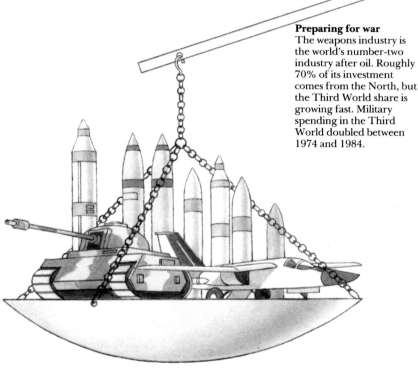

Preparing for war
The weapons industry is the world's number-two industry after oil. Roughly 70% of its investment comes from the North, but the Third World share is growing fast. Military spending in the Third World doubled between 1974 and 1984.

Count out 60 seconds and 30 of the world's children will have died for lack of food and adequate health care. Count out another 60 seconds: in this short space of time, the world will have spent $1.4 million on its military. Indeed, we are currently (1984) spending $750 billion a year on the instruments of death – and, in the process, opening up a new battlefield of social neglect. Between 1945 and 1983, it is estimated that 16 million lives were lost in war. We now lose a similar number every year due to various forms of social neglect. We have got our priorities drastically wrong. The $100 billion or so now spent by developing countries on weapons is three times what it would have cost to provide essential health care, medicines, vaccinations, clean water, and sanitation for all.

The Romans were among the first to insist that the only way to secure peace was to prepare for war, regardless of the cost. But around the world the cost is mounting. In Iran, the war with Iraq had resulted in war damage valued at $100 billion by 1983. In Afghanistan, where 4 out of 5 adults are illiterate, nearly 2,000 schools have been destroyed since the Soviet invasion.

Spending vs aid
There is a huge and growing gap between world military expenditure and world spending on development aid (see graph, right). Military expenditures of developed countries are now 30 times larger than their aid budgets for the developing countries. The tragedy is that sustainable economic development could remove many pre-war tensions.

☐ World military expenditure

▨ World foreign economic aid

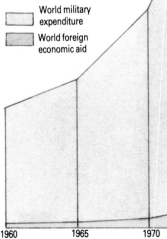

1960   1965   1970

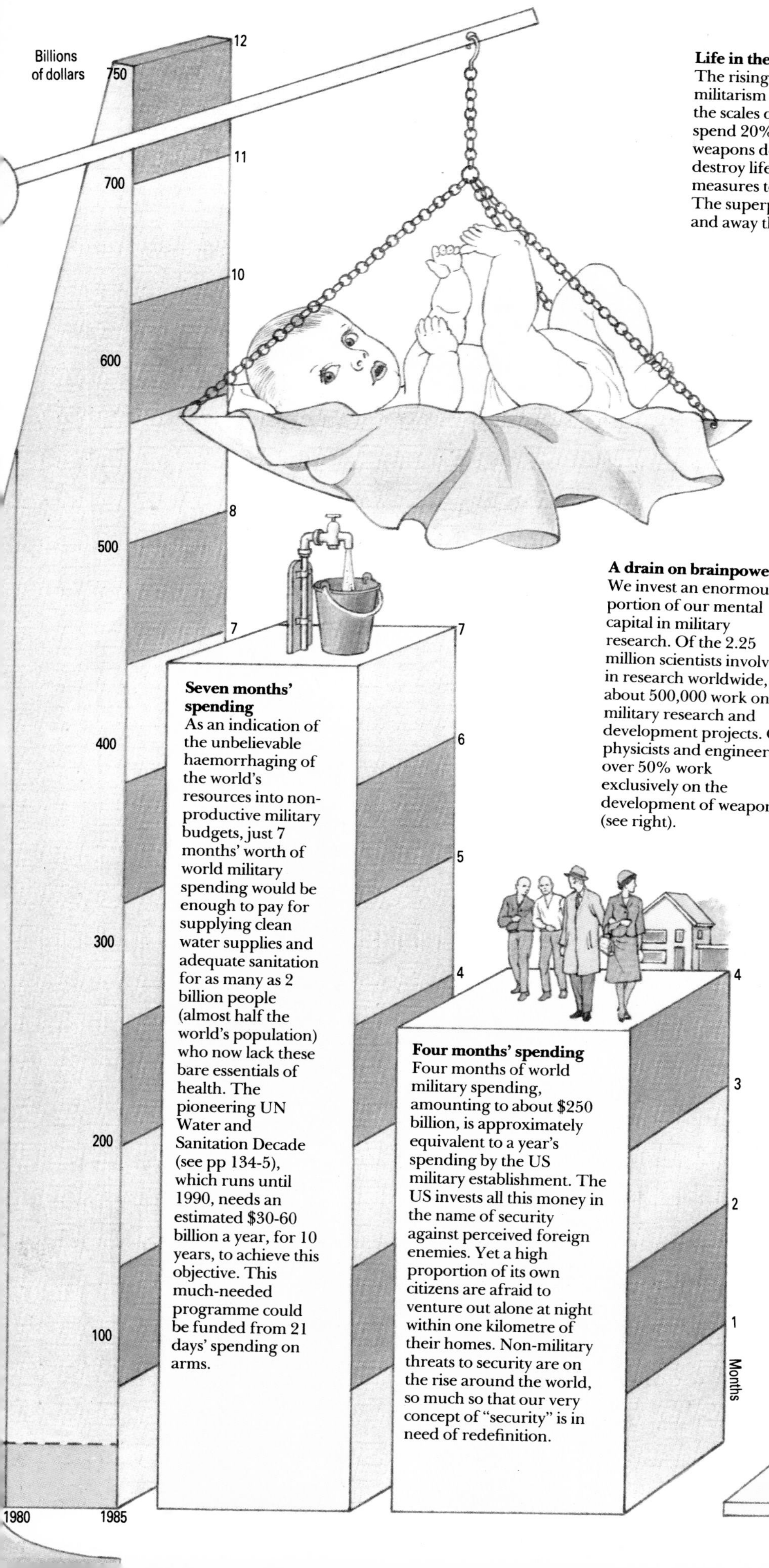

Billions
of dollars

750

700

600

500

400

300

200

100

12

11

10

8

7

6

5

4

3

2

1

1980   1985

Life in the scales
The rising cost of militarism is highlighted by the scales diagram, left. We spend 20% more on weapons designed to destroy life than on health measures to preserve life. The superpowers are far and away the biggest military spenders – but a study published in 1980 ranked the US a poor ninth among 142 countries in per capita economic and social spending. The USSR trailed even this meagre performance, coming in as low as 25th.

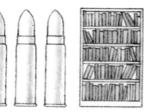

Bombs or books?
In our wrong-headed list of global priorities, we give the military equal weight with education. A single nuclear submarine costs as much money as the annual education budgets of 23 developing countries with 160 million school-age children.

A drain on brainpower
We invest an enormous portion of our mental capital in military research. Of the 2.25 million scientists involved in research worldwide, about 500,000 work on military research and development projects. Of physicists and engineers, over 50% work exclusively on the development of weapons (see right).

Seven months' spending
As an indication of the unbelievable haemorrhaging of the world's resources into non-productive military budgets, just 7 months' worth of world military spending would be enough to pay for supplying clean water supplies and adequate sanitation for as many as 2 billion people (almost half the world's population) who now lack these bare essentials of health. The pioneering UN Water and Sanitation Decade (see pp 134-5), which runs until 1990, needs an estimated $30-60 billion a year, for 10 years, to achieve this objective. This much-needed programme could be funded from 21 days' spending on arms.

Four months' spending
Four months of world military spending, amounting to about $250 billion, is approximately equivalent to a year's spending by the US military establishment. The US invests all this money in the name of security against perceived foreign enemies. Yet a high proportion of its own citizens are afraid to venture out alone at night within one kilometre of their homes. Non-military threats to security are on the rise around the world, so much so that our very concept of "security" is in need of redefinition.

Months

Eight hours' spending
If we could divert just 8 hours of military spending, worth $680 million, we might eradicate malaria. Some 200 million people worldwide suffer from this debilitating disease.

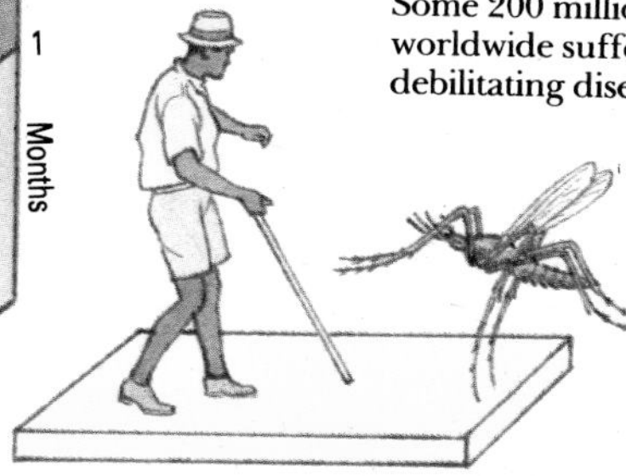

of the primitive spirit that says "If you do not agree with me, I shall kill you to prove my conviction", but it also undercuts our very means of long-term livelihood, providing damning evidence of our short-sightedness. If only we would suspend our squabbles and adopt a broader view, we would see that benign landscapes are still open to us.

The ultimate foolishness

The ultimate horror of nuclear war is becoming more probable every day. How many readers of this book believe they will die peacefully in their beds? The superpowers and their allies continue to add to their arsenals, now rated at 15,000 megatons. One megaton is equivalent to 80 Hiroshima-type bombs, so present arsenals contain explosive power equivalent to 1.2 million Hiroshimas.

As if that were not enough, the present rate of build-up means that stockpiles will soon reach 20,000 megatons. Even more worrying is the fact that the superpowers are now talking about nuclear war as a phenomenon to be survived, even "won".

Until the mid-1970s, nuclear stockpiling was geared to the concept of mutually assured destruction (or MAD, for short), with missiles primarily targeted on enemy cities. But now, as weapon-delivery systems become ever-more accurate (the latest NATO missiles can reputedly hit an area the size of a tennis court in the USSR), the MAD strategy has been superseded by the dominant aim of destroying missile silos and other mainly military targets. Just conceivably, it is thought, one side could "take out" the other's nuclear capability with a carefully timed and targeted strike.

Nuclear deterrence, in short, is giving way to a far more frightening concept, that of nuclear war fighting, sometimes termed the "nuclear utility targeting strategy" (or NUTS). So significant is this "advance", that the US will spend almost $500 billion on it during the 1980s.

Proponents of NUTS argue that nuclear weapons will continue to maintain a constructive balance of terror. This, they insist, is a stable situation – and they point to the fact that there have been no nuclear exchanges since 1945. Yet the proliferation of super-sophisticated, unimaginably destructive technology may serve to make the delicate balance of terror even more delicate, and hence less stable than it has been.

As recently as the late 1950s, both superpowers were asserting that their nuclear arsenals (then relatively small) would be enough to assure an intolerable retaliation if a nuclear strike were ever to be launched. Is there now no limit to the amount of "overkill" we need to enforce the "peace"?

By going along with an accelerating increase in nuclear arsenals, political leaders have implicitly asserted that they have full confidence in the command-and-control capacities of their weapons systems – despite multiple malfunctions during test firings. They have also assumed a degree of

One million Hiroshimas

"The stone age may return on the gleaming wings of science, and what might now shower immeasurable blessings upon mankind may even bring about its total destruction. Beware, I say; time may be short."
WINSTON CHURCHILL

The nuclear payload carried by a single Trident submarine is equivalent to *eight* times the total firepower expended during World War II. Today's nuclear arsenals contain the combined potential firepower of over one million Hiroshimas. The nuclear fireball, right, gives a striking impression of the degree of "overkill" now afforded by the world's nuclear weapons. The warheads carried by a single Trident submarine have the explosive capacity to destroy all the major cities of the northern hemisphere. There has been a dramatic change, in fact, in the nuclear arsenals of both the US and USSR, both in terms of quantity and quality. "Quality" is important, since the accuracy, reliability, and flexibility of nuclear warhead delivery systems help determine their destructive potential. Indeed, the ever-increasing accuracy and sophistication of the world's missiles make the degree of overkill achieved to date look even more ridiculous.

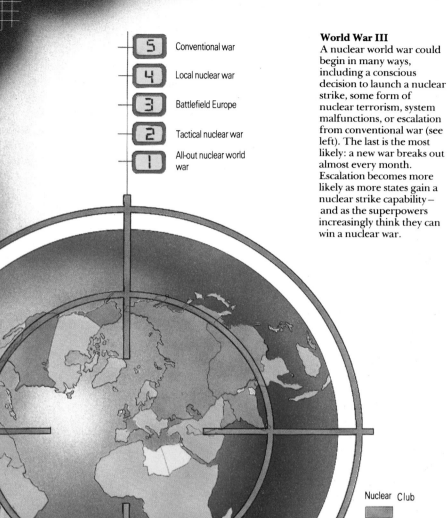

5 — Conventional war

4 — Local nuclear war

3 — Battlefield Europe

2 — Tactical nuclear war

1 — All-out nuclear world war

World War III
A nuclear world war could begin in many ways, including a conscious decision to launch a nuclear strike, some form of nuclear terrorism, system malfunctions, or escalation from conventional war (see left). The last is the most likely: a new war breaks out almost every month. Escalation becomes more likely as more states gain a nuclear strike capability – and as the superpowers increasingly think they can win a nuclear war.

Nuclear Club

Full members

Almost members

Next in line

Awaiting political decision

Acquiring political option

Hiroshima: 0.013 megatons
The first military use of the atomic bomb came with the dropping of the 13-kiloton "Little Boy" bomb in 1945, killing nearly 100,000 people.

World War II: 3 megatons
A single square, left, is equal to the total firepower used in WWII.

Poseidon: 9 megatons
The three squares shown, left, represent 9 megatons, equal to three WWIIs. They are also equivalent to the firepower of a single Poseidon submarine. The US has 33 strategic nuclear submarines.

Trident: 24 megatons
The eight squares, left, represent 24 megatons, the firepower equivalent of a single modern Trident submarine. Enough to destroy every major city in the North.

Goodbye to cities
A hundred squares equal 300 megatons, enough to destroy all the world's cities.

The nuclear escalator
The number of states now riding the escalator towards full membership of the nuclear club is increasingly ominous. There is still no effective control over club membership. The Nuclear Non-Proliferation Treaty, signed in 1970, ostensibly restricts the sale of nuclear weapons to non-nuclear states and restricts the total number of nuclear states. But, although the treaty has been ratified by 121 states, it has turned out to be dangerously weak in practice. Its signatories do not necessarily fulfil all the treaty's promises, and many important states have never actually signed the treaty. These include France, China, Argentina, Brazil, Israel, India, Pakistan, South Africa, and Spain. Almost all of these are riding high on the nuclear escalator (see world map, above). The more states that have such a nuclear capability, the harder it will be to preserve the current fragile stalemate.

Target Earth
Enormous ingenuity has been expended to ensure that nuclear warheads land on particular sites or cities. By 1979, US missiles were so accurate that they could destroy Russian missiles in their silos. Indeed, the policy of deterrence, based on the idea of mutually assured destruction, is now giving way to new strategies based on nuclear war fighting. By 1990, the whole US strategy will be geared to a policy of nuclear war fighting. By the mid-1990s, once the new wave of technologies now being developed begins to be deployed, including anti-ballistic missile systems, anti-submarine warfare systems, and anti-satellite weapons, the superpowers may actually believe that nuclear war is winnable. Theoretically, one side might develop its targeting capability to such a degree that it could pre-empt retaliation.

rationality in whatever new leaders come along. What happens when nuclear weapons get into the hands of members of the international community who may be even less predictable and "rational" than the present nuclear club?

Nuclear winter or environmental collapse?

Even a limited nuclear war would inflict almost unlimited injuries to our planet: a bang to end all bangs. We are now learning that only a fraction of our present nuclear arsenals needs to be detonated to lift so much smoke, soot, dust, and other debris into the atmosphere that sunlight would be all but eliminated over the combatant nations (plus all by-stander nations) of northern Eurasia. The result would be darkness, day and night, for months on end, halting photosynthesis, the basic process that sustains this green planet. And, as the sun's warmth was lost, so temperatures would plunge as low as minus 20-40°C, making it all but impossible for crops, large animals, and humans to survive.

Nor would the nuclear winter be confined to the mid-latitudes of the northern hemisphere. The cloud would gradually extend into the tropics. Although the pall would thin out as it dispersed, its impact would not necessarily fall at the same rate—since tropical ecosystems are unusually sensitive to even minor climatic fluctuations.

Bang or whimper?

We are already engaged in World War III, to paraphrase Professor Raymond Dasmann of the University of California, a war against our Earth—and we are winning it.

In the South, we have successfully gutted large portions of tropical rainforest, and allowed good soil to be washed uselessly away. In the North, the Earth's river arteries and ocean life-tides carry untold poisons, while rain, that life-giver from the skies, sometimes proves to be as acid as vinegar.

And, just in case our straightforward ecological assaults should fail, we have recourse to the alternative strategy of nuclear war. We could trigger a "nuclear winter" with less than 1% of our current nuclear arsenal. We may convince ourselves that we are "secure", but globally we have never been more threatened.

Eventually the cloud would cross the Equator, reaching deep into the South. The consequences would be compounded by the explosion of some 200 megatons on targets in the tropics, such as oil fields, military bases, and nuclear power plants.

A "nuclear winter" would grip the Earth. By the time it was all over, modern agriculture would have been eliminated, and there would be little prospect of re-establishing even rudimentary agriculture for at least another growing season. While World War III could readily kill two billion people, at least as many could die through freezing and starvation.

So our civilization could go out with a multi-megaton bang. Meanwhile, the fear of nuclear war blinds us to a parallel threat already upon us—as we devote more and more of our resources to the potential destruction of our natural base. If we do not learn to live in harmony with our environment, we shall experience the laws of nature in full force—the backlash of a resource failure. On this course, human society seems destined to go out with a whimper—or, rather, a prolonged wail.

Environmental degradation is like a cancer, or many forms of cancer, spreading silently, unseen, through the body of our planet. If it were like a heart attack, its effect would be all too apparent, and we would swiftly take steps to remedy the problem. But it isn't and we don't.

UNDER NEW MANAGEMENT

We are a privileged generation, faced with an opportunity for creative endeavour on a scale which surpasses that required of any earlier society. After setting ourselves apart from nature, we must become a part of nature again: truce, treaty, and reconciliation. *Homo sapiens* must advance from a pioneer species, which is aggressive, prolific, and greedy for resources, into a climax species, which recognizes ecological constraints, swaps assertiveness for co-operation, and expresses self regulation as the golden mean. By saving our biosphere and ourselves, we may attain a degree of humanity not known before: through a caring attitude towards our one-Earth home, we become "human kind".

Sustainable management

We are moving into a totally new phase of the human adventure. Instead of ransacking the Earth without thought for tomorrow, we must guard and use it on a sustainable basis. This is the great transition we must make which will demand a management exercise of a scale unequalled in human history.

Before we make the switch from runaway growth to sustainable management, it is vital that we calculate the productive capacities of our human and natural resources. At present, our observation, measurement, and monitoring of environmental change is grossly inadequate. We are now destroying crucial planetary resources of species, forests, and fisheries without knowing the full consequences of our actions. Ironically, we do have the expertise to calculate these productive capacities, and, as we have seen, there already exists the communications power and a diverse institutional framework to bring effective planet management within our grasp.

Perhaps our most turbulent transition will be the establishment of equity among ourselves – the only basis on which the transition to sustainable management of our natural environment can succeed. We must move beyond talk of you *or* me, North *or* South, us *or* them – the language of conflict – for the planet offers enough resources for all, provided they are equitably shared.

Transition is far from impossible. Already, **definite patches** of light can be seen at the far end of the population tunnel. And industrial designers are coming up with cleaner resource-efficient products and processes which generate less waste and less pollution. A quarter-tonne satellite now carries

The great transition

Although we live in the finite environment of Earth, we continue to exploit its resources as if they were infinite, as if we had another planet out there in space. We cannot continue in this way for long. Sooner rather than later (when events may act for us in a manner not to our liking), we will have to bring under control the current dangerous trends of, for example, over-population, energy depletion, environmental abuse, and spending on "security" (see right). This is already beginning to happen in some parts of the world. China, for example, is making a determined effort to control its population growth and thus to maintain an acceptable standard of living. Before we are able on a global scale to make the transition to sustainable and equitable living patterns, we must first determine exactly what the long-term productive capacities of our planet are – both its limits and its untapped potential. We can begin with the fact that many current capacities are over-stretched and will require a substantial climb-down from such excessive growth rates as those shown here.

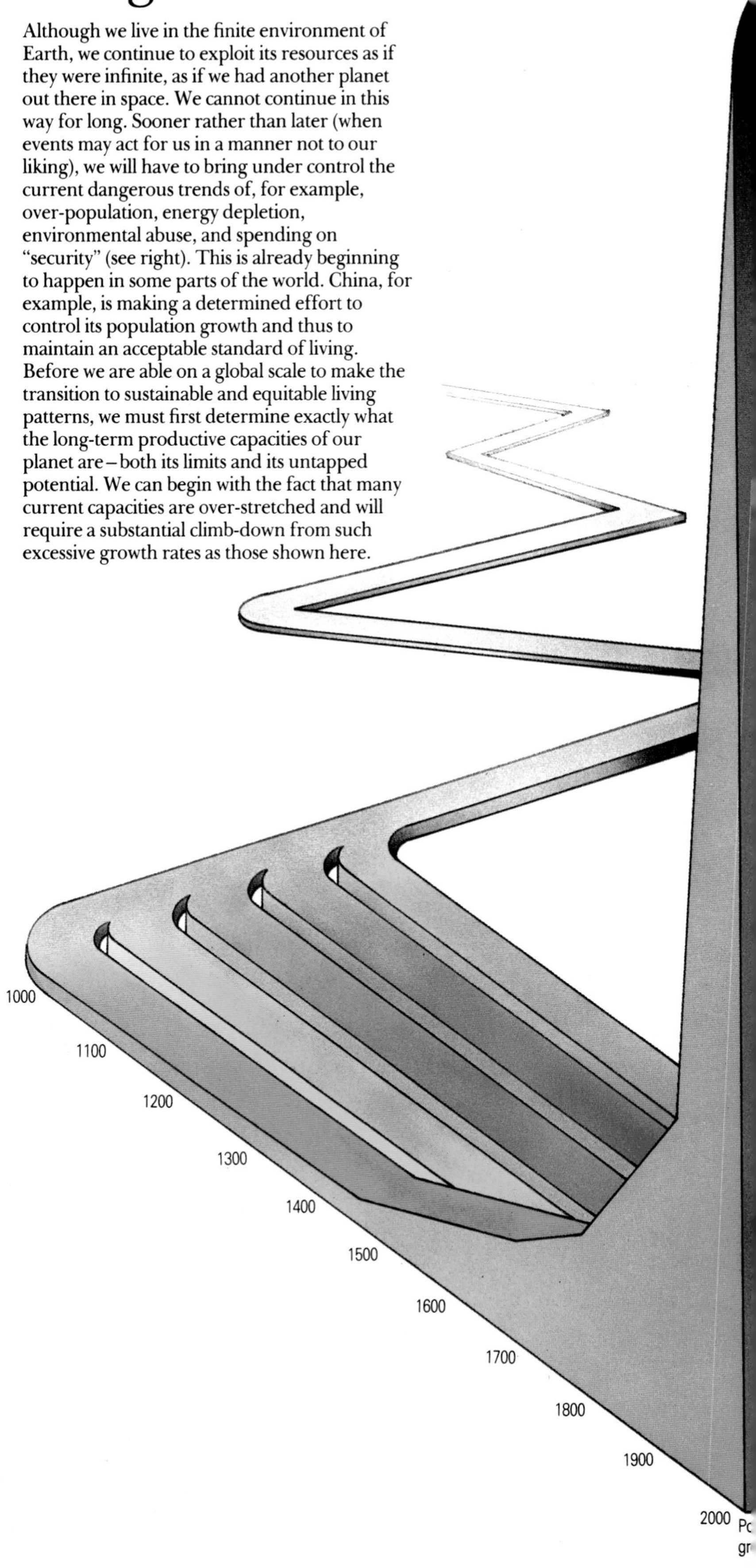

1000
1100
1200
1300
1400
1500
1600
1700
1800
1900
2000 Po
gr

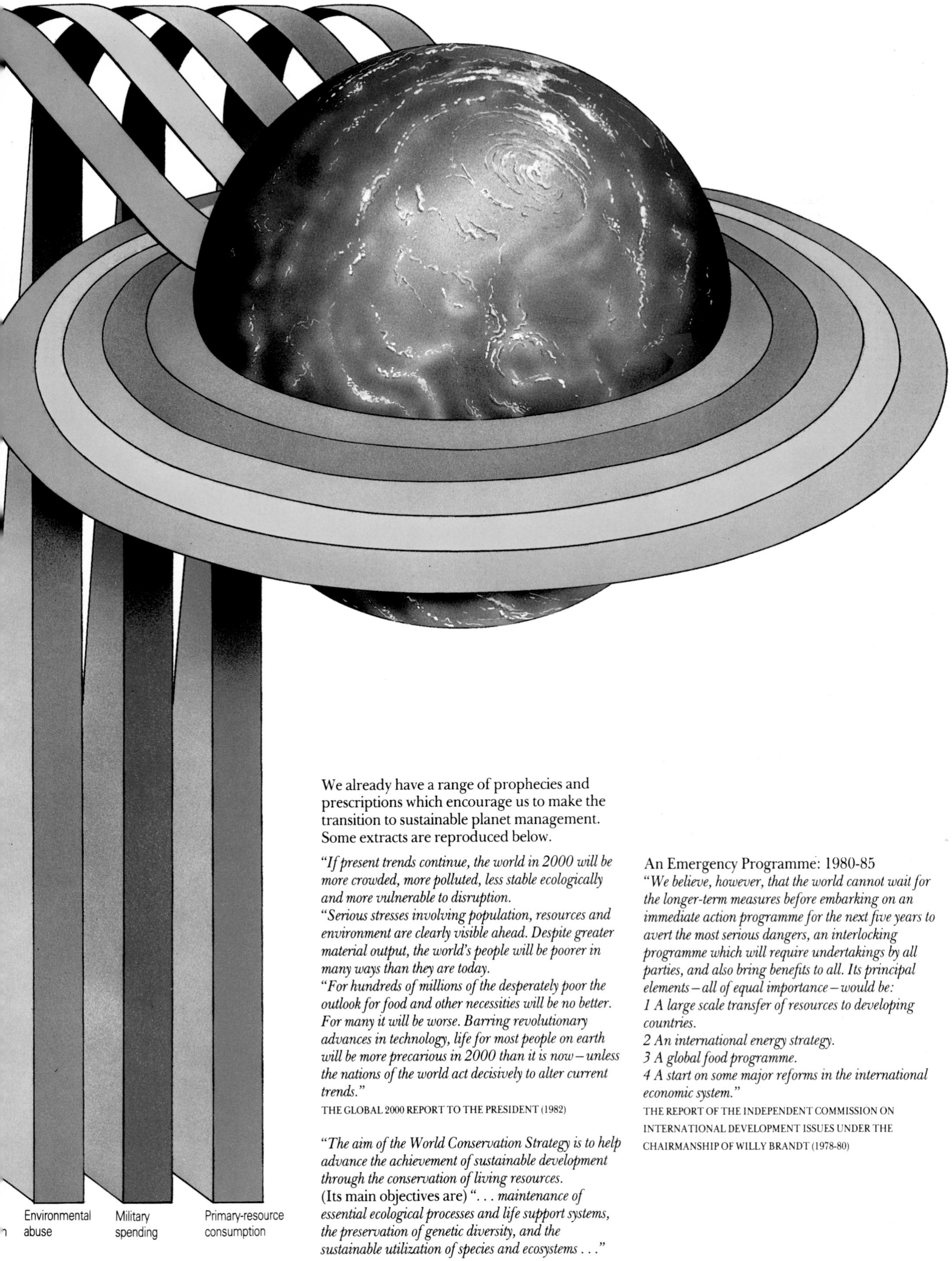

Environmental
abuse

Military
spending

Primary-resource
consumption

We already have a range of prophecies and prescriptions which encourage us to make the transition to sustainable planet management. Some extracts are reproduced below.

"If present trends continue, the world in 2000 will be more crowded, more polluted, less stable ecologically and more vulnerable to disruption.
"Serious stresses involving population, resources and environment are clearly visible ahead. Despite greater material output, the world's people will be poorer in many ways than they are today.
"For hundreds of millions of the desperately poor the outlook for food and other necessities will be no better. For many it will be worse. Barring revolutionary advances in technology, life for most people on earth will be more precarious in 2000 than it is now – unless the nations of the world act decisively to alter current trends."
THE GLOBAL 2000 REPORT TO THE PRESIDENT (1982)

"The aim of the World Conservation Strategy is to help advance the achievement of sustainable development through the conservation of living resources.
(Its main objectives are) "... *maintenance of essential ecological processes and life support systems, the preservation of genetic diversity, and the sustainable utilization of species and ecosystems* ..."
WORLD CONSERVATION STRATEGY (IUCN, WWF, AND UNEP, 1980)

An Emergency Programme: 1980-85
"We believe, however, that the world cannot wait for the longer-term measures before embarking on an immediate action programme for the next five years to avert the most serious dangers, an interlocking programme which will require undertakings by all parties, and also bring benefits to all. Its principal elements – all of equal importance – would be:
1 A large scale transfer of resources to developing countries.
2 An international energy strategy.
3 A global food programme.
4 A start on some major reforms in the international economic system."
THE REPORT OF THE INDEPENDENT COMMISSION ON INTERNATIONAL DEVELOPMENT ISSUES UNDER THE CHAIRMANSHIP OF WILLY BRANDT (1978-80)

more transatlantic telecommunications than a 175,000-tonne copper cable. These efforts must be brought together, given a new priority, and communicated to the widest audience. We might even build ourselves a *global* "think tank", turning our own expertise into a springboard ready for our greatest transition yet.

Repairing the biosphere

The transition to sustainable society accomplished, *Homo sapiens* will embark on a new and exciting phase of growth. It will demand from each of us a high sense of responsibility for our planet, and for each other. It will also be an infinitely rewarding and enriching experience.

Our first expression of global responsibility will be to launch a worldwide reconstruction programme. Based on initiatives already taken in some fields and on new ecological understanding, the overriding aim of this programme will be to restore biological diversity everywhere. It will mean safeguarding the powerhouses of diversity (the various ecological biomes), giving priority to wild as well as domesticated species, and often choosing diverse, plant-rich landscapes in preference to monocultures.

Diversity must also be the codeword for the way we manage ourselves. Not only shall we need to draw from a wide range of cultural and minority options to improve the quality of our lives, but also to draw upon a broad, participatory power base in our political systems to oppose and reverse present trends towards homogeneity, over-centralization, the abuse of power, and an uncaring society.

It will fast become obvious that with the global repair programme under way, the world neither needs nor can afford to spend $750 billion every year on its military machine. A realistic argument for de-militarization is not hard to build. We have already seen how modern concepts of security are broadening to include economic and social welfare, outgrowing the narrow definition of military defence. We have also seen how the world nuclear arsenal has outgrown its strategic usefulness to the point where it threatens life on Earth. Add to this the economic liability of military spending, and the case is complete. Both the USSR and the US have performed less well than expected in the global marketplace in recent decades partly as a result of excessive military spending. The US share of production among the top OECD countries, for example, slipped from 60 percent in 1955 to 45 percent in 1978. At the same time, it is hardly a coincidence that Japan and West Germany – both largely free of the military-spending "albatross" – achieve high economic performance: these smaller countries rank third and fourth behind the superpowers in the world rankings for GNP.

Though we will not easily escape our own aggressive and rapacious qualities, we are already recognizing that the repair and safety of our planet is our highest common interest.

Coming of age

When we begin to take full responsibility for the management of our planet, our first job will be to repair our damaged environment. Many of the most delicate repair operations will be carried out by the Earth itself, if we give it time. For despite our technology we cannot reconstruct a coral reef or replant an intricate wetland ecosystem.

Our second task will be to develop in sustained harmony with our planet's life-support systems. If the human individual continued to grow for 70 years at the same rate of growth experienced in the first months of life, it would grow to gigantic proportions. Obviously this does not happen. After adolescence, growth develops along a different path of mental, emotional, and spiritual advancement. Our species has reached the same crossroads as a human individual on the brink of adulthood. There is slight apprehension at first, but like the first dive into water, fear gives way to fascination once the breakthrough is made.

"The unleashed power of the atom has changed everything except our way of thinking . . . we need an essentially new way of thinking if mankind is to survive".
ALBERT EINSTEIN

I have a high regard for our species, for all its newness and immaturity as a member of the biosphere. As evolutionary time is measured, we arrived here only a few moments ago and we have a lot of growing up to do. If we succeed, we could become a sort of collective mind for the Earth, the thought of the Earth. At the moment, for all our juvenility as a species, we are surely the brightest and brainiest of the Earth's working parts. I trust us to have the will to keep going, and to maintain as best we can the life of the planet."
LEWIS THOMAS

*"Nobody made a greater mistake than he who did
nothing because he could do only a little".*
EDMUND BURKE

Safeguarding the fragile miracle

Alone among species, humankind has been able to leave the biosphere and study it from the outside. We are now able to "look in" on the fragile miracle, Gaia, and on our own behaviour, with a sharpened perception. And as our vision clears, and our danger becomes apparent, we increasingly question our role in an otherwise harmonious world.

We have acquired great power; that much is obvious. We have already seen how human handiwork has altered some of the major chemical cycles of the biosphere, notably increasing the flow of carbon, nitrogen, and sulphur. This effect of accelerating existing processes is widely evident: we have increased the flows of energy exchange, information transfer, and "pollution" (that is, materials transfer); we have hastened both the geographical spread of species and their concentration, also their extinction and multiplication; and we have boosted both soil erosion and soil replenishment. We have increased violence at the same time as we have raised hope of organization, order, and interdependence in global society. And most of all, we have increased the rate of change.

Most Gaian feedback systems to cope with change are slow – whether to stabilize through positive feedback, or to exploit the opportunity for new experiments. They have a long lead-in time, so that changes we initiate now may produce a backlash we cannot yet see coming. Among the few elements of the living planet that can act quickly in response to danger to global systems – quickly enough to forestall major perturbations, even a shift to a wholly new set of conditions – is humanity itself.

There is no going back now. We cannot rely on "all powerful" Mother Nature to repair all our errors. We are grown up. We have acquired the power of life and death for our planet and most of its inhabitants.

For more than three decades, it is our nuclear power to destroy that has increasingly dominated our world view. The loss of self-respect produced by evidence of our cruelty and folly as a species, and the looming threat of nuclear holocaust, have darkened our horizons, entrenching the view that we can be a blight, a cancer on the face of the Earth. But along with this undeniable destructive power, we have also acquired the power to protect and sustain life – a gift we sadly undervalue. Consider what role we might now assume – not as destroyers

but as life-givers, as caretakers of a flowering world. Our "satellite vision" means that all the planet's resources – soils, forests, rivers, oceans, minerals – can be not only mapped in fine detail, but vetted for pollution, erosion, or drought; for changes in albedo or humidity; for populations of species from plant life to parasites or disease organisms; for movements of shoaling fish or migratory creatures; for minerals or geothermal energy; and for human mismanagement, from soil damage to military build-up.

We have the capacity to process this data at high speed, analyse it, and communicate it around the world in seconds. Two-way communication means we can gather "on the ground" information widely, and respond to it quickly.

Our diversifying power structure, with ever-multiplying special interest groups, village organizations, regional groupings, and transnational bodies, means that we can *effect action*, all at once and globally, to a concerted aim and by a diversity of means. We can even tailor solutions and actions in the smallest locality to meet the situation, and yet contribute correctly to a wider programme.

Our skills in genetics, engineering, and ecology mean we can now work with natural systems to derive benefit from them, without destroying their integrity and ability to renew themselves. We can live off the biosphere's income, rather than using up its capital. We can increase its income, too.

With the power of life in our hands, we could, for instance, make forests spring up on bare lands, safeguard species against the pressures for extinction, restore diversity to our landscapes and fields, refertilize the soil, restart the greening cycle in arid lands, reverse the pollution of the oceans and atmosphere, recycle our wastes to useful ends, harness the energy of the sun, wind, and water, and redeploy the genetic wealth of evolution to *craft* organisms to work in partnership with us – new crops, microbes, medicinal plants, natural oils, and a host of other materials. And just as we have long controlled the populations of many other species, we could control our own, at a sustainable level.

It is time for humanity to use this power, and use it well. We must have the courage to face ourselves, to admit our power of life and death, and bring it under permanent, watchful control. Now we must take sides with life.

Epilogue

"The most beautiful object I have ever seen in a photograph, in all my life, is the planet Earth seen from the distance of the moon, hanging there in space, obviously alive. Although it seems at first glance to be made up of innumerable separate species of living things, on closer examination every one of its working parts, including us, is interdependently connected to all the other working parts. It is, to put it one way, the only truly closed ecosystem any of us knows about. To put it another way, it is an organism. It came alive, I shall guess, 3.8 billion years ago today, and I wish it a happy birthday and a long life ahead, for our children and their grandchildren and theirs and theirs."
LEWIS THOMAS, FEBRUARY 1984

In the course of writing tens of thousands of words for this book, I have had much time to ponder old issues anew.

First of all, I have found that I hardly know this planet – and I am in good company. Scientists do not even agree, within 50 percent either way, on how much vegetation there is on Earth, crucially important as that is to our understanding of where we can grow crops, support livestock, or harvest wood. They know even less about our wild habitats, upon which we make greater and greater demands. We are extinguishing species not yet even discovered – indeed, we have only conflicting estimates of Earth's total complement of different life-forms. As for our knowledge of the effects of human action, very few nations establish the true rates of soil loss, deforestation, or pollution; some cannot accurately count their hungry, poverty-stricken, or workless populations. In the oceans, we do not know the size of the fish stocks we are depleting, nor the rate of spread of the toxins we pour out. Our ignorance is so vast, in fact, that we are not aware of it.

Our understanding of our planet is also sadly deficient. True, we have grown familiar with spacecraft photos of that lonely-looking globe hanging in the void, covered with a life-sustaining biosphere that makes our planet uniquely beautiful and leaves it uniquely fragile. Yet we know next to nothing about the workings of Earth's ecosystem. While we are now unlocking the secrets of DNA and life's molecules, we have only begun to grasp the nature of planetary life as an organic whole. Scientists are only just formulating questions such as "To what extent does the network of all living things actively control the make-up and temperature of the atmosphere, to maintain our biosphere as a single life-support system?" What, in other words, is the nature of the Gaian functioning of our planet?

Far from supplying essential answers, we are not even sure what are the right questions to ask. And despite our primitive understanding, we pursue unwitting experiments of global scope, altering Earth's climate in a manner we barely recognize and with results that will irreversibly affect every citizen of the planet.

I find it increasingly difficult to conceive of the speed at which we are over-loading Earth's ecosystem. Our numbers have almost doubled in 35 years, and are still growing fast. We are "consuming" entire regions – forests, grasslands, arable zones – at a pace that should remind us of the image of lily pads extending across a pond. If the pads double in area each day, and if the pond is to be entirely covered in 30 days, on which day is the pond half-covered? Answer: the 29th day.

Still more worrying, the degradative processes underway have built up so much momentum that they cannot be halted overnight. Our situation is like that of the captain of a supertanker. If he decides he wants to turn around, he will need several *miles* to slow his ship, let alone to head in a basically different direction. Time is not on our side.

The consequences of our impact on Earth's ecosystem are already so pervasive and profound that they will surely persist for a long stretch into the future. The toxic chemicals we pour into our environment could well leave their poisoning impact until long after our children are gone. The desertlands we are creating will still be apparent in several centuries' time. The green band of forests around the Equator is being transformed into a bald ring that will probably endure for millennia. The extinction spasm we are imposing on wildlife species may not be made good for millions of years.

But by far the most significant finding of all that I have come across while working on this book is that we are making a start on the road towards sensible stewardship of our planet. While population grows and grows, and habitats continue to be degraded on every side, there has been an extraordinary outburst of awareness during the past few years. There are hundreds of environmental agencies at official levels, and at grass-roots levels there are thousands of citizen groups, all seeking to come to grips with our problems.

Were I to write an Epilogue like this in the year 2000, I could well look back on the present time as a point when signs of hope were springing forth in all kinds of unexpected places. We have the chance, quite simply, to be the first to live in final accord with our Spaceship Earth – and hence in final harmony with each other. The Ancient Greeks, the Renaissance communities, the founders of America, the Victorians, enjoyed no such challenge as this. What a time to be alive!

Norman Myers
August 1984

Appendices

Maps and data

In our familiar view of the world, we have learned to think of the North Pole as the "top" and the South as the "bottom". This, in itself, conditions much of our thinking. Worse still, since it is impossible to convey both accurate *areas* and accurate *shape* outlines of our curved continents on a flat map, every projection sacrifices one or the other. The most well known projection is the Mercator, which tends to show land masses increasingly larger as it approaches the North Pole. The result is to create a "Eurocentric" Northern view of the world, with the Southern continents (which actually straddle the centre of the globe, around the Equator) reduced in significance and size.

In this book, we have often used a projection devised by Gaia, based mainly on Gall's cylindrical projection, but viewed in a different perspective, bringing the South into prominence, and countering the Eurocentric view of the world. We have also used numerous other projections (see sources) to alert the reader to different views of the planet, and to convey data in the clearest graphic form. The more recent Peters projection, used in the later chapters of this book, represents the true land mass of the continents, thus emphasizing Latin America and Africa, but distorting their familiar shapes and patterns.

The "broken-up" maps, where the continental outlines are rearranged under tables of visual data, along graphs, or raised to different heights, are all based on statistical groupings.

Just as maps can never be entirely free of distortion, so global statistics always mask wide variations. The "average" calorie intake of the poorer South is much lower than that of the North, for instance; but this level, itself adequate, conceals the plight of around half a billion starving people. Statistics rely, too, on nations' capacity to collect and willingness to admit to, reliable data about themselves. FAO figures, for example, though "authoritative", can only be as good as the contributing national statistical services. LANDSAT will, eventually, give us clearer data on global resources, but its work is only beginning. To offset global uncertainties, we have used case studies, informed analysis, and research data as a countercheck wherever possible.

The base year for current data in this book is 1980/2 unless otherwise stated. Future projections are mostly carried through to 2025. Past studies are more rare, as the correlation of world data is relatively recent. Even 15 years ago, categories used in UN statistics were very different from those in use today.

Despite all such caveats, however, the data are overwhelmingly clear in their import. Most devastating are those which show rates of soil erosion, desertification, deforestation, species loss, pollution, as well as the very fully documented facts on militarization, increasing violence, income division, human suffering, and wasted potential. Even if some estimates vary – for instance, between 10 and 15 million people are counted as refugees – they are still dreadful. And most of them are more likely to be under, rather than over estimates.

Essential reading

There is an enormous amount of reference material now published in the field of environment and development. Many strongly argued polemical or philosophical popular books are also available, and more come every month as the world's conscience is aroused. Out of this mass of information, there is a handful of books which every thinking person should now have on their bookshelf – books which are entirely outstanding as pioneers and information sources. We recommend:
Lester R. Brown *State of the World 1984*, A Worldwatch Institute Report on Progress Toward a Sustainable Society, W.W. Norton (1984).
P. R. Ehrlich, A. H. Ehrlich, J. P. Holdren *Ecoscience: Population, Resources, Environment*, W.H. Freeman, San Francisco (1977).
Paul Harrison *Inside the Third World*, Penguin Books (1979) and *The Third World Tomorrow*, Penguin Books (1980).
J. E. Lovelock *Gaia, a New Look at Life on earth*, Oxford University Press (1979).
North-South: A Programme for Survival, Pan Books (1980) and *Common Crisis North-South: Cooperation for World Recovery*, Pan Books (1983), Reports of the Independent Commission on International Development Issues.
Peter Russell *The Awakening Earth*, Routledge and Kegan Paul (1976).
Jonathan Schell *The Fate of the Earth*, Jonathan Cape (1982).
Alvin Toffler *The Third Wave*, Collins (1980).
The World Development Reports, 1978 to 1984, The World Bank, Oxford University Press.
World Conservation Strategy, IUCN, UNEP, WWF (1980).

The following, just as vital and informative, comprise an important bibliography:
Agriculture: Toward 2000, Economic and Social Development Series, Food and Agriculture Organization of the United Nations, Rome (1981).
Robert and Christine Prescott Allen *Genes from the Wild*, Earthscan (1983).
R. Chambers *Rural Development; Putting the Last First*, Longman (1983).
P. Chilton and C. Aubrey, eds. *Nineteen Eighty-four in 1984*, Comedia Publishing Group (1983).
Jacques-Yves Cousteau and the staff of the Cousteau Society, *The Cousteau Almanac, An Inventory of Life on our Water Planet*, Doubleday and Company, Inc. (1981).
Erik P. Eckholm *Down to Earth, Environment and Human Needs*, W.W. Norton (1982).
John Elkington, *Sun Traps, The Renewable Energy Forecast*, Penguin Books (1984).
N.C. Flemming, ed. *The Undersea*, Cassell (1977).
The Global 2000 Report to the President, Penguin Books (1982).
Paul Harrison and John Rowley *Human Numbers, Human Needs*, International Planned Parenthood Federation (1984).
Ronald Higgins *The Seventh Enemy, The Human Factor in Global Crisis*, Pan Books (1980).
M.W. Holdgate, M. Kassas and G.F. White, eds. *The World Environment 1972-82*, A Report by the United Nations Environment Programme,

Tycooly Ltd., Dublin (1982).
Anthony Huxley *Green Inheritance*, campaign book of the World Wildlife Fund plant conservation programme (forthcoming, Collins).
Hazel Johnson, Henry Bernstein with Raúl Hernán Ampuero and Ben Crow *Third World Lives of Struggle*, The Open University, Heinemann Educational Books (1982).
Pat Roy Mooney "The Law of the Seed", *Development Dialogue* (1983): 1-2 Dag Hammarskjöld Foundation, Uppsala.
Norman Myers *The Sinking Ark*, Pergamon Press (1979) and *A Wealth of Wild Species*, Westview Press (1983).
Kathleen Newland *The Sisterhood of Man*, W.W. Norton (1979).
Colin Norman *The God that Limps – Science and Technology in the Eighties*, W.W. Norton (1981).
D. and M. Pimentel *Food, Energy and Society*, Resource and Environmental Science Series, Edward Arnold (1979).
Paul Sieghart ed. *Micro-chips with Everything*, Comedia Publishing Group (1982).
Ruth Leger Sivard *World Military and Social Expenditures 1983*, World Priorities Inc (1983).
The State of the World's Children 1984, UNICEF, Oxford University Press.
Tom Stonier *The Wealth of Information: A Profile of the Post-Industrial Economy*, Thames Methuen (1983).
Third World Atlas, Open University (1983).

Abbreviations

ACP African Caribbean and Pacific Countries
AFP Agence France Presse
AP Associated Press (US)
ASEAN Association of South East Asian Nations
BODA British Overseas Development Administration
CARICOM Caribbean Common Market
CCAMLR Convention on the Conservation of Antarctic Marine Living Resources
CITES Convention on International Trade in Endangered Species
COMECON (or Comecon) Council for Mutual Economic Aid, or Assistance (Communist Nations)
COPES Convention on the Protection of Endangered Species
DNA deoxyribonucleic acid (see Glossary)
ECOWAS Economic Community of West African States
EEC European Economic Community
EEZ Extended Economic Zones
EIA Environmental Impact Assessment
ERR Earth Resources Research
FAO Food and Agricultural Organization (specialized Agency of the United Nations)
GDP Gross Domestic Product
GGP Gross Global Product
GNP Gross National Product
GRP Gross Regional Product
IBPGR International Board for Plant Genetic Resources
IIED International Institute for Environment and Development
ILO International Labour Organisation (specialized Agency of the United Nations)
IMF International Monetary Fund (specialized Agency of the United Nations)

IMMP International Multi Media Promotions
INFACT International Formula Action Coalition
INGOs International Non-Governmental Organizations
IPPF International Planned Parenthood Federation
IT Information Technology (see Glossary)
ITDG Intermediate Technology Development Group
IUCN International Union for the Conservation of Nature
IWC International Whaling Commission
LDCs Less Developed Countries (see Glossary)
MARPOL International Conventions for the Prevention of Pollution from Ships
NASA National Aeronautics and Space Administration (US)
NATO North Atlantic Treaty Organization
NCS National Conservation Strategies
NGOs Non Governmental Organizations
NICs Newly Industrialized Countries
NIEO New International Economic Order
OAS Organization of American States
OAU Organization of African Unity
ODA Overseas Development Administration
OECD Organization for Economic Cooperation and Development
OPEC Organization of Petroleum Exporting Countries
OTEC Ocean Thermal Energy Conversion (see Glossary)
OXFAM Formerly, Oxford Committee for Famine Relief. International Charity formed in World War II, to bring aid to poverty and famine-stricken countries.
PADIS Pan-African Documentation and Information System
PHC Primary Health Care (see Glossary)
PQLI Physical Quality of Life Index (see Glossary)
PREST Programme of Policy Research in Engineering, Science & Technology (University of Manchester
SCAR Scientific Committee on Antarctic Research
SEWA Self-employed Women's Association (India)
SITE Satellite Instructional Television Experiment (India)
UN United Nations
UNCLOS United Nations Conference on the Law of the Sea
UNEP United Nations Environment Programme (organ of the United Nations)
UNESCO United Nations Educational, Scientific and Cultural Organization (specialized Agency of the United Nations)
UNFPA United Nations Fund for Population Activities
UNHCR Office of the United Nations High Commissioner for Refugees (organ of the United Nations)
UNICEF United Nations Children's Fund (organ of the United Nations)
UPI United Press International (US)
WCS World Conservation Strategy
WHO World Health Organization (specialized Agency of the United Nations)
WIPO World Intellectual Property Organization
WWF World Wildlife Fund

Glossary

Albedo effect When the "shininess" of the planet increases, as a result of deforestation for example, it radiates more of the sun's energy back into space.

Appropriate technology Low-cost technology for small-scale use. The idea originated with Gandhi in relation to rural India.

Bio-gas A methane-rich gas produced by the fermentation of animal and human dung and crop residues, used as fuel or as fertilizer by many developing countries.

Biogeography The science of distributing species and ecosystems.

Biomass Scientific term used to describe the dry animal and plant matter found on the face of the planet.

Biomes Major regional ecological communities of plants and animals extending over a large natural areas.

Biosphere The thin covering of the planet that contains and sustains life.

Biotechnology The application of biological organisms, systems, or processes, to manufacturing industry.

Bottom-up development Theory of development that focuses on targeting poverty and meeting basic human needs (as opposed to "trickle down").

Brandt Commission An independent commission on international development issues, created in 1978, under the Chairmanship of Willy Brandt.

Brown-outs A form of "black-out" which occurs in cities when washed-up forest sediments silt up hydro-electric dams.

Cash crops Crops which generate funds for the producer countries through their export value, as opposed to crops providing staple foods for the local population.

Deficit financing Financing current operations on overdraught.

Desertification Term used when deserts increase as a result of human action.

Desertization The natural process by which deserts increase.

DNA Deoxyribonucleic acid, a compound found in the chromosomes of plants and animals, is the inherited material of almost all living things.

Double burden Double work load of unpaid domestic work plus external work, paid or unpaid; especially in the case of women.

Eco-development Development which takes environmental impact into account and holds sustainable management as its ultimate aim.

Ecosystem A community of organisms and their environment. It can apply equally to a geographical area of land or ocean or to the entire planet.

First world The developed world: the West and developed Oceania (Australia, Japan, New Zealand).

Fossil energy Solar energy biologically stored over the millennia, such as oil and coal.

Freedom House New York based survey of nations' political and civil rights.

Genetic diversity A measure of natural genetic variation, which can apply either within or between species. It is vital to the functioning of ecosystems and is the basis of biological wealth.

Genetic engineering The transfer of genes between organisms of different species.

Genetic erosion The loss of genetic variability and with it, the ability to change. Applies to individual and to communities of species.

Geostationary orbit Common path of satellites orbiting Earth at the same speed as the rotating planet.

Group of 77 Originated in 1964 as a group of 77 developing countries, to express Third World views on economic and monetary affairs. Now consists of about 120 members.

Infant mortality The number of deaths of children aged 0-12 months, per 1,000 live births.

Information technology (IT) Combination of electronic computing techniques and electronic communications.

Least developed countries UN category of 29 developing countries, low-income commodity exporters with low industrial bases.

Less developed countries (LDCs) Broad category covering all developing countries.

Low-income countries World Bank category of 30 countries with annual GNP per capita of less than $410.

Megacorps *see* transnationals.

Monoculture When a genetic make-up is replicated to provide a uniform crop.

Narrowcasting Broadcasting, or other communication, with a restricted group such as the licensed audience of cable TV.

New Japans Newly industrialized countries.

Ocean Thermal Energy Conversion (OTEC) A system producing power by exploiting the temperature difference between the warm surface and cool bottom layers in tropical seas.

Physical Quality of Life Index (PQLI) Index of general national well-being, based on averages of infant mortality, literacy, and life expectancy (devised by the Overseas Development Council, US).

Phytomass Term used to measure an amount of dry plant material. Combined with zoomass, it comprises biomass.

Primary Health Care (PHC) Community-based strategy for health for all, involving health monitoring and education.

Satellite footprint Practical reception area of a satellite's transmission.

Schumpeter's cycles Schumpeter, in 1939, showed that cycles of economic activity in the industrial world are related to technological innovation.

Second World USSR and Eastern Europe.

Stabex system A system of compensations for loss of export earnings, devised by the Lomé Convention.

Sundown industries Formerly successful heavy industries in the West – such as steel, heavy engineering, ship-building, textiles etc.

Third World Less developed countries (the South).

Transnationals Also called megacorps or multinationals. Huge business corporations with activities in two or more countries.

Trickle-down development Theory of development by which investment at the top, in industry and high-technology projects, creates wealth which will trickle down to the poor.

Underemployment Unproductive employment for little reward.

Zoomass Term used to measure an amount of dry animal matter. Together with phytomass, it comprises biomass.

Sources and credits

INTRODUCTION
Overall consultants: David O. Hall, Norman Myers, Joss Pearson.
pp12-13 The fragile miracle
Artist Chris Forsey
Sources Visual based on the Gaia principle after James E. Lovelock *Gaia: a New Look at Life on Earth*, Oxford University Press (1979); and J. Donald Hughes "Gaia: an Ancient View of our Planet", *Environmental Review*, Vol.6, No.2, 1982; atmospheric gases, data from Dorion Sagan and Lynn Margulis "The Gaian Perspective of Ecology", *The Ecologist*, Vol.13, No.5, 1983, and P. Cloud "The Biosphere", *Scientific American*, Sept. 1983; further sources, P.R. Ehrlich, A.H. Ehrlich, J.P. Holdren *Ecoscience: Population, Resources, Environment*, W.H. Freeman (1977); *Concise Atlas of the Earth*, Mitchell Beazley (1973); A. Huxley, *Green Inheritance* Collins (in press).
pp14-15 Accelerating evolution
Artist Bill Donohoe
Sources Peter Russell *The Awakening Earth*, Routledge and Kegan Paul (1979), and personal communication; James E. Lovelock, op.cit.; John Platt "The Acceleration of Evolution", *The Futurist*, February 1981; R. Buckminster Fuller *Critical Path*, Hutchinson (1981); *Concise Atlas of the Earth*, op.cit.
pp16-17 Latecomers to evolution
Artist Gary Marsh
Sources Sparks and milestones in evolution and science from Peter Russell (personal communication); exponential growth in human population from J.R. Weeks *Population, an Introduction to Concepts and Issues*, Wadsworth (1978) plus *Demographic Yearbook 1981*, UN, and *Encyclopaedia Britannica*; rise in energy consumption from Mitchell Wilson *Energy*, Time-Life (1969), and Earl Cook, *Scientific American*, September 1971; scientific journals from D.J. de Solla Price *Science since Babylon*, Yale University Press (1961); mobility from *Encyclopaedia Britannica* and John Platt, op.cit.
pp18-19 The long shadow
Artist John Shipperbottom
Sources Main visual sources from Crises sections throughout this book; data for population growth, J.R. Weeks, op.cit. and *Demographic Yearbook 1981*, op.cit.; military expenditure from R. Leger Sivard *World Military and Social Expenditures 1983*, World Priorities Inc.; species loss, data from World Wildlife Fund and N. Myers.
pp20-21 Crisis or challenge?
Photograph Daily Telegraph Colour Library and NASA
Sources James E. Lovelock *Gaia: a New Look at Life on Earth*, op.cit.; Peter Russell *The Awakening Earth*, op.cit.; Jonathan Schell *The Fate of the Earth*, Jonathan Cape (1982); *World Conservation Strategy*, IUCN, UNEP, WWF (1980).

LAND
Overall consultants: Norman Myers, David O. Hall, Erik Eckholm. **Research co-ordination**: Ken Laidlaw, Colin Hines. **Contributors**: Roy Baishley, Barry Barclay, Joss Pearson. **Principal data sources**: FAO, World Conservation Strategy. **Principal map projection**: Gaia's own.

pp24-5 The fertile soil
Artist Bill Donohoe
Map Gaia projection, divided by continent
Sources *FAO Production Yearbook 1981*; *World Conservation Strategy*; P. Colinvaux *Introduction to ecology*, John Wiley; *The State of Food and Agriculture 1977*, FAO, Fig.3.1
pp26-7 The green potential
Artist Bill Donohoe
Map Gaia projection; vegetation zones amended from *The Times Atlas of the World*.
Sources Biomass data from G. L. Ajtay, P. Ketner and P. Duvigneaud *The Global Carbon Cycle*, John Wiley, New York (1979); climate/vegetation diagram from P. Ehrlich, A. Ehrlich and J. P. Holdren (1979) *Ecoscience: Population, Resources, Environment*, W. H. Freeman (1977).
pp28-9 The global forest
Artist Bill Donohoe
Map Gaia projection; zones designated forest land from *The Times Atlas of the World* (with N. Myers' amendments).
Sources *FAO Yearbook of Forest Products 1981*; R. Persson *World Forest Resources*, Royal College of Forestry, Stockholm (1974); A. Sommer "Attempt at an assessment of the world's tropical forests", *Unasylva*, 28:112.
pp30-1 Tropical forests
Artist Bill Donohoe
Map Nordic projection by John Bartholomew, open and closed forest zones by N. Myers.
Sources D. J. Mabberley *Tropical Rain Forest Ecology*, Blackie (1983); *Tropical Forest Ecosystems*, UNESCO. Goods and services diagram *Forestry: Sector Policy Paper*, World Bank (1978). Forest regeneration from *Natural History*, 4/83, pp 72-3.
pp32-3 Humans on the land
Artist Chris Forsey
Map Gaia projection, continents grouped according to economic blocs.
Photographs *from left to right* R. Woldendorp/Susan Griggs Agency; Adam Woolfitt/Susan Griggs Agency; Barbara Parkins/Susan Griggs Agency
Sources *FAO Production Yearbook 1981*.
pp34-5 The world croplands
Artist Bill Donohoe
Map Gaia projection, map zones amended from *Fighting World Hunger*, FAO. Production statistics grouped regionally, not geographically.
Sources *FAO Fertilizer Yearbook 1981*; *FAO Production Yearbook 1981*; P. Ehrlich, A. Ehrlich and J. P. Holdren *Ecoscience: Population, Resources, Environment*, W.F. Freeman (1977); D. Crabbe and S. Lawson *The World Food Book*, Kogan Page (1981).
pp36-7 The world's grazing herd
Artist Chris Forsey
Map Gaia projection; vegetation zones after Fig. 52 in C. Barnard *Grasses and Grasslands*, Macmillan (1964). Livestock statistics grouped regionally, not geographically.
Sources *FAO Production Yearbook of 1981*; T. Lodge *The Farm*, Collins (1983); A. Buchanan *Food, Poverty and Power*, Spokesman (1982).
pp38-9 The global larder
Artist Bill Donohoe
Map Gaia projection divided by economic blocs
Sources *FAO Production Yearbook 1981*; *FAO Yearbook of Fishery Statistics 1981*; D.G. Coursey

and P.H. Haynes "Root crops and their potential as food in the tropics" *World Crops*, July 1970. Estimates for potential populations were calculated by assuming that 1 million calories meets the yearly requirement of one person. The calorific value of 1 kg of root crops (harvested wet weight) was taken to be 1,000 calories; and 1 kg (harvested dry weight) of cereal was 3,500 calories.
pp40-1 The disappearing soil
Artist Chris Forsey
Photographs *left* Arthur Rothstein/Peter Newark's Western Americana; *right* Ivan Strasburg/Alan Hutchinson Library.
Map Gaia projection with data supplied by D. Hall and N. Myers from various sources.
Sources Global land loss pie-chart from P. Buringh in M.W. Holdgate, M. Kassas and G.F. White, eds. *The World Environment 1972-1982*, Tycooly, Dublin (1982), Table 7.3, with amendments by N. Myers and D. Hall; US erosion map from P. Ehrlich, A. Ehrlich and J. P. Holdren *Ecoscience; Population, Resources, Environment*, p258; annual soil loss due to water erosion from Dusan Zachar *Soil Erosion*, Elsevier (1982).
pp42-3 The shrinking forest
Artist Chris Forsey
Photograph Victor Englebert/Susan Griggs Agency
Map Gaia projection with zones as on pp 30-1; fronts of forest destruction supplied by N. Myers
Sources Earthscan briefing documents; *The Global 2000 Report to the President*, Penguin (1982); *World Conservation Strategy*; World Wildlife Fund data; fuelwood and industrial wood projections from N. Myers and *World Forest Products Demand and Supply 1990 and 2000*, FAO (1982).
pp44-5 Destroying the protector
Artist David Ashby
Photographs *left* Alan Hutchinson Library; *right, top* Jean Pierre Dutilleux/*Observer Magazine*, *bottom* OXFAM
Sources *World Conservation Strategy*, World Wildlife Fund, Earthscan, N.Myers.
pp46-7 The encroaching desert
Artist Eugene Fleury
Photograph Horst Munzig/Susan Griggs Agency
Map Gaia projection with zones adapted from the *World Map of Desertification*.
Sources *World Map of Desertification* UN Conference on Desertification 1977 UNEP-FAO-UNESCO-WMO; Alan Grainger *Desertification how people make deserts how people can stop them and why they don't*. Earthscan, IIED (1982); *World Conservation Strategy* IUCN, UNEP, WWF (1980).
pp48-9 Hunger and glut
Artist Eugene Fleury
Map Gaia projection divided North/South according to UN classification of developed/developing nations; map zones from *World Food Report 1983*, FAO.
Sources *Agriculture: Toward 2000*, FAO (1981); D. O. Hall "Food versus Fuel, a world problem" in *Energy from Biomass*, Applied Scientific Publishers (1982).

pp50-1 The cash-crop factor
Artist Eugene Fleury
Photograph Horst Munzig/Susan Griggs Agency
Map Gaia projection
Sources Trade flows adapted from *FAO Trade Yearbook 1981* and *FAO Commodity Review and Outlook 1982-3*; malnutrition symbols placed against those countries where nutritional requirements are less than 100% – taken from *World Food Report 1983*, FAO. Commodities' purchasing power taken from *South* magazine, November 1983.

pp52-3 The global supermarket
Artist Chris Forsey
Sources *New Internationalist*, February 1982, pp 16-17; Coffee Marketing Board; *Empty Breadbasket?*, The Cornucopia Project

pp54-5 Harvesting the forest
Artist Chris Forsey
Photographs *top* Ken Saiven/WWF; *bottom* Duncan Poore/WWF
Map Gaia projection
Sources *Yearbook of Forest Products Statistics* (1983); *FAO Commodity Review and Outlook 1982-83*; *FAO Trade Yearbook 1961*

pp56-7 Forests of the future
Artist Bill Donohoe
Photographs *top* Kotoh/Zefa; *bottom* BBC
Sources Earthscan; *Tropical Forest Ecosystems* UNESCO; David O. Hall; P.K.R. Nair *Agroforestry Species: a crop sheets manual*, International Council for Research in Agroforestry (1980); D.J. Mabberley *Tropical Rainforest Ecology*, Blackie (1983); N. Myers.

pp58-9 Managing the soil
Artist Chris Forsey
Sources L. Berkofsky, D. Faiman and J. Gale eds. *Settling the Desert*, Jacob Blaustein Institute for Desert Research (1981); *Ecological Aspects of Development in the Humid Tropics*, National Academy Press (1982); P.K.R. Nair "The Re-Marriage of Crops and Trees", *International Agricultural Development*, July/August 1983. A. Rapp, H.N. Le Houerou and B. Lundholm eds. *Can Desert Encroachment be Stopped?* Swedish Natural Science Research Council (1976); Earthscan; D.O. Hall and N. Myers.

pp60-1 Green revolution?
Artist Bill Donohoe
Map Gaia projection
Sources *FAO Production Yearbooks* 1975, 1976, 1978, 1981 and 1982; D. Pimentel and M. Pimentel *Food, Energy and Society*, Edward Arnold (1979); "Revolution in a Rice Bowl", Channel 4 series *Utopia Limited*, first shown on 1st November, 1983; *Ecoscience*, Table 7.16; L.R. Brown *State of the World 1984*, Norton (1984).

pp62-3 The Chinese model
Artist Bill Donohoe
Photographs Arts Council of Great Britain
Sources S. Aziz *Rural Development: Learning from China*, Macmillan (1978); Walter Shearer "Integrated Systems in Rural Communities. A Chinese example: The UNU Approach" UNU. Visual ideas from *China Today*.

pp64-5 Agriculture in the balance
Artist Chris Forsey
Sources L.R. Brown *The State of the World*, W.W. Norton (1984); D. Pimentel and M. Pimentel *Food, Energy and Society*, Edward Arnold (1979); *World Development Reports 1982* and *1983*; David O. Hall.

pp66-7 The new agricultural revolution
Artist Chris Forsey
Sources P. Ehrlich, A. Ehrlich and J. P. Holdren *Ecoscience*; A. Huxley *Green Inheritance*, Collins (in press); WWF Information pack for Plant Conservation Programme "Crops"; N. Myers *A Wealth of Wild Species*, Westview Press (1983); *Time* magazine, May 1984.

OCEAN
Overall consultants: Sidney Holt, Norman Myers, Erik Eckholm. **Contributors:** Patricia W. Birnie, Sidney Holt, Donald J. Macintosh, Barbara Mitchell, Viktor Sebek, Jonathan I. R. Simnett, with the assistance of PREST, University of Manchester. **Principal map projection:** Lambert zenithal equal-area.

pp70-1 The world ocean
Artist Chris Forsey
Map Lambert zenithal equal-area projection, with details from The Open University Oceanography Maps (see below), human population density statistics from *The Times Atlas of the World*, currents schematized by S. Holt.
Sources B. C. Heezen and M. Tharp *World Ocean Floor* Oceanography Maps, The Open University (1977); N.C. Flemming, ed. *The Undersea*, Cassell (1977); P. Tchernia, *Descriptive Regional Oceanography*, Pergamon Press (1980).

pp72-3 The living ocean
Artist David Mallott
Map Lambert zenithal equal-area projection; with data on phytoplankton production areas adapted from FAO *Atlas of the Living Resources of the Sea* (1981); human claims on ocean from *World Oceans and Seas* Transemantics Inc., amended by N. Myers.
Sources Ocean life and Antarctic convergence diagrams devised by Sidney Holt; other data from N. C. Flemming, ed. *The Undersea*, Cassell (1977); R. D. Ballard and J. F. Grassle, "Return to oases of the deep", *National Geographic* (Nov 1979); C. F. Hickling and P. Lancaster-Brown, *The Seas and Ocean*, Blandford Press (1973); B. N. Marshall, *Ocean life*, Blandford Press (1971).

pp74-5 The vital margins
Artist David Mallott
Photographs *top* Erica Coleman/Des Barrett; *bottom left* Fredrik Ehzenstrom; *bottom right* Donald J. Macintosh.
Map Lambert zenithal equal-area projection; with data adapted from World Conservation Strategy IUCN-UNEP-WWF (1980) and *The Times Atlas of the Oceans*.
Sources P. R. Ehrlich, A. H. Ehrlich and J. P. Holden, *Ecoscience: Population, Resources, Environment*, W. H. Freeman (1977); V. J. Chapman, ed. "Wet coastal ecosystems" *Ecosystems of the world*, Elsevier Scientific (1977); *The Readers' Digest Great World Atlas;* data on area/productivity from D. J. Macintosh.

pp76-7 The global shoal
Artist Chris Forsey
Map Lambert zenithal equal-area projection, with fishing zones adapted from FAO *Atlas of the Living Resources of the Sea* (1981).
Sources FAO ibid; additional data K. Laidlaw.

pp78-9 Ocean technology
Artist Chris Forsey
Map Lambert zenithal equal-area projection with data adapted from *The Times Atlas of the Oceans* and sources following.

Sources Data and visual reference supplied by PREST, University of Manchester. Additional information from Ken Laidlaw and Jonathan I.R. Simnett.

pp80-1 The polar zones
Artist Eugene Fleury
Maps Azimuthal equal-area projection from the *CIA Polar Regions Atlas*, supplied by Sidney Holt; fish resources data adapted from FAO *Atlas of the Living Resources of the Sea*; ice development from *The Times Atlas of the Oceans*. Additional details provided by Sidney Holt.

pp82-3 The empty nets
Artist Eugene Fleury
Map Lambert zenithal equal-area projection with fishing fleets details from *The Times Atlas of the Oceans*. Other data amended by Sidney Holt from sources following.
Sources *World Conservation Strategy*, IUCN-UNEP-WWF (1980); *Ecoscience*, ibid.

pp84-5 Polluting the ocean
Artist Chris Forsey
Maps World map: Lambert zenithal equal-area projection, with data adapted from *The Times Atlas of the Oceans*, including oil tanker routes and polluted areas; also on Mediterranean map. Other information from sources following:
Sources "Main oil movements by sea", *BP Statistical Review of World Energy* (1982); New York Bight diagram information from *The Amicus Journal* (Fall 1983) supplied by N. Myers; oil pollution in the Mediterranean sea from *Ambio* Vol.N No.6 (1977). Additional data on land and sea-based oil pollution from Viktor Sebek; also UNEP, Greenpeace, PREST.

pp86-7 Destruction of habitat
Artist Eugene Fleury
Photographs *left* R. Eugene Turner/University of Louisiana; *right* Field Studies Council.
Maps World: Nordic projection by John Bartholomew, with data adapted from *Global Status of Mangrove Ecosystems*, and IUCN Commission on Ecology, Papers No 3; Chesapeake Bay, *The Times Atlas of the Oceans*; other data adapted from the following:
Sources E. D. Gomez "Perspectives on coral reef research and management in the Pacific" *Ocean Management* (1982-3), C. Roger, "Caribbean coral reefs under threat" *New Scientist* (Nov 5 1981); B. Salvat, "Trouble in Paradise" *Parks* 3(2), 1.4.

pp88-9 Whose ocean?
Artist David Mallott
Map Lambert zenithal equal-area projection, with data supplied by Sidney Holt. Other information amended from the following:
Sources *Ecoscience* (ibid); *The Times Atlas of the Oceans*; N. Meith, "Saving the small cetaceans", *Ambio* Vol XIII No 1 (1984); B. Mitchell and R. Sandbrook, "The Management of the Southern Ocean", IIED (1980); *Oceanas* 82/3 Vol 23.

pp90-1 Harvesting the sea
Artist Chris Forsey
Map Lambert zenithal equal-area projection, with information adapted from FAO (ibid).
Sources Food chain diagram after J. R. Beddington and R. M. May, "The harvesting of interacting species in a natural ecosystem", *Scientific American* 247 (5) (1982); other data adapted from R. Laws, "Antarctica: a convergence of life", *New Scientist* (Sept 1, 1983); "Management of multispecies fisheries" *Science* Vol 205 (1979).

pp92-3 Clean-up for the oceans
Artist Eugene Fleury
Map Lambert zenithal equal-area projection, with data from Greenpeace, UNEP, and IMO, supplied and amended by Viktor Sebek.
Sources "The international conference on tanker safety and pollution prevention 1978", Inter-Governmental Marine Consultative Organizations; *Briefing document on ocean dispersal of radioactive wastes*, Greenpeace (1983); "UNEP's ten regional seas programme", *Ambio*, Vol XII No 1 (1983), with advice from N. Myers.

pp94-5 Managing Antarctica
Artist Eugene Fleury
Map Azimuthal equal-area projection from the *CIA Polar Regions Atlas*, supplied by Sidney Holt; data from FAO and IIED (with amendments).
Sources FAO, *Atlas of the Living Resources of the Seas*; Barbara Mitchell, *Frozen Stakes: the Future of Antarctic Minerals*, IIED (1983); *The Times Atlas of the Oceans* plus input from N. Myers.

pp96-7 The laws of the seas
Artist David Mallott
Map Lambert zenithal equal-area projection, with UNCLOS data supplied by the UN Information Centre.
Sources *The Times Atlas of the Oceans* and information from Patricia Birnie, and N. Myers.

pp98-9 Future ocean
Artist Aziz Khan
Photographs *top* National Maritime Institute; *bottom* J. Roessler, Planet Earth Pictures/Seaphot.
Map Adapted from Athelstan Spilhaus whole ocean map.
Sources Details adapted from *The Times Atlas of the Oceans*, plus data from J. Elkington.

ELEMENTS

Overall consultants: Norman Myers, David O. Hall, John Elkington. **Contributors**: Hugh Miall, P. Mick Kelly, Graham Farmer, Robin Stainer, Trevor Davies, David Baldock, John Valentine, David Olivier, Brian Price. **Principal map projection**: Gaia's own.

pp102-3 The global powerhouse
Artist David Mallott
Sources *left*: M. King Hubbert "The energy resources of the Earth" *Scientific American* September 1971, pp 62-3; *right*: D. Deudney and C. Flavin *Renewable energy*, W. W. Norton, New York (1983); P. B. Stone *14 Sources of New and Renewable Energy*, Earthscan (1981).

pp104-5 The energy store
Artist Bill Donohoe
Map Gaia projection, divided into economic blocs
Sources BP Statistical Review of World Energy (1982); FAO; G. Leach *Energy and Food Production*, IPC (1976); *National Geographic Special Report on Energy*, pp 20-1 (Feb 1981); UN energy statistics.

pp106-7 The climate asset
Artist David Mallott
Map Interrupted Mollweide's homolographic projection by George Philip & Son Ltd
Sources Agroclimatic zones on map adapted from A. N. Duckham and G.B. Masefield *Farming Systems of the World*, Chatto and Windus (1970). R. B. Bunnett *Physical Geography in Diagrams*, Longman (1976); P. R. Ehrlich, A. H. Ehrlich and J. P. Holdren, *Ecoscience: Population, Resources, Environment*, W. H. Freeman (1977); *The Times Atlas of the World*.

pp108-9 The freshwater reservoir
Artist David Mallott
Map Gaia projection
Sources *The Global 2000 Report to the President*, Penguin (1982); R. Ambroggio "Water" *Scientific American*, Vol. 243, p.92 (September 1980); M. Falkenmark and G. Lindh *Water for a Starving World*, Westview Press; Farooque Ahmed "Design parameters for rural water supplies in Bangladesh" (1981); *The Demand for Water*, UN Natural Resources, Water Series No. 3 (1976); M.W. Holdgate, M. Kassas and G.F. White eds. *The World Environment 1972-1982*, Tycooly Ltd, Dublin (1982); P.R. Ehrlich, A.H. Ehrlich and J.P. Holdren *Ecoscience: Population, Resources, Environment*, W.H. Freeman (1977).

pp110-1 The mineral reserve
Artist Bill Donohoe
Map Gaia projection
Sources *Metal Bulletin Handbook*; US Federal Emergency Management Agency; Shearson/American Express's *Annual Review of the Metal Markets, 1982/3*; US Bureau of Mines; M. Shafer "Mineral Myths", *Foreign Policy*, no.47, 1982.

pp112-3 The oil crisis
Artist Aziz Khan
Map Gaia projection
Sources BP Statistical Review of World Energy (1982); J. Elkington *Sun Traps: the Renewable Energy Forecast*, Pelican Books (1984); R. Leger Sivard *World Energy Survey* 2nd ed., World Priorities, Leesburg, Virginia 22075.

pp114-5 The fuelwood crisis
Artist Ann Savage
Map Nordic projection by John Bartholomew
Sources *Map of the Fuelwood Situation in the Developing Countries*, FAO (1981); D.O. Hall, G.W. Barnard, and P.A. Moss *Biomass for Energy in the Developing Countries*, Pergamon (1982); Erik Eckholm *UNICEF and the Household Fuels Crisis*, UNICEF (1982); Phil O'Keefe "Fuel for the People; Fuelwood in the Third World" *Ambio*, Vol.12 (2), 115-17 (1983).

pp116-7 The greenhouse effect
Artist Alan Suttie
Map Gaia projection
Sources Energy flows taken from *Ecoscience*, p.47 Table 2-14; W. Kellogg and R. Schware *Climate Change and Society: Consequences of Increasing Atmospheric Carbon Dioxide*, Westview Press (1981); S. Schneider and R. S. Chen "Carbon dioxide warming and coastline flooding" *Annual Review of Energy*, Vol.5 pp 107-140; N. Myers "The Carbon Dioxide Connection", *J. Social Biol. Struct.* (1983); Bette Hileman "Recent Reports on the Greenhouse Effect" *Environ. Sci. Technol.*, 18(2) (1984).

pp118-9 The invisible threat
Artist Bill Donohoe
Map Oblique azimuthal equidistant projection by George Philip & Son Ltd
Sources I. Billick *et al.* in *Clear* newpaper (The Campaign for Lead-free Air) No.1, p.3; *Ecoscience* pp 48, 555. Russ Hoyle "The silent scourge" *Time* (November 9 1982); "Downwind: the acid rain story" (1982) Ministry of Supply and Services, Canada; *Acidification Today and Tomorrow*, Swedish Ministry of Agriculture Environment '82 Committee pp32-42; M. J. Gittins *Pollution*, National Survey for Clean Air (1983); *Acid Rain a review of the phenomenon in the EEC and Europe* by Environmental Resources Ltd., Graham & Trotman (1983).

pp120-1 Water that kills
Artist Chris Forsey
Map Gaia projection
Sources R.P. Ambroggio "Water" *Scientific American* (September 1980) pp100-1; *Water, Sanitation, Health – for All?*, Earthscan.

pp122-3 Widening circle of poison
Artist Chris Forsey
Sources David Bull *A Growing Problem: Pesticides and the Third World Poor*, OXFAM (1982); R.D. Hill "Controlling the Epidemic of Hazardous Chemicals and Wastes" *Ambio*, Vol.12, pp 86-90; Lewis Regenstein "The Toxics Boomerang", *Environment*, Vol.25, No.10, December 1983; Marcus Linear "Gift of Poison – the Unacceptable Face of Development Aid", *Ambio*, Vol.11, No.1 (1982).

pp124-5 The nuclear dilemma
Artist Bill Donohoe
Map Gaia projection
Sources Greenpeace "What's wrong with nuclear power?" (leaflet); C.P. Alexander "Pulling the Nuclear Plug", *Time* (February 13 1984); Greenpeace Ltd *The Windscale File*.

pp126-7 An energy efficient future?
Artist Chris Forsey
Photograph Harwell Laboratories
Sources Cathy King *Energy for All A Look at Centralised Energy Systems and the Practical Alternatives*, Greenpeace, London (1983); *New and Renewable Energies 1 and 2*, Earthscan; Graham Freeman "Get to Grips with your Fuel Bills", *Modern Purchasing*, October 1978; "The Demand for Energy: Sharp Reaction to Second Oil-Price Shock" *OECD Observer*.

pp128-9 Managing energy in the South
Artist David Cook
Photograph Erik Eckholm
Sources *New and Renewable Energies 1 and 2*, Earthscan; *UNICEF Energy Activities*; *China Now* Jan/Feb 1981; G. Foley, P. Moss and L. Timberlake *Stoves and Trees*, Earthscan.

pp130-1 The climate factor
Artist John Potter
Map Interrupted Mollweide's homolographic projection by George Philip & Son Ltd.
Sources *Climate Monitor* (June 1983-Aug 1983), Vol.12, No.3, p.94; F. Philibert Nov 1983 "L'enfant du diable" *Geo* No.57, p.27; M. Kelly and J. Palutikof "Facing up to the weather" *Marxism Today* (March 1982); "El Nino's ill wind" *National Geographic*, Vol.165, No.2 (Feb 1984) pp 162-3; J. Stuller "El Nino stirs up the world's weather" Readers Digest, December 1983.

pp132-3 Managing water
Artist Alan Suttie
Map Gaia projection
Sources Per capita water availability, 2000 *The Global 2000 Report for the President*, Penguin (1982) *World Conservation Strategy*; J.A. Allen "High Aswan dam is a success story", *Geographical Magazine*, March 1981; "The Demand for Water: procedures and methodologies for projecting water demands in the context of regional and national planning", Natural Resources/Water Series No.3, UN.

pp134-5 Clean water for all
Artist Alan Suttie
Map Nordic projection by John Bartholomew
Photograph Anne Charnack
Sources Sumi Krishna Chauhan *Who Puts the Water in the Taps?*, Earthscan. *Water, Sanitation, Health – for All?*, Earthscan.

pp136-7 Waste into wealth
Artist Alan Suttie
Map Gaia projection
Sources Jon Vogler *Jobs from Junks How to create employment and tidy up derelict cars*, Intermediate Technology (1983); Christine Thomas *Material Gains*, Earth Resources Research (1979). William V. Chandler "Materials Recycling: The Virtue of Necessity", Worldwatch Paper 56 (1983).

EVOLUTION
Overall consultants: Erik Eckholm, David O. Hall. **Contributors**: Pamela M. Berry, Julian Caldecott, Peter Evans, Stephen Mills, Jane Thornback, Gillian Kerby, Simon Lyster, Karl G. Van Orsdol.
pp140-1 The life pool
Artist Bill Donohoe
Sources Evolution of life diagram adapted from D. Attenborough *Life on Earth*, Collins and BBC (1979); other details from *World Conservation Strategy*; G.H. Dury, *An Introduction to Environmental Systems*, Heinemann (1981); Jack McCormick *The Life of the Forest*, McGraw Hill; plus input from Stephen Mills and N. Myers.
pp142-3 Life strategies
Artist Shirley Willis
Sources Biomes diagram after H. Walter *Vegetation of the Earth*, Springer Verlag (1979); bio-communities from IUCN, plus input from D. O. Hall and N. Myers; also data from G. L. Ajtay, P. Ketner and P. Duvigneaud *The Global Carbon Cycle*, Wiley (1979).
pp144-5 Partners in evolution
Artist John Potter
Map Gaia projection
Sources Information on livestock and crop production from *Production Yearbook 1982* Ministry of Agriculture, UK; the WWF *Book of Plants*; other data adapted from G. W. Beadle "The ancestry of corn", *Scientific American*, Vol 242 (1980); J. Harlan "The plants and animals that nourish man" *Scientific American*, Vol 235 (1976).
pp146-7 The genetic resource
Artist David Salariya
Sources Schematized from R. and C. Prescott-Allen *Genes from the Wild*, Earthscan (1983); *World Conservation Strategy*; *The Global 2000 Report to the President*; N. Myers *A Wealth of Wild Species*, Westview (1983).
pp148-9 Keys to the wild
Artist Norman Barker of Linden Artists
Sources WWF Mark Plotkin *Plant Pack for Plant Conservation Campaign on Ethnobotany;* Green Medicine; N. Myers *A Wealth of Wild Species*, Westview Press (1983); A. Huxley *Green Inheritance*, Collins (in press).
pp150-1 Fellowship with wildlife
Artist David Salariya
Sources N. Myers op.cit., D. Pimentel and M. Pimentel *Food, Energy and Society*, John Wiley, New York; *BioScience*, Vol 30 No 11 plus data supplied by G. Kerby, D. O. Hall, N. Myers.
pp152-3 The irreplaceable heritage
Artist George Thompson
Sources UK habitat data adapted from FAO; *World Conservation Strategy*; WWF; IUCN. Chart of disappearing soil from P. Buringh (1981) in *The World Environment 1972-1982* and amended by N. Myers; Council for the Preservation of Rural England; Swedish Society for the Conservation of Nature.

pp154-5 The destruction of diversity
Artist Ann Savage
Sources Species destruction data adapted from WWF *Annual Report 1983*; *The Global 2000 Report to the President*; additional data from IUCN *Red Data Book on Mammals* and Robert Allen *How to Save the World*, IUCN-UNEP-WWF (1980), amended by N. Myers; species extinction data from "Geological time" *Science* Vol 215.
156-7 Genetic erosion
Artist John Potter
Map Gaia projection, with details of threatened crop areas adapted from *World Conservation Strategy*, IUCN-UNEP-WWF, and IBPGR.
Sources *The Global 2000 Report to the President*; N. Myers *The Sinking Ark*, Pergamon Press (1979); R. and C. Prescott-Allen *Genes from the Wild*, Earthscan; *Development Dialogue*, Dag Hammarskjöld Foundation, Uppsala (1983:1-2).
pp158-9 Towards a lonely planet
Artist Roger Stewart
pp160-1 Conserving the wild
Artist Eugene Fleury
Map Equal area homolosine projection by Miklos D.F. Udvardy, with information based on IUCN Paper No.18 prepared for UNESCO; other data from *World Conservation Strategy*. Antarctic map adapted from Polar regions Atlas, CIA (1978)
Sources IUCN Conservation Monitoring Centre, Kew; World Conservation Centre, Gland, also from J. Harrison, K. Miller and J. McNeely "The world coverage of protected areas", *Ambio*, Vol.II No.5 (1982).
pp162-3 Harvesting the wildlife
Artist George Thompson
Sources IUCN Conservation Monitoring Centre; G. Nilsson *et al.* (1980) Facts about furs, Animal Welfare Institute, Washington DC. WWF US Annual Report 1983. *World Conservation Strategy;* TRAFFIC (USA), Channel 4 Television. Additional data supplied by K. Van Orsdol, J. Caldecott, N. Myers.
pp164-5 Preserving the genetic resource
Artist Ann Savage
Map Gaia projection, with data from J. Harlan op. cit., amended by N. Myers.
Sources Earthscan; IUCN Conservation Monitoring Centre; World Wildlife Fund/IUCN data for Plant Conservation Programme; *Development Dialogue*, op.cit.; R. and C. Prescott Allen "Park your genes", *Ambio*. Vol.12 (1) 1983; N. Myers *The Sinking Ark*, op.cit.
pp166-7 Laws and conventions
Artist Alan Suttie
Maps Gaia projection, with information from IUCN, Environmental Law Centre, Bonn; wildlife trade data and migratory routes from WWF US.
Sources Wildlife Trade Monitoring Unit, IUCN, Cambridge; TRAFFIC, UK; *World Conservation Strategy*; IUCN *Red Data Book* Vol 1; plus data supplied and amended by S Lyster.
pp168-9 Towards a new conservation
Artist Martin Camm of Linden Artists
Map Adapted from UN map symbol with data from *World Conservation Strategy*.
Sources After C. Bass *National Conservation Strategy for Nepal*, IUCN (1983), with details from World Conservation Centre, Gland; *National Conservation Strategies*, IUCN's CDC (January 1984); IBPGR; Unesco Courier (April 1981) *World Conservation Strategy*.

HUMANKIND
Consultants: Norman Myers, David O. Hall, John Elkington, Ken Laidlaw **Contributors**: John Rowley, Stewart Ainsworth, Harford Thomas, Uma Ram Nath, Peter O'Neill, Raúl Hernán Ampuero, Derrick Knight, Stephanie Leland, Kaye Stearman
pp172-3 People potential
Artist Alan Suttie
Sources Cultivable land area from P. R. Ehrlich, A. H. Ehrlich, J. P. Holdren *Ecoscience: Population, Resources, Environment*, W. H. Freeman (1977). Global statistics and case-study material from *UNESCO Statistical Yearbook* (1983); *1983 World Population Data Sheet*, Population Reference Bureau; *Report on the World Social Situation 1982*, Dept. of International Economic and Social Affairs, UN; *Freedom at Issue*, Freedom House (1978); Ruth Leger Sivard *World Military and Social Expenditures 1983*, World Priorities; *World Development Report 1983*, World Bank.
pp174-5 Working potential
Artist Eugene Fleury
Maps Gaia projection, after UN regions
Sources Workforce statistics from *Labour Force Estimates and Projections 1950-2000*, ILO (1977); labour distribution triangle from *Third World Atlas*, The Open University (1983); wage labour trends from *ILO Yearbook of International Statistics* (1980); *World Labour Report*, ILO (1984).
pp176-7 Homo sapiens
Artist George Thompson
Sources *UNESCO Statistical Yearbook* (1983), Table 2:11; G. T. Kurian *The New Book of World Rankings*, Facts On File Publications (1984), Tables 292, 321; D. J. de Solla Price *Science since Babylon*, Yale University Press (1961).
pp178-9 A sense of identity
Artist Aziz Khan
Maps Peters projection
Sources Distribution of races adapted from *Third World Atlas*, The Open University (1983); official languages from *Atlas of Mankind*, Mitchell Beazley (adapted); case study material from S. Wallman, "Identity options" *Minorities: Community and Identity*, Springer-Verlag (1983).
pp180-1 Population crisis
Artist Eugene Fleury
Maps Peters projection
Sources Population pyramids 1980 and 2000 from R. Leger Sivard *World Military and Social Expenditures 1983*, World Priorities p.27; infant mortality from *1983 World Population Data Sheet*; forecasts from *Long-Range Population Projections of the World and Major Regions, 2025-2150, Fine Variants as Assessed in 1980*, UN (1981); current population by continent, *1983 World Population Data Sheet*, Population Reference Bureau; land pressure from *People*, International Planned Parenthood Federation, "Earthwatch" section no 13, 1983; population density from *Demographic Yearbook 1981*, UN; world population graph from J. R. Weeks *Population, an Introduction to Concepts and Issues*, Wadsworth Publishing Company (1978), amended by N. Myers; also P. Harrison and J. Rowley, *Human Numbers, Human Needs*, IPPF (1984).
pp182-3 The work famine
Artist Chris Forsey
Map Peters projection
Sources Labour force figures from *Labour Force Estimates and Projection 1950-2000*, ILO (1977);

percentage employed and underemployed, North and South, from *People*, Vol.6 No.3 (1979) (Northern figures adjusted) economic rankings from *World Development Report 1983;* discrimination in employment study from *World Labour Report* (1984); further information "The most basic need", *New Internationalist*, April, 1983; *Demographic Yearbook 1981*, UN.

pp184-5 Sickness and stress
Artist George Thompson
Map Peters projection
Sources Population pyramids from L. F. Bouvier "Planet Earth 1984-2034: a democratic vision", *Population Bulletin*, Population Reference Bureau Vol. 39, No. 1, February 1984; estimate of drug imports in the South from *IFDA Dossier* January/February 1983; deaths from social neglect, and world health budgets from R. Leger Sivard *World Military and Social Expenditures 1983;* new deaths from P. O'Neill *Health Crisis 2000*, WHO (1983); the new outcasts from *Public Health in Europe* No. 21, WHO (1983); infant mortality and child killers from *The State of the World's Children 1984* (UNICEF), Oxford University Press; medical personnel from *World Health Statistics Annual 1983* WHO.

pp186-7 The literacy chasm
Artist John Potter
Map Peters projection
Sources Primary and secondary enrolment from *Demographic Yearbook 1981*, UN; *UNESCO Statistical Yearbook* (1983); access to media, *UNESCO Statistical Yearbook*; world literacy, ibid.; male/female literacy from *World's Women Data Sheet*, Population Reference Bureau (1980); aboriginal poem from *Bunji*, December 1971, reprinted in the *New Internationalist*, October 1983; "Higher education and development", *Third World First*, May, 1983.

pp188-9 Outcasts and refugees
Artist John Potter
Photograph Adam Woolfitt/Susan Griggs
Map Peters projection
Sources Famine threat areas from P. R. Ehrlich, A. H. Ehrlich, J. P. Holdren *Ecoscience, op. cit;* directions of refugee exodus from M. Kidron and R. Segal *The State of the World Atlas*, Pan Books (1981); refugee numbers from UN High Commission for Refugees; further information from the Minority Rights Group, OXFAM, Amnesty International.

pp190-1 Managing numbers
Artist John Potter
Map Peters projection
Sources Government positions on family planning from *Fertility and Family Planning* wallchart, *People* (1982) Vol.9, No.3; conceptions and abortions from *Population Misconceptions*, Population Concern (May 1984); literacy, longevity, and infant mortality from *1983 World Population Data Sheet*, Population Reference Bureau; UN Fund for Population Activities; Physical Quality of Life Index, G. T. Kurian *The New Book of World Rankings*, Facts On File Publications (1984); IPPF.

pp192-3 The voice of women
Artist John Potter
Map Peters projection
Photographs *top* Philip Howard *centre* Amnesty International *bottom* Ed Barker
Sources "The integration of women in African development", UN Commission for Africa (1974); "Women in agriculture" FAO

Information Note; "Arab Women", Report No. 27, Minority Rights Group (1983); women in national legislatures from S. McLean (Minority Rights Group UK) "The role of women in the promotion of friendly relations between nations", and World Conference of the UN Decade for Women (Copenhagen 14-30 July 1980), Statistical extract Table 17, amended by N. Myers; women's work, incomes, ownership from UN Decade for Women information pack.

pp194-5 Health for all
Artist George Thompson
Sources Norway case study from *Report No 11 to the Storting* (1981-82), Royal Ministry of Health and Social Affairs and *The State of the World's Children 1984*, (UNICEF), Oxford University Press; alternative medicine from A. Huxley, *Green Inheritance*, Collins (forthcoming); Sudan case study from *World Health* magazine, July, 1981; further information, P. O'Neill, *Health Crisis 2000*, Heinemann (1983); D. Morley, J. Rohde, G. Williams, *Practising Health for All*, Oxford University Press, 1983; and M. Mesarovic and N. Myers, "The Global Possible: what can be gained?" in *The Global Possible*, World Resources Institute, May 1981.

pp196-7 Tools and ideas
Artist Norman Barber of Linden Artists
Sources Distance learning data from the International Centre for Distance Learning, Open University; International Cooperatives Alliance, Geneva; also G. Rumble and K. Nauy, eds. *The Distance Teaching Universities*, Croom Helm (1981); *World Labour Report*, ILO (1984); Sesame St.; "Global employment and economic justice: the policy challenge", K. Newland, Worldwatch Paper 28, April 1979; Intermediate Technology Development Group review, March, 1984; B. Stokes "Local responses to global problems: a key to meeting basic human needs", Worldwatch Paper 17, February, 1978.

pp198-9 A polycultural world
Artist David Cook
Photograph David Pearson
Sources Minority Rights Group reports; J. Benthall in *The Traveller*, Vol.14, No.2, summer 1984; "Plotting the peoples", *New Internationalist*, December, 1976; "National identity and foreign domination", Ngugi Wa Thiong'o, *Unesco Courier*, 1982.

CIVILIZATION
Overall consultants Norman Myers, David O. Hall, John Elkington, John Bowers
Contributors David Satterthwaite, Peter Marsh, Adrian Norman, Melvin Westlake, Simon Maxwell

pp202-3 The world city
Artist Ann Savage
Map Peters projection
Sources Populations in cities from the *New Internationalist* (1982); principal world air routes from *The Times Atlas of the World* (1981).

pp204-5 The world factory
Artist Roger Stewart of Virgil Pomfret Agency
Map Peters projection
Sources Global distribution of R & D expenditure from *UNESCO Statistical Yearbook* (1983); services compared to agriculture from *The World Development Report 1983*, Oxford University Press, and G.T. Kurian, *The New Book of World Rankings*, Facts on File (1984), Table 112; $ value added in manufacturing from

World Development Report 1983, pp114-15; number of R & D scientists from *UNESCO Statistical Yearbook* (1983); use of the global R & D budget from Colin Norman, "Knowledge and power: the global research and development budget", Worldwatch Paper No.31 (July 1979) p.6, Table 1; technological waves from *The Conservation and Development Programme for the UK*, Kagan Page (1983), p.41, Fig.1. Further information from Colin Norman *The God that Limps* and T. K. Derry and Trevor I. Williams *A Short History of Technology*, Oxford University Press (1960).

pp206-7 The power of communications
Artist Chris Forsey
Map Mollweide's interrupted homolographic projection.
Sources The geostationary orbit, distance, from J. Elkington, *Sun Traps*, Penguin Books (1984); submarine cables from *The Times Atlas of the Oceans*, pp 200-1. Further information *From Semaphore to Satellite*, International Telecommunication Union (1965), and Eryl Davies, *Telecommunications: a Technology for Change*, Science Museum, HMSO (1983).

pp208-9 The world market
Artist Chris Forsey
Map adapted from Peters projection
Sources Structure of merchandise, imports, and exports, *World Development Report 1983*, pp166-69; value of exports, 1982, from *Monthly Bulletin of Statistics*, UN (June 1983) p.xviii; OPEC share of world oil production from *Third World Atlas*, The Open University Press, Oxford University Press (1983) pp 66-69; nationality of multinationals, ibid., p.61; value of manufactures graph from *Monthly Bulletin of Statistics*, p.xviii; percentage of primary products in exports from *World Development Report 1983*, pp 166-7; financial exchanges, *Wall Street Journal*; regional share of world exports from *Monthly Bulletin of Statistics*, pp xxx-xxxiii.

pp210-1 The world's wealth
Artist Clive Spong of Linden Artists
Map adapted from Peters projection
Sources Gross Regional Product and GNP data from R. Leger Sivard *World Military and Social Expenditures*, World Priorities (1983), pp 32-35; resource endowment data adapted from *Third World Atlas*, The Open University Press, Oxford University Press (1983), pp 66-7; balance of payments deficits from *World Development Report 1983*, Oxford University Press, pp 174-5; "Banking on the Fund – the IMF", Third World Studies, Case study 9, The Open University Press (1983).

pp212-3 Chaos in the cities
Artist Aziz Khan
Map Peters projection
Photographs *top* Brian Anson, *bottom* UNICEF
Sources city population data from David Satterthwaite; urban population 1980 and 2000, *New Internationalist* (1982).

pp214-5 Monopolies in media control
Artist Roger Stewart, Virgil Pomfret Agency
Map Oblique azimuthal equidistant projection
Sources T. Y. Canby "Satellites that serve us", *National Geographic* (September 1983); media per capita, by region, from G. T. Kurian *The New Book of World Rankings*; press agencies from "The big four", *New Internationalist* (June 1981), pp 12-14; also Paul Sieghart, ed., *Micro-chips with Everything*, Comedia Publishing Group (1982).

pp216-7 Market tremors
Artist Clive Spong of Linden Artists
Map adapted from Peters projection; North/South division after Brandt
Sources Regional shares of world trade from *Monthly Bulletin of Statistics*, UN (June 1983), pp xxx-xxxiii, 106-127; OECD; trends in world trade from *World Development Report 1982*, p.11, Fig.2.3; weighted index of commodity prices, ibid., p.28 Fig.306; further information from *World Development Report 1983* and *Crisis Decade in the Eighties*, ICDA.

pp218-9 Haves and have-nots
Artist Aziz Khan
Map Peters projection; North/South division after Brandt
Sources Third World debt from R. Leger Sivard *World Military and Social Expenditures*; GNP per capita per country, and by world regions, from *World Development Report 1983*, Table 1, p.27; income distribution, ibid., pp200-201, Table 27; further material from *North-South: A Programme for Survival*, Pan Books (1980); case-studies from *Time*, 2 July 1984, *The Guardian*, 10 February and 8 July 1983, *The Sunday Times*, 17 July 1983.

pp220-1 The poverty bomb
Artist Ann Savage
Photograph WHO/ILO
Map Peters projection; North-South division after Brandt
Sources Population in absolute poverty from G. T. Kurian, *The New Book of World Rankings*, Table 69; low income countries from *World Bank Atlas 1983*, The World Bank; people without basic needs, see pp 172-3 sources; further material, R. Chambers, *Rural Development: Putting the Last First* and Paul Harrison, *Inside the Third World*, Penguin Books (1979).

pp222-3 Urban regeneration
Artist David Cook
Map Peters projection
Sources City regeneration schemes, North and South, from David Pearson and John Bowers; *Learning by doing*, The World Bank (1983); "Sites and services" projects, *World Development Report 1983*, Oxford University Press. Further material from R. Cassidy, *Livable Cities A Grass-Roots Guide to Rebuilding Urban America*, Holt, Rinehart and Winston (1980) and *Accelerated Development in Sub-Saharan Africa*, World Bank (1981).

pp224-5 The will to communicate
Artist Bill Donohoe
Sources Reversing the flow data from Inter Press Service, Rome, and *New Internationalist*, June, 1981, pp 12-14; SITE data from L. K. Sharma "After the end of SITE", *The Times of India*, (6 August 1976); further information, T. Stonier, *The Wealth of Information*, Thames Methuen (1983) and Paul Sieghart, ed., *Microchips with Everything*, Comedia Publishing Group (1982).

pp226-7 Technology transfer
Artist Nicky Snell, Virgil Pomfret Agency
Sources Appropriate technology from ITDG, and from P. Harrison, *The Third World Tomorrow*, Penguin Books (1980); also *Blending of New and Traditional Technologies*, case studies (ILO), Tycooly Publishing Ltd (1984), *Common Crisis: North-South: Cooperation for World Recovery*, Brandt Commission, Pan Books (1983). "Experiments in modes of development communication", IFDA dossier (February, 1984); background material from Keith

Holroyd, also Colin Norman *The God that Limps – Science and Technology in the Eighties*, W.W. Norton and Company (1981).

pp228-9 Growing interdependence
Artist Clive Spong of Linden artists
Map Peters projection
Sources Export statistics from *Monthly Bulletin of Statistics*, UN (June 1983), pp xxx-xxxiii, 106-127; *World Labour Report*, ILO (1984), p.57, Table 2.10; further material from *Third World Atlas*, The Open University Press (1983), *World Development Report 1983* and *Crisis Decade in the Eighties*, ICDA.

pp230-1 Closing the gap
Artist Ann Savage
Map Peters projection
Sources SDR holdings from IMF and G. T. Kurian *The New Book of World Rankings*, Facts on File (1984), Table 90; development assistance, ibid., Table 49; international aid data, ibid., Table 50; World Bank Annual Reports 1979-1983; GNP data from *1983 World Bank Atlas*; further material from the Lome Convention, and R. Chambers *Rural Development: Putting the Last First*, Longmans (1983).

MANAGEMENT
Overall consultants: Erik Eckholm, D. O. Hall, John Elkington. **Contributors**: Frank Barnaby, Dr. A. John R. Groom, Peter Russell, V. Tarzie Vittachi, Peter Willetts, Thomas Wilson.

pp234-5 The family of nations
Artist Rob Burns
Map Peters projection
Sources Nation states from *Third World Atlas*, The Open University Press (1983).

pp236-7 The reluctant internationalists
Artist Alan Suttie
Sources *UN Image and Reality*, UN Dept. of Public Information (1984).

pp238-9 Voice of the world
Artist Francesca Pelizzoli
Sources *Yearbook of International Organizations 1984*, Vol I, p.905. Peter Willetts ed. *Pressure Groups in the Global System: The Transnational Relations of Issue-Orientated Non-Governmental Organizations*, Frances Pinter Publishers (1981). IPPF.

pp240-1 The voice of the village
Artist Francesca Pelizzoli
Sources "The Cooperative World", *New Internationalist*, February 1977.

pp242-3 Breaking points
Artist Aziz Khan
Map Peters projection
Sources Antarctic territories from *The Times Atlas of the World*, Plate 5; additional data from R. Leger Sivard *World Military and Social Expenditures 1983*, World Priorities, and M. Kidron and Dan Smith *The War Atlas*, Pan Books (1983); further material from D.M.A. Leggett and C.M. Waterlow *The War Games that Superpowers Play*, The Centre for International Peacebuilding, London (1983) and F. Barnaby, "Where Wars Happen", *Future War: Armed Conflict in the Next Decade*, Michael Joseph (1984).

pp244-5 Towards a violent planet
Artist Ann Savage
Map Peters projection, adapted
Sources War deaths from R. Leger Sivard, op.cit.; military expenditure, ibid.; governments, ibid.; US and USSR bases from M. Kidron and Dan Smith *The War Atlas*, Pan Books (1983).

pp246-7 The cost of militarism
Artist Norman Barber of Linden Artists
Sources Military versus social expenditure from R. Leger Sivard, op.cit.; also *The State of the World's Children 1984*, UNICEF, M. Mesarovic and N. Myers "The Global Possible: what can be gained?", *The Global Possible*, World Resources Institute, May 1981.

pp248-9 One million Hiroshimas
Artist Eugene Fleury
Map Oblique azimuthal equidistant projection
Sources F. Barnaby *Future War: Armed Conflict in the Next Decade*, Michael Joseph (1984); *Nuclear Weapons Databook*, Natural Resources Defense Council, Inc.; R. Leger Sivard, op.cit.; *The Nuclear Casebook*, Polygon Books (1983); J. Schell *The Fate of the Earth*, Jonathan Cape (1982).

pp250-1 Bang or whimper?
Artist Roger Stewart of Virgil Pomfret Agency
Sources P. Ehrlich "When Light is Put Away: Ecological Effects of Nuclear War", *The Counterfeit Ark: Crisis Relocation for Nuclear War*, J. Leaning and L. Keyes eds., Ballinger (1984); F. Barnaby op.cit.; "Long-Term Biological Consequences of Nuclear War", *Science*, Vol 222, No 4630, 23 December 1983; P. Ehrlich "The Nuclear Winter" *The Amicus Journal*.

pp252-3 The great transition
Artist Gary Marsh
Sources *North-South: A Programme for Survival*, Pan Books (1980); *World Conservation Strategy*, IUCN, UNEP, WWF (1980); *Toward a Steady-State Economy*, Herman E. Daly ed., W.H. Freeman and Company (1972); R. Buckminster Fuller *Critical Path*, Hutchinson (1981).

pp254-5 The coming of age
Artist John Shipperbottom of Virgil Pomfret
Sources James E. Lovelock *Gaia: A New Look at Life on Earth*, Oxford University Press (1979); Peter Russell *The Awakening Earth*, Routledge and Kegan Paul (1976); Thomas Wilson *An Expanded Concept of Security* (forthcoming) *World Conservation Strategy*, op.cit.

pp256-7 The fragile miracle is safeguarded
Artist Jim Channel of Linden Artists
Sources James E. Lovelock, op. cit. Pirages *Global Ecopolitics*; Peter Russell, op. cit.; Thomas Wilson, op. cit.; *World Conservation Strategy*; J. Platt "The Acceleration of Evolution", *The Futurist* (February 1981).

Index

Publisher's Acknowledgements
Gaia Books extends warmest thanks and appreciation to all the many, many individuals who gave their time unstintingly to the research and preparation of this book, and first and foremost to Norman and Dorothy Myers, without whom the project could never have been carried through. We also give special thanks to David Hall, for his patient guidance and advice, to Erik Eckholm, for his work as US reader and consultant, to Ken Laidlaw, for his two years of work and loyalty to the task, to John Elkington, for setting aside all his many commitments to join the team in the final months, to James Lovelock and Peter Russell for their inspiration, to Peter Brent, for his help on Evolution, to Barry Barclay, Bryan Poole, and Yvette van Giap for their early work on the concept and approach; to Uma Ram Nath and Melvin Westlake for their work on the later chapters; to Sidney Holt for his long work on Ocean, to Colin Hines for his research on Land; to Tom Burke of Green Alliance, Jon Tinker of Earthscan, and Paul Wachtel of WWF International, for their support and advice on the content; also to Maureen Keaveney, Maureen McNeil, Derek Pryce, Graham Henley, Benno Glauser, Joss Lemmers, Roy Laishley, David Kardish, and Susan Leigh for invaluable assistance in the first months' preparations; to Kyle Cathie and Phil Pochoda for their faith in the book; to the patient staff of Earthscan, ICDA, *South*, IIED, *New Internationalist*, the Central Reference Library (Westminster), ILO (London), the Museum of Mankind (British Museum), the UN Information Service, the IUCN Conservation Monitoring Centre at Kew, the World Conservation Centre at Gland, Manchester University's PREST department, the Climatic Research Unit at the University of East Anglia, King's College, London University, and many other academic and research establishments. We would also like to thank the following for their assistance and support: Jonathan Hilton, Christopher Pick, Caroline Simpson (cartography); Sue Burt and Lesley Gilbert for controlling manuscript production and keying; Imogen Bright and Lucy Lidell for help and support; Giovanni Caselli for early illustration work; Keith Holroyd, Chris Schumacher, and Dr Sandra Wallman; Sara Mathews, Viv Pover, Mat Cook, Brenda Breslan, Jean Stevens, Sasha Devas, and Fred Ford for assistance on design and paste up; David Thomas for research assistance; John Brewer, Alan Woodcock, and Barry Smith of Marlin Graphics; Michael Burman and Bob Gray of F. E. Burman Ltd; Anita Porcari of Mondadori Ltd; On Yer Bike; the staff of many picture agencies, in particular Aspect, Susan Griggs, and the Alan Hutchinson Library; and the host of unknown people who answered our telephone queries on data around the world, without complaint, and were unfailingly helpful.
Most of all, we should like to thank our artists, who worked long and cheerfully, checking and rechecking all the minutiae of maps and diagrams, and creating the body of this Atlas.

GAIA
AN ATLAS
OF PLANET
MANAGEMENT

GAIA BOOKS LIMITED

General editor
Dr NORMAN MYERS

ANCHOR BOOKS
ANCHOR PRESS/DOUBLEDAY & COMPANY INC.
Garden City, New York 1984

A GAIA ORIGINAL

Conceived by Joss Pearson

Written by Norman Myers
with Uma Ram Nath and Melvin Westlake

Direction	Joss Pearson
	Patrick Nugent
Editorial	Michele Staple *Project editor*
	Roslin Mair
	John Spayne
	David Black
	Erik Ness
	Cecilia Walters
Design	Chris Meehan
	David Cook
	Marnie Searchwell
Picture Research	Elly Beintema
Production	Robert K. Christie

Copyright © 1984 by Gaia Books
Limited, London

All rights reserved

Published by Anchor Press, Doubleday & Company Inc.,
Garden City, New York

First Edition

Library of Congress Cataloging in Publication Data
    Main entry under title:
    GAIA, an atlas of planet management
        Bibliography: p
        Includes index
        1. Environmental policy. 2. Human ecology. I. Gaia
Books Ltd. II. Myers, Norman. III. Title: G.A.I.A.,
an atlas of planet management.

HC79.E5G32 1984 333.7 83-20837

ISBN 0–385–19071–9

ISBN 0–385–19072–7 (pbk)

Filmset by Marlin Graphics Ltd Orpington, Kent

Reproduction by F.E. Burman Ltd London

Printed and bound in Italy by Mondadori, Verona

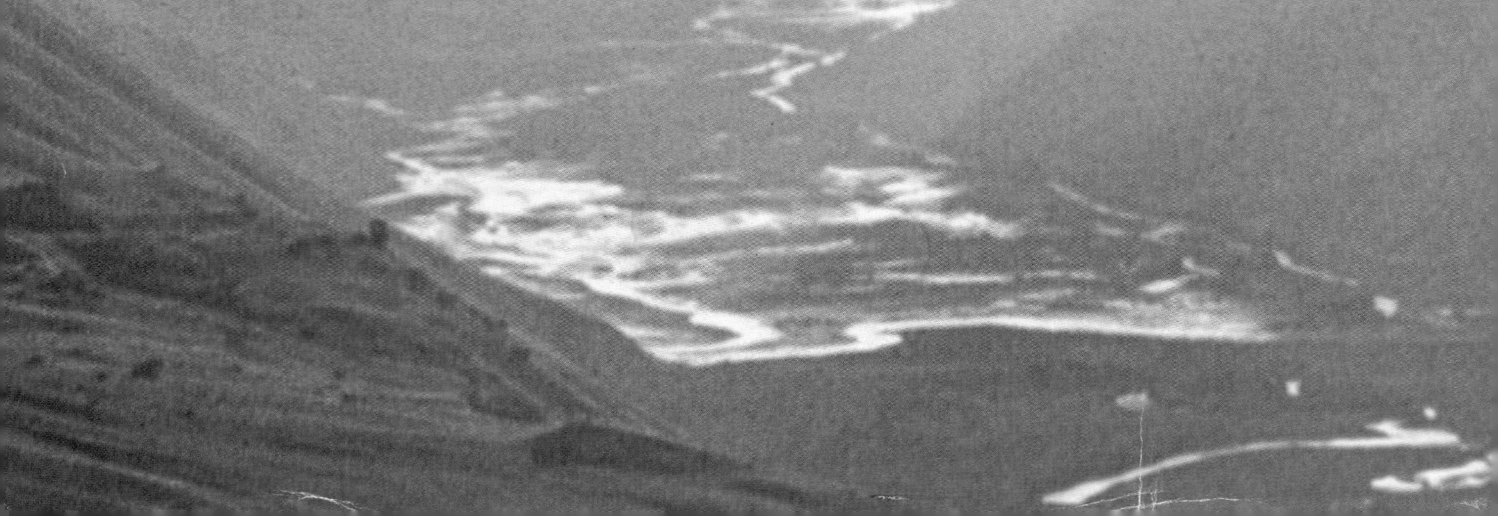